Property of Lois Meredith

Christmas gift from my son, Ronald Meredith, & his wife, Jo;

# Kentucky Pioneers
# and
# Their Descendants

*Compiled by*

ILA EARLE FOWLER
For the Kentucky Society,
Daughters of Colonial Wars

GENEALOGICAL PUBLISHING CO., INC.

*Baltimore*                                    *1988*

Originally published: Frankfort, Kentucky, ca. 1951
Reprinted: Genealogical Publishing Co., Inc.
Baltimore, 1967, 1978, 1988
© 1967
Genealogical Publishing Co., Inc.
Baltimore, Maryland
All Rights Reserved
Library of Congress Catalogue Card Number 67-16864
International Standard Book Number 0-8063-0150-3
*Made in the United States of America*

# Table of Contents

## COUNTY RECORDS

## FAMILY RECORDS

# PREFACE

The Daughters of Colonial Wars of the State of Kentucky, mindful of the need for more printed records to aid research, have furnished the material for this volume. It has been a labor of love and the Kentucky Daughters trust that it will be helpful to all patriotic societies who are devoted to the preservation of accurate and reliable records of our ancestors. At no time in our history has this been more needed than in this day of severe trial of our modern patriots, men and women. We pray that we may be so guided by Divine Providence that we may measure up to the full stature of our forbears whose lives and deeds we record in these pages.

Great credit is due those whose labor furnished the material. To this end the name of the donor of each group of data appears at the head of her contribution. It is with earnest appreciation that each item has been received and included.

The proof-reading on this book has been careful and painstaking and it is hoped that few mistakes will be found.

The work of the printer has been carefully and thoughtfully done and it is due to him to state that the vagaries of spelling and punctuation are those of the original records which have been reproduced as nearly as possible in the form in which they are found.

ILA EARLE FOWLER

# FOREWORD

It is a lamentable fact that Kentucky records are, for the most part, arranged according to counties and there is no general index. For this reason it is difficult to find information on a family if the county location is not known. When a compilation such as this is issued, however, a wealth of data is made available to the genealogist and researcher. Only three other compilations containing similar Kentucky records have been published, so there is a wide open field in this type of work.

*Kentucky Pioneers and Their Descendants,* sponsored by the Society of Colonial Wars of Kentucky, contains from thirteen to fifteen thousand names taken from Bibles, tombstones, obituaries, birth certificates, vital statistics, tax books, deeds, wills, marriage and census records, principally of the counties of Caldwell, Christian, Fleming, Hopkins, Jefferson, Livingston, Lincoln, Larue, Hardin, Fayette, Jessamine, Mason, Woodford, Calloway, Mercer, Bourbon and Franklin.

With the enormous interest in genealogy and the strict requirements of patriotic societies for correct lineages, this book will prove a boon to those tracing their ancestry. To the historical societies and genealogical libraries faced with the problem of directing research and answering numerous queries by mail, it will often mean the saving of many hours of research.

Mrs. W. T. Fowler is to be congratulated for compiling these hitherto unpublished Kentucky records. They will in this way be made available to the researcher and will be preserved for the future. Mrs. Gretna Cobb Davis is due her share of credit for compiling the index, because a book of this sort without an index is of little value.

BAYLESS E. HARDIN, *Secretary*
Kentucky Historical Society

# Kentucky Pioneers
# and Their Descendants

## BARTLETT

### FRANKLIN COUNTY, KENTUCKY, COURT RECORD

(Formed from Woodford, Mercer and Shelby counties, 1794)
Copied by Mrs. Lula Reed Boss

DEED BOOK K.—Page 168

Dated May 22, 1822

(In part) "WHEREAS Lewis Craig and John Sanders executed deed to Henry Bartlett junior, Thomas Bartlett and James Wood of Fayette county, 1791, for 408 acres of land in Woodford county".........."Henry Bartlett junior died without issue".........."his father, Harry Bartlett, became his heir, and died intestate leaving the following persons his children and heirs at law, to-wit: Thomas Bartlett; Elizabeth Gale, wife of Josiah Gale; Phoebe Sanders, wife of James Sanders; Polly Hickman, widow of Thomas Hickman; Sally Banks, widow of James Banks; Frances Hardin, widow of Wesley Hardin, and children of deceased daughter, Ann Alsop, namely: Sarah Alsop, Elizabeth Alsop, Guilford Alsop and others"...............Above mentioned heirs sell land to Lewis F. Stephens.

\* \* \* \* \*

Major Harry Bartlett (also called Henry) of Spotsylvania county, Virginia, married ca 1752, Sarah Crane, daughter of Col. John and Elizabeth Crane of Spotsylvania county. Major Harry Bartlett and wife, Sarah Crane Bartlett, died in Franklin county, Kentucky before May 22, 1822.

Note: Consult the Will of Henry Bartlett junior recorded in Fayette County, Kentucky.

Ann Bartlett, born in Virginia, 1768; married in Caroline county, Virginia, March, 1786, George Alsop (born 1763). They removed to Franklin county, Kentucky in 1815.

Their children were: (Records from the Bible of Guilford Dudley Harris* in the possession of Mrs. Mary (Harris) Davis, of New London, Missouri.)

Sally M. Alsop, born 1-8-1787
Betsy C. Alsop, born 4-15-1788
Henry Bartlett Alsop, born 3-14-1791
Guilford Dudley Alsop, born 5-16-1792
Parmelia Alsop, born 11-11-1794
George T. Alsop, born 3-9-1799
Louisiana Bartlett Alsop, born 11-9-1805
Nancy Alsop, born 4-15-1808

Louisiana Bartlett Alsop married Samuel Wilson Mayhall in Franklin county, Kentucky, 11-14-1826. Removed to Missouri in April, 1830, and located in New London.

Their children were:

Margaret Ann Mayhall, born 9-13-1827; died 8-16-1892, New London.
Jefferson Alsop Mayhall, born 2-5-1829; died 7-12-1897.
Elizabeth Jane Mayhall, born 10-30-1830.**
Sarah Caroline Mayhall, born 5-9-1832.**
John Walker Mayhall, born 6-4-1833.**
George Elliott Mayhall, born 9-24-1834; died 1-11-1922.
Augusta Gold Mayhall, born 1-20-1836; died 3-16-1899.
Louisiana Cornelia Mayhall, born 7-17-1837.
Clay Crittenden Menefee Mayhall, born 4-15-1839; died 10-17-1898.
Frances Merial Mayhall, born 8-8-1840; died 1921.
Samuel Wilson Mayhall jr., born 9-19-1842; died June, 1843.
Laura Wilson Mayhall, born 8-3-1845; died December, 1923.
William Slosson Mayhall, born 8-23-1850.
Margaret Ann Mayhall married 4-1-1842, Elliott Harris (born 8-1-1819) in Madison county, Kentucky; died 1-29-1906, New London, Missouri.

### FAYETTE COUNTY, KENTUCKY, COURT RECORD (In abstract)

(Formed from Kentucky county in 1780)

Will of "Henry Bartlett of Fayette county, Kentucky."
Dated: 7-25-1792. Proven: December Court, 1794.
Witnesses: Jas. M. Crosky and Sucky M. Crosky.

"I lend unto my brother, John Crane Bartlett, my three negroes, viz.: Jenny, Gabriel and Delphenny, during my father, Harry Bartlett's and my mother, Sarah's life, and all the rest of my estate be it of whatever

---

*Guilford Dudley Harris was born 2-29-1864; died New London, Missouri, 10-24-1942.
**These three children died the same day, date unknown, of Cholera.

kind, and the proceeds arising from my said estate lent my brother, John Crane Bartlett, during my father's and mother's life to be disposed of as they think proper, and after the death of my said mother and father, that my whole estate then be divided equally with the increase of the said negroes aforesaid, between my brother, John Crane Bartlett, and my five sisters, viz.: Elizabeth, Phebe, Polly, Sally and Franky ................."

"Lastly I appoint my brother, Thomas Bartlett, and William Wood," executors.

Note: William Wood married Ann Crane, sister of Sarah Crane, mother of the said Henry Bartlett.

## NICHOLAS COUNTY, KENTUCKY, COURT RECORDS (Abstracts)

(Formed from Bourbon and Mason counties, 1793)

### DEED BOOK B.—Page 31
### Dated January 4, 1802

William Bartlett of Nicholas county purchases 1,200 acres of land in Nicholas county from Humphrey Marshall.

### DEED BOOK 4.—Page 402
### Dated .................., 1816.

Phoebe Buchanan, widow and relict of James Buchanan, deceased, and James Buchanan, heir at law of the said Buchanan, deceased, and Nancy, his wife, sell land in Nicholas county to William Bartlett.

### DEED BOOK H.—Page 368—BARTLETT HEIRS AGREEMENT

"THIS CONTRACT made June 5th, 1822 between Joseph Bartlett, James Wilson and Dorcas Wilson his wife, Dorcas was Dorcas Bartlett, Ashford Prather and Polly Prather his wife, Polly was Polly Bartlett, James Buchanan and Nancy Buchanan his wife, Nancy was Nancy Bartlett, Benoni Duncan and Phebe his wife, Phebe was Phebe Bartlett, George Swarts and Betsy Swarts his wife, Betsy was Betsy Bartlett, Samuel Bartlett, children and heirs and legal representation of William Bartlett, deceased, late of the county of Nicholas in the State of Kentucky, of the first part, and Ebenezer Bartlett, of Fleming county, in the same State, of the second part.

"WHEREAS, the said William Bartlett, deceased, departed this life having first made a Will, and he left said Joseph Bartlett, Dorcas Wilson, Polly Prather, Nancy Buchanan, Phebe Duncan, Betsy Swarts, Samuel Bartlett, and the said Ebenezer Bartlett, and also William Bartlett and Ann Foster, who was Ann Bartlett, (the two latter of whom have departed this life) his children and heirs and legal representation. That the said William Bartlett, last named, left two children, who are now living and entitled to his portion of the estate of his deceased father. That the said Anna Foster, also left seven children, who are now living and are entitled to their mother's portion of her father's estate. And, WHEREAS, also the widow of the said William Bartlett first named, to-wit: Phebe Bartlett, is entitled to one-third part of the estate of the said William Bartlett, deceased, and the said Ebenezer Bartlett has purchased out her interest in the said estate..........she has become dissatisfied with the contract and wishes and is attempting to set aside the said Contract that the said Ebenezer Bartlett agrees to give the said Phebe Bartlett, one thousand dollars for her interest in the said estate, and the parties of these presents have agreed and now agree that they will not take under the will of the said William Bartlett, their ancestor, but that they will take as his heirs and distribute according to the Statute of distribution, each one an equal share and part of the estate, real, personal, and mixed, in the same manner as if the said William Bartlett, intestator, that the parties of the first part are and shall be equally interested with the said Ebenezer Bartlett in the purchase of the interest of the aforesaid Phebe Bartlett, in and to the estate as aforesaid............ The said Joseph Bartlett has now sold out his entire interest in the said estate to Ebenezer Bartlett, whereby Ebenezer is entitled to two parts thereof............"

Written on the margin of the Contract is:
"September 30, 1829 delivered to Ebenezer Bartlett,

Ebenezer Bartlett our Attorney in Fact to compromise with the said Phebe Bartlett in relation to the Contract made with her by him for her interest in the estate of aforesaid on the best terms he can and if he shall pay or agree to pay her any other, or further sum of money, the parties of the first part agree to pay the said Ebenezer Bartlett one-tenth part each, and the parties empower the said Ebenezer Bartlett........."

*     *     *     *     *

William Bartlett married 1st.........................; married 2nd "on the .... day of ................., 181.., Phebe ..............," who survived him.

Issue by first wife: (no issue by 2nd wife, Phebe ..............)
(Not arranged according to dates of birth)

1. Ebenezer Bartlett—died Hancock county, Illinois, 12-2-1843; married before 1-10-1799, Rebecca Standiford (born Baltimore county, Maryland, 7-27-1782; died Hancock county, Illinois, 1845)
   The Will of Ebenezer Bartlett is recorded in Will Book G, pages 6-7-8, Carthage, Hancock county, Illinois. Dated 10-30-1843; proven December Court, 1843. Witnesses: William Darnall and Nathan H. Grafton.
2. Samuel Bartlett.
3. Dorcas Bartlett md. James Wilson.
4. Ann Bartlett (deceased by 1822) md. Harrison Foster and "left 7 children," namely: Polly, William, Aaron, Harrison, Phoebe, Lettice and Dorcas Foster.
5. Polly Bartlett married Ashford Prather, 1810.
6. Nancy Bartlett married James Buchanan, 1815.
7. Phoebe Bartlett (Marriage Bond reads "Feaby") married Benoni Duncan in Adams county, Ohio, 11-21-1811.

8. William Bartlett jr. (deceased by 1822) married Rachel Hildreth in Adams county, Ohio, 8-16-1815. He left "two children," one of whom was Squire Bartlett for whom Robert L. G. Edwards (md. Susan Hildreth in 1824) was serving as his guardian in 1828.
9. Betsy Bartlett married George Swarts, 9-30-1819.
10. Joseph Bartlett (under age in 1803 when a suit was filed by his father, William Bartlett senior).

\* \* \* \* \*

June Court, 1822 (Circuit Clerk's office, Nicholas county) a suit was filed "Phebe Bartlett, widow and relict of William Bartlett senior, deceased, vs. Ebenezer Bartlett, admr. of estate of said deceased."

(in part) Phebe Bartlett "respectfully saith that on the . . . . . . . day of . . . . . . . . . . . . . . . . . ., in the year 181. .," she "intermarried with a certain William Bartlett, senior". . . . . . . . . . . . . . .that "the . . . . . . day of . . . . . . . . . . . . . . . ., 1820, the said William Bartlett departed this life," . . . . . . . . . . . . . . . . .Phebe renounces the Will of William Bartlett. And "in pursuance of the law in such case, the said County Court of Nicholas County, then setting, did appoint Henry Roberts, Zeb Moore, L. Amatt, Daniel Ballengall and Hiram Metcalfe, commissioners to assign and allow to her dower of all real and personal estate of the deceased, including the slaves, which estate also consists of land at Lower Blue Licks, and land adjoining the same which the said William Bartlett had purchased of James Buchanan, also the lands of the home farm and Mansion house. . . . . . . . . . . ." stating that her "dower interest amounts to about $7,000.". . . . . . . . . . . . .speaks of a "certain Ebenezer Bartlett, son of her deceased husband" as being the administrator of estate. . . . . . . . . .states she is "being stripped of her dower in said estate by the acts of said Ebenezer, and a certain Samuel Bartlett, his brother," further stating that "Ebenezer and Samuel Bartlett treated her in a most shameful manner, and so did the rest of the children of the said deceased, and more particularly the said Samuel Bartlett."

Ebenezer Bartlett as administrator of the estate of William Bartlett senior, answered the suit of Phebe Bartlett, widow and relict, July 2, 1822. He stated he "admits that the Complainant Phebe intermarried with William Bartlett, deceased, and before his death the deceased attempted to make a Will which after his death was rejected by the Nicholas County Court for want of legal proof. . . . . . . . . ." March 1823 court records show that the Case was dismissed against Ebenezer Bartlett and Phebe Bartlett was ordered to pay all court costs.

\* \* \* \* \*

William Bartlett senior is buried on the old Bartlett plantation in Nicholas county. This land is now known as the Hammond farm and is located about four miles from the once famous Blue Lick Spring. On his tombstone is this simple inscription:

"WILLIAM BARTLETT, PIONEER

Died 1820"

Carlisle Mercury, Nicholas County, Kentucky.

September 23, 1926

(In part) "The Famous Blue Lick Springs, noted all through 'Dixieland' and far into the north, as being in its time the most fashionable summer resort in the south, has been the subject of litigation in the Courts of Kentucky for many years.

".........William Bartlett, a rugged pioneer from Virginia, stopped on Stoner Creek, Bourbon county..............he followed a buffalo trail and located Blue Lick Springs, secured a grant of an extensive body of land from Virginia State Government, which included famous Blue Lick Springs. With his wife, son, and son-in-law, James Buchanan, lived at the springs and made salt. He divided a part of this land into town lots, built cabins, and called it 'Bartlettsburg.'

"The hearing of this case will come up in the November Term of Court, for possession of this, the most historic Springs in the United States, the home site of the first and only genuine Blue Lick Springs, which was originally granted to William Bartlett."

In the Will of George Michael Bedinger, dated Dec. 7, 1843, Nicholas county, he leaves to "wife Henrietta, the family plantation partly on the plat of Bartlettsburg."

D. P. Bedinger, son of George M. Bedinger, was appointed "sole executor" under the Will of William Bartlett senior, which for "lack of legal proof" was not permitted to be recorded.

Children of Ebenezer Bartlett and his wife, Rebecca (Standiford) Bartlett: (Not arranged according to dates of birth)

1. Eliza Bartlett married Josiah W. McCabe, 1826.
2. Franklin J. Bartlett.
3. Elizabeth Bartlett married 3-14-1822, Aquilla Hildreth (killed 1-27-1864 while serving in the War Between the States. He was a member of Company K, 118th Illinois Infantry.)
4. Sarah Bartlett married ................ Lapham.
5. Lucinda Bartlett, born 11-30-1807; died Mason county, 11-15-1867; married 5-11-1824, Robert Fristoe (born 4-4-1801; died Mason county, 6-16-1873.)
6. Mary Jane Bartlett married James Legrande Sanford (1819-1889.)
7. Silas Bartlett married Barbara McDaniel in Mason county, 1837.

Tombstone Inscription, Bath county, Kentucky:

"Barbara Bartlett, 1812-1902"

8. Sally Ann Bartlett married .................. Craender.
9. Henry J. Bartlett, born 3-7-1818.
10. Malinda Bartlett, born 11-12-1820; died November, 1903; married 12-13-1838, her 1st cousin, William Preston Duncan (born 9-27-1815.) Malinda (Bartlett) Duncan married 2nd, Elias Bower, 3-4-1851. Lived La Harpe, Illinois.

## FUNERAL NOTICES

"Died—In Fresno, April 9th, 1887, Edwin L. Sanford, a native of Illinois, aged 19 years, 7 months and 14 days. Funeral to take place at Centennary Church, Madera, on Sunday, April 10, at 2 o'clock, p. m. Friends and acquaintances of the family are requested to attend.
"Died—James L. Sanford, a native of Connecticut, aged 70 years, 4 months. In Fresno, February 9th, 1889. The funeral will take place from Centenary Church, Madera, today, Sunday, February 10, at 2:30 P. M. Friends of the family are respectfully invited to attend."

## MASON COUNTY, KENTUCKY COURT RECORDS (Abstracts)

"Second Town established by Act of Virginia Legislature in Mason County, Kentucky (then Bourbon county) was in 1787, Charles Town on 80 acres of land belonging to Ignatius Mitchell on the Ohio River at the mouth of Lawrence's Creek."

### DEED BOOK C-1.—Page 422
### Dated November 17, 1802

Ignatius Mitchell and Mildred his wife, of Mason county, sell land "granted Ignatius Mitchell by Patent bearing date of February 8, 1780."
Note: In some of the deeds Mildred, wife of Ignatius Mitchell, is called "Milly."

### DEED BOOK J.—Page 419
### Dated September 13, 1807

Ignatius Mitchell and Mildred his wife, of Mason county, to Francis (or Frances) Mitchell and Susan W. Mitchell, both of Baltimore, Maryland. Deed land "for 5 lbs. Maryland money to him advanced some years ago to locate land in partnership with James W. Mitchell."

### COURT ORDER BOOK E.—Page 245
### March Court, 1805

Ignatius Mitchell granted license to operate a public ferry from his lands at Charlestown to the opposite shore; boat 40 feet long and 8 feet wide and two good hands to attend the same. John Chambers surety.

### COURT ORDER BOOK F.—Page 68
### April Court, 1807

Ignatius Mitchell appointed Justice of the Peace for Mason county.

### WILL BOOK F.—Page 388

Will of "Ignatius Mitchell of Mason county and State of Kentucky." Dated: 3-4-1825. Proven: March Court, 1826.
Witnesses to Will: David V. Rannels, Caroline Fowke, and John J. Crosby.
Leaves "to son Richard Mitchell land in Mason county and land in Brown county, Ohio"........speaks of "Mitchell's Ferry on the Ohio

river." (Son Richard had no issue at date of Will, and had wife, Monica Mitchell.) Leaves to son Charles S. Mitchell; son-in-law, John Forsythe, "land where he now lives in Brown county, Ohio;" daughter Mildred Forsythe, wife of John Forsythe; son Ignatius Mitchell jr.; daughter Patsy Allen, wife of Charles W. Allen of Henderson county, Kentucky. (No mention of wife Mildred in Will.)

Executors of estate: 'sons Charles S. Mitchell and Ignatius Mitchell, jr."

\* \* \* \* \*

Issue of Ignatius Mitchell, senior and his wife Mildred (Smith) Mitchell: (Not arranged according to dates of birth.)

1. Col. Charles Smith Mitchell md. in Mason county 9-2-1821, Elizabeth Fowke, with Susan Fowke signing the marriage bond.
2. Mildred E. Mitchell md. 1st in Mason county, John Forsythe, 6-16-1813; md. 2nd before 1854, .......... Robinson.
3. Richard B. Mitchell. Died Mason county, 1854; married Monica ................ before 1825. The Will of Richard Mitchell is recorded in Will Book Q, page 330, dated 4-20-1854; proven November Court, 1854. He makes no mention of wife Monica and leaves to niece Martha M. Best, late Mastin; sister Mildred E. Robinson; brother Ignatius S. Mitchell land in Ohio; desires "to be buried in the Catholic Cemetery, Washington, Mason county, Kentucky."
4. Martha (called "Patsy") Mitchell md. in Mason county, 1-14, 1819, Charles W. Allen. In 1825 they were residents of Henderson county, Ky.
5. Ignatius S. Mitchell jr., born in Mason county, 1-9-1799; died 3-3-1882; md. Ann Bumby Fowke (born 10-19-1800 in Virginia; died July 1891.)

### DEED BOOK 80.—Page 509
#### Dated May 31, 1852

Ignatius S. Mitchell and Ann B. Mitchell his wife, sell land in Mason County to Nimrod H. Robinson.

Note: Mason county court records show that Elizabeth Fowke who married Charles Smith Mitchell, and Ann Bumby Fowke, who married his brother, Ignatius S. Mitchell, jr., were the children of Roger and Susannah Fowke. Roger Fowke died in Mason county. Will Book D., page 310, dated 11-9-1818; proven December Court, 1818, gives the Will of Roger Fowke. Court Order Book N., page 249, July Court, 1841, gives the estate of Susan Fowke, deceased. Philip R. Triplett, admr. John Masterson (or Masters) surety.

### COURT ORDER BOOK X.—Page 115
#### February 26, 1887

Charles Mitchell Smith, On Petition—Ex Parte
Charles Mitchell Smith "changes name to Gerrard Fowke."
Sibella, daughter of Col. Charles Smith Mitchell and wife, Elizabeth

Fowke, married in 1854, John D. Smith, and their son, Charles Mitchell Smith, born 6-25-1854 in Charleston Bottom, Mason county, changed his name to "Gerrard Fowke." On Feb. 26, 1887, by action of the Mason County Court he took the name of "Gerrard Fowke, borne by the first American ancestor of his grandmother, Elizabeth Fowke, wife of Charles Smith Mitchell." "Her father, Roger Fowke, left Fauquier county, Virginia, for Kentucky in 1804." "He was fifth in descent from the immigrant, the family having lived in the Northern Neck of Virginia and in Charles county, Maryland, since 1651."

> Reference: Page 6, taken from Reprint from the Ohio Archacological and Historical Quarterly for April 1929, printed by the F. J. Heer Printing Company, Columbus, Ohio, page 5, of Booklet in the Public Library, Maysville, Kentucky, entitled "Gerrard Fowke."

> See: "The Register of the Kentucky State Historical Society," Frankfort, Kentucky, Vol. 38, No. 124, July, 1940, pages 270-271, Bourbon Circuit Court Records (in abstract) by Julia Spencer Ardery.

> DEED BOOK 58—Page 468 (Mason county court record)

Dated May 25, 1852, gives the issue of Col. Charles Smith Mitchell and his wife, Elizabeth Fowke Mitchell, as follows:

> Charles Smith Mitchell; Richard P. Mitchell; Sibelle S. Mitchell (md. John D. Smith); Susan C. Mitchell; Ignatius W. Mitchell; David R. Mitchell; Theobald Mitchell; Harrison Clay Mitchell; Joseph O. Mitchell and Elizabeth Mitchell.

MARYLAND SERVICE, Revolutionary War, Ignatius Mitchell.
References:
> "Maryland Archives," Volume XVIII, page 137, gives:
> "Muster Roll and Other Records of Maryland Troops in the Revolutionary War, 1775-1783."

> Maryland Troops, Volume 1, Maryland Lines, gives:
> "Mitchell, Ignatius (sometimes abbreviated Igns), Sergt., enlisted May 16, 1777; discharged May 16, 1780."
> "Mitchell, Ignatius, Sergt. August 1, 1777; discharged July 25, 1778. Remarks: 'promoted'."

## MASON COUNTY, KENTUCKY COURT RECORDS (Abstracts)

### WILL BOOK K.—Page 193

Will of Thomas Browning of Mason county, Kentucky.

Dated: 6-15-1830. Proven: July Court, 1835.

Mentions wife (does not give her name); sons, Theoderic L. Browning, Ludwell Yancey Browning, Edmund Woodville Browning, and daughter, Harriet LeWright Browning.

Witnesses: W. B. Lurty and Samuel Howison.

### DEED BOOK C.—Page 216
### Dated May 24, 1796

John Gaskins and Sarah his wife, of Mason county, convey land to Thomas Browning, of same place, land located "on the waters of Little Bracken."

### DEED BOOK A.—Page 257
### Dated April 29, 1804

Robert B. Morton and Mary his wife, of Mason county, convey to Thomas Browning, of same place, "100 acres on waters of Cabbin creek adjoining lands of Edmund Browning." Witness to deed: William Bronough, sr., William Bronough and Peter D. Myer.

### DEED BOOK J.—Page 9
### March 27, 1806

Thomas Marshall and Fanny his wife, of Mason county, convey to Thomas Browning, of same place, 100 acres of land.

### DEED BOOK J.—Page 12
### March 27, 1806

Thomas Browning and Elizabeth his wife, of Mason county, execute mortgage to Thomas Marshall, of same place, to secure purchase price of land.

Note: Hon. Thomas Browning married Elizabeth LeWright.

### WILL BOOK B.—Page 22

Will of "Acquilla Standerford of Mason county, Kentucky." (The Will is signed Aquilla Standiford.)

Dated: 1-10-1799. Proven: 6-24-1799.

Witnesses: John Gaheagan, Squire Hildreth, and Samuel Hawkins.

Names "daughters Hannah Hawkins, Sarah Hildreth, Mary Smith and Rebecah Bartlett," to whom he gives "one shilling each and no more"; son, Nathan Standiford, "one shilling and no more"; daughter Milcah Little, "750 acres of land on the waters of Eagle Creek, being part of land bought by Richard Masterson and John Tebbs of a certain Thomas Cavan and Absolem Craig"; son, George Standiford, "750 acres being part of the same survey as above mentioned, likewise to my said son George, for three years the residue of my servant Pompy's time, he to pay unto Samuel Hawkins 42 lbs. in order to discharge a debt due him the said Hawkins;" son, Elijah Standiford, "354 acres being the residue of the land above mentioned, likewise one gray horse and likewise my carpenter and joiner tools"; son Aquilla Standiford, "110 acres of land, part of the land I now live on, the upper end adjoining Hildreth's and to be laid off as not to injure the residue of the survey. My said son Aquilla likewise one black horse"; son John Standiford "the residue of my land on Licking, the place I now live on and adjoining his brother, Aquilla, to be the property of my said son John at the death of his mother and her widowhood." To "well beloved wife Sarah Standiford, all the residue of my personal property of every kind to be at her own disposal and likewise the residue of the land and plantation I now live on during her lifetime and widowhood, and at her death to be equally divided among all children." "I desire at my death that Joseph my servant may be a freeman. Pompy, my servant, is to serve George Standiford three years, said three years to commence the first day of January, 1799, and after that he is a freeman."

## COURT ORDER BOOK C.—Page 254
### June 24, 1799

Last Will and Testament of Acquilla Standiford, deceased, was produced in court and proven by the Oaths of John Geoheagan, Squire Hildreth and Samuel Hawkins witnesses thereto and ordered to be recorded. Sworn to by George Standiford, executor, who with Thomas Dobyns, Squire Hildreth, John Geoheagan and Samuel Hawkins, his surety, acknowledged Bond for one thousand pounds.

## COURT ORDER BOOK C.—Page 256
### June 24, 1799

William Bartlett, William Millar, David Ballengall and Mathew Stewart, or any three of them, being first sworn, are ordered to appraise in current money the personal estate and slaves, if any, of Aquilla Standiford, deceased, and report to the next court.

Note: Aquilla Standiford was born in Baltimore county, Maryland. 8-25,1741; married 12-27-1764, Sarah Clark (born 6-10-1744.)

Reference: Register of St. John's and St. George's Churches, Baltimore and Harford counties, Maryland, pages 90, 104, 155, 188, 201, 221, 227, 342 and 386.

Aquilla Standiford signed the petition, September 19, 1787, as a "settler of Limestone country" to the Virginia Assembly for the division of Mason county from Bourbon county.

## DEED BOOK E.—Page 241
### February 25, 1799

Daniel Hillman, guardian of William Craig and Violet Craig, heirs of Absalom Craig, deceased, all of Mason county, lease to Robert B. Morton, of same place, for term of eleven years from date, land on Lawrence creek.

## DEED BOOK L.—Page 285
### February 14, 1810

Daniel Hillman and Heathy his wife, late Heathy Craig, William Ballinger and Violet his wife, late Violet Craig, heirs and representatives of Absalom Craig, deceased, all of Mason county, appoint James Lounsdale, of same place, their attorney.

Note: Absolem Craig also owned land on Eagle creek in Adams county, Ohio, in 1829.

# BAYLES

## BAYLES FAMILY BIBLE
Bourbon County, Ky.

(Contributed by Mrs. James McLeod)

### BIRTHS

Nathan Bayles was born Sept. 30, 1801.

Hannah Middaugh (his wife) was born July 3, 1805.

Phoeby M. Bayles (daughter of the above couple) was born Nov. 22, 1821.

Mary Bayles (2nd daughter of above couple) was born May 4, 1825.

Elizabeth Bayles (3d daughter of above couple) was born May 3, 1827.

Nancy Cogswell Bayles (4th daughter of above) was born Mar. 30, 1830.

Nathan Bayles (son of above couple) was born May 18, 1832.

Hannah Margaret Bayles (5th daughter of above couple) was born April 22, 1835.

Hiram Winburn Alexander was born Nov. 8, 1830.

Mary E. Alexander (wife of above) was born Nov. 14, 1852.

John Madison Alexander (son of above) was born July 26, 1871.

Nancy Winburn Alexander (daughter of above) was born Nov. 8, 1875.

Elizabeth Buckner Alexander (2nd daughter) was born May 23, 1880.

Thomas Mayhen Alexander (twin to Elizabeth Buckner Alexander) was born May 23, 1880.

Cratis Bowles Alexander was born Sept. 9, 1883.

Mary Prescott Alexander was born Sept. 9, 1883 (twin to above).

Elizabeth Jean McLeod was born June 19, 1901.

Margaret Elizabeth Alexander was born Aug. 22, 1902.

John Thomas Alexander was born Oct. 16, 1908.

Francis Winburn Alexander was born Jan. 9, 1911.

Virgil Carter Steed and James McLeod Steed were born May 1, 1937.

Anne Perry Patterson was born June 12, 1940.

### MARRIAGES

Nathan Bayles was married to Hannah Middaugh March 4, 1820.

Phoebe Bayles was married to John Desha Sept. 6, 1838.

Mary E. Bayles was married to John S. Grimes Feb. 3, 1842.

Nancy Cogswell Bayles was married to Socrates Bowles Nov. 18, 1851.

Nathan Bayles was married to Rebecca Roseberry July 22, 1852.

Mary E. Grimes married J. W. Prescott Nov. 16, 1875.

Jessie Bowles was married to Hannah Perkins in Gouchland Co., Va. March 1713.

Robert Letcher Bowles married Ann Forman in Bourbon County, Ky. (Above was father of Socrates Bowles.)

Mary Elizabeth Bowles (daughter of Socrates Bowles) was married to Hiram Winburn Alexander, Oct. 19, 1870.

James McLeod and Nancy Winburn Alexander (daughter of Hiram Winburn Alexander) were married Nov. 2, 1899.

John Madison Alexander (son of H. W. Alexander) married Sarah Catharine Cropp Nov. 27, 1901.

Thomas M. Alexander (2nd son of H. W. Alexander) married Mary Estelle Burgess Oct. 15, 1904.

Elizabeth Buckner Alexander (2nd daughter) married James Iran Patterson June 5, 1912.

Elizabeth Jean McLeod married Virgil Carter Steed April 21, 1930.

James Alexander Patterson married Ann Payne Perry Jan. 15, 1938.

## DEATHS

Nathan Bayles, Sr., died July 9, 1848.

Hannah M. Bayles, died April 4, 1839.

Elizabeth Bayles, died July 9, 1848.

Mary Bayles, died Sept. 19, 1824.

Nathan Bayles, Jr., died Nov. 14, 1855.

Nancy Cogswell Bowles, died April 11, 1865.

Hannah M. Bayles, died Sept. 16, 1872.

Daniel Bayles, died April 10, 1886.

Socrates Bowles, died March 30, 1897.

Thomas P. Bowles (son of Socrates) died Jan. 17, 1886.

Robert Bowles, died October 25, 1892.

Mary E. Prescott, died March 30, 1908.

Nathan B. Bowles, died Sept. 21, 1913.

Hiram Winburn Alexander, died Feb. 24, 1903.

Mary Elizabeth Alexander, died June 5, 1927.

Thomas Mayhen Alexander, died Oct. 6, 1908. .

Elizabeth Buckner Alexander Patterson, died April 7, 1931.

James McLeod, died Feb. 6, 1932.

James I. Patterson, died April 21, 1925.

John Madison Alexander, died Oct. 11, 1935.

## BOURLAND-REESE

### CHRISTIAN-TRIGG-MARSHALL-CALLOWAY COUNTIES

(Descent from EARLE: John; Samuel I; Samuel II; Samuel III; BAYLIS, NANCY EARLE REESE, whose daughters, Damaris and Mary, both married Bourland)

### BOURLAND

(Furnished by Mrs. Shelton Lamar (Rebecca Waitt) Washington, D. C.)

### CENSUS OF 1840—TRIGG COUNTY

Page 296—Slaton Bourland: 1 male under 5; 2 males 5-10; 1 male 10-15; 1 male 20-30; 1 male 40-50; 2 females under 5; 1 female 5-10; 1 female 15-20; 1 female 20-30.

Page 296—Tandy Bourland: 1 male 15-20; 1 female 20-30.

Page 298—Moses McWaters, Sr.: 1 male 15-20; 1 male 30-40; 1 male 60-70.

Page 298—Wyatte McWaters: 1 male 20-30; 1 female under 5; 1 female 10-15.

Page 298—Hugh McWaters: 1 male 70-80; 1 female 10-15; 1 female 60-70.

Page 301—John Ford: 1 male under 5; 1 male 20-30; 1 female under 5: 1 female 10-15: 1 female 20-30.

Page 288—Joseph B. Reese: 1 male 10-15; 1 male 15-20; 1 male 40-50: 1 female under 5; 1 female 5-10; 1 female 30-40.

Page 290—Will Fowler: 1 male under 5; 2 males 5-10; 1 male 30-40: 1 female under 5; 1 female 20-30.

Page 290—Andrew K. Bourland: 1 male 30-40; 1 female 5-10; 1 female 10-15; 1 female 30-40.

Page 290—Thomas Wadlington: 1 male under 5; 1 male 5-10; 1 male 40-50; 1 female under 5; 2 females 10-15; 1 female 20-30.

Page 291—David Jennings: 2 males under 5; 1 male 40-50; 1 female 5-10; 3 females 10-15; 2 females 15-20; 1 female 20-30; 1 female 40-50.

Page 293—Will McWaters: 1 male under 5; 1 male 5-10; 2 males 10-15; 1 male 40-50; 2 females under 5; 1 female 20-30.

Page 285—Daniel Ford: 1 male 50-60; 1 male 70-80; 2 females 5-10; 1 female 10-15; 1 female 15-20; 1 female 40-50.

Page 293—J. C. Wadlington: 1 male 30-40; 1 female 20-30.

Page 294—Samuel McWaters: 1 male 20-30; 1 female 15-20.

Page 295—James Baylis: 2 males 15-20; 1 male 30-40; 1 female 10-15; 1 female 30-40.

Page 278—Moses McWaters: 2 males 15-30; 1 male 30-40; 1 female 5-10; 1 female 10-15.

Page 279—Thomas Wadlington: 1 male 5-10; 2 males 20-30; 1 male 30-40; 1 male 50-60; 1 female under 5; 1 female 20-30; 1 female 30-40.

Page 279—Anthony Wadlington: 1 male 20-30; 1 female under 5; 1 female 20-30.

Page 283—James M. Ford: 1 male 5-10; 1 male 40-50; 1 female 5-10; 2 females 10-15; 1 female 20-30.

Page 285—Mordecai Ford: 1 male 15-20; 1 male 60-70; 2 females 10-15; 1 female 50-60.

## TRIGG COUNTY CENSUS, 1850

Page 297—Elizabeth Jennings, 52, b. Tenn. Rachel Jennings, 31, b. Ky. Melisha Boaz, 24, b. Ky. Eliz. Jennings, 21; Ann (?) E. Jennings, 19, f.; Rebecca Jennings, 16; John Jennings, 13; Peter Jennings, 11; Robert Boaz, 6.

Page 312—Thomas Theron Reese, 23, b. Carolina, farmer.

Page 312—Joseph B. Reese, 50, b. Carolina; Mariam C. Reese, 18, b. Ky.; Zaria A. Reese, 12, b. Ky.; Asphasia Reese, 10, b. Ky.

Page 313—Thomas Wadlington, Jr., 30, b. Ky.; Phoebe Wadlington, 36, b. Ky.; Mary Wadlington, 9, b. Ky.

Page 313—Thomas Wadlington, Sr., 68, b. N. C.; Rhoda Wadlington, 47, b. Va.; Wm. B. Wadlington, 17; Sebra Wadlington, 14; Eveline Ross, 40; Mary Ross, 16; O. G. McGinnis, 24.

Page 320—William Fowler, 43, b. S. C.; Nancy Fowler, 38, b. Ky.; James C. Fowler, 18; West Fowler, 16; Martha E. Fowler, 13; Wm. B. Fowler, 10; Sarah D. Fowler, 6; David R. Fowler, 5; John B. Fowler, 2.

Page 322—Andrew K. Bourland, 45, b. Ky.; Medis Bourland, 43, b. Tenn.; Sarah Bourland, 20; Rebecca F. Bourland, 19; Samuel Bourland, 21.

Page 323—Albartis Prince, 51, farmer, b. Ky.; Mary Prince, 50; Thomas H. Prince, 19; Prudence Prince, 12; Mary Prince, 10; Enoch Prince, 8.

Page 326—Eliza Wadlington, 22, b. Ky. in house with the Mitchells.

Page 326—Thomas Wadlington, 52; Frewy Wadlington, 39; Celia Wadlington, 15; Felix Wadlington, 16; Wayman Wadlington, 10; Ann Wadlington, 8; Mark Wadlington, 6; Lee B. Wadlington, 1; Miriam Wadlington, 30, b. Ky., in house with Saxon.

Page 329—Ferdinand Wadlington, 32; Lerlarh (?) Wadlington, 24; Anthony Wadlington, 2; Mary F. Wadlington, 3 months.

Page 350—Alfred Prince, b. Tenn., 23; Eliza Prince, b. Tenn., 23; Louisa Prince, 4, b. Ky.; America J. Prince, 2, b. Ky.

## BOURLAND

By Mrs. Shelton Lamar (Rebecca Waitt)

### CALLOWAY COUNTY CENSUS RECORDS, 1840

Page 67—Wm. Bourland: 1 m. 5-10; 1 m. 30-40; 1 f. under 5; 1 f. 5-10; 1 f. 10-15; 1 f. 30-40.

Page 69—James Bourland: 1 m. 5-10; 1 m. 10-15; 1 m. 15-20; 1 m. 40-50; 1 f. under 5; 1 f. 10-15; 1 f. 30-40.

Page 67—Samuel U. Bourland: 2 m. under 5; 1 m. 5-10; 1 m. 20-30; 2 f. 5-10; 1 f. 20-30.

Page 79—Dabney Bourland: 1 m. 10-15; 1 m. 40-50; 1 f. 5-10; 1 f. 30-40.

Page 79—Joseph Bourland: 1 m. under 5; 1 m. 5-10; 2 m. 10-15; 1 m. 40-50; 1 f. under 5; 1 f. 10-15; 1 f. 15-20; 1 f. 30-40.

Page 78—Sarah Bourland: 1 m. under 5; 1 m. 5-10; 1 m. 15-20; 1 f. 10-15; 1 f. 15-20; 1 f. 40-50.

### CALLOWAY COUNTY CENSUS, 1850

Page 862—B. Bourland, 31, b. Ky.; Nancy L. Bourland, 35, b. Ky.; James B. Bourland, 9; Wm. S. Bourland, 6; Elia C. Bourland, 4; Sara Ann, 1; James M. Bourland, 18.

Page 861—Slaton Bourland, 57, b. S. C.; Eliza, 34, b. Ky.; Andrew Bourland, 15; Evaline Bourland, 13; Mary H. Bourland, 11; Jno. R. Bourland, 9.

Page ...—Wm. T. Bourland, 31, b. Ky.; Lydia Bourland, 34; Wm. S. Bourland, 9; H. M. Bourland, 7 (male); C. G. Bourland, male, 5; Susan C. Bourland, 2; Harriet Bourland, 1; Sarah Ann Price, 15.

### CALLOWAY COUNTY CENSUS, 1870

Baylos E. Bourland, age 52, male; Nancy L. Bourland, 54; Celia C. Bourland, 23; Sarah A. Bourland, 29; Mary E. Bourland, 19; Joseph Rodgers, 11, b. Tenn.; Wm. S. Bourland, 26, saddle manufacturer; Mary E. Bourland, 25, wife.

## MARSHALL COUNTY CENSUS, 1850

James Bourland, 58, b. S. C., wheelwright; Hester Bourland, 48; James E. Bourland, 17, b. Ky.; Elizabeth A. Bourland, 17; Miles B. Bourland, 9.

Joseph Bourland, 53, b. S. C., blind; Susanna M. Bourland, 45; Reuben W. Bourland, 24; Wm. M. Bourland, 22; Andrew J. Bourland, 21; Newton J. Bourland, 11; Mary B. Bourland, 18; Luisa E. Bourland, 13; Lucy T. Bourland, 9.

## MARSHALL COUNTY CENSUS, 1860

J. Bourland, 68, b. S. C.; H. A. Bourland, 58, b. S. C.; M. B. Bourland, 20, male, b. Ky.

## BOURLAND-REESE (Christian Co., later Trigg)

### By Mrs. Ila Earle Fowler

Deed Book H., p. 249.—1817, 11/28-1818, 11/2.—Ephraim Reese and wife, Nancy, to James Lindsay, $1,300, land on Little R., S. side of "large spring about ¾ miles above the mill," crossing the river. Wit. Samuel Northington; Wm. Northington.

Deed Book I, p. 347—Archibald Reese to John Davis.

Deed Book I, p. 360—Otway C. Reese to John Davis.

Deed Book I, p. 379—Willis J. L. Reese to John Davis.

Deed Book I, p. 421, 9/19/1818.—Samuel Reese of Dallas county, Ala., to Michael Northington, $1,800, 360 A., Little R. part of 400 A. survey made for Reese by virtue of a Christian Co., court cert. 2384. Mentions Northington's line. wit. James Coleman, J. W. Cooke.

Deed Book F, p. 120, 2/1/1816.—Edward Hampton Reese and wife, Catherine, to Laban Taylor Rascoe, for $150, 170 A. on Little R., mentions corner of Samuel Earle's survey. wit. Michael Northington, Ephraim Reese.

Book A—Will book, Christian county, 1808.—p. 165: Ephraim Reese attested will of Joseph Willbanks, July Court, Christian county, in 1804 he was one of the appraisers of the estate of Thomas Prince Earle.

## FROM MARRIAGES, CHRISTIAN CO., KY.

1/13/1816.—Damaris Reese, daughter of Capt. Ephraim Reese md. Andrew Bolling, Edward E. Reese, bondsman.

10/10/1815.—Polly C. Reese, daughter of Ephraim Reese, md. Slayter C. Bowlen, return made by Dudley Williams. In another entry, Slayton C. Bourland md. Polley C. Reese, daughter of Ephraim Reese, Edw. H. Torrance, bondsman, date 10/9/1815.

4/29/1810.—Willis Millbanks (or Willbanks ?) md. Mariam Reese, Laban Rascoe bondsman, father Ephraim Reese.

1/17/1804.—Laban Rascoe md. Sally Reese; Jesse Fort, minister. (This minister md. a cousin of the bride, daughter of William Prince of Caldwell county.)

1. Edwin Earle Bourland, md. Cara Thornton: their children: (1) Pauline Bourland md. (2) Laurette Bourland md. Graves Sledd; (3) Leon Bourland; (4) Marjorie Bourland.
2. Effie Bourland md. T. E. Garland; their children: (1) Clifford Garland, md., had one son; (2) Bernie Bourland md. Eugene Moore, had 1 daughter; two sons, Joe Moore and Jean Moore; (3) Edwin Garland, md. Fern .........., Tommy Garland; (4) Ford Garland, md ........
3. Willie Queen Bourland, still living in Marshall co. Ky., md. Robert Lee Shemwell who died Benton, Ky., April 1919. Their children: (1) Mary md. John A. Harton, lives in Arlington, Va., children, Mary, Margaret and John Harton; (2) Helen, md., lives in Ky.; dau. Rebecca and Dixie. (3) Adeline Shemwell unmarried works for U. S. in Washington, D. C.; (4) Julia Garland md. John Cotton, dau. Donna, living in Arlington, Va. (5) Robert Lee Shemwell, Jr. lives in Wash., md. Zella Gray Bacon, dau. Rilla Bacon. (6) Dorothy Shemwell, lives Marshall county, Ky., md. V. G. Wagoner; sons Joe and Bob Wagoner. (7) Albert Shemwell, lives in Marshall co., Ky. (8) Elizabeth Shemwell.

## BOURLAND (variously spelled)

(Copied by Mrs. Ila Earle Fowler)

### CALLOWAY COUNTY, KY., MARRIAGES

1825: Jan. 31, Miles Bourland to Artinecy Bourland, consent of father, witnesses: Francis H. Clayton, John S. Clayton.

1827: Feb. 2, Andrew Gillmore to Seabury Bourland, consent of Benj. Bourland, father; wit.: John M. Bourland.

1827: Mch. 21, Erasmus G. Bearden to Dicey Bourland, father Benj. Bourland, witnesses: John M. Bourland, John Griffin.

1828: June 23, Isaac Floyd to Hulda Bourland, consent of father (not named) witness, Thos. Bourland.

1828: Oct. 25, Wm. Duncan to Sarah Bourland, R. Bourland father, wit. Thurston Grubbs.

1830: Jan. 6, Samuel M. Bourland to Lucinda Wright, consent of father, witness, Francis H. Clayton.

1832: Ap. 16, Wm McLean to Harriet H. H. Bourland, father Slaton Bourland, witness: Ephraim T. Rees.

1834: Mch. 24, Slaton Bourland to Eliza Burnham, father Fed Burnham, witness, McLean.

1835: Asa Collie to Maria L. Bourland, consent of mother, witnesses: J. Copeland, Thruston Grubbs, latter the minister.

1835: March 20, James Shearing to Matilda Bourland, consent mother: witness: Jos. Shearing.

1841: Aug. 3, Edmund Holloway to Susan Bourland, both of age, solemnized by H. Darnell.

1843: Sept. 21, Jas. R. Bourland to Mary Grubbs, consent of mother, sol. by Ephraim Owings, M.G.

1845: Thos. H. McQuistons to Martha Ann Stilly.

1841: Dec. 4, Hiram C. Bourland, to Urrisa Candue Stice, consent of father verbally, sol. by H. Gilbert.

## CALLOWAY COUNTY DEEDS

1834: Bourland & Waddy from G. W. Frazer, town lot, $317.14, Dec. 9
B, 2
1833:Dec. 24, Slaton Bourland to Peter Kesniger, land $160.........B, 23
1837: Jan. 15, James Bourland from Levi Strand, $103, land...... C. 80
1836: Mch. 4, R. Bourland to Trustees M. E. Church, land, $15.... B. 396
1836: Mch. 30, Ben Bourland to J. F. Dunn, land, $250........... B. 431
1836: Oct., S. Bourland to E. Grady, land, $1,000................ C. 16
1839: Nov. 25, D. B. Bourland from Isaac Floyd, land, $100....... C. 436
1840: May 12, D. B. Bourland from Wm. Rice, land.............. D. 42
1838: Mch. 15, James Bourland to Thos. Watson, land, $212.50.... C. 113
1840: Sept. 8, D. B. Bourland to Jas. Clark, land, $850........... C. 187
1839: Dec. 5, Hiram Bourland to W. J. Clark, land, $100......... C. 442
1840: Mar. 22, D. B. Bourland, from Thos. Dark, land $50.83-¾... D. 231
1850: Apr. 15, B. E. Bourland to Duncan & Dailey, lot, $90....... G. 1
(Baylis Earle B.)
1840: April 2, S. Bourland from H. W. Pool's heirs by land com'r. F. 473
1852: B. E. Bourland from B. P. Pool, land, $400................ G. 543
1854: S. Bourland, from H. P. Pool, com'r, $500 (Jan. 9)......... G. 244
1854: Oct. 9, Slaton Bourland to A. J. Beale, land, $250......... H. 501
1854: May 13, I. G. Bourland to T. C. Wilson, land, $50.......... H. 383
1856: Jan. 28, I. G. Bourland to J. W. McCord, land, $300........ J. 179
1859: Ap. 16, B. E. Bourland to G. A. C. Holt, lot, $185.......... K. 485
1860: Feb. 4, B. E. Bourland to B. Harding and J. Z. Sledd, town
lots L. 40
1823: Reuben E. Bourland a minister solemnizing mrgs. in Calloway Co.

## MARRIAGES

1825, Aug. 16, Francis H. Clayton to Elizabeth Bourland, father's consent,
by A. H. Davis, J. P. wit. Jno. Bourland, Miles Bourland.
1823: Mch. 31, Hiram Perkins to Elizabeth Bourland, consent of Jacob
Bourland.

## BROWNFIELD-BRUMFIELD

(Contributed by Mrs. Ila Earle Fowler)

These two names have been so often confused in copying Hardin county and Larue county records, by being used one for the other that care is necessary to make the distinction. There were families of both names and it is sometimes necessary to consult the original records.

(The following may be found in Jillson's Land Grant Index: Edward; William; James; Job; John.)

### Larue County Census, 1850, Brownfield.

George W. Brownfield, 33, male, blacksmith; M. J. Brownfield, 29, female; Allen Newton, 18, male; Charles Hagan, 17, male; J. F. Brownfield, 9, male; Isabelle Brownfield, 7, female; .... M. Brownfield, 4, male; James Brownfield, 1, male; ....................

Jefferson Brownfield, 35, male; Nancy Brownfield, 24, female; Empson Brownfield, 38, male; Lucinda Brownfield, 39, female; C. A. Brownfield,

33, male; Wm. Brownfield, 20, male; Henry Brownfield, 23, male; Martha Brownfield, 23, female; George Brownfield, 16, male; .......... Brownfield, 12, male; Sarah Brownfield, 10, female; Jacob Ashcraft, 68, male.

### Page 655

### Brownfield, Larue County Census, 1850—p. 670-1

John Brownfield, 36, farmer; E /or/H.A./ Brownfield, female, 34; M. C. Brownfield, 22, female; ..............; Isaac Ashcraft, 60.

### p. 657

John Brownfield, 36; Sarah Brownfield, 32, female; Jane Brownfield, 24, female; M.    Brownfield, 15, female; John F. Brownfield, 14, male; Sarah Brownfield, 10, female; Fielding Brownfield, 8, male; Rosetta Brownfield, (25?) female; L.    Brownfield, 20 or 2, female; S. E. Brownfield, 17 / or 12/ female.

### 1814 Tax Lists: Hardin County

George Brownfield, 1 male, 3 horses, $240
Wm. Brownfield, 250 acres, Nolin creek, 4 horses, 1 white male, $1,080
Wm. Brownfield, 1 wh. male, 6 horses, $200
Wm. Brownfield, 300 acres, Nolin creek, surveyed for Polly Martin,
          6 horses, $300
          545 acres, surveyed for Peter Body
          400 acres, Rolling Fork
Charles Brownfield, 20 acres 3rd rate land
1815..Wm. Brownfield, 400 acres Rolling Fork; 500 Nolin creek; (Huston's C); 6 horses, $2,375

### Hardin County Tax Lists, 1815

Philip Creel, 230 acres 3rd rate land on Nolin creek; John Creel; Jacob
          Creel; Henry Creel, 100 acres 3rd rate, Nolin & Green
George Brownfield, 100 acres 3rd rate, Nolin & Green
Wm. Brownfield, Sr., 254 acres 3rd rate land, 4 horses
Wm. Brownfield, Jr., 5 horses
Charles Brownfield, 1,050 acres Otter creek, 1 horse
Wm. Brownfield, 400 acres, Rolling Fork, survey Brown, 500 acres on
          Nolin, survey Martin.
1811
Wm. Brownfield, 6 horses; Richard Brownfield, 140 acres 3rd rate on
          Cedar creek, 7 horses.
Richard and Elijah Crail

### Nelson County Tax Lists, 1793:

Richard Brownfield, 174 acres; Edward Brownfield 200 acres; William
          Brownfield, ............
Benjamin Fowler listed.
From a mss. found in bundle of old papers received in Historical Society at Frankfort from estate of George D. Todd, dec'd. (Mrs. Cannon says Geo. D. Todd died in the 1890s.) The paper is yellow and old, gives

Brownfield history in Pennsylvania, traced to Ireland and one who was in Cromwell's Horse troops, later came to America, to Fayette Co., Pa. Charles and Betsey Brownfield in 1769 settled on the Redstone. They had 8 sons and 1 daughter: (Betsey Bird of Winchester, Va.)

Edward; Charles, Jr.; Robert; Thomas;

Empson; Richard; William; Benjamin; Sally. Of these Wm. and Richard came to Ky., according to this mss.
Brownfield—

Hardin county, Ky. marriages:

4/12/1797/James Fowler and Mary Shakles
5/22/1816/David Herndon and Polly Moreman, daughter of Jesse
12/2/1819/Thomas Lincoln and Mrs. Sarah Johnson, George L. Rogers
9/3/1803/George Brownfield and Nelly Ashcraft, also 3/5/1803 (return of license)
12/13/1806/George Brownfield and Catherine Husk, return 12/21/1806
5/5/1803/James Brownfield and Mrs. Sally Pirtle
Larue County, Tax list: 1850
John Brownfield, 1 white voter, 135 acres @ $800; 120 acres @ $480; 1 wh. m.; 1 wh. m. over 20; 9 cattle; 10 worth over $50; 3 children between 5 and 15; $1,550.
John Brownfield, no land, no children
Field Brownfield, no land
Henry Brownfield, 200 acres, one child
Reuben Brownfield, no land, one child, lot in Hodgenville
Thomas Brownfield, no land, no children
Empson Brownfield, no land, no children
George Brownfield, 800 acres on S. Fork, 3 children, horse and cattle, $4,400
Jeff Brownfield, no land, no children
Another list, Geo. W. Brownfield, 103 acres, S. Fork, one child
Census Larue county, 1850:
Thomas J. Brownfield, 23, clerk;
Reuben Brownfield, 26, tailor;
E. A. Brownfield, 3;
Wm. I. Brownfield, 3;
....B/Brownfield, female, 2;
J. J. Brownfield, 1;
Reuben Brownfield, 40;
(R) A Brownfield, 27, female;
Wm. I. Brownfield, 2.

. . . . . . . . . . . .

(William Brownfield was ensign in Clark's Illinois Regiment, in 1781, T-DV2 P. 501)

From Harrodsburg Order Book, of 1799-1814, p. 71.—James Brownfield had land adjoining John Berry, John Shelby and Andrew Patterson.
p. 77.—Richard Berry took up 455½ acres of land on warrant 13803, adjoined his survey of 200 acres, Doran's line mentioned.

From Ky. Vital Statistics cards
Larue county

Births: Emmie E. Bennifield, born 6/10/1857, father James Bennifield; mother, Elizabeth H. Pryor.

Henry Bennifield, b. 2/2/1854, father Henry Bennifield; mother, Eunice Bryant.

Jesse R. Bennifield, b. 9/18/1877; father, J. C. Bennifield, mother, Mary Howell.

John C. Bennifield, b. 1/16/1852, father Henry Bennifield, mother Eunice Bryant.

Mary C. Bennifield, b. 6/7/1851; father D. I. Bennifield; mother, Margaret Reed.

Hensley Bennifield, b. 10/28/1859; father, D. T. Bennifield; mother, Margaret L. Reed

Joel Washington Bennifield, b. 10/10/18....; father, James S. Bennifield; mother, Elizabeth Puryear.

George Ellis Brownfield, b. 3/15/1857; father, Empson Brownfield; mother, Elizabeth E. Crop.

male child, b. 11/9/1853; father John Brownfield; mother, Alcy Ann Brown.

Benton F. Brownfield, b. 10/16/1854; father, Thomas J. Brownfield; mother, Mary E. Newton.

Anna E. Brownfield, b. 7/28/1862; father Thos. J. Brownfield; mother Mary E. Newton.

Susan C. Brownfield, b. 12/2/1854; father, Jefferson Brownfield; mother, Martha Kirkpatrick.

Mary C. Brownfield, b. 9/2/1854; father R. Brownfield; mother, Elizabeth J. Brownfield.

........ Brownfield, b. 9/2/1859; father, George W. Brownfield; mother, not given.

Martha Brownfield, b. 6/4/1862; father, James S. Brownfield; mother, Elizabeth Pryor.

Wm. P. Bennifield, b. 2/3/1853; father Daniel Bennifield; mother, Margaret E. Reade.

Edward Brownfield, b. 7/31/1859; father, Henry Brownfield; mother, ........Thompson.

Edmond Bramfield, b. 7/11/1859; father, John Brownfield; mother, ........Brawn.

Edwine Brownfield, b. 8/2/1857; father, Jeff Brownfield; mother, Martha Kirkpatrick.

A. A. Bunnifields, b. 11/13/1862; father, ........Bunifields; mother, Mary J. Skaggs.

George Bunifield, b. 10/23/1860; father, Henry Bunnifield; mother Narcissa Henderson.

Brownfield, Fielding L., b 3/22/1859; father, George W. Brownfield; mother, Mary J. Hogan.

Perlina Brownfield, b. 6/15/1859; father, Empson Brownfield; mother, ........Crop.

Marshall county births: J. F. Brumfield, b. 9/24/1877; father, J. F. Brumfield; mother, E. C. Cabbell. (This should be John Cabell Brownfield, b. father, John Franklin Brownfield; mother, Eliza C. Cabbell.)

Larue.—Bennifield, Miss E. (?); b. 5/16/1857; father, Alex Bennifield; mother, Mary J. Skaggs.

Brownfield Deaths: Susan Brownfield, 20 days old, daughter of Jeff and Martha Brownfield. (no date copied)

Elizabeth Brownfield, 27 years old, 1857; child bed fever; b. Green Co., daughter of E. and Mary Thompson.

James Brownfield, son of George and Mary Brownfield, 8 years. no date copied.

Elizabeth Brownfield, 1 year; daughter of Jas. and E. Brownfield. (no date copied.)

Sally Brownfield, 60 years, b. East Tenn., daughter of Louis and Nancy Tadlock. (no date copied)  All these vital statistics dates of Ky., except a few, are between 1850 and 1862.

1830—George Brownfield to Chas. C. Beatty          Deed Book M 95
Charles Brownfield to George Brownfield, shares of the following heirs mentioned:  Harriet Brownfield; Hays Brownfield; Patton Brownfield; Robert Brownfield; Simpson Brownfield; Jane Brownfield; Sarah Brownfield; Ann Brownfield; Theron Brownfield— Page 384, Book 1817-1835.

## WILLS

Nancy Ashcraft to son, Jacob, all goods; grand-daughter, Elizabeth, daughter of Andrew Walters mentioned.
Witnesses:    John Ashcraft; Elisha Adams;
Joseph Kirkpatrick.

Will Book B. Page 144, April 1, 1812
Pro. April 18, 1829

Thomas Brownfield, wife Rebecca; sons: Richard, having had a portion of land entailed to him by his grandfather, Richard Brown; Charles Brownfield, "land willed to me by my father, Charles Brownfield"; mentions "other heirs." June 20, 1840. Exec. wife, Rebecca Brownfield; Alexander Brownfield; N. R. Walker, Book                                                                    E 107

Will Book D, Page 260, Richard Brownfield, grand-daughter, Fanny Brownfield; wife Mary Brownfield; oldest son, James Brownfield; other children: Patterson Brownfield; Samuel H. Brownfield; Thomas Brownfield; Casander Brownfield; William Brownfield, July 13, 1834.

Will Book C—Isham Enlow, youngest daughter, Malvina Enlow, under 21.  Children mentioned:  Abraham Enlow; Thomas Brooks; Polly; Lyda; Bedsy; Malvina.
Witnesses:    James Wallace, Jacob Ashcraft,
Taylor Bard; Thos. W. Rathbone.

### Feb. 12, 1816

Enoch Berry, Will Book A, Page 310, wife, Elizabeth; children, Benjamin, Samuel, Nancy, Peggy, Betsey. Sole executor Wm.

Ventrees—13 Aug. 1807, Pro. 8 Aug. 1808
Jediah Ashcraft, Will Book B, Page 8. Wife, Nancy; children; Nancy, John, Nelly, Jacob. Wife executrix.

April 19, 1793
Pro.————————————

*Chas. Brownfield* of George Township, Fayette Co. Penn., wife Ruth Brownfield yearly rents from all lands east of Morgantown Road, whereon I now reside, and all tracts adjoining thereto.

Son, Thos. Brownfield, tract in Hardin Co., Ky., purchased of Walter Carlisle.

Son, Robt. Brownfield, rents from the place that Alex Brownfield now lives.

Son, Alexander Brownfield premises he now resides on, being the farm bought of the heirs of John Scacklet, together with all the land I bought of Jas. Page and Woodbridge.

Son, Zadoc Brownfield "to Creek to Caldwell's line; thence by Washington Reed's lot to the Haydon Town Road; thence along said road to the mouth of the lane; thence down said lane to the spring *drean;* thence down *drean* to the creek at mouth of spring *drean,* including the tanyardy; thence up the creek to beginning.

Son, Chas. Brownfield, the land *seuded* to me by Andrew M. C. Caven in Whatton Township, 200 acres and $200 in such movable property needed to improve the said land.

Daughter, Ruth Brownfield, her maintenance to be recd. out of the profits and rents of the lands her mother receives her dowry from.

Daughter, Mary Ann Evans, 10 acres of land to be run out of the meadow parallel to David Evans line to the post oak and rail fence on Moses line, and 5 acres timber land to be run from the creek to the *meader* and to join the lands. Mentions Dan. Rebekah Goff.

Son, Boerll Brownfield. Aug. 19, 1827.

Hardin County, Kentucky, Record—ELIZABETHTOWN

*Index to Deeds*

| | |
|---|---|
| 1816—Wm. Brownfield, Jr. to Wm. Brownfield, Sr. | E 518 |
| 1813—Richard Brownfield to Wm. Hicks | E 10 |
| 1813—Wm. Brownfield to Daniel Morgan—Bond | E 274 |
| 1818—Wm. Brownfield to John Ashcraft | G 31 |
| 1821—Wm. Brownfield to James Brown | H 98 |
| 1821—Wm. Brownfield to Wm. Cassna | H 166 |
| 1827—Richard Brownfield to David Carr | K 285 |
| 1837—Alfred Brownfield to Thos. Chilton—Mortgage | M 419 |

## CARSON FAMILY

York County, Penn.; Washington County, Va.
and Lincoln County, Kentucky
Furnished by Mrs. S. Peyton Welch

Bible-Records of Ransom Carson of Lincoln County, Ky.

Ransom Carson, born Mar. 30, 1816, died Dec. 10, 1886
Jaila Carson, born Sept. 29, 1811, died May 9, 1861
Mary Carson, born June 29, 1837
Sarah Catherine Carson, born Apr. 23, 1839
Cynthia Carson, born May, 1841, died Feb., 1890
Charles Carson, born May 10, 1843
Margaret Carson, born Sept. 29, 1845, died Nov. 20, 1869
Martha C. Carson, born Aug. 29, 1851, died Sept. 21, 1876
Willie Brown Carson, born July 25, 1863
Thomas M. Carson, born July 7, 1865
Lettie Carson, born Jan. 12, 1866
Marriages:
Ransom Carson married Miss Jaila H. Curtis, Sept. 15, 1836
Ransom Carson married 2nd Mrs. Sophia James, Aug. 14, 1862
Mary E. Carson, daughter of Ransom and Jaila Carson married Oct. 4, 1855, Simeon Hicks.
Sarah Catherine Carson, daughter of Ransom & Jaila H. Carson married Jan. 25, 1858, Samuel Rice Welch.
Margaret A. Carson, daughter of Ransom & Jaila H. Carson married Nov. 11, 1867, Chas. Rochester.
This old Bible was published in 1849 and has been handed down to Mrs. Allene Welch Myers, Springfield, Mo., the granddaughter of Ransom and Jaila H. Carson.

\*     \*     \*     \*     \*

Ransom Carson was one of twelve children, all of whom were born in Kentucky. His Will is found in Lincoln Co. Ky., Will Book 4, page 44, Written Nov. 1, 1884 and probated Jan., 1887. Ransom Carson was the son of David Carson, Jr. (b. Aug. 28, 1780 in Washington Co., Va., died 1844) and his wife Cynthia Meek, (born Aug. 10, 1783 in Washington Co., Va., died in Lincoln Co., Ky. on Jan. 26, 1850). David Carson, Jr., and Cynthia Meek were married at her father's home, Cedarville, Va., on Sept. 26, 1799 by Rev. Edward Crawford. She was the daughter of Maj. Samuel Meek, who served in the Virginia Legislature from 1797 to 1803 inclusive. He died July 9, 1812, aged 52 years. His wife Elizabeth Allen Meek died May 21, 1831, aged 70 years. Both are buried at Old Glade Spring, Va. Samuel and Elizabeth Allen Meek reared a large family at Cedarville, Va., and during the 40's they all sold out and emigrated to Kentucky, Tennessee and Missouri. David Carson, Jr., was the son of David Carson, Sr., and his wife, Elizabeth Dysart. He came to Washington Co., Va., in 1772 and died near Liberty Hall, Washington Co., Va. in 1803-4. He is buried in Old Moor Cemetery.

David Carson, Sr., (of age in 1762) was the son of Samuel Carson, who left will in York Co. Penn. Will Book A, page 216. He named three sons: David Carson of age, William Carson, a minor, and Samuel Carson, a minor. Executor, David Carson; Executrix, Jannet.

Ransom Carson and his wife Jaila H. Carson are buried in the Buffalo Cemetery at Stanford, Kentucky. Tombstones in good condition. Samuel R. Welch, born in Jessamine Co., Ky., June 10,1819 and died Oct. 31, 1883. He married Sarah Catherine Carson (b. 1839, died Sept. 27, 1925) and they are buried in the Nicholasville, Kentucky (Jessamine Co.) Cemetery. Their graves are well marked.

## CALDWELL

### Walter Caldwell of Bath County, Ky.
### Furnished by Mrs. S. Peyton Welch

Walter Caldwell, born in Virginia, Dec. 12, 1777, married in Bath County, Kentucky, Dec., 1799, Mary Breckenridge, born in Virginia, September 13, 1778. They removed to Ralls County, Missouri, where she died September 28, 1841, he surviving until May 16, 1842—Ref. William Clark Breckenridge—His Life Lineage and Writings"—Pub. by James Malcolm Breckenridge—1932, page 127.

Mary Breckenridge was a daughter of Robert Breckenridge and his wife Mary Doak of Montgomery County, Va., and Bath Co., Ky. Walter Caldwell and family left Bath Co., Ky., about 1827 and settled in New London, Mo., where he was Major of the Militia and County Judge for a number of years.

Children of Walter and Mary (Breckenridge) Caldwell:

1. Larue Caldwell, b. 12-12-1800, in Bath Co., Ky., d. 5-25-1879, in Ralls Co., Mo., married 6-25-1821, in Bath Co., Ky., John Helms, b. 5-19-1799, in Montgomery Co., Ky., d. 10-12-1870 in Ralls Co., Mo. They had seven children.

2. Green V. Caldwell, b. 1-15-1803, in Bath Co., Ky., settled in Ralls Co., Mo., and died there in 1831, married Mary Gray (dau. of Capt. Isaac Gray) b. 8-24-1808 in Bath Co., Ky., and died 1-5-1882 in Trimble Co., Ky. They had two daughters, Mary (Gray) Caldwell married 2nd Tabner Young.

3. James D. Caldwell, b. 11-8-1804 in Bath Co., Ky., died 6-7-1841, in Mo. He was a doctor. Married 1-1-1825 Eliza L. Briggs, born 11-18-1805, dau. of Ebenezer and Phoebe (Gilkey) Briggs. 8 children.

4. Samuel Kincade Caldwell, settled in Ralls Co., Mo., died 1868, married 1st 8-31-1830 in Mo. Barbara Briggs. Married 2nd 1-18-1842 Catherine Barkley, mother of his children. Married 3rd, 4-26-1863, Mary Ann Barkley, sister of Catherine.
5. William Y. Caldwell, settled in Lewis Co., Mo., died before 1887. Married Dec. 15, 1836, Mrs. Jane (Jamison) Fisher, d. 1890.
6. Robert Breckenridge Caldwell, settled in Ralls Co., Mo., born 3-12-1810, married 1st 6-3-1841, Rosanna Splawn, d. 1857. Mar. 2nd 6-15-1858 Catherine Floweree. Had issue.
7. John Preston Caldwell, settled in Lewis Co. Mo. born 3-17-1815 in Ky., died 1911 in Mo. married 2-2-1841 Elvira C. Reddish, (1823-1893). They had issue.
8. Matilda Ann Caldwell, b. 10-8-1813 in Bath Co. Ky. married Kemp Floweree. They settled in Ralls Co. Mo. and had one child, Daniel Floweree.
9. Mary Caldwell, b. 10-20-1818, in Bath Co. Ky. died 6-23-1876 in Pike Co. Mo. married her cousin Harmon Caldwell (1811-1898). They had three children. Harmon Caldwell was the grandson of William Caldwell and wife Elizabeth Kennedy of Bath Co. Ky.

## ABSTRACT OF DEED BOOK A—CHRISTIAN COUNTY, KENTUCKY

(Abstracted by Mrs. Ila Earle Fowler)

Pages 1-2. 6th July, 1797. Wm. Roberts of Shelby County, Ky., to Jonathan Logan of Christian County; for 96£ current money of Ky.; 135 A. patent of Mch. 18, 1797 on N. Fk. of W. Fk. of Red River. Mentions: Corner of Wm. Croghan's 2600 A. survey line of Vandew Vall's 207 A. survey. Wit: George Robinson, Robt. Logan, Dc. Logan, Matthew Logan.

Page 3. Sept 5, 1798. Robert Harrison to Brewer Reeves; Negro girl, age 13 Yrs.; for $300; name not given. Teste: Samuel Bradley.

Pages 4-5-6. Oct. 16, 1798. Deborah Ferguson, lately Deborah Dans, Exr. of Will of James Davis, dec'd., to Brewer Reeves, by power given in Will of s—d Davis 300 A. land, sold in lifetime to Brewer, and on which Brewer lived, 100£ pd. to Davis in lifetime, West Fork of Red River. Peter Ferguson, husband, gave his consent, and signed with her. Wit: Young Ewing, Samuel Hardin, Jesse Cornelius.

Pages 7-8-9. Oct. 24, 1799. Joseph Garrison, to son, Arter Garrison; for love & affection, one bright bay horse, 9 head of cattle, 2 breeding sows, 1 pot & 1 bake oven, 2 setts plow irons with other farming & cooker tools, 3 bedsteeds & furniture & all rest of household furniture, subject to a reasonable maintenance for self & wife during life. Wit: Jas. Garrison, John X Garrison, Isaac Stroud. Sig., Joseph Garrison, son.

Page 10. Dec. 14, 1799. John Cotton to Elizabeth Jones; 120 Spanish milled dollars; 9 head of hogs; household furniture of sd. John Cotton *containing* of beds, *puter,* crockery ware, knives and forks and also kitchen furniture *containing* of pots, kettles, ovens & also hoes, axes and plow. Teste, David Markey.

Pages 11-12-13. Dec. 10, 1799. Benj. Menees & Ann, wife, Robinson Co., Tennessee to Brewer Reeves; 50£, 50 A. survey date 21 June 1793 in district set apart for officers and Soldiers of Va. Line in Christian Co., on West Fk. Little River. Mentions: Mouth of Rains Lick Creek; head of the Spring. Teste: Saml Bradley, W. Z. Anderson (signed).

Page 14. John Clark & Benj. Clark; Bond of John Clark as Co. Crt. Clerk, to James Garrard, Esq. Gov. 1000£, July 16, 1799.

Pages 15-16-17. 21 Feb. 1800. Jacob McFaddin to Joshua *Caitz* 150 A. where sd. McFaddin lately lived. Mentions: where Jones line intersects McFaddins, Montgomery & Roberts survey. Wit: Young Ewing, Just*n* Cartwright, John Campbell, Matthew Adams.

Page 18. June 17, 1800. Samuel X Goodwin, goodwill & affection to niece Lear Goodwin & nephew John Griffith Goodwin, one cow & calf.

Page 19. David Brown, goodwill & affection to grand dau. Lydia Goodwin, feather bed & furniture, ½ doz. peuter plates, 1 dish; also to Nancy Goodwin, one 2 yr. old heifer; also to Lear Goodwin 1 feather bed & furniture, 1 Dutch oven, 2 iron potts, ½ doz. peuter plates, one peuter dish & Bason. Wit: Wm Henry, Samuel X Goodwin, Benj. Clark.

Pages 20-21-22. Elizabeth x Nishinger to (Aug. 1, 1800); Conrad Lear x (Planter), power atty.; especially to convey land in N. C. on Catawba R. which came to her by her bro. Christopher Nishinger, dec'd. Wit: M. Wilson, JP, Thos. Arthur, Abner Robinson.

Pages 23-25. Samuel Davis, Nov. 8, 1800. To Samuel Penick, 100 £, land in Warren Co., 100 A. being ½ of a settlement sight granted to Stephen Harding as his own headright, lying & being in the grove called the blackberry pond. Wit: Matthew Adams, John Campbell, Jane Davis relinquished her dower.

Page 26. Nov. 26, 1799. Robert Stevenson to Jacob McFaddin, one negro girl, Lucy. Att: Young Ewing. Joshua Caitz to Jacob McFaddin, one negro man named Tom, abt. 20 yrs old. Nov. 26, 1799.

Pages 27-29. Feb. 16, 1800. Jacob McFaddin to David McFaddin, of Montgomery Co., Tenn., $200, 100 acres, Lick Branch of West Fork of Red River, below the Big Crossing, pt. of Doraty Hunter's head right.

Page 30. Oct. 21, 1800. Thos. Morris to Chas. Grant, stock of 100 head of hogs or more, marked with 2 smooth crops & an under bit out of left ear & some few with only 1 crop out of left ear, 1 bay horse, 1 red cow & calf, 2 beds & what belongs to them, all household goods & farming tools & crop, $260.

Page 32. John Kuykendall & Joseph Kuykendall to Joshua Caits, negro boy Toney, Feb. 2, 1801. Wit: Young Ewing, John Clark.

Page 32. Silas McBee, Adm. John Clark, dec'd., to Young Ewing negro girl Peggy, $180, Feb. 2, 1801. Wit: John Clark, Joshua Caits. *Bill of Sale*

Page 33. Silas McBee, adm. John Clark, dec'd. sold to John Clark, negro girl Rachel, $196. Att: Young Ewing, Joshua Caitz. Feb. 2, 1801.

Page 34.   Dennis Sullivan to John Thompson, Sr., a bay gelding, Branded C T on buttock, 6 yrs old, now under attachment & $50. Nov. 27, 1800.   If horse not redeemed Bill of Sale void. Wit: John Thompson Sr., Jas. Thompson.

Page 35.   Wm. Dryden to Sally Easley, negro woman Rachel $200, Nov. 28, 1800.   Teste. Thos. Lester.

Page 36.   Brewer Reeves to John Irwin of Davidson Co. Tenn, negro man Stephen, abt. 20 yrs. old, 100£.   Aug. 30, 1798.   Wit: Young Ewing, Wm. Warring.

Page 37.   Sept. 22, 1800.   John North of Norfolk Co., Va. to Sally Ervine of Ch. Co., 37£, 32¼ A., N. Fk. of W. Fk. Red R, part of Military Claim of 369 A. in name of NORTH.   Wit: Young Ewing, John Campbell, Matthew Adams.

Page 39-51.   Husbands deed to Husbands, Emy Husbands of Henderson Co., relict of Herman Husbands, Sr., late of Summerset Co. Pa-; Wm Husbands, Christian Co-; David Sheaffer, Shelby Co- Ky. & Mary, wife, late Mary Husbands-; Peter Kimmel late of Summerset Co- Pa. in right of his wife Pheebe Husbands, dec'd.-; Evans Bennett of Henderson Co. in right of wife lately Emy Husbands-; Herman Husbands, Sr. & Jr.-; Coxes Crk. in Mileford Township (now Somerset Co., Pa.)   Warrant of Mch 1, 1775.   Wit: John Stump of Pa, Isaac Husbands; June 25, 1803.

Page 52-55.   Nov. 4, 1798.   James Wilson, to Young Ewing; John Irwin obtained a deed in equity against heirs of John Montgomery, dec'd; $376 and costs, at Court of I. Sessions, Logan Co.; David Caldwell, Clk. Logan; Jas. Wilson, Sheriff Ch. Co.   Wit: Wm Shannon, Wm Roberts; $1,100 A.

Page 56.   14 Feb. 1801.   Dorathy x Hunter, to Jacob McFaddin $200; 100 A. on Lick Branch of W. Fk. of Red R. below Big Crossing; part of Doraty Hunter's head right; Wit: David x McFaddin, John x Hunter.

Pages 59-60.   1802, Aug. 4.   James Davis, to Sam'l Hardin, $100; 100 A. part of a 1120 acre survey on W. Fk. Red River.   Corner Jas. Hicks survey.   Wit: John Campbell, Jos. Davis, Jas. Hicks.

Pages 61-62.   1802, Aug. 4.   Jas. Davis, to Absolom Hicks, $100, 100 A. pt. of 1120 acres on W. Fk. Red R; Wit: John Campbell, Sam'l Hardin, Joseph Davis.

Pages 63-65.   23 Oct. 1802.   James Davis to Jas. Hicks, $100, 100 A. pt of 1120 A. survey W. Fk. Red R; Matthew Adams, Absolom Hicks.

Pages 65-67.   June 15, 1803.   Sarah x Wallace of Henderson Co. Ky. to John Gordon, Patsy Gordon, Robert Gordon & Ambrose Gordon, heirs & legatees of Ambrose Gordon, dec'd. £ 150; 200 A. in Christian Co. on W. Fk. of Pond R; Wit: Lonza Martin (Louiza ?), Wm Gordon, John Wilson.

Page 68.   James Jeffrey, to Jesse Jeffrey, 1 negro man named Abraham abt 25 yrs old & 1 negro woman Suey, 45 yrs. $600; 8th Feb. 1803. Wit: Sam'l Hardin, Willis Hicks.

Page 69.  Mch 11, 1803.  Richard C. Anderson & Salley, wife, of Jefferson Co. Ky. to Wm Daniel $1500, land in Ch. Co., on W. Fk. of Red R; 400 A.  Mentions: Young Ewing's survey; 1100 A. survey of Shannon, Montgomery & Roberts.  Worden Pope, Clk. Jefferson.

Page 73.  Andrew Rogers, Appd. John Rogers Atty., to recover from Thos. P. Earle the deeds to 2 tracts, 23rd May, 1803.  Teste: John Mills, Asa Easter.

Page 74.  John Cotton Appts Samuel Earle true & lawful Atty., to recover 300 A. land, from State, all in Ky, and to deliver to Joseph Bonnds deed to tract on Little River whereon sd. Bonnds (Boonds) (Bounds?) lives; Teste: LLL Hawking, Adam Linn (Limn).

Page 76.  Dec. 22, 1803.  Joshua Cates to Dabney Finley $20, land on Dry Branch of W. Fk. of Red River, 75 A., An old Lick corner of a 200 A. survey of Jas. Armstrong's, 26th Dec. 1803.

Page 78.  Feb. 29th, 1801.  Minny x Farrs & John Portmann, Binds her children, Judy, George, Michael & Sarah Farrs to be learnt the common trade of farming, & the girls common housekeeping; board & lodging; humane treatment; Judy abt 11; George 7, Michael 5, Sarah 3; boys till 21; girls till 18.  Chas. Hamilton, John Portman.

Pages 79-80.  July 6, 1797.  William Roberts of Shelby Co. Ky. to John Corday for 60 £ 200 Acres, patent dated Mch 18, 1795; on Rienco lick creek, branch of N. Fk. of W. Fk.  Jonathan Logan, Geo. Robinson, Robt. A. Logan.

Page 81.  26th July 1803.  John Luttrell & Daniel Fristoe for 60 £; land on lick branch of W. Fk. of Rcd R. below Bigg Crossing; 100 A. pt. of Doraty Hunter's head right.

Page 83.  Sept. 14, 1803.  James Bone to Samuel Lewis & Azanah Bone, 500 £, a tract of Military land on Muddy R. near Logan C. H., 121 Acres, together with a water grist mill & saw mill, Corner to Wilson; Sharpshin.  Teste: Jas. Campbell, Lewis Cornelius, Joseph Armstrong.

Page 85.  9th Feb. 1803.  Wm Davis to Joshua Cates.  Wit: John Clark, George Brown; sold to him; Cates turned over his Warrant as follows: Georgia: Agreeable to an Act of the General Assembly passed the 23rd day of October 1787 for the raising of State troops, Joshua Cates having enlisted himself a soldier in Capt. Bacon's Co. & well & truly served the time of his enlistment he is hereby discharged & for his Services aforesaid is justly entitled to six hundred & forty acres of land to be obtained in the first purchase made by the Legislature. Given under my hand at office this 8th day of April, 1791.

Page 86.  Oct. 30, 1800.  George Wilson Humphreys of Pickering Co. Miss. Tenn appt's. David Smith of Christian Co. atty. in fact for the sale of 500 Acres of land in Hardin Co. Ky. on Buffalo Crk.  Wit: Wm Cavenaugh, John Thompson, Polly Dillingham.

Page 88.  9th June 1803.  Samuel Smyley of Nelson Co. Ky. to David Young of Same; for $300; 100 Acres, survey date 15th July 1799; Christian Co. on Little R. & granted to Smyley (Similey) by Gov. Garrard.  Wm Rogers, Jno. Campbell.  Teste: Ben Grayson, Wm A. Rogers, J. Lewis, J. P. S. C. Nelson Co.

Page 92. 22 Sept. 1803. Ferdinand Wadlington, planter, to Thos. Wadlington, planter, for $500, 200 A. on Little R, on both sides. Mentions Dunscombe's Line.

Page 95. Aug. 9, 1902. Jacob McFaddin to John Luttrell £60; Lick Branch, W. Fk. of Red R, below Big Crossing, pt. Doraty Hunter's head right, 100 A. M. or L.

Pages 96-97. Thomas x Parker, for goodwill and esteem to son Joseph Parker, negro wench, Jenny, & boy named Tolliver, 12th July 1803. Wit: Wm. Stroud, Sally x Stroud, Valentine Rachels.

Page 98. 18th Nov. 1799. Tucker M. Woodson & Patsy, his wife, to Golson Stepp of Lincoln Co. Ky. £400, land on West Fk.

Page 100. May 13, 1801. Martha Reeves & Samuel Bradley, Adm. Brewer Reeves, to Hananiah Davis & Azariah Davis & James Dunn Davis, 50 A. on W. Fk.; a contract for mill. Wit: David Stuart, John Stuart, John Wilson.

Page 104. James Coleman mortgaged to David Mackey, Robert Fryatt's headright of 200 A. on both sides Little R, near mouth of Casey's Crk. Wit: Thos. Isbells, Nov. Term 1803.

Page 105. John Dempsey, power of Atty. to Ephriam Reese. Wit: Wm Pyle, John Campbell, 10th June 1802.

Page 106. 2nd Jan. 1804. Richard Taylor & Sarah his wife of Jefferson Co., Ky. to Robert Abernathe of same, £ 750; 1,000 acres land; the other 430 pt. in name of Wm. Roberts, assignee of Gabriel Long, & being in part set apt. Etc., middle Fk. Little River, Mth. of Barren Fk. Worden Pope, Clk., Jefferson Co.

Page 107. Robert x Wyatt relinquished title to his warrant, June 10, 1804.

Page 111. Feb. 14, 1801. John and Zechariah Johnson, exrs. of Zechariah Johnson, of Rockbridge Co. Va. to Robert McKinsey (or McChesney) of Rockbridge, £500, a tract of survey, date of 7th Nov. 1797; Pat. 27 May 1799. Mentions: Marks on trees: M. S. and G. Bell & R. Nelson; month of a Spring Branch, West Fk. Red R, where the Carolina line crosses it. (Carolina then, being Tennessee later.) Wit: John J. Prendergrast, David Hutchison, Alex'r Hanna.

Page 113. From Va. the copy of right from Will. Chas. Campbell, Clk. Rockbridge.

Feb. 11, 1802. Same to Joseph White, land on S. side Cumberland River, 1,000 A. of Rockbridge Co. survey, June 1785, Pat. 10th June 1800. Mentions: Carolina line (Tennessee.) Wit: John J. Prendergrast, Sam'l Hatton, Robt White, Andrew Reid, Rockbridge C. C. (Va.?); 13th July 1802.

5 head horses, 18 head cattle, 52 head hogs, 4 head sheep; all my beds, chairs, chest, plates, dishes & every kind of household furniture; & all my stock. Wit: James Campbell, Lin Cornelius, Joseph Armstrong.

Page 124. Jesse Jeffrie $1000 to Abraham Stuart, negro man Abraham & woman, Lucy, 26. Wit: John Clark, Michel Dillingham; Mch. 1804.

Page 126. 23 Feb. 1796. Thomas Boals & Thos. x Carlin of Shelby Co., Ky. to Elizabeth Boals, Jun. dau. to James Boals of Same Co. young bay mare 3 yrs, old, for £25. Wit: Thos. Thursby, Martha Cyphers, Wm Davis, Jefferson Co. justice, W. White, J. P.

Page 128.   Martia Reeves & Sam'l. Bradley, Adm. Brewer Reeves, sold & delivered at public auction to Vachel Dillingham negro girl, *Nantz*, Ap. 14, 1800.  Teste. Robt. Coleman.

Stacy Babcock sold to John Moore negro wench, Ann & negro girl Mary, negro boy Chas.  Wit: V. Dillingham, John Clark.  27 July 1802.

Page 129.   Apr. 28, 1804.   Patrick Callahan bound out to David Wood his 2 children Mary Innis Callahan, 8 yrs. old 9th day of next Sept. & David Callahan, 16 yrs. old 9th Jan. next; boy in usual business of field; girl usual occupation of sewing, knitting, weaving & spinning; to supply food & clothes; to teach girl to read English distinctly & to write a decent hand; Boy to read & write & cypher thru the common rules including what is commonly called "The Rule of Three".  Wit: Wm. Armstrong, James Dixon.

Page 131.   May Court 1804.   Benj. x Garvis & Martha Starks mortgage contract.  Marriage abt. to take place between Benj. Garvis & Martha x Starks.  Sd. Benj. deems it just to convey, make over & deliver one negro girl, between 12 to 20, bay horse, cow & calf, 1/2 plantation he lives on, and when he dies, use of all during her life; $100 to her son Reubin Starks, also to pay State price on land she is living on and to give her son Jesse Starks one cow & calf in or on March 1 next.  To give Reubin & Betsy Starks 1 Yr. Schooling apiece; provided sd. Martha marries & continues to live with him during their lives; to give dau. Betsy a horse & saddle.  Teste: Wm. Bradford.

Page 133.   Oct. Term, 1801.   Wm. Padfield, sold to Wm. Husbands a water grist mill & everything belonging thereto & all interest in lands adj. sd. mill on Barren Fk. of Little River for value rec'd.  Wit: John Clark, Christopher Carpenter.

Page 134.   29th July 1799.   Wm. Story, a certain black horse taken up by Wm. McClure is his, made out and signed Wm. Story. John Jones.  Teste: Adam Lynn, J. P.

Page 134.   V. Dillingham to Wm. Padfield negro boy Harvey, abt. 5 yrs. old.  22 July 1801.

Page 135.   Jan. 28, 1801.   Wm. Sugg of Robertson Co. Tenn., $150, to V. Dillingham, 1 negro boy named Harry, 5 or 6.  Wit. Benj. McClendon.

Page 137-139.   Earle; Rogers Deed.

Page 140-141-142.   LINE AS SURVEYED BETWEEN LOGAN & CHRISTIAN COS.; August 22, 1797; John Campbell, S.C.C., Aug. 8, 1803. Plat shows location of State line, County lines, Road from Horans to Simon's Mill as Thomas Boran's; Stuart's; (Whippoorwill Breathitt's Creek); A. Adams; Benj. H. Hardin; John Boran's; Dickerson's; David Smith; Elk Fork; Hugh Surley and Edwd. Pannell, C. C., Young Ewing, S.C.C.; Nicholas Lockett, D. S. for Wm. Reading, Logan Co.

Page 144.   *Plan of Elizabeth* (Town later called Hopkinsville.)

Page 145.   Bond of John Caruthers and John Gray to John Weldon Williams, Armstrong Long & Asa Estes, Trustees for heirs of John Dyer, dec'd., $800.  9th Feb. 1802.

Page 146.   Robt. and Jeremiah Cravens bond to John Weldon, Wm. Armstrong and A. Estes or successors in office, $700.  Feb. 9, 1802.

Page 147.   Thos. Reddick of Nansemond Co., Va.; bond to the sum of $750 to Jesse Cravens of Ohio Co., Ky. land in Christian Co.; 300 acres; Military survey; part of warrant 2140 on 3 forks of Little River; June 14, 1802.   Wit: Young Ewing, Joshua Cates (Cats), John Parish, John Campbell.

Page 149.   Dec. 7, 1804.   Hans x Black power of atty. to Jacob Black of Greenville Co., S. C. for all *accts.*, etc. of Henry Brasher, Blake Colton, Adam Andrews, Benj. Pollard, Wm. Cockran, Jas. Cockran, Noel Hide, James Hide, Benj. Armstrong, Moses Cork, Hezekiah Cockran, Albert Roberts.

Page 151.   James Adams & Agnes Adams, wife; power Atty. to James McGinley of Adams Co., Pa.   Collector debts, etc. & entitled estate Matthew Wilson of Adams Co. father to sd. Agnes Adams; Jan. 14, 1805.   Wit: Matthew Adams, John Gray.

Page 153.   David Smiley of Davidson Co., Tenn. for $10 & love, etc. to beloved friend Austin Boals, son of Jas. Boals of Christian Co. sorrel mare, age 5 yrs.   Oct. 7, 1805.

Page 155-157.   Eli Crow for $200 to Valentine Rashels, land on Pond River, Jan. 14, 1805; David Campbell's line.   Wit: Wm. Stroud, Thos. Hogans, Less Stroud.

Page 157.   Jan. 8, 1805.   Thos. Black to Joseph Lewis, $400, Cert No. 3012, from Ky. in 1798; 200 A. survey, Mch 29, 1799.   Wit: Joseph Gamble, & Wm. Husbands.

Page 160.   8th Jan. 1808.   David Clark to John Pugh, $300; Cert. 3403 Ky. 1798 to Peter Club; survey 29th June 1799 W. Fk. Pond River.   Wit: Joseph Gamble, Joseph Hines.

Page 162.   Jan. 14, 1806.   John P. Finley, power of Atty. to Joseph Barrons, to recover from Wm. Finley, Exr. & Judith Finley, Extr'x. (now Judith Holsey, wife of Thos. Holsey) of Wm. Finley, Wythe Co., Va.   Wit: Isaac Clark, Henry Clark.

Page 163.   Dec. 14, 1805.   Wm. Finley of Wythe Co., Va. appts. Dabney Finley of Christian Co., Ky. to sell tract in Madison Co.   Wit: Zeba Howard, Sam Younglove, James Bradley, Asa Finley, Jerey Lewis.

Page 164.   Peter Thompson to Thomas Reddick, $400 E. sinking Fk. of N. Fk. of Red River.   Wit: J. Cravens, Young Ewing, Joshua Caits, John Campbell.

Page 166.   Abraham Scott appoints Russell Jones of Jackson Co., Ga. Atty. espec. claim against David Criswell for work and labor and to sell any lands in that State, particularly 1000 acres on Broad River, adj. Byings.   Jan. 27, 1806.

Page 169.   June 16, 1804.   Wm. Croghan & wife Lucy of Jefferson Co. to Geo. Pemberton, Christian Co., for $1520, 500 acres land in Ch. Pat. by Croghan, May 19, 1800, on Sinking Branch of Middle or Muddy W. Little River.   Mentions: Large Spring; George Flynn's Old Encampment.   Worden Pope, Jefferson Co., Clk.

Page 172.   8th April 1805.   William L. Findley of 1st pt. to Daniel Campbell, heir at law of Angus Campbell & Matthew Wilson William Stroud & Paul Castleberry, Comrs. appt'd. by Court of Christian Co.

$15, pd. by Angus C. for tract on Castleberry's Fork of Tradewater, 300 acres. Wit: Benj. Lacey, Jas. M. Johnston, Wm. Cravens.

Page 174. Feb. 11, 1804. Matthew Adams, Christian Co., to Samuel Reid of Warren, $100; land on Pond River.

Page 175. June 30, 1804. Hardyman Dunning to Shadrack x Dunning for $500; 200 ac. Wit: Abraham Morris, Winiford Dunning, Selah Dunning.

Page 177. Mch. 14, 1804. John Kuykendall & Martha, his wife, of Henderson Co., to Benj. Talbot for £ 100, W. Fk. Pond River; 200 A. Wit: John Gordon, Thos. G. Davis, Isham T. Wright, George Gordon.

Page 179. Sept. 25, 1804. Geo. Underwood of Hanover Co., Va., to Adam Linn and Ferdinand Wadlington of Christian, 400 A. for $700. Mentions: Blue Spring Creek and Nathaniel Burwell's Line. Wit: Abm. Boyd, Chas. Linn, Thos. McLaughlin.

Page 180. June 12, 1800. To Shadrack Dunning, Christian Co., from John Handley (reverent) of Ohio Co., $1000; Little River, W. side, 1st large fork of Muddy Fk. of Little River, emptying in on W. side above the mouth. Wit: Philip Taylor, Willis x Odom, James Roberts, John Roberts, Andrew Donoson, Winyfred Dunning, Hardyman Dunning.

Pages 182-183 May 15, 1804. John Dempsey late citizen of Christian Co., (Ephraim Reese his true & lawful Atty.) & Thomas Prince Earle for $200, pd. by Thomas P. Earle land on Casey's Crk. of Little River, granted to John Dempsey, 16th Feb. 1803, 200 A. John Rogers, Edw. Hampton Reese.

Page 184. Dec. 29, 1804. Thomas Wadlington, John Mills & Maria M. Mills, David Cooper and Elizabeth Cooper of Christian Co., & Wm. Brown & Sara Brown & wife of Livingston Co., of 1st pt. & Elizabeth Wadlington, wife of Thos. Wadlington, dec'd. who in his life gave verbally to Ferdinand Wadlington 200 A. where sd. Thos. Wadlington lived, on Island for $550 and deed to carry this out. Signed: Wit: Asa Estes, David Wood, John Potts.

Page 187. Mch. 5, 1804. Peter Thompson to Jesse Brooks and the Church of Christ for $6.00; for meeting house and burial ground; successors; Wm. Wallyce's Line; Military Line of Peter Thompson, buildings, etc. Wit: Josiah Fort, Jno. Riggs, Wm. Brooks, Jesse Brooks.

Page 189. Apr. 4, 1803-23rd May. James x Reeves & Nancy Reeves, wife; to John Jennings for $460; on Sinking Fk. of Muddy Fork of Little River Fielding Woolf's line; Granted to sd. Reeves by Cert. No. 3361. Wit: Wells Griffith, Samuel Means, Jesse Jeffrey.

Page 191. 4th Sept. 1804. Michael Dillingham & Wm. Wood, sold to John Campbell; Inez, May and Charles for $600.

Page 192. Dec. 4, 1804. Timothy Riggs to Silas Riggs, one black mare, one sorrel horse & colt, 2 cows & calves, 2 heifers, 1 feather bed & furniture, one iron kettle, 1 Dutch oven. Wit: Jesse Clark, Jacob Riggs.

Page 192. John Strong to Benj. Campbell for $500, woman Lucy, 16 & child Grace. Wit: Paul x Patrick, John x Patrick; 18th Apr. 1805.

Page 193. Larkin Rogers, Appt'd. John Breathitt Atty. to use his name in land certificate for 200 A., Nov. 7, 1804. Wit: John Vance, Richard Stanford.

Page 194. Oct. 8, 1804. Wm. M. Hall Appd. John Breathitt Atty., to draw land certificate for 200 A. Teste: James M. Johnson.

Page 195. Sept. 10, 1805. Wm. Lindley to Jas. Fruit, $330, Land warrant No. 158; 400 A. on waters of Pond River, now in possession of James Fruit. Wit: Wm. Stroud, Joseph Gamble, Powers Lambkin, Chas. Kavanch (Kavanah ?).

Page 197. Feb. 19, 1805. Robt. Abernathy, planter, for $16, to Wm. Nichols land on headwaters of "Little River" pt. of land I now live on, 4½ acres. Wm. Dupuy, Joseph Dupuy, Jas. Nichols. *Plat* 199.

Page 199. 6th Feb. 1806. Joseph Dupuy to Joseph Gamble for $600; warrant No. 274 for land on Little River; 200 A. Jas. Bradley, Jacob Gonterman.

Page 201. Nov. 25, 1802. John Cotton sold to Elijah Simpson of Sumner Co., Tenn. on Little River, on N. E. side of his plantation, 100 A. $100. Wit: Sam'l. Johnston, John Cotton.

Page 203. 9/9/1805. Wm. Lindley to Wm. Thompson for $600, on Castleberry's Fk. Trade Water River; 300 A. Mentions: Paul Castleberry's line. Wit: Robert Coleman, John Lindley, Benj. Thompson.

Page 204. Motion before Justices of the Peace for Rockingham Co., Va. at the C. H. May 24, 1790. Brewer Reeves by his Atty., brought notices against Geo. Randle at next court to move for a judgment against Randle for Amt. of a judgment against *us* on Randle's Replevin Bond given to Alexander White for 69 £ 1s. 10d. with costs; Reeves being Security for Randle; Court adjudged Pltff. 71£ 4s. 2d. Teste: Henry Ewen, C. R. C. Copy Test: S. McWilliams, C. R. C.

John Wayne, J. P. for Rockingham (Co.); Certified to copy 2/21/1795; in the 19th Yr. of C.wlth. .25 costs, 1.00 Co. seal, .63 Certif—$1.88.

Page 206. Jan. 4, 1800. Samuel Deason sold to Absolom Humphreys 200 A.; mentions line of Jesse Wall; binds against any prior claim (no water course.) Articles of Agreement & Order for transfer of certificate instead of deed. Wit: John Templeton, Jesse Wall.

Page 207. Joseph x Davis to Clement Davis the headright of Wm. Davis lying between Little & Big Flat Lick Timber; 200 A. one bull 4 yrs. brindled and speckled; Red Rone Horse, 14 yrs. old; 12th Mch. 1804. Wit: Jonathan Chandler, Wm. Davis, Jeremiah Davis. Oct. Crt. 1804.

Page 207. Charles Thompson of S. C. Union Dist. (Logan Co. ? Ky.) $300; by hand of Powers Lampkins of Christian Co.; delivered, negro girl, 12, Sylvia. Wit: Jacob Fuler; Bill of Sale; Wm. x Lamkins.

Page 208. John G. Robbins to Henry Gibson, woman, Raney and her 3 children, Daphney, Parris & Juno and also James, brother of sd. Raney, $1,000, Jan. 30, 1805. Teste: Robt. Coleman, July 12, 1806.

Page 209. William x Hush for $300 to David Black, girl Narcisse between 5 & 6, Dec. 9, 1805. Wit: Allin Bobbitt, Andrew Jamison.

# COX

(Supplied by Mrs. Reba Brownfield Fowler)

## GREEN COUNTY TAX LISTS

1795—John Cox, 1 male over 21; Robert Cox, 1 male, 2 horses, 19 cattle, 5 town lots; Robert Cox, 1 male, 2 horses, 19 cattle, 5 town lots.

1796—Robert Cox, 1 male above 16, 1 horse, 11 cattle.

1797—Robert Cox, 1 white male over 21, 2 horses, 11 ordinary license, — town lots.

1799—David Cox, 1 male over 21, 1 over 16, 1 horse; Samuel Cox, 1 male over 21, 1 horse; Robert Cox, 200 acres, 3rd. rate land, on Trammel's creek, 1 male, 2 horses.

1802—Robert Cox, 100 acres 2nd. rate land, Clover creek, 1 male, 2 horses.

1803—Robert Cox, 100 acres 2nd. rate land, Cloverlick creek, 1 male, 2 h.

1804—Robert Cox, 100 acres, Cloverlick creek, 1 male, 2 horses.

1805—Robert Cox, 100 acres, Cloverlick creek, 1 male, 1 horse; Thomas Cox, 1 male, 1 horse.

1807—Littleberry Cox, Robert Cox, Thomas Cox.

1808—Thomas Cox, Samuel Cox.

1809—John Cox, 350 acres land, 1 male, 2 blacks, 3 horses. Also Thomas Cox. Robert Cox, 100 acres, etc.

1810—Littleberry Cox, Robert Cox.

1811—Robert Cox; John Cox, 100 acres, etc.

1814—John P. Cox, 250 acres, value $3,236.

1823—John P. Cox, 250 acres; Archibald Cox.

1827—John P. Cox; Frederick Cox; Archibald Cox; Samuel Cox.

1830—John Cox, 100 acres; John Cox, Caleb Cox, Jacob Cox; Archibald Cox, 65 acres, 6 town lots, $3,450; Robert Cox; Robert Cox, Sr., 100 acres on Cloverlick; John P. Cox, 60 acres, $860; Elizabeth Cox, 250 acres, $7,163; Archibald Cox, 5 lots in Greensburg, $1,900; Robert Cox, Caleb Cox, Joshua Cox, Jacob Cox, Will Cox, John Cox, Frederick Cox, Samuel Cox.

1835—John P. Cox and Robert Cox.

1837—Robert Cox, 100 acres, Clovelick creek; Robert Cox, Jr.; Elizabeth Cox, 200 acres, $1,200, 8 blacks $2,775, 2 horses $100; Casteen Cox, William Cox, Charles Cox, Littleberry Cox, Caleb Cox, Jacob Cox, John Cox, Archibald Cox.

1834—Archibald Cox, 100 acres, 1 house and lot in Greensburg, $2,150; John Cox, 100 acres; Frederick Cox, $1,350; John P. Cox, 150 A., $4,370; John Cox, Jr., 60 acres, $685.

## From the Old Cox Family Bible, in possession of Mrs. Reba B. Fowler

John P. Cox and Elizabeth H. White were married Feb. 12, 1795. Their children were:

Nancy Cox and Jackson G. Winton were married December 23, 1819.

Archibald Cox and Sallie W. Howe were married May 2, 1822.

Samuel Cox and Anna Carden were married December 21, 1824.

Elizabeth B. Cox and John Shreve were married July 20, 1826.

Judith P. Cox and Francis Cowherd were married Jan. 6, 1829.

John P. Cox, Jr. and Regina D. Patteson were married May 2, 1833.

Frederick Cox and Precious L. Halsell were married Aug. 14, 1834.

Archibald Cox was married the second time to Harriet Buckner, Jan. 14, 1835.

Lucy Ann Cox and Thomas Jefferson Cabell were married April 6, 1837.

Lucy Ann Cox, born May 1, 1815, died at Campbellsburg, Kentucky Dec. 22, 1874; was a widow 20 years.

Lucy Ann Cox and Thomas J. Cabell married April 6, 1937.

1. Ermine Catherine Cabell born Dec. 1837, married John (Jack) Brownfield
2. John Cabell married Birdie Ray
3. Martha Cabell married Willis Chelf (Harrodsburg).
4. Benj. Francis Cabell, born June 6, 1850 at Mannsville, Ky., Taylor county, married Ellen Patterson.

Thomas J. Cabell was the son of Joseph Cabell who came to Taylor, then Green county from Va.

Benjamin Francis Cabell, above, was Prof. "Frank" Cabell, who spent his life in the teaching profession, Potter College, Bowling Green. "Cabell Hall", the central building of Western Ky. Normal School at Bowling Green was named for him.

## GREEN COUNTY, KY., MARRIAGES

p. 38

Samuel Cabell and Sarah Mann, May 15-18, 1810, daughter of Moses Mann and Fanny Mann. James Hill, Minister, Bondsman Joseph Cabell.

p. 9

Joseph Cabell and Rachel Mann, —— 20, 1802, minister James Hill

p. 109

Archibald C. Cox and Sally W. Howe, May 2, 1822, minister John Howe

Wm. Mann and Nancey Wilcoxen, dau. Wm. Wilcoxen, Ap. 4, 1808
note Geo. Wilcoxen

Joseph Mann and Betsey Hill, Dec. 21, 1799, dau. of Jas. and Mary Hill.
Moses Mann bondsman

James Herod and Nancy Burks—— 16,1799, dau. John Burks, Silas Burks
bondsman

John Herod and Nancy Peace, May 31, 1798, Simon Peace (James Herod, B)

Theron Brownfield, and Susannah Murry, dau. of Jas. Murry (Wm. Murray, bondsman)

Wm. Mann and Elizabeth White, Oct. 15, 1839

H. G. Mann and Mary E. Powell, Sept. 26, 1835

Moses Mann and M. Penn, Dec. 21, 1837

Benj. F. Chelf and Lumida Pryor, Jan. 20, 1848

Wm. Cabell and Priscilla Cox, Mch. 12, 1845

Dr. Geo. W. Cabell and E. L. Crouch, Aug. 17, 1842
Samuel Cabell and J. Louisa Montgomery, Nov. 26, 1839
Archibald G. Cox and Harriett Buckner, Jan. 13, 1835
Dallas Brownfield and Rebecca Moody, Feb. 1, 1844
Robert Brownfield and Nancy Morris, Jan. 3, 1842

## DENTON-LEER (LEAR) FAMILY
### (Contributed by Mrs. Matilda Leer Denton)

John Denton of Garrard County, Kentucky, born ——, died October 1821. Married Nancy, and had James Thompson Denton, born April 5, 1805, married Josephine C. Harris, born March 4, 1818, Garrard County, Kentucky, died January 7, 1875—issue:

John Tyree Denton, born December 25, 1848, in Russell County, Kentucky married America Jane Jones of Jessamine County, Kentucky, October 12, 1875—issue:

John Will Denton, born November 25, 1884; died May 5, 1943.

(The above John Will Denton was the son of John Tyree Denton, born December 25, 1848 and his wife America Jane Jones.

———

Matilda Lear Denton, born October 12, 1885, wife of John Will Denton, was the daughter of James Monroe Leer, born May 11, 1841 and his wife Amelia Turner, born December 13, 1851.

John Will Denton and wife Matilda Leer Denton were married April 29, 1908; issue—

1. Anne Thomas Denton, born August 9, 1909; married October 10, 1934 William Hubert Buckles, born Aug. 7, 1907, and had issue:
    Anne Carol Buckles, born October 14, 1937
    Bettie Sue Buckles, born March 19, 1942
2. John Tyree Denton, born April 25, 1911; married August, 1937 Anne Elizabeth Fishback, born March 3, 1917. No issue.
3. Corday Buckley Denton, born October 10, 1913; married April 9, 1934 Barton Kinkead Battaille, born January 3, 1914; issue:
    Matilda Fontaine Battaille, born March 8, 1935
    Elizabeth Barton Battaille, born August 13, 1940
    Shelby Leer Battaille, born September 16, 1946
4. Lura Amelia Denton, born May 9, 1915; married November 8, 1937 Thomas James Kay, born December 5, 1910; and had issue:
    Thomas Denton Kay, born February 23, 1940.
5. Matilda Jane Denton, born March 9, 1917; married June 23, 1940 Gordon Hoover Sympson, born August 23, ——; and had issue:
    Gordon Hoover Sympson, Jr. born December 3, 1942
    Jane Leer Sympson, born August 23, 1944
    Amelia Denton Sympson, born May 25, 1947.

Henry Leer (Lear) married Ann ? ——. He owned property in town of Liberty, state of Maryland. Had children—
    Rebecca, wife of Aaron Smedley; David Leer; Abraham Leer; John Leer; Mary Leer. His widow was Ann Leer.

David Leer, son of Henry, born June 11, 1769; married December 2, 1794, Elizabeth Leer, born December 11, 1770. Issue:

David Leer, born January 15, 1803; married June 10, 1830 Charlotte Corday Kenney, born December 12, 1809. Issue:

James Monroe Leer, born May 11, 1841; married October 29, 1874 Amelia Turner, born December 13, 1851. Issue:

Matilda Leer, born October 12, 1885; married April 29, 1908 John Will Denton, born November 25, 1884

## ELKIN

(Furnished by Mrs. S. A. Glass, Lexington, Ky.)

Descent from EARLE—John; Samuel I; Samuel II; Samuel III; Elizabeth Earle married Benjamin Elkin of Frederick Co., Va.

1818/Nov. 12.—Benjamin Elkin of Woodford and Jessamine Co. gave to his younger daughter, Marian Rosetta Elkin, one negro girl.

Children of Benjamin Elkin and Elizabeth Earle Elkin:
(data from Mrs. S. A. Glass)

1.—Atlantic Ocean Elkin, b. March 27, 1785, in Va., d. March 1, 1874, md. (1) Mr. Harris; (2) Benjamin Kearby. Buried in Lexington Kentucky Cemetery.

2.—Marian Rosetta Elkin, b. 1797, d. Aug. 1, 1855, md. Obadiah Prewitt (b. 1788, d. 1844) buried at Nicholasville, Ky.

3.—Baylis Elkin, his wife's name unknown.

4.—Alfred Elkin md. Polly (Mary) Hunt.

5.—Frederick Sapphira Elkin.

6.—Harriet Elkin md. John Walker. (descendants in Miss. and Memphis, Tenn.

7.—Elizabeth Reese Elkin.

8.—Martha Elkin md.......... Reynolds.

9.—Wilhelmina Elkin, name of husband unknown. (she had one brown eye and one blue.)

———

1.—Isaiah Elkin md. Anne McClanahan in Va., in 1792 was paying taxes in Woodford county, Ky.; Lived in Clover Bottom, that county: children:

1.—McClanahan Elkin, in tax books of Woodford in 1815, d. a bachelor.

2.—Strother Elkin.

3.—Amanda Elkin md. Wm. Gollop in Jessamine county, Ky., Nov. 26, 1822; went to Miss.

4.—Adonijah Elkin md. Adelia Lucas Elkin, widow of his cousin, Thomas Elkin; went to Miss. after 1828.

5.—Merriman Elkin md. Susan A. Bailey of Bourbon county, Ky.

6.—Sydney S. Elkin md. Jane Ashford, his second cousin, Sept. 6, 1830, in Woodford county; went to Nebraska.

7.—Anastasia Elkin.

8.—Narcissa Elkin md. Thomas Bayes.

2.—Benjamin md. Elizabeth Earle in Va. (Frederick county); came to Jessamine county, Ky.

3.—Amanuel Elkin.
4.—Lucy Elkin md. Wm. Barbee.
5.—Cassarina Gollop Elkin md. John Hawkins, May 31, 1812, in Woodford county, Ed Waller officiating.
6.—Linda Elkin md. John W. Campbell.
        .... children of Amanda and Wm. Gollop Elkin:
1.—Joseph Berry Elkin md. Nancy Love.
2.—Thomas Elkin md. Louise Thenster.
3.—Anne Elkin md. Joseph Thomas; many descendants of these three in Miss.

## CROMWELL
### (Compiled by Mrs. Ila Earle Fowler)

Fayette Co. Orphan Book, 1846-1852, p. 88, Alvin W. Cromwell, his children: Isabella and Mary Ann Cromwell. p. 88, John and Susan Cromwell, orphans of Patsy Cromwell, (late Watts) father Joshua Cromwell.
Orphan Book, 1835-1846, p 118, Oliver and Vincent Cromwell, bond $3,-000, 3/2/1838, Oliver Cromwell guardian of James; Mary; David; Catherine; and Rachel Lauderman, orphans of Frederick Lauderman. (the widow, Rachel Lauderman.)

(Of these: Mary Lauderman married Williams Adams, had son John Adams, and daughter who married Charles Erd. Dyke Hazelrigg in this line. James Lauderman was killed in 1872 at Mill & Third street; David Dyke Lauderman was city treasurer of Lexington, according to Mr. Ollie Randolph, 1947). Ky. V. S. Oliver Cromwell, aged 58, b. Fayette county, d. Fayette, 3/15/1855, will, wife Elizabeth; children not named except daughter, Jane L. O. Cromwell. exrs. J. H. Lauderman and son Edward Cromwell.

In 1830s, Vincent Cromwell, will, wife Nancy, son William; daughters Stevenson and Tyler.

Benjamin Cromwell, wife Jane, children not named except son Marquis, brother Oliver Cromwell, exr.

Jane Cromwell, son Vincent, son Wm. B., daughter Nancy Montague, son Alvin, son Marcus.

Oliver Cromwell, C. M. Keiser, and Johnson Haley signed appraisement of estate of Henry Buford, widow Betty Buford. In Certificate name is Thompson Haley, **Thompson** underscored.

(See McAdams—Fayette Co. Hist., p 115).

## HALEY
### (Compiled from Records by Mrs. Ila Earle Fowler)

(See also Burns' copies of marriages, Fayette Co.)
Randolph Haley married Susan B. Lilly, 2/7/1831; Gabriel Lilly, bondsman.
Randolph Haley married Lucy White, 11/27/1849, bondsman, Percival Gaugh.
Randolph I. Haley married Mary Bunnell 12/7/1848, bondsman, John Chrisman.

Will Book A, p. 79, William Haley; wife Henrietta; son Benjamin; dau. Ofrida Ourton.

June, 1849, Randolph Haley's will.

Feb. 1817, Susannah Haley's will. D, 176.

1804, Melinda Haley's will. Book P, 106.

March 1877, Mary Heley will.

Randolph Haley, will, 6/5/Aug. 1885.

1849, Ambrose Haley, Book S, p. 219, wife Mary; grand daughter Mary Elizabeth Weathers; son Wm. D. Haley; dau. Lucinda Weathers; dau. Mary Parish; son-in-law Wm. Weathers.

1830, Feb. James Haley, Will Book I, p. 345.

Keiser Vital Statistics:

Keiser, Mrs. B. C., age 55, 9/12/1859, Typhoid, b. Pa., d. Lexington.

Keiser, J. N., age 98, 5/21/1856, b. Md., d. Lexington, gastritis.

## LAUDERMAN
### (Compiled by Mrs. Ila Earle Fowler)

Lauderman, Jacob, Will Book J, p. 442. Fayette, d. 1830, wife Catherine; 2 sons, Frederick and William Lauderman; dau. Mary Harp; dau. Katherine Cromwell.

Had advanced money to John, Geo. W., David, Joseph and Smith Lauderman.

Lauderman, Frederick, d. 1833, inventory.

Joseph Lauderman, d. 1833, no heir's names given.

Sophia Lauderman, d. 1848 husband John, dau. Georgeann; Oliver Cromwell, exr.

Catherine' Lauderman, d. 1850-51.

John Lauderman, d. 1854-5.

George W. Lauderman, d. 1841, wife Sarah; son Robert Holland; daus. Susan and Frances, both under age. Geo. W. Lauderman's mother living, Book W, p. 299.

(See Staples "Pioneer Lexington" for further on Jacob Lauderman).

From Gazette: Died of cholera 1833:

In ward 4, Lexington, Joseph Lauderman.

In ward 4, Susan Lauderman, wife of George W. Lauderman.

Ad, Gazette, 1833: Geo. W. Lauderman, Saddling & Harness & Boot and Shoe making. The firm had been Laudermann & Stevenson.

(Abraham Lauderman, private, 9/18/1812 to 10/30/1812, Capt. Caleb Hardesty's Co., 2nd Reg. Ky. mounted militia.

Vital Statistics:

Johnson, Nancy, aged 89, b. N. J.; d. Lexington, 12/31/1855.

Shyrock, John Frederick, 94, d. 12/25/1856, b. Md.

Gazette, cholera victims, 1833:

Judith, widow of Gov. Charles Scott, d. at B. Gratz.

Mrs. Jane Byrne, wife of John Byrne, Ward 2.

Samuel, servant of Capt. Fowler, Short Street, also Bob Coleraine.

Thomas Sprake and wife, Ward 4.

From Kentucky tax lists: 1814 Fayette county:

Spraike, James (Ayers agent).

Spraiks, Thomas, occurs twice.

1815:

Spracks, Jr. and Sr.

(see page 816 Perrin's Fayette Co. for Sprake sketch).

(Burns' copies of wills:)

Thomas Chambers married Rachel Maguire, 4/1/1817, Edward Maguire bondsman. (See p. 171, McAdams).

Guardian Book Fayette, 1846-1856.

John B. Wilgus and Wm. G. Moore, Guardians, bond $100, 10/16/1851, for Mary E. Fowler, orphan of Daniel H. Fowler, deceased.

## RANDOLPH

(Contributed by Mrs. Ila Earle Fowler)

Vital Statistics, Kentucky.

Randolph, Moses, died April 8, 1854, aged 77 (b. 1777), New Jersey, cause, old age, parents unknown. Fayette county.

Randolph, Sarah, d. Feb. 11, 1858, aged 80 (b. 1778), Fayete county, paralysis, parents unknown.

Randolph (or Randall), Susan. d. June 6, 1856, aged 85 (b. 1771), b. Maryland, pneumonia, parents unknown.

(By comparing dates of Moses Randolph's will it is seen that this is card indexed wrongly as Randall).

Fayette county records.

Moses Randolph, inventory and settlement, will book V, p. 294-473, April 8, 1856. C. M. Keiser and Moses Randolph Adm. amount personal property $4,385.18. Balance due estate $993.95. Page 474, heirs who received same amounts of $86.47: Wm. H. Randolph, ex. estate of Wm. Chambers; Mary Ford; James and Rachel Maguire; John and Julian Springer; Sarah Randolph; John H. Randolph; Adam H. Hanna; C. M. Keiser; and received $43.23, David Maguire and E. D. Maguire. (C. M. Keiser married Nancy Randolph, daughter of Moses) John H. Randolph, moved to Newcastle, Ind. (real estate seems not to be inventoried.)

Book U: inventory, August 30, 1854, Dec. 12, 1854, names slaves. Milky, old woman, $100; Western, 40, $600; John, 30, $900; Bolden, 26, $900; Andrew, 18, $900. estate inventoried $7,149; sale proceeds, $4,362; deed to heirs of graveyard, from Alex Brand, B. 30, p. 358, heirs' powers of attorney, B. 32, p. 325.

Moses Randolph, Jr., will, B. 9, p. 42, August 10, 1894, probated Aug. 20, 1900. Daughter, Sally B. Keiser; John L./or/S. Randolph; W. E. Randolph; Ollie D. Randolph. Grandchildren: K. E. Hurst; Addie Hurst. Adm. Ollie D. Randolph.

Orphan Book, 1835-46, p. 410, Margaret Ann Randolph, orphan of John H. Randolph, Joseph A. Moore, gdn., April 14, 1846.

(See Burns copy of Fayette records: )

John H. Randolph married Mary Ford, 2/14/1844, Wm. Ford, bondsman.

Moses Randolph married Rachel Lauderman, 12/6/1848, Owen (Oliver) Cromwell, guardian.

John Randolph married Paulina Valendingham, 1/12/1835: Henry Oustin, Bondsman.

John H. Randolph married Nancy C. Moore, return 7/14/1830, married in July. (son of Moses Randolph, Jr.)

(other Randolph data, p. 855, Fayette county History, Perrin).

(For extended article on Fitz-Randolphs of New Jersey, see Genealogical and Historical Register of New England, July, 1943.)

### FLEMING COUNTY, KENTUCKY RECORDS

(Compiled by Mrs. Lula Reed Boss, Maysville, Kentucky)

FLEMING COUNTY, KENTUCKY COURT RECORDS (in abstract)

(Formed from Mason County in 1798)

DEED BOOK A-1.—Page 226—DEED OF GIFT

Dated March 14, 1799

Jacob Reed of the county of Mason and State of Kentucky, deeds to "my son, Isaac Reed," 255 acres of land located "on the headwaters of Indian and Farrow creeks branches of the North Fork of Licking river, being a part of the land purchased by the said Jacob Reed of a certain Richard Masterson and now laid off to the aforesaid Isaac Reed, beginning at a stone in the line of Thomas Owsley's survey" and "running thence to the line of Zazarus Maddux." Witnesses to deed: Zazarus Maddux, Thomas Maddux, John Harris Hayman, James Alexander, Joshua Taylor and Rowland Alexander.

DEED BOOK A-1.—Page 220—DEED OF GIFT

Dated June 26, 1799

Jacob Reed and Nancy his wife of the county of Fleming and State of Kentucky, convey to Samuel Stevens, of the county of Mason, . . . . "all that tract of land lying and being on the waters of Indian Lick creek in the county of Fleming and Commonwealth of Kentucky," . . . . . "to corner of Rowland Alexander's" . . . . . containing 200¾ acres.

(Signed) Jacob Reed

Nancy Reed(**)

Witnesses to deed: Joshua Taylor, Joseph Powers and Thomas Treacle.

(**) Webster's Collegiate Dictionary gives:

"Ann—diminutive of Nancy."

In all other court records the 2nd wife of Major Jacob Reed is called "Ann Reed."

### MARRIAGE BOND

Samuel Stevens and Rebecca Reed were married 11-6-1798.

Copy of note of consent: "I Jacob Reed of the county of Fleming am willing for the clerk of the said county to grant a license to Samuel Stevens of Mason county, and my daughter Rebecca Reed to join in the banns of Holy matrimony. Given under my hand this 31st of Oct., 1798." Witness: Isaac Reed.

## DEED BOOK B.—Page 88
### Dated January 27, 1801

"Isaac Reed of the Northwest Territory, Hamilton county, Ohio," conveys to William Piper, of Fleming county, Kentucky, . . . . . . "land granted by the Commonwealth of Virginia to Richard Masterson and by him conveyed to Jacob Reed, and by Jacob Reed conveyed to the aforesaid Isaac Reed."

Note: This is the last record of Isaac Reed in Fleming county, Kentucky. He is not listed among the heirs of Major Jacob Reed, deceased.

## DEED BOOK G.—Page 25—POWER OF ATTORNEY

"Know All Men By These Presents: that I, Enoch Furr senior, of Loudoun county, State of Virginia, having a matter of controversy now pending and unsettled; Now Know Ye that I appoint and nominate James Reed senior, of the county of Fleming and State of Kentucky, my true and lawful attorney for me and in my name, to transact all such business as he the said James Reed senior may think reasonable, just, and right, and to do all such business as I myself might do were I personally present, hereby ratifying and confirming all such business bargains or contracts as the said James Reed senior may deem proper to make.

"In Testimony Whereof I have hereunto set my hand and affixed my seal this 24th day of May, 1816."

Witnesses: James Reed and John D. Stockton.

## DEED BOOK L.—Page 415
### Dated February 11, 1822

Enoch Furr and Sarah his wife, of Loudoun county, Virginia, convey to William DeBell, of Fleming county, for $3,036, 253 acres of land located "on waters of Fleming creek being part of an 800 acre tract surveyed and patented for Edwin Furr and deeded by Commissioners appointed by the Fleming County Court in pursuance to an Act of Assembly concerning the conveyance of lands and agreeable to the title Bond held by said Enoch Furr against said Edwin Furr for 5/16th of the said 800 acres and this part sold contains 253 acres," and bounded as follows: " . . . . . near James Reed's house and including the improvement formerly owned and occupied by Jasper Seybold . . . . . . "

(Signed) Enoch Furr<br>Sally Furr

See: Pension Claim No. W-11030 for more complete information on Enoch Furr.

## DEED BOOK F.—Page 479
### Dated February 3, 1816.

James Reed and Sibby his wife, of Fleming county, convey to John Downs, of same place, "land on waters of Fleming creek."

## DEED BOOK O.—Page 346
### Dated November 9, 1827.

James Reed of Fleming county, Kentucky, and William Reed, of Mason county, Kentucky, convey to Severn Pollitt, of Fleming county, "land in Fleming county on the waters of Indian creek and the North Fork of Licking, being part of a tract of land formerly belonging to Jacob Reed, deceased, the said James Reed and William Reed being two of said heirs." Land bounded as follows: "Beginning at Edwards survey of 7,000 acres . . . . thence to Kendall Moss' line . . . . thence to Thomas DeBell's . . . thence to William Eubanks, jr. line . . . to the original survey this 24th day of May, 1816."
Witnesses to deed: Alexander H. Pollitt and James Pollitt.

## DEED BOOK J.—Page 207
### Dated April 9, 1819

Deed from James Reed senior to Appollos C. Dobyns, both of Fleming county, Kentucky.

### Page 494
### Dated April 26, 1820

Deed from James Reed senior to Thornton F. Dobyns, James R. Dobyns and Lewis Craig Dobyns, all of Fleming county, Kentucky.

## DEED BOOK H.—Page 166
### Dated September 28, 1818

James Dobyns of Fleming county conveys to Charles Dobyns and Silas P. Duvall, of Mason county, "my remaining interest in and to dower slaves assigned to our mother, Frances Brown, late Frances Dobyns, widow of our deceased father, Edward Dobyns, late of Mason county, Kentucky."

## DEED BOOK P.—Page 216
### Dated June 23, 1829

George W. Dobyns and Rebecca his wife, of Bath county, Kentucky, and Edward Dobyns and Ann his wife, of St. Louis county, Missouri, convey land in Fleming county to G. B. Moss.

## COURT ORDER BOOK B.—Page 222
### Monday, October 3, 1803

On Motion of William Reed who made oath thereto and together with Alexander Daugherty and James Reed his security entered into and acknowledged their Bond in the penalty of five hundred pounds conditioned agreeably to law. Certificate is granted William Reed for obtaining Letters of Administration of the estate of Jacob Reed, deceased, in due form."

### Page 222

Ann Reed, widow and relict of Jacob Reed, deceased, came personally into court and relinquished her rights of administration of the estate of her deceased husband.

Page 222

Ordered that Jasper Seybold, John Hart, William DeBell and Thomas Treacle, or any three of them being first duly sworn before a Magistrate of this county, do appraise in current money the personal estate and slaves, if any, of Jacob Reed, deceased, and make report to the next court.

Page 295

Ordered that John Hart, Nathaniel Foster and John Jones, Esquires, or any two of them, do examine and settle with William Reed his administration accounts of Jacob Reed, deceased, and make report thereof to the next court.

## COURT ORDER BOOK C.—Page 39
### December Court, 1807.

"The report of the Reviewers of the road from Mason county line the nearest and best way to intersect Clover road near Thomas Treacles returned and ordered to be recorded which is in these words, to-wit: (Endorsed on the back of a copy of the order.) "In obedience to the within order we the undersigned subscribers having been duly sworn agreeably to the direction of said order and have proceeded to review the said road so report that the road will run through the lands of Thomas Housley's and striking there on the land of the heirs of Major Jacob Reed**, deceased, and through the claim of James Dobbins (Dobyns) striking the Stone Lick road and then entering into the lands of the heirs of Robert Young and others...................."

(Signed) Joseph Powers, James Reed, Thomas Treacle
7th of Dec., 1807."

Note: James Dobyns md. Sarah Cooper, 9-2-1794. Sarah was the daughter of Mary Reed and her 1st husband, Lieut. Appollos Cooper (killed at the Battle of Brandywine.) Mary Reed Cooper was the daughter of Major Jacob Reed. Mary Reed Cooper md. 2nd William Stoker.

**Note: Jacob Reed, Gent., Member of the Loudoun County (Virginia) Committee of Correspondence, 1774-1775; Captain in 1779, and Commissioned Major of the Third Battalion, Loudoun County Militia, 1781; married 1st Rebecca Claypole (died Loudoun county, Va. 1785-1787) and Major Jacob Reed married 2nd Ann Taylor, who survived him.

## COURT ORDER BOOK C.—Pages 208 & 209
### August Court, 1810

"And that William Furr be appointed overseer thereof.........from thence to James Reed's and that he be assisted in keeping the road in repair by John Hart, John Hart junior, Reuben Goslin, Nathaniel Goslin, Nathan Goslin, Benjamin Goslin, Joseph Goslin, Alexander Young, John White, Sampson Furr, John Downs and William Furr, and that James Reed be appointed overseer thereof from thence to the Lewis county line, and that he be assisted in keeping the same in repair by John Reed, Jacob Reed, William Foxworthy senior, William Foxworthy junior, Joel DeBell, Andrew Wright, Scioto Evans, W. DeBell, Ben DeBell, George

Glascock, James Edmonson and hands, Thomas Edmonson, Benjamin Mosely and hands, ———— Morris, Ben Burriss, Daniel Oneal, John Hinton, Ben Plummer, Abraham Plummer, John Olliver, William Griffith, Zadock Burriss, Alexander Henderson, James Leeper, David Henderson and hands, Joseph Henderson, W. Clancy, Joseph Burriss, George Beeler, Thomas Veach, W. Plummer and George Truitt and ordered that the said overseers keep that part of the said road assigned to them respectfully forty feet wide."

## COURT ORDER BOOK D.—Page 13
### December Court, 1817

"Ordered that Aaron McIntyre be and he is hereby appointed overseer of the road leading from the forks near James Reed's to Farrow's Mill and that he keep the same in good repair as far as John Goddard's and have the following hands, to-wit: Caleb Asbury, William and John Raybourne, James Tillett, Lander Tatman, Edward Turner, Famous Mortimer, David Blue, Famous Blue, William Goddard, Thomas Goddard, William Farrow junior, Thomas Davenport, William Reed, John Owens, Jacob Reed and John Goddard junior."

## COURT ORDER BOOK D.—Pages 179-180
### September Court, 1811
### (Circuit Clerk's Office)

"John Doe, ex dem, William Bryant, Plt.

vs

James Dobyns, Dft.

(in part).......... "This day came the plaintiff by his attorney, and the defendant Rowland Alexander, in proper person, as the defendants, William Reed, James Reed, Jacob Reed, William Stoker and Mary his wife, and the infant heirs of Joseph Reed, deceased, the heirs and legal representations of Jacob Reed, deceased............"

## COURT ORDER BOOK E.—Pag 141
### July 28, 1829

"A report of a way to turn the road from James Reed's 'old place to Farrow's Mill was returned..........the "road leading from James Reed's old place on the State road to Farrow's Mill........" (Signed) J. DeBell.

Note: By 1830 James Reed had returned to Mason county. See: Mason County court records.

## WILL BOOK A.—Page 37

Will of "Edward Furr, of Fleming County, Kentucky."

Dated: 4-10-1801. Proven: 7-10-1801.

Witnesses: John DeBell, Thomas Greade, James Bishop and Louis Davis.

Leaves to "sons, William Furr, Sampson Furr and Stephen Furr; to sons-in-law, Aaron (or Amos) Watson, Thomas Harrison, James Reed, and James Downing. Makes no mention of wife."

Issue, with marriages, of the children of Edward (also called "Edwin") Furr taken from court records. Not arranged according to dates of births.

1. Charity Furr md. in Mason county, 8-31-1793, James Downing. Removed to Fayette county, Ky.
2. William Furr, born 1765, md. in Mason county 11-8-1794, Sinae Edwards. Removed to Fountain county, Indiana.
3. Sabina Furr, born 1768-69; died Mason county, 1849; md. in Loudoun county, Virginia, 8-30-1784, James Reed (born 1759; died Mason county, 1835.)
4. Leah Furr md. in Mason county, 8-10-1794, Aaron (or Amos) Watson.
5. Margaret Furr md. in Mason county, 7-16-1796, Thomas Harrison.
6. Stephen Furr—died Fleming county, 1802. James Reed, appointed administrator of estate (Will Book A., page 67.)
7. Sampson Furr, md. in Mason county, 2-14-1801, Sally Cantwell.

Inscriptions on grave stones from cemetery on farm of A. J. Sloop located on Hussey road, about 4½ miles from Flemingsburg, Fleming county, Kentucky. Copied by Krickle K. Carrick, of Brookline, Mass., June 15, 1939.

John Hart, Esqr, born April 19, 1742 and died April 25, 1832, aged 90 yrs: & 6 ds.

Col. David Hart, born August 15, 1770 & died April 2, 1835 aged 65 Yrs. 7 ms & 18 ds.

In Memory of Matilda Hart, consort of D. Hart. Died Aug. 25, 1842, ag'd 70 years.

In Memory of Polly S. consort of L. D. Browning, born Sept. 29, 1798 and died June 22, A. D. 1840 in the 42nd year of her age.

In Memory of Lydia Lewellin, consort of John A. Lewellin, who died April 19, 1835, agd. 32 years, 8 ms & 26 ds.

> From adverse blasts & lowring storms
> Her favour soul he bore
> & with yon bright angelic forms
> She lives to die no more

Margaret T. daughter of T. & M. Shanlin, born April 28, 1844; died Dec. 3, 1863 (Should the name be Shanklin?)

> O do not weep or grieve for me,
> You know I must go home,
> I was upon a visit here,
> And now I must return

In Memory of Mary S. daughter of Thomas & Margaret Shanklin & consort of Geo. Ivens. Died May 15, 185.., aged 20 yrs., 4 mo., 20 dss

Addison S., son of M. T. & H. Evans. Born March 21, 1843; died May 19, 1843.

Jane S., wife of T. L. Turner. Born Dec. 18, 1836; died May 23, 1857.

In Memory of Simon Carpenter, born Oct. 8, 1775; died May 11, 1859.

——————of ..on Carpent...., born Aug. 15, 1793; died June 3, 1870.

In Memory of Susan M., daughter of G. M. & Ann J. Lauman. Died Dec. 14, 1840 aged 2 yrs. 7 mo. & 13 ds.

Lucinda, wife of J. H. Evans. Born Sept. 23, 180.. (3 or 8); died _____.

Adalade H., dau. of M. T. & H. Evans. Born Apr. 11, 1844; died May 29, 1844.

Mary Evans wife of Joseph Evans & daughter of David & Katharine Thomas, born May 21, 1772; died July 17, 1830.

> Beloved in life & lamented in death
> Yet could she speak she now would say
> Weep not for me God's voice obey
> (all that was visible)

In Memory of Margaret S. Tibbs, consort of Wm. Tibbs, departed this life Dec. 18, 184...

## FRISTOE
### Mason County, Kentucky, Court Records

*FRISTOE FAMILY*

(Compiled by Lula Reed Boss, Maysville, Kentucky)

**MASON COUNTY, KENTUCKY COURT RECORDS** (abstracts)

(Formed 1789 from Bourbon county)

DEED BOOK A.—Page 198—Dated September 7, 1789.

Richard Graham of Prince William county, Virginia, to John Fristoe of county of Bourbon, District of Kentucky ... Whereas Richard Graham stands bound unto John Fristoe for three several bonds or obligations in the sum of 832 lbs. 15 shillings and 6 pence each to be paid on or before September 7, 1794, all dated September 7, 1789, and are to be discharged in gold at 5 shilling and 4 pence the pennyweight or dollars at 6 shilling each agreeable to the present Standard of Virginia currency. In consideration of said debt, Richard Graham mortgages to John Fristoe land in District of Kentucky and county of Mason containing 13,470 acres, survey bearing date of June 2, 1783, two-thirds of which said tract was patented 16th of June, 1786, and granted by the Commonwealth of Virginia unto Richard Graham, and the other one-third unto the said John Fristoe assignee of Thomas Lee assignee of John Edwards who was assignee of the said Richard Graham. Land located on the waters of North Fork of Licking river. Witnesses to mortgage: Peter Ringo, Joseph Ringo, Major Ringo, Lewis Lee, Carty Wells, William Farrow and Hugh Forbes.

(The mortgage of John Fristoe, dated July 6, 1789, to Thomas Lee Sr., is recorded in Deed Book X, page 255, Prince William County, Virgini court records.)

### DEED BOOK B-1—Page 218
#### Dated June 2, 1794

John Fristoe of Bourbon county, District of Kentucky and State of

Virginia, to Richard Graham of Dumfries (Prince William county) and State aforesaid . . . Whereas John Fristoe did some years ago purchase from Richard Graham one-third part of a tract of land containing 13,470 acres being 4,493 acres for which the said Fristoe (as assignee of Thomas Lee who was assignee of John Edwards who was assignee of said Graham) obtained a patent from the Land Office . . . Now this Indenture . . . John Fristoe conveys to Richard Graham all that one-third part of the tract of land lying and being on Cabbin Creek and North Fork of Licking in Mason county, District of Kentucky, containing 13,470 acres. Witnesses to deed: Peter Ringo, Joseph Ringo, Major Ringo, Lewis Lee, Carty Wells, William Farrow, Thomas Young and Hugh Forbes. Recorded in Mason county February 24, 1795.

### DEED BOOK C-1—Page 45
### Dated April 24, 1800

John Fristoe of Fairfax county, Virginia, conveys to Henry Disbrow and John Graham, both of Mason county, Kentucky, for 292 lbs. two parcels of land in Mason county . . . "beginning at the n. e. cor. of Richard Graham's survey originally granted to John Edwards assignee of James Thompson attorney for Richard Graham. . . . "

### DEED BOOK A-C—Page 14—DEED OF TRUST
### Dated April 18, 1803

Between John Edwards, Sr., of Bourbon county, Kentucky, of the first part, and William Lamb of Mason county, Kentucky, Asa Bealle of Mason county, Haden Edwards of Franklin county, and John Fristoe of Mason county, and John Edwards, Jr., of Bourbon county, of the second part, and David Davis, Jacob Spears, Damovel Talbot, Daniel Vertner, Haden Edwards, Sr., and John Edwards, Jr., James Hutchison, James Carter, . . . . . . . . . . Brooks, Charles Spears, William Chessman, George and Edward Thompson, Thomas Hocheley, Samuel and Daniel Tebbs and Simon West, of the third part . . . That John Edwards, Sr., for divers good causes hereunto moving and more particularly in consideration of the sum of 5 shillings . . . doth by These Presents convey to William Lamb, Asa Bealle, Haden Edwards, Jr., John Fristoe and John Edwards . . . all the land tenements and hereditaments whatsoever situated either in the State of Kentucky or Military land in the State of Ohio . . . they to sell land for debts of John Edward, Sr., due the parties of the third part . . .

### DEED BOOK H—Page 326—RELEASE
### Dated April 19, 1804

John Fristoe of Mason county, State of Kentucky, releases and forever quit claims the mortgage executed by Richard Graham to John Fristoe September 7, 1789.

### DEED BOOK O—Page 337
### Dated May 4, 1815

John Fristoe and Jemimia his wife, convey to Thomas Peck, all of Mason county, "land on Limestone road adjoining the town of Washington in Mason county, State of Kentucky." (This property had been purchased April 10, 1811. Deed Book M., page 113).

### COURT ORDER BOOK H—Page 161
#### December Court, 1817

"On motion of William C. Rawls, it is ordered that a summons be issued against James Mattocks and Jemima his wife, late Jemima Fristoe, executor of the will of John Fristoe, deceased, to appear at the January Court and show cause why the said James Mattocks shall not give security for the execution of the will."

### DEED BOOK 36—Page 414
#### December 2, 1831

Charles Humphreys, deputy for William Reed, Sheriff of Mason county, of the one part, to Thompson Fristoe, of Mason county . . . Thompson Fristoe was the high bidder for the property of the estate of Thomas McKee "in the hands of John Griffith and Samuel Fitzgerald, his administrators, that had come into the hands of Thomas McKee and Columbus McKee his heirs at law. Thompson Fristoe purchased lot fronting 29 feet on Plumb street."

### DEED BOOK 39—Page 86
#### March 19, 1833

Jesse Fristoe of Maysville, Kentucky. to Thompson Fristoe, of same place . . . party of the first part conveys to party of the second part for $900 lot on Third street adjoining lot now owned by Jesse Fristoe and on which he now resides, and which was sold to said Jesse Fristoe by John Marshall. Witnesses to deed: Richard Fristoe and Benjamin Willett.

### DEED BOOK 39—Page 1
#### June 1, 1833

James W. Moss and Mary his wife, of Boone county, Missouri, to Richard Fristoe, of Mason county, Kentucky . . . convey for $1434.16 land "on Limestone creek being part of May's 800 acres and part of a parcel of John and Thomas Millers' survey . . . thence to James Wilson's line . . . "

### COURT ORDER BOOK M—Page 424
#### December Court, 1836

Estate of Silas Fristoe, deceased. Richard Fristoe administrator. Moses Dimmitt surety in the sum of $1,000.

### DEED BOOK 49—Page 81
#### June 4, 1839

James W. Moss and Mary his wife, of St. Louis county, Missouri, convey to Richard Fristoe, William Fristoe and Benjamin Willett, all of Mason county, Kentucky, for $750 "land on Limestone creek."

## DEED BOOK 55—Page 141
### March 28, 1846

Richard Fristoe of Mason county, to Jesse Fristoe, of same place, "land on Limestone creek" . . . to Benjamin Jacob's cor. . . . thence to Lewis Jacob's cor. . . . "

(Signed)   Richard Fristoe, Sarah Fristoe

## COURT ORDER BOOK P—Page 207
### October Court, 1852

Sarah Maria Higdon, infant orphan of Levi Higdon, deceased, with Catherine Higdon, now Catherine Bowman, wife of Joshua B. Bowman, acting as guardian.

## DEED BOOK 63—Page 213
### March 9, 1854

Richard Fristoe of Mason county, to Robert Fristoe, of same place, conveys for one dollar to Robert Fristoe "land on Flemingsburg pike beginning at the n. e. cor. of Robert Fristoe's farm . . . "

## DEED BOOK 72—Page 99
### December 18, 1865

"Heirs of Thomas Fristoe, deceased." . . . "confirm to Jacob and Elizabeth H. Reed, R. B. Case, Robert Fristoe and Alfred McAtee, their heirs and assigns, or either of them forever, the right of way to pass and repass over the lands which we inherited from said Thomas Fristoe, deceased, along the way or road as now used by said parties in coming down the hollow of the Maysville and Mt. Sterling turnpike, striking the said turnpike near the birdge across the branch putting into Limestone creek the side (toward Maysville) of the late residence of said Thomas Fristoe, deceased, and near the line of Hiram T. Pearce, said way or road to be of sufficient width for a wagon."

This Indenture, "Heirs of Thomas Fristoe, deceased," was signed by: Robert Fristoe, Barnette Fristoe, Mahala Mackey, Richard Fristoe, Malinda Higdon and Jesse Fristoe. (Thomas Fristoe left no wife or children so his heirs were his brothers and sisters).

## DEED BOOK V—Page 202
### November 9, 1819

Charles Ward, deputy Sheriff of Mason county, and acting for Samuel Baldwin, High Sheriff of said county, conveys to John Higgins, of Mason county, Inn Lot No. 105 . . . according to a "writ issued from the Clerk's office of the Montgomery County Circuit Court and bearing teste of Micajah Harnson, clerk thereof on the 9th day of October, 1819, directed to the Sheriff of Mason county came to the hands of the said Sheriff of Mason county on October 11, 1819, commanding that the estate of Jemima Mattocks, late Jemima Fristoe, and James Mattocks her husband, as far as the derived estate either real or personal by devizee from John Fristoe, deceased, and Thomas Starke, late of the sheriff's baliwick . . . "judgment in the sum of $1840 rendered in a decree of the Montgomery Circuit Court" . . . "John Peebles recovered against said parties for the value of 184 acres of land in the said decree mentioned whereof the said Jemima Mattocks, James Mattocks and Thomas Starke are convicted as appears of record" . . . therefore "a lot in the town of Washington, Mason county, known as lot No. 105 and a mulatto slave named Fanny, as the property of the said Jemima Mattocks and James Mattocks, devised to the said Jemima by the said John Fristoe, deceased, was sold to satisfy the debt. John Higgins was the high bidder and purchased the lot mentioned.

### DEED BOOK 28—Page 328
### March 2, 1825

Henry Williams of Mason county, mortgages to Jesse and Richard Fristoe, of same place, slaves Mary, Hester and David, to secure them for money Henry Williams owed Marshall Key.

### DEED BOOK 54—Page 303
### January 4, 1838

Richard Fristoe of Mason county, gives Right of Way through his land and use of rock thereon to the Mt. Sterling Turnpike Company.

### DEED BOOK 48,—Page 123
### September 23, 1839

William K. Wall executor of estate of Samuel January, deceased, to Richard Fristoe, of Mason county . . . "lot on Limestone creek on the south side of the turnpike leading from Maysville to Flemingsburg."

### DEED BOOK 49—Page 191
### July 20, 1840

Daniel Fristoe of Maysville, Kentucky, purchases Lot No. 36 fronting on Third street from the Commissioners of Mason County.

### DEED BOOK 50—Page 352
### September 11, 1841

Alfred Fristoe of Mason county from Francis Cobb and Ann, his wife, Lot No. 37.

### DEED BOOK 58—Page 552
### Dated March 19, 1849

Jesse Fristoe and Hannah his wife, of Mason county, convey to Barnett Fristoe, of same place, land on Limestone creek.

## EARLY LAND WARRANTS OF ADAMS COUNTY STATE OF OHIO

Entry No. 1786
200 acres
Watercourse: Lick Fork
Warrant No. 3996
John Fristoe
Date: September 30, 1800
Surveyor: John Beasley

Virginia Military Bounty Land Warrant No. 3996 for 200 acres of land was issued November 15, 1785 to Benjamin Smither in consideration of his services for the Revolutionary War as a soldier in the Virginia Continental Line. John Fristoe, assignee, located the warrant on a tract of land described as Survey No. 1786 in Adams County, Virginia Military District, Ohio. The tract was patented to John Beasley, assignee of John Fristoe. (Vol. 3, page 349—U. S. Department of The Interior, General Land Office, Washington, D. C.)

## 1790 CENSUS RECORDS OF STAFFORD COUNTY, VIRGINIA

John Fristoe, 3 in family
John Fristoe, 9 in family
Richard Fristoe, 7 in family
William Fristoe, 8 in family

## WILL BOOK D—Page 170

Will of "John Fristoe of Mason county, Kentucky." "Old and infirm of body, but of sound and retentive mind and memory." After just debts and funeral expenses are paid "I give and bequeath unto my beloved wife Jemimah as an evidence of my affection and token of gratitude for her affectionate attention to me in my old age, and as the little which I leave has been obtained in a great measure by her own industry, I hope and trust that my children and grandchildren will not think hard of this my disposition of it, and the more especially as most of them have been assisted by me in my prosperous days" . . . leaves entire estate to wife. Wife Jemimiah, executrix. Witness to will: Samuel Taylor, James Byers and John Chambers. Dated: December 3, 1810; probated July Court, 1817.

James Mattocks was granted license August 25, 1817, to marry Mrs. Jemima Fristoe. Reuben Ringo signed as bondsman.

(According to "Overwharton Parish Register, Old Stafford County Virginia, 1720-1760," by William F. Boogher, John Fristoe was born June 6, 1741. Jemima ———— Fristoe was the second wife of John Fristoe and not the mother of any of his children. See: Clift's "History of Maysville and Mason County." pages 149 and 150.)

## COURT ORDER BOOK H—Page 109

The will of John Fristoe was proven July 14, 1817 by the oaths of John Chambers and James Byers, two of the subscribing witnesses.

Page 170, January Court, 1818.

Administration of the estate of John Fristoe, with will annexed, is granted Joshua C. Laws and Elizabeth his wife. Joseph Frazee surety in the sum of $4,000. "Jemima Mattocks, late widow of the said deceased, having been regularly summoned to appear here on this day and show cause why she should not give security, and she having refused to do so, and it also appearing to the court that the estate of John Fristoe, deceased, hath been greatly wasted."

## WILL BOOK J— Page 363

Will of "Jesse Fristoe of Mason county, State of Kentucky." "Being sick and weak in body, but of sound mind and disposing memory." Leaves to son, Thompson Fristoe; son Daniel Fristoe and son John Fristoe, "balance to rest of children who shall then be living or to their heirs." Son Thompson Fristoe and John Wilson, executors. Witnesses to will: George Grant, James Jacobs and Lewis Jacobs. Dated: February 22, 1833; probated September Court, 1833.

## WILL BOOK R.—Page 33

Will of "Richard Fristoe of Mason county, Kentucky." Leaves to beloved wife Sarah Fristoe during her natural life all estate real, personal and mixed, what is left at her death to go to: Thomas Fristoe (requests that he live with his mother); Son Barnette; granddaughter Elizabeth Mackey; and other children, namely: Robert, Richard, Jesse, Fanny Willett, Malinda Higdon and Mahala Mackey. Sons Thomas and Barnette Fristoe, executors. Witnesses to will: James P. Wilson, J. N. Wilson and Robert A. Cochran. Dated September 3, 1856; probated January Court, 1857.

## DEED BOOK 66.—Page 578
### November 25, 1858

Barnett Fristoe and Margaret his wife, to James P. Wilson, all of Mason county, Kentucky,............parties of the first part convey to party of the second part land "deeded and willed to the party of the first part by Richard Fristoe."

## MARRIAGE RECORDS

Thomas Fristoe married Margaret L. Lawrence October 3, 1815. (Copied from old Marriage Book. Bond is missing.)

John Wilson granted license to marry Mary Fristoe, August 9, 1821. Jesse Fristoe, bondsman.

Benjamin Willett granted license to marry Frances (called Fanny) Fristoe, February 14, 1822. Richard Fristoe, bondsman.

William Mackey granted license to marry Mahala Fristoe, February 16, 1826. Richard Fristoe, bondsman.

Levi Higdon granted license to marry Malinda (called Linney) Fristoe, August 14, 1831. Richard Fristoe, bondsman.

John Jacobs granted license to marry Ann Fristoe, June 25, 1832. Jesse Fristoe, bondsman.

Daniel Fristoe granted license to marry Lorando Holiday, April 10, 1840. Frederick Weedon, bondsman.

## WILL BOOK O.—Page 16
### September Court, 1847

Dower in slaves and land allotted to Malinda Higdon, widow of Levi Higdon, deceased, and children, namely; Joanna Higdon, wife of Ebenezer Brittain; Nancy Higdon; Elizabeth Higdon; Emily Higdon; Catherine

Higdon, wife of Joshua B. Bowman; Leonard Higdon; Jesse Higdon; Mary Frances Higdon; Sarah Maria Higdon and Levi Dent Higdon.

October, 1852, Joshua B. Bowman and wife Catherine, were residents of Harrison county, Kentucky. (Court Order Book P, page 207).

## COURT ORDER BOOK T.—Page 373
### July Court, 1873

An Instrument of Writing bearing date of January 14, 1871, purporting to be the last Will and Testament of Robert Fristoe, deceased, was this day produced in court and filed. On motion of Silas F. Fristoe and Elizabeth H. Reed, it is ordered that they be, and are hereby entered of record as contestants of said will.

### Page 504—July Court, 1874

On motion of James B. Fristoe, Silas F. Fristoe and Jacob Reed, it is ordered that administration upon the goods, chattels, credits, and effects of Robert Fristoe, deceased, be, and the same is hereby granted unto them. Sureties for same: W. P. Watkins, James Curtis and W. H. McGranaghan.

*     *     *     *     *

Robert Fristoe and his wife, Lucinda (Bartlett) Fristoe had issue:
1. Elzabeth Hildreth Fristoe, born August 20, 1826, wife of Jacob Reed.
2. James B. Fristoe, born April 10, 1828.
3. Silas Franklin Fristoe, born April 30, 1833.

### MAYSVILLE EAGLE

Copy of newspaper on file in the Maysville Public Library, Maysville, Kentucky.

Died May 8, 1850 Miss Ruth Fristoe after a brief illness.

### 1850 CENSUS RECORDS OF MASON COUNTY

Richard Fristoe, 75 years of age, farmer, born in Virginia.
Sarah Fristoe, 72 years of age, born in Virginia.
Thomas Fristoe, 40 years of age, born in Kentucky.
George Fristoe, 27 years of age, born in Kentucky.
Barnette Fristoe, 31 years of age, born in Kentucky.
Margaret Fristoe, 18 years of age, born in Kentucky.
Robert Fristoe, 50 years of age, born in Kentucky.
Lucinda Fristoe, 43 years of age, born in Kentucky.
Alfred Fristoe, 42 years of age, born in Kentucky.
Elizabeth Fristoe, 38 years of age, born in Kentucky.
Eliza A. Fristoe, 14 years of age, born in Kentucky.
William T. Fristoe, 13 years of age, born in Kentucky.
George Fristoe, 7 years of age, born in Kentucky.
Richard H. Fristoe, 4 years of age, born in Kentucky.
Lewis A. Fristoe, 2 years of age, born in Kentucky.
Caroline E. Fristoe, 1 year of age, died in 1850.
Jesse Fristoe, 35 years of age, born in Kentucky.
Hannah Fristoe, 25 years of age, born in Ohio.

Andrew A. Fristoe, 6 years of age, born in Ohio.
Richard H. Fristoe, 4 years of age, born in Ohio.
Sally A. Fristoe, 6 months of age, born in Ohio.
Mahala Mackey, 45 years of age, born in Virginia.
Malinda Higdon, 49 years of age, born in Virginia.
James B. Fristoe, 22 years of age, born in Kentucky.
Silas F. Fristoe, 17 years of age, born in Kentucky.
Elizabeth H. Harding, 23 years of age, born in Kentucky.
Lucinda V. Harding, 4 years of age, born in Kentucky.
Benjamin Willett, 62 years of age, born in Virginia.

Old pages from Fristoe Bible pasted in Martin-Johnson Bible in the possession of Mrs. M. Peale Collier, of Paris, Kentucky, and copied by Mrs. William B. Ardery, of Paris.

Daniel Fristoe was born December 7th, 1739.
Mary Fristoe was born September 11, 1735.
Susannah Fristoe, daughter of Daniel Fristoe and Mary his wife, was born June 29, 1760.
Lydia Fristoe was born November 17, 1761.
Mary Fristoe was born May 22, 1765.
Thomas Fristoe was born November the 27th, 1767.
Thomas Fristoe was born January 17, 1770.
Ann Fristoe was born March the 13th, 1772.
Catherine Fristoe was born June 19, 1774.
Henry Williams, son of George and Mary Williams, was born March the 10th, 1779.
George Williams was born April the 1st, 1781.
The first daughter of Rhodin and Catherine Hord was born March the 23rd, 1801 and survived 8 days.
Mary Hord was born May the 7th, 1802.
Thamar Hord was born the 7th of January, 1805.
William Henry Hord was born December the 9th, 1807.
Daniel Thomas Fristoe Hord was born April 10, 1810.
William Grinstead was born August the 18th, 1772.
Rhodin Hord was born January the 1st, 1777.
Prudence Grinstead, daughter of William and Ann Grinstead, was born the 5th of October, 1793.

## MARRIAGES

William Grinstead and Ann his wife were married the 7th of January, 1793.

Rhodin Hord and Catherine his wife were married September the 9th, 1800.

## DEATHS

Daniel Fristoe departed this life November 3, 1774 in the 35th year of his life.

George Williams Senr. departed this life the 4th day of July, 1791.

James Grinstead departed this life on Sunday evening, April the 6th, 1807, aged 84 years and 4 months.

Thomas Fristoe departed this life April the 23rd, 1815.

Edmund Martin and Susannah his wife married the 10th of March, 1788.

Elijah Martin and Rebecca Boggs were married November 27, 1791.

## HARROD DATA

(Contributed by Mrs. Ila Earle Fowler)

1. Harrodsburg, Mercer County, Ky. Book 17, page 339-408 11/29/1831—John Fauntleroy trusted to sons Wm. K. and James H. 500 acre tract on which he and Ann Harrod lived on Harrod's Run—place known as Harrod's Station.

   Slaves—Eleven—Allin, Nelly, Frank, Ellen, Susan, Isabela, Joseph, Abraham, Sarah—also equity of redemption in girl

   Gabriella mortgaged to Joseph Weisiger;

   George mortgaged to Joseph Weisiger;

   George mortgaged to Jawb Chaplin.

2. Trusteeship to provide maintenance of wife and children as he was deeply involved and feared the loss, etc.—and paying his (John's) debts—page 408. He and his wife to have services of one negro man and woman their life time and minor children to be educated.

3. Mercer County—Book 1, page 1:

   1786-1811—John Willis of Mercer County to Beverly Mann of same— 75 pounds—land on Salt River—200 acres—part of Grant of Joseph Willis, 6/15/1784—mentions corner of David Caldwell.

4. Mercer County, Book 1, page 11.

   Mary Fauntleroy appointed Wm. and Richard Keene of Maryland, Attorney in all her matters and as Executrix of Thos. Stephens, deceased—and estate of late husband, John Fauntleroy.

   Book 1, page 34

   Jas. Harrod to John Mahan 100 acres for 10 pounds—part of tract on which Harrod lived.

   Mentions Wm. Lawrence's Corner—John Cowan's (J. H. signed) line 4/27/1787.

5. Mercer County, Book 1, page 93

   Peter Casey and Nancy—wife—105 pounds sell to Nathan Neil—land on Salt River—202 acres—part of 1 survey of 1,000 acres—and 1 of 300 acres by Sd. Casey 8/20/1786—all houses, etc.—Wit. Stephen Ashby, Robt. McAfee, (Ashby removed to Hopkins Co. and Casey moved on to Union County and settled Caseyville.)

   Boyle County, Kentucky, Records, DANVILLE. Copied March 12, 1941, by Mrs. Ila Earle Fowler

   Abstract of the will of Ann Harrod, widow of James Harrod of Harrod's Fort and Harrodsburg. Written Nov. 24, 1842, probated May term Boyle County Court, 1843.

   Mentions grand-daughter, Mary Ann Ray, with bequest of $1.00; grand-daughter, Eliza Davis, with $1.00; great-grandson, John Fauntleroy, Jr., $1.00; great-grandson, Edward Moore, $1.00; grand-daughter, Nancy Fauntleroy, one negro woman, Jane, at $250 to be taken out of her part of estate; grandson, Griffin T. Fauntleroy, one negro boy, Manuel, at $200, to be taken out of his part of her estate; grandson, Jas. H.

Fauntleroy, one negro, Ned, at $150, to be taken out of estate; great-granddaughter, Elizabeth Ray, 50c; remainder of estate to be divided among the other grand-children hereinafter named: John H. Fauntleroy, David E. Fauntleroy, Maria W. Martin, Margaret Beckett, Robert Fauntleroy, Samuel Fauntleroy. W. H. Martin and her grand-son, John H. Fauntleroy, named Executors. Witnesses: John D. Terhune and Wm. M. Brown. Duff Grenn, Clerk B. C. C. Book 1, p. 39.—Power of Atty. John H. Fauntleroy to Jas. Burnett.

This names eleven of the children of Margaret Harrod and her husband, John Fauntleroy. A later deed mentions that Margaret Harrod's estate was divided into twelvths. The 12th child was evidently a daughter who married .... Moore. (I have seen a statement that Margaret Harrod Fauntleroy had 13 children. Eleven of them survived her, and the 12th left a son, Edward Moore.—I.E.F.)

Abstracts of some later deeds that give more information on the marriages of the children of Margaret Harrod Fauntleroy.

Deed Book 1, Boyle Co., page 66; David E. Fauntleroy of Platte Co., Missouri, power of attorney (to sell all his inherited lands except "The Harrod Station Farm") to John H. Fauntleroy and W. H. Martin.

Oct. 12, 1842.

Book 1, page 39; Margaret Fauntleroy's heirs, power of attorney to John H. Fauntleroy, to sell lands, etc.

Page 153; Nancy Fauntleroy, power of attorney to Wm. H. Martin, her brother-in-law, June 24, 1842.

Page 158; David E. Fauntleroy, power of attorney to A. J. Caldwell, July 13, 1843.

Page 188; James H. Fauntleroy, power of attorney to A. J. Caldwell.

Page 452; John H. Fauntleroy, to Robert Montgomery, deed to land, received $100, part of third payment, and other had been secured.

Isham Ray and wife, Mary Ann (Fauntleroy), Charles Davis and wife, Mary (Fauntleroy); James H. Fauntleroy; Wm. Bickett and wife, Mary (Fauntleroy); Griffin T. Fauntleroy; David E. Fauntleroy; Nancy Fauntleroy; Robert W. Fauntleroy; Samuel Fauntleroy; all appoint John H. Fauntleroy and Wm. H. Martin Attys. with power, etc.

Book 2, page 1; Griffin T. Fauntleroy to Robert Montgomery, Sept. 13, 18—.

Book 3—Oct. 23, 1849, it appears that Samuel K. Fauntleroy had been an infant at his mother's death, and the Court had sold his land, and Commissioners had collected, etc. At this date he signs deed to Robert Montgomery who had moved to Louisville, for his part of 300 acres and 1 rood. The final payment had been $682 or ½ the whole price of his part, and receipt is given for $172 more.

Book 3, page 417—Sept. 11, 1850, the heirs: Wm. S. and Nancy F. Slaughter; Isham and Mary Ann Ray; Charles and Eliza Davis; Wm. H. and Maria Martin; Samuel, Griffin T., James H., John H. Fauntleroy—and great-grandchildren: Edwin R. Moore; grand-daughters, Margaret Fauntleroy and Rebecca Fauntleroy. Also daughter Margaret Bickitt and husband, Wm. G. Bickett. The land had been sold for $35 an acre, 316½ acres, brought $11,068.75.

## HOPKINS COUNTY, KY., MARRIAGES

(Furnished by Mrs. Ila Earle Fowler)

(2nd dates are those of the return of the marriage by the minister to county clerk)

The first marriage in Hopkins county was that of William Oates and Elizabeth Earle. They were of Muhlenberg county and the license was granted there and returned in Hopkins. She may have lived in Hopkins. Her father was Baylis Earle, Jr., son of Judge Baylis Earle and Mary Prince Earle of Spartanburg, S. C. Further notice of this marriage in Rothert's History of Muhlenberg County, Ky.

Other marriages in 1807 were:

July 27—James Davis and Jane Lovin

Oct. 14—James Howell, Esther Cardwell; John Bourland, minister

Date Blank—John Harvey and Anna Hewlett

August 3—Henry Neely and Sally Christian; John Bourland, minister

Dec. 20—John Mendsor and Rebecca Clark. (This may be Jonas Menser or John Menser, surely Menser)

Oct. 8—John Robertson and Patsey Davis; John Bourland, minister

1808:—

Feb. 19—John Jones and Ruth Carroll

Feb. 1-2—Joseph Kuykendall and Betsey M. Morrow, John Bourland, minister

March 13—Nathaniel Harding and Rachel Branson

April 27—Solomon Summers and Mary Earle (widow of Thomas Prince Earle, who came from S. C. 1800, d. 1802-3) by John Bourland

June 1—Nathan Hibbs and Polly Bourland; John Bourland

Sept. 14—James Taylor and Catherine Barker; John Bourland

Sept. 27—Alexander Miller and Rebecca Bishop; John Bourland

June 8—James Rash and Delilah Bone; John Bourland

Nov. 1—John Hibbs and Elizabeth Campbell

Oct. 31—Araham Eastwood and Jemima Merritt; John Bourland

Nov. 8—John Chapel and Martha Carter; John Bourland

Dec. 5—George Hooker and Nancy Orton; John Bourland

Dec. 30—Alexander M. Henry and Nancey Richards; John Bourland

Feb. 25-28—John Daughterty and Susannah Parker; Thos. Adams, J. P.

1809:—

Jan. 23-26—John Nants and Margaret Kennedy; W. R. Weir, J. P. (Nance ?)

Jan. 24-26—James Moore and Margaret Todd; John Bourland

Feb. 6, Mch. 18—James Prather and Nancy Timmons; Thos. Adams, J. P.

Mch. 6-July 30—James Murphy and Elizabeth Bone

Feb. 27-Mch. 9—Eli Bishop and Mary Gill; John Bourland (Progenitor of perhaps all the Bishops of the county. I have often heard him spoken of, he must have lived to a good old age. IEF)

March 10—Richard Baker and Betsey Tier

Mch. 8-9—Jacob Wolf and Milly Meredith; Rev. J. Bourland
April 12-13—Martin Dyal and Polly Redmon; Rev. J. Bourland
May 20-25—Ishman Conner and Anne Shepherd; Rev. J. Bourland
Aug. 3—Pearson Newsom and Mary or Nancy Davis; Rev. J. Bourland
Aug. 7-10—Michael Harmon and Bethany Parker; Thos. Adams, J. P.
Aug. 18-24—Richard Brown and Nancy Palmer; John Bourland
Sept. 12—Stephen Timmons and Sarah Laffoon; J. Bourland
Nov. 24-26—Franklin E. Owen and Eliza T. Berry; W. R. Weir, J. P.
Dec. 23-24—John Bailey and Patsey Sisk; J. Bourland

1810: —
Jan. 6-7—Daniel Shemate and Delilah Ashby; Thos. Adams, J. P.
Feb. 24—John Walker and Charity Palmer; John Bourland
Feb. 26—Joseph Rogers and Rachel Howell; John Bourland
Apr. 4-7—Daniel C. Quinn and Sarah Littleton; J. Bourland
Apr. 24—Henry Harman and Nancy Murphy; Samuel Harvey, J. P.
Apr. 24-25—Aaron Reynolds and Nancy Crowley; Thos. Adams, J. P.
June 13, Sept. 4—James Edmiston and Mary Matthews; W. R. Weir
June 18-21—Daniel Campbell and Letty Orton; John Bourland
June 21, Jul. 1—James Harrell and Biddy Scroggin; W. R. Weir, J. P.

On July 23, 1947—Claiborne R. Baker, aged 64, died in Madisonville Hospital. Had been interested in mining, etc. Night clerk at Madison Hotel. (His mother was Bettie Knox, daughter of John Knox. She married brother of Viola Baker, who married Dr. Eldred Glover Davis. Her husband died. She came to live with William and Elizabeth Earle when Claiborne was a little boy.

1812: —
Oct. 16-17—Lefford French and Jane Blackwell
Dec. 8-19—Moses Brown and Edith McKinney

1813: —
Jan. 15—James Leiper and Sarah Ashby
Feb. 9-13—Samuel Phillips and Rebecca Childress Whitesides; Sam'l. Brown, M. G.
Apr. 19-29—Cabet Long and Hannah Bishop; John Bourland (Caleb ?)
Mch. 13-17—John Burkhalve and Catherine Timmons; John Bourland
Mch. 13—Stephen Timmons and Polly Settles
Mch. 13-May 4—George Timmons and Elizabeth Minor; Thos. Adams, J. P.
Mch. 24—Isaac Dial and Rebecca Fike; Thos. Adams, J. P.
Apr. 13-15—John Edwards and Patsey Phipps; Thos. Adams, J. P.
May 19-20—John Newman and Jane Gardner; E. Givens, J. P.
June 4—Isaac Thompson and Lenna Garis; T. Adams, J. P.
June 8-10—Charley Wyat and Phebe Tidlock; John Bourland
June 26-28—John Goard and Rachel Bourland; John Bourland
June 26—Lewis Welch and Sarah G. Guime
June 29-July 1—Colgate Scott and Phereby Parker; T. Adams, J. P.
July 9-11—Thomas Foley and Patsey Brown; Thos. Adams, J. P.
July 14-15—Cabb Litton and Polly Hawkins; John Bourland
July 20-22—Isaac Coffman and Marah Harber; John Bourland

Aug. 6-10—William Bradshaw and Susan Wyatt
Aug. 11-12—James Kennedy and Rachel Sloan; E. Givens, J. P.
Sept. 13—George Adams and Peggy McKinney; E. Givens, J. P.
Blank Date—Stephen Houseman and Ann Esom
Oct. 4—Samuel Adams and Mary Bishop; E. Givens, J. P.
Oct. 16-17—Joseph Robertson and Elizabeth McNary; T. Adams, J. P.
Oct. 18-20—Wm. Easley and Rebecca Clayton; Daniel Brown
Oct. 21-22—Isaiah Cheek and Caty Thompson; E. Givens, J. P.
Nov. 2—John Bennett and Betsey Wade
Nov. 6-7—Chas. Cavanah and Lucy E. Owen; E. Givens, J. P.
Nov. 13-14—Joseph Trumble and Betsy Adams; T. Adams
Nov. 13-14—Thomas Robards and Nancy Timmons; T. Adams, J. P.
Nov. 30—Stephen Gray and Nancy Hill
Nov. 27—John Patterson and Jane Ramsey; Samuel Brown, M. G.
Aug. 11-14—Richard Parker and Polly Davis; E. Givens, J. P.

1814:—

Jan. 3—Robert Adams and Smitha Cates; E. Givens, J. P.
Jan. 12-13—Green Brown and Ann Brown; E. Givens, J. P.
Jan. 15-20—James Campbell and Annis Long; Thos. Adams, J. P.
Jan. 21—Stephen Parker and Catherine Ashby; Thos. Adams, J. P.
Feb. 2-4—James Finley and Patsey Dobyns; John Bourland
Feb. 7—Jesse Herrin and Rebecca Bourland
Feb. 7—Alfred Herrin and Elizabeth Littlepage; Rev. Lemuel Harvey
Feb. 21-24—David Herrin and Sally Herrin; Rev. John Bourland
Mch. 21-23—David Menser and Phebe Swinney; Rev. Paxam
Mch. 7-20—Joseph Davis and Lucy Herrin
Feb. 7-9—Joseph Crawley and Eleanor Ramsey; John Bourland
Mch. 15-17—Reading Barfield and Nancey Esom; John Bourland

1825:—Benjamin Knox to Ann C. P. Earle, Dec. 28

1828:

Peter Goad to Amanda Wilkins, April 25/May 1, Rev. E. W. Earle

1829:—

     Needham Dailey to Eliza T. Smith, June 18/25   Rev. E. W. Earle
Edward A. Pennington to Emaline ——————, Sept. 24/Oct. 4, Rev.
E. W. Earle

1830:—

John M. Johnson (Dr.) Elizabeth P(rince) Earle, Oct. 6/7. Rev. H. B.
     Hill

1832:—

Josephus White to Elizabeth Slaton, Mar. 31-April 5—Rev. E. W. Earle

1833:—

David Berry to Lenora A. Earle Sept. 30/Oct. 2, Silas B. Davis

1835:—

Hamilton Tomlinson to Margaret Reynolds, Feb. 2/5, Rev. E. W. Earle,
     M. G.

Felix G. Johnson (Dr.) to Matilda J. Davis, Oct. 19. (He died).
    She married (?) Turbeville, was called Jane
Isaiah Clark to Jane Page, Sept. 15/26, E. W. Earle
Wilson A. Hunt to Martha Ann Barr, Apr. 13/16, E. W. Earle
Alderson W. Sisk to Polly Price, June 14

1837:—
Stephen D. Rash to Eliza Wilson, Ap. 5/6, Rev. S. L. Edgar
Stanley G. West to Tildann Almon, Aug. 22/24, E. W. Earle
George Bowman to Minerva Smith, Sept. 30/31, E. W. Earle
Stanley Hester to Lucy Amos, Apr. 9/9, E. W. Earle

1938:—
George Waetzel to Hetty Sisk, May 30/30, E. W. Earle
Emsley C. Bobbett to Mary W. Rash, Oct. 8/11, E. W. Earle

1839:—
Samuel W. Almon to Mary W. Gunn, Jan. 31/31, E. W. Earle, M. G.
Samuel Rorer to Josephine S. C. Earle, May 29/30, John W. Kelly, M. G.
John W. Hooker to Narcissus Hankins, June 6/6, E. W. Earle
Robert Sisk to Ceily Sisk, July 16/16, E. W. Earle
Rutherford Sisk to Susan Williams, Oct. 14/14, E. W. Earle

1840:
Daniel G. Denton to Orlena Agnes Almon, May 19/July 3, E. W. Earle
......Wesner to Trecy Grady, Sept. 21/22, E. W. Earle
Richard Littlepage to Delilah Shaw, Aug. 14/Sept. 14, E. W. Earle
A. J. Sisk to Sabrina Clark, July 6/6, E. W. Earle

1841:—
Edward T. Williams to Rhoda Ann Earle, Apr. 12/13, James Nisbet
John Price, to Eleanor Sisk, June 7/8, E. W. Earle
Joseph D. Morton to Deborah C. Robertson, Aug. 25/26, E. W. Earle
Madison Gamblin to Emaline L. Fox, Apr. 7/8, E. W. Earle

1842:—
Chas. E. Oates to Nancey H. Earle, Sept. 29/29, Rev. S. M. Wilkins
David C. Turbeville to Matilda J(ane) Johnson, Jan. 14

1844:—
Earle W. Davis to Mary Ann Adkins, Jan. 1818, John Bobbitt

1849:—
John B.(aylis) Earle to Sarah C. Woolfolk, Oct. 1/1, A. Boyd

1849:—
Oct. 1—John B. Earle, Sarah C. Woolfolk, A. Boyd, M. G. return
    Oct. 1, 1850

1861:—
Nov. 30—U. B. Earle, Paulina Gregory, by O. Collins, M. G.
    witnesses: H. S. Goodloe, A. W. Earle, at home of R. Gregory

1866:—
May 25—M. V. Earle to Miss M. F. Coleman, Thos. E. Young, M. of C. C.
    witnesses: B. C. Coleman, Alexander Teague, home of B. C. Coleman

## COUNTY RECORDS, HOPKINS COUNTY

1816.—Administration of Baylis Earle, Jr., Wife Ann Earle, Elizabeth Oates and her husband Wm. Oates; Polly Wickliffe and her husband Benjamin Wickliffe; S. B. Earle (Samuel Baylis); Jane Earle, under guardianship of Ann Earle, her mother.

1832.—Nancey Holland Earle, widow of John Earle, deeded land to Mr. Boggan; also gave her daughter, wife of Jeremiah Cravens, and her grandchildren: young Jere Cravens, John Cravens and Elizabeth N. Cravens, a negro slave.

1813, Dec. 31.—Inventory of Thomas Prince Earle (soldier of 1812), appraisers: Samuel Harvey; Elisha G. Smith; John Bone.

### Gravestones at Grapevine Cemetery near Madisonville

Josephine, wife of Samuel Rhorer, b. Feb. 14, 1820; died April 20, 1861.

Samuel Rhorer, died July 6, 1880, aged 70 years.

E. A. Almon, born June 29, 1837, died March 12, 1807.

Nancy C. Cargile, daughter of J. R. and E. M. Cargile, born March 5, 1856. (stone sunken below ground.)

Aspasia William Earle, born Sept. 25, 1815, died March 23, 1893.
Bettie, wife of A. W. Earle, born Sept. 26, 1826, died April 29, 1891.

John B. Knox, born Nov. 15, 1829, died March 4, 1910.

George W. Fowler, aged 47 years and 11 months, died Nov. 19, 1894.
George Leslie Fowler, son of George and S. I. (Susan Isabel) Fowler, b. Sept. 10, 1877, d. Feb. 15, 1879.

Fannie T. Stidham, dau. of John G. W. and Sophia W. Morton, b. Jan. 28, 1870, d. June 30, 1905. "Faithful to her trust even unto death."
Sophia W. Morton, b. June 10, 1831, d. Aug. 7, 1917.

John G. W. Morton, b. Aug. 20, 1822, d. Aug. 1, 1917. "Gone but not forgotten" on both stones.

P. M. Martin, b. April 7, 1843, d. Feb. 29, 1884.
Willie B., daughter of Josie R. and P. M. Martin, b. Jan. 16, 1876, d. May 21, 1876.

Josephine B., dau. M. C. and N. B. Earle, b. Aug. 10, 1856, d. April 26, 1878.

Mary W., wife of T. B. Earle, b. Sept. 6, 1851, d. June 22, 1882. (nee Mary King.) "Meet me in heaven" and Verse of Asleep in Jesus . . . this and Rock of Ages sung at her funeral.

Louisa M. Todd, b. July 2, 1859, d. May 18, 1881. (nee King.) Weeping willow on stone.

Capt. Wm. Inglish, departed this life March 12, 18..-. "In life beloved, in death lamented."

Thomas R. Cardwell, 1824-1915. Mexican War Veteran. (Middle name Risdon, called "Riz").

Paulina Robertson, dau. of R. and S. F. Gregory, b. Aug. 11, 1845, d. July 5, 1888. "I shall be satisfied to wake in his likeness."

## EARLE-DILLINGHAM RECORDS

(Furnished by Mrs. Charles Klapproth of Midland, Texas from the
Family Bible of John O. and Mary M. Dillingham Earle
of Hopkins county, White Plains)

John O. Earle, son of Edward H. and Susan Earle, b. Nov. 1818.

Mary M. Earle, dau. of Ephraim R. and Mary J. Dillingham, b. Jan. 1, 1827.

Manlius Valerius Earle, son of J. O. and Mary M. Earle, b. Dec. 28, 1842.

Florence Vitula Earle, dau. of J. O. and Mary M. Earle, b. Sept. 15, 1844.

Norman Robert Earle, son of J. O. and Mary M. Earle, b. July 15, 1846.

Edward Ephraim Earle, son of J. O. and Mary M. Earle, b. Nov. 27, 1848.

Mary Susan Earle, dau. of J. O. and Mary M. Earle, b. May 1, 1851.

Richard Franklin Earle, son of J. O. and Mary M. Earle, b. Aug. 17, 1853.

John Orville Madison Dillingham Earle, son of J. O. and Mary M. Earle, b. March 17, 1856.

Una Rosaline Earle, dau. of J. O. and Mary M. Earle, b. Nov. 1, 1860.

Margaret Melvina Earle, dau. of J. O. and Mary M. Earle, b. Dec. 24, 1863.

Ida R. Sophia Earle, dau. of J. O. and Mary M. Earle, b. Oct. 14, 1867.

### MARRIAGES

John Orville Earle and Mary Melvina Dillingham married Oct. 7, 1841.
Moses Alexander Denton and Florence Vitula Earle md. May 12, 1863.
Manlius Valerius Earle and Martha Frances Colman md. May 25, 1866.
A. M. Blaine and Mary Susan Earle md. Feb. 18, 1875.
Richard Franklin Earle and Laura Florence Laffoon md. Nov. 6, 1875.
Thomas Jefferson Denton and Una Rosaline Earle md. Oct. 5, 1876.
Mack Vanover and Ida S. Earle md. Oct. 14, 1867.

### DEATHS

Margaret Melvina Earle d. Feb. 17, 1863.
Norman Robert Earle d. May 6, 1864.
Martha Frances, wife of M. V. Earle, departed this life June 21, 1871.
Infant daughter of M. F. and M. V. Earle d. June 21, 1871.
Manlius Valerius Earle d. Jan. 12, 1873.
John Orville Madison Dillingham Earle d. Nov. 12, 1873.
John O. Earle d. May 14, 1895.
Mary Melvina Earle d. Feb. 1, 1912.
Abram Monroe Blaine d. Sept. 13, 1901.
Mary Susan Blaine d. Dec. 28, 1940.
Moses Alexander Denton d. Dec. 26, 1884.
Florence Earle Denton d. March 19, 1918.

(Certified by Nora Blaine Teague, Grant Co., New Mexico, who
received the Bible from her mother, Susan Earle Blaine, and handed
down to her by her parents, J. O. and Mary M. Earle, sworn before
T. M. Rivera, N. P.)

## DENTON FAMILY

(From the Family Bible of Alex and Florence Earle Denton, sworn to by Laura Bell Denton Pierce, before J. E. Rockett, N. P., Dallas county, Texas.)

### BIRTHS

Moses Alexander Denton, son of Jesse Denton, b. Feb. 25, 1837.

Florence Vitula Earle, dau. of John O. and Mary M. Earle, b. Sept. 15, 1844.

Rena Demaris Denton, dau. of Moses Alexander Denton and Florence Vitula Earle Denton, b. Jan. 29, 1864.

Francis Marion Denton, son of Moses Alexander Denton and Florence Vitula Earle Denton, b. March 15, 1866.

Laura Bell Denton, dau. of Moses Alexander Denton and Florence Vitula Earle Denton, b. Feb. 15, 1868.

Edward Byron Denton, son of Moses Alexander Denton and Florence Vitula Earle Denton, b. Aug. 24, 1870.

Barnie Demetress Denton, son of Moses Alexander Denton and Florence Vitula Earle Denton, b. May 19, 1873.

Charlie Elbert Denton, son of Moses Alexander Denton and Florence Vitula Earle Denton, b. March 31, 1876.

William Wallace Denton, son of Moses Alexander Denton and Florence Vitula Earle Denton, b. Sept. 14, 1878.

Alice Monica Denton, dau. of Moses Alexander Denton and Florence Vitula Earle Denton, b. May 4, 1881.

Moses Alexander Denton, Jr., son of Moses Alexander Denton and Florence Vitula Denton, b. Feb. 17, 1885.

### MARRIAGES

Moses Alexander Denton and Florence Vitula Earle Denton md. May 12, 1863.

Francis Marion Denton and Lucy Alice Hoag md. Nov. 19, 1891.

### DEATHS

Moses Alexander Denton d. Dec. 26, 1884.

Florence Vitula Earle Denton d. March 9, 1918.
(Added by Mrs. Klapporth)

Rena Denton Campbell Ross d. Sept. 5, 1942.

Francis Marion Denton, d. June 1, 1932.

Edward Denton d.

Charles Elbert Denton d. May 11, 1942.

Wallace Denton d.        Alice Denton Simonds d.

Moses Alexander Denton, Jr. d. in infancy.

Lucy Alice Hoag Denton d. July 4, 1940 (she was from the family of Benjamin S. Hoag of Cochocton, N. Y.)

## EARLE-DILLINGHAM-DENTON
### (By Mrs. Klapporth)

Laura Denton Pierce, dau. of Alex and Florence Earle Denton, b. Feb. 15, 1868, St. Charles, Ky., baptized at Brock, Texas, married at Dallas, Texas, March 24, 1900 to W. M. Pierce, son of John P. Pierce and Ann Elizabeth Pierce who was b. at Bloomingdale, Ill., Nov. 5, 1869.

Charles Elbert Denton, son of Moses Alexander Denton and Florence Vitula Earle Denton, b. Weatherford, Texas, March 31, 1876, died in Los Angeles, Calif., May 1, 1942.

Wallace Denton, son of Alex and Florence Denton, b. Sept. 14, 1879, d. Anadarko, Okla., md. Fay Hall in Okla.

Children of Laura Denton Pierce:

Willa Louise, b. March 22, 1901.

John Wentworth Pierce, b. Nov. 4, 1902.

William Wilner Pierce, b. Feb. 26, 1908.

.......... Louise Pierce (above) never md. is an M.D.

John Wentworth Pierce and his wife Mignon Pierce have two daughters: Elizabeth and Martha Louise.

William Pierce has a dau., Laura Jean.

## LAFFOON FAMILY
### (Contributed by Mrs. Ila Earle Fowler)

John Bledsoe Laffoon, b. April 12, 1833, md. Nov. 15, 1854 Martha Henrietta Earle, b. Jan. 2, 1833, d. Aug. 1, 1907. Their children:

1. Susan Isabelle Laffoon, b. Aug. 17, 1855, living 1950; md. (1) George W. Fowler in Hopkins county, Jan. 12, 1875; one son, George Leslie Fowler, b. Sept. 10, 1877, d. 1879, aged 18 months. She md. (2) James Polk Nuckols, b.           d.

2. Amma Walker Laffoon, b. Nov.; md. Joseph W. Rash Nov. 23, 1881.
   1. Mary Belle Rash b. Oct. 23, 1882, md. Jacob W. Wells, Dec. 9, 1903. He died
      1. Joe Rash Wells, b. June 15, 1906.
      2. Frank Garnette Wells, b. Dec. 31, 1907.
      3. Mary Ruby Wells, b. Jan. 5, 1912, md. Wm. Kaufman.
      4. Jacob Maurice Wells, b. Feb. 27, 1914; md. Freda Franklin, daughter of Charles G. Franklin and Minnie (Sugg) Franklin.
   2. Martha Ruby Rash, b.         ; d.         ; md. Roy Hall, d.     .  Their son, Earle Crawford Hall b. Sept. 12, 1913.
3. Ruby Laffoon, b. Jan. 15, 1868; md. Mary Nisbet,        Common wealth's Attorney, Circuit Judge Fourth Judicial District, Ky., Governor of Kentucky. Their children:
   1. Laura Isabel Laffoon, b. Feb. 15, 1895, married Harry Boyd, Feb. 15, 1919.
   2. Martha Lou Laffoon, b. Jan. 1, 1900, md. Wm. Reese Robinson June 1, 1920; their children: (1) R. W. Robinson, b. March 20, 1921, served as parachuter in World War II; md.        ; (2) Thomas Robinson, b.
   (3) Lelia Holeman Laffoon, b. March 21, 1904; md. Edd Lindsay.

## OTHER LAFFOON DATA

John Bledsoe and —— Henson Laffoon had these children:

1. William Laffoon
2. John Bledsoe Laffoon, Jr., b. Jan. 12, 1833, d. Jan. 29, 1895.
3. Hardin Laffoon, md. Bettie O'Brien, dau. of Rev. John O'Brien.
4. Polk Laffoon, md. Hattie Parker, dau. of Wm. Parker.
    1. Guy Laffoon, died unmarried
    2. Lena Laffoon md. Wallace Crenshaw
    3. Emma Laffoon md. Watt Nisbet
    4. Polk Laffoon, Jr., Covington, Ky.
5. Irene Laffoon md. Dr. Green Nance
6. Sallie Laffoon md. John Young
7. Mollie Laffoon md. James Young.

## LAND—JESSAMINE COUNTY

(Records contributed by Mary Rees Land (Mrs. William F. Land),
228 Desha Road, Lexington, Ky.)

Consisting of:

1. Three sworn affidavits as to contents.
2. Seven marriage records from the lost Marriage Books of Jessamine County, Kentucky.
3. Copy of Marriage Bond of Lewis Neal and Miss Louisa Lowry.
4. The following Bible Records:
    a. From the Bible of Isaac Rees
    b. From the Bible of Lewis Neal.
    c. Records from the Bible of J. S. Baskett.
    d. From the Bible of Fountain Land, and the Willis Bible.
    e. From the Bible of William L. and Maggie P. Land.
5. Abstracts of copies of attached wills and Baskett Indenture.
6. Copy of the Baskett Indenture, 1815.
7. Copies of the following wills:
    a. William Baskett, Fluvanna County, Virginia.
    b. Will of John Shepherd, Fluvanna County, Virginia.
    c. Will of Daniel Singleton, Orange County, Virginia.
    d. Will of Toliver or Taliaferro Craig, Woodford County, Kentucky.
    e. Will of Margaret McDowell, Woodford County, Kentucky.
    f. Will of John Craig, Boone County, Kentucky.
    g. Will of John Ford, Shelby County, Kentucky.
    h. Will of James Baskett, Shelby County, Kentucky.
    i. Will of George O'Neal or Neal, Jessamine County, Kentucky.
    j. Will of Elizabeth Singleton Neal or O'Neal, Jessamine County, Kentucky.
    k. Will of Melvin Lowry, Jessamine County, Kentucky.
    l. Will of Fountain Land, Jessamine County, Kentucky.
    m. Will of William L. Land, Fayette County, Kentucky.

State of Kentucky
County of Fayette

The affiant, Mary Rees Land, states that she is a resident of Fayette County, Kentucky, and that the following is a true and exact copy of seven ministerial certificates of marriage between the parties thereto, which were recorded in one of the books containing records of marriages in the office of the County Court Clerk of Jessamine County, Kentucky, which book has since been misplaced or stolen from the said Clerk's office:

George Knight to Phebe Hiter, Dec. 20, 1821, by E. Waller.
Jas. B. Walker to Sally Lowery, Dec. 7, 1819, by E. Waller.
Jas. Hiter to Ann Singleton, May 27, 1801. Certificate proven by Mason Singleton.
Hawkins Craig to Patsy Singleton, Jan. 27, 1814, by E. Waller.
Melvin Lowery to Phoebe Hiter, Oct. 28, 1800, by George S. Smith.
Lewis Singleton to Rebecca Robards, Jan. 16, 1814, by John Metcalf.
John Neal to Esther Livingston, June 12, 1823, by E. Waller.

The affiant further states that she personally copied the foregoing certificates of marriage from the above mentioned book of records before the same disappeared from the Jessamine County Clerk's office.

Witness my hand at Lexington, Kentucky, this 11th day of December, 1948.

MARY REES LAND

Subscribed and sworn to before me by Mary Rees Land, personally known by me to be the affiant herein, this the 11th day of December, 1948.

CATHERINE S. MITCHELL,
Notary Public, Fayette County, Kentucky

My commission will expire the 2nd day of April, 1952.

State of Kentucky
County of Fayette

The affiant, Mary Rees Land, states that she is a resident of Fayette County, Kentucky, and that she is familiar with the family Bible records of J. S. Baskett, James Baskett, Isaac Rees, William L. Land, Fountain Land, Henry Willis and Lewis Neal; that she owns and has in her possession all of such Bibles except the Bibles of Lewis Neal and Henry Willis, and that the copies of records attached hereto, from the Bibles of J. S. Baskett, James Baskett, Isaac Rees, William L. Land and Fountain Land are accurate and correct.

The affiant further states that she personally copied the records from the Bible of Henry Willis, and knows her copy to be accurate; that she has a copy of records from the above mentioned Neal family Bible which was prepared by her mother, Nannie Baskett Rees Jones, and known by this affiant to be accurate and correct; copies of each of said records are attached hereto.

The affiant further states that she personally copied the will of William L. Land from the records of the County Court Clerk of Fayette County, Kentucky, and the wills of Margaret McDowell and Toliver or Taliaferro Craig from the records of the County Court Clerk of Woodford County, Kentucky, and the wills of George Neal or O'Neal, Elizabeth Neal or O'Neal, Melvin Lowry and Fountain Land, and the Marriage Bond between Lewis Neal and Miss Louisa Lowry from the records of the County Court Clerk of Jessamine County, Kentucky, and that the attached copies of the above mentioned wills and Marriage Bond are accurate and correct.

The affiant further states that the will of James Baskett is of record in the Shelby County Court Clerk's office, Kentucky, and that the will of John Shepherd is of record in Fluvanna County, Virginia, and that the attached copies of these wills are accurate and correct copies of copies of said wills left to this affiant by her grandfather, James S. Baskett; that the will of Daniel Singleton is of record in Orange County, Virginia, and that the copy of said will hereto attached is a correct and accurate copy of a copy sent to this affiant by a cousin, Mrs. Woods, of California.

Witness my hand at Lexington, Kentucky, this 11th day of December, 1948.

MARY REES LAND

Subscribed and sworn to before me by Mary Rees Land, personally known by me to be the affiant herein, this the 11th day of December, 1948.

CATHERINE S. MITCHELL,
Notary Public, Fayette County, Ky.

My commission expires the 2nd day of April, 1952.

State of Kentucky
County of Fayette

The affiant, Mary Rees Land, states that she is a resident of Fayette County, Kentucky, and that she personally copied the will of John Ford from the records of the County Court Clerk of Shelby County, Kentucky, and that the attached copy of said will is accurate and correct.

The affiant further states that the will of John Craig is of record in the Boone County Court Clerk's office, Kentucky, and that the will of William Baskett is of record in the office of the Clerk of the County Court of Fluvanna County, Virginia, and that the deed from Warren Cash et al., to James Baskett and Robert Baskett, is of record in the office of the Clerk of the County Court of Fluvanna County, Virginia, and that the attached copies of these wills and this Indenture are accurate and correct copies of copies of these wills and this Indenture, which were made from the originals and left to this affiant by her grandfather, James S. Baskett.

Witness my hand at Lexington, Kentucky, this 14th day of December, 1948.

MARY REES LAND

Subscribed and sworn to before me by Mary Rees Land, personally known by me to be the affiant herein, this the 14th day of December, 1948.

CATHERINE S. MITCHELL,<br>Notary Public, Fayette County, Kentucky

My Commission expires the 2nd day of April, 1952.

### Copy of Marriage Contract Between Lewis Neal and Miss Louisa Lowry, Found in File Box, Jessamine County, Kentucky.

"Know all men by these presents that Lewis Neal and James H. Lowery are held and firmly bound into the Commonwealth of Kentucky in the just and full sum of fifty thousand pounds current money, the payment of which will and truly to be made, we bind ourselves, our heirs, etc., jointly and severally firmly by these presents sealed with our seals and dated the 18th day of February, 1824. The condition of the above obligation is such that whereas there is a marriage shortly intended to be solemnized between the above bound Lewis Neal and Miss Louisa Lowery of this County. Now if there be no lawful cause to obstruct said marriage then the above obligation to be void also to remain in full force and virtue.

Signed: Lewis Neal<br>Jas. H. Lowery"

Magistrate Daniel B. Price, Clerk of Jessamine County Court, is hereby authorized to issue license to Mr. Lewis Neal to marry my daughter, Louisa Lowery. Given under my hand and seal this 18th day of Feb. 1824.

Melvin Lowery

Witnesses:
Jas. H. Lowery
John P. Lowery

### Records from Bible of Isaac Rees

Note: This Bible was given to me, (Mary Newton Rees Land, Mrs. Wm. F. Land) by my aunt, Fannie Rees Hall.

### FAMILY RECORD: MARRIAGES

Isaac Rees and Ealeonar Brite were married together this November 22 day 1801.

John Adams and Pasha Rees were married together August the 26th, 1820.

Abram Rees and Nancy J. B. Jones was married April the 26th, 1838.

## BIRTHS

Isaac Rees born the 11 day of July 1776.
Ealeoner Brite Rees was born July 13 .......
Their children ages:
Pasha Rees born May the 17 day 1804.
Abram Rees born May the 10 day 1806.
John Adams born July 21, 1892.
Susannah Ellen Adams was born November the 1, 1835.
Nancy J. B. Rees was born August 22, 1816.
William Allen Rees was born May the 28th, 1840.
Elizabeth Eleanor Rees was born October the 22th, 1842.
Isaac Milford Rees was born November the 8, 1844.
John M. Rees was born May 19th, 1848.

## MARRIAGES

Abram Rees and Nancy J. B. Jones were married April 26, 1838.
W. Y. Warford and E. E. Rees were married Feb. 3, 1870.
Joseph T. Rees and Nannie Baskett were married June 2, 1880.
Edgar B. Hall and Fannie D. Rees were married Nov. 2, 1887.
A. L. Rees and Rosa B. Dowden were married April 6, 1892.
W. A. Rees and Bird Long were married Oct. 6, 1897.

## BIRTHS

Joseph Talbot Rees was born November 12th, 1850.
Mary J. Rees was born June 12th, 1853.
Arattus L. Rees was born January 20th, 1856.
Fannie D. Rees was born Mar. 8, 1859.
Mary Newton Rees was born June 1st, 1881.
Isaac William Adams born June 8th, 1821.
Marandy B. Adams was born Feb. 4th, 1823.
Grandison Adams born October 26th, 1824.
Abram R. Adams born the 3rd day of January, 1827.
Mary Adams born Feb. 14th, 1829.
John B. Adams born March 26th, 1831.
Frances D. Adams born September 7, 1833.
The births and deaths of nine slaves are also therein recorded.

## BIRTHS

Lelah Warford was born Nov. the 18th 1870.
Fannie May Warford was born Dec. 5th, 1874.
Fannie D. Rees was born Nov. 22nd, 1897.
Mary Frances Duncan was born March the 26th, 1900.
William Duncan Frye was born December 7th, 1905.
Dudley J. Hall was born August 3rd, 1889.
Elizabeth Land was born April 9, 1904.
Mary Elizabeth Frye was born May 3, 1908.
Mary Rees Land was born June 14, 1916.
Evan Rogers Rees was born March 17th, 1893.
Bird Long Rees was born March 19th, 1871.
William Allen Rees was born May the 28th, 1840.

## MARRIAGES

Mary Newton Rees and William Fontaine Land, November 12, 1902.
Elizabeth Land and William Henderson Smith, June 15, 1929.

## DEATHS

Abram Rees died Wednesday morning, November the 10th, 1875, aged 69 years and 6 months.

Joseph T. Rees died October 29th, 1881, Saturday morning at ten o'clock.

Nancy J. B. Rees died nine o'clock Friday morning, December 13, 1889.

Isaac M. Rees died nine o'clock and ten minutes, Thursday morning, June 1, 1893.

Jamie Rees Yeager died October 27th, 1809.

J. N. Rees died January 13th, 1910.

William A. Rees died October 30th, 1913.

Edgar B. Hall died February 8th, 1928.

Fannie Rees Hall died January 17th, 1938.

A. L. Rees died April 8th, 1938.

Nannie B. Rees Jones died November 17th, 1944.

M. Barrett Cox, husband of Fannie D. Rees, died May 17, 1944.

Isaac Rees departed this life Thursday. morning about two o'clock, January, 1816.

Eleanor Rees departed this life Tuesday morning about two o'clock, August 7th, 1838.

John Adams departed this life, Saturday morning about three o'clock, August 24th, 1839.

Isaac W. Adams departed this life on Tuesday evening, six o'clock, June 28th, 1823.

Samuel Adams departed this life on Sunday evening, about five o'clock, April 29th, 1838.

Grandison Adams departed this life on Sunday morning, about nine o'clock, August 29th, 1829.

### Record of Lewis Neal and Family, from Neal Bible

Lewis Neal, born April 20, 1799, died May, 1868; married February 19, 1824 by Elder William Sterman, to Louisa A. Y. Lowry, born December 20, 1804, died November 3, 1847.

Children:

Mary E. Neal, born December 8, 1824, died July 4, 1848; married December 19, 1844 to George Smith by Elder Younger Pitts.

William F. Neal, born April 25, 1826; died ———; married May 1, 1851 to Rebecca Davenport, of Texas.

Elizabeth J. Neal, born October 16, 1827; died June 13, 1899; married December 16, 1849, to Bryant Sloan by Elder Smith Thomas.

John L. Neal, born May 25, 1829; died July 27, 1901; (bachelor).

George M. Neal, born January 28, 1831; died June 28, 1857 (bachelor).

Phebe L. Neal, born December 22, 1832; died August 7, 1906; married January 25, 1855 to J. S. Baskett by Elder Jordan Walker.

Jesse Neal, born May 19, 1834; died August 5, 1834.

Martha W. Neal, born May 29, 1835; died February 13, 1868; married January 25, 1855, to James Middleton by Elder Jordan Walker.

Nannie K. Neal, born June 23, 1837; died June 15, 1906; married March 15, 1857, to Dr. G. M. Phillips, by Elder Jordan Walker.

Margaret F. Neal, born August 5, 1839; died January 30, 1910; married December 1, 1858, to Ed Drane, by Elder Robert Rice.

Louisa Ruth Neal, born February 24, 1841; died November 16, 1919; married C. Hoskins on June 28, 1864, by J. F. Johnson.

Bina Todd Neal, born January 9, 1843; died May 25, 1896; married December 6, 1860; to Merrit Drane, by W. S. Giltner

Tomson Ann Neal, born November 12, 1844; died September 28, 1855.

James D. Neal, born September 16, 1846; died January 11, 1870.

Lewis Neal and Nancy E. Kent married October 26, 1848, by Elder George Bristow.

Nancy E. Neal, died April 23, 1888.

Note: Phebe Lowry Neal and J. S. Baskett and Martha W. Neal and James Middleton had a double wedding. Margaret F. Neal and Bina (Melvina) married brothers. Nancy E. Kent (a widow) was Lewis Neal's second wife. No children.

### Records from Bible of J. S. Baskett

This certifies that James S. Baskett and Phebe Lowry Neal were solemnly united by me in the Holy Bonds of Matrimony at the residence of Lewis Neal on the twenty-fifth day of January (Thursday) in the year of our Lord One Thousand, Eight Hundred and Fifty-five, conformably to the Ordinance of God and the Laws of the State.

### FAMILY REGISTER

Mary Newton Rees, born June 1, 1881, married William F. Land (b. April 17, 1881) November 12, 1902.

Their Children:

Edna Elizabeth Land, born April 9, 1904.

Mary Rees Land, born June 14, 1910.

Elizabeth married William Henderson Smith, June 15, 1929.

Their Children:

William Henderson Smith, Jr., born October 30, 1934.

Mary Rachel Smith, born March 17, 1937.

Family Record of J. Baskett:

James Baskett was born March 4th, 1787. Mildred Baskett, wife of James Baskett was born December 16th, 1789.

Children of James & Mildred Baskett:

Sarah Elizabeth Baskett was born August 26th, 1814.

Mary Ann Baskett was born August 5th, 1817.

Frances Jane Baskett was born August 13th, 1821.

William Christopher Baskett was born February 22, 1826.

Lucy Mildred Baskett was born July 23rd, 1828.

James Semple Baskett was born February 17th, 1852.
Nancy Martin Baskett was born March 30th, 1835.
James Baskett and Mildred Shepherd were married Feb. 9th, 1813.

## DEATHS

Nancy Martin Basket Kinkead died November 21, 1852.
James Baskett died March 28, 8 o'clock P. M., 1863.
Mildred Baskett died May 14th, 1874.
W. C. Baskett died June 27th, 1901.
Mary A. Baskett Bayne died July 1st, 1878.
Lucy M. Baskett Bohannon died July 20th, 1903.
Sarah E. Jesse died October 1st, 1864.
Frances Jane Baskett Hartford died September 24, 1910.

## MARRIAGES

Nancy E. Baskett to J. T. Rees, June 1st, 1880.
Mary L. Baskett and Thos. L. Hornsby were married Nov. 8th, 1882.
Margaret D. Baskett and Clarke N. Rowland were married April 27, 1885.
Florence L. Baskett and B. F. Snyder were married October 20th, 1886.
Minnie S. Baskett and R. J. King were married Sept. 16th, 1890.
Loran B. Baskett married (1st) Virginia Martin, Jan. 16th, 1901. (2nd) Margaret Maddox, Sept. 19, 1942.

## BIRTHS

James Semple Baskett was born February 17th, 1832.
Phebe Lowry Neal, wife of James Semple Baskett, was born December 22nd, 1832.
Nancy Elizabeth Baskett was born April 14th, 1856.
Mary Louisa Baskett was born August 31st, 1860.
Mildred Samuel Baskett was born December 29th, 1861.
Florence Low Baskett was born September 30th, 1865.
Loran Baldwin Baskett was born October 20th, 1870.

## DEATHS

Phebe Lowry Neal Baskett, wife of J. S. Baskett, died August 7th, 1906.
J. S. Baskett died January 18, 1920.
Virginia Martin Baskett, wife of Loran B. Baskett, died January 3, 1942.
Nannie Baskett Rees Jones died 11-17-1944.
Margaret Drane Baskett Roland died 6-26-1945.
Florence Law Baskett Snyder died June 19, 1947.

### Bible Record of Fountain Land

Parents Record:
Fountain Land was borne January 2, A. D. 1815.
Martha M. Land was borne September the 22d, A. D. 1819.

## BIRTHS

Mary Ellin Land was borne May the 27th, A. D. 1848.
Henry B. Land was borne April the 8th, A. D., 1851.
William Luther Land was borne July 22, A. D., 1854.
Albert Melvin Land was borne February 13th, 1857.
John Milton Land was borne March 27th, 1861.
Infant was borne March 27th, 1861, died March 27th, 1861.

## MARRIAGES

Fountain Land and Martha M. Willis were married June the 10th, A D., 1847.

## DEATHS

John Milton Land died April 13th, 1862.
Fountain Land died January 3rd, 1899.
William Luther Land died April 17th, 1901.
Mary E. Land Baker died January 7th, 1908.
Martha Land (wife of Fountain Land) died March 31, 1918.
Henry B. Land died March —— 1920.
Albert Melvin Land died February 16, 1932.

Willis Bible Record:
Henry Willis born November 8th, 1791.
Elizabeth Hagin (Willis) born April 6, 1794.

Their Children were:
Jackson S. Willis, born December 25, 1816.
Josiah T. Willis, born December 22, 1817.
Martha M. Willis, born September 22, 1819.
William I. Willis born October 1st, 1821.
Mary L. Willis, born August 16, 1823.
Lucinda J. Willis, born October 30, 1823.
Silas R. Willis, born March 12, 1828.
Benjamin F. Willis, born January 31, 1834.

## DEATHS

William J. Willis, died April 8, 1903, aged 82 years.
Mary Willis Mathews died October 13, 1909.
Bettie Lemon Willis died December ——, 1920.

### Records from Bible of William L. Land and Maggie P. Land

This certifies that the rite of Holy Matrimony was celebrated between Wm. L. Land of Jessamine Co., Ky. and Maggie P. Mathews of Jessamine Co., Ky., on the 24th of October, 1878.

## MARRIAGES

Wm. L. Land and Maggie P. Mathews married Oct. 24th, 1878.
William Fontaine Land and Mary Newton Rees, Nov. 12, 1902.
Sara Edna Land and Charles Jacob Bronston, June, 1907.

LeRoy Mathews Land and Ethel Reasor, September 3, 1914.
Luther McDowell Land and Hettie Martin Frazee, May 19, 1916.
Joseph Porter Land and Dorothy Duncan, Nov. 8, 1917.
Edna Elizabeth Land and William Henderson Smith, June 15, 1929.
Marjorie McDowell Land and James Link Jefferson, July 3, 1940.
Ann Elizabeth Land and Hill Maury, May 12, 1943.
Martha Frazee Land and Emmet Lawrence Chiles, August 7, 1946.

## BIRTHS

William Luther Land, July 22, 1854.
Maggie Porter Land, May 18, 1852.
Mattie Mathews Land, August 18th, 1879.
Will Fontaine Land, April 17th, 1881.
LeRoy Mathews Land, May 1, 1883.
Sarah Edna Land, May 13, 1886.
Joseph Porter Land, August 18, 1890.
Luther McDowell Land, December 4th, 1893.

Grandchildren and Great-Grandchildren:

Edna Elizabeth Land, April 9, 1904.
Mary Rees Land, June 14, 1916.
Marjorie McDowell Land, September 24, 1917.
Ann Elizabeth Land, March 13, 1921.
Martha Frazee Land, April 3, 1928.
William Henderson Smith, Jr., October 30, 1934.
Mary Rachel Smith, March 17, 1937.
Dianne Frazee Jefferson, November 22, 1942.
James McDowell Jefferson, May 15, 1945.
Patricia Land Jefferson, August 1, 1946.
Shreve Maury, 1947.
Lawrence McDowell Chiles, July 21, 1948.

## DEATHS

William L. Land, April 17, 1901.
Shreve Maury, son of Hill and Ann Land Maury, March 7, 1948.

### Abstract of Attached Copies of Wills

Will of Daniel Singleton, Will Book 3, page 314, Orange County, Virginia. Dated November 10, 1790, probated October 27, 1794. Witnesses, William Bennet Webb, Samuel Mason, Goodrich L. Grasty. Legatees: Son Manoah Singleton; Daughters, Lois Looker, Susanna Lancaster; grand-daughters (children of Susanna Lancaster "her present three youngest daughters") Sarah, Susannah and Elizabeth; daughters, Joannah Lancaster, Mary Perry; children (of testator) Manoah Singleton, Edmond Singleton, Martha Proctor, Joannah Lancaster. Executors, friend Rich'd C. Webb and sons-in-law Uriah Proctor and Rich'd Lancaster.

Will of George Neal or O'Neal, Will Book E, page 317, Jessamine County, Kentucky. Dated August 5, 1836, probated November Court, 1836. Witnesses, John Garrison, Ezekiel Haydon. Legatees: Wife, Elizabeth Neal; son, James Neal (230 acres in Shelby County); sons, Lewis Neal (100 acres in Shelby County); Elijah Neal (95 acres in Jessamine County), George Neal (93 acres in Jessamine), Creath Neal (87¼ acres in Jessamine), David Neal (97½ acres in Jessamine; daughter, Mary Forbes; tract deeded to son John Neal has reverted to testator's estate since death of John; daughter, Mary Forbes; sons, Elijah Neal, George, Creath and David Neal. Executors, sons Elijah, George, and David, they all living in Jessamine County.

Will of Elizabeth Singleton O'Neal (Widow of George O'Neal or Neal.) Will Book H, page 359, Jessamine County, Kentucky. Dated October 17, 1850, probated May Court, 1852. Witnesses: Thos. W. Foster, William Campbell. Legatee: Daughter, Mary Forbes (negro girl, Lydia.) Executor, son Elijah Neal.

Will of Melvin Lowry, Will Book F, page 88, Jessamine County, Kentucky. Dated April 24, 1838, probated August Court, 1838. Witnesses: Jacob Wilmore, C. F. Howard. Legatees: Wife, Phebe Lowry, farm and personal property "together with all the money which I have on hand for the schooling and raising of my children, William C., Melvin T., and Phebe H. Lowry;" to sons, James II. Lowry, John P. Lowry; to daughters, Elizabeth Singleton, Louisa Neal, Jane Grimes, Malvina Todd, Nancy Knight, and Martha West and Mary E. Lowry; sons Charles F. Lowry, William C. and Melvin T. Lowry; daughter, Phebe H. Lowry; children, James H. Lowry, Elizabeth Singleton, Louisa Neal, John P. Lowry, Jane Grimes, Nancy Knight, Martha West, Mary E. Lowry, William C. Lowry, Charles F. Lowry, Melvin T. and Phoebe H. Lowry. Executors, wife Phebe Lowry and son Charles F. Lowry.

Will of Margaret McDowell, Will Book E page 65, Woodford County, Kentucky. Dated March 2, 1816, probated July Court, 1816. Witnesses: L. Wilkinson, John P. Porter. Legatees: sons, Henry H. McDowell and Joseph Jefferson McDowell; daughters, Clarissa Mira McDowell and Elizabeth Porter. Executors, not named. Will proved by Lyddale Wilkinson and John P. Porter.

Will of John Shepherd, Fluvannah County, Virginia (mentioned in "Virginia Wills," p. 382.) Dated December 16, 1796, probated February 2, 1797. Witnesses: Thomas T. Davis, David Johnson, Jesse Perkins. Legatees: To daughters, Joanna and Annis; to wife, Mary Shepherd; to sons, Augustine Shepherd, and John Shepherd; to daughter, Annis Shepherd; to son, Augustine Shepherd; to daughters, Mary Perry, Elizabeth Cocke, Joanna and Annis, Nancy Perkins, Frances Baskett. Executors, sons David and Christopher Shepherd.

Will of James Baskett, Shelby County, Kentucky, Dated August 1, 1860, probated April Court, 1863. Witnesses: J. M. Bullock, Shelby Vannatta. Legatees: To wife; to son, J. S. Baskett; to daughters, Sarah Jesse, Mary A. Bayne and Frances J. Hartford; to sons, W. C. Baskett (including land bought of D. Perry), and James Baskett; to daughter, Lucy M. Bohannon; to son, James S. Baskett. Executors, Sons, William C. Baskett and James S. Baskett.

Will of Fountain Land, Will Book L page 732, Jessamine County, Kentucky. Dated December 3, 1888, probated January 16, 1899. Witnesses: Dent Hoover, B. M. Arnett. Legatees: Wife, Martha M. Land (including land at Hanly, purchased by testator from Hardin Masters, Richard Phillips, and Alex Walker); to sons, Henry B., William L., and Albert M. Land; to daughter, Mary E. Baker (land on which she and her husband, John A. Baker reside, bought by testator and John A. Baker, from Cassa Robards et al.); to son, Henry B. Land. Executors, Sons, Henry B. Land and William L. Land.

Will of William L. Land, Will Book 9, page 112, Fayette County, Kentucky. Dated April 17, 1901, probated April 27, 1901. Witnesses: George L. Shanklin, David Barrow, A. L. B. Blanding. Legatees: Wife, Maggie Porter Land; son, William Fountaine Land (the oldest son); wife, Maggie Porter Land appointed Executrix; if she dies before estate is settled, sons, William F. Land and LeRoy M. Land to act as Executors.

Will of Toliver or Taliaferro Craig, Will Book B page 79, Woodford County, Kentucky. Dated December 15, 1790, probated August 5, 1799. Witnesses: John Cooke, Anthony Lindsey, Daniel Baldwin. Legatees: My beloved wife, Mary Craig; children, John Craig, Toliver Craig, Lewis Craig, Joseph Craig, Elijah Craig, Benjamin Craig, Jeremiah Craig, Jossie Faulkner and Elizabeth Cave; John Sanders and Sarah Singleton. Executors, sons, John Craig, Toliver Craig, and Lewis Craig.

Will of William Baskett, Fluvanna County, Virginia. Dated September 1, 1812; probated May 22, 1815. Witnesses, David Shepherd, Nancy Shepherd, and Polly Shepherd. Legacies: To my thirteen children. Executors, my two sons, Abraham and Jesse Baskett. The bondsmen were Benjamin Bowles, James Currin, Walter Timberlake and Joel Parrish .

Will of John Ford, Will Book 1, p. 227, Shelby County, Kentucky. Dated April 13, 1803, probated October Court, 1803. Witnesses: Oswald Thomas, David Denny, David Thomas. Legacies: To Davit Barnett (in fulfilment of contract); to my son Samuel (335 acres being part of a preemption granted to George Thompson and partially bordered by lands of Benjamin Yates, S. Spencer, William Ford, and Daniel Barnett); to son, Edward; to wife, Catherine; to son, Elisha, for his services in selling my land in Carolina; to son Samuel and daughter Linney; to son Spencer and daughter Ann; Executors, My three sons, William, Elisha, and Samuel.

Note: John Ford's wife, Catherine, is a second wife, and son, Edward, her child.

Will of John Craig. Dated February 4, 1811; probated December Term, 1815. Witnesses: James Hammonds, Sam'l Craig, Nath'l Craig, Richard L. Sparrow, Toliver Craig, Jr. Legacies: to my dear wife, Sally Craig; to my sons, Elijah Craig, Benjamin Craig, Francis Craig, Phillip Craig; to my sons-in-law, Cave Johnson, John Cave, and John Bush; to wife, Sally Craig; to son-in-law, Thomas M. Prentiss; to sons, John H. Craig and Lewis Craig. Executors: Friend, John Craig, of Scott County (Son of Toliver), and sons, John H. Craig and Lewis Craig. Probated in Boone County, Kentucky.

## A BASKETT INDENTURE, 1815

This Indenture made this twenty-second day of November in the year of our Lord one thousand eight hundred and fifteen, between Warren Cash and Susanna, his wife, of the County of Hardin and State of Kentucky, John Baskett of the County of Shelby and the State aforesaid, Thomas Baskett and Dicey, his wife, of the County of Shelby and the State aforesaid, John Shepherd and Nancy, his wife, of the County of Shelby and the State aforesaid, Abraham Baskett and Frances, his wife, of the County of Fluvanna and the State of Virginia, Jesse Baskett and Salley, his wife, of the County of Fluvanna and State of Virginia, John Kent and Elizabeth, his wife, of the said County of Fluvanna and State aforesaid, Joel Parrish and Mildred, his wife of the said County of Fluvanna and State of Virginia, Job Baskett and Salley, his wife, of the County of Shelby and State of Kentucky, Jesse Dale and Anne Nixon, his wife, of the County of Woodford, and State of Kentucky, aforesaid, and William Connelly and Peggy, his wife, of the County of Shelby and State of Kentucky aforesaid (which said Susanna, wife of Warren Cash and formerly Susanna Baskett, John Baskett, Thomas Baskett, Nancy, wife of John Shepherd, and formerly Nancy Baskett, Abraham Baskett, Jesse Baskett, Elizabeth, wife of John Kent and formerly Elizabeth Baskett, Mildred, wife of Joel Parrish and formerly Mildred Baskett, Job Baskett are children, Legatees and Co-heirs of William Baskett, deceased, late of the said County of Fluvanna and State of Virginia, and which said Peggy wife of William Connelly and Jesse Dale are Grandchildren and also Legatees and co-heirs of said William Baskett, deceased, they being the children of the late Mary Dale, deceased daughter, who was formerly Mary Baskett, a daughter of the said William Baskett, deceased, (not legible on account of worn fold of paper) James Baskett and Robert Baskett of the County of Fluvanna and State of Virginia aforesaid of the other part,

Witnesseth: That said Warren Cash and Susanna, his wife, John Baskett, Thomas Baskett and Dicey, his wife, Abraham Baskett and Frances, his wife, John Shepherd and Nancy, his wife, Jesse Baskett and Salley, his wife, John Kent and Elizabeth, his wife, Joel Parrish and Mildred, his wife, Job Baskett and Salley, his wife, Jesse Dale and Anne Nixon, his wife, and William Connelly and Peggy, his wife, for and in consideration of the sum of One Thousand Eight Hundred Dollars Current money of Virginia by the said James Baskett and Robert Baskett to them in hand paid at or before the ensealing and delivery of these presents, the receipt is hereby acknowledged, Have and each of them hath granted, bargained and sold and by these presents do and each of them doth grant, bargain and sell unto the said James Baskett and Robert Baskett and to their heirs and assigns, all their several and respective proportions and shares or dividends, in and of all the Lands late the property of the said William Baskett, deceased, which said Lands are situated in the County of Fluvanna and State of Virginia aforesaid on Kent's Branch and Lilly's Creek, are in three several Tracts all adjoining each other and containing in the whole by estimation seven hundred and eighty-six and one-fourth acres, be the same more or less, together with the appurtenances unto the said hereby bargained and sold shares, proportions or covenants in and of said shares, as yet undivided between or in any wise appurtaining.

To Have and To Hold the said several and respective shares, proportions or covenants in and of said lands and premises and appurtenances unto them, the said James Baskett and Robert Baskett and their heirs and assigns forever, to the only proper use and behoof of them, the said James Baskett and Robert Baskett and their heirs and assigns forever.

And the said Warren Cash and Susanna, his wife, John Baskett and Thomas Baskett and Dicey, his wife, John Shepherd and Nancy, his wife, Abraham Baskett and Frances, his wife, Jesse Baskett and Salley, his wife, John Kent and Elizabeth, his wife, Joel Parrish and Mildred, his wife, Job Baskett, and Salley, his wife, Jesse Dale and Anne Nixon, his wife, William Connelly and Peggy, his wife, for themselves and the said several and respective shares or covenants in of the said lands herein before covenanted and with—with the appurtenances unto the said James Baskett and Robert Baskett and to their heirs and assigns forever and against the claim or demands of themselves or either of their heirs and also from and against the claim or demand of all and every other person or persons, whomsoever shall and will warrant and forever defend by these presents.

In Witness whereof the parties hereto have to these presents set their hands and affixed their seal this day and year hereinbefore written.

Signed, sealed and delivered in presence of:

| | | | |
|---|---|---|---|
| Warren Cash | (Seal) | John Kent | (Seal) |
| Susanna Cash | (Seal) | Elizabeth Kent | (Seal) |
| by Warren Cash, | | Joel Parish | (Seal) |
| her attorney-in-fact | | Mildred Parrish | (Seal) |
| John Baskett | (Seal) | Job Baskett | (Seal) |
| Thomas Baskett | (Seal) | Salley Baskett | (Seal) |
| Dicey Baskett | (Seal) | by Thomas Baskett, | |
| John Shepherd | (Seal) | her attorney-in-fact | |
| Nancy Shepherd | | Jesse Dale | (Seal) |
| by John Shepherd | | Ann Nixon Dale | (Seal) |
| her attorney-in-fact | | William Connelly | (Seal) |
| Abraham Baskett | (Seal) | Peggy Connelly | (Seal) |
| Frances Baskett | (Seal) | by John Shepherd, her | |
| Jesse Baskett | (Seal) | attorney-in-fact | |
| Salley Baskett | (Seal) | | |

## WILL OF WILLIAM BASKETT

I, William Baskett, of the County of Fluvanna and State of Virginia, being weak in body but of sound and disposing mind and memory, do constitute, make and ordain this writing following my last Will and Testament; that is to say, it is my will and desire that my just and lawful debts be first paid.

Item: It is my will and desire that my estate after my decease be equally divided among my thirteen children or their lawful representatives as the law prescribes where persons die intestate, with this exception: That whatever part or parts of my estate my children or their representatives has received from me heretofore the same shall remain with them as a fee simple and shall not by them nor any of them be accounted for in the division of my estate by virtue of this my last will and testament.

And lastly I do appoint and constitute my two sons, Abraham and Jesse Baskett as Executors to this my last will and Testament, utterly revoking all former wills and testaments heretofore by me made.

In testimony therof, I have hereunto set my hand and seal this first day of September, 1812.

WILLIAM BASKETT (Seal)

Published, acknowledged and signed, sealed as my last will and testament in presence of:

David Shepherd<br>Nancy Shepherd<br>Polly Shepherd (her X mark)

At a Court of monthly sessions held for Fluvanna County on Monday the 22nd day of May, 1815. This will was this day presented in Court and proved by the oath of Nancy Shepherd and David Shepherd, two of the witnesses thereto and ordered to be recorded; and on the motion of Abraham and Jesse Baskett, the executors therein named, who made oath thereto as the law directs and enters into and acknowledged bond in the penalty of Twenty Thousand Dollars with Benjamin Bowles, James Currin, Walter Timberlake and Joel Parrish, as their securities, conditioned as the law directs, certificate is granted them ror obtaining a probate thereof in due form.

Teste: John Timberlake, C. F. C.
A copy—Teste: M. W. Perkins, Clerk.

WILL OF JOHN SHEPHERD<br>Fluvanna County, Virginia<br>Probated February 2, 1797

In the name of God Amen. I, John Shepherd of the County of Fluvanna, being at this time of sound mind and disposing memory, do make, constitute, and ordain this to be my last will and testament, in manner and form following: Imprimis, I give to my daughters, Joanna and Annis, one negro girl each, one feather bed and furniture, one cow and calf, one ewe and lamb each, to be delivered by my executors at their marriage or as they arrive at lawful age. I lend unto my beloved wife, Mary Shepherd, the plantation and land whereon I now live (except my son Augustine Shepherd should go to Kentucky and be inclined to purchase land in that part, then it is my will that part be sold for him so as not to interfere with the plantation by my executors in order for him to purchase land in that country) with all my stock of horses, cows, hogs, and sheep, to be by her freely enjoyed as also my household and kitchen furniture, plantation and blacksmith's tools during her natural life, and the whole of my negroes except one to each of my two daughters as in before mentioned.

Item: I give to my son, John Shepherd, after the division of my estate the sum of forty one pounds, eight shillings more than an equal part with the rest of my sons. I give and bequeath unto my daughter, Annis Shepherd, one woman's saddle and bridle, to be delivered to her by my executors when called upon, to her and her heirs forever.

Item: If my son, Augustine Shepherd, should choose to live on the land whereon I now live, I give and bequeath to him after the death of my wife one hundred and fifty acres to be laid off at the lower part of my land including all houses to him and his heirs forever.

Item: I also give and bequeath to my son, Augustine, when he arrives to lawful age, one feather bed and furniture, one cow and calf, and one man's saddle to be delivered to him by my executors to him and his heirs forever.

Item: I give and bequeath to my daughters, after the death of my wife, Mary Perry, Elizabeth Cocke, Joanna and Annis, Fifty pounds current money to be raised out of my estate by my executors to them and their heirs forever.

Item: I give and bequeath to my daughter, Nancy Perkins, one negro girl named Lucy, now in her possession, also I give unto my said daughter after the death of my wife, fifty pounds current money to be raised out of my estate by my executors to her and her heirs forever.

Item: I give and bequeath to my daughter, Frances Baskett, the land whereon she now lives to be enjoyed by her and her heirs forever.

Item: It is my will and desire, if after all my just debts are paid, there should be any remainder either by bill, bond, or otherwise, the same be equally divided amongst all my children or their legal representatives.

Item: It is my will and desire that if either of my children should die not having lawful issue or representatives of children alive at that time of his or her death, that then in that case, all and every part or parts of my estate hereby given them, shall revert to the surviving brothers or sisters or their legal representatives.

Lastly I do constitute my sons David and Christopher Shepherd executors to this my last will and Testament hereby revoking all other wills by me heretofore made. In testimony whereof I have hereunto set my hand and affixed my seal this sixteenth day of December, One thousand and seven hundred and ninety-six.

John Shepherd (Seal)

Signed, sealed, published and declared by the Testator to be his last will and testament in presence of:

Thomas T. Davis
David Johnson
Jesse Perkins

At a court held for Fluvanna county, February the 2nd, 1797. This will was this day in open court proved by the oathes of Thomas T. Davis, David Johnson and Jesse Perkins the witnesses thereto and ordered to be recorded. And on the motion of David Shepherd and Christopher Shepherd the executors therein named who made oath thereto and entered into bond with William Basket and Benjamin Clarke their securities in the penalty of Ten Thousand Dollars, conditioned as the law directs, certificate is granted them for obtaining probate thereof in due form.

Teste John Timbulake, C. C.

## THE WILL OF DANIEL SINGLETON

In the name of God Amen. I, Daniel Singleton of Orange County and Colony of Virginia, being in health and of sound mind and perfect memory (Blessed be God) do make and ordain this my last will and testament and form following (that is to say) my Will and desire is that my Body be buried in a decent and Christian like manner at the Descretion of my Executors hereafter named and Secondly all such debts as I shall justly owe at the time of my death be paid out of my Estate by my Executors. As to my Estate both real and personal I dispose thereof as follows:

Item. I give unto my son Manoah Singleton a tract of land adjoining to that Tract I gave to my son Manoah Singleton containing one hundred and ninety-eight acres, which he has already had in possession and since became my property.

Item. I give to my Daughter Lois Looker the same tract of Land that I gave to my son Edmond Singleton already been in her possession and agreed to take it for her portion or full part of my Estate, But I now further add and present her with Fifteen Pounds Cash to be paid out of my Estate by my Executors.

Item: I give to my Daughter Susanna Lancaster one feather bed, one cow and two sheep already had in Possession and for the further part of my Estate in lieu of giving to my said Daughter, Susanna Lancaster, I give unto her present three youngest Daughters, namely, Sarah, Susannah and Elizabeth, Fifteen Pounds each to them and their heirs and assigns forever but should any of either of the above named children die before they come to age or marry that my desire is that the Surviving take the part allotted to the Deceased.

Item: I give to my daughter Joannah Lancaster one cow already in possession and also Five Pounds Cash to be paid as above.

Item: I give to my Daughter Mary Perry twenty pounds cash as above. The above Legacies I give and confirm unto the above children and to their heirs and assigns forever, and the Residue of my Estate of every kind so ever I desire may be sold by my Exors as they shall think proper and the money Divided amongst my children hereafter named equally or their heirs should either one die before such Division, Manoah Singleton, Edmond Singleton, Martha Proctor, Joannah Lancaster.

I do hereby constitute and appoint my friend Rich'd C. Webb and my two sons in law Uriah Proctor and Rich'd Lancaster Exors. of this my last will and hereby make null and void all of every Will and Wills heretofore made by me Declaring this to be my last Will and Testament.

In Witness Whereof I have hereunto set my hand and seal this tenth day of Nov. one thousand seven hundred and ninety.

Daniel Singleton (Seal)

Signed, sealed and acknowledged in
presence of

William Bennet Webb
Samuel Mason
Goodrich L. Grasty.

At a Court for Orange County the twenty-seventh of October, 1794, This last Will and Testament of Daniel Singleton Dec'd was presented into Court by Richard C. Webb and Richard Lancaster two of the Exors therein named and proved by oaths of William B. Webb and Sam'l Mason two of the Witnesses thereto and ordered to be recorded and on the motion of the Exors who made oaths according to law certificate is granted them for obtaining a probate thereof in due form whereupon they with William E. Webb their Security Executed bond according to Law.

In Orange Circuit Court Clerk's office, Virginia, June 21, 1930, I do hereby certify that the foregoing is a true and correct copy of the Will of Daniel Singleton, recorded in this office in Will Book No. 3 on page 314.

Given under my hand and the seal of this Court, this 21st day of June, 1930.

(Seal) Katherine B. Brown,
Deputy Clerk, Circuit Court
Orange County, Virginia

## THE WILL OF TOLIVER OR TALIAFERRO CRAIG

Will Book B, page 79, Office of the Clerk
of the County Court of Woodford County, Kentucky

In the name of God, Amen. I, Toliver Craig, of Woodford County, being in a low state of health but of perfect disposing mind and memory, calling to mind the uncertainty of this mortal life, do constitute this my last will and testament in manner and form following:

First and principally I recommend my soul to God that gave it, and my body to be interred after my death at the discretion of my Executors hereafter named.

Secondly and as for the worldly estate the Lord has blessed me with, I lend two negroes named Warrick and Teanor and a horse and a best bed and furniture unto my beloved wife, Mary Craig, during her natural life and after her death to be equally divided among my children hereafter named as the rest of my estate.

Thirdly I desire that my children all be made equal with the one that received the most of my estate; that is, what it was worth when they received it.

Fourthly I desire that the balance of my estate both real and personal be equally divided between my nine children, namely: John Craig, Toliver Craig, Lewis Craig, Joseph Craig, Elijah Craig, Benjamin Craig, Jeremiah Craig, Jossie Faulkner and Elizabeth Cave.

Fifthly it is my will and desire that my above named children make John Sanders and Sarah Singleton part equal with theirs in property at the praise value.

Sixthly, it is my desire that my sons, John Craig, Toliver Craig, and Lewis Craig do execute this my last will and testament.

Witness my hand and seal this fifteenth day of December one thousand seven hundred and ninety (December 15, 1790.)

his

Toliver X Craig      (Seal)

mark

Teste:   John Cooke
        Anthony Lindsey
        Daniel Baldwin


At a Court held for Woodford County at the Courthouse thereof on Monday the 5th day of August, 1799, this last will and testament of Toliver Craig, deceased, was presented in Court and proved by the oathes of John Cooke, Anthony Lindsey, and Davie Baldwin three subscribing witnesses thereto and was ordered to be recorded.

Teste T. Turpin, Clk.


## WILL OF MARGARET McDOWELL

Will Book E, Page 65, Woodford
County Court Clerk's Office,
State of Kentucky

In the name of God, Amen. I, Margaret McDowell, being weak and low in bodily strength but of sound mind and memory do make and ordain this my last will and testament.

I will and bequeath to my son, Henry H. McDowell, that part of the land on which I now live, which I deeded to him last summer, also a good bed and bedcloathing. I will and bequeath to my son, Joseph Jefferson McDowell, the balance of the land on which I now live, including all the appurtenances thereto belonging; also a good riding horse and bed and bed cloathing. I will and bequeath to my daughter, Clarissa Mira McDowell, two hundred dollars in cash, a good riding horse, saddle and bridle and a good bed and bed cloathing. I will and bequeath to my daughter, Elizabeth Porter, a good bed and bed cloathing.

My will and desire is that the property I possess exclusive of the above legacies should be equally divided among all those of my children now living. I include in the above all lands and real estate to which I have a right.

In Testimony I have hereunto set my hand and affixed my seal this 2nd day of March, 1816.

(Signed)    Margaret McDowell (Seal).

Teste:
L. Wilkinson
John P. Porter

Woodford County Sct.
July County Court, 1816.

The Last Will and Testament of Margaret McDowell was produced in Court and was proven by the oaths of Lyddale Wilkinson and John P. Porter, subscribing witnesses thereto, and ordered to record. Atteste.

John McKinney, C. C. W. C.

Note:    The interesting point about this will is the fact that the testatrix refers to "my daughter, Elizabeth Porter." In all other references Elizabeth is given as the wife of her cousin, Caleb Wallace McDowell, who died in 1811; she evidently married twice. Margaret McDowell was widow of Colonel Joseph McDowell, Jr., and daughter of Colonel George Moffett.

## WILL OF JOHN CRAIG

In the name of God, Amen.  I, John Craig of the County of Boone and State of Kentucky, being of sound mind and disposing memory, but calling to mind the uncertainty of human life and being desirous to dispost of all such worldly estate as it has pleased God to bless me with, do hereby give and bequeath the same in the following manner, (towit):

First, to my dear wife, Sally Craig, I give in fee simple forever all my personal estate and all my slaves (except my negro Jim) during her natural life.  It is my desire that at my death, my negro man, Jim, should be free and at the death of my said wife, the balance of my slaves shall also be free.

2.    It is my will and desire that my real estate shall be the funds out of which all my just debts shall be paid.  To this end I hereby devise to my executors hereinafter mentioned all my real estate in fee trust to sell the same or part thereof for the payment of my said debts and desire the residue (if any there be) in the manner hereinafter mentioned, my executors will exercise their discretion in selecting such parts of my real estate for sale as they may think fit; having regard the general and best interest of all the devisers; and may sell at public or private sale on prompt payment, or on credit with such security as they may approve and judge most advantageous to all concerned so far as may be consistent with the laws of the country and the rights of creditors.

3.    To my sons, Elijah Craig, Benjamin Craig, Francis Craig, Philip

Craig and my sons-in-law, Cave Johnson, John Cave, and John Bush, I give one shilling each to be paid them by my executors, they, and each of them, having been sufficiently advanced and provided for before the execution of this will.

4. My debts being paid pursuant to article second of this will, it now remains to dispose of the residue of my real estate and for this purpose it is my will and desire that all my land, tenements and hereditaments, may be divided into seven equal parts to be disposed of as follows: To my dear wife, Sally Craig, I give in fee simple forever one of the said parts. To my son-in-law, Thomas M. Prentiss, I give in fee simple one other of said parts. To my son, John H. Craig, and Lewis Craig, I give in fee simple the balance of my estate to be equally divided.

5. I do hereby constitute and appoint my friend, John Craig, of Scott County (son of Toliver), my sons, John H. Craig, and Lewis Craig, my executors of this my last will and testament hereby revoking all other or former wills or testaments by me hereunto made. In Testimony whereof, I hereunto set my hand and affix my seal this 4th day of February in the year Eighteen hundred and eleven.

John Craig (Seal)

Signed, sealed and delivered  
as my last will and testament  
in presence of  
James Hammonds  
Sam'l Craig  
Nat'l Craig  
Richard L. Sparrow  
Toliver Craig, Jr.

December Term, 1815

Boone County Court

This last will and testament of John Craig, deceased, was exhibited in Court and proved by the oathes of James Hammonds and Samuel Craig, two subscribing witnesses and ordered to be recorded.

Att: Willis Graves, Clk.

January Term, 1816

Boone Co. Court

Certificate of the probate of the estate of John Craig, Sr., deceased, is granted unto John H. Craig, one of the Executors named in the will of the deceased (with leave reserved to the other executors named in said will to join in the probate when they may think fit) who took the oath by law required and entered into bond with Cave Johnson and Thomas M. Prentiss his securities in the penal sum of Fifty Thousand dollars conditioned pursuant to law.

Willis Graves, Clerk

Commonwealth of Kentucky
Boone County. To-wit:

I, J. G. Hamilton, Clerk of County Court for County aforesaid, do certify that the preceeding is a true copy of the last will of John Craig, deceased, order proving the same, and certificate of the probate of Executor qualified, etc., as now of record in my office. Given under my hand this 6th day of March, 1844.

J. G. Hamilton, Clerk

## WILL OF JOHN FORD

### Will Book 1, p. 227, Shelby County, Kentucky

I, John Ford, of the Commonwealth of Kentucky, being weak of body but of sound and disposing mind, do make, ordain, constitute, and appoint this my last Will and Testament in manner and form following:

First, my desire is that all my just debts be paid and further my desire is that my executor convey to Davit Barnett an hundred and fifty acres of land agreeable to a bond given by me to said Barnett.

Item: I give and bequeath unto my son Samuel, and his heirs, a certain parcel of land supposed to contain 335 acres (be the same more or less) being part of a settlement and preemption granted to George Thompson, which parcel of land lieth in the Northwestwardly part of said settlement and preemption on which the said Samuel now lives and bound as follows: Northwestwardly and Westarly by the preemption lines, Southwardly by Benj. Yates' land, and 100 acres lot of mine whereon I now live; Eastwardly by S. Spencer and William Ford's land and thence around with Daniel Barnett's land where it shall be conveyed to him according to the above mentioned land.

Item: I give and bequeath to my son, Edward, his heirs and assigns, 100 acres of land which lieth whereon I now live, with this exception, that all the land of S 100 acres which lieth on the west side of the branch I live on, I give the use of to my wife, Catherine, during her continuance in a state of widowhood and also keeping her residence thereon, but on her removal of the same or marriage, to revert to my said son Edward.

Item: I give and bequeath to my said wife my sorrel horse, or young gray mare, which soever of them she may choose; also the bed and furniture whereon I now lie and one cow and calf, her choice of my stock, one sow and pigs, and three suitable hogs to kill for pork, 2 ewes, 20 barrels of corn, 10 bushels of wheat and 20 lbs. in cash to be paid, when my last will shall take effect.

Item: My will and desire is that the residue of my estate of every species be sold at public vendue of ready money or in credit as my executors shall think best and the money arising therefrom shall be divided as follows: I give to my son Elisha $30 for his services in selling of my land in Carolina; I give to my son Samuel $50 and to my daughter Linney 25 lbs. I give to my son Spencer 24 lbs. and to my daughter Ann 20 lbs.

Item: My desire is that all the residue of my estate not hereby disposed of be equally divided between all my children and I do hereby constitute and appoint my three sons, William, Elisha and Samuel, executors of my last will and testament. In Testimony whereof I have herein set my hand and seal this 13th day of April, 1803. Signed and acted in presence of:

Oswald Thomas
David Denny
David Thomas

John Ford

Shelby County, October County Court, 1803.

This last will and Testament of John Ford, Dec'd., was produced in Court and proved by the oath of Oswald Thomas and David Denny, two of the subscribing witnesses thereunto and ordered to be recorded and on the motion of William, Elisha, and Samuel Ford, the Exec's named in said Will and having made oath thereto, certificate is granted them for obtaining a probate thereof in due form and thereupon entered into and ask'd bond in the sum of Lbs. 1000 with John and Spencer Ford, their securities conditioned as the law directs.

James Craig

Note: John Ford's wife, Catherine, is a second wife, and son, Edward, her child.

## WILL OF JAMES BASKETT

I, James Baskett of the County of Shelby and the State of Kentucky, do hereby make my last will and testament in manner and form following, to-wit:

First, I desire that all my just debts and funeral expenses be paid.

Second I give to my wife for and during her life under the restrictions herein named, my home farm, the dividends that may acc. on my Ashland bank stock, all of my slaves, all of the live stock of any kind, on said farm, all the crops on said farm whether gathered or in the field, mature or unmatured. The farming utensils and the household and kitchen furniture. It is my wish, however, that my son J. S. Baskett remain with his family on the said home farm with my wife and that they live together as one family and that he act as manager of said farm, slaves, etc., for his mother and for his services he shall have one fourth of the profits of the said farm and my wife three fourths thereof and the expenses of the family shall be paid in like, viz: three fourths to be paid by my wife and one fourth by said son. But if any difficulty arise between my wife and my said son and they should agree to live separately then in case of their separating my wife shall have for her life that portion of said farm lying South of the big road running through said farm with the dividend of said bank stock, said slaves and personal property as herein above devised, to her in the same manner as above given to her, viz: for and during her natural life, and my said son shall have immediate and exclusive of that portion of said home farm on the north of said road.

Third: I have heretofore advanced to my daughter, Sarah Jesse, two slaves, also some money and personal property amounting in value to Two Thousand Dollars with which sum she shall be charged in the future distribution of my Estate. I have also given her One Thousand and Twenty Seven Dollars which I designed as an absolute gift and in way of advancement and with which she is not to be charged in the distribution of my Estate.

Fourth: I have advanced to my daughter, Mary A. Bayne, about One Hundred and Thirty-Six Acres of land on which she now lives, and a negro girl and some personal property all worth at the time of the gift Two Thousand Dollars with which same she shall be charged in the future distribution of My Estate and I hereby ratify and confirm to her and her heirs forever the said gift of the said land and slaves, etc.

Fifth, I have advanced to my daughter, Frances J. Hartford, a negro girl and some personal property and about One Hundred Acres of Land on which she now lives all of which at the time of the gift was worth Two Thousand Dollars with which sum she shall be charged in the future distribution of my Estate and I hereby ratify and confirm to her and her heirs forever the said gift of land, slaves, etc.

Sixth: I have advanced to my son, W. C. Baskett, a title bond for the conveyance of Fifty-Five acres of land lying on the North side of the Road leading from Consolation to Shelbyville. I now ratify and confirm said gift of said land to him and to his heirs forever. I have also advanced to him a slave named Moses and some personal property which Land, Slave, and Personal Property worth at the time of the gift Two Thousand Dollars with which sum he shall be charged in the future distribution of my Estate. I now give to my son, W. C. Baskett, and his heirs forever ninty-one and a half acres of land which I bought of D. Perry on which his dwelling house stands but with the encumbrance of Two Thousand and Seven Hundred Dollars (Although it is now worth twice as much) which sum of $2700 he is to be charged with and to account for in the future distribution of my Estate without interest thereon and should there be a sufficiency of my Estate left at the death of my wife undevised specifically herein to give each of my said children Two Thousand Seven Hundred dollars, he, W. C. Baskett, shall pay over to my Executor the difference betwene the Two Thousand Seven Hundred Dollars and the amount he may be entitled to in accordance with the provision of this will.

Seventh: I have advanced to my son, James S. Baskett, a slave named Marshall and some personal property worth at the time Five Hundred and Fifty Dollars with which sum he is to be charged in the future distribution of my Estate. I now give and devise to him and his heirs forever my home farm together with its appurtenances supposed to contain two hundred and ninety-eight acres with which, or its value, he is not to be charged as advancement or otherwise in the distribution of my Estate, subject, however, to the life Estate devised to my wife as herein above set forth. I have given to my son, James S. Baskett, a larger portion of my Estate than to any other child. I have done so partly because I had made advancements to my other children years before. I had given him a much smaller amount and because he has always lived with me and has ever been a dutiful and obedient son.

Eighth: I have advanced my daughter, Lucy M. Bohannon, the tract of land I bought from John Davis for which I paid said Davis two thousand and eighty three dollars with which sum she shall be charged in the future distribution of my Estate.

Ninth: It is my will and desire that upon the death of my wife all the property devised to her for life except the land herein devised to my son, James S. Baskett, shall be equally divided among all my children after they are all made equal in as to advancements made to each as herein above charged against them and to make such division my Executor shall select three respectable and disinterested men of good judgment each of whom shall receive five dollars per day for his services.

Tenth: If I should not sell my lands herein devised my Executor is hereby authorized and empowered to sell and convey the same the proceeds of which he will divide equally among my children.

Eleventh: And lastly I hereby nominate and appoint my sons, William C. Baskett and James S. Baskett Executors of this my last will and testament and direct the County Court to require no security of them as such. In witness whereof I hereby set my hand and seal the First day of August 1860.

Signed, Sealed and Acknowledged.

James Baskett, Seal

In presence of
J. M. Bullock
Shelby Vannatta


Kentucky Shelby County Court
April Term 1863.

A writing purporting to be the last will and testament of James Baskett, deceased, was produced in Court and proved by the oathses of J. M. Bullock and Shelby Vannatta subscribing witnesses thereto whereupon said will was ordered to be recorded and time is given the Executors mentioned therein to qualify as such.

Att: John T. Ballard Clerk
Shelby County Court

## WILL OF GEORGE O'NEAL OR NEAL
### Will Book E, Page 317

Jessamine County Court' Clerk's office, Kentucky.

In the name of God, Amen, being the fifth day of August, 1836, I, George Neal of the County of Jessamine, State of Kentucky, being weak in body but of sound mind and disposing memory do make this my last will and testament in manner and form following (that is to say):

First: That all my lawful debts are to be paid out of my estate.

Second: I give and bequeath unto my beloved wife, Elizabeth Neal, one-third part of all my estate both real and personal during her natural life in which third it shall be included all the negro slaves in my possession and at her death said negro slaves shall be equally divided amongst all my children.

Third: I give and bequeath to my son, James Neal, the tract of land on which he lives in Shelby County, Kentucky, which I have deeded him, containing 230 Acres, also the movable property which he has received as charged to him in my memorandum book.

I also give and bequeath the rest of my sons movable property to the same value as that charged to my son James (if they have not received it). Also I give and bequeath to my son Lewis Neal the tract of land on which he lives in Shelby County Kentucky, containing 100 acres which I have deeded to him. Also I give and bequeath to my son Elijah Neal the tract of land on which he now lives in Jessamine County, Kentucky, containing 95 acres which I have deeded to him. Also I give and bequeath to my son George Neal the tract of land on which he now lives in Jessamine County, Kentucky, containing 93 acres which I have deeded to him. Also I give and bequeath to my son Creath Neal the tract of land on which he now lives in Jessamine County, Kentucky, containing 87¼ acres which I have deeded to him. Also I give and bequeath to my son David Neal the tract of land which I deeded to him in Jessamine County, Kentucky, containing 97½ acres.

I do hereby devise and decree that all the rest of my lands in Jessamine County (not named) to be equally divided among my six sons above named, share and share alike (I wish them to be engaged themselves in the division, a majority to rule); furthermore they may sell or buy to and from each other but it is not to pass out of the family but as brethren such division to be by them and their heirs forever.

I also heretofore give to my daughter Mary Forbes $2500 which I consider as her portion of my estate which was then equal to the portion of the land which I deeded to each of my sons, but the tract of land which I deeded to my son John Neal having reverted back to my estate since his death I have bought the entire interest of his widow in said tract of land and received her deed for the same. It is therefore my will that my daughter, Mary Forbes, shall receive in money the value of a child's part of the said tract of land upon a final division of my estate. It is my will that immediately after my death and in the first division of the lands that each of my three sons, Elijah Neal, George Neal, and Creath Neal receive as much more land as will make each of them equal in lands as my son David Neal.

Also I do hereby nominate and appoint my three sons, Elijah, George, and David my executors (they all living in the County of Jessamine and State of Kentucky) of this my last will and testament, and I do hereby ordain and appoint this to be my last will and testament hereby revoking and disannulling all wills herefore made my me.

In witness whereof I hereunto put my name, this 5th day of August, 1836, and in the presence of the subscribing witnesses.

George Neal (Seal)

Attest: John Garison
Ezekiel Haydon

In Jessamine County Court (November Court, 1836) I certify that the foregoing writing was produced in Court and proven to be the last will and testament of George Neal, deceased, by the oaths of John Garrison and Ezekiel Haydon and ordered to be recorded which is done.

Test: Daniel B. Price, Clk.
by A. M. Poage, D. C.

An inventory and appraisement of the estate of George Neal follows on page 319 Will Book E.

## WILL OF ELIZABETH SINGLETON O'NEAL
(Widow of George O'Neal or Neal)
Will Book H, Page 359
Office of the Clerk of the County Court
Jessamine County, Kentucky

In the name of God, Amen, I, Elizabeth Neal, of the County of Jessamine and State of Kentucky, considering the uncertainty of life and being of sound mind and memory, do make and publish this my last will and testament.

First: I bequeath my negro girl Lydia (abt. five years of age) to my daughter Mary Forbes to have and to hold during her natural life and at her death to descend to her daughters Caroline and Mary Forbes; My reason for making the above request is that Mary Forbes did not get an equal share in the first division.

Second: It is my wish that the remainder of my property be sold and the proceeds thereof be distributed equally among my children. In case of the death of any one of these children, I devise that the share of such descendant shall go to his or her children. I do hereby appoint my son Elijah Neal sole executor of this my last will and testament. I request the court not to require security of my executor.

In Testimony Whereof, I hereunto set hand and seal and decree this my last will and testament in presence of the witnesses named below this seventeenth day of October, One Thousand Eight Hundred and Fifty.

Elizabeth Neal     (Seal)

Keene, Jessamine County, Kentucky.

Teste: Thos. W. Foster
       William Campbell

Will probated May Court, 1852.       Melvin T. Lowry, County Clerk.

## WILL OF MELVIN LOWRY

Will Book F, Page 88

County Court Clerk's office of Jessamine County, Kentucky

I, Melvin Lowry, of the County of Jessamine and State of Kentucky, low in health but of sound mind and disposing memory, do make and establish this my last and only will and testament in manner following:

It is my will that all my just debts be paid and secondly it is my will that my wife Phebe Lowry retain the farm on which I now live together with the following negroes: Mary, a woman, and her four children, Elijah, Nancy, Sam, and Lenah, and Tom, a man, and Joe, a boy, and such of the stock of all kinds as she may think proper and all or such of the household furniture and farming utensils as she may think proper, together with all the money which I have on hand for the schooling and raising of my children, William C., Melvin T., and Phebe H. Lowry, and at her death the farm and negroes to be sold and equally divided between all my children in manner and form hereafter provided.

I give to my son, James H. Lowry, Dennis, a boy, at $500. I give to my son, John P. Lowry, Andrew, a boy, at $500. I have given to my daughters Elizabeth Singleton, Louisa Neal, and Jane Grimes, Malvina Todd, Nancy Knight and Martha West, all a negro and other property each to the amount of $500 which together with the amount I gave James and John is to be deducted from their proportional part of my estate at the death of my wife.

It is my will that all of my negroes not herein bequeathed be sold together with such other property as my wife does not keep with the exception of Manoah, whom I give to my daughter, Mary E. Lowry at $300 and to include a horse which she may select in the amount and at her marriage to be made equal with my other daughters and out of the money arising from the sale. It is my will that my son Charles F. Lowry be paid $500 and as my sons William C. and Melvin T. Lowry at age to be paid the like amount of $500, and as my daughter Phebe H. Lowry to be paid the like sum of $500 should she marry during the lifetime of my wife, and at her death, the farm and negroes to be sold and divided equally between my children, James H. Lowry, Elizabeth Singleton, Louisa Neal, John P. Lowry, Jane Grimes, Nancy Knight, Martha West, Mary E. Lowry, William C. Lowry, Charles F. Lowry, Melvin T.

and Phoebe H. Lowry after deducting the amount each have and may receive, and lastly nominate and appoint my wife Phebe Lowry and my son Charles F. Lowry executor and executorix of this my last will and testament, and it is my will that they be not required to give security for the performance of the duty and executing the provisions of my last will and testament.

In witness whereof I have hereunto subscribed my name and affixed my seal this 24th day of April, 1838.

Melvin Lowry  (Seal)

Acknowledged in the presence of
Jacob Wilmore
C. F. Howard

Jessamine County Court, August Court, 1838

I, Daniel B. Price, Clerk of the County Court of Jessamine County, do certify that the foregoing last will and testament of Melvin Lowry deceased was this day produced in Court and proved by the oaths of Jacob Wilmore and C. F. Howard, the subscribing witnesses to be the act and deed of the said Lowry. Whereupon the same was ordered to be recorded which is accordingly done.

Test. Daniel B. Price, Clerk<br>by Alex M. Poage, D. C.

## WILL OF FOUNTAIN LAND

### Will Book L, Page 732

### Jessamine County Court House

I, Fountain Land, of the County of Jessamine, State of Kentucky, do make and constitute this instrument my last will and Testament and I hereby revoke all wills heretofore made by me.

1st. I will to my beloved wife, Martha M. Land, absolutely all of my personal property of every description, except my cash and the claims owing to me by note or otherwise, and of my cash and claims due owing me, I will her one-third thereof. Also I will to my wife during her life the farm on which we reside consisting of about one hundred and fifty acres including the store room at Hanly, the lot on which it is situated and all the improvements thereon, and which was purchased by me from Hardin Masters, Richard Phillips, and Alex Walker.

2nd. I have advanced to my son, Henry B. Land, Twenty-five Hundred ($2500) Dollars, and for said sum he is to account on a final division of my estate, and I will devise him 222 acres 2 roods and 23 poles of land in the said County of which I have heretofore caused to be surveyed for him in two parcels, and I estimate said land at the value of Fifteen Thousand Five Hundred ($15500) Dollars and with said sum he is to be charged in the settlement of my estate.

3rd. I will to my son, William L. Land, the 309 acres 2 roods and 17 poles of land in Jessamine County on which he now resides and I heretofore caused to be surveyed by me for him in two parcels, and I estimate said land at the value of Fifteen Thousand Five Hundred ($15,500) Dollars and with said sum he is to be charged in the settlement of my estate.

4th. To my son, Albert M. Land, I will 314 Acres, 1 rood and 11 poles in said County of Jessamine which I have heretofore caused to be surveyed for him, and which I estimate to be of the value of Eighteen Thousand ($18,000) Dollars, and which sum is to be charged to him in the final settlement of my estate, but for the use of my family is reserved the graveyard on the land last mentioned, 3 by 4 roods square.

5th. To my daughter, Mary E. Baker, I will all my undivided right, title, and interest in and to the tract of land in Jessamine County on which she and her husband, John A. Baker, reside, containing 300 acres 3 roods and 10 poles and which was conveyed to me and said John A. Baker by deed of Cassa Robards and others. This interest in said land I estimate as of the value of Eighteen Thousand ($18,000) Dollars and on a final division of my estate, she is to be charged with the said sum.

6th. Should any or either of my children die without heirs of his or her body living at the time of his or her death, whether the death of such child shall occur before or after my death, then and in that event, the land above willed to the child or children so dying, I will and devise to his or her surviving brothers and sisters, and to the descendants of such of them as may be dead.

7th. Excepting the $2500 advancement to my son, Henry B. Land, I make no charge of advancements to any of my children. The advancements I have made with them are small, and exclusive of said $2500 my children are to be considered equal in the advancements I have made them.

8th. After the death of my wife I will and direct that my Executors shall sell the land willed to her for life, and all the land and estate I may own and not disposed of, and to convey the same. The sale to be made at such time and on such terms as they may deem most beneficial to all interested and the net proceeds arising from the sale they will divide equally among my four children mentioned above. All other assets of my estate not specifically devised, are in like manner to be divided equally among my said children.

I hereby nominate and appoint my sons, Henry B. Land, and William L. Land, Executors of this will and direct that no security be required of them as such.

Given under my hand this 3rd day of December, 1888.

Fountain Land.

Signed by Fountain Land in our presence, and by us in his presence and at his request.

Dent Hoover
B. M. Arnett

State of Kentucky
County of Jessamine, January term 1899, January 16th.

I, Curd Lowry, Clerk of Jessamine County Court, do certify that the foregoing instrument of writing purtaining to be the last will and Testament of Fountain Land, deceased, was on this day produced and filed in open Court, and offered for probate and being proven by the oath of B. M. Arnett, one of the subscribing witnesses thereto, and the signature of Dent Hoover, the other subscribing witness, but now dead, being proven as genuine by the said B. M. Arnett, and the signature of the testator being also further proven by the oath of William L. Land, the said instrument was allowed confirmed and established as and for the last will and Testament of said Fountain Land, deceased, and as such duly admitted to record which together with the certificate, is duly recorded in my office.

Attest, Curd Lowry, Clerk.

## WILL OF WILLIAM L. LAND
Will Book 9, Page 112
Dated April 17, 1901
Recorded April 27, 1901
County Court Clerk's office of Fayette County, Kentucky

I, William L. Land, a resident of Fayette County, Kentucky, being of sound mind and disposing memory do make and publish this my last will and Testament hereby revoking all others by me heretofore made.

Item 1. I direct all my just debts to be paid including funeral expenses and expenses of administrating my estate.

I bequeath to my beloved wife, Maggie Porter Land, all my household and kitchen furniture of all kinds and all my farming implements. I also devise to her the two gray horses, one bay work horse and one bay work mule and one driving mare, the surrey and surrey harness.

Item 3. I bequeath my home farm known as Richland to my wife during her natural life with remainder to my children or descendants *per stirpes.*

Item 4. I devise my executrix to sell my Fayette County farm known as Grassland, provided that a suitable price can be obtained for it, within three years and she is empowered to convey same in fee simple title to the purchaser. If the Grassland farm be not sold in three years then I direct that it be divided between my children and their descendants per stirpes, giving an equal portion to each child, the descendants of any child that may die before that time taking their parent's portion.

Item 5. I direct that my Jessamine County, Kentucky, lands be held and managed by my estate or Executrix for the benefit of my estate until my youngest child arrives at 21 years of age and then to be divided among all my children equally per stirpes, the descendants of any child that may die taking the equal portion of their parent.

Item 6. All my personalty not specifically devised is to pass to my executrix and by her to be disposed of when ready for market or when she may be able to sell same for proper value. The proceeds of such property she is to pay to my creditors and from time to time as she is able out of the estate or sale of the Grassland farm she is directed to pay on my debts until all are paid.

Item 7. I devise my oldest son, William Fountain Land, to assist his mother in the management of my property, and from the time he reaches twenty-one years of age until my estate is divided, I direct that my Executrix pay him for his services at rate of fifty Dollars per month.

Item 8. I appoint my wife, Maggie Porter Land, as my Executrix without any bond to be required of her. I direct that there shall be no public sale of my personalty and no inventory of my property required by the Court. The words "of my estate" were inserted or interlined on the second page of this Will before signing.

Item 9. In event of my wife dying before my estate is divided, I direct my two sons, William Fountain Land and Leroy M. Land to act as my Executors without bond.

In testimony whereof I have hereunto set my hand this 17th day of April, 1901.

William L. Land.

Signed by William L. Land in our presence and acknowledged by him in our presence to be his last will and we at his request and in his presence and in the presence of each other hereunto set our hands as witnesses This 17th day of April, 1901.

George L. Shanklin
David Barrow
A. L. B. Blanding

I, Claude Chinn, Clerk of the Fayette County Court of Fayette County in the State of Kentucky do certify that on this day the foregoing Instrument of writing was produced to me in my office and was fully proven on oath of George L. Shanklin and David Barrow, admitted to probate and with my certificate has been duly recorded in my office.

Witness my hand this 27th day of April, 1901.

Claud Chinn, Clerk
by Otto Fincher, D. C.

### LEER—BOURBON COUNTY

(Contributed by Mrs. Corday Leer Buckley)

### FAMILY RECORD OF DAVID LEER AND CHARLOTTE CORDAY KENNEY

David Leer born in Bourbon Co., Ky., January 16, 1803.
Charlotte Corday Kenney born in Bourbon Co., Ky., Dec. 12, 1809.
Married in Bourbon Co., Ky., June 10, 1830.

### Children

Margaret, born May 21, 1831; died February 2, 1835.
Elizabeth, born May 27, 1833; died March 13, 1918.
Charles Carroll, born February 11, 1835; died June 10, 1922.
Catherine, born July 17, 1840; died April 19, 1873.
James Monroe married Amelia Turner Oct. 29, 1874.

### Marriages

Elizabeth married John L. B. Alberti May 26, 1853.
Charles Carroll married Adelia Ewing August 19, 1866.
Catherine married John Lewis Ringo February 19, 1867.
James Monroe married Amelia Turner Oct. 29, 1874.

## FAMILY RECORD OF JAMES MONROE AND AMELIA TURNER LEER

Infant daughter born August 6, 1875, died August 6, 1875; a son, born July 29, 1879, died August 4, 1879; Corday, born February 19, 1877; Vernon, born October 31, 1880; Davereau, born January 19, 1882; Matilda, born October 12, 1884; Roe Cora, born November 4, 1885, died November 30, 1886; Junior, born April 28, 1887, died February 20, 1888; Amelia, born January 8, 1889; Loura, born March 25, 1891; James Monroe, born February 6, 1894.

### Marriages

Corday married Benjamin Franklin Buckley January 22, 1896.
Vernon married June 30, 1914 Bessie Tribble.
Davereau married February 12, 1907 Katherine Fox.
Matilda married April 29, 1907 John Will Denton.
Amelia married August 28, 1913 Alfred Caruthers.
Loura married March 5, 1912 Roger Randolph Early.
James Monroe married February 22, 1918 George McDaniel.

## CHILDREN OF CORDAY LEER AND BENJAMIN F. BUCKLEY

Benjamin Franklin Buckley, Jr., born May 12, 1901.
Monroe Leer Buckley born February 2, 1905.
Benjamin F. Buckley, Jr., married Oct. 16, 1929 Beulah Mae Saunders, born March 27, 1900.

### Children

Benjamin Franklin Buckley III born Sept. 27, 1924.
Betty Saunders Buckley born Dec. 28, 1931.
Benjamin Franklin Buckley III married Feb. 12, 1949 Rosemary Dummitt.
Monroe Leer Buckley married April 20, 1933 Amelia Pickrell King.

*Contributed by Mrs. Benjamin F. Buckley*

Mason County, Kentucky Book 1, page 519.

Know all men by these presents that we, James Whaley, John Whaley, Benjamin Whaley, Daniel Whaley, James Nichols, in behalf of his wife, Nancy, late Nancy Whaley and Reason Talbott in behalf of his wife, Jane, late Jane Whaley, do for ourselves and our heirs hereby make over Grant and release to Sary Whaley our sister a full and equal share of all negroes and their increase now belonging to us by virtue of a Deed of Gift from John Whaley our father to us and recorded in the County of Mason as· Full and ample manner as if the said Sary Whaley had been mentioned in said Deed of Gift the said Sary having been born since Deed was made which said Grant we and each of us bind ourselves, our heirs execute and administrators firmly by these presents to the said Sary Whaley and her heirs and assigns forever. In testimony whereof we have hereto set our hands and seals this thirteenth of October 1807.

James Whaley
Benjamin Whaley
John Whaley
William B. Whaley
Mark Wallingford
Daniel Whaley
James Nichols
Reason Talbott.

Mason County Ct.

I Thomas Marshal, Clerk of the County aforesaid do certify that the within agreement was produced before me and proved by the Oath of Joseph Doniphan and James Key witnesses thereto before according to law and the same is duly recorded.

Given under my hand the ninth day of November 1807.

Thomas Marshal

### Contributed by Mrs. Benjamin F. Buckley

Thomas Buckley was born August 15, 1843.
Elizabeth Weimer was born August 12, 1845.
Thomas and Elizabeth Weimer Buckley were married Aug. 29, 1862.

### Children

Benjamin Franklin Buckley was born August 12, 1863.
Ellen, born July 2, 1865.
Elizabeth, born June 12, 1867.
Florence, born January 26, 1871.
Ann Eliza, born January 12, 1875.
Julia, born May 22, 1877.
John Lewis, born August 25, 1878.

Bible Record of Simon and Ann Nichols.

John H. Nichols, born May 10, 1756.
Thomas Nichols, born Sept. 22, 1758.
Margareth Nichols, born Feb. 10, 1761.

Wm. Nichols, born June 13, 1763.
Esther Nichols, born Sept. 12, 1766.
Simons Nichols, born Dec. 8, 1768.
Nicholas H. Nichols, born June 7, 1770.
Ann Nichols, born Jan. 13, 1772.
Ann departed this life Feb. 10, 1774.
Joseph Nichols, born May 23, 1774.
James Nichols, born Jan. 26, 1777.
Ann Nichols, born April 9, 1779.

The above are the sons and daughters of Simon and Ann Nichols who were married Aug. 10, 1755.

Simon Nichols died May 29, 1813 in the 89th year of his age.
Simon Nichols was from Scotland.
From Bible record owned by Miss Julia Moneyhon, Augusta, Ky.

From Bible of Miss Julia Moneyhon, Augusta, Ky.
Record of James and Nancy Whaley Nichols.
Julia Nichols, born Jan. 14, 1803.
Nancy Nichols, born May 22, 1805.
Nany Nichols, died July, 1806.
Mary, born Jan. 14, 1807.
Mary, died March 1, 1809.
Alfred, born Sept. 14, 1808.
John, born June 4, 1810.
Mary, born Nov. 9, 1811.
Eleanor, born Sept. 12, 1813.
James Nichols, born Nov. 2, 1815.
Willis Nichols, born Dec. 6, 1817.
Jeremiah Nichols, born Jan. 27, 1820.
Matilda Nichols, born Jan. 11, 1822.

### Family Record of Simon Nichols

Nicholas Nichols, born April 14, 1824
Aliza and Joseph Nichols, born Nov. 24, 1825.
Joseph Nichols, died Dec. 1825.
Eliza Nichols, died July 31, 1831.
Isaac Nichols, born Oct. 18, 1828.
Nancy Nichols, wife of James Nichols died Feb. 17, 1840.
James Nichols, consort of Nancy Nichols, died Dec. 14, 1855.
Louisa Nichols, wife of Nicholas Nichols, died April 1855.
James Nichols, son of N. Nichols, born Feb. 4, 1849.

Copied in 1856, Lexington, Mo., by L. F. Weimer,
consort of Julia Nichols Weimer of Bracken County, Ky.

Rachel, wife of Alfred Nichols, born May 28, 1813.
Marian, wife of Alfred Nichols, Jr., born Dec. 17, 1822.
Julia Weimer died May 14, 1866.

## BIBLE RECORD

From a Bible now in possession of Mrs. Margaret Leete
of Prestonsburg, Kentucky
Furnished by Mrs. Claude P. Stephens

"Ironton, Ohio.
April 1897—

Ralph Leete of Burlington, Ohio, and Harriet Elizabeth Hand, daughter of Rev'd. William Thomas and Francis Hand, married at Gallopolis, Ohio, Nov. 24, 1848.

The offspring of their marriage are—

William Hand Leete, born at Burlington, Ohio, Oct. 12, 1849.
Edith Ives Leete, born Ironton, Ohio, Nov. 11, 1852.
Frederick Guilford Leete, b. Ironton, Ohio, July 14, 1860.
Elizabeth Francis Leete, b. Ironton, Ohio, June 17, 1865.
Ralph Herman Leete, b. Ironton, Ohio, Aug. 12, 1872.

In the paternal line of ancestry the above is a registration of a portion of the 8th generation of the descendants of William Leete, an English Lawman, who migrated from Huntington England in April, 1639, and was one of the Founders of the Commonwealth of New Haven;— Was Governor of the Commonwealth for twelve years after the connection of New Haven with the Royal Colony of Connecticut;—Was several times chosen Governor and held that position at the time of his death 1683.

This done at my home in Ironton, Ohio, April 18, 1879—in the 76th, year of my life.

Ralph Leete.

————————

p—2

Rev. William T. Hand and Elizabeth Francis married in the Parish Church of Grantham in the County of Lincoln, England, by Rev'd Wm. Patchet Vicar of Said Parish, June 13, 1828. In the year 1834 they migrated to Cincinnati, Ohio.

Rev. William T. Hand, died at Ironton, Ohio, May 9, 1860.
Mrs. E. F. Hand died at Ironton, Ohio, April 7, 1841.

### Children

Harriet E. (Elizabeth) born at Grantham England, April 2, 1829, died at Ironton, Ohio, May 14, 1879.

Ella Lenore, born at Rohoboth, Clermont Co. Ohio, Dec. 12, 1836; died at Ironton, Ohio, March 21, 1891.

————————

Edith Ives (Leete Hamilton, d. Jan. 30, 1903 at Ironton, Ohio; buried at Woodland Cemetery, aged 50 years.

Ralph Leete, died July 15, 1905, at Ironton, Ohio, buried Woodland Cemetery, aged 83 years.

William Hand Leete, died March 6, 1927, at Lima, Ohio.

Ralph Herman Leete, died Feb. 14, 1926, buried at Prestonsburg, Ky., his home.

(This Bible—presented to Ralph Herman and wife Margaret Leete, by their Father, Ralph Leete, 1897)

## LOGAN COUNTY
### (Contributed by Mrs. Ila Earle Fowler)

Notes:

9/17/1824—Elisha Herndon's Will, Logan county, Ky. Estate left to wife Betsey; $800 to John Aingel (son of Wm. Aingel) and Wm. Hannington, son of Agnes Hannington; exrs., Brother, Joseph Herndon, and John P. Bush. . . . . witnesses: Philip Washburn, John Hickman. Probated 8/8/1826. B. 6, p. 298.

6/2/1809—Will James Herndon, probated 7-20-1815.

3/5/1823—William Aingel, estate to wife, Ann Aingel and children: Wm. Henry Aingel; George Aingel; Paisley Aingel; John Ripley Aingel. Exrs. Wm. Mallory; Wm. Farbush; Ben Proctor. Witnesses: John Boyd, John Hickman, John W. Hickman.

3/31/1838—Joshua Cales, estate to Hiram B. Withers and Ephraim Ewing, guardians for family. Exr. Hiram B. Withers . . . wits. Richard Higgins, J. M. Perry.

1/14/1830—Logan county, Ky.—Thos. Foster, Vincent Higby, Drury H. Poor, trustees to incorporate Union Meeting House in Logan county, in an addition to the town of Russellville.

Ky. Acts of 1837—For benefit of Union Baptist church in Logan county, legal title to 130½ poles of land conveyed by Thos. Rodman to Union Baptist church at Little Whippoorwill, to be vested in Reuben Morgan, Henry Miller, Richard West and Asa Greer, trustees.

Deed Book, 74, p. 277—Elizabeth Riley and her husband; F. L. Riley, Maggie Grinter and her husband, Oscar Grinter, on Dec. 20, 1895, deeded 133 acres of land jointly to John and James Fowler; also deeded, Oct. 30, 1893, 43 acres to Henry Fowler, D. B. 71, p. 584.

Book D, p. 415, Robert B. Herndon, guardian for heirs of Robert Poor, dec'd.: on Dec. 12, 1828, paid Richard Burnett $9.50 for tuition for Elizabeth Frances, Sally Ann and Drury W. (Poor).

## HERNDON MARRIAGES FROM LOGAN COUNTY RECORDS

James D. Alcock married Anna Herndon, 5/22/1837.
Parmelia Herndon married Richard Burnett, 1/7/1824.
Mary Jane Herndon married Henry Browder, 3/11/1835.
Harriet E. P. Herndon married Christopher T. Browder, 4/1/1846.
Mary Jane Herndon md. R. N. Beachamp, 10/2/1851.
Sally Herndon md. Robert B. Dudley, 2/23/1815—their son md. his cousin, Catherine Haden, daughter of Isabella Herndon Haden (Earle).
Elizabeth Herndon md. Zachariah Edgar, 9/25/1802.
James Herndon md. Polly West, 6/25/1814.

Robert B. Herndon md. Ellen Crewdson, 9/25/1813.
John Herndon md. Rhoda Furbush, 9/12/1812.
Hiram Holcum (Holcomb) md. Isabella West, 1/18/1813.
Elisha Herndon md. Betsey Aingel, 3/12/1805.
Samuel Page md. Polly Herndon, 3/12/1816.
Levi C. Roberts md. Franky Herndon, 5/1/1814.
Joseph Herndon md. Arena Harris, 2/14/1819.
John Maben md. Nancey Herndon, 2/24/1819.
William Herndon md. Ellen Crewdson, 1/17/1825.
George R. Herndon md. Marry Annah Chasteen, 1/23/1825.
Joseph Herndon md. Catherine Washblown, 3/25/1829.
John B. Herndon md. Barsha Ann Browning, 9/28/1831.
Henry Browder md. Mary Jane Herndon, 3/11/1835.
Arena Herndon md. James D. Acock, 5/22/1837.
George Herndon md. Frances Holcomb 7/24/1837.
Wilson Page md. Susan Ann Hodges, 8/30/1843.
Elizabeth Bishop md. Cornelius Burnett, 6/26/1813.

1866, March 6—Rev. E. W. Earle deeded land on the line of Dade and Cedar counties, Mo., to Ben P. Earle, Thomas Buck Earle; P. J. Bailey; deed produced Aug. 10, 1868, Test. J. B. Herndon, Jr., D. Clerk to Haddox.

1872, Jan. 18—1873, Nov. 7—E. W. Earle and wife Elizabeth, deeded land in Logan county to Ben P. Earle; mentions fork of Muddy River, Bailey's line, E. T. Bailey; John W. Christy, clerk of Hopkins county, by R. C. Speed, D. C., to W. Winlock, clerk of Logan by W. A. Newman, D. C. (No. 568, p. 538).

1875, Feb. 1-April 17, Ben P. Earle of Hopkins Co., sold this land to John B. Page, Logan Co.; mentions Edward and Lucy Bailey and P. B. Edwards, D. C. (decd No. 136, p. 191, Logan Co.)

1844, Sept. 3 Ezias W. and Isabella Earle to George Earle and D. W. Poor, "land on which we live" on Whippoorwill creek, given by Geo. Herndon to Robt. Poor; Marmaduke Morton, clerk. (Book Z, p. 509 and 529).

1844, Nov. 6—E. W. Earle and Isabella Earle for one dollar and love and affection, negro boy, Monroe, and negro girl, Titia Ann, to George Earle and Catherine Dudley, they to retain same their lifetime, deed to apply to any other child born of their lawful wedlock. Also to Catherine Hayden and her after born children, negro girl Mimi.

(Note: Data from Family Bible of Isabella Herndon—Poor-Haden-Earle and other Family Bible sources regarding these children.)

Isabel Herndon married Walter Poor, 9/17/1818; announcement also in Kentucky Gazette.
Isabel Poor married James Haden, 5/17/1826.
Isabel Haden married Ezias Earle 5/18/1842.
Elizabeth Frances Poor, b. Oct. 17, 1819, md. Dr. George Holcomb, 3/23/1837.
Sarah Ann Poor, b. Oct. 26, 1821.
Drury Woodson Poor, b. Oct. 1, 1822.

Catherine Haydon, b. Sept. 17, 1827, married her cousin Robert Dudley.

Elizabeth Frances Poor Holcomb died April 1, 1838.

Drury Woodson Poor died June 24, 1883, at Henderson, Ky.

Catherine Dudley died Dec. 30, 1906.

Sarah Ann Poor died 9/21/1835.

George Robert Earle, born May 24, 1843, killed in Confederate service, Dec. 2, 1862.

Benjamin Prince Earle, b. April 22, 1846; died April 30, 1918.

James Reuben Herndon married Martha Ellen Burnett, Nov. 11, 1852, by John H. Gammon, in presence of William Herndon, D. W. Poor, Jr., Robert Herndon, Elisha Herndon, and Cornelius Burnett, at home of Richard Burnett.

In Christian county, the following Herndon marriages from the records.

John Cook and Martha W. Herndon, Dec. 29, 1823, Stephen Woodward, bonds.

Henry Edwards married Polly Herndon, daughter of James, Benjamin Herndon, bondsman.

(See p. 321—Holcomb Family by Compton)

(See Earle Family, printed by Guelff Printing Co., Marquette, Mich. 1934, pp. 76-108.)

## MILAM

Family Records from Photostats which will be placed in Ky. Historical Society, contributed by Mrs. John B. Trivett, 68 Norman Drive, Birmingham, Alabama.

### Births

John Tecumseh Milam born at Benson, Franklin County, Ky., March 17th, 1832.

Elizabeth Morgan, born at Jeffersonville, Ia., Feb. 19th, 1836.

John Morgan Milam, son of J. T. and Elizabeth Milam, born at Jeffersonville, Ia., May 26, 1856.

Anna Belle Milam, daughter of J. T. and Elizabeth Milam, was born at Benson, Franklin Co., Ky., July 15th, 1859.

James William Milam, son of J. T. and E. Milam, born at Benson, Franklin Co., Ky., July 30th, 1861.

Katie Milam, daughter of J. T. and E. Milam, born at Benson, Franklin Co., Ky., Dec. 20th, 1863.

Charles Clark Milam, son of J. T. and E. Milam, born at LaGrange, Oldham Co., Ky., Feby. 15th, 1865.

Emma Waide Milam, daughter of J. T. and E. Milam, born at LaGrange, Oldham Co., Ky., Dec. 8th, 1867.

Bettie Pennington, daughter of J. T. and E. Milam, born at LaGrange, Oldham County, Ky., January 20th, 1874.

Ben Tecumseh, son of J. T. and E. Milam, born at La Grange, Oldham County, Ky., on Nov. 20th, 1875.

Catherine Wilson Milam—Cassady, daughter of Bettie Milam and El Cassady, born August 1, 1887.

## Marriages

John Howard and Elizabeth M. Doom were married by the Rev. E. L. Wilson at Middlesboro, Ky., Feb. 10, 1904.

Lily Mac Leod Doom and William J. Kinnaird were married May 21, 1902, at Cincinnati, Ohio.

Harry (Harriet) Beard Kinnaird and John Blevins Privett were married April 20, 1921 in Middlesboro, Ky., by Rev. J. V. Logan.

Patsey Wilson Kinnaird and Wilmer Dickens Webb were married February 9, 1924 in Birmingham, Ala., by Rev. W. R. Dobyns.

Wm. Kinnaird Privett and Katherine Speaks Binford were married January 11, 1944 in Birmingham by Dr. R. P. McGregor.

Annie Belle Webb and W. E. Chatham, Jr., were married July 6, 1946, in Birmingham, Ala.

Wm. J. Howard and Mary Hodges were married Nov. 15, 1945 in Annapolis, Md.

John Tecumseh Milam and Elizabeth Morgan were married by the Rev. R. H. Allen, at Jeffersonville, Ia., on the 17th day of Oct., 1854.

Jno. P. Doom and Annie B. Milam were married Feb. 6th, 1877.

Jno. M. Milam and Katie M. Moore were married October 24th, 1882.

Bettie P. Milam and Edward Cassady were married February 8, 1896, at Jeffersonville, Indiana.

## Deaths

Katie Milam, daughter of J. T. and E. Milam, died at Benson, Franklin County, Ky., aged 3 months and 15 days, on the 5th day of April, 1864.

J. T. Milam died at Hot Springs, Ark., Nov. 5, 1875, aged 43 years, 8 months and 14 days.

Emma Waide Milam died at LaGrange, Oldham Co., Ky., aged 12 years, 4 months and 5 days on the 13th of April, 1880.

Elizabeth Milam died at La Grange July 26th, 1898, aged 62 years, 5 months and 7 days.

Ben T. Milam died October 1, 1936, Middlesboro, Ky.

Mary Howard died February 22, 1937, Hartford City, Indiana.

Julian Meredith Howard died June 14th, 1941, Middlesboro, Ky.

John M. Milam, son of J. T. and E. Milam, died at Louisville, Ky., Sept. 22nd, 1903, aged 47 years, 3 months and 27 days.

John Tecumseh Milam died at Pittsburgh, Pa., June 20th, 1907, son of J. M. Milam.

James William Milam, son of J. T. and E. M. Milam, died at Memphis, Tenn., June 13, 1915.

Lily Doom Kinnaird, daughter of J. P. and Annie M. Doom, died April 13, 1925 at Birmingham, Ala., aged 47 years, 5 months, 8 days.

John Philip Doom, husband of Annie Milam Doom, died November 16, 1927, age 76 years and 12 days, Middlesboro, Ky.

Annie Milam Doom died Nov. 7, 1932, age 73 years, 3 months 23 days —Middlesboro, Ky.

*Miscellaneous*

Lillie MacLeod Doom, daughter of Jno. P. and Annie B. Doom was born at La Grange, (Ky.) Nov. 5th, 1877.

Sallie Doom, daughter of Jno. P. and Annie B. Doom, was born at La Grange, Ky., April 3rd, 1880.

Elizabeth Doom, daughter of Jno. P. and Annie B. Doom, was born at La Grange, Ky., Sept. 26, 1882.

Harry Beard Kinnaird was born April 19, 1903 at Cincinnati, Ohio (Harriett).

Mary Howard, daughter of Elizabeth D. and John Howard, born June 17, 1905, Middlesboro, (Ky.)

John Doom Howard, son of Elizabeth D. and John Howard, born March 30, 1907.

William J. Howard, born November 18, 1915.

Julian Meredith Howard, born March 11, 1918.

Elizabeth Howard born January 1, 1920.

Patsy Milam Kinnaird, daughter of Lily Doom and W. J. Kinnaird, born July 1, 1905.

William Kinnaird Privett, son of Harry (Harriett) Kinnaird and John B. Privett born September 3, 1922.

John Blevins Privett, Jr., born December 24, 1930 at Birmingham.

Annie Belle Webb, daughter of Patsy Kinnaird, and W. D. Webb, born January 28, 1925, Birmingham.

Wilmer Dickens Webb, Jr., born December 16, 1927, Birmingham, Ala.

Patsy Kinnaird Webb, daughter of Patsy L. Webb and W. D. Webb, born July 11, 1931, Mobile, Ala.

Harriett Doom Privett, daughter of Harry (Harriett) Beard Kinnaird and John B. Privett, born April 7, 1933, Birmingham, Ala.

## BRACKEN BAPTIST CHURCH 1799-1836

Copied by Mrs. Ann Delia Yellman, Maysville, Ky.

Deed at Brookville, Bracken County, Kentucky

Nov. 21, 1808 — Trustees to Patterson

Trustees of the Bracken Accadamy, State of Ky. to Nathaniel Patterson 200.00 paid to them......by said Patterson, a certain parcel of land lying County of Christian, Ky. granted by the Commonwealth of Ky. by Patent bearing date 12 day of June 1800 for 200 Acres

Trustees of Bracken Accadamy of Bracken Co. Ky.
Philip Buckner
Robert Davis
James Wells
James Armstrong
Martin Marshall
Thomas Nelson          Signed by John Payne
Will Buckner
J. Blanchard                    Nov. 21 1808

## Methodist Trustees Of Meeting House

Ferdinand Dora and his wife Ann to Trustees of Methodist Meeting House
William Robinson
Casper Bownan
Robert Tevis          Bracken County, Ky Aug 1819
James Carter
John Leathan

Minutes of the Bracken Association of Baptists begun at Bracken Meeting House on Saturday the 20th of May, 1799, Mason County, Kentucky.

Our aged and beloved Br. David Thomas, Br. James Turner, Moderator, Br. Donald Holmes, Clerk.

### Churches and Messengers

Washington—David Thomas, Jas. Turner, Jno. Corwine, Wm. Cheeseman.

Mays Lick—Donald Holmes, Thos. Young, Ruben Payne.

Bracken (near Minerva)—Lewis Craig, Phn. Thomas, Steven Hiott, Wm. M. Curry.

Stone Lick (near Orangeburg)—Wm. Byram, Aaron Houghton, Wm. Been.

Lees Creek (near Dover)—Philip Drake, Chas. Anderson.

Ohio Locust—Jos. Wright, Jas. Thompson.

Licking Locust—Laur. Triplet.

Richland Creek (near Burtonville)— Joshua Singleton, Roland Parker,

### Suppliers

Licking Locust—Brothers L. Craig, David Thomas, Philip Drake, Wm. Holton, James Thompson, Jos. Morris.

Richland Creek—Brothers Anderson, Jas Thompson, Wm. Holton, David Thomas, Philip Drake.

Adjourned—Jas. Turner, Sec.

From Baptist Church Minutes, Washington, Ky.

12-13-14 of October 1799, Saturday the 12th, 11 o'clock

### Churches and Messengers

Washington—David Thomas, Rich. Carwin, Thos. Sentony, Thos. Sloe.

Mays Lick—Donald Holmes, Wm. Allen, Nat'l. Hickson.

Bracken—Jos. Morris, Wm. Holton, Stephen Hiott.

Stone Lick—Wm. Byram, Wm. Bean, Wm. Harper, George Brown.

Lees Creek—Philip Drake, Robert Elrod.

Ohio Locust—Chas. Smith, Jas. Thompson, Tob. Stout.

Licking Locust—Laurence Triplett, Henry Hunt.

Richland Creek—Joshua Singleton, Stephen Lee.

Licking—Jonathon Jackson, Joe Washburn.
Mays Lick, second Saturday, October on to Monday, 13th, 1800.
Washington—Miles W. Conway, Sampson Tolbert.
Mays Lick—Donald Holmes, Wm. Allen, Thomas Young, Nathaniel Hixson.
Stone Lick—Aaron Houghton, Wm. Bean, Jas. Lawson, Wm. Byram.
Lees Creek—Philip Drake, Griffin Evans, Charles Anderson.
Ohio Locust—Jas. Thompson, Job. Stout.
Licking Locust—Lawrence Triplett, James Sanders, John Winn,
Richland Creek—Joshua Singleton, Stephens Lee.
Licking—Macsy Mannerief, Jonathan Jackson.
Foxes Creek—James Wright, William Markwell.
Bracken—Lewis Craig, William Holton.

Copied from Minutes of the Bracken Association of Baptists
Held at Stone Lick Church Sept. 19, 20, 21, 1801,
Mason County, Ky.

### Churches and Messengers

Washington—Miles W. Conway, Jas. Turner, Wm. Cheeseman, Amos Corwine.
Mays Lick—Donald Holmes, Wm. Allen, Thomas Longly.
Bracken—Wm. Holton, Thos. Mills, John King.
Stone Lick—Hiram M. Currey, Wm. Bean, Thomas Elrod, Wm. Byram.
Lees Creek—Philip Drake, Chas. Anderson, Griffith Evans.
Ohio—Jas. Thompson.
Licking Locust—John Winn, Laurence Triplett, Jas. Johnston, Jas. Dunlap.
Rich. Creek—Joshua Singleton, Aaron Owens, Stephen Lee.
Licking—Jas. Burns, Jonathan Jackson.
Foxes Creek—Joel Havens, Jas. Wright, David Beadle.
Johnston—Charles Metcalf, John Stout.
Salt Lick—Samuel Cox, Wm. Haven.

### Minutes, Sept. 18, 19, 20, 1811—(217)

Washington—Wm. Payne, Nicholas Devore, Jas. Turner, Lewis Gorden.
Mays Lick—Donald Holmes, Wm. Allen, John Johnston, Jas. Morris.
Bracken—Stephen Hiott, Lewis Craig, Philemon Thomas.
Stone Lick—Wm. Bean, Wm. Byram, Thomas Elrod, Aaron Houghton.
Lees Creek—Philip Drake, Charles Anderson.
Ohio Locust—Zac. Thompson, Job. Stout, Thomas Powers.
Licking Locust—Laurence Triplett, John Winn, Jas. Dunlap, Jas. Sanders.
Richland Cr.—Stephen Lee, Roland Parker.
Licking—John Burns, Jonathan Jackson.
Foxes Creek—David Beadle, Joel Havens, Sam. Powel.

Johnstons—John Stout, Ishmael Davis.

Salt Lick—Wm. Harper, Wm. Canington (Carrington?), Landan Calbert.

Cedar Hill—James Carson.

Indian Run—John King, Samuel Allison.

Wilson Run—John Debell, James Reed.

### At Bracken Meeting House, Sept., 1803

#### Churches and Messengers

Washington—Wm. Payne, Jas. Turner, Miles W. Conway, Amos Turner.

Mays Lick—Jacob Griff, Nat. Hixon, Wm. Allen, Wm. Hiter.

Bracken—Lewis Craig, Phil M. Thomas, Wm. Holton, Jos. Morris.

Stone Lick—Aaron Houghton, Wm. Been, George Brow (Boon), Wm. Byram.

Lees Creek—Philip Drake, Richard Robinson, Griffith Evans.

Ohio Locust—Jas. Thompson, Josiah Harbert, Peter Mirrell (Minell?).

Rich. Creek—Joshua Singleton, Murdock Cooper, Stephen Lee, John Owens.

Licking—John Routt, John Jackson.

Fox's Creek—Wm. Estil, Sepe (Jepe) Foster, Nat. Foster.

Salt Lick—Wm. Harper, Landan Calvert, Samuel Cox.

Cedar Hill—John Gutteridge.

Indian Run—John King, Thos. Mills.

Wilson Run—John Williams, Wm. Scott.

Soldier Run—Nat Foster, David Thomas.

Three Mile—Eli Oxley, Wm. Stephens.

Clover—Wm. Smith, James Howard.

### 1804

Washington—Wm. Payne, Miles W. Conway, Amos Carwine, Henry Putman.

Mays Lick—Jacob Grigg (Griff), Nat'l Hixon, Laurence Crail, John Singleton, Wm. Allen.

Bracken—Lewis Craig, Wm. Holton Sen., Samuel Frazer, Wm. Holton, Jr.

Stone Lick—Wm. Byram, Philip Drake, Charles Anderson, Griffon Evans.

Lees Creek—Rich'd Robinson.

Ohio Locust—Jas. Thompson, Amos Miller.

Richland Cr.—Joshua Singleton, Stephen Lee, John Owens, Aaron Owens.

Licking—Jonathan Jackson, Henry Man.

Fox Cr.—Jos Wright, Joel Havens.

Salt Lick—Wm. Harper, Wm. Davis, Sam'l Cox.

Cedar Hill—Jas. Lawson, John Gutteridge.

Johnson—Chas. Metcalf, George Fasiguker (?).

Indian Run—John King.

Wilson Run—Joseph Power, Jas. Johnston, John Williams, John Debell.

Three Mile—Eli Oxley, Wm. Stephenson.

Clover—David Bedle, Castor Shrout.

Soldier run—Bart 'is Anderson, Jas. Carson, David Thomas.

South Fleming—John Passons, Ishmael Davis, James Sanders, Laurence Triplett.

Licking Locust—Henry Hurst.

## COPY OF THE RECORDS OF THE SOUTH HALF OF THE MAYSVILLE, KY., CEMETERY CO. (OLD PART)

H. H. Barkley, *Pres.*

(Contributed by Mrs. Ann Delia Yellman)

(Names of people buried in Maysville Cemetery. Dates given are year of death; some graves have no date)

Lot 1, Sec. 2.—George Adamson, 1879; Mary Adamson, 1879; Sarah Cunningham, 1895; William Adamson, son of Moses and Eliz. Adamson; Moses Adamson; Elizabeth Ingram Adamson; Lucy Adamson.

Lot 2, Sec. 2.—Hannah Wilson; Mary Wilson; John M. Wilson; Sarah King; Samuel Strode; Margaret Wilson, 1913; Nelson Clift; Edward King; Henry M. King; Spohr; Dora King, 1878; Kate King, 1889; Mary King.

Lot 3, Sec. 1.—Mrs. Samuel McDonald, 1907; Isaac Nelson, 1892; Mary J. Nelson, 1867; Dr. Wm. Nelson, 1884; Mary M. Nelson, 1885; Thadius Jacobs, 1863; T. M. Adamson, 1905; J. A. Nelson.

Lot 4, Sec. 2.—George Nelson, 1873; Simon Nelson, 1865; John Nelson; Lettia Nelson, 1886; Simon Nelson, 1922; Nannie Nelson, 1938; Roy Nelson, 1936; Wm. J. Boles, 1945.

Lot 5, Sec. 5.—Wm. McGranaghan, 1853; Mary McGranaghan, 1849; Charles McGranaghan; Florence McGranaghan, 1860; Jane Ellis, 1873; Mary Coryell, 1866; Ella McG. Nute, 1898; W. H. McGranaghan, 1891; Jane Ellis McGranaghan, 1892; Frank McGranaghan, 1891; Dr. Will McGranaghan, 1916.

Lot 6, Sec. 2.—Jane Nelson, 1879; W. R. Wood, 1859; Mary P. Wood, 1875; Mary T. Wood, 1879; Sallie Davis, 1860; Elizabeth Sumrall Davis, 1909.

Lot 7, Sec. 2.—Delia Lane Makay; Herman Wood, 1889; Richard M. Wood, 1859; George T. Wood, 1896; Harry T. Wood, 1898; James F. Wood, 1867; R. C. Wood, 1863; Sallie Wood, 1909; Delia Wood Lyon, 1911; Mrs. Geo. T. Wood, 1914.

Lot 8, Sec. 2.—Wm. Ballenger, 1864; Susan C. Taylor, 1844; Wm. C. Ballenger, 1822; Margeretta Ballenger, 1892; Elizabeth M. Pratt, 1887; Wm. Erb, 1867; Nancy Dickman; Elizabeth Ballenger; Jane Carruthers, 1840; John F. Ballenger, 1889.

Lot 9, Sec. 2.—Henry Willett; Bertha Willett; Dayton Willett; Mrs. Dayton Willett. (10 graves on lot.)

Lot 10, Sec. 2.—Henry L. Newell, 1912; Ella G. Newell, 1881; Richard Newell, 1869; Birdie May Newell, 1873; Frank Newell, 1880; Harry L. Newell, 1869; W. W. Newell, 1900; Lizzie L. Newell, 1874; Hans Newell, 1890; Mary Newell, 1879; James Newell, 1909; Stonewall J. Newell, 1916; Sarah F. Newell, 1926; Claud Newell; Nettie Spain, 1937; Elizabeth Newell, 1940; Mary Newell, 1879; Mary M. Newell, 1939; Annie B. Newell, 1940.

Lot 11, Sec. 2.—(Wm. Hancock.)—George S. Hancock; Nannie W. Hancock, 1885; Frank Easum, 1884; Sallie Easum, 1892; Mary Elizabeth Smith; Mary S. Hancock, 1866; John Hancock; John W. Hancock, 1900; Julia Hancock, 1911; Elizabeth T. Hancock, 1897; John W. Hancock, 1834. (15 graves on this lot.)

Lot 12, Sec. 2.—Joseph Ryan, Sr., 1894; John Ryan; Anna Ryan, 1910; Jos. T. Ryan, 1915; Mrs. Jos. T. Ryan, 1911.

Lot 13, Sec. 2.—(Godfry Miller, Henry Bode.)—Henry Bode, 1865; Elizabeth Bode, 1897; Joseph Bode, 1898; Frederick Bode, 1903; Harry A. Miller, 1890; Barbera Miller, 1896; Godfry Miller, 1937; Margeret Cablish, 1930; Jack Cablish, 1922; Louise Vantine, 1918; George W. Vantine, 1930.

Lot 14, Sec. 2.—John Lowery; Joseph Lowery, 1928; Mary Lowery, 1932; Alice B. McDaniel, 1937.

Lot 15, Sec. 2.—(Peter Miller, John T. Bendell.)—Peter Miller, 1865; Sarah Miller, 1894; Wm. Miller, 1902; Henry Miller; John Miller, 1890; Fred B. Miller, 1908; Catherine F. Miller, 1911; Peter Miller, 1934; Johannah Bendell; Catherine Bendell, 1890; 1. J. F. Bendell; F. A. Bendell; 2. J. F. Bendell; Fred Mendell, 1934; Kate Mendell, 1943; Elizabeth Mendell, 1915; C. I. Bendell; Caroline Bendell, 1889.

Lot 16, Sec. 2.—Christian F. Zweigart, 1897; Mary Zweigart, 1914; Henry Weiand, 1861; Fred Weiand; Dorthory Weiand, 1900; Louise R. Weiand, 1893; Jacob Weiand, 1901; Anna M. Weiand, 1905; Lulie Zweigart, 1907; John Zweigart, 1910; Mary Frances Zweigart, 1913; Mary Zweigart, 1914; Mrs. Christian Zweigart, 1914; Rosenie F. Zweigart, 1926; VeMiette M. Zweigart, 1923; Christian Zweigart, 1931; Caroline Zweigart, 1947; Lillie B. Roden, 1944.

Lot 17, Sec. 2.—Abraham R. Pearce; Mrs. A. R. Pearce; Bert L. Smith, 1894; Lucie Smith, 1889; Charles Smith; Mrs. Charles Smith; Harry B. Smith, 1912; Mary Smith, 1912; Charles E. Smith, 1927.

Lot 18, Sec. 2.—James C. Brookover, 1886; Rachel Brookover, 1882; H. A. Brookover, 1880.

Lot 19, Sec. 2.—(John J. Sparks trans. part of lot, Susan J. Bliss.)— Martha Sparks, 1863; Leslie Adamson, 1900; Ella J. Adamson, 1921; Wm. H. Bliss, 1914; Steven Bliss, 1871; Susan J. Bliss, 1882.

Lot 20, Sec. 2.—Wm. Wood, 1885; Mary F. Wood, 1865; Laura J. Wood, 1837; Thomas P. Wood, 1897; Emma B. Wood, 1892; Phoebe C. Wood, 1887; Wm. C. Wood, 1894; Letitia Wood, 1903; Joseph T. Wood, 1912; J. James Wood, 1927; Elizabeth Wood, 1946.

Lot 21, Sec. 2.—(Railroad Lot, all graves removed from L. & N. Depot.)—Joseph Edwards; Moses Trever; J. W. Roten; Caroline Crowell; Eugene John Murphey; Henry Krimmel.

Lot 22, Sec. 2.—(Railroad Lot.)

Lot 23, Sec. 2.—(Railroad Lot.)

Lot 24, Sec. 2.—(Railroad Lot.)

Lot 25, Sec. 2.—(Mrs. Ann M. Byers sold N. ½ to Mrs. James H. Rogers.)—Lorena Evans, 1898; Willie Clark, 1891; Mrs. Charles Turner, 1902; James H. Rogers; Lida Clark Rogers; E. M. Tolle, 1912; Nancy D. Tolle, 1914; Mary Turner, 1937; Wm. E. Howard, 1923; James H. Rogers, 1920; John Clark Rogers, 1934; Horace J. Rogers, 1909.

Lot 27, Sec. 2.—(J. M. Breeden and Wm. Cummings.)—Anna Whittington; John M. Whittington, 1891; John Whittington; Johanna Tolle, 1901; Elvira Tolle, 1893; Jarvis G. Cady, 1875; Charles Cady, 1900; Mary Cady, 1908.

Lot 26, Sec. 2.—(Bardsley.)—Sarah Ellen Parry, 1901; Needam Parry, 1891; Emma Wood, 1914; Elizabeth Wood Parry, 1939.

Lot 28, Sec. 2.—(W. S. Reed; ½ sold to John Schmidt.)—John G. Smith, 1884; Joshua Smith, 1886; Henry Fresh; Catherine Fresh; Florence McDaniel, 1901; J. W. Sawyer, 1866; J. L. Sawyer, 1861; Fannie McDaniel, 1918.

Lot 29, Sec. 2.—(Robert H. Baldwin.)—Wm. H. McAtee, 1902; Lee B. McAtee, 1923; Robert H. Baldwin, 1863; Sallie T. Baldwin, 1862; J. G. Baldwin, 1831; Nancy M. Baldwin, 1840; John A. Baldwin, 1845.

Lot 30, Sec. 2.—(W. W. Baldwin.)—Mary M. Ranson, 1880; Bessie Ranson, 1888; Betty B. Ranson; Simon Cartmell, 1891; Robt. L. Baldwin, 1897; W. W. Baldwin, 1906; Mrs. Sallie Baldwin (nee Darnell), 1913; A. C. Respess, 1926; Nannie (Mrs. A. C.) Respess; W. Baldwin Respess, 1943; W. W. Baldwin, Jr., 1931; Lucie Baldwin, 1923; Anna Cartmell, 1936; Baldwin Cartmell, 1936; Lutie Cartmell (mother), 1938.

Lot 31, Sec. 2.—(Andrew T. Wood.)—Thomas McMillin, M.D., 1873; Elizabeth Webb Yancy, 1889; James McMillin, 1857; Jusel Wood, 1837; John G. Avery, 1849; Dr. J. D. Collins, 1908; Sadie M. Collins, 1903; Laura Bell Wood, 1857.

Lot 32, Sec. 2.—(George W. Tudor.)—Thomas J. McCarty, 1874; Charles P. Adams, 1934; George W. Tudor, 1910; Harriet M. Tudor, 1872.

Lot 33, Sec. 2.—(Edward Bell.)—James D. Bell, 1869; Edward W. Bell, 1911; Margaret Bell, 1920. (Six other graves.)

Lot 34, Sec. 2.—(David Brown.)—Clarence Brown, 1891; David Brown, 1865; Sabathiel Brown, 1871; John Willett, 1874; J. R. Rudy, 1891; Joseph F. Owens, 1882; Lizzie S. Owens, 1877; Caroline Rudy, 1921.

Lot 35, Sec. 2.—(A. J. Browning.)—Six graves not marked; Frank King; Johnie O. Lauby, 1899; A. J. Browning; Francis Browning; Rufus Browning; Judith Browning; Mary Jane Browning, 1913; John G. Browning, 1917.

Lot 36, Sec. 2.—(Leroy W. Kenner.)—This lot trans. to Mrs. Sallie Froman, 1874. The west of said lot trans. to Robert Sously, 1883. The half of same trans. to Mrs. Clara D. Clark of Vansburg, Ky. John Clark, 1902; Charles Froman, 1879; James Froman, 1880; Presilla Froman, 1894; Wilson Froman; Henry Froman, 1891; Thomas H. Carty, 1912; Cynthia Carty, 1910; Annie Froman, 1916; Sarah Crowell, 1823; Clara Clark, 1943; George S. Carter, 1928.

Lot 37, Sec. 2.—Vacant.

Lot 38, Sec. 2.—Vacant.

Lot 39, Sec. 2.—(Sabrina Mangan. West side lot 39 sold to John Cox, Vanceburg, Ky.)—Wheeler Cox, 1884; Jimmie Cox, 1880; Jonnie Cox, 1877; Albert Cox, 1865; Sabrina Mangan, 1882; Roxanna White; James Cox, 1862; John Cox, 1914; Elizabeth Cox, 1940; Alice Cox, 1923.

Lot 40, Sec. 2.—(Keith Berry. E. side of lot sold to John Wheeler.) —Mrs. Keith Berry; Eliza Keith Berry; Darius Berry; George Ann Berry, 1907; Frank Berry; Eliza Bullock Berry; Thomas Keith Berry, 1872; Susan E. Berry, 1897; Lottie Keith Berry, 1941; Morris Hugh Milliken, 1939; Sudie B. Milliken, 1947; Marie W. Milliken, 1940.

Lot 41, Sec. 2.—(Thomas Biggers.)—George W. Rea, 1875; Henry Rea, 1869; George Rea, 1875; Susan Rea, 1868; Susan Rea, 1864; Mary E. Rea, 1909; Thomas M. Rea, 1908. (Other graves.)

Lot 42, Sec. 2.—(Charles Clark.)—Eliza McClure Clark, 1878; C. Clark, 1855; S. D. Clark, 1846; H. M. Clark, 1852; Cep Clark. (5 other graves.)

Lot 43, Sec. 2.—(B. Whiteman Wood. ½ of lot sold to John S. Means; ½ sold to Wm. Wallingford.)—Margeret Duke, 1892; Joseph Spencer; Mary Spencer; Nellie Means; Edgar Means; Maggie Means; Clarence Means; Frank Means, 1894; Lucille Tweed, 1932; Wm. H. Wallingford, 1909; Mrs. Wm. H. Wallingford, 1907; Lottie Adele Smith, 1911; Wilson Smith, 1926; Mary E. Smith, 1945; Dr. T. H. Smith, 1940.

Lot 44, Sec. 2.—(Josiah Brenner [owns] North ½, John Zeck South half.)—Jas. Gunn, 1894; Jos. Brenner, 1899; Mrs. Jos. Brenner, 1906; Johanna Lipp, 1883; John Zeck; Charlett Zeck, 1883; Birdie Brenner, 1900; Lulie D. Schmidt, 1889; Adam Zeck; .... Zeck; Samuel Otto, 1889; Carrie F. Trapp, 1892; Mrs. Minnie Gunn, 1909.

Lot 45, Sec. 2.—(J. H. Keerans.)—J. A. Keerans, 1888; Martha Keerans, 1886; Teft Keerans, 1873; Maguire Keerans, 1872; Anna Pollitt; James Ensor, 1904; Bert Pollitt; Mary Ensor, 1921; B. O. Keerans, 1900; Sarah Williams, 1903; Thomas A. Williams, 1895; Mary Williams, 1893; Betie Sweet; Joseph Howard; John Roe, 1906; Mrs. John Roe, 1906; Elmer Rudy; Bertie Rudy.

Lot 46, Sec. 2.—(Wm. Broadwell.)—Other Graves; Sarah Ellen Turnipseed, 1889; George Broadwell, 1906; Nancy J. Broadwell, 1894; Gilbert Broadwell, 1888; Ruby Broadwell, 1890; Charles Broadwell, 1865; T. T. Emmons, 1901; Charles Deal, 1912; Mrs. Charles Deihl; Mrs. W. H. Ginn, 1898; Clarence Broadwell, 1904; Jacob Turnipseed; John Dryden, 1916; Mary Dryden, 1930; Carrie Dryden, 1938; Earle Dryden, 1920.

Lot 47, Sec. 2.—(Washington Fire Co.)—J. W. Bridges; Edward Harrocks; Samuel Outton, 1922; Mrs. Julia Ficlin (Mrs. Dr. Harover), 1923; Mrs. Frankie Matthews, 1924; Edwin Matthews, 1942; Joe Matthews, 1937; Dr. S. R. Harover, 1930; Nora Frakes, 1932.

Lot 48, Sec. 2.—(Neptune Fire Co.)—Three graves; James A. Wallace, 1839; Belle F. Wallace.

Lot 49, Sec. 2.—(Sarah Stevenson.)—Thomas B. Stevenson, 1868; Nat Woods' boy; Hiram Hendrixson; Margeret Hendrixson.

Lot 50, Sec. 2.—(Mason Lodge.)—Mrs. J. F. Lee, 1874; J. F. Lee, 1897; T. F. Stevens, ....; Willie Wilson, 1883; S. B. Nicholson, 1882; Wm. C. Jenkins, 1869.

Lot 51, Sec. 2.—Margeret A. Creighbaum, 1900; Samuel Creighbaum, 1901; Margeret Creighbaum, 1857; Allen and Mary Creighbaum, 1857; James Creighbaum, 1901; R. G. Lynn, 1905; James Clark, ....; Mrs. James Black, 1882; Eliza Margan, 1888; James Morgan, 1874; Elizabeth Lynn, 1868; Mary Watkins, 1872; Ellen McKinley, 1896; Jane Clark, 1882; Mary Clark, 1918; Lida Creighbaum, 1937.

Lot 52, Sec. 2.—(Hiram T. Pearce.)—James Threlkeld, 1906; James Threlkeld, 1877; Little Moss; B. G. Moss, 1872; A. Moss, 1868; Belville Moss, 1885; Richard M. Threlkeld; Octavia Threlkeld, 1901.

Lot 53, Sec. 2.—(Louis C. Pearce.)—Louis C. Pearce, 1891; Eliza Pearce, 1861; Hiram McI. Pearce, 1878; Willimena Pearce, 1890; Samuel Pearce, 1916; Phoebe Pearce, 1843; Edny M. Pearce, 1837.

Lot 54, Sec. 2.—(Mrs. Ann Robertson.)—W. C. Selashmoot, 1847; Ann Robertson, 1864; Agnes Rogers, 1852; Theressa D. Rogers.

Lot 55, Sec. 2.—(Mrs. Mary Powling.)—Lousisa Powling, 1900; Thomas Powling, 1860; Mary A. Powling, 1876; John Powling, Sr., 1843; Mary Williams & E. Powling; Thomas Bell, 1841; Thomas Oridge, 1863; Louie Oridge, 1880; Kate Oridge, 1880; Thomas W. Oridge, 1881; John Powling, Jr., 1849; Mrs. Rebecca Oridge, 1908; Anna King, 1932.

Lot 56, Sec. 2.—Hannah Rickett; Jacob Outten; James Rosendall; F. N. R. Outten, 1871; Jane R. Outten, 1898; Conrad Rosendall, 1858; Susan Rosendall, 1861; ...... Outten; Phoebe Bell Outten, 1926; Horace Outten, 1910.

Lot 57, Sec. 2.—(Mrs. Eliza McClung.)—Rev. John A. McClung, 1859; A. L. Baldwin, 19...; Ann Baldwin, 1943.

Lot 58, Sec. 2.—(R. H. Stanton.)—Judge Stanton, 1891; Asenath T. Stanton, 1894; Asenath S. Forman, 1936; William Forman, .....

Lot 59, Sec. 2.—A. C. Respass; Jane Respass, 1882; Augustine Respass, 1849; Thomas A. Respass, 1919; ......

Lot 60, Sec. 2.—(Martha E. Cobb.)—Harris King, 1917; Alice Roe King, 1909; Margeret Trimble; Elizabeth Haney; Elizabeth Haney; John B. Orr, 1904; Emma O. Rice, 1939; Thomas H. Rice, 1925; Louise Trimble; Papa.

Lot 61, Sec. 2.—(Charles White and R. Dawson.)—John White, 1811; C. C. White, 1888; Charles White, 1897; John G. Waugh, 1823; Sophia A. Waugh; S. A. Waugh; Eliza Jones, 1859; Nancy White, 1896.

Lot 62, Sec. 2.—(Thomas Ross.)—Dr. Wilson Coburn, 1853; Ann W. Coburn, 1897; Carrie Coburn, 1858; John Coburn, 1896; Cornelia Coburn, 1859; Kate C. Ross, 1906; Thomas A. Ross, 1885; Nellie Ross, 1866; Mary E. Ross, 1859; Watson A. Ross, 1858; Maurice Waller, 1908; Lewis Collins Ross, 1943.

Lot 63, Sec. 2.—(Alex Calhoun and David Atkinson.)—John M. Calhoun, ....; Celistine Calhoun, ....; Ann Calhoune, 1874; Alex Calhoune, 1859; P. M. McCarthey, 1909; Mrs. P. M. McCarthey, 1899; John Alex Atkinson; .............; David B. Atkinson, 1847; Kate Atkinson; Francis Atkinson, 1862; Anna M. Atkinson; Mr. Atkinson; Lucy Atkinson; David Calhoun.

Lot 64, Sec. 2.—(Ruth Tolle.)—Four Graves; Ruth Shouse, 1887; Cora B. Shouse, 1887.

Lot 65, Sec. 2.—(Thomas Gurney.)—Thomas E. Gurney, 1838; Grave; William & Sallie Powling; Grave; Emma F. Guerney; Ann Gurney, 1862; Thomas Guerney, 1883; Lucy Guerney, 1904.

Lot 66, Sec. 2.—(Robert Adair.)—Sarah Adair, 1860; Bertie Adair, 1858; Robert D. Adair, 1935; James Adair, 1940; Two graves; George Dodson, 1890; Florence Dodson, 1891; Mary Elizabeth Dodson, 1912; Omar Dodson, 1919; Grave.

Lot 67, Sec. 2.—(H. Gosling.)—Stanley Finirty, 1901; James L. Finirty, 1934; Lottie Finirty, 1943; Two graves; Jennie Burrows Flowers, 1905; Bettie Burrows Britten; Norma W. Flowers, 1923; Margaret Flowers, 1916; Anna Burrows, 1891; Ella Burrows, 1894; Charlette Burrows, 1897; William Burrows, 1882; Maggie Burrows; Mollie Burrows; Sallie Burrows, 1924; Julia Lurtie, 1885; Grave.

Lot 68, Sec. 3.—(R. C. Grundy.)—Dr. John H. Holton, 1891; Garret H. Holton, 1889; Mrs. Annie Holton, 1925; John W. Wroten, 1873; John Cambies, 1898; William Taylor, 1853; Julia B. Paddock, 1896; Estene Paddock, 1918.

Lot 69, Sec. 3.—(Wm. Huston.)—Four graves; two graves; Clara Huston; Laura Huston; Ann Huston; Emily Huston; Charles H. Huston; Deborah Lee; Francis Lee Huston, 1886; James A. Huston, 1885; Matilda Huston, 1849; Clara Huston Johnson, 1908; Thomas Johnson, 1922.

Lot 70, Sec. 3.—(A. M. January.)—Eliza Spillman, 1866; Alexander Logan, 1854.

Lot 71, Sec. 3.—(William Hodge.)—Deborah Watt; Mary Newman; Lizzie Ross; William Hodge, 1860; Isabella Hodge, 1865; ........; Nannie Cartmell, 1904; Simon M. Cartmell, 1896; Lucretia T. Cartmell, 1908; Charles Cartmell, 1913; Robert M. Cartmell, 1925; Charlette W. Cartmell, 1941; Elizabeth M. Cartmell, 1942; Dr. John W. Cartmell, 1936.

Lot 72, Sec. 3.—(Hugh Power and Ezekiel Dimmitt.)—Levinia Cooper Power, 1863; Hugh Power, 1878; Dyas Power, 1908; Marion Cooper Power, 1936; Martha E. Moore Power, 1921; Ann Delia Power Yellman, 19...; Wm. L. Yellman, 1932; Charles Power, 1887; ............; Ezekiel Dimmitt, 1874; Martha Dimmitt, 1884; Thomas & Ann Dimmitt, 1848; Mariah Dimmitt, 1890; Jennie Dimmitt, 1885.

Lot 73, Sec. 3.—(Mary Morrison.)—Unmarked graves; Lidia Traxel, 1936; Wm. L. Traxel, 1925; Martha Traxel, 1917; Esculine Traxel, 1935.

Lot 74, Sec. 3.—(Simon Nelson.)—Sarah McDonald; M.........
M.........; Margeret Tudor, 1868; Luella Young, 1871; Rulif M. Ricketts, 1875; Minerva Ricketts, 1899; Alice Clark Buck, 1941; Olivia Martin, 1873; Wm. Martin, ....; Willie Martin; Robert Martin, 1875; John A. Martin, 1869; Martha Martin, 1903; Wilber Martin, 1903; James Martin, 1882; Wm. A. Martin, 1898; Catherine Martin, 1903; Lillie A. Martin, 1874; Will T. Martin, 1931.

Lot 75, Sec. 3.—(M. Stanley and T. K. Ricketts.)—James S. Martin, 1830; America Ricketts, 1835; Lea Martin, 1859; Violet Ricketts, 1866; Thomas Kerr Ricketts, 1906; Wm. Ricketts, 1897; Fannie Holmes, 1936; Rulif Ricketts, 1848; Mary Ricketts, 1850; T. K. Ricketts, 1905; Mary Ricketts, 1903; Permilia Ricketts, ....; John P. Ricketts, 1883; Sallie N. Ricketts, 1925; Minerva Ricketts, 1941; Anna Poyntz Ricketts, 1928; Elizabeth Ricketts, 1925.

Lot 76, Sec. 3.—(Lewis Collins.)—Eleanor Owens, 1877; H. J. Collins; S. J. Collins; S. P. Collins; Lewis Collins, 1870; Mary E. Collins, 1881; Valentine Peters Peers, 1830; Margeret Hawes, ...54; James Curtis Owens, 1908; Maria Collins Owens, 1910; M. T. McClanahan, 1945.

Lot 77, Sec. 3.—(A. D. Hunter.)—R. B. Case, 1898; Susan Case, 1885; Sarah Case, 1917; McAtee Case, 1943; Emma Case, 19...; Thomas W. Case, 1932; Kate Case, 1920; Mrs. Eliza B. Harover, 1901; Eliza Lee Harover, 1911; Charles W. Geisel, 1851; Louise Geisel, 1910; Esther Herbst, 1840; Mrs. Alice Cooper, 1909; George Herbst, 1848; Eliza Herbst, 1838.

Lot 78, Sec. 3.—(George W. Blatterman.)—Fannie Blatterman, 1891; Eleanor Collins Blatterman, 1901; Lewis Collins Blatterman, 1909; Elizabeth Blatterman, 1864; Edward Brooks, ....; George W. Blatterman, 1912; G. W. Blatterman, Jr., 1909.

Lot 79, Sec. 3.—(R. N. Collins.)—Edward Cox Collins, 1859; Mary Collins, 1880; Richard H. Collins, 1888.

Lot 80, Sec. 3.—(Henry Rudy.)—Jefferson Childs, 1931; Simon Childs, 1875; Margeret Rudy, 1874; Amelia Clarkson, 1934; Jennie Rudy, 1930; Samuel G. Rudy, 1904; Elmer L. Rudy, 1903; Newton Rudy, 1914; Mrs. Newton Rudy, 1914; Mrs. Margeret Childs, 1916; Wm. C. Rudy, 1918; Anna E. Rudy, 1939; George W. Rudy, 1930.

Lot 81, Sec. 3.—(B. P. McClanahan.)—Henry Johnson, Sr.; Sarah Ann Power; B. P. McClanahan, 1923; Mrs. B. P. McClanahan, 1925.

Lot 82, Sec. 3.—(Conrad Rudy.) Several Graves, Perry Rudy, 1920; Mother, 1892; ...... Barker; Anna Barker; James Fristoe; Mrs. J. B. Fristoe; Mildred Frances Barker; Newton Rudy; Mrs. Newton Rudy; Joseph K. Brady, 1923.

Lot 83, Sec. 3.—(Mrs. Mary Rudy and E. C. Wisenall.)—Eleanor Wisenall, 1893; John Wisenall, 1858; Josephine Wisenall, 1916; Mary C. Wisenall, 1923; John Rudy, 1847; Margeret Rudy, 1863; Oletha Rudy, ........; J. J. Easton, 1924; Simon E. Childs, 1902.

Lot 84, Sec. 3.—(Wm. & John H. Richeson.)—John B. Richeson, 1855; Mildred Richeson, 1850; Mary Todd Richeson, 1881; W. W. Richeson, ........; J. H. Richeson, 1876; Eliza Richeson, 1899; Ragsdale Richeson, 1899; Holt Richeson, 1898; Mollie Richeson; Minnie Richeson; Sue Richeson, 1928; Ed Richeson, 1941; Mary Eliza Richeson, 1936; Mary Alice Richeson, 1939.

Lot 85, Sec. 3.—(Michael Ryan.)—Mildred Ryan; Michael Ryan, 1879; Maria Louise Ryan, 1890; Elizabeth Ryan, 1860; Henry Ryan.

Lot 86, Sec. 3.—(M. Culbertson and Wm. F. Wilson.)—Milton Culbertson, 1874; Margaret Culbertson; Jane M. Byrne, 1851; M. C. Wilson, 1897; W. F. Wilson, Jr., 1896; T. P. Wilson, 1893; W. F. Wilson, Sr., 1910; Amelia D. Wilson, 1913.

Lot 87, Sec. 3.—(John Triplett.)—Elizabeth Clark Triplett, 1850; Sarah Jones Triplett, 1854.

Lot 88, Sec. 3.—(Wm. Newell.)—George W. Wardell; Wm. Wardell, 1849; Isabelle Newell, 1864; Sarah B. McMillan; Laura E. Wardell, 1874; Wm. Newell; Andrew J. Newell, 1869; Two graves; Mariam Stubblefield, 1913; Judith Howe Newell, 1913; Mrs. James Bland, 1916; James Bland, 1916; Mrs. Will Stubblefield, 1916; Will Stubblefield, 1929; Chester Bland, 1919; Belle Bland, 1940.

Lot 89, Sec. 3.—(Isaac Morford and J. D. Roach.)—Isaac N. Morford, 1886; Mary E. Morford, 1900; Elizabeth Seaman; Charles Seaman; Willie Beace; A Son of W. J. Morris, 1864; Five other graves.

Lot 90, Sec. 3.—(John G. and R. G. Stewart.)—Esther Stewart; Alonzo H. Downing, 1849; Francis Ravencraft, 1849; Margeret Ravencraft, 1859; Johny, Jr., 1867; .............. Ravencraft, 1868; Mrs. Margeret Ravencraft, 1907; John J. King; Sarah King; Reuben King.

Lot 91, Sec. 3.—(Goldenburg, Thomas Wallace & Clara Newdigate.) —Graves 1-8, .................; 9. W. H. Loughbridge, 1862; 10. Thomas Wallace; Graves 11-19, ................; 20. Mary E. Wallace; 21. Sarah J. N. Wallace; 22. Annie M. Wallace, 1928.

Lot 92, Sec. 4.—(Armistead Purnell.)—Armistead Purnell, 1894; Comfort Julia Purnell, 1866; Wm. H. Purnell, 1860; Lucy Purnell, 1859; Isaac Purnell; Charles Purnell; May Wayne, 1866; Grave; Mary Purnell Campbell, 1934; James H. Purnell; Julia Purnell.

Lot 93, Sec. 4.—(Hamilton Gray.)—Andrew Gray, 1847; Elizabeth Gray; Hamilton Gray; Six other graves; Rosa Pickett McDowell, 1936.

Lot 94, Sec. 4.—(J. A. Bierbower.)—Susan Keighley, 1875; Father, 1858; Mother, 1894; R. C. Bierbower, 1870; Frederick Bierbower, 1910; Frank Bierbower, 1927; Ellen Bierbower, 1927; Agnes Bierbower, 1924; Fannie Bierbower, 1940; Grace Bierbower, 1944; Mary O. King, 1907.

Lot 95, Sec. 4.—(James Johnson.)—James A. Johnson; Robert Johnson; Charley Johnson; Hamilton Johnson; Mary Johnson; Mrs. Elizabeth Johnson; Miss Bessie Johnson; James A. Johnson, Jr.; Ethel (Johnson) Owens (Mrs. Cleon C.); Alpheos Bascom, 1859; Patsy Bascom, 1859.

Lot 96, Sec. 4.—(A. A. Wadsworth.)—Sullivan Duvall, 1849; Prudence Ramsdale, 1851; Adna Anson Wadsworth, 1853; Martha Wadsworth, 1891; Wm. H. Wadsworth, 1893; Charley Wadsworth, 1906; W. H. Wadsworth, 1908; Ida Power Wadsworth, 1936; John Gray Wadsworth, 1930.

Lot 97, Sec. 4.—(B. C. Larew.)—14 graves in this lot. Mary Ann McNeely, 1860; Joseph F. Thompson; Mrs. Joseph Thompson; Francis Clark; George Graham; Jane Graham.

Lot 98, Sec. 4.—(Joseph H. Frank.)—John Frank, 1851; Anna Frank, 1856; Joseph Frank, 1886; Eliza Frank, 1881; William S. Frank; Theresa Scott, 1858; Bettie Byrne, 1930; William A. Byrne, 1906.

Lot 99, Sec. 4.—(David Clark.)—Levi Fleming, 1898; Elizabeth Fleming, 1803; H. Clay Triplett, 1874; Fleming Daulton; Phil Triplett, 1895; David Clark, 1882; Mary Ann Clark, 1882; John Fleming, 1914; Mary T. Lilleston; Mary Ann McNeely, 1860 (Same name and date in lot 97.)

Lots 100 and 101, Sec. 4.—(Odd Fellows.)—Chas. Sunier; John C. Wallace, 1846; Alfred Moss, 1852; Wm. B. D. Baker; Wm. Schnelle, 1885; James Miller, 1897; August Bergman; Allen Dodson, 1947; Flora Miller, 1923.

Lot 102, Sec. 4.—(Sons of Temperence.)—Elisa Pickering; Elizabeth E. Farley; Wescott Farley; Thomas J. Farley; John W. Farley, 1903; Mary Farley, 1929; James A. Frost, 1941; Dora F. Frost, 1929.

Lot 103, Sec. 4.—John W. Lane, 1899; T. Boyce Lane, 1899; Father, 1861; Mother, 1871; Julia A. Dryden, 1891; John Geiss, 1891; Mrs. John

Geiss (Elizabeth Athep), 1913; Wilson Lane, 1921; J. W. Farley's Children; Anna Dudley Muse; Robt. A. Lane, 1937; Elizabeth Lane, 19.....
Lot 104, Sec. 4.—(John M. Duke.)—Lucy B. Morton; Mary Morton; Hannah Morton Duke; John M. Duke; James W. Duke, 1867; J. R. Duke; John M. Morton; John M. Duke; Sarah Dewees Duke, 1902; Mary Duke; J. M. Lashbrooke, 1892.
Lot 105, Sec. 4.—(O. D. Davis.)—15 graves on lot. Deborah Burgoyne, 1905; Katherine Schatzmann, 1942; Eva Daugherty, 1946; Wm. M. Daugherty, 1939; L. W. Galbraith, 1904; Mary Galbraith, 1905; Mrs. Joshua Holliday; Joshua Holliday, 1908; O. D. Burgoyne, 1916; Matilda H. Burgoyne, 1925.
Lot 106, Sec. 4.—(Joseph H. Taylor.)—10 graves on lot. Robinson Weeden; Anna Weeden; Lizzie Weeden, 1872; Frederick Weeden, 1872; Elizabeth Weeden, 1858.
Lot 107, Sec. 4.—(Roswell Grant.)—Lennen Purnell, 1930; Mollie Grant Purnell, 1931.
Lot 108, Sec. 4.—(John Thompson and Margeret McCollough.)—Wm. McCollough, 1899; A. Buley McCollough, 1897; Hugh McCollough, 1888; Hugh McCollough, 1866; Margeret McCollough, 1872; Mary T. McCollough; Ann M. McCollough; Susan Dern; Jennie McCollough Baird; Mary Thompson, 1848; John Thompson, 1862; James Thompson; Delitha Thompson.
Lot 109, Sec. 4.—(Episcopal Church.)—Kate Harlow, 1855; Babe K. Harlow; James Nash, 1840; Lizzie Nash, 1845; Harry Ziegler Guern, 1944.
Lot 110, Sec. 4.—(James Smith.)—Samuel Smith; Mary Smith; Elizabeth Smith Topping, 1851; Richard Smith Jones, 1849; Jane Smith Clarkson, 1896; Thomas Smith, 1849; Ann Smith, 1859; Henry Smith, 1896; Ann Smith, 1895; James Smith, 1897; Harriet Elizabeth Smith, 1849; Sarah Ann Smith, 1850; Elizabeth Bullin Smith, 1857; Henry Sherman Smith, 1866; three graves; Lillie Smith Tash, 1921; John D. Tash, 1935.
Lot 111, Sec. 4.—(Andrew Mitchell.)—John Andrew Mitchell; Martha Mitchell, 1912; Andrew Mitchell, 1864; Mary L. Cady, 1888; Mattie Mitchell, 1865; Lizzie Mitchell, 1864; Dickey Mitchell, 1860; Alex M. Rogers, 1890; Belle Rogers; Walter Allen Peterson, 1947; Oscar Clay Mattingly, 1947; Earl Wayne Roe, 1947; two other graves.
Lot 112, Sec. 5.—(E. D. Anderson.)—Angeline Mayhugh, 1905; Anderson children; two graves; Eloise Mayhugh, 1879; Isabella Mayhugh, 1885; J. D. Mayhugh, 1903; Jane Mayhugh, 1872; Nancy J. Mayhugh, 1872; Fielding Mayhugh, 1852; Oscar Mayhugh, 1863; Carrie Mason; Mrs. Laura Wells, 1910; Mrs. Alex Mayhugh; William T. Mayhugh; Jennie Ziegler Mayhugh, 1923.
Lot 113, Sec. 5.—(Wm. Stillwell.)—Mary E. Stillwell, 1849; Wm. Stillwell, 1857; Phoebe Dye Stillwell, 1865; Evert Stillwell, 1853.
Lot 114, Sec. 5.—(Charles B. Anderson.)—Mary Eliza Anderson, 1852; George Ann Anderson, 1853; Charles B. Anderson, 1897; Chas. V. Anderson, 1849?; Rachel Anderson, 1873?; Paul D. Anderson, 1885; Dr. L. D. Anderson, 1857; Mary J. Anderson, 1844; one other grave.
Lot 115, Sec. 5.—(John Pelham.)—14 graves on lot; Charles Pelham, 1829; Isabella Pelham, 1851; Wm. Pelham, 1914; Mrs. William Pelham, 1928; Louis Pelham, 1942.

Lot 116, Sec. 5.—(William Corwine.)—Mary A. Corwine, 1859; William Corwine, 1852; Amanda Corwine, 1842; John C. Pecor, 1914; Mrs. John C. Pecor, 1917; Clayton Pecor, 1918.

Lot 117.—(J. H. Pecor and Christopher Russell.)—Jeremiah Russell, 1848; Simeon Russell, 1843; Christopher Russell, 1894; Mary Ann Russell, 1892; Margeret Russell; George Pecor, 1860; Jane Pecor, 1902; John Pecor, 1887; J. H. Pecor, 1907; W. B. Pecor, 1915; Rachel Pecor, 1944.

Lot 118, Sec. 5.—(Benjamin F. Thomas.)—Benjamin F. Thomas, 1865; Louisa Thomas, 1872; Sarah Lizzie Thomas, 1861; Catherine Flinn, 1858; Andrew T. Cox, 1886; Mrs. A. T. Cox, 1908; Ben Cox, 1912; Dr. D. C. T. Franklin, 1913; Elizabeth Cox Franklin, 1931.

Lot 119, Sec. 5.—(H. J. Hickman.)One grave; Mary A. Ashbrook, 1879; W. Joseph Ross, 1872; Julia Hotze, 1897; George C. Pemperton; Catherine Pemperton, 1876; Curtis J. Pemperton, 1861; Wm. A. Pemberton, 1868; Sallie W. Ross, 1863; George C. Ross, 1863; Susan Nicholson, 1919; C. H. Nicholson, 1902.

Lot 120, Sec. 5.—(Confidence Lodge; must have been from L. & N. Depot.)—Asa Lyons, 1812; Thomas J. Barrere, 1832; F. M. Taylor, 1869; Onesimus Atherton, 1857; 12 graves on lot.

Lot 121, Sec. 5.—(Augustus Sunior and Wm. Ort.)—William Ort, 1902; Catherine Ort; James Ort; William Ort; Paul Ort, 1861; Katherine Ort, 1873; Mrs. Wm. Ort; Frances Davis, 1887; Nora Davis, 1889; Augustus Sunior, 1865; Mrs. Augustus Sunior, 1913; Robert Sunior, 1884; two graves; seven graves; Elizabeth Burbage Garten, 1929; Julia Burbage, 1879.

Lot 122, Sec. 5.—(J. and M. C. Harover.)—15 graves on lot. John G. Harover, 1853; Matilda Harover, 1883; Marion Harover; Children of G. W. Dixon; Mary Luman, 1872; Henry B. Luman, 1879; Thomas M. Luman, 1911; Emma C. Luman, 1927; Alberta Cravey, 1940.

Lot 123, Sec. 5.—(Peter B. Jones.)—Peter B. Jones, 1850; Elizabeth Jones, 1898; Mattha Jones, 1834; Mary Jones, 1837; Catherine Jones, 1844; A. B. Jones, 1891; Emona L. Jones, 1909; Eliza Davis, 1845; Hannah Davis, 1852; Martha Davis, 1854; John S. Jones, 1912.

Lot 124, Sec. 5.—(Robert Payne.)—17 graves. H. P. McIlvaine, 1891; Mrs. H. B. McIlvaine, 1922; Lena McIlvaine, 1941; S. Charles Vicroy, 1899; Wesley Vicroy, 1903; Ethel McLaughlin, 1913; Robert Payne, 1848; Susan Payne; Melvina Higgins, 1893; Wm. Higgins, 1891; F. Higgins; Margeret Jane Vicroy, 1933; Lula Vicroy, 1918.

Lot 125, Sec. 5.—(Dudley A. Richardson.)—Dudley A. Richardson, 1890; E. W. Richardson, 1843; Wm. H. Richardson, 1895; Annie D. Keith, 1888; Mrs. Dudley Richardson, 1907; Thomas Arbuthnot Keith, 1930; Annie Dudley Richardson Keith; Thomas Arbuthonot Keith, Jr., 1943.

Lot 126, Sec. 5.—(Jacob Joerger.)—Grand Ma, 1856; Tillie Joerger, 1902; Jacob Joerger, Jr., 1895; Jacob Joerger, 1894; Mother Joerger, 1899; Wilhelmina Joerger, 1906; Louie Joerger, 1913; Sallie, 1922; Julia, 1935.

Lot 127, Sec. 5.—(Mack Wallingford.)—Celia Hopkins, 1860; Arthur G. Wallingford, 1878; Nolie Wallingford, 1873; Matha Wallingford; Webster Power, 1864; James R. Mills, 1898; Elizabeth Lamar Goodman, 1933; Buckner W. Goodman, 1926; Henry Boyd, 1918.

Lot 128.—(A. P. Stewart and H. W. Thompson.)—H. W. Thompson, 1866; Elizabeth Thompson, 1899; Andrew M. Thompson, 1890; Mattie Thompson, 1880; John W. Thompson, 1927; John B. Gibson, 1898; J. B. Gibson, Jr., 1877; Mary L. Gibson, ....?; Katie L. Gibson, ....?; Jimmie Stewart, 1859; Jane C. Stewart, 1854; Achiseth Miller, 1849; Mary Jane Rounds, 1840.

Lot 129, Sec. 5.—(Basil L. Williams.)—Rebecca Williams, ....; Horace Williams, ....; Elizabeth Stephens, 1885; Leeann Stewart, 1883; James Stewart, 1892; Lucy Stewart, 1877; Ida M. Moran, 19...; John H. Moran, 1947; W. L. Moran, 1930; Sallie E. Moran, 1933.

Lot 130, Sec. 5.—(Fred Schatzmann and John Dinger.)—Amelia Schatzmann, 1854; Frederick Schatzmann, 1902; Regina Schatzmann, 1891; Joseph Schatzmann, 1935; Lillie Schatzmann, 1940; Louisa Schatzmann, 1942; Julia Schatzmann; Alton Schatzmann, 1945; John Dinger, 1876; Mary Dinger, 1867; two other graves.

Lot 131, Sec. 5.—(Charles B. Hill.)—Nannette C. Wilson, 1925; Mattie Hill Lovel, 1921; Duke Hill, 1892; Charles B. Hill, 1887; Mother, 1895; Sudie Hill, 1896; Charlie Hill, 1902; Mary Smith, 1861; David Smith, 1841; three other graves.

Lot 132, Sec. 5.—(P. V. Vanden.)—Charles F. Vanden, 1841; Charles C. Vanden, 1850; George B. Vanden, 1853; P. B. Vanden, 1883; Mrs. P. B. Vanden, 1910; Edna Farrow; Cyrus Canfield; Sarah Jane Wolford; Mrs. Ben Fleming; Charles Sweet's Child; Sam T. Farrow, 1916; Luella Farrow, 1935.

Lot 133, Sec. 5.—Robert F. Means, 1907; James Hall Means, 1859; Susan Means, wife of A. H. Means; Anna Bell Means; Alvin H. Means, 1932; Ida C. Means, 1929; R. F. Means, 1907; Mrs. R. F. Means, 1907; George B. Means, 1934; Leslie Means, 1880; Mattie Power, 1866; Sarah Shackleford, wife of Marcus Shackleford; Millard Foxworthy.

Lot 134, Sec. 5.—James H. Hall, 1886; Mary C. Hall, 1815; Wm. F. Hall, 1936; Tillie D. Hall, 1940; John N. Brooks, 1867; Charlette T. Brooks, 1870.

Lot 135, Sec. ...—Leander Collins, 1882; Milo G. Collins, 1875; Thos. D. Collins, 1865; Lillie G. Collins, 1865; Frank S. Collins, 1884; H. H. Collins, 1897; Martha J. Collins, 1937; Thomas T. Stone, 1883; Nancy Stone, 1908.

Lot 136, Sec. 6.—(S. S. Miner.)—Wm. C. Miner, 1898; Chas. S. Miner, 1892; Selden N. Miner, 1849; Ariminta Miner, 1894; Samuel S. Miner, 1844; Elizabeth Brooks, 1877; Fannie S. Graham; Etta F. Graham, 1886; Henry G. Smoot, 1882; Mrs. Betty Smoot (wife of H. G. Smoot), 1912; Julia S. A. Emma Hulett.

Lot 137, Sec. 6.—John Brosee, 1884; Frederick Brosee, 1901; Fred Brosee; Mary L. Brosee; John Brosee; H. C. Campbell; John Jacob Bartruft; Lucinda Newdigate, 1895; Sarah Bell Alexander, 1896; Lizzie Myers; Fanny M. Campbell, 1938; Sarah M. Case, 1931; Ernest Brosee, 1900; Percy N. Brosee; Amy Brosee, 1891; Wm. Brosee, 1936.

Lot 138, Sec. 6.—(Wm. Cuttenden.)—One grave not marked; Emily Cuttenden, 1837; Electa Cuttenden, 1845; Julia A. Robinson, 1852; George W. Lloyd, 1874; Harriet Lloyd; Susan Lloyd, 1899; James Lloyd, 1916; Lloyd Best.

Lot 139, Sec. 6.—(Charles W. Franklin.)—Elizabeth Franklin, 1851; Grave; Daniel Spaulding, 1849; Mary E. Spaulding, 1852; Daniel G. Spaulding, 1852; James G. Spaulding, Jr., 1854; James G. Spaulding, 1880; Mary R. Spaulding, 1897; Daniel Spaulding, 1855; Margeret Spaulding, 1833; John Spaulding, 1838.

Lot 140, Sec. 6.—(Charles B. Coons.)—Charley B. Coons, 1866; Nancy Coons, 1863; Martha Coons; Nancy Coons, 1849; H. A. Coons, 1856; T. M. Coons, 1856; Nancy Poynts Coons, 1882; Emma Maltby, 1905; Charles C. Maltby, 1907; Ada Coons; four graves.

Lot 141, Sec. 6.—(John Macher.)—Charles Macher, 1922; Henry Macher, 1828; Martha Macher, 1822.

Lot 142, Sec. 6.—(Nat. Poynts.)—Mary C. Smith; James and Anna Pemberton; three others.

Lot 143, Sec. 6.—Hettie Harbin, 1854; John Harbin, 1865; Samuel L. Blaine, 1883; Samuel Blaine, 1910; Anna Coons Blaine, 1899; George C. Blaine; E. Robert Blaine, 1911; Fannie Owens Blaine, 1943; Samuel Blaine, 1910.

Lot 144, Sec. 6.—(Charles H. White and Littleton Hill.)—Mary A. Watkins, 1871; Richard W. Watkins, 1877; Grave; John Bridges, 1905; Martha Bridges, 1833; Lavina Bridges, 1846; Jennie Bridges Bromley, 1843; Anna Frazer Crockett; Mary Frazer; Elizabeth Clark, 1863; Robert White, 1861; Isaac Watkins, 1821; two graves; Dillie Watkins, 19....; Uncle Dick Watkins; Earle Watkins.

Lot 145, Sec. 6.—(Solomon Shockley and Wm. Bridges.)—John L. Shockley, 1847; Mrs. Ella Clark, 1902; Wm. S. Bridges, 1870; Mrs. Amanda Bridges, 1907; Bettie K. Bridges, 1855; Mary C. Bridges, 1848; John D. Bridges; six other graves.

Lot 146.—(Mrs. Kate Taylor.)Five graves; Fannie Grant, 1866; Ely Grant; Hattie E. Grant; Elizabeth Grant, 1892; John L. Grant, 1924; Stephen L. Grant, 1883; Mrs. Penelope Grant, 1903; Anna Nell Knapp, 1920; Geo. Knapp, 1919; Frangivus? Cooper, 1903.

Lot 147, Sec. 6.—(John Bridges.)—E. Whitaker, 1910; Nelson Whitaker; Mrs. Mary Colson Whitaker; Harlan P. Whitaker, 1908; Emma S. Whitaker, 1909; Kerrilla Whitaker, 1910; Dr. Emery Whitaker; John L. Whitaker, 1924; Mrs. Mary Cox Whitaker, 1940; two graves.

Lot 148, Sec. 6.—Elizabeth Greenwood, 1901; Henry Greenwood, 1873; Wm. Ramsey, 1879; Aug. Miller; John L. Skinner; Peter Sapp; Geo. Stull.

Lot 149, Sec. 6.—(Single Rights.)—David Clutter; Wm. Ramsay; S. F. Fowler; Mary A. Bridges; Mrs. Eleanor Ramsey; Mary Poth, 1863; Ida Grover, 1869; John M. Levi; Edw. Gillespie; Alice B. Clark.

Lot 150, Sec. 6.—Mattie F. Adams; Claud Meyers, 1867; Mollie and James Bridges, 1868-70; Mary Ann Fisher; Andrew May; Mary May, 1871; Maggie Smith, 1866; Jas. Manning; R. N. Fowler; E. G. Bridges; seventeen graves unknown.

Lot 153.—(Singles.)—Henry Sensfelder, 1851; John T. Heiser, 1857; Geo. W. Morris; Abraham Stouger? 1856; Geo. Menderson, 1850; Jacob Stephar..?, 1856; James Adams, 1853; Geo. W. Walker, 1853; L. J. Childs.

Lot 154.—John Hettick, 1866; Jno. Kohlor, 1865; Henry Kinsler; Louise Ketring; ...... Clark; Louisa Eheans.

Lot 156, Sec. 6.—(Julia A. Hudnut.)—Lizzie Hudnut, 1872; Elias P. Hudnut, 1882; Julia A. Hudnut, 1883; V. O. Pinchard, 1895; Grace Pinchard, . . . .; Miss Tillie Pinchard; Bertha Pinchard; Elizabeth Nayes.

Lot 157, Sec. 6.—Henry Clay Barkley, 1897; Isabella Howell Barkley, 1897; Charley Barkley, 1865; Howell Finch Barkley, 1894; Eliza J. Barkley, 1899; Cora Belle Barkley, 1896; Mrs. Harry Barkley, 1924; Frank Owens Barkley, 1936; Roberta Robinson Barkley, 1938.

Lot 158, Sec. 6.—(Edw. Bell.)—Dr. A. G. Browning; Mrs. Dr. A. G. Browning; Clinton Browning; Lucy Browning, 1863; Charlie Browning, 1847; Dr. W. McG. Browning, 1866.

Lot 159, Sec. 6.—Abigail Throop Browning, 1894; Dr. Duke Jefferson, 1943; Dr. T. J. Robb, 1931; Jennie D. Key, 1886; Nannie Key, 1910; Wm. R. Key, 1922; J. D. Evans, 1926; Clara Vivian Cole, 1893; Allen D. Cole, 1929; Alfred E. Cole, 1903.

Lot 160, Sec. 6.—H. C. Tureman, 1850; Amanda Tureman, 1893; Peyton Tureman, 1892; Wm. Tureman, 1851; Ann, wife of Wm. Tureman, 1895; Amanda Tureman; Charles Tureman, 1844; Edwin Tureman, 1848; T. Y. P. Tureman, 1891; J. R. Alexander, 1859; Mary Alexander; Henrietta Tureman.

Lot 161, Sec. 6.—Carrie Phister, 1857, Frank Phister, 1806; Elijah C. Phister, 1887; Thomas R. Phister, 1911; Jane A. Phister, 1923; Lucy W. Phister, 1943; Conrad M. Phister, 1922; Eleanor H. Phister, 1927.

Lot 162, Sec. 6.—Ann Eliza Phister; Eva C. Lawry; Dr. Morris Phister, 1892; Anna Cahil Phister, 1910; Margeret J. Phister, 1904; Charles P. Phister, 1903; Malnor C. Blaine, 1896; Mary C. Blaine, 1897; Mary Phister Blaine, 1896; Walter Wood, 1898.

Lot 163, Sec. 6.—Jacob Phister, 1839; Jas. H. Phister, 1851; Benjamin Phister, 1886; Ann Eliza Phister, 1851; Mary W. Phister; Conrad M. Phister, 1881; Charity C. Phister, 1840.

Lot 164, Sec. 6.—Dempsey Carrell, 1865; Carlista Carrell; Sanford Carrell; Carrie Carrell; Jennie Carrell; two graves; Emma Young, 1901; Had a small school in the eighties. Jerry Young, 1872; Bettie Young, 1939.

Lot 165, Sec. 6.—Jos. Antes, 1860; Paul Smith; Clarence Nichols, 1939; Vannie Nichols, 1943; Margeret C. Smith, 1903; N. B. Smith, 1893; America Smith, 1891; Ruben B. Smith, 1868; five unmarked graves.

Lots 166 and 167, Sec. 6.—Elizabeth Shackleford, 1921; John Shackleford, 1885; Ann Shackleford, 1893; Ann Armstrong Shackleford, 1859; Mary Shackleford, 1848; James Shackleford, 1903; Laura A. Shackleford, 1902; Mary E. Shackleford, 1889; Wm. Chambers, 1882; Orlena Shackleford, 1901; Aunt Prusilla Col.; Hiram Clark, 1853; Cornelia Clark, 1868; Charles Shackleford, 1909.

Lot 168, Sec. 6.—Chas. Ammon, 1864; Chas. O. Ammon, 1900; Charlotte Ammon, 1891; Willie Ammon, 1886; Henry Dersch, 1913; Margeret Dersch, 1862; Augusta Dersch, 1917; Kayie B. Dersch, 1937; Wm. H. Dersch, 1935; Lillie M. Dersch, 1927.

Lot 169, Sec. 6.—Thomas Mountjoy, 1850; Deborah Mountjoy; Maria Mountjoy, 1846; John T. Mountjoy; W. L. Mountjoy; Jas. A. Fleetwood, 1863; Mary Sedden, 1875.

Lot 170, Sec. 6.—Rev. Harrop, 1924; Daniel Bonniwell, 1886; L. S. Bonniwell, 1853; Rosanah Bonniwell, 1852; Louvisa Bonniwell, 1920; Geo. Hancock; Lillie W. Wise; Geo. Wise, 1920; Maria Harrop, 1913; Nannie J. Wise, 1927; William B. Wise, 1930; grave.

Lot 171, Sec. 6.—Henry Tolle, 1877; W. J. Tolle; Henry Tolle, 1890; grave, 1898; Robt. C. Tolle, 1890; Myrtle B. Tolle, 1890; Mr. and Mrs. Thos. Tolle (one grave), 1935-1913; Thos. Duke Tolle, 1901; Addie H. Curtis, 1939; Frank Hill, 1898; Robert Green; Mr. and Mrs. John Childs; Betty Tolle; Jane Holiday; Jennie Harning; Mutin Horning, 1916; six graves.

Lot 172, Sec. 6.—Wm. S. Rand.

Lot 173, Sec. 6.—Elizabeth Bertram, 1869; Chas. Bertram; Jacob Bertram; W. S. Bertram; Henry Bertram, Sr., 1891; Vivian Bertram; Henry Bertram, 1907; Allie Bertram, 1909; Mrs. Henry Bertram, 1913; Elizabeth Osborn, 1904; Leslie Osborn; Ed. A. Kelley, 1885; Margaret Eitel, 1876; Wm. C. Eitel, 1882; E. M. ......; John Eitel; Thomas Royce, 1869.

Lot 174.—(Thos. Wise.)—H. S. Outten; M. W. Outten; Caroline Wise, 1853; Willie W. Gibson, 1929; four graves.

Lot 175, Sec. 6.—Parthenia Frame, 1843; Hannah Mastin, 1848; Wm. S. Case; Anna Case Birney, 1858; Sprig Case, 1878; Rubin Case, 1876; Narcissa Case, 1880; Hannah Mastin Bland, 1906.

Lot 176, Sec. 6.—Charles Thomas, 1863; Elizabeth Thomas, 1899; Jacob Thomas, 1885; Amanda Thomas, 1871; Alice J. Thomas, 1851; Richard Thomas, 1854; John N. Thomas, 1896; James C. Thomas, 1917; Jacob Thomas, 1932.

Lot 178, Sec. 6.—(A. Casto; Casto Street in Maysville.)—W. T. Casto, 1862; Susan Casto, 1835; Obijah Casto; Nancy Casto, 1855; Almira Oldham; Clarence Oldham, 1909; Mrs. George Oldham, 1914; George Oldham, 1913; Willie Oldham, 1924; Maria D. Jacobs, 1868; James Jacobs, 1902; Martha A. Jacobs, 1883; Susan Mitchell, 1836; Andrew Mitchell, 1835; Henry Gorman, 1900; Harry Bell.

Lot 179, Sec. 6.—(Robert Power.)—Anna B. Jacobs, 1862; Minnie Power, 1856; E. B. Buffield, 1884; Robt. Brutherton; Ada Calhoun, 1922; Ella Calhoun, 1934; Alex Calhoun, 1931; one grave.

Lot 180, Sec. 6.—Wm. Hunt, 1892; Thos. Hunt, 1864; Mrs. Wm. Hunt, 1913; Geo. A. Mitchell, 1903; Angie K. Mitchell, 1916; Clarence L. Salee, 1908; Lula Mitchell Salee; Daniel Kirk, 1871; Mary W. Kirk, 1908.

Lot 181, Sec. 6.—(Wm. Wormald.)—Wm. Wormald, 1901; Lottie B. Wormald, 1889; Charlette Wormald, 1929; Walter C. Wormald.

Lot 182, Sec. 6.—(Jos. C. Mendell.)—Rachel Mendell, 1931; Thos. Mendell; Timothy Mendell; Anna Mendell; seven other graves.

Lot 183, Sec. 6.—Jas. H. Conrad, 1864; Taylor Conrad, 1902; Stanley Conrad, 1916; Mary Lena Conrad, 1919; Nannie B. Jones, 1924; Elizabeth E. Conrad, 1932; W. H. Conrad, 1934; Susan B. Wallingford, 1922.

## MASON COUNTY

TOMBSTONE INSCRIPTIONS—MASON COUNTY KENTUCKY
CEMETERIES

Compiled by Mrs. Lula Reed Boss, Maysville, Kentucky

"All that tread
The globe are but a handful of the tribes
That slumber in its bosom

The majestic and courtly roads which monarchs pass over, the way that the men of letters tread, the path the warrior traverses, the short and simple annals of the poor, all lead to the same place, all terminate, however varied in their routes, in that one enormous house which is appointed for all living."

Sacred to The Memory of Worsham Anderson who departed this life July 11th, 1833, aged 72 years, 7 months and 19 days. Of the deceased he was a soldier of the Revolutionary war. He sustained through life the relative duties of citizen, husband, father and friend. He was a father to the fatherless and a friend to the widow. His heart, his home, his all was the common property of friend and neighbor. A short time before his death he gave himself up to the Lord. He sought Him by prayer and supplication and did not seek in vain.

* * * * *

Sacred to the Memory of Missaniah Anderson relict of the late Worsham Anderson, who departed this life March 20th, 1834, aged 69 years, 1 month, 18 days. Of the deceased was truly an ornament to the circle in which she moved. As a wife, she was a helpmate indeed. As a mother she was tender, kind and always alive to the interests of her family and neighbors. She was loved and respected by many. She gave satisfaction to her friends that all well expressed her willingness to die and said how sweet it is to die in Jesus.

* * * * *

Marcus B. Brooks. Born July 8, 1840. Died March 24, 1851.

* * * * *

Elizabeth J. Jenings. Formerly consort of Thomas Lewis. Born August 18, 1794. Died February 14, 1854. 59 years, 5 months, 26 days. Blessed are the dead who die in the Lord.

* * * * *

Mrs. Susan S. Anderson. Born February 3, 1778. Died March 18, 1854.

In Memory of Misaniah W. daughter of John W. & Susan S. Anderson who died June 1, 1844, aged 17 years, 10 months and 4 days. She sleeps in Jesus Christ.

* * * * *

Sacred to the Memory of Capt. John W. Anderson, who departed this life July 22, 1834, aged 42 years, 8 months and 3 days. Of the deceased it may be truly said that he possessed in an eminent degree all those qualities of head and heart that render man interesting in this world and fit him for that which is to come. By his most scrupulous integrity and honorable deportment in life he endeared himself in a singular manner to his friends and succeeded effectually in disarming his foe; and in his death he gave a cheering evidence of his entire confidence in the saving influence of the Christian religion. Blessed are the dead who die in the Lord.

\* \* \* \* \*

Prudence Anderson died July 28, 1848 in the 45th year of her age.
'Tis finished, the Conflict is over.
The Heaven born spirit is fled;
Her wish is accomplished at last;
And now she is entombed with the dead

\* \* \* \* \*

The foregoing tombstone inscriptions were found in a family grave yard on the farm of Dan H. Lloyd in Mason county, Kentucky. The farm is situated on the Germantown road about eleven miles from Maysville.

\* \* \* \* \*

Tombstone inscriptions from the Old Stone Baptist Church Cemetery on Lawrence Creek, Mason county, Kentucky.
Sacred to the Memory of Elizabeth Reed. Died October 31, 1856, aged 66 years. A member of the Baptist Church for fifty years.
Sacred to the Memory of Jacob Reed. Born 1785. Died 1869.

\* \* \* \* \*

Stone Lick Cemetery, Mason county, Kentucky
Sabina Reed, consort of Marshall Curtis, died 1845, aged 43 years

\* \* \* \* \*

Tombstone inscriptions from Union Cemetery located on the Hebron Salem Pike near Germantown, Mason county, Kentucky:
Elijah Hayden—born Jan. 8, 1763; died Nov. 15, 1845.
Elizabeth, wife of Elijah Hayden, born July 2, 1770; died March 14, 1860.
Richard P., son of John and Ollie Rees—Dec. 17, 1878; Sept. 7, 1888. Another little Angel Before the Heavenly Throne.
Mary Lizzie, daughter of J. W. and O. F. Rees, born Dec. 6, 1876; died June 12, 1879. God gave, He took, He will restore. He doeth all things well.
Daniel Rees, born August 10, 1806; died Jan. 5, 1877.
Mary Evans Rees, born Dec. 25, 1813; died March 8, 1895.
John W. Rees, born June 7, 1835; died July 3, 1882. An honest man is the noblest work of God.
In Memory of Jane Cooper, who died July 6, 1812 in the fifty-eighth year of her age.
Charles Barrett, born October 5, 1826; died March 15, 1888.
Thomas S. Kilgore, born Sept. 20, 1799; died June 24, 1835 (or 1885).

Samuel K. S., son of J. and M. Kilgore—died Oct. 25, 1842.

Joseph Kilgore—died Dec. 22, 1841.

Dedicated to the Memory of Sarah Taylor, wife of Rev. Caleb J. Taylor, by her affectionate children. Died Aug. 29, 1851, aged 77.

Lydia Williams. 1891-1902.

Elizabeth M. Rees, daughter of D. and M. Rees. Died Aug. 9, 1858.

Kate L. Rees, wife of D. J. Rees, born July 19, 1852; died June 1, 1877.

Mary Lizzie Rees, daughter of D. J. and M. B. Rees, died July 3, 1886, aged 2 years 7 months. Gone like the sweet flower 'neath death's fearful power.

\*   \*   \*   \*   \*

Tombstone inscriptions from May's Lick Cemetery, Mason county, Kentucky.

Sarah C. Summers, consort of Thomas Summers, born Jan. 5, 1807; married Dec. 22, 1829; died March 10, 1833.

Walter Mathews, native of Warrickshire, England. Died July 29, 1852.

Moses Myall, Native of Stamhurst England, born 1797; died 1871.

Elder Walter Warder died April 6, 1836 in 49th year of age. Pastor of Baptist Church Mayslick 22 years.

Daniel Bell, a Soldier of the Revolution, died Jan. 21, 1849 in 87 year of his age.

Mary Runyon, wife of Asa R. Runyon, died August 30, 1832 aged 36 years.

Asa R. Anderson, died June 20, 1829.

Philip Wagoner, native of York County, Pennsylvania, died June 3, 1841.

Charity Morris died Feb. 18, 1816 in 28th year of age.

Nathaniel Roff died Feb. 14, 1825 in 70th year of his age.

Jane Isabel Mackey, wife of William Mackey, died May 21, 1827, aged 24 years.

Oce Taylor, wife of Robert Taylor, died June 1806, aged 21 years.

George Burroughs, born May 7, 1792; died June 8, 1813, aged 21 years.

Desire Drake died Jan. 30, 1812 aged 59 years. Wife of Abraham Drake.

Abraham Drake died December 23, 1805, aged 54 years.

John Drake died Aug. 7, 1800, aged 21 years.

James Drake, son of R. and Jane Drake, died October, 1800.

William Drake died February, 1828.

Mary Thornborough died Aug. 3, 1812 in 29th year of her age.

Harriet Jameson died Dec. 17, 1839, aged 21 years.

David Jameson died Feb. 11, 1851, aged 71 yrs. & 19 days.

Peter Harrison died Nov. 8, 1841 in 38th year of his age.

\*   \*   \*   \*   \*

Tombstone inscriptions from the Shannon Cemetery, Mason county, Kentucky.

Gen. William Reed, died Feb. 26, 1837, aged 67 years and 2 days.

The slab over his grave reads:

Farewell vain world for I have gone
From all thy cares to rest;
Into the bosom of my God
And be forever blessed.

\* \* \* \* \*

In Memory of Mary M. Reed, consort of William Reed Sr. Died of Cholera June 21, 1835, aged 65 years & 11 days.

The slab over her grave reads:

Adieu my friends and children dear
Pray for me dont shed a tear,
Your loss is my eternal gain,
A world of bliss and free from pain.

There has been erected at the graves of General William Reed and Mary Moore Reed, his wife, a more recent monument, which reads:
Gen. William Reed died Feb. 26, 1837, aged 67 years and 2 days.
Mary M., his wife, died June 21, 1835, aged 65 years and 11 days.
Erected by their daughter, Julia A. Browning.

\* \* \* \* \*

General William Reed served with distinction in the War of 1812. On the Honor Roll of Kentuckians who fought in Perry's ships in the Battle of Lake Erie, September 10, 1813, his name appears. (See: Clift's "History of Maysville and Mason County," Volume 1, page 311.)

\* \* \* \* \*

Francis Baker, murdered Nov. 2, 1824 in 31st year of his age.

Simeon West died June 10, 1835 aged 71 years 5 months and 15 days.

Judith L., consort of Captain John M. Reed, died July 14, 1841, aged 48 years, 6 mos. & 28 days.

Joseph James, son of John and Judith L. Reed, Volunteer in Mexican War, died March 14, 1848 aged 20 yrs. 5 mos. & 18 days.

Isaac D. Craycraft died Nov. 8, 1832 in 25th year of age.

Lawrence Wheeler died Nov. 5, 1832 in 50th year of his age.

In Memory of Mrs. Brown Consort of David Brown, died December 4, 1824, aged 30 years.

David Brown died February 22, 1836 in 58th year of his age.

Sydney K. Reed, Consort of William Reed jr., born January 7, 1808; died of cholera, June 17, 1835.

Ludwell Yancey Browning, born July 19, 1807; died April 5, 1845.

Julia Ann Reed Browning, born December 14, 1814. Died (date not filled in.) (Her estate was administered in Mason county, April 4, 1899. Court Order Book No. 1, page 221.)

William McDonald died July 25, 1839 aged 74 years 10 mos. & 10 days.

Matilda Ann, Consort of James M. Troutman, died March 11, 1835, aged 34 years & 5 mos.

Elizabeth Reed Cowgill, born Sept. 28, 1829; died May 1, 1833.

\* \* \* \* \*

Maysville Cemetery, Maysville, Mason county, Kentucky.

Sergt. Richard H. Fristoe, Co. A. 40th Kentucky Mounted Infantry. (There are no dates on tombstone.)

Corporal William T. Fristoe, Co. D. 10th Kentucky Cavalry. (There are no dates on this tombstone.)

The two graves are side by side and a standard reads: "Post G.A.R."

\* \* \* \* \*

Tombstone inscriptions copied from a family grave yard on the farm of Charles Franklin Reed. This land is located on the south side of the Maysville and Mt. Sterling turnpike, about two miles from Maysville in Mason county, Kentucky.

Lucinda Fristoe died November 15, 1867 aged 59 years 11 mos. & 15 days.

> Go home my friends
> Dry up your tears
> I must lie here
> Till Christ appears

Robert Fristoe born April 4, 1801; died June 16, 1873.

> Rest Father Rest, Sleep Dear one Sleep
> From Pain and Sorrow free
> Though at thy grave we grieve and say
> Tis Sweet to know there is rest for thee

\* \* \* \* \*

Tombstone inscription from Washington Cemetery, Mason county, Kentucky.

Ann Grinstead, wife of Rev. William Grinstead, died Oct. 30, 1817, aged 45 years.

(According to "Overwharton Parish Register—Old Stafford County Virginia—1720 to 1760," by William F. Booghes, Ann (Fristoe) Grinstead was born March 13, 1772.)

\* \* \* \* \*

Tombstone inscriptions from old cemetery located back of the Maysville Public Library, Maysville, Mason county, Kentucky:

Charles Erb Wolf, born Easton, Pennsylvania Jan. 1, 1800; died July 25, 1833. First mayor of Maysville.

Mrs. Mary Lee, wife of Captain Stephen Lee, and daughter Margaret M. Lee, aged 6 months, both of whom died April 15, 1818.

William Sumrall died 1819, aged 10 years.

Walter Case, born March 5, 1792; died May 4, 1820.

Isiah Wilson, born Feb. 14, 1785; died July 22, 1821.

Pleasant H. Baird, son of P. H. and Mary Baird, born Jan. 8, 1819; killed June 29, 1824 by "going on a tread mill."

Nathan Gulick died Oct. 2, 1826, aged 49 years 5 months 22 days.

Thomas Duncan died 1826.

Micajah Bland died 1826, aged 49 years.

Jacob Boone died May 4, 1827.

Mary Boone, consort of Jacob Boone, died July 30, 1828.

Peter Grant drowned at the mouth of the Great Kanawha river on Jan. 10, 1829, aged 47 years 2 months 6 days.

Peter McQuality died 1832, aged 24 years.

Nancy A., consort of William Little, died March 8, 1833, aged 26 years 3 months 17 days.

John Hobson Langhorne died 1834.

Nancy Duncan, relict of Thomas Duncan, died 1842.

Samuel Culberson, born in Maysville Sept. 25, 1800; died April 30, 1844.

Mary McCullough, consort of James McCullough of Pittsburg, died April 10, 1847.

John Armstrong, born in Ireland Feb. 21, 1787; died May 29, 1838.

## MASON COUNTY

### COPY OF THE RECORDS OF MAYSVILLE & MASON COUNTY CEMETERY "NEW PART"—LETTERS A THROUGH G

1892    Archdeacon, John H.—5-15-1892—Sec. L, Lot 19
Adams, Henry—12-23-1892—Sec. H, Lot 110

1893    Adams, Mrs.—1-2-1893—Single Lot 110

1895    Allspaugh, Mrs. Kate—8-12-1895—Sec. E, Lot 64

1896    Adams, John—1-2-1896
Adamson, Mrs. Alice K. (Keith)— 6-22-1896—Sec. J, ½ Lot 6

1897    Alexander, Joseph—12-31-1897—Sec. E, Lot 67

1898    Armstrong, Mrs. Lizzie (Col.)—Lot 107
Archdeacon, Mrs. Jane—4-30-1898—Sec. L, Lot 19

1899    Anderson, V. T.—1-9-1899—Sec. H, Lot 4
Alexander, Joseph M.—8-9-1899—Sec. S, Lot 74
Armstrong, John—10-6-1899—Sec. J, Lot 1

1900    Allsbaugh, Sr. Jacob—1-4-1900

1901    Augnebower, John H.—11-9-1901—Sec. H, Lot 52

1903    Allen, Eliza—11-7-1903—Samaritan Lot

1905    Alexander, Mrs. Ann C.—4-2-1905—Sec. L, Lot 74
Alexander, J. W.—8-4-1905—Sec. L, Lot 74

1906    Adams, Henry—7-24-1906—Sec. H, Lot 110

1907    Auther, James H.—8-24-1907—Sec. A, Lot 7

1908    Allen, Mrs. George M.—3-23-1908—Oval 7
Anderson, Harriet—6-8— (Col.)
Alexander, Wm.—9-19-1908—Sec. L, Lot 74

1909    Aikman, Mrs. Abbie—3-5-1909—Single 305

1910    Adams, Mrs. Elizabeth—6-25-1910—Sec. H, Lot 110
Applegate, Celia—11-25-1910—Single Sec. A, No. 11

1911    Armstrong, Mrs. Martha A.—2-3-1911—Sec. J-C, Lot 1

1912    Adamson, H. K.—10-11-1912—Sec. J-D, Lot 6

1913    Applegate, Carrie C.—1-27-1913—Single A, No. 43
       Allen, Mrs. D. R.—9-6-1913—Sec. L, Lot 75
1914    Arn, Martha—1-12-1914—Sec. A, Lot 16
       Abbott, Nannie Thompson—8-3-1914—Sec. L, Lot 5
       Allison, Thomas—9-13-1914—Sec. L, Lot 9
1915    Auther, Jennie R.—1-22-1915—Sec. A, Lot 7
       Alexander, Mary B.—2-5-1915—Sec. L, Lot 74
       Arn, Ella—6-11-1915—Sec. A, Lot 16
1916—Altmeyer, John Robert—10-21-1916—Sec. G, Lot 16
1917    Applegate, Ida Estelle—1-3-1917—Single A, No. 21
       Allen, David R.—2-7-1917—Sec. L, Lot 75
1919    Applegate, Tully—10-2-1919—Single A, No. 9
1920    Adkins, Agnes E.—2-5-1920—Single A, Block No. 2, No. 261
       Adkins, Milissa—2-20-1920—Single A, Block No. 2, No. 262
       Adkins, J. A.—Removed to St. Paterick Cemetery
1921—Adkins, Catherine—1-17-1921
1922—Archdeacon, Mrs. Margaret—1-2-1922—Sec. L, Lot 19
       Archdeacon, William—4-4-1922—Sec. L, Lot 19
       Adair, G. W.—4-18-1922—Sec. H, N. ½ Lot 64—Removed from Old
         Cemetery
       Alton, G. W.—4-25-1922—Sec. E, ½ Lot 92
       Altmeyer, John J.—5-0-1922—Sec. G, Lot 16
       Allspaugh, Jacob—7-25-1922—Sec. E, Lot 64
       Applegate, Charley—8-15-1922—Single A, No. 8
       Anderson, Mrs. Adelaide—10-19-1922—Sec. E, Lot 25
       Anderson, Langhorn Tabb—11-5-1922—Sec. E, Lot 26
       Applegate, Richard—11-18-1922—Sec. A, No. 46
       Anderson, Thomas P.—11-24-1922—Sec. E, Lot 25
1923    Anderson, Mrs. Mack—10-3-1923—Sec. H, Lot 44
1924    Arn, May Belle—2-6-1924—Sec. A, Lot 16
1924    Aikman, James—2-10-1924—Sec. K, No. 306
       Armstrong, Elizabeth Chansler—10-10-1924—Sec. J, Lot 10.
1925    Arn, Sherman—6-16-1925—Sec. A, Lot 16
       Allison, James—9-24-1925—Single K, No. 571
1926—Anderson, Ella Carr (Augusta, Ky.)—1-
1925    Anderson, Elsie—12-20-1925
1926—Adams, Rosa H.—9-10-1926—Sec. H, Lot 110
       Alexander, Geo.—12-30-1926—Sec. L, Lot 55
1927    Allison, Elizabeth—6-2-1927—Sec. L, Lot 9
       Applegate, Ida—11-12-1927—525

## B

1891    Bierley, Emma—11-12-1891—Sec. H, Lot 99
1892    Burk, Wilhelm—4-5-1892—Sec. H, Lot 145
       Bradley, Charles—8-28-1892—Sec. L, Lot 65
       Boman, Frank—11-2-1892—Single Lot
1893    Burrows, Geo.—9-16-1893—Sec. L, Lot 21
1894    Burgle, Andrew—2-17-1894—Sec. H, Lot 100
1895    Burgess, Mrs. Sarah—7-5-1895—Sec. L, Lot 2

1896    Barcraft, Geo.—1-3-1896—Sec. E, Lot 4
        Boyce Infant
        Burrows, Nettie—8-31-1896—Sec. L, Lot 21
1897    Burger, Mrs. James—1-3-1897—Sec. H, Lot 108
        Browing, J. L.—4-3-1897—Triangle Lot 1
        Brown, Mrs. Dora—9-5-1897—109
        Bendel, H. C.—11-20-1897—Sec. L, Lot 30
1898    Boughner, Mrs. Mary—1-31-1898—Sec. J, Lot 3A
        Bramble, Mrs. John W.—2-7-1898—Sec. K, Lot 17
        Bissett, Robert—7-5-1898—Sec. J, Lot 4
        Berry, Auther—10-22-1898—Sec. L, Lot 128
        Bolling, J. J.—11-20-1898—Sec. H, Lot 158
1899    Barcroft, Mrs. Lon H.—1-7-1899—Sec. E, Lot 4
        Baldwin, Henry—2-7-1899—Lot 147
        Blaisdell, H. R.—3-16-1899—Sec. L, Lot 75
        Berger, Nicholas—3-30-1899—Sec. 8, Lot 111
        Burgle, Mrs. Theresa—4-30-1899—Sec. H, Lot 100
        Bramel, Wm. H.—7-2-1899—Sec. O, Lot 6
        Burke, Leslie M.—7-8-1899—Sec. H, Lot 145
        Berry, Mable—12-20-1899—Sec. L, Lot 28
1900    Blanton, Ben—6-9-1900—Lot 192
        Brown, Mrs. Susan K.—11-17-1900—Sec. H, Lot 131
1901    Bradley, Selton M.—1-17-1901—Lot 185
        Baker, Mrs. Lee Ann—2-13-1901—Sec. H, Lot 156
        Baird, Mrs. Amanda—7-18-1901—Sec. H, Lot 112
        Bierley, Duke—9-10-1901—Sec. H, Lot 99
        Ball, Mrs. Nancy—10-20-1901—Sec. H, Lot 16
1902    Beckett, Mrs. Boone—5-25-1902—Lot 193
        Burgess, J. B.—7-23-1902—Oval Lot 4
        Bramel, Henry—8-23-1902—Sec. L, Lot 21
1903    Burrows, Dollins Rudy—2-11-1903—Sec. L, Lot 21
        Bramel, Turner—3-18-1903—Sec. O, Lot 25
        Bratton, Mrs. Charles H.—3-25-1903—Lot 224
        Bullock, Kate Preston—4-19-1903—Sec. A, Lot 6
        Blanton, J. M.—5-6-1903—Lot 186
        Bradley, John W.—8-1-1903—Sec. H, Lot 28.
        Bradford, Mrs. Ellen—8-4-1903—Lot 221
        Brown, J. H.—12-13-1903—Sec. H, Lot 129
1904—Bradley, Iva—1-14-1904—Lot 217
        Baldwin, Wm. P.—7-29-1904—Sec. H, Lot 7
        Bramel, Mrs. Wm.—10-3-1904—Sec. O, Lot 6
1905—Bierley, Katie—4-1-1905—Sec. H, Lot 99
        Blythe, Wm.—7-31-1905—Lot 235
1906—Browing, Judith K. Browning—4-9-1906
        Baldwin, Harriet—4-16-1906—Sec. H, Lot 7
        Bradley, Hattie—5-21-1906, Lot 216
        Burns, James M.—6-16-1906—Sec. H, Lot 19
        Baird, W. W.—6-29-1906—Sec. H, Lot 112
        Blythe, Nellie—12-25-1906—Lot 258
        Bendel, Charles F.—12-26-1906—Sec. L, Lot 30

1907    Baird, J. H.—2-15-1907—Sec. H, Lot 112
        Bryant, Mrs. Edward—3-4-1907—Sec. O, Lot 26
        Baldwin, Miss Belle—3-15-1907—Sec. H, Lot 7
        Bradley, Mrs. Frances—4-29-1907—Sec. H, Lot 28
        Britten, Wm.—5-8-1907—Sec. O, Lot 6
        Brown, Ambrose—5-25-1907—Lot 109
        Butcher, Mrs. George—8-10-1907—Lot 255
1908    Butler, John—2-26-1908—Lot 254
        Barr, Mrs. Jennie—4-27-1908—Sec. H, Lot 135
        Bradford, Mrs. Joseph—8-4-1908—Lot 284
        Burk, Louis A.—11-3-1908—Sec. H, Lot 145
        Brodt, John—12-6-1908—Sec. H, Lot 14
        Bratton, Chas.—12-1908—Lot 223
1909    Brown, Jennie—1-6-1909—Lot 303
        Bullock—7-16-1909—Sec. L, Lot 11
        Bowling, Sarah—7-25-1909—Sec. H, Lot 158
1910    Barbour, James—3-16-1910—Sec. L, Lots 82, 83
        Brodt, Mrs. John G.—4-18-1910—Sec. H, Lot 108
        Burke, Mrs. Henry—5-15-1910—Sec. H, Lot 145
        Bissett, Mrs. Mary A.—6-22-1910—Sec. J, Lot 4D
        Beasley, Charles—9-25-1910—Sec. O, Lot 19
1911    Brown, Mrs. Minerva—1-27-1911—Lot 314
        Burger, Mrs. Elizabeth—2-11-1911—Sec. H, Lot 111
        Bramel, Mrs. Martha A.—8-3-1911—Sec. O, Lot 25
        Bacon, Mrs. Margeret P.—8-4-1911—Sec. E, Lot 10
        Bouldin, Mrs. Eddie—10-29-1911—Sec. O, Lot 20
        Bierley, Janett E.—12-27-1911—Sec. A, Lot 28
1912    Bruer, J. D.—1-1-1912—Sec. E, Lot 91
        Beckett, Nevil Lee (infant)
        Burgess, Asa R.—3-3-1912—Sec. L, Lot 2
        Blythe, Eliza Jane—4-27-1912—Lot 234
        Bullock, ..........—?-18-1912—Sec. G, Lot 13
        Brown, Geo. W.—11-5-1912—Sec. K, Lot 304
        Bolinger, Sallie (From Louisville)—11-15-1912—Sec. A, Lot 1
1913    Bryant, M. T.—1-19-1913—Sec. A, Lot 42
        Blaisdel, Agnes—4-22-1913—Sec. L, Lot 75
        Brown, Sarah Ann—7-1-1913—Sec. O 5½, Lot 4
        Bacon, L. T.—7-9-1913—Sec. L, Lot 7
        Burrows, Jane Atherton—7-21-1913—Sec. L, Lot 21
1914    Bramel, Minnie Bell—2-3—Sec. O, Lot 25
        Burgess, Mary C.—6-27-1914—Sec. L, Lot 2
        Bruns (Burns?), Bernard—7-2-1914—Sec. H, Lot 120
1914    Ball, Alice P.—8-22-1914—Sec. A, Lot 107
        Ball, Jas. M.—9-9-1914—A. No. 106
        Blythe, Howard—7-10-1914—Sec. K, No. 233 (on Pearl Blythe Lot)
1915    Bacon, Margaret—2-23-1915—Sec. E, Lot 10
        Bacon, Jacova Reynolds—2-23-1915—Sec. E, Lot 10
        Bradford, Jos.—8-30-1915—Sec. K, Lot 350
        Biggers, Charles E.—9-1-1915—Sec. L, Lot 59
        Burr, Geo. W.—9-24-1915—Sec. A, No. 137

Beasley, Amanda—12-23-1915—Sec. O, Lot 19
Bowling, Laura—12-27-1915—Sec. H, Lot 158
1916 Bauer, Mary E.—3-11-1916—Sec. H, E. ½ Lot 20
Bridges, Sam P.—8-19-1916—Sec. H, W. ½ Lot 93
Burgess, Parthenia—1-19-1916—Oval lot 4
Brady, Belle Mefford—10-26-1916—Sec. A, Lot 165
Bramel, A. Wood—11-9-1916—Sec. O, Lot 6
Bradford, Martha A.—12-15-1916—Lot 177
1917 Bouldin, John E.—5-31-1917—Sec. O, Lot 20
Bradford, Ambrose—6-16-1917—Sec. A, Lot 201
Browning, J. W.—12-2-1917—Sec. H, Lot 20
1918 Bierley, John C.—3-8-1918—Sec. H, Lot 67
Bauer, Mary—8-30-1918—Sec. H, Lot 125
Bradford, Geo.—9-9-1918—Sec. K, Lot 359
Barbour, Jr. James Foster—10-8-1918—Sec. L, Lot 83
1919 Bouldin, Nannie Keith—1-26-1919—Sec. O, Lot 20
Bradley, Eliz.—1919—Sec. A, Lot 236
Branch, Wm.—1919—Sec. H, Lot 27
Baldwin, Edmon—10-24-1919—Sec. H, Lot 7
Bramel, Wm. P.—11-17-1919—Sec. O, Lot 6
Bright, John—11-18-1919—A No. 253
1920 Bradley, Mary (Paris, Ky.)—1920
Beckett, Woodrow—6-1-1920—K 410
Browning, Mrs. Lida—7-13-1920—Sec. H, Lot 133
Butcher, John Samuel—8-6-1920—Sec. H, Lot 90
1921 Bridges, L. M.—4-7-1921—K No. 442
Bramel, J. T.—6-3-1921—Sec. L, Lot 9
Brubaker, Owen Lee—12-11-1921—Sec. H, Lot 60
1922 Boling, A. J.—6-3-1922 K Nos. 447 & 448
Brubaker, James K.—6-14-1922—Sec. H, W 52
Burke, Henry—8-25-1922—Sec. H, Lot 145
Boyd, E. F.—9-25-1922—Sec. H, W Lot 50
1923 Boyce, Matilda—1923—A. No. 349
Boyd, Sallie Kirk—3-5-1923—Sec. H, Lot 50
Branch, Mary D.—3-11-1923—Sec. H, Lot 27
Blanton, Rose—1923—K No. 184
Bruer, Mary G.—5-18-1923—Sec. E, Lot 91
Bowling, Katherine M.—1923—K, No. 447
Brodt, John R.—11-16-1923—Sec. H, Lot 59
Bouldin, Martha—11-29-1923
1924 Bradford, Bessie—2-4-1924
Bridges, Elizabeth B.—3-1-1924
Bailey, U. G.—4-11-1924
Barbour, Minnie Phillips—5-29-1924
Bayles, Parthey—6-5-1924
Bruns, Elizabeth—6-11-1924
Bullock, Nannie R.—6-22-1924
Barrett, Walter—7-27-1924
Bennett, Geo.—8-6-1924
Broadway, Claton—9-11-1924

Butcher, Lettie—9-27-1924
Burton, J. B.—10-6-1924
Berry, Bertie—11-1-1924
Breeze, R. G.—12-10-1924
Bright, Mary Frances—12-27-1924
1925 Breeze, Thos.—1-12-1925
Blake, Nancy Jane—2-11-1925
Bell, Blanch—3-10-1925
Blythe, Clara—5-6-1925
Beasley, Zach—5-20-1925
Barbour, George T.—6-15-1925
Bradley, Mary Ann—1925
Bean, John L.—2-11-1925
Bramel, John W.—12-8-1925
1926—Berry, W. T.—1-15-1926
Bradford, Martha—1-29-1926
Brown, Charles, Jr.—3-8-1926
Boyd. Joe R.—3-27-1926
Breeze, Chas. H.—8-2-1926
Bonner, Bessie L.—9-24-1926
Berger, Jas.— 10-20-1920
Britton, Catherine M.—10-29-1926
Beckett, Boone—12-7-1926
Bell, H. C.—12-21-1926
1927—Bierlin, Amanda—1-7-1927
Baldwin, Sam B.—2-14-1927
Berry, Wm.—2-28-1927
Bramel, Amelia—3-5-1927
Bean, Chas. P.—4-10-1927
Bennett, Mary B.—6-5-1927
Bishop, Geo.—6-6-1927
Browning, Margeret (or Marion)—6-28-1927
Brooks, H. N.—8-16-1927—(Wilson, N. C.)
Brubaker, Bertha L.—8-29-1927
Bonser, Margeret—9-24-1927
Bendel, Geo.—11-9-1927
Barbour, Mrs. John—11-30-1927

C

1891 Clark, W. B.—12-25-1891
1892 Carr, Thomas—4-14-1892
Cox, Lizzie—10-21-1892
1893 Chamberlain, Wm. L.—12-1-1893
1896 Cochran, R. A.—1-14-1896
Clay, Mary—3-24-1896
Cooper, Sarah P.—4-7-1896
Cochran, Mrs. Hattie J.—9-19-1896
Carr, Mrs. Mary—10-26-1896
Carnahan, John T.—11-21-1896
1897 Colledge, Rev. A. B.—3-18-1897

1898 Coburn, Mrs. Ben W.—9-14-1898
Chenoweth, Mrs. Julia—9-20-1898
1899 Chamberlain, Clarence S.—9-4-1899
1900 C.........., Lafayette—5-4-1900
1900 Clutter, Aron—8-16-1900
Campbell, Mrs. Eliza J.—8-30-1900
Cahill, Mrs. Anna W.—11-2-1900
Cobb, John—12-5-1900
1901 Calvert, Wm.—4-11-1901
1902 Cummings, Anna—2-1-1902
Childs, Mrs. Grace B.—2-4-1902
Cochran, Mary Duffield—7-7-1902
Coburn, Ben W.—8-5-1902
Campbell, Eliza—12-24-1902
1903 Calvert, Mrs. W. T.—2-21-1903
Carr, Mr. and Mrs.—9-26-1903
C......., Harry—1-8-1904
1905—Claypool—4-22-1905
Cummings, Edward—10-13-1905
1906 Cobb, Louisa N.—1-22-1906
Crawford, Geo. N.—9-10-1906
College, Mrs. E. A.—9-11-1906
Crawford, Chas.—10-17-1906
Crawford, Joseph—10-24-1906  (Removed from Old Cemetery)
1907 Childs, Mrs. G. W.—4-4-1907
1909—Crosby, Mrs. J. A.—4-4-1909
Claypool, John W.—7-23-1909
Cummings, R. T.—8-29-1909
Clark, S. O.—8-31-1909
1910 Carpenter, Henry—2-10-1910
Coffee, Geo. G.—2-19-1910
Caldwell, John L.—5-2-1910
1911 Case, James W.—2-13-1911
Cochran, Mary Underwood—4-24-1911—(Poyntz Reserve)
Carr, Ellen Jane—5-2-1911
Cahill, James E.—6-22-1911
Childs, Geo. W.—12-5-1911
1912—Cobb, James—7-4-1912
Claybrook, Jos. L.—1-12-1912
1913 Carr, F. M.—3-20-1913
Calvert, Alexander H.—5-14-1913
Colburn, Elizabeth—8-21-1913
Cooper, Geo. E.—10-10-1913
Calvert, Kate Lindsay—11-15-1913
Cox, Albert Bernard—10-13-1913
1914 Coffee, Susan E.—2-18-1914
Cummings, Wm. H.—3-5-1914
Cummings, Mary—5-8-1914
Colledge, John A.—6-30-1914
Cummings, James H.—11-7-1914

1915   Chamberlain, John L.—1-31-1915
Chamberlain, Clarence—9-4-1899
Core, Bovee D.—3-17-1915
Calvert, Pierce T.—4-5-1915
Chard, Lucretia Belle—5-21-1915
Chenoweth, Thos. J.—6-18-1915
Cunningham, Eleanor Foster (Moved from Charleston Bottom)—
10-15-1915
1916   Cochram, Joseph—10-1916
Carr, R. A.—10-31-1916
Chamberlain, James—12-29-1916
1917   Crane, John—1-21-1917
Collis, Emily—2-15-1917
Case, Yancey—2-19-1917
Colburn, Rosa—2-24-1917
Cobb, Jos. R.—3-8-1917
Caldwell, Mary Eliza—4-19-1917
Chollar, Mildred Clair—6-26-1917
Cochran, George Welsh—7-24-1917
Crosby, John A.—11-2-1917
Cord, T. P.—11-16-1917
Cone, Amelia—12-7-1917
1918   Colburn, Levi, 3-28-1918
Collins, Mrs. (m. Old Cemetery)
Curran, Thomas B.—10-21-1918
Cole, Effie—10-21-1918
Chenowith, Mary E. P.—11-1-1918
1919   Carr, Andrew J.—1-27-1919
Cochran, Wm. D.—2-11-1919
Calvert, Catherine—4-7-1919
Cooper, Milton H.—4-17-1919
Cummings, Richard—5-22-1919
Cobb, Rose (Col.)—6-13-1919
1920   Crawford, Bertha—3-3-1920
Coulter, Mrs. M. W.—9-11-1920
Cook, Frank—10-11-1920
1921   Coulter, M. W.—1-9-1921
Carrigan, Mrs. Elmer—2-11-1921
Cox, Wm.—6-10-1921
Candell, Susan—1921
1922   Clark, Ora B.—3-18-1922
Carrigan, Omar—6-4-1922
Cox, Agnes—7-13-1922
Chamberlain, Alice, Miss—1922
Cooper, Wm.—7-29-1922
Cracraft, R. C.—8-21-1922
Craig, Andy—8-21-1922
Cline, A. G.—11-13-1922
Casey, A. M.—2-7-1922
Carr, Virginia R.—12-24-1922

1923   Cockrell, Addie—1-14-1923
       Curran, Hannah C.—2-15-1923
       Campbell, Harold—4-19-1923
       Cox, Emily C.—5-28-1923 (from Vanceburg, Ky.)
       Clark, Emrich G.—5-28-1923
       Colledge, Lida N.—6-24-1923—(Hamilton County, Ohio)
       Collins, Mary—6-24-1923
       Cochran, Frances J.—9-18-1923
       Chenault, John B.—9-23-1923
       Cord, Robt. B.—11-9-1923
       Carpenter, Virg.—4-19-1923
1924—Cox, Josephine—4-24-1924
       Calbert, Chas.—6-2-1924
       Cord, Louise—7-11-1924
       Cuttis, Wm. G.—11-4-1924
1925—Crawford, Elizabeth—5-18-1925
       Childs, Henry—5-31-1925
       Chard, Wm.—6-25-1925
       Curtis, Lida O.—7-5-1925
       Collins, J. T.—8-9-1925
       Cash, Nathan—10-14-1925
1926—Carpenter, Samuel—4-2-1926
       Chenoweth, Hiram P.—4-16-1926
       Carr, Andrew C.—6-1-1926
       Curtis, Wm. N.—6-25-1926
1927—Conrad, Loyd E.—2-20-1927
       Carrigan, Minerva—3-21-1927
       Carr, Amelia A.—7-25-1927
       Cobb, Jno. J.—9-20-1927
       Cochran, James H.—10-1-1927
       Collins, Catherine—10-20-1927
       Chollar, C. L.—11-8-1927
       Colburn, Carl—11-26-1927

# D

1891—Dawson, Mrs. Mary—12-21-1891
1892—Dimmitt, Mrs. Sinclair—3-26-1892
       Dietrich, Jr. Henry—7-5-1892
       Downing, Ellis—9-14-1892
1893—Dimmitt, Mose—11-1-1893
       Downing, Mrs. Robt.—2-18-1893
1894—Dietrich, Mrs. Henry—4-24-1894
1895—Dodson, Mrs. C. M.—3-33-1895
       Dietrich, C. P.—8-6-1895
1897—Dodson, Lutie—9-20-1897
1898—Downing, Robert—4-30-1898
1899—Davis, Geo. W.—7-27-1899
1900—Davis, Mrs. Carrie Maddox—4-24-1900
       Dawson, Richard—9-28-1900

1901—Downing, Charles—8-28-1901
    Davis, Mrs. Ann E.—12-12-1901
1902—Downing, Mrs. Lucinda—2-15-1902
    Dawson, Mrs. Larman—2-21-1902
    Dimmitt, Hal W.—11-12-1902
1903—Dodson, Mrs. R. H.—6-8-1903
    Dimmitt, Mrs. Laura—10-5-1903
1906—Dugan, Mrs. J. T.—3-20-
    Downton, John—6-18-
    Dobyns, Mrs. Jennie K.—11-19-
    Dinger, John C.—11-27-
1907—Dieterich, Mrs. Charles P.—3-7-'07
    Dugan, Della—4-17-
    Dugan, Anna Lou—4-17-
    Dugan, Louise—4-17-
    Davis, Rebecca—12-12-
1908—Dieterich, Henry C.—4-5-
1909 Duley, Wm.—12-19-
1910—Dimmittl, Mrs. E. C.—6-2-
    Davis, Jos.—9-0-
1911—Davis, James—2-24-
    Dinger, Wm. A.—3-2-
    Dodson, Charles—3-17-
    Dinger, Katherine Weaver—4-4-
    Downton, Mrs. John—12-31-
1912—Daulton, Mrs. Margaret A.—1-31-
    Durrum, Louise Alexander—4-6-
    Durrum, Harvey Alexander—6-19-
    Davis, W. H.—10-10-
    Dickens, Bettie Ross—11-21-
1913—Douglas, Agnes—6 23-
    Dimmitt, Hal. W.—7-19-
    Drennen Lona—9-12-
    Dudley, Gerald, W.—12-18-
1914—Durrum, Harvey R.—4-11-
    D    , Laura Pogue—7-27-
1915—Daugherty, Sarah J.—3-23-
    Davis, Mary—4-6-
    Dickson, Thos.—10-3-
    Davenport, Mary O.—11-28-
    Dieterich, Anna—12-13-
1916—Dieterich, Lutie—5-16-
    Daulton, John L.—11-21-
    Dawson, Larman—11-25-
    Dinger, Charles—12-21-
1917—DeBold, J. W.—10-5-
    Daulton, Emily—11-29-

1918—Denton, Nettie—4-20-
    Duzan, John—9-5-
    Devine, J. T.—9-28-
1919—Duley, Frances—7-14-
    Dale, Robt.—12-17-
    Durrett, Wm. H.—9-8-
    Duncan, Nellie—11-28-
1920—Davis, Harry A.—3-1-(From Lexington) Ky.
    Dimmitt, E. C.—10-17-(Germantown) Ky.
    Dresel, Mrs. Clarence—1-5-
1921—Dickson, Marvin—1-6- (Lewisburg)
    Downing, James E.—5-23-
    Dryden, Robt. L.—6-30-
1922—Dryden, Daisy T.—3-14-
    Dryden, Harrison—4-29-
    Dryden, Edna M.—12-24-
    Denton, V.—10-22-
1923—Dickson, Mrs. Jesse—1-14-
    Dearing, John—1-26-
    Dunnington, Wm.—3-29-
    Duzan, Kate—4-17-
    Davis, Thos.—5-11-
    Duzan, Bonnie Brown—6-18-
1924—Duzan, Annie—1-4-
    Dorsey, Mary L.—9-4-1923
1924—Dawson, W. B.—9-24-
    Dale, Henry—9-26-
    Dunn, Julia—12-13-
    Dickson, Mary F.—12-29-
1925—Dieterich, Henry C.—1-5-
    Durham, Wilford A.—1-26-
    Dickson, Alcon—1-27-
    Dodson, George A.—1-29-
    Dye, Mary V.—2-17-
    Dickson, Edna E.—5-19-
    Darnall, James—8-24-
    Davis, Edward H.—11-3-
1926—Dimmitt, Mary A.—1-7-
    Duzan, Edith—2-26-
    Dale, Julia—9-2-
    Davis, Nannie B.—9-5-
    Dryden, Rufus—10-4-
1927—Dinger, Catherine—3-10-
    Davenport, Ellen—7-4-
    Dawson, Margaret E.—9-12-
    D......, Charles E.—9-24-
    Duzan, Owen H.—10-5-
    Dunbar, Mae—11-28-
    Davenport, M. N.—12-13-

## E

1896—Edgington, John K.—8-7-
1904—Edgington, Parris D.—2-16-
1908—Eitel, John—4-6-
1809—Evans, Shelton—2-22-
   Ethell, Mrs. J. E.—3-29-
1910—Elliott, Mrs. Amanda—8-9-
1911—Evans, Geo.—6-25-
   Ellis, Simon B.—12-1-
1913—Ewing, Luella—12-8-
1915—Edgington, Wm.—6-21-
   Evans, John W.—10-10-
1916—Ellis, Richard Allen—7-14-
1917—Elliott, Harry—4-4-
   Eitel, Matilda—6-16-
1918—Easton, Edith—10-17-
   Estept, Phoebe—10-29-
1919—Ellis, W. H.—2-15-
   Emmonds, Harvey—2-28-
   Emmonds, Anna Delle 3-1-
   Emmonds, Mrs. Hattie—3 3
1921—Edwards, Elizabeth—2-15-
   Ennis, Shas. E.—3-23-
   Ennis, Lottie K.—6-2-
   Erwin, Wm. H.—7-11-
   Evans, Isabelle—10-29-
1922—Ewing, George—1-25-
   Eakins, Dora L.—11-7-
1923—Elliott, J. H.—3-21-
   Electria, Lettia—3-29-
   Emmons, Thom.—5-23-
   Eakins, Henry—12-7- (Connersville, Ind.)
1925—Ellis, Minnie—6 12-
   Ellis, Beatrice—6-12-
   Ellis, Marshall—6 12-
   Easton, Mary E.—10-25-
1926—Edgington, Cyanthia Ann—8-15-
1927—Ellis, Anderson N.—1-29- (Cambridge, Mass.)
   Evans, Ella Mae—3-10-
   Evans, James—3-21-
   Elliott, James—9-8-

## F

1892—Fitzgerald, Lawler—3-11-
   Flora, Wm.—3-15-
   Fossett, Ben—4-19-
   Finch, Anderson—3-13-
   Frazee, Miss Jennie—9-5-

1894  Fleming, Wm. Lee—5-15-
1895—Fristo, Alfred—12-7-
1896—Mrs. Marie Fristo—6-5-
　　　　Fansler, Mrs. Lidia—8-15-
1898—Filson, Mrs. Elizabeth J.—2-27-
　　　　Fuller, infant
1899—Fant, Mrs. James P.—10-17-
1900—Fristo—12-16-
1901—Frakes, Jos.—3-5-
1903—Fant, James P.—12-15-
1904—Flora, Geo.—7-23-
1906—Fristo, Mary—1-13-
　　　　Fischter, Charles L.—2-29-
　　　　Fulton, Julia or Lithia—7-19-
1908—Ficklin, Robert—2-7-
　　　　Ficklin, Alice—3-10-
1909—Fansler, John—3-30-
1910—Fleming, Mrs. John T.—11-13-
1913—Fleming, John T.—5-5-
1915—Foster, Isaac Newton—8-17-
1915—Foster, Isaac Newton—10-15-

　　　Removals from Charleston Bottom Cemetery—10-15-1915—

　　　　Foster, Edmond—10-15-
　　　　Foster, Wm. T. B.
　　　　Foster, Martha J.
　　　　Foster, Jr. Edmond
　　　　Foster, Sarah M.
　　　　Foster, Lutie B.
1916—Farrell, J. H.—2-14-
1917—Fuller, Amos—1-28-
　　　　Ficklin, Horacio N.—2-24-
1918—Forman, Susan—8-7-
　　　　Frederick, Austin H.—10-27-
1919—Fyffe, Elizabeth—2-14-
　　　　Forman, M. M.—7-10-
1920—Frederick, Lewellyn—1-13-
　　　　Finch, Mrs Bettie M.—11-1-
1921—Follmer, Alberta—1-6-
　　　　Fitch, Maggie Davis—3-17-
　　　　Fowler, Mattie Lee—3-27-
1921—Forman, Anna M.—8-2-
　　　　Forman, Harry P.—11-2-
1922—Fant, Charles F.—2-4-
　　　　Fullmer, Mrs. Nannie—2-16-
　　　　Fichter, John—3-15-
　　　　Frederick, W. H.—11-4-
　　　　Fowler, Eva—12-3-

1923—Foster, Eliza Jane Watkins—1-17-
    Fowler, Laura May—2-24-
    Farrow, Nannie—5-10-
    Frazee, Mary Lee 6-13- (Lexington, Ky.)
    Frazee, Dr. J. M.—8-2-
    Frame, Eli C.—8-15-
1924—Fulmer, Paul—10-5-
1925—Foster, James A.—1-10-
    Forman, Geo. W.—3-2-
    Fowler, Sam—3-6-
    Forman, Wm.—4-10-
    Fristo, Wm. T.—8-15-
    Fristo, Clarence—11-25-
1926—Fraysur, Rachel—5-30-
    Forman, Lolo—8-26-
    Fergeson, Anna B.—9-17-
    Fyffe, Henry T.—12-4-
    Farrow, Howard—12-11-
1927—Fleming, Benjamin—10-16-
    Fleming, Geo.—10-19-
    Frame, Bert N.—12-27-

# G

1894—Goodpaster, Miss—2-3-
1898—Greenlee, Eli—11-10-
1899—Gray, Mrs. Emily Bobyns—5-1-
1900—Goodpaster, L. A.—8-12-
1902—Miss Gill—4-13-
1904—Groves, Blackstone—1-14-
    Gill, John—11-27-
1907—Galbreath, Geo. E. B.—2-27-
    Gaither, Mrs. R. J.—12-23-
1909—Gault, M. W.—8-31-
1014—Griffon, Geo. W.—2-4-
    Groppenbecker, Helen II.—11-1-
1915—Green, Julia B.—6-5-
    Gaither, Richard J.—7-20-
    Green, Amos—12-4-
1916—Galbreath, Annie L.—2-12-
    Grigsby, Winona O.—4-6-
1921—Geisel, G. W.—2-3-
    Griffith, Mollie—2-3-
    Grant, Mrs. John T.—6-4-
1922—G......, Mrs. Margaret—1-13- (Morristown, N. J.)
    Gettis, John C.—5-18-
1924—Geisel C. Edw.—4-25-
    Goodwin, Andrew—12-26-
    Goodwin, Charles C.—10-27-
    Goodman, C. A.—1-22-

Goodwin, T. F.—5-30-
Grant, Charles—7-1-
1924—Green Carol—10-5-
Goodwin, Mrs. Charles—11-23- (Manchester, O.)

## COURT AND OTHER RECORDS
## MASON COUNTY

(Compiled by: Mrs. Lula Reed Boss, Maysville, Ky.)

MASON COUNTY COURT RECORDS (ABSTRACTS)
Deed Book B-1, Page 50—Dated October 5, 1793

Richard Masterson and Sally his wife, of Fayette county, Kentucky, convey to Jacob Reed, of Mason county, Kentucky, land in Mason county "on the headwaters of Indian and Farrow creek and branches of the North Fork of Licking, being part of said Masterson's survey of 1,270 acres and running to the line of Thomas Ousley's survey, containing 680 acres." Witnesses to deed: Daniel Fagan, Edwin Furr, David Broderick and John Roe. Recorded June 24, 1794.

Deed Book C, Page 448—Dated September 6, 1796

Philip Buckner of Mason county, Kentucky, conveys to Jacob Reed, of the same place, land in Mason county "on the waters of the North Fork of Licking, containing 200 acres." Witnesses to deed: George Lewis, Michael Cassidy, Stephen Treacle and Isaac Reed.

Deed Book C, Page 450—Dated September 6, 1796

Philip Buckner of Mason county, Kentucky, conveys to Jacob Reed, of the same place, land in Mason county "situated on both sides of the North Fork of Licking river, containing 1,000 acres." Witnesses to deed: George Lewis, Michael Cassidy, Stephen Treacle and Isaac Reed.

Deed Book E, Page 324—Dated August 16, 1798

Henry Owsley and Martha his wife, of County of Lincoln, State of Kentucky, convey to William Reed, of Mason county, land in Mason county being "two-thirds of survey of 450 acres patented in the name of Henry Owsley by virtue of a Land Office Treasury Warrant, situated and lying on the waters of the North Fork of Licking river joining Hugh Shannon's Settlement." Witnesses to deed: Pearce Lamb, John Williams and Isaac Bunnell.

Deed Book E, Page 328—Dated October 21, 1798

Henry Owsley of Lincoln county, Kentucky, appoints James Dobyns, of Mason county, his Attorney to settle with Simon Kenton as locator of certain lands upon Land Warrant from the State of Virginia. Witnesses to Power of Attorney: Thomas Marshall jr. and James Walker.

Deed Book R, Page 409—Dated September 18, 1810

William and Daniel Owsley of Lincoln County and State of Kentucky, executors of the Will and Testament of Thomas Owsley, deceased, convey to Henry Mauzy, of Garrard county, Kentucky, land in Mason county.

Deed Book E, Page 509—Dated April 2, 1799

John Williams of the county of Lincoln and State of Kentucky, conveys to William Reed, of Mason county, land in Mason county "being part of a Treasury Warrant survey in the name of John Williams situated and lying and being in Mason county on the waters of the North Fork of Licking river, beginning at Shannon's most westerly corner of his Settlement" . . . thence to Owsley's northwest corner . . . thence with Owsley's line . . . containing 100 acres. Witnesses to deed: Robert Flora sr., Thomas Jones, Thomas McCatney, William Pickett and John Hauger.

Deed Book C, Page 506—Dated December 27, 1796

DEED OF GIFT

Edwin Furr of the county of Mason and State of Kentucky, to James Reed, of the same place, for "the natural love and affection which I bear unto the said James Reed" deeds land in Mason county containing by survey 170 acres . . . "Beginning at the most Easterly corner of said Edwin Furr's survey of 800 acres of land made agreeable to an entry made on the twenty-fifth day of May, 1780 in the name of the said Edwin Furr."

(James Reed married in Loudoun county, Virginia, August 30, 1784. Sybill also called "Sibby and Sabina" (Furr, daughter of Edwin) called Edward Furr, with Jacob Reed signing the marriage bonds.)

Survey Book "C", Page 428—Fayette County Clerk's Office, Lexington, Kentucky

"March 26, 1784 surveyed for Edwin Furr 800 acres of land by virtue of a Treasury Warrant No. 4387 agreeable to an entry made May 25, 1780, lying on waters of North Fork of Licking river on south side of said creek." Speaks of "ash and two sugar trees at a corner of George Brent's survey of 500 acres" . . . "thence south 37 E along Joseph Jackson's line."

Rich. Masterson signed as Deputy Surveyor. Examined by Thomas Marshall, Surveyor Fayette County. Chain Carriers: Amour Batterson and George Puff.

Deed Book E, Page 189—Dated June 29, 1798

William Reed and Mary his wife, of the county of Mason and State of Kentucky, convey to Robert Glenn, of same place, "land in Mason county on a draught of Shannon Run the waters of the North Fork of

Licking river, it being part of a survey patented in the name of Henry Owsley" . . . sell 110½ acres. Witnesses to deed: John Hager, John Jones.

### Deed Book D, Page 185—Dated August 7, 1797

Richard Masterson and Sally his wife, of Bourbon county, Kentucky, convey 100 acres of land in Mason county located "on North Fork of Licking river" to Sarah Emily Edwards. Witnesses to deed: Robert Rankin and Edwin Furr.

### Deed Book B-1, Page 68—Dated December 29, 1797

Robert Cooper of Montgomery county, Tennessee, appoints Lewis Moore of Mason county, Kentucky, his Attorney to see about a "certain Military Warrant No. 4338, which I, Robert Cooper, obtained as heir of Appollos Cooper, deceased, for his services in the Virginia Line on Continental Establishment."

This Power of Attorney was signed and acknowledged in Montgomery county, Tennessee, by Robert Cooper in the presence of Robert Dunning and Hayden Wells, Justices for Mongomery county, Tennessee.

### Deed Book J., Page 355—Dated June 10, 1807

William Fields of Mason county, Kentucky, "for love and affection" deeds "to my daughters, Martha and Malinda Fields" eighty-one acres of land in Mason county adjoining lands of Michael and Samuel Fenton, Samuel Reeves and James Patterson; also deeds household and kitchen furniture and "bond in the hands of Ben Powell, of Loudon county, Virginia."

### Deed Book M., Page 143—Dated August 31, 1811

James Hughey and Mary his wife, convey to William Reed and Daniel Rees, all of Mason county, Kentucky, "285½ acres, being part of an entry and survey of 9,922 acres of land made for Cleon Moore, situated and lying in Mason county, State of Kentucky."

### Deed Book C, Page 225—Dated September 13, 1814

James Hughey and Mary his wife, of Franklin county, Kentucky, convey to Elisha Cowgill, of Mason county, "75 acres of land located in Mason county on waters of Shannon Run being part of a survey for Cleon Moore which contained 9,922 acres." Witness to deed: George Cowgill.

### Deed Book P, Page 64—Dated February 25, 1815

Samuel J. McDowell and Nancy his wife, of Mason county, Kentucky, convey to William Reed, of same place, "all that part of a survey of 9,922 acres in Mason county, which is on the waters of Shannon, and which was deeded to Samuel J. McDowell by James Hughey and Mary his wife." Witness to deed: John Keel. (Deed is signed) Samuel J. McDowell and Ann McDowell.

### Deed Book 33, Page 242

James P. Price, attorney for William D. Price, Alex H. Price, John H. Price and Ann P. Price, all of Richmond, Virginia, convey to William Reed, of Mason county, Kentucky, "fifteen hundred acres of land on waters of Shannon." (Signed) James Pope Price. Witnesses to Power of Attorney: Emerson Summers, David Brown, Alexander Anderson and Robert Anderson.

### Deed Book 34, Page 217—Dated April 17, 1830

James Curtis and Elizabeth his wife, to James Reed and Marshall Curtis, all of Mason county, Kentucky, one certain lot or piece of ground adjoining the city of Maysville in the county of Mason on the south side of Third street commonly called the Tan Yard lot on which is situated a tan yard, Stano bark house and brick dwelling house adjoining N. Hixon's lot.

### Deed Book 47, Page 427—Dated November 20, 1830

James Ragsdale of Mason county, Kentucky, conveys to William Reed, of same place, "land located on north side of Shannon creek, it being part of Cleon Moore's survey of 9,922 acres." Witness to deed: George Cowgill, Ebenezer Linn and Elridge Waller.

### Deed Book 37, Page 352—Dated August 25, 1831

James Reed and Sabina his wife, of the county of Mason, convey to Titus Harris, of same place, lot in Mason county "being part of the ground conveyed to said James Reed and Marshall Curtis by James Curtis, April 17, 1830 and by the said Marshall Curtis conveyed to the said James Reed by deed dated June 17, 1830."

### Deed Book 51, Page 519—Dated July 26, 1842

Zadock Mullikin of Mason county, became indebted to Martha and Malinda Fields of Bracken county, Kentucky, in the sum of $108 for past due rent; also indebted to John M. Reed for two notes; also to Isaac Reed for note which said Isaac Reed assigned over to John M. Reed . . . Now to secure the payment of said debts, Zadock Mullikin mortgages crop of corn, oats, hemp, and tobacco to Martha and Malinda Fields and John M. Reed.

### Deed Book 116, Page 226—Dated December 17, 1913

"This Indenture between Elizabeth H. Reed, widow of Jacob Reed, deceased, of the one part, and Charles F. Reed, party of the second part, both residents of Maysville, Mason county, Kentucky." "For natural love and affection that the party of the first part bears for the party of the second part, her son, conveys all right, title, and interest, as widow of Jacob Reed, her life interest in and to lands of Jacob Reed in Mason county, Kentucky, to Charles F. Reed."

## COURT ORDER BOOK A
### Page 450—December Court, 1793

Robert Slaughter, Esq., came into Court and produced a license to practice law and took the oath of allegiance of office.

### Page 458—January Court, 1794

Bertram Ewell, Esq., came into Court and produced a license to practice law in the several county courts in this state.

### Page 477—March Court, 1794

Upon the motion of Peter Machir, he is permitted to take the Oath of Allegiance and Fidelity to this State and also the United States.

### Page 98—July Court, 1795

Thomas Dobyns commissioned Sheriff of Mason county by the Governor of Kentucky. Signing as sureties for the faithful performance of his duties were: Joseph Berry, Joel Berry, Withers Berry, Elijah Berry, Robert Rankin, Daniel Carroll, William Roe, Lewis Craig, William Reed, James Dobyns, and George Berry, Jr.

## COURT ORDER BOOK B
### Page 296—August Court, 1796

Upon motion of Dillard Collins, Michael Cassidy, Winslow Parker, Jacob Reed and Patrick Allison are appointed Commissioners to take depositions for perpetuating Testimony for the establishment of land made in the name of Samuel Brockman, Sr., of one thousand acres on the North Fork of Licking and make report to the next court.

(Orange county, Virginia. Book 21, page 13, dated February 22, 1796, gives: John Brockman of Orange county and State of Virginia, appoints "my friend Dillard Collins of Clark county and State of Kentucky" attorney to handle "my lands in Kentucky.")

(Heirs of Dillard Collins settled later in Hopkins Co., Ky.)

### Page 380—December Court, 1796

Thomas Dobyns, Gentleman, Sheriff of this county, together with James Dobyns, Jacob Reed, William Burke, James Reed, Philip Donoven, Daniel Carroll and John True, his sureties, acknowledged bond in penalty of 3,000 pounds for his true and faithful collecting and accounting for the levies of this county for the year 1797.

### Page 392—December Court, 1796

Jasper Seybold, James Reed, John Newman, and Henry Worstell, or any three of them, first sworn, are appointed to view a way proposed for a road from Edwin Furr's Settlement on the Fleming (creek) to Charles Pelham's mill and make report to the next court.

### Page 417

"At a Court Continued and held for Mason County the 24th of January, 1797

#### PRESENT

George Mitchell                         Winslow Parker
and John Gutridge, Gentlemen Justices:

Report of the way proposed for a road from Edwin Furr's Settlement on Fleming to Charles Pelham's mill returned as follows:—To wit, Beginning near said Furr's Plantation then by Sypoles from thence thro Major Reed's lane thence by David Worstells plantation from thence taking the dividing ridge between the North Fork of Licking and Mill creek to Shipley's Plantation thence the present road to the said Pelhams Mill; and it is ordered that the Sheriff Summon the Different proprietors of Land thro which said road is proposed to appear at the next Court and shew cause if any why the Same may not be Established."

### COURT ORDER BOOK C
#### Page 1  February Court, 1797

"Upon motion of Edward Furr setting forth that he holds the bed and north side of Fleming Creek at the mouth of Logan's Run and that he is desirous of building and erecting a water grist mill thereon and it is ordered that a writ be issued agreeable to an Act of General Assembly for viewing the place whereon he is about to erect the same, and it is further ordered that this writ be complyed the second Thursday in April next."

### Page 64—July Court, 1797

Upon motion of William Kenton, guardian of the orphans of Jacob Lockart, deceased, John Gutridge, Patrick Hunter, and Robert B. Morton, are appointed Commissioners, or any two of them, to take depositions to perpetuate Testimony to establish an entry of 500 acres made in a Military Warrant in the name of Jacob Lockart.

### Page 341—February Court, 1800

Administration of the estate of James Nelson, late a Captain in the Battalion for the protection of the frontier of the State of North Carolina, is granted John Blanchard.  Sureties: Philip Buckner and David Bell.

### COURT ORDER BOOK D
#### Page 155—June Court, 1801

John Nichols this day personally appeared in Court and made oath that sometime in the year 1791 he was possessed of a Certificate for

Clark's or Logan's Company which he delivered to Thomas Warring then sheriff of Mason county to whom he was indebted, part of the amount for taxes and took his due Bill for the balance and that he has since recovered the following Certificate to the amount of said Balance in exchange, to-wit: No. 521 to John Wood for £ 3:12 for services as an Ensign in Logan's expedition, dated the 10th day of August, 1787; No. 529 to John Clifford for £ 2:8:4 for services as a soldier in Clark's Campaign, dated the 10th day of August, 1787; also No. 582 to Spencer Reeves for seventeen shillings and seven pences for services as a soldier in Logan's expedition, dated the 10th day of August, 1787 and further that the said Certificates were always considered by him as the bona fide property of the said John Nichols and his brother, Thomas Nichols, and that he never sold or paid in Taxes the balance of his above mentioned Certificates.

### Page 209—October Court, 1801

Samuel Logan, Jr., produced a Certificate No. 536 for 17 shillings and 7 pence for services as a soldier in Logan's Campaign bearing date of August 10, 1787 and made oath that the same is his property and never has been discharged by way of taxes.

James McKinley presented Certificate No. 543 for 17 shillings and 7 pence for services as a soldied in Logan's Campaign bearing date of August 10, 1787 and made oath that the same is his property and never has been discharged by way of taxes.

### Page 287—March Court, 1802

Thomas Dougherty produced his license and took the several oaths prescribed by Law and he is admitted to practice as Attorney at Law in this Court.

### Page 349—June Court, 1802

Richard L. Wheatley produced his license and took the several oaths prescribed by Law and he is admitted to practice as an Attorney at Law in this Court.

### COURT ORDER BOOK E
### Page 155—June Court, 1804

Upon motion of William Hull he is licensed and permitted to vend any merchandise as a Peddler within the State for one year agreeable to law.

### COURT ORDER BOOK F
### Page 58—April Court, 1807

John G. Heith produced his license and took the several oaths prescribed by Law and he is admitted to practice as an Attorney at Law in this Court.

### Page 110—November Court, 1807

David Brown produced his license and took the several oaths pre-scribed by Law and he is admitted to practice as an Attorney at Law in this Court.

### Page 204—October Court, 1808

John Reed, infant son of William Reed, being over the age of four-teen years, came into court and made choice of William Reed, his father, as his guardian, who being appointed by the court upon his giving se-curity, whereupon he together with DeVall Payne, James Chambers, Alexander Daugherty, and Edward Settle, his sureties entered into bond in the penalty of six hundred dollars.

### Page 205—October Court, 1808

William Reed also appointed guardian for his infant sons, Jacob Reed, William Reed, Joseph Reed and James Reed, all under fourteen years of age. Sureties: DeVall Payne, James Chambers, Alexander Daugherty, and Edward Settle in the penalty of $2,400.

### Page 300—September Court, 1809

William Reed is appointed guardian of Fenton Russell, Washington Russell, William Russell, and John Russell, infant orphans of George Russell, deceased. Sureties: Alexander Daugherty, Elisha Cowgill and Sarah Russell in the sum of $2,000.

(Will Book H., Page 31. Loudoun county Virginia court records, shows that John Moore, of Loudoun county, in his will left money to his grandsons named in the foregoing records. His will is dated 7-27-1806, and was probated 9-8-1806.)

### WILL BOOK C, Page 174

Will of "John B. Moore, of Mason county, Kentucky." Dated November 15, 1811; probated December 9, 1811.

Leaves "to youngest brother, William Moore, legacy coming to me from my grandfather, John Moore, the exact sum I know not; house-hold furniture in the care of Joseph Moore to be given to my oldest brother; Joseph to keep bed and give tea kettle to aunt Clow Moore" . . . further stating: "money in the hands of my uncle, William Reed, Esq., to pay last expenses." Witnesses to will: Charles B. Smith, James Layton, and Daniel Rees.

(William Reed, Esq., had married Mary Moore, daughter of John Moore, of Loudoun county, Virginia.)

### COURT ORDER BOOK J
### Page 4—June Court, 1819

Upon motion of Bodine Bailey it is ordered that John Waugh, Rich-ard Ritter, James Ireland and Peter Degman, or any three of them being sworn be appointed to view a way for a road from Ritterville to the mouth of Cabin creek and make report to this court of the convenience and inconvenience attending the opening of said road.

### Page 223—October Court, 1821

Satisfactory evidence was adduced to the Court to shew that David Duncan is the father and heir at law of Thomas Duncan, deceased, late a soldier in the First Regiment of Infantry in the service of the United States.

## COURT ORDER BOOK K

### Page 76—December Court, 1823

"Ordered that a whipping post be erected on the public grounds in Washington and that John Chambers, John Johnston and Thomas Ellis be appointed to have the same erected."

### Page 367—January Court, 1827

William Reed is appointed guardian for Mary Reed, Rebecca Reed, Nancy Ellen Reed and Joseph Reed, infant heirs of Jacob Reed, deceased, and upon his giving security with Sanford Mitchell and Levi Van Camp entered into and acknowledged bond in the sum of $500.

## COURT ORDER BOOK L

### Page 312—April Court, 1830

Administration of the estate of William Stoker, deceased, is granted William Reed, Jr., William Reed, Sr. surety. Jonathon Kennard, Asa Watson, Elijah Martin and Britton Chandler appointed to appraise the slaves, if any, of William Stoker, deceased.

### Page 348—October Court, 1830

"Ordered that William Reed and John Brown be recommended to the Governor of this State as proper persons to Commission one of them Sheriff of Mason county, they being the two senior Magistrates in said county. A majority of all the Justices being present and concurring in said nomination."

### Page 349—October Court, 1830

Upon motion of Christian Schultz and John M. Morton, purchasers of five of the nine heirs of Moses Daulton, deceased, it is ordered that Joseph Forman, William B. Phillips, William L. McCalla and George Corwine, or any three of them, being first duly sworn, be appointed to lay off and assign the dower of Mrs. Mary Daulton in the lands of her late husband, Moses Daulton, deceased, and make report to the next court.

Page 383—February Court, 1831

"William Reed produced a Commission from the Governor of this State appointing him Sheriff of Mason County, and thereupon he came into Court and took the several oaths prescribed by law and entered into and acknowledged bond for the performance of said office, with Charles Ward, Septimus D. Clark, Charles Clarke, Robert Humphrey, Charles Humphrey, Benjamin Bayless, Richard Soward, Thomas Mountjoy, Winslow Parker, Abner Hord, James K. Marshall, Walter Calvert, Thomas Hord, John Marshall, John M. Reed, William Reed, Jr., and George Cowgill as his sureties in the penalty of $10,000 as conditioned by law."

Page 521—July Court, 1832

Report of the road from Germantown by John Reeve's to General Reed's mill was returned in court and ordered to be recorded.

COURT ORDER BOOK M

Page 5—September Court, 1832

Estate of Joseph Moore, deceased. William R. Beatty, administrator. Adam Beatty surety.

Page 172—April Court, 1834

This day Amos Shroufe, one of the heirs of Adam Shroufe, deceased, came into court and it appearing to the satisfaction of the court, by the affidavit of Rice Boulton that notice in writing of the proceding has been given to Mary Shroufe and Sebastian L. Shroufe, two of the heirs of said Adam Shroufe, deceased, and to Thomas Worthington another of the heirs of the said Adam Shroufe, deceased, and to John Cornick, husband of Nancy Cornick, late Nancy Shroufe, and to Robert Booth, husband of Elizabeth Booth, late Elizabeth Shroufe, and it appearing to the satisfaction of the court that the said Amos Shroufe, Mary Shroufe, Sebastian Shroufe, Sarah Shroufe, Nancy Cornick, late Nancy Shroufe, and Elizabeth Booth, late Elizabeth Shroufe, are the only children and heirs of the said Adam Shroufe, deceased. Commissioners are appointed to go upon the lands lying in Mason county on the Ohio river which the said Adam Shroufe died possessed of and divide the same into six equal parts having due regard to quantity and quality and allot one of the said parts to each of the heirs.

Deed Book N., page 9, dated December 13, 1812, shows that Adam Shroufe had wife, Hannah Shroufe. The noncupative will of Adam Shroufe (Will Book J., page 287) states that he "died 2-19-1833."

Page 277—August Court, 1835

The Will of James Reed, Sr., was produced in court and proven by the oaths of Nicholas D. Coleman and Lucy A. Coleman and ordered to be recorded.

George Cowgill, William Tanner, William Reed, and A. A. Wadsworth appointed by the court to appraise the personal estate and slaves, (if any) of James Reed, Sr., deceased, and make report to the next court.

### Page 283—August Court, 1835

William S. Reed qualified as Executor of the last Will and Testament of James Reed, Sr., deceased.

### Page 297—September Court, 1835

Sophia Ann Waugh, infant orphan of John Waugh, Jr., deceased, being over the age of 14 years, came into court and made choice of John Pelham as her guardian. Eliza Jane Waugh, over fourteen, made choice of John Pelham as her guardian; also Mary Waugh. John Pelham was appointed guardian for Nancy Waugh, under 14, and Winslow Parker signed as surety.

### Page 417—December Court, 1836

Estate of George Cowgill, deceased. William Reed, Sr., administrator. Sureties: Ludwell Yancey Browning and John M. Reed. "Nancy Cowgill, the widow of George Cowgill, deceased, personally came into court and relinquished her rights to serve as administratrix."

### Page 445—March Court, 1837

Last Will and Testament of William Reed, Sr., proven by the oaths of Richard Soward, Leondias M. Laws and Harrison Richardson. Bond given for $30,000 to secure the proper administration of the estate by Ludwell Yancey Browning.

### Page 455—April Court, 1837

Upon motion of Agnes Rogers it is ordered that a Ferry be granted her from her lands at the mouth of Cabin creek across the Ohio river; also a Ferry across Cabin creek. Upon her giving bond and surety whereupon she executed and acknowledged bond with Thornton Hord surety in the penalty of $1,000 as conditioned by law and it is ordered that she be allowed the same rate of ferriage as John Waugh was allowed at the same place.

### Pages 493 and 494—September Court, 1837

Records give the administration of the estates of Jacob Reed, deceased, and Joseph Reed, deceased, with John M. Reed being appointed administrator of both estates. Ludwell Y. Browning, surety.

### COURT ORDER BOOK N
### Page 9—April Court, 1838

Samuel Musgrove and Nancy Cowgill, administrators of the estate of George Cowgill, deceased, "appointed in the State of Missouri where the said George Cowgill departed this life," came into court and gave bond to administer the estate of the said George Cowgill, deceased, in the State of Kentucky. Surety: James W. Waddell.

### Page 249—July Court, 1841

Estate of Susan Fowke, deceased. Phillip R. Triplett, administrator. John Masterson, surety.

### Page 469—September Court, 1844

Upon motion of John S. C. Waugh, Sophia A. Waugh, Eliza Jane Waugh, Mary Jane Waugh and Charles White and Nancy his wife, it is ordered that Edward Bullock, John Pelham and Julius C. Degman, or any three of them, be appointed to procession the tract of land lying in Mason county which descended to them from their father John Waugh, deceased, and that the surveyor of Mason county attend said processioners and that they make report to the next court.

### COURT ORDER BOOK O
### Page 264—September Court, 1849

Administration of the estate of Robert Bridwell is granted to Richard Peckover, who made oath and acknowledged bond in the amount of $100. James Jacobs, surety.

Richard Peckover is appointed guardian for Elizabeth Bridwell, infant orphan of Robert Bridwell, deceased. James Jacobs, surety. Richard Peckover is also appointed guardian of Charles Bridwell.

### Page 274—October Court, 1849

John M. Reed appointed guardian of Benjamin Clark, infant son of Leondias Clark. Calvin Blan, surety, in the sum of $2,000.

### Page 421—May Court, 1850

Thomas Daulton is appointed guardian of Sally, Harvey, William and Martha Daulton, infant children of George W. Daulton. A. A. Wadsworth, surety.

### Page 450—October Court, 1850

Administration of the estate of Agnes Rogers, deceased. William W. Rogers, administrator. Hezekiah Jenkins surety in the sum of $600.

### Page 497—May Court, 1851

Ordered that David Bronough, a senior Justice of this County, sign and the Clerk of the Court countersign and affix the Seal of the County to 20 bonds for $1,000 each, numbers from one to twenty, and deliver the same to the President and Directors of the Maysville and Lexington Railroad Company as part of the subscription of $150,000 of stock taken in said company on the part of the said county.

### COURT ORDER BOOK 45 (Circuit Clerk's Office)
#### Page 425—November Court, 1849

"Nancy Cowgill, William Reed, Samuel Musgrove and Elizabeth his wife, Joseph Reed and ........Kyle and Mary his wife, are not now inhabitants of this Commonwealth.........."

### COURT ORDER BOOK 48 (Circuit Clerk's Office)
#### Page 598—February Court, 1855

"John M. Reed has departed this life and it is ordered that Isaac S. Reed be appointed to take charge of the affairs of Mary Reed, daughter of General William Reed, deceased, with John R. Fields and Wyatt Weedon sureties in the sum of $4,000."

### COURT ORDER BOOK 52 (Circuit Clerk's Office)
#### Page 430—April Court, 1860

Estate of Armedda O. Glidewell, deceased. William Reed Browning, administrator.

### COURT ORDER BOOK 53 (Circuit Clerk's Office)

Pages 348-349, dated July 25, 1861, lists all the living heirs (in 1861) of General William Reed and his wife, Mary Moore Reed.
The suit is styled:

James Cowgill, admr. of estate of Nancy Reed Cowgill, Plt.
vs.
Mary Reed's administratrix & others, Defts.

Mrs. Julia Ann (Reed) Browning was serving as the admrx. of the estate of her deceased sister, Mary Reed. In this suit Emery Whitaker was appointed by the court "attorney to defend the non-resident defendants."

### From: THE NATIONAL ARCHIVES, Washington, D. C.
#### JAMES REED—Pension Claim R 8676 (of heirs)

"The Revolutionary War record of James Reed (of Loudoun county, Virginia) has been found and is given herein, the data for which were obtained from the papers on file in Revolutionary War Pension Claim R 8676, based upon his military service in that War.

The Revolutionary War record shows in the effort of the heirs of James Reed to obtain a pension based upon his service in the Revolutionary War, a sworn statement was filed in their behalf which was made by one William Furr on April 17, 1855, at which time he was aged ninety years and a resident of Fountain county, Indiana.

William Furr stated that James Reed enlisted sometime in 1776, served under Captain John McGeth in the Virginia Troops and continued in service until the close of the war and that a part of his service was as a teamster engaged in hauling provisions for the army.

He stated further that the soldier, James Reed, married his sister, Miss Sabina Furr, and that they were married at their father's (his name not given) home in Loudoun county, Virginia. The Marriage Bond, which was recorded on the records of Loudon county, Virginia, bears date as of August 30, 1784. On this Bond her name is given as Miss Sybill Furr. One Jacob Reed signed the bond with James Reed.

William Furr stated that about six years after their marriage, James Reed and his wife moved from Loudoun County Virginia to Mason county (later Fleming county) Kentucky, and that he accompanied them and resided in their home.

The soldier died about 1835 in Maysville, Kentucky, and was buried with Honors of War. His age, place of birth and names of his parents not given. His widow, Sabina or Sybill, died about 1849, at the same place, of an attack of Asiatic Cholera, at which time she was aged about eighty years.

In 1855, the only surviving children were Jacob, James, Stephen and William Reed. Their ages and places of residence are not stated."

### WILL BOOK K—Page 191

Will of "James Reed senior of the city of Maysville, Mason county, Kentucky." Leaves to son Jacob Reed; son James Reed; son Stephen Reed, he "to add to the advancement he may make his son, Sampson Reed, when Sampson comes of age;" daughter Sabina Curtis, wife of Marshall Curtis; son William S. Reed. "I will and bequeath unto my wife Sabina the whole of my estate, real, personal, and mixed, to be held and owned by her during her natural life and at her death to be distributed among my children according to the foregoing provisions of my will." Wife Sabina Reed and son William S. Reed, executors.

Dated: September 23, 1834. Probated: August Court, 1835.

Witnesses to Will: N. D. Coleman, Lucy A. Coleman, and Joseph D. Barker.

### WILL BOOK L—Page 58

Will of "William Reed senior of Mason county and State of Kentucky." Leaves to "my five granddaughters, daughters of David and Sarah Brown, namely: Charlotte Glenn, Mary Ann Soward, Nancy Throop, Sophia and Elizabeth Brown, to whom he bequeathes land in Lewis and Clark counties, Missouri; to grandson, William R. Brown; to four grandchildren, children of Jacob Reed, land in Lewis and Clark counties, Missouri, namely: Mary R. Kile, Rebecca Reed, Nancy Ellen Reed and Joseph Reed; daughter Polly Reed; daughter Rebecca Fields; daughter Nancy R. Cowgill; daughter Elizabeth Reed Musgrove; son William Reed and his daughter, Sally Reed, land in Lewis and Clark counties, Missouri; daughter Julia Ann Browning to whom he "gives and bequeaths the plantation which I now live on including all lands on the north side of the south branch of Shannon;" to son John M. Reed . . . then states: "to Amanda Baily I bequeath one cow, horse, etc.," . . . "this is in full for all demands against me" . . . (no relationship stated to this Amanda Baily); to granddaughter, Sally R. Fields. (No mention of wife in will).

Appoints Ludwell Yancey Browning executor of estate.

Witnesses to Will: Richard Soward, S. M. Lawson, Margaret Williams, and Harrison Richardson.

Dated: January 31, 1837. Probated: March Court, 1837.

### WILL BOOK L, Page 509—Dated July 19, 1939

Administration of the estate of Greenberry Fields, deceased. Rebecca Fields, widow, and John Adamson, administrators.

(Greenberry Fields married Rebecca Reed in Adams county, Ohio, March 18, 1810.)

### WILL BOOK Q—Page 357

Will of "John M. Reed of county of Mason and State of Kentucky." Dated: November 7, 1854. Probated: February Court, 1855.

Leaves to son, Isaac S. Reed the use of $1,000 during his life, and at death of Isaac same to descend to and be equally divided among "my daughters, Armedda Glidewell, Nancy Frampton, Mary Ball and Judith Weedon, or to their heirs." To children of daughter, Susan Wheeler, late wife of Aaron H. Wheeler, "eight in number, when each arrives at the age of 21 years." To two children of deceased daughter, Elizabeth Lacy, Ann and Judith Lacy, when of age of 21 years; daughter Nancy Frampton the use of $1,000, and at her death to be equally divided among all "my children;" to daughter Mary Ball, and at her death to go to her heirs; to daughter, Armedda Glidewell "the house and lot in the town of Sardis (Mason county) Kentucky, in which I now live, household furniture, etc., on the condition that she lives with me during my natural life" . . . speaks of "her now living daughter, Frances Glidewell;" to daughter Judith Weedon; grandson Benjamin Leonidas Clark when he reaches 21 years; to brother William Reed, now living in Clark county, Missouri.

Appoints son Isaac Shelby Reed and Emery Whitaker, executors.

Witnesses to Will: Luke Dye, James Vardinburg, James S. Bratton and Emery Whitaker.

### WILL BOOK Q.—Page 588

Will of "Isaac S. Reed of the county of Mason and State of Kentucky."

Dated: August 30, 1856. Probated: September Court, 1856.

States: "the sum of $1,000 bequeathed me by my father is to be paid first as directed by his will," . . . mentions "beloved wife Jane Reed." "The farm on which I reside containing 150 acres and my tract of land over Shannon known as the Field's tract to be sold," . . . proceeds to be equally divided between my sisters who are living and the heirs of those who are dead . . . other half to "my wife giving her the right of disposing of it at her death to her brothers and sisters and their heirs, but out of her half she shall pay the following bequests: to Alice Calvert $50; to Walter Calvert, son of Walter Calvert senior, deceased, one horse when he arrives at 21 years; to John James Calvert, youngest son of Walter Calvert, deceased, $50 when he arrives at 21 years; to Catherine and Isaac Calvert, children of Clifton Calvert, deceased, $200 each, to be paid them when they marry; to May Susan Brown, daughter of Mrs. Walter Calvert, $50 when she marries or arrives at 21 years; to Charles Calvert one roan horse."

Appoints Allen Baker and Henry S. Jefferson, executors.

Witnesses to Will: Addison Dimmitt and Emery Whitaker.

## WILL BOOK I—Page 409

Will of "Elizabeth H. Reed, of Maysville, Mason county, Kentucky." States she "is nearing ninety years of age." Mentions farm she ownes and on which "she and her late husband lived until his death, November 26, 1913, located on the south side of the Maysville and Mt. Sterling turnpike, about two miles from Maysville in Mason county, Kentucky," and gives same to her "beloved son, Charles F. Reed." Leaves to "my three granddaughters, Elizabeth H. Reed, Nora May Reed and Lula Reed Boss, who are the three daughters of my said son, Charles F. Reed," . . . to "my grandson, James B. Reed, son of my said son, Charles F. Reed." Leaves to Clarence and John Jolly who are the sons of my deceased granddaughter, Elizabeth E. Jolly, and who both reside in Fleming county, Kentucky, the sum of five hundred dollars each.

Date of Will: June 17, 1916. Probated: December 8, 1919.

The Will of Elizabeth Hildreth (Fristoe) Reed was proven by the oaths of J. Foster Barbour and George T. Barbour and ordered to be recorded.

## DEED BOOK Y, Page 24—Power of Attorney

Dated: January 14, 1829.

John J. Fields of Loudoun county and Commonwealth of Virginia, appoints Jonathan Reed, now of the county and state aforesaid, but who is about to go to the State of Kentucky "my true and lawful attorney" . . . to attend to property "I may be entitled to in the State of Kentucky, especially a negro man named Peter and a negro woman named Patt and her children, and a tract of land containing 80 acres and all my interest in and to my father's estate, meaning William Field's estate, the land aforesaid being situated in Mason county, Kentucky."

## DEED BOOK E—Page 277

"Washington, Mason county, Kentucky, April 12, 1799.

Agreement between William Bishop of Fairfax county Virginia, of the one part, and Obediah Fuqua of Kanawha county Virginia, of the other part . . . "the said Fuqua agrees to do for and attend to a certain claim of the said Bishop and every interest necessary to be done for said Bishop in the premises respecting said claim at his the said Fuqua's only proper charge and expense . . . Fuqua to obtain the interest of said Bishop "in land as heir of John Bishop, the claim including the mouth of Gwyandotte river and running up and down the Ohio river for quantity granted to savage and others, being their Bounty in Braddock's War, and it is agreed on the part of the said William Bishop that the said Fuqua is to pay him $100 for the said claim."

Witnesses to Agreement: Chas. Tathom, B. B. Stith and Thos. C. Lewis.

## MASON COUNTY KENTUCKY COURT RECORDS

Marriages: (date represents the date the license was issued.)

David Brown and Sarah Reed, 8-21-1812.

Thomas Marshall, bondsman.

According to tombstone inscription in the Shannon Cemetery, Sarah Reed Brown "died Dec. 4, 1824, aged 30 years." David Brown "died Feb. 22, 1836, aged 58 years."

John Moore Reed and Judith Leake, 10-6-1812.

Walter Leake, bondsman.

Tombstone inscription in the Shannon Cemetery gives: "Judith Reed died July 14, 1841, aged 48 years, 6 months and 28 days."

George Cowgill and Nancy Reed, 3-18-1819.

D. B. Hickman, bondsman.

George Cowgill was born 3-3-1797; died Clark county, Missouri, 8-26-1836.

Nancy Cowgill died in Clark county, Missouri, 6-4-1859.

Marshall Curtis and Sabina Reed were married 9-17-1822.

(Curtis Bible record)

William Reed Junior and Sidney Kennard, 4-10-1827.

Willis Ballenger, bondsman.

Tombstone inscription in the Shannon Cemetery states Sidney Reed was "born 1-7-1808; died of Cholera, 6-17-1835."

Samuel Musgrove and Elizabeth R. Reed, 4-6-1829.

William Reed signed as the father of Elizabeth. John M. Reed, bondsman.

Richard Soward Junior and Mary Ann Brown, 5-18-1829.

David Brown, bondsman.

William S. Reed and Maria Mott, 12-3-1830.

Joseph Roseman, bondsman.

William S. Reed was born 3-31-1810 in Fleming county, Kentucky; died Fountain county, Indiana. Maria Mott Reed was born in Ohio, 11-25-1812. Died Fountain county, Indiana. (This information was contributed by their son, the late Henry Clay Reed, born in Mason county, 10-5-1847; died in Indiana.)

Ludwell Yancey Browning and Julia Ann Reed, 6-18-1832.

William Reed signed as father. Robert Curtis, bondsman.

Tombstone inscription in the Shannon Cemetery gives that Ludwell Yancey Browning was "born 7-19-1807 and died 4-5-1845." Tombstone inscription shows that Julia Ann Browning was "born 12-14-1814." The date of her death is not on the stone. Her estate was administered April 4, 1899 (Court Order Book No. 1, page 221.)

Joseph Glenn and Charlotte Brown, 8-13-1832.

David Brown, bondsman.

Aaron H. Wheeler and Susan Reed, 7-28-1832.

John M. Reed, bondsman.

(Susan Wheeler was deceased by 11-7-1854.)

Benjamin B. Throop and Ann (Nancy) R. Brown, 5-16-1836.

Richard Soward, bondsman.

William Reed Brown and Harriet Arthur, 4-9-1838.

Harrison Richardson signed as the guardian of William Reed Brown. R. I. Hughey, witness.

Charles C. Lacy and Elizabeth S. Brown, 3-27-1838.

James W. Waddell, bondsman.

Walter L. Lacy and Sophia R. Brown, 10-1-1839.

Charles C. Lacy, bondsman. Cornelius Waller signed as the guardian of Sophia. James Waller, witness.

Isaac Shelby Reed and Jane Calvert, 3-5-1840.

Walter Calvert, bondsman.

(Jane Calvert Reed was born 1826 according to 1850 census of Mason county).

DEED BOOK 55, Page 102—Deed of Gift—Dated March 27, 1846

Isaac S. Reed of Mason county "to well beloved daughter, Eleanor C. Reed, one piano with cover and stool and one ingrain carpet containing 30 yards." This daughter is not mentioned in the will of Isaac Shelby Reed.

John F. Wilson and Sabina Reed, 2-7-1840.

Joseph Reed, bondsman.

Edward Valentine and Rebecca Reed, 4-6-1840.

Jacob Reed, bondsman. Henry Valentine, father. George McFee and Richard Brown, witnesses.

Mason Ball and Mary Moore Reed, 11-21-1842.

John M. Reed, bondsman. Samuel Owens, witness.

Oliver Hazard Perry Wheeler and Elizabeth Reed, 5-28-1843.

Jacob Reed, bondsman.

Elizabeth Reed was born 8-6-1820 and died 5-20-1873. (Wheeler Bible record.)

Stephen C. Frampton and Nancy L. Reed, 6-17-1844.

John M. Reed, bondsman.

James Lacy and Elizabeth Reed, 9-4-1845.

John M. Reed, bondsman.

John Ball and Mary Jane Reed, 12-31-1845.

Craven Lane, bondsman. Jacob Reed, father. A. A. Wadsworth, witness.

Abraham Glidewell and Armedda O. Reed, 12-24-1845.

Joseph F. Jones, bondsman.

Byram Harding Junior (of Stafford county, Virginia) and Elizabeth Hildreth Fristoe, 10-21-1845. Benjamin Willett, bondsman.

Jacob Reed and Mrs. Elizabeth H. Harding married by Rev. J. W. Warder, 4-17-1855. Mary Lockridge and Mr. and Mrs. Robert Fristoe, witnesses.

John L. Scott, bondsman.

William Shackleford and Sarah L. Reed, 11-12-1845.

John F. Dunnington, bondsman. Consent of Isaac Reed.

Leonidas Clarke and Judith Ann Lacy Reed, 1-25-1846.

John M. Reed, bondsman.

Leonidas Clarke died in Misosuri, 5-5-1848, and Mrs. Judith Ann Lacy Clarke married 2nd before 11-7-1854, Wyatt Weedon. Wyatt Weedon married 1st, 9-24-1832, Avi Peddicord.

William King and Eliza Jane Reed, 12-12-1848.

William S. Reed, bondsman.

Eliza Jane Reed was born 2-6-1832.

William Reed Browning and Mary Ann Ball, 12-21-1854. They were married by Milton Pyles at the residence of Leonard Pyles in Mason county.

William Reed Browning died 10-2-1886. Mary Ann Browning died 3-2-1914.

Woodville W. Browning, born 9-22-1840; died Alvin, Texas, 11-14-1908; married 6-28-1864, Susan Franklin Mitchell (born 5-28-1842; died Alvin, Texas, 11-28-1910.) Both are buried in the Shannon Cemetery, Mason county, Kentucky. (This information contributed by Mrs. T. J. Johnson, Route No. 3, Box 81, Mission, Texas. Mrs. Johnson is a descendant of General William Reed and his wife, Mary Moore Reed, and has in her possession the epaulets worn by General Reed during the War of 1812.)


Records from the Reed Bible in the possession of Mrs. Robert Lincoln Holbroook (nee Queen Azile Reed) of Lewiston, Idaho.

## BIRTHS

John M. Reed was born March 10, 1792.

Judith Leake, consort of John Moore Reed, was born 22nd Dec., 1792.

Isaac Shelby Reed was born the 28th of Sept., 1813.

Susan Reed was born the 22nd Aug., 1815.

Armida O. Reed was born Feb. 3, 1817.

Mary Reed was born Nov. 13, 1818.

Nancy Reed was born June 14, 1820.

Sarah W. Reed was born Aug. 14, 1822. Died June 22, 1845.

Elizabeth Reed was born April 22, 1824. Elizabeth Lacy died Aug. 31, 1851.

Juliann Reed was born May 19, 1826. Died Oct. 2, 1826.

Joseph James Reed was born Sept. 25, 1827. Died March 14, 1848.

Judith A. Lacy Reed was born July 25, 1829. Died Jan. 24, 1914.

Judith L., consort of Captain John M. Reed, departed this life July 14, 1841.

Ben Daniel Leonidas Clark, son of Leonidas and Judith Ann Clark, born July 11, 1847, died May 24, 1927.

Leonidas Clark departed this life May 5, 1848.

Aunty Frampton died Nov. 11, 1902.

## MARRIAGE RECORDS

John M. Reed and Judith Leake married Oct. 12, 1812.

Aaron Wheeler and Susan Reed were married July 31, 1832 by H. Baker.

Isaac S. Reed and Jane Calvert were married March 5th, 1840 by Mason.

Mason Ball and Mary M. Reed were married Nov. 22, 1842 by H. Baker.

Stephen C. Frampton and Nancy L. Reed were married June 20, 1844 by H. Baker.

James Lacy and Elizabeth Reed were married Sept. 4, 1845 by H. Helon.

Abraham Glidewell and Armida O. Reed were married by H. Baker Dec. 25, 1845.

Leonidas Clark and Judith Ann Reed were married by H. Baker Jan. 26, 1846.

Bible Records—Family of William Reed and Sidney Kennard his first wife:

Sarah Ann Reed was born February 22, 1828.

Family of William Reed and Margaret Ann Gaines Reed his second wife:

William Reed was born Jan. 31, 1839.

Delilah Elizabeth Reed was born Feb. 6, 1841.

Louise Josephine Reed was born March 23, 1843.

Mary Catherine Reed was born July 23, 1845.

James W. Reed was born Dec. 3, 1847.

Julia Ann Reed was born Oct. 20, 1850.

John M. Reed was born May 5, 1853.

Lizza Reed was born June 22, 1855.

Alice B. Reed was born June 13, 1857.

Ida Virginia Reed was born Oct. 17, 1859.

Susan M. Reed was born Oct. the 15th, 1861.

Agnes Lee Reed was born April the 4th, 1864.

## DEATHS

William Reed departed this life March the 12th, 1887.

Delilah Elizabeth Reed departed this life July 24, 1853.

John M. Reed departed this life August 24, 1854.

Ida Virginia Reed departed this life Dec. 2, 1860.

Julia Ann Reed departed this life July the 15th, 1879.

James W. Reed departed this life March the 12th, 1887.
Louise Josephine Reed Tall departed this life 1889.
Susan Margaret Reed Breedon departed this life 1889.
Alice B. Reed Kincaid departed this life 1884.
Agnes Lee Reed Pliter departed this life 1938.

## MASON COUNTY KENTUCKY COURT RECORDS

### DEED BOOK 45, Page 455—February 22, 1841

Wyatt Weedon of county of Mason and State of Kentucky, purchases 163 acres of land in Mason county "on Clark's Run" from James B. Claybrooke.

### DEED BOOK 62, Page 604—March 1, 1854

Jane Peddicord of Mason county, conveys land in Mason county for $4,528 to Wyatt Weedon . . . Jane Peddicord retaining lien on said land until full purchase price is paid. Witnesses to deed: Jacob Slack, J. B. Claybrooke.

### DEED BOOK 66, Page 263—April 15, 1858

Wyatt Weedon and Judith Ann his wife, and Jane Peddicord, all of Mason county, sell to Benedict Kirk, of same place, land "where Wyatt Weedon now lives on the waters of Clark's Run."

### WILL BOOK T, Page 247

Will of "Jane Peddicord of Mason county, Kentucky."
Dated 9-27-1859. Proven. March Court, 1864.
Leaves to "grandchildren Charles Henry Weedon, Jane Weedon and Marie Weedon."

### DEED BOOK 71, Page 405—April 19, 1866

Jennie Weedon and Marie E. Weedon of Shelby county, Missouri, convey land in Mason county "willed to us and our desceased brother by Jane Peddicord."

### COURT ORDER BOOK S, Page 92—February Court, 1866

Estate of Charles H. Weedon, deceased. J. B. Claybrooke, admr.

### COURT ORDER BOOK R, Page 528

Marie E. Weedon, over the age of 14 years, made choice of James B. Claybrooke as her guardian. April court, 1864.

The following records are in the possession of Missouri descendants and were copied by Mrs. E. B. Wall, of Los Angeles, California.

Elisha Cowgill senior married Martha Cowgill, 1-22-1767.
Elisha Cowgill senior died 10-25-1804 in Mason county, Kentucky.

The old Cowgill Bible gives that "Martha Cowgill senior died 1-26-1834, aged 88 years." Therefore, she was born in 1746 and was 21 years of age when she married.

Their issue:

1. Rachel Cowgill, born 11-2-1767
2. Ewing Cowgill, born 7-22-1769
3. Elisha Cowgill jr., born 2-14-1771; died Putman County, Indiana 1855; md. 3-18-1794, Nancy (Ann) Stanton Tarvin, daughter of George Tarvin and his wife, Sarah Cracraft. George Tarvin died in Bracken county, Kentucky, 1-5-1811. Sarah (Cracraft) Tarvin died between 10-18-1794 and 9-17-1798. (Consult Hampshire county, Virginia [now W. Va.] Court records.)
4. John Cowgill, born 3-8-1775
5. Eleazar Cowgill, born 11-7-1776; md. in Mason County, 12-10-1797, Jane McFarland
6. Martha Cowgill, born 1-15-1779; md. in Mason county, 6-26-1799, Joseph Tarvin
7. Henry Cowgill, born 1-5-1782
8. Alexander Cowgill, born 2-9-1784
9. Ann Cowgill, born 10-3-1786; died 7-31-1828
10. Abner Cowgill, born 5-14-1789; died 8-3-1824
11. Hannah Cowgill, born 8-4-1794

(3) Issue of Elisha Cowgill junior and Nancy (Ann) Stanton Tarvin:

1. Martha, called "Patsy" Cowgill, born 9-4-1795; md. in Mason county 3-26-1811, Reuben Bartholomew Smith jr.
2. George Cowgill, born 3-3-1797; died Clark county, Missouri, 8-26-1836; md. in Mason county, 3-18-1819, Nancy Reed, daughter of Gen. William Reed. Nancy Reed Cowgill died Clark county, Missouri, 6-4-1859
3. Ruth Cowgill, born 1-11-1799; died 1-24-1819; md. in Mason county, 12-24-1816, Allison Gray
4. John Cowgill, born 10-1-1800; md. in Mason county (1st) 11-27-1828, Mary Glenn. She died 10-18-1839 and John Cowgill md (2nd) in Putman county, Indiana, 1-25-1840, Rachel Thompson. Hon. John Cowgill died 3-25-1868 in Chillicothe, Livingston county, Missouri.
5. Patty Cowgill, born 5-4-1802
6. Sally Cowgill, born 6-27-1804 and was living in Putman county, Ind., 1887; md. in Mason county, 3-2-1829, Lucius Chapen
7. Mary Cowgill Tarvin married George Tarvin 1-18-1832 (son of Richard Tarvin, born 1775; died Campbell county, Kentucky, October, 1822, and his wife Sarah Armstrong, whom he married in Mason county, 8-3-1796)
8. Lucinda Cowgill, born 3-17-1808; died 11-25-1811
9. Henry E. Cowgill, born 10-6-1809; md. in Putman county, Indiana, 9-5-1833, Joanna Stevenson. They had a son Alexander C. Cowgill.
10. Tarvin W. Cowgill, born 8-4-1811; md. Agnes F. Tarvin, 5-25-1837
11. Andrew Cowgill, born 11-20-1815; died 9-23-1816

12. William M. Cowgill and
13. Thomas M. Cowgill (twins, born 7-21-1817)
    William M. Cowgill md. in Putman county, Indiana, Rhodanna C. Lewis, 3-24-1842.
14. Charles S. Cowgill, born 6-25-1818; died 5-3-1819
15. Elisha P. Cowgill, born in Mason county 7-4-1819, was living in Putman county, Indiana in 1887; md. there 8-1-1839, Mary F. Talbott (born 1820 in Shelby county, Kentucky)
    Rachel Thompson, 2nd wife of John Cowgill, was born 6-5-1810; died Chillicothe, Missouri, 10-30-1897.

(Putman County, Indiana, marriages from Washington County Chapter, D. A. R., Greencastle, Indiana.)

Elisha P. Cowgill md. Mary F. Talbott, 8-1-1839
Henry E. Cowgill md. Joanna Stevenson, 9-5-1833
John Cowgill md. Rachel Thompson, 1-26-1840
William M. Cowgill md. Rhoda Ann C. Lewis, 3-24-1842

(For further information consult "History of Putman County, Indiana," published in 1887 by Lewis Publishing Company, 113 Adams Street, Chicago, Ill., page 328.)

Hon. John Cowgill and Tarvin W. Cowgill were members of the first Board of Directors of DePauw University, Greencastle, Putman county, Indiana.

(Excerpts from Obituary published in the Chillicothe (Missouri) Spectator of April 2, 1868):

"In our last week's issue we noted the death of Hon. John Cowgill ......The deceased was born in Mason county, Kentucky, October 1800 and at near the age of thirty years moved to Indiana, and at the town of Greencastle commenced the study and practice of law, and after sometime thus engaged successfully, we are well assured, he was chosen Judge of the Court of Common Pleas for the District, which place he held for eight years......While thus engaged he was chosen Law Professor of Grencastle University......Judge Cowgill was one of the many hundreds of our self-made men......his loss will fall heavily upon the church of which he was, in health, a constant attendant......The members thereof will miss his stalwart form, massive forehead, mild pleasing countenance, his fine blue eyes......will miss his calm, lucid, elegant prayers......Judge Cowgill has left us a history important to the legal profession, in this; that a lawyer can be a good christian gentleman; that he can be honest; that he can be modest; that he can move through the profession with all its conflicts and asperities, and through society without jostling anybody with a rudeness or unkindness; that he can be dignified without being pompous or stiff mannered; that he can be gentle and kind without being insulted or runover; that he can entertain positive opinions without being bitter and hostile to those who entertain different opinions; that he can pass around the jagged points in society without bruises, or ever having even his pride wounded; that he can be liberal and yet be closely economical............"

(Signed) "By a Brother Lawyer"

This glowing tribute is followed by a series of Resolutions by the members of the Chillicothe Bar. And also elsewhere in the paper is the Call of the School Board for a meeting to fill the membership, a vacancy occurring through the death of Hon. John Cowgill.

Children of John and Rachel Thompson Cowgill:

Martha Agnes, born Feb. 24, 1841 at Greencastle, Indiana
Henry Cowgill, born Oct. 28, 1842 at Greencastle; died Aug. 25, 1895
 Chillicothe, Missouri
Sarah Stevenson Cowgill, born Sept. 27, 1844 at Greencastle
Clara Baxter Cowgill, born Aug. 2, 1847 at Greencastle; died Sept.
 6, 1920 Chillicothe, Missouri
James M. Abshire and Clara Baxter Cowgill married Dec. 18, 1869
 at Chillicothe, Missouri
Frank P. Hearne and Sarah Stevenson Cowgill married at Chilli-
 cothe, Missouri (1st wife)

## MASON COUNTY, KENTUCKY COURT RECORD
### Deed Book 60, Page 253—April 4, 1850

Nancy R. Cowgill, E. T. Cowgill, James Ellison and Martha his wife, William C. White and Mary his wife, B. F. Hagerman and Ann his wife, James Cowgill and Susan his wife, and T. Cowgill by Nancy R. Cowgill his guardian, all of Clark county and State of Missouri, convey to Emanuel Mallenee, John T. Wilson and H. R. Dobyns, officers of Masonic Lodge No. 33, Independent Order of Odd Fellows, of Mayslick, Mason county and State of Kentucky, and their successors, lot of ground in the town of Mayslick on east side of Lexington road on which stands a large frame house. The deed is signed:

James Cowgill
Susan Cowgill
William C. White
Mary R. White
James Ellison and Martha Ellison,
 both of St. Louis, Mo.
Nancy T. Cowgill

B. F. Hagerman
Ann S. Hagerman
Nancy R. Cowgill
Elisha T. Cowgill by his mother
 and guardian, Nancy R. Cowgill

## MINISTERS' BONDS
## MASON COUNTY KENTUCKY COURT RECORDS

(Compiled by Lula Reed Boss, 480 West Second Street,
Maysville, Kentucky)

### June 22, 1790

"On Motion of the Reverend John McClatchey, a minister of the church of England, who entered into and acknowledged bond with John Kenton and David Broderick, sureties."

### November 25, 1790

"On Motion of Henry Burchett, a Methodist Minister, he is permitted to join in holy matrimony such persons as shall apply according to Law; he to give bond and security in the Clerk's Office for his performance. Samuel Strode, surety."

(Wording of all licenses similar to the above)

### December 28, 1790

Isaac Edwards. Baptist Minister. No surety given.

### November Court, 1793

John King. Baptist Minister. No surety given.

### August 23, 1794

Richard Bird (Byrd). Methodist Minister. Robert Armstrong, surety.

### March Court, 1796

John Campbell. Presbyterian Minister. Alexander K. Marshall, surety.

### May Court, 1796

Robert Smith. Baptist Minister. Philemon Thomas, surety.

### July 25, 1796

Benjamin Northcutt. Methodist Minister. Francis Taylor and R. Armstrong, sureties; R. Smith, witness.

### July 26, 1796

Philip Drake. Baptist Minister. Cornelius Drake, surety.

### August Court, 1796

"George Tarvin produced credentials of his Ordination and also of his being in regular Communion with the Dunkard Church took the Oath of Allegiance to this Commonwealth required by an Act of Assembly entitled an Act to regulate the solemnization of marriage and that he is hereby authorized to celebrate the rites of matrimony agreeable to the forms and customs of the said church between any persons to him regularly applying therefor within this State upon his giving security in the Office." Jacob Hoensaker, surety.

October Court, 1796

Simon (Simeon) Walton. Baptist Minister. Lewis Craig, surety.

October Court, 1796

Lewis Craig. Baptist Minister. Simeon Walton, surety.

October Court, 1796

Joseph Moore. Methodist Minister. Simon Fields, surety.

June Court, 1797

Jeremiah Lawson. Methodist Minister. Frederick Dyke (Dike), surety.

September Court, 1797

William Holton. Baptist Minister. No surety given.

October Court, 1797

Thomas Scott. Methodist Minister. This record states that this is a copy, the original being in Lincoln county.

December Court, 1797

Richard McNamara. Presbyterian Minister. No surety given.

December Court, 1797

John Dunlevy. Presbyterian Minister. Sebastian Shrofe, surety.

April Court, 1799

David Thomas. Baptist Minister. James Dobyns, surety.

September Court, 1799

Caleb Jarvis Taylor. Methodist Minister. Austin Reeves and John Petticord sr., sureties.

December Court, 1799

William Ratcliff. Methodist Episcopal Minister. Elijah Hayden and Pearce Lamb, sureties.

July Court, 1800

Charles Anderson. Baptist Minister. Matthew Anderson, surety.

February Court, 1801

John E. Finley. Presbyterian Minister. Richard Applegate, surety.

February Court, 1801

Aaron Stratton, a Justice of the Peace, is appointed to celebrate the Rites of Matrimony agreeable to an Act of Assembly. William Aisles, surety.

March Court, 1802

Robert Wilson. Presbyterian Minister. Thomas Marshall jr., surety. John Campbell and Edward Harris, Elders.

### February Court, 1803

Jacob Greggs (Griggs). Baptist Minister. Nathaniel Hixson, John Johnston, Thomas Young, Cornelius Drake and Donald Holmes, of May's Lick, Kentucky, sureties.

### June Court, 1803

Joshua Singleton. Baptist Minister. William Byram, surety.

### July Court, 1804

Thomas Elrod. Baptist Minister. Samuel Lucas and L. Murdock Cooper, sureties.

### August Court, 1805

William Williamson. Presbyterian Minister. Robert Robb and George Fearis, sureties.

### January Court, 1809

Archibald Alexander. Methodist Minister. Jesse Pepper and Samuel Pickerell, sureties.

### March Court, 1811

William Grinstead. Baptist Minister. James W. Moss and Edmund Martin, sureties.

### March Court, 1812

Henry McDonald. Methodist Minister. Eli Truitt and George Kirk, sureties.

### January Court, 1813

Jesse Holton. Baptist Minister. Thomas Robinson, surety.

### October Court, 1813

Hugh Barnes. Methodist Episcopal Minister. John Merrick and Walker Reed, sureties.

### June Court, 1817

Thomas Erskine Birch. Lutheran Reformed Church. William Bickley and Samuel W. Holloway, sureties.

Samuel West. Methodist Minister. Austin S. Reeves and DeValt Cooper, sureties.

### December Court, 1818

John Allen. Baptist Minister. Benj. B. Hieatt and John vanBuskirk, sureties.

George Mitchell. Methodist Episcopal Minister. Ennis Duncan jr., and Michael Wilson, sureties.

### April Court, 1819

Walter Griffith. Methodist Minister. Austin S. Reeves and Benj. B. Kirk, sureties.

### December Court, 1820

Burwell Spurlock. Methodist Episcopal. William Duff, surety.

January Court, 1821

James Elrod. Baptist Minister. Thomas Robinson and John Chambers, sureties.

May Court, 1821

John T. Edgar. Presbyterian Minister. No surety named.

October Court, 1821

John Pollard. Methodist Episcopal Minister. William Anno and Lorimer Chowning, sureties.

March Court, 1822

Mathew Gardner. Christian Minister. William Jenkins and Edward Railsback, sureties.

April Court, 1823

Timothy McMann. Baptist Minister. Walker Reed and Aaron Houghton, sureties.

October Court, 1823

James Savage. Methodist Episcopal Minister. James W. Coburn and Walker Reed, sureties.

December Court, 1824

Stephan Lindsley. Presbyterian Minister. John Johnson and David V. Rannells, sureties.

January Court, 1825

Thomas Williams. Baptist Minister. Thomas Robinson and Benjamin Flinn, sureties.

November Court, 1825

John Bailey. Baptist Minister. William Byram, surety.

June Court, 1826

Jilson Hambrick. Baptist Minister. Samuel Owens and William Reed, sureties.

November Court, 1827

John W. Riggen. Methodist Episcopal Minister. Simon R. Baker and Enos Woodward, sureties.

January Court, 1829

Thomas J. M. (or A.) Mirres (or Mines). Presbyterian Minister. Lowman L. Hawes and James Ward, sureties.

March Court, 1830

Hector Sanford. Methodist Episcopal Minister. John Orange, surety.

October Court, 1830

John Jacobs. Baptist Minister. William Bean and Walker Reed, sureties.

December Court, 1830

William L. Brackenridge. Presbyterian Minister. William Tinker and Thomas Dye, sureties.

### October Court, 1831

Thomas Hall. Methodist Episcopal Minister. William Tinker and James Byers, surety.

### January Court, 1832

James Phillips. Baptist Minister. Daniel Spalding and Walker Reed, sureties.

### May Court, 1832

Alexander Logan. Episcopal Minister. Thomas Y. Payne and Charles Ward, sureties.

### August Court, 1832

David S. Burnett. Baptist Minister. Walker Reed and Samuel January, sureties.

### January Court, 1832

Lewis D. Howell. Presbyterian Minister. Lewis Collins and Thomas Newman, sureties.

Francis A. Savage. Methodist Episcopal Minister. James Ellis and John W. Franklin, sureties.

Clairbourne Purtle. Methodist Episcopal Minister. Francis A. Savage and Perry Jefferson, sureties.

### May Court, 1833

Richard C. Ricketts. Church of Christ. John Senteney and James Shackleford, sureties.

### November Court, 1833

Richard Deering. Methodist Episcopal Minister. David R. Bullock and Otway P. Peck, sureties.

### December Court, 1833

Aglett (or Aylett) Rains. Church of the Disciples of Jesus Christ; "Ancient Gospel." Walker Reed and Winslow Parker, sureties.

### December Court, 1834

Benjamin Hill. Methodist Episcopal Minister. Francis A. Savage and Alfred H. Pollock (or Pollard), sureties.

### January Court, 1835

John O. Kane. Baptist Church. "Minister of the Ancient Gospel." Larkin A. Sandidge and Levi Vancamp, sureties.

### July Court, 1835

Mason Owens. United Baptist Church. John L. Kirk and Samuel Wells, sureties.

### September Court, 1835

John M. Holton. Church of Christ. William Perrine and Joseph Sprigg Chambers, sureties.

### January Court, 1836

Paradise L. McAboy (or McAvoy). Presbyterian Minister. John Hunter and Charles W. Ritchey, surety.

### July Court, 1836

Robert C. Grundy. Presbyterian Minister. Francis T. Hord and John W. Anderson, sureties.

### September Court, 1836

George W. Sincoe. Methodist Episcopal Minister. George Poynter and John Green, sureties.

### October Court, 1836

Gilbert Mason. Baptist Minister. Jasper S. Morris and Walter Calvert, sureties.

### COURT ORDER BOOK M.

### Page 374—June Court, 1836

"Upon motion of Francis Savage, it is ordered that Richard Soward, Athelstan Owens, William P. Thomas, and Julius G. Coleman be appointed Commissioner to divide the lot on which the Wesleyan Chapel at Minerva is built between the trustees of said church who hold title to part of said land and the heirs of Jacob Winter, to-wit: Jacob M. Winter and Martha Winter, and make report thereof to the next Court."

### December Court, 1838

Stephen A. Rathburn. Methodist Episcopal Minister. Jacob P. Downing and Milton Kirk, sureties.

### January Court, 1839

John Collins. Methodist Episcopal Minister. Otway P. Peck and Richard J. (or I.) Hughey, sureties.

### February Court, 1839

George Harding. Methodist Episcopal Minister. Edward L. Bullock and Marshall Curtis, sureties.

### March Court, 1841

Jasper I. Moss. "Church usually called the Disciples of the Lord." John W. Franklin and Francis T. Hord, sureties.

### November Court, 1841

Ezekiel Forman. Presbyterian Minister. Francis Chambers and John James Key, sureties.

### October Court, 1842

Ezra M. Boring. Methodist Episcopal Minister. James Savage and Samuel Worthington, sureties.

### December Court, 1842

John T. Brooks. Christian Minister. John W. Franklin and Peter Gordon, sureties.

### May Court, 1843

Lewis Jacobs. "Particular Baptist Church of Jesus Christ." Jacob White and Rowland Parker, sureties.

## August Court, 1844

William Hill. Methodist Episcopal Minister. Edward L. Gault and Charles Gordon, sureties.

## September Court, 1844

William Finnelly. Catholic Church. Walker Reed and John Henry, sureties.

The foregoing records were copied from Court Order Books A to N, inclusive, and from Ministers' Bonds in file box, County Clerk's office, Maysville, Mason county, Kentucky.

The following list was copied from old Marriage Book No. 1. Column entitled: "By Whom Married." Listed after each name is the year first appears of record. No. Bonds have been located for same (and some may have been Justices of the Peace.)

| | | | |
|---|---|---|---|
| William Wood | 1793 | Eleazor Johnson | 1812 |
| Richard Durrett | 1795 | William Warder | 1813 |
| James O'Cull | 1796 | James Thompson | 1813 |
| Aquilla Standiford | 1796 | A. G. Houston | 1813 |
| Donald Holmes | 1797 | Hezekiah Smith | 1813 |
| Richard Thomas | 1800 | Joel H. Haden | 1814 |
| David Scott | 1802 | Richard Tilton | 1814 |
| Joseph Morris | 1802 | Eli Truitt | 1814 |
| Peter Hastings | 1802 | Walter Warder | 1815 |
| Stephen Bovell | 1803 | Jonathon Wilson | 1816 |
| William B. Moss | 1804 | Daniel Moss | 1817 |
| William Payne | 1805 | Samuel Helms | 1817 |
| John Parsons | 1806 | Absalom Hunt | 1819 |
| Alexander Monroe | 1808 | James Blair | 1819 |
| Baldwin Clifton | 1808 | Samuel Parker | 1819 |
| Bethwell Riggs | 1811 | William Holman | 1819 |
| Abbott Gedobiad (?) | 1812 | Edward Pattison | 1820 |

## MASON COUNTY, KENTUCKY COURT RECORDS

### Declaration of Pensioners

COURT ORDER BOOK J., Page 24—July Court, 1819

Satisfactory proof was adduced to the Court to show that John Purcell, Jane Pritchard, late Jane Purcell, Mary Hill, late Mary Purcell, Catherine Bergen, late Catherine Purcell, Margaret Gilkerson, late Margaret Purcell, Charles Purcell, Nancy Pritchard, late Nancy Purcell, George Purcell, Malinda Purcell, and Alfred Purcell are the legal heirs and representatives of George Purcell, deceased, late an officer in the Revolutionary War. The said George Purcell was the reputed half-brother of Col. Charles Simms, of Alexandria; that he is the same George Purcell whose Will is of record in this court bearing date of the 5th day of August, 1804. All of which is ordered to be certified to the Secretary of War.

WILL BOOK B., Page 428

Will of George Purcell "of Mason county, Kentucky." Dated: 8-5-1804. Probated: April Court, 1805.

Mentions wife Peggy; daughters, Jane Tevis, Polly, Caty, Nancy, Peggy, Malinda; sons, John, Charles, George, and Alfred Purcell. Wife Peggy and John Randolph and William Bryan, executors. Witnesses: Winslow Parker and Gabriel Phillips.

Jane Purcell married 1st in Mason county, Peter Tevis, 9-1-1802.

Peter Tevis died in Mason county. Estate administered March 19, 1816. (Court Order Book G, pages 423-424) Mrs. Jane (Purcell) Tevis married James Pritchard in Mason county, 9-20-1816.

Deed Book V, page 138, dated March 27, 1819, shows that the widow of George Purcell had married a Mr. ........ Chandley.

### Page 47—October Court, 1819. (War of 1812)

Satisfactory evidence was adduced to the Court to show proof that Margaret Jones, was the widow of the late William Johnson who was enlisted in the army of the United States in the 17th regiment of infantry, and died at Cleveland in the State of Ohio on the 16th day of June, 1813, whilst in the service of the U. S. and that Mary Johnson born on the 23 day of April, 1804, Elizabeth Johnson born 10th day of January, 1805, Nancy Johnson born 4th day of March, 1810 and Lavena Johnson born 8th day of May, 1812, are the children and legitimate heirs of the said William Johnson, deceased. Whereupon the said heirs being all infants under the age of 16 years, William Murphy is appointed their guardian, upon his giving security whereupon he together with Athelstan Owens his security, executed and acknowledged bond in the penalty of $500 conditioned by law which is ordered to be certified to the Secretary of State.

### Page 75—January Court, 1820

Daniel Morgan came into court and proved that Armstead H. Morgan, and Susannah Fike, late Susannah Morgan, who is the present wife of Elijah Fike, are the reputed children and only children and heirs at law of Jeremiah Morgan, deceased, an officer in the Revolutionary War, and who was the reputed brother of General Simon Morgan, deceased, which is ordered to be certified to the Secretary of War.

### Page 103—June Court, 1820

Gives the same information, with this additional: The Will of Jeremiah Morgan, dated June 17, 1795, is recorded in Logan county, Kentucky, and copy of same was produced in court and that Jeremiah Morgan died intestate as to any Revolutionary Bounty Land he might have been entitled to for his services as an officer in that war all of which is ordered to be certified to the Secretary of War.

### Page 135—September Court, 1820

Benjamin Fitzgerald produced in open court a declaration in conformity with the Act of Congress in that case made and provided; which, having been duly sworn to in open court it is ordered to be filed among the records of this court. It is further ordered that it be certified to the Secretary of War that this court is of the opinion from the evidence produced by said Benjamin Fitzgerald that the property set forth in the schedule is of the value of $25.

Pension Claim No. S 35931 gives that Benjamin Fitzgerald was aged 65 in 1818; that he enlisted from Montgomery county, Maryland, 2-11-1777; was discharged at Fredericktown, Maryland. In 1820, he stated that his wife was lame and very old.

### Page 163—January Court, 1821

Francis McDermed (McDermitt) produced in open court a declaration in conformity with the Act of Congress in that case made and provided, which having been duly sworn to in open court is ordered to be filed among the records of this court. It is further ordered that it is to be certified to the Secretary of War that this court is of the opinion from the evidence of the said Francis McDermed and George Shepherd, sworn in open court, that the property set forth in the schedule is of the value of $73.

### Page 174—February Court, 1821

Abiah Hukill produced in court a declaration in conformity with the Act of Congress in that case made and provided, which was sworn to in open court and ordered to be filed among the records of this court. It is further ordered that it be certified to the Secretary of War that this court is of the opinion from the evidence of the said Abiah Hukill sworn in open court that he possesses no property other than as is stated in his said declaration.

### Page 193—June Court, 1821

Satisfactory proof was adduced to the court shewing that Sally Collins, wife of Edmund Collins, late Sally Kenton, is the heir-at-law and only child of Mark Kenton, deceased. It was also proven to the Court that the said Mark Kenton was a commissioned officer, but of what grade not ascertained, and that he served at least five years, and was discharged at the close of the Revolutionary War and that he died in the year 1785 all of which is ordered to be certified to the Secretary of War.

Sally Kenton married in Mason county, 4-17-1800, Edmund Collins. Elizabeth Kenton signed as the mother of Sally. Samuel Dunham signed as bondsman.

### Page 204—July Court, 1821

Abiah Hukill produced in open court his declaration which had been formally certified to the Secretary of War and proved by William Reed and Squire Frazee that the property contained in the said schedule is not worth more than the sum of $77.87½ and the court being satisfied that the sum is the full value of said property it is ordered that the same be certified to the Secretary of War.

Abiah Hukill was aged 62 years in 1821. Enlisted from Virginia in Lee's Legion of Horse. In 1818, he was residing in Bracken county, Kentucky; in 1821 he was living in Mason county. Pension Claim: No. S 35439, Maryland.

### Page 222—October Court, 1821

Samuel DeHart produced in court his certain declaration of service whilst in the army of the United States in the late Revolutionary War and swore to the same in open court which is ordered to be certified to the Secretary of War.

### Page 242—January Court, 1822

George Maines produced in court a declaration in conformity to the Act of Congress in that case made and provided and swore to the same in open court, which is ordered to be filed and it is ordered to be certified to the Secretary of War that the court is of the opinion from the evidence of Phillip Maines, sworn to in open court, that the property contained in said declaration is of the value of $107.87½.

### Page 242—January Court, 1822

James Rice produced in court a declaration in conformity to the Act of Congress in that case made and provided and swore to the same in open court, which is ordered to be filed and it is further ordered to be certified to the Secretary of War that this court is of the opinion from the evidence of Samuel Rice, sworn to in open court, that the property contained in said declaration is of the value of $00.

### Page 323—February Court, 1823

James Rice produced in court a declaration and schedule in conformity to the Act of Congress in that case made and provided for the purpose of obtaining a pension from the United States and swore to the same in open court, which is ordered to be certified to the Secretary of War. It is further ordered that it be certified that this court is of the opinion from the evidence of Samuel Rice, sworn to in open court, that the property stated in said schedule is of the value of $50.12½.

## COURT ORDER BOOK K

### Page 149—September Court, 1824

Satisfactory proof was introduced to the court showing that Samuel DeHart, late a private in the army of the Revolution, and inscribed on the pension list, Roll of the Pennsylvania Agency, at the rate of $8 per month, departed this life on the 21st day of May, 1824, and that administration of his estate was this day granted to Jacob Boone, which is ordered to be certified to the Secretary of War. See: Pension Claim No. 335892, Pennsylvania.

## COURT ORDER BOOK H

### Page 19—July Court, 1816 (War of 1812)

Satisfactory evidence was adduced to the court to shew that John Hamilton is brother of and legitimate heir-at-law of Benjamin N. Hamilton, late a soldier in the first United States Rifle Regiment, which is ordered to be recorded and certified to the Secretary of War.

### Page 19—July Court, 1816 (War of 1812)

Satisfactory evidence was adduced to the court to shew that Margaret Tible is the widow and the heir-at-law of Richard Tible, late a soldier of the first regiment of Riflemen in the United States Army, which is ordered to be recorded and certified to the Secretary of War.

### Page 19—July Court, 1816 (War of 1812)

Satisfactory evidence was adduced to the court to shew that Henry Riely is son of and legitimate heir-at-law of Jesse Riely, late a soldier of the First U. S. Rifle Regiment, which is ordered to be recorded and certified to the Secretary of War.

### Page 39—October Court, 1816 (War of 1812)

Satisfactory evidence was adduced to the court to shew that Finetta Murrah is the daughter and legitimate heir-at-law of Joseph Murrah, deceased, late a soldier in the First Regiment of Riflemen in the service of the United States which is ordered to be recorded and certified to the Secretary of War.

### Page 40—October Court, 1816

Administration of the estate of Joseph Murrah, deceased, granted Margaret Murrah. Charles Purcell, surety in the sum of $200.

### Page 123—October Court, 1817 (War of 1812)

Satisfactory evidence was adduced to the court to shew that Harry Martin is father of and legitimate heir-at-law of Fields Martin, late a soldier of the First Regiment of U. S. Infantry, who it would appear died at Erie in September, 1815, while in the service of the U. S. and who enlisted in said service for five years with Captain Henry R. Graham in Washington, (Mason county) Kentucky on the 18th day of May, 1812. All of which is ordered to be recorded and certified to the Secretary of War.

### Page 135—October Court, 1817 (War of 1812)

Satisfactory evidence was produced to the court to shew that Margaret Botts is the widow of Richard Botts, deceased, and that John Botts, Nancy Botts, Lucy Botts, Benjamin Botts and Barnabas Botts are the children and legitimate heirs-at-law of said Richard Botts, late a soldier of the 17th Regiment in the service of the U. S. enlisted to serve during the War, and that said Botts died at Niagara while in the service which is ordered to be certified to the Secretary of War.

### Page 137—October Court, 1817 (War of 1812)

Satisfactory evidence was adduced to the court to shew that John Betty is the father of and the legitimate heir-at-law of John Betty, deceased, late a soldier in the First Rifle Regiment in the U. S. service; that he died in the service of the U. S. and the same is orderd to be certified to the Secretary of War.

### Page 147—December Court, 1817 (War of 1812)

Satisfactory evidence was adduced to the court to shew that John McCew, Selina McCew, Edward McCew, and William McCew, infant children under the age of 16 years are four of the legitimate children and heirs-at-law of Edward McCew, late a soldier in the service of the U. S. belonging to the 19th Regiment, and that said McCew was killed at Ft. Meigs and that John Hughey is their guardian, which is ordered to be certified to the Secretary of War.

### Page 175—February Court, 1818 (War of 1812)

Satisfactory evidence was adduced to the court to shew that Joseph Robb is father of and legitimate heir-at-law of William Mac or McRobb, late a soldier of the army of the U. S. and who enlisted with Captain Henry R. Graham in Washington, (Mason county) Kentucky on the 13th day of May, 1812, for five years and who died whilst in the service of the U. S., which is ordered to be certified to the Secretary of War.

### Page 186—March Court, 1818 (War of 1812)

Satisfactory evidence was adduced to the court to shew that Jacob Applegate is father of and legitimate heir-at-law of Nicholas Applegate, deceased, a soldier in the U. S. Army, who enlisted with Captain Henry R. Graham in Washington, (Mason county) Kentucky on the 26th day of March, 1812, to serve for five years, and who died in the service of the U. S. at Belfontaine on the Missouri about February, 1814, whilst attached to the company of Captain Hamilton of the First Infantry, all of which is ordered to be recorded and certified to the Secretary of War.

### Page 231—July Court, 1818 (War of 1812)

Satisfactory evidence was adduced to the court to shew that Mary Jefferson is the widow and legitimate heir-at-law of James Jefferson, late a soldier in the First Rifle Regiment of the U. S., and that the said James Jefferson was killed while in the service of the U. S. at Dudley's Defeat near Ft. Meigs in May, 1813, which is ordered to be certified to the Secretary of War.

### Page 254—October Court, 1818 (War of 1812)

Mary Kilpatrick, widow of Hugh Kilpatrick, late a private soldier in the Company of Militia of Mason County commanded by Captain John Baker of the 10th Regiment of Kentucky Militia commanded by Colonel ........ Boswell, proved her marriage with said Kilpatrick by the oaths of John Reed and William Reed who were present at the marriage and Major John Baker, late Captain, that the said Kilpatrick died upon his return from the army in the year 181-, having served his tour of six months, that he the said Captain, was not present at his death, but passed the place where he was buried on the road from Ft. Meigs to Kentucky a few days after his death. The said witnesses proved that said Mary Kilpatrick had two children living, one about 8 and one about 5 years of age. All of which is ordered to be certified to the Honorable Secretary of War.

## COURT ORDER BOOK K

### Page 13—April Court, 1823 (War of 1812)

Satisfactory proof was introduced to court shewing that Alexander Bratton is the only child and heir-at-law of Davis Bratton, deceased, late a soldier in the Army of the U. S. and who enlisted at the town of Washington, (Mason county) Kentucky, under Captain Henry R. Graham all of which is ordered to be certified to the Secretary of War.

### Page 73—December Court, 1823

Samuel DeHart produced his declaration and schedule and swore to the same in open court which is ordered to be filed and it is ordered that a copy thereof be certified to the Secretary of War. He also proved by the oath of Jacob Boone that he the said DeHart is destitute of any property of any kind which is also ordered to be certified to the Secretary of War.

### Page 336—August Court, 1826

Satisfactory proof was introduced to the court shewing that Rachel Reardon, Philip Reardon, Milton Reardon and Ann Reardon, are children and only heirs-at-law and legal representatives of James Reardon, deceased, who was entitled to 50 acres of land by virtue of a Virginia Military Warrant and entered and surveyed, which is ordered to be certified. Military Warrant No. 12442.

## COURT ORDER BOOK L

### Page 445—September Court, 1831

Satisfactory evidence was adduced to the court to prove that Thomas Young, Robert Young, Willoughby T. Young and Margaret Cooke, late Margaret Young, are the children and heirs-at-law of Robert Young, deceased, and who was said to be an officer in the Virginia Continental Lines during the Revolution, and who died intestate, which is ordered to be certified accordingly. See Pension Claim No. S 11921—Virginia.

### Page 529—August Court, 1832

Thomas Morris, John Salmon and William Devin respectfully produced in Court and subscribed and swore to the following written statement or declaration of their respective services as soldiers in the war of the Revolution, in order to obtain the benefits of the provision made by the Act of Congress passed June 7, 1832, which was ordered to be certified to the Secretary of War of the United States. And sundry witnesses being sworn and examined, the court does hereby declare its opinion that the said applicants were soldiers of the Revolution and served as stated by them.

## COURT ORDER BOOK M

### Page 2—September Court, 1832

Satisfactory proof was introduced to the court shewing that William I. Barker, Edmund B. Barker, Lucinda C. Barker, Joseph D. Barker, Simon M. Barker, and Maria M. Barker are the only heirs of William Barker, deceased, and that William Barker intermarried with Mary Ann Seal Markham, daughter of the late Captain James Markham, and it is ordered that the same be certified to the proper office.

### Page 3—September Court, 1832

Satisfactory proof being introduced to the court shewing that Captain James Markham, deceased, had four children, to-wit: Elizabeth Markham who intermarried with Nimrod Combs; Mary Ann Seal Markham who intermarried with William Barker; Anna M. Markham who intermarried with George Goode, and James L. Markham. And that Mary Ann Seal Barker is now living in Mason county, Kentucky, and that all the other children are dead, which is ordered to be certified to the proper office.

### Page 4—September Court, 1832

Abraham Williams produced his declaration with the deposition of George Briarly attached and the certificates of Walker Reid and Conquest W. Owens attached thereto, which were sworn to in open court; and the court after an investigation of the matter is of the opinion that he said Abraham Williams was a Revolutionary officer and served as he stated. And George Briarly, Walker Reid and Conquest W(yatt) Owens are credible persons, and their statements are entitled to credit.

Abraham Williams, born 1747 Baltimore (now Harford) county, Maryland; served as 2nd Lieut. 1776 under Capt. Benjamin Amos. See: Pension Claim "Maryland Survivor."

### Page 4—September Court, 1832

George Brierley (Briarly) produced his declaration with deposition of Abraham Williams and the certificate of Thomas Mountjoy and George Mefford attached thereto, which were sworn to in open court. And the court after an investigation of the matter is of the opinion that the said George Brierly was a Revolutionary soldier and served as he states, and that the said Abraham Williams, Thomas Mountjoy and George Mefford are credible persons and their statements are entitled to credit.

George Brierly, born 1757; died Bracken county, Kentucky, 9-30-1833; enlisted from Harford county, Maryland, and served under Capt. Benj. Amos and Second Lieutenant Abraham Williams. In 1853 Mary, widow of George Brierly, was living in Bracken county, Ky. George Brierly married 3-27-1793 Mary Garrison (born 1761) Mary Brierly was living as late as 11-22-1856 (Pension Claim No. R 1196, Maryland)

### Page 7—October Court, 1832

Thomas Kirk produced his declaration with the depositions of William Kirk and Benjamin Kirk attached thereto, which were sworn to in open court, and the court after an investigation of the matter is of the opinion that the said Thomas Kirk was a Revolutionary soldier and served as he states, and that William and Benjamin Kirk are credible persons and their statements are entitled to credit. Which is ordered to be certified to the proper office.

Thomas Kirk, born 1759; enlisted from Frederick county, Maryland in 1776. (See: Pension Claim No. S 31188—Maryland)

### Page 25—January Court, 1833

Michael David produced his declaration with the deposition of Marshall Key and Charles Ward attached thereto, which were sworn to in open court, and the court after an investigation of the matter is of the opinion that the said Michael David was a Revolutionary soldier and served as he stated and that the said Marshall Key and Charles Ward are credible persons and their statements are entitled to credit.

Michael David, born 1763 in Frederick county, Maryland; enlisted from Shenandoah county, Virginia. (Pension Claim No. S 12729—Virginia)

### Page 111—October Court, 1833

Satisfactory proof was this day, Oct. 14, 1833, made in open court by the oaths of Marshall Key, Conquest W. Owens and John S. David, that Michael David, deceased, late a pensioner of the U. S. departed this life on the 3rd day of June, 1833, and that the said Michael David was the identical person named in an original certificate, now here shewn to the court, bearing date of May 13, 1833, and signed by Lewis Cass, Secretary of War, granting to said Michael David a pension of $26.66 per annum and numbered ..... And it is further satisfactorily proven to the satisfaction of the court that Celia David is the widow of the said Michael David, deceased, and that she is now living.

### Page 29—January Court, 1833

Jarrett Burton produced his declaration with the deposition of Anderson Doniphan, and the certificate of George Grant and Charles Ward attached thereto, which were sworn to in open court. And the court after an investigation of the matter is of the opinion that the said Jarrett Burton was a Revolutionary soldier and served as he stated. And that the said Anderson Doniphan, George Grant and Charles Wilkerson are credible persons, and their statements are entitled to credit.

Note: In one place the record gives Charles Ward—at the end says "Charles Wilkerson." Pension Claim gives Charles Wilkerson.

Jarrett Burton, born 1759; served from Virginia. Pension Claim No. R 1517—Virginia.

### Page 30—January Court, 1833

James Ireland produced his declaration with the deposition of Elizabeth Waugh, and the statements of Winslow Parker and George Grant attached thereto, which were sworn to in open court. And the court after an investigation of the matter is of the opinion that the said James Ireland was a Revolutionary soldier and served as stated and that the said Elizabeth Waugh, Winslow Parker, and George Grant are credible persons and their statements are entitled to credit.

Page 32—January Court, 1833

Peter Hargate produced his declaration with the deposition of Thomas P. Thomas (clergyman) and Lewis Craig attached thereto, which were sworn to in open court, and the court, after an investigation of the matter, is of the opinion that the said Peter Hargate was a Revolutionary soldier and served as he states. And that Thomas P. Thomas and Lewis Craig are credible persons and their statements entitled to credit.

Sgt. Peter Hargate, born 7-25-1754 in Liberty county, S. C.; removed to Mechlenburg county, N. C., in 1764. A letter written from Paris, Kentucky on 10-10-1849, stated that he died 11-24-1837, and that he married Molly Ford Easton on 2-26-1817. Pension Claim No. S 31096, North Carolina.

COURT ORDER BOOK M, Page 517—December Court, 1837

Last Will and Testament of Peter Hargate, deceased, produced in court and sworn to by Mary Hargate, the executrix.

COURT ORDER BOOK M, Page 530—February Court, 1838

Mrs. Mary Hargate the executrix named in the last Will and Testament of Peter Hargate, deceased, offered to prove in court by Mrs. Elizabeth Gray, one of the subscribing witnesses to said Will, the same so as to admit the Will of record, which proof was objected to by John H. Craig, Mary T. Craig and David W. McGhee and Nancy his wife, who claim part of the estate of the said Peter Hargate as his heirs-at-law, and contested the validity of said Will, and upon their motion the question of admitting the said Will to record is continued until the next court at their costs. And upon their motion it is ordered that a dedimus be awarded them to take the deposition of Mrs. Mary Pattie, Mrs. Mary Craig, and Mrs. Mary Levi, to be read in evidence in this case, upon their giving to the said Mary Hargate reasonable notice of the time and place of taking same. And upon the further motion, it is ordered than an attachment issue herein against Mrs. Hannah Levi and Mrs. Mary Elrod, directed to the sheriff of Bracken county, Kentucky, for a contempt offered the court in failing to attend as witnesses when summoned by the sheriff and that they be held to bail in the sum of $50 each with one security each.

WILL BOOK L—Page 217

Will of Peter Hargate. Dated: 3-20-1837—Probated: Dec. Court, 1837.

Leaves to "wife Mary during her natural life or widowhood" all real and personal estate "except as much as is hereafter bequeathed." In case Mary should marry then she is to have but one-third of estate; to daughter, Judith Helen Frazee; son Henry Augustine Hargate; daughter Nancy McGhee one dollar. Witnesses: F. A. Savage and Elizabeth Gray.

David McGee and John H. Craig orders the Sheriff to take charge of the estate of Peter Hargate until further notice as it is their intention to contest the Will. January Court, 1838.

## COURT ORDER BOOK N—Page 4

David McGee and Nancy his wife, and John H. Craig and Mary T., his wife, paid to Robert Elrod $1.50; Polly Elrod $1.94, and Hannah Levi $1.00 for serving as witnesses.

## COURT ORDER BOOK M

### Page 33—January Court, 1833

Satisfactory proof was produced in court that Thomas Williams, Sarah Fox, late Sarah Williams, and Elizabeth Faw are the legal heirs and only representatives of Thomas Williams, deceased, late of the town of Washington, Mason county, Kentucky, which is ordered to be certified.

### Page 42—February Court, 1833

William Peck produced his declaration with the deposition of John Peck and the certificate of James Ward and Charles Ward attached, which were sworn to in open court, and the court, after an investigation of the matter, is of the opinion that the said William Peck was a Revolutionary soldier and served as he states, and that the said John Peck, Charles Ward, and James Ward are credible persons and their statements are entitled to credit, which is ordered to be certified to the proper office.

### Page 42—February Court, 1833

John Lancey produced his declaration with the certificate of James Taylor and Stephen Wilson attached thereto, which were sworn to in open court, and the court, after an investigation of the matter, is of the opinion that the said John Lancey was a Revolutionary soldier and served as he states and that James Taylor and Stephen Wilson are credible persons and their statements are entitled to credit.

### Page 53—April Court, 1833

Satisfactory evidence was adduced to the court to prove that John A. Bean, Harrison Bean, William G. Bean, John Crutcher and Letitia his wife, formerly Letitia Bean, Joseph Tolle and Charlotte his wife, formerly Charlotte Bean, Frank McClure and Matilda his wife, formerly Matilda Bean, and Fanny Bean are the children of Leonard Bean and Eda his wife, deceased, formerly Eda Kilgour, are the only heirs at law in fee to William Kilgour, late a private with the First Maryland Regiment of the Revolutionary War.

Leonard Bean also was a Revolutionary soldier. He was born in 1758; enlisted from Maryland in 1777. His wife, Eda Kilgour, was born in 1760. See: Pension Claim S. 35189—Maryland and Sea Service.

COURT ORDER BOOK P, Page 8—June Court, 1851

Estate of Leonard Bean, deceased.

William G(allenous) Bean and John A(lbert) Bean, administrators.

## COURT ORDER BOOK M

### Page 56—April Court, 1833

John A. Bean and James Ireland personally appeared in open court and made oath that Benjamin Cole whose name is inscribed on the pension list of the Kentucky Agency, and whose certificate signed by I. C. Calhoun and dated July 21, 1819, is hereto annexed; departed this life on the 12th day of July, 1832, at his residence in the county of Mason, and that Elizabeth Cole, who has assigned the annexed Power of Attorney to John A. Bean, is the widow of the said Benjamin Cole.

Benjamin Cole, born 1750; died 7-12-1832; enlisted from Fredericktown, Maryland in 1778; married in Washington county, Maryland, 11-15-1784, Elizabeth Long (born 1760) and was living as late as 7-1-1848. See: Pension Claim W 3000, Maryland. Bounty Land Warrants 13441-160-55.

### Page 58—May Court, 1833

John Salmon produced in addition to his declaration made at the last August court, and swore to the same in open court. And it is ordered to be certified that there is not now and was not at the last August term, any clergyman residing in the town of Washington, and that Thomas Morris, Moses Fowler and Thomas Peck, whose testimony is appended to the above declaration of John Salmon made at the last August term subscribed and sworn to the same in open court, and that they were persons of good character and entitled to full credit as witnesses.

John Salmon, born 1754; died Mason county, 9-21-1841; enlisted from Monmouth county, N. J. He came to Kentucky in 1795. See: Pension Claim No. S 30686 New Jersey.

### Page 58—May Court, 1833

Thomas Morris produced an addition to his declaration made at the last August term of court and swore to the same in open court. And it is ordered to be certified that there is not now, and was not at the last August term any Clergyman residing in the town of Washington and that John Salmon, and Titus Bennett, whose testimony is appended to the above declaration, of the said Thomas Morris made at the last August court, gave, subscribed, and made oath to their statements in open court and that they are persons of good character and are entitled to full credit as witnesses.

Thomas Morris, born 1750; enlisted from New Jersey. Came to Kentucky about 1788-1789. See: Pension Claim No. S 30597, New Jersey.

### Page 72—July Court, 1833

Moses Fritter produced his Declaration with the deposition of Elizabeth Thornton ("she knew the pensioner in Stafford county Virginia") and the affidavit of Robert Thornton and John W. Franklin attached thereto which were sworn to in open court. And the court after an investigation of the matter, is of the opinion that the said Moses Fritter was a Revolutionary soldier and served as stated, and that the said Elizabeth Thornton, Robert Thornton and John W. Franklin are credible persons and that their statements are entitled to credit.

Moses Fritter, born Stafford county, Virginia, 1755; served from Stafford county, 1778; removed from that county to Pennsylvania, thence to Kentucky; later removed to Ohio, and then back to Mason county. See: Pension Claim No. S 1201, Virginia.

### Page 95—September Court, 1833

John Love produced his Declaration with the affidavit of Thomas Newman and Nicholas D. Coleman and John V. Lovely attached thereto, which were sworn to in open court. And the court after an investigation of the matter, is of the opinion that the said John Love was a Revolutionary soldier and served as stated, and that the said Thomas Newman, Nicholas D. Coleman and John V. Lovely are credible persons and that their statements are entitled to credit.

### Page 160—February Court, 1834

William Allen produced his declaration with the certificate of Walter Warder and Jasper S. Morris attached thereto, which were sworn to in open court. And the court after an investigation of the matter, is of the opinion that the said William Allen was a Revolutionary soldier and served as stated, and that the said Walter Warder is a clergyman, resident of the county of Mason and that the said Walter Warder and Jasper S. Morris are credible persons and that their statements are entitled to credit.

William Allen, born 1758, died Mason county, Kentucky, May, 1839; married "August 8, after the close of the Revolutionary War," Frances Pepper in Fauquier county, Virginia. Frances Pepper was born 1762. See: Pension Claim No. W 8318— Virginia.

### Page 174—April Court, 1834

John Baldwin produced in court his declaration with the affidavits of Richard C. Ricketts and John Ricketts and the deposition of Joshua Davidson, resident of Fleming county, Kentucky, attached thereto, which declaration and certificate were sworn to in open court. And the court after an investigation of the matter is of the opinion that the said John Baldwin was a Revolutionary soldier and served as stated, and that the said Richard C. Ricketts and John Ricketts are credible persons and that their statements are entitled to credit.

John Baldwin, born 1762, Amelia county, Virginia; enlisted from Virginia in 1780; re-enlisted 1781 from Amelia county, Va. See: Pension Claim No. S 37733—Virginia.

### Page 175—April Court, 1834

Samuel Strode and Ann Strode came personally into court and proved that they are well acquainted with David Williams, late an officer in the Virginia lines in the Revolutionary War and with Thomas Williams, late of the town of Washington (Mason county), and that the said David Williams and Thomas Williams are brothers, and they know them from their boyhood up to the time of their death; that David Williams died without children many years ago; that Thomas Williams died in the town of Washington about two years ago, leaving Thomas Williams, Sally Fox, late Sally Williams, and Elizabeth Faw, daughter of Nancy Faw, late Nancy Williams, as his heirs.

### Page 200—October Court, 1834

William Reed and James Reed appeared in open court and proved that Apolos Cooper, late a Lieutenant in the Revolutionary War, was killed at the Battle of Drandywine (September 11, 1777) and that at the time of his death he left a widow named Mary and three children to-wit: Robert Cooper, Sarah Cooper, and Jacob Cooper; that Robert Cooper died many years ago without any legitimate children, leaving Jacob and Sarah his heirs-at-law; that Sarah intermarried with James Dobyns; he died in the month of July, last, and that Jacob Cooper and Sarah Dobyns are both living in the State of Kentucky; that Mary the widow of the said Appollos Cooper intermarried with one William Stoker; that both Stoker and his wife have been dead several years. Upon motion of the said Jacob Cooper and Sarah Dobyns it is ordered that the above proof be certified to the proper office.

Lieut. Appollos Cooper married Mary Reed, sister of William and James Reed. The heirs of Lieut. Cooper were awarded 2666 2/3 acres of land (Land Office Military Warrant No. 4338). The balance of pay due Lieut. Cooper after his death, was paid to Col. Levin Powell, of Loudoun county, Virginia, to be given to Cooper's heirs.

Mary (Reed) Cooper was the daughter of Major Jacob Reed and his wife, Rebecca (Claypole), of Loudoun county, Virginia.

### Page 207—November Court, 1834

Satisfactory evidence was produced in open court that William B. Lurty, Moore Lurty, Robert Lurty and Mary Ann Proctor, were the only heirs of John Lurty, a Lieutenant in the Virginia State Navy, that Robert Lurty is dead and left two heirs, William and Elizabeth Lurty; that Mary Ann Proctor is dead and left ten heirs, namely: Notley, Newton, William, George, John, Larkin, Patsey and Hannah Proctor and Fanny Stephenson and Lucy Ann Wood, wives of ——— Stephenson and Baker G. Wood; that Moore Lurty is dead and left children in

Virginia, and that these are the only heirs of Lieut. John Lurty of the Virginia Navy, and the same is ordered to be certified.

Captain John Lurty, Navy, was awarded 4,000 acres of land. He served as Lieut. on the Dragon April 17, 1777 to May 3, 1778, and was commissioned 1st Lieut. of the Page, August 2, 1776. He married Rose Bronough, daughter of Captain David Bronough (born ca. 1700; died 1774, King George county, Virginia). David Bronough was Captain of King George County Militia, 1752.

### COURT ORDER BOOK L, Page 115—October Court, 1828

Estate of John Lurty, deceased.
John Reed, administrator. William Reed, surety.

### COURT ORDER BOOK M

#### Page 273—July Court, 1835

Daniel Bell produced his declaration and swore to the same in open court, also the deposition of George M. Bedinger and the certificate of Walter Warder, Levi Vancamp, Marshall Key, Daniel Runyan and Winslow Parker, all sworn to in open court, which is ordered to be certified to the Secretary of War.

#### Page 290—September Court, 1835

Satisfactory evidence being produced to the court that John Harle, William Harle, George W. G. Harle, Hippocrates Harle, Baldwin Harle, Leander Harle and Noah Harle are the legal heirs and representatives of John Harle, deceased, and that the same be certified to the proper authorities.

#### Page 353—March Court, 1836

Daniel Bell produced his declaration and the same having been sworn to at a former Court by him and that the statement of George M. Bedinger, Walter Warder, Levi Vancamp, Marshall Key, Daniel Runyan and Winslow Parker was also sworn to at the same time. The court is of the opinion that the said Daniel Bell is entitled to a pension and that the statements of the said George M. Bedinger and others are entitled to full credit all of which is ordered to be certified to the proper office of the Government.

Daniel Bell, born Stafford County, Virginia, 4-14-1765; died Mason county, Kentucky. Enlisted from Stafford county, Virginia, 1779. See Pension Claim No. S 30271, Virginia.

Tombstone Inscription from May's Lick cemetery, Mason county, Kentucky: "Daniel Bell, a Soldier of the Revolution—died Jan. 21, 1849 in 87th year of his age."

#### Page 403—September Court, 1836

Satisfactory proof was made in open court by the oaths of John Hall and Marshall Rankin that William Rankin, late a pensioner of the U. S., departed this life on the 12th day of April, 1836, and that the said William Rankin was the identical person named in an orginal certificate, now here to the court shewn bearing date the 18th day of December, 1833, and signed by Lewis Cass, Secretary of War, granting to said William Rankin a pension of $80 per annum and numbered 25274, and it was further proved to the satisfaction of the court that Mary Ann Rankin, the widow of the said William Rankin, died on the 29th day of July, 1836. It was also proven in court that Harrison Rankin, Blackstone H. Rankin, James M. Rankin, John L. Rankin, Robert P. Rankin, Thomas Rankin, Elizabeth who intermarried with John Hall, Sarah Rankin who has intermarried with James Rankin, Harriett Rankin who has intermarried with George D. Stockton, Ann who has intermarried with Wyatt Webb and Caroline who has inter-married with George W. Stockton, are children of the said William Rankin, deceased, above described, which is ordered to be certified to the Secretary of War.

William Rankin, born 1758/59; served from Berkeley county, Virginia; married Mary Ann Reed (born 1768—died 7-29-1836) about 1790. See: Pension Claim No. S 31315 and Bounty Land warrant No. 1483.

### Page 409—October Court, 1836

Satisfactory evidence was produced to the court by the oaths of George Shepherd and Alexander R. Bullock that George Shepherd, a pensioner of the U. S., departed this life on the 6th day of May, 1836, and that the said Mary Ann Shepherd is the widow of the said George Shepherd, and that he is the same person named in a certificate issued from the War Office dated the 13th day of November, 1832, which is ordered to be certified to the Secretary of War. See: Pension Claim No. W 8723, Virginia.

### Page 410—October Court, 1836

John McAdow produced his declaration to obtain a pension under the Act of June 7, 1832, with the certificates attached thereto of William Turner and Benjamin Bean which were sworn to by the said John McAdow, William Turner and Benjamin Bean. And the said court do hereby declare their opinion after the investigation of the mat-ter and after putting the questions prescribed by the War Department, that the said John McAdow was a Revolutionary soldier and served as he states. And the court further certifies that it appears to them that William Turner and Benjamin Bean, who have signed the foregoing certificates are residents of Mason county and are credible persons and that their statements are entitled to credit, which is ordered to be cer-tified on the back of said declaration to the Secretary of War. See: Pension Claim No. 6581, Maryland: John McAdow.

### COURT ORDER BOOK N, Page 31—August Court, 1838

Administration of the estate of John McAdow granted John McAdow, Larkin A. Sandidge and David Lindsay, surety as conditioned by law.

## COURT ORDER BOOK M

### Page 521—January Court, 1838

Satisfactory evidence has been exhibited to the court that William Peck was a pensioner of the U. S. at the rate of 20 dollars per annum, was a resident of Mason county and State of Kentucky and died in the said county on the 15th day of February, 1837, and that he left a widow who still survives him and whose name is Susan Peck.

## COURT ORDER BOOK N

### Page 2—March Court, 1838 (War of 1812)

Satisfactory evidence was produced to the court to prove that James Martin who enlisted in the army of the U. S. in the year 1812 in a company then or afterwards commanded by Capt. Augus Sangan resided at the time of his enlistment in the county of Adams, State of Ohio and enlisted at Bainbridge, county of Ross and State of Ohio, and that he left a family at his residence when he went into the service. That the said James Martin has never returned, that he died in the service or was killed at the Battle of River Raisin and that John G. Martin is the son and only child and heir-at-law in fee of the said James Martin, late a private of the 19th Regiment of U. S. Infantry. All of which is ordered to be certified to the proper office in the city of Washington.

### Page 29—July Court, 1838

Edward Dulin came into court and proved that James B. Carter, now of the City of Maysville, is one of the heirs of Dr. Thomas Carter, deceased, late of Virginia, who was a surgeon in the Revolutionary War and he is personally cognizant that the said James B. Carter has heretofore received his proportion of half pay as one of the heirs of the said Dr. Thomas Carter, dec.

### Page 78—April Court, 1839

Mary Ann Shepherd produced a declaration under the pension law of the U. S. and swore to the same in open court, she also produced the statement of James O'Cull, Rowland T. Parker and George Shepherd, which were all sworn to in open court. The court is of the opinion that the facts stated in the foregoing papers are true and that the said Mary Ann Shepherd is entitled to a pension which is ordered to be certified to the Secretary of War.

Pension Claim shows that Mary Ann Shepherd was Mary Ann McDermed (McDermitt)

### Page 144—January Court, 1840

Mary Ann Shepherd produced a declaration under the pensions law of the U. S. and swore to the same in open court; she also produced the statements of Rowland T. Parker, George Shepherd and Henry Lee, which were all sworn to in open court. The court is of the opinion that the facts stated in the foregoing papers are true and that the said

Mary Ann Shepherd is entitled to a pension which is ordered to be certified to the Secretary of War.

### Page 148—January Court, 1840

Satisfactory proof was this day made in open court by the oath of————, that John Love of Mason county, Kentucky, late a private of the U. S. departed this life on the 9th day of March, 1839, and that the said John Love was the identical person named in an original certificate now here shown in court bearing date of February 2, 1836, and signed by Lewis Cass, Secretary of War, granting the said John Love a pension of $40 per annum and it was further proved to the satisfaction of the court that the said John Love departed this life leaving no wife and that Edward L. Bullock was appointed administrator of the said deceased for the purpose of drawing the balance of his pension that was due up to the day of his death.

### Page 190—September Court, 1840

Satisfactory proof was made to the court by the oaths of John Chambers and Marshall Key that William Bickley, late of Mason county, Kentucky, was a pensioner of the U. S. and departed this life on the 13th day of August, 1840, and that the said William Bickley is the identical person named in a pension certificate, now before them, signed by Lewis Cass, Secretary of War, dated 4th day of February, 1834, for the sum of $80 per annum. That the said William Bickley died without any wife living and left William Bickley, Jr., his child his heir-at-law, which is ordered to be certified.
See: Pension Claim No. S 30864.

### Page 228—April Court, 1841

Satisfactory evidence was introduced to the court by the evidence of Mrs. Lucinda Garrison, who proved that John Baldwin, an old soldier and lately a pensioner on the Government of the U. S., died at her house in the county on the 30th day of January, last, which is ordered to be certified to the Secretary of War.

### Page 310—June Court, 1842

The Declaration of Justinian Jefferson for the purpose of obtaining the benefit of the Act of Congress of June 7, 1832, was this day produced in court together with the certificate of John McCarthy, a justice of the peace for Mason county, certifying that the same had been sworn to before him together with the statement of Hiram Baker, Samuel Cracraft and John McCarthy, which were sworn to by the said Baker, Cracraft, and McCarthy, the court is of the opinion that the said Justinian Jefferson is entitled to a pension and that the said Hiram Baker, Samuel Cracraft and John McCarthey are entitled to full credit which is ordered to be certified to the proper office of Government.

### Page 326—September Court, 1842

It being proven to the satisfaction of the court in open court by the affidavit of Eliza B. Langhorne, Joseph C. Farrin and Jacob Rardin that Captain Thomas Young, a Revolutionary Officer of the Virginia State line of the army of the Revolution, and late a resident of Mason county, departed this life on the 22nd day of April, 1837, intestate, without leaving widow or children or any legal heirs, that he had neither brother or sister living or who left surviving issue save and except his brother Robert Young who departed this life in said county many years ago leaving as his only heirs four children, to-wit: Thomas, Robert, Margaret, now widow of L. Cooke, and Willoughby T. Young; and the said Thomas, son of Robert, departed this life before his uncle, the said Capt. Thomas Young, leaving four sons as his only heirs, to-wit W. H. Young, James M. Young, Thomas M. Young, all of lawful age and William C. Young, now under the age of 21 years of age. That the said Willoughby T. Young departed this life intestate since the death of the said Capt. Thomas Young, leaving one child as his only heir, to-wit: Ann Maria, wife of George M. Proctor, of Maysville, in said county.

And the said court doth order it to be certified that Robert Young, the nephew, and Margaret Cooke, the niece, and W. H. Young, James M. Young, Thomas L. Young and William C. Young, the children of the said Thomas Young, deceased, the nephew, and Ann Maria, wife of George M. Proctor, the daughter of William T. Young, deceased, another nephew, are the only heirs of the said Captain Thomas Young, deceased.

### Page 358—March Court, 1843

Satisfactory proof was introduced into court by the testimony of Conquest W. Owens and Henry R. Reeder, who were sworn in open court, that Mary Salmon of Mason county, Kentucky, is the widow of John Salmon, a Revolutionary pensioner and that the said Mary Salmon is still living in Mason county, Kentucky; that the said John Salmon departed this life on the 21st day of September, 1841, all of which proof is ordered to be certified to the War Department of the U. S.

### Page 364—May Court, 1843

Satisfactory evidence was produced to the court that Philip Rice, was a pensioner of the U. S. at the rate of $67 per annum, was a resident of the county of Bracken in the State of Kentucky, and died in Dover, Mason county, Kentucky, on April 24, 1841, and that he left a widow whose name is Martha M. Rice.

### Page 380—July Court, 1843

Frances Allen produced in open court her Declaration under the pension laws of the U. S. and subscribed and swore to the same in open court, attached thereto she also produced the statement of William Holton which was sworn to in open court by the said William Holton, and the court having examined the same is of opinion that the said Frances Allen is entitled to a pension under the Act of Congress granting pensions to the widows of Revolutionary pensioners and it is ordered that the same be certified to the Secretary of War.

## Page 398—November Court, 1843

Frances Allen, widow of William Allen, deceased, a Revolutionary pensioner again produced in court the deposition of William Holton attached to the Declaration, which was certified at the last July term of court. She also on this day produced in open court the deposition of George Shackleford, and the court now orders and directs that it be certified to the Secretary of War that the said William Holton and George Shackleford, the latter of whom has since departed this life, are men of respectibility and credibility and that their statements are full faith and credit and that the said William Holton and George Shackleford are and were personally known to the court.

## Page 407—January Court, 1844

Richard Applegate produced an affidavit in writing and swore to the same in open court, and made oath to said affidavit or declaration, for a pension as a volunteer or spy in the last War, as stated in his Declaration and the disability as therein set forth was occasioned from exposure while in the line of duty, and that he served as he stated. And it is ordered that the clerk of this county certify the same to the War Department of the U. S.

## Page 413—March Court, 1844

Satisfactory evidence was produced to the court that Col. James McDowell, a pensioner of the Revolutionary War, died in this county on the 31st day of December last and that Mary McDowell is his widow and now living in this county, and the same is ordered to be certified to the Secretary of War.

## Page 425—May Court, 1844

Satisfactory evidence was produced in open court by the oaths of Abner Hord and Charles T. Marshall, that James McDowell died in the county of Mason, and State of Kentucky, on the 31st day of December, 1043, and that he was the identical person named in an original certificate shown to the court, No. 4340, bearing date of January 19, 1833, and signed by Lewis Cass, Secretary of War, granting to said James McDowell $61.66 per annum during his life. It was also proven to the satisfaction of the court by the oaths of Abner Hord and Charles T. Marshall that Mary McDowell is the widow of the said James McDowell and that she is still living.

## Page 470—September Court, 1844

Satisfactory evidence was introduced to the court that William Allen, late of Mason county, Kentucky, and who was a Revolutionary pensioner and entitled to a pension of $40 per annum under an original certificate now produced in open court, dated March 14, 1834, signed by Lewis Cass, Secretary of War, and recorded in the Pension Office in Book E., Volume 7, page first, departed this life on the 20th day of May, 1839, at his residence in Mason county, Kentucky. Satisfactory proof was also introduced to the court that Frances Allen is the widow of said William Allen, deceased, and that she is still living in the county of Mason, State of Kentucky, all of which is directed to be certified to the office of the Secretary of War.

### Page 503—January Court, 1845

The Declaration of Thomas Brightwell was produced in court and the same is ordered to be certified to the Secretary of War. The deposition of Captain Moses Dimmitt was produced in open court and the same is ordered to be certified to the Secretary of War. The foregoing deposition and declaration was sworn to by Dimmitt and Brightwell in open court and it appearing to the satisfaction of the court that the disease called the King's-evil, or scrofula, originated as set forth in said affidavit and the same is ordered to be certified to the Secretary of War.

## COURT ORDER BOOK O

### Page 8—June Court, 1845

The declaration of Thomas Brightwell was produced in open court and sworn to at the January Court, 1845, and the deposition of Moses Dimmitt was also taken and sworn to in open court, and on this day the attorney of the said Thomas Brightwell also produced in open court the affidavit of Doctor John M. Duke and Doctor Samuel K. Sharpe, and it is ordered to be certified to the Secretary of War of the U. S., that the court is of the opinion that the said Thomas Brightwell came by the disease under which he now labours whilst in the actual service of the U. S. in the line of his duty.

### Page 84—November Court, 1846

Satisfactory proof was introduced in open court that John Ward, a Revolutionary soldier pensioner of the U. S. departed this life in the county of Mason on the 26th day of October in the year 1846, and that Dotia Ward is the widow of the said John Ward; is still living in the county of Mason, State of Kentucky, all of which is ordered to be certified to the War Department of the United States.

### Page 122—July Court, 1847

Theodocia Ward, the widow of John Ward, deceased, a Revolutionary pensioner of the U. S., produced her declaration to obtain the benefits of the provision of the Act of Congress of July 7, 1838, entitled an "Act granting half pay and pensions to certain widows," and swore to the same in open court, which is ordered to be certified to the War Department of the U. S. Satisfaction was also made to the court by the oaths of Jesse Turner and Ostrander Coburn two of their body, who proved that they are well acquainted with the said Theodocia Ward, that the said Theodocia Ward is the widow of John Ward, deceased, late of Mason county, Kentucky, who was a Revolutionary pensioner of the United States, which is also ordered to be certified to the War Department of the United States.

### Page 122—July Court, 1847

Parmelia J. Hodges, widow of William Hodges, deceased, produced an affidavit in writing in open court and swore to the same, and also the certificate of James Artus, Abner Hord and Joseph Frazee, Justices of this county, which is ordered to be certified to the Secretary of War of the U. S.

William Hodges was granted license in Mason county, Kentucky, to marry Parmelia Jones, 7-21-1801. James Jones, father.

### Page 148—January Court, 1848

Satisfactory proof having been exhibited to the court by the affidavits of Elijah C. Phister and William H. Wadsworth, who are persons entitled to credit, that William B. Parker of the city of Maysville, Mason county, Kentucky, is the father of the late Rowland Simpson Parker, who was a volunteer in the U. S. Service, and that Rowland Simpson Parker was an unmarried man and had no child or children at the time of his death, and that he died about the ——day of July, 1846, and it is now ordered that the same be certified to the Secretary of War, or to the proper office of Government.

### Page 199—August Court, 1848

It is hereby certified that satisfactory proof has been established before the County Court of Mason county, Kentucky, on this day by the affidavits of Col. Stephen Lee and Elijah C. Phister, that Patrick Moran, a citizen of the city of Maysville, Mason county, Kentucky, is the father of James Moran, who was a private in the company of Captain Ewing of the Regiment of Kentucky volunteers commanded by Col. Manlius V. Thompson, and who was killed in the vicinity of Mexico while in the service of the U. S., and that said James Moran was never married and left no widow or children and that said Col. Stephen Lee and Elijah C. Phister are citizens of the said city of Maysville and are entitled to credit.

### Page 271—September Court, 1849

Satisfactory proof was introduced in open court that Mary Ann Shepherd, widow of George Shepherd, deceased, late a pensioner of the U. S., departed this life in the county of Mason, State of Kentucky, on the 14th day of February, 1849, having made a Will and Testament, by which she appointed Alfred Cooper her executor, who was regularly qualified as such. It was proven that said Mary Ann Shepherd, as the widow of said George Shepherd, deceased, was a pensioner of the U. S., all of which is ordered to be certified to the War Department.

### WILL BOOK O—Page 151

Will of Mary Ann Shepherd. Dated: 4-28-1847. Proven: **March** Court, 1849.

Leaves to: "grandchildren, George W. Browning, Sarah Ann Woodsmall, Lavinda Eaton, Elias Browning and Margaret Browning the sum of $250, this bequest includes a note I hold on Sarah Browning and George W. Browning for the sum of $30." My children, namely: George, John, Robert, Anna D. Brewer (Brewes), Fanny Boyd . . . states that Fanny Boyd has been left a widow with a family to raise and educate . . . mentions deceased daughter, Sarah Browning. Executors: sons John,

George and Robert and friend Alfred Cooper. Witnesses: W. G. Bullock and Cordelia Bullock.

## COURT ORDER BOOK O
### Page 432—June Court, 1850

It being proved to the satisfaction of the court that Judith Young, who was a pensioner of the U. S. at the rate of $320 per annum, departed this life on the 30th day of May, 1849, and that she left a daughter whose name is Margaret Cooke and that she is still living and upon motion of the said Margaret Cooke the same is ordered to be certified to the War Department.

## COURT ORDER BOOK P
### Page 114—April Court, 1852

The Court being fully satisfied in the premises it is ordered to be certified that John B. Richeson, son of Col. Holt Richeson, deceased, of the Revolutionary War is entitled to one-sixth part of the estate of the said Holt Richeson, deceased. That Bettie Fleet is entitled to one-twelfth part and that Mary E. W. Quarles is entitled to one-twelfth part of said estate and that the said John B. Richeson, Mary E. W. Quarles and Bettie Fleet are the only heirs in this county (Mason) of the said Holt Richeson, deceased.

### Page 128—May Court, 1852

On motion of William H. Pollitt, administrator of the goods and chattels, rights and credits of Captain James Markham, deceased, is granted unto him. Whereupon the said William H. Pollitt took the oath required by law and with John Pelham, David L. Bradley, William D. Coryell and Samuel W. Pollitt as his sureties entered in and acknowledged bond to the Commonwealth of Kentucky in the penalty of $10,000 conditioned according to law and it is ordered that certificate of administration be granted to him in due form. (See: Court Order Book M, pages 2 and 3).

### Page 133—May Court, 1852

The court being fully satisfied in the premises, it is ordered to be certified that the following persons are the heirs and the only living heirs of Col. Holt Richeson, deceased, late of King William county, Virginia. Viz:

First: John B. Richeson of Maysville, Kentucky, who is the only living child of the said Holt Richeson, deceased.

Second: James Francis Row and Thomas Row, infants, in the care of William Martin of King & Queen county, Virginia, who are children of Thomas Row, who was a son of Mary Row (formerly Frazer), deceased, who was a daughter of Mary Frazer (formerly Richeson), deceased, who was a daughter of the said Col. Holt Richeson, deceased, and the wife of William Frazer; also Elizabeth Truehart, wife of Peter G. Truehart of Richmond, Virginia; Agnes Messinger, wife of Francis G. Messinger of Camden, Maine; Helen Cutting, wife of William H. Cutting of Boston,

Mass.; John D. Frazer of Boston, Mass., and Mildred W. Frazer of Richmond, Virginia, all children of Alexander Frazer, deceased, who was a son of said Mary Frazer (formerly Richeson), deceased, who was a daughter of the said Col. Holt Richeson, deceased, and wife of William Frazer aforesaid.

Third: Mary E. C. Quarles, infant, (with her mother Mrs. Mary E. W. Quarles in Maysville, Kentucky), who is a daughter of Francis West Quarles, deceased, who was a son of Frances Quarles, deceased, (formerly Richeson), who was a daughter of the said Col. Holt Richeson, deceased, and the wife of Benjamin Quarles; also Thomas D. Quarles of Richmond, Virginia, Susan Pemberton, wife of Thomas Pemberton of Richmond, Virginia, who are children of the said Frances Quarles, deceased, (formerly Richeson), who was a daughter of the said Col. Holt Richeson, deceased, and the wife of Benjamin Quarles, as aforesaid.

Fourth: Mrs. Mary E. W. Quarles of Maysville, Kentucky, the widow of Francis West Quarles, and who is the only child of Francis West Richeson, deceased, a son of the said Col. Holt Richeson, deceased.

Fifth: Cornelius Eubank and Ann E. Eubank, infants (living with Mrs. Mary E. W. Quarles of Maysville, Kentucky), who are children of Eliza Eubank (formerly Mattox) deceased, who was a daughter of Jane Pearcy Mattox (formerly Richeson), deceased, who was a daughter of the said Col. Holt Richeson, deceased, and the wife of John Mattox; also James B. Mattox of Essex, Virginia, John H. Mattox of Richmond, Virginia, William West Mattox of Petersburg, Virginia, Edwin A. Mattox of St. Louis, Missouri, and Francis Mattox of near St. Louis, Missouri, children of said Jane Pearcy Mattox (formerly Richeson), deceased, who was a daughter of the said Col. Holt Richeson, deceased, and the wife of John Mattox as aforesaid.

Sixth: Four children, names unknown, of Mary———, deceased, who was a daughter of Elizabeth Fleet (formerly Richeson), deceased, who was a daughter of the said Col. Holt Richeson, deceased, and the wife of John W. Fleet; also Miss Betty Fleet of Maysville, Kentucky, and Edwin Fleet of King & Queen county, Virginia, children of the said Elizabeth Fleet (formerly Richeson), deceased, who was a daughter of the said Col. Holt Richeson, deceased, and the wife of John W. Fleet as aforesaid.

## Page 151—June Court, 1852

This day personally appeared in open court David Wood and Conquest W. Owens and made oath that they were long well acquainted with Peter W. Holmes and Martha his wife, and that they are the same persons mentioned in the foregoing marriage certificate of Reverend James Savage. That they knew them both at the time of their marriage and were well known to the fact of their marriage though they were not present at their marriage; and about the year——— the said Peter W. Holmes went to Texas and after some years returned to Kentucky. They learned from Holmes himself, that he was living in Texas. He remained here (Mason county) a short time and returned to Texas as they always understood, and afterwards died, or was killed in the Mexican

War. Of course they know nothing of his death but from rumors. His wife Martha Holmes continued to reside in Washington, Mason county, Kentucky, where she died in April, 1851, never having married again. They have living only one child, Mary Ellen Holmes, a minor about 15 years old who is living in Washington and is maintained by two aunts, who are very poor. She having no property of any kind in this county, which is ordered to be certified.

### Page 263—March Court, 1853

This day Rice Bolton well known to the court to be a credible witness, came into court and upon his solemn oath made the following statement which is duly entered on record, viz.:

Rice Boulton states: That he is about 65 years old and is from the State of Virginia, and knew James Pemberton of King & Queens county, Virginia. This affiant moved out to Kentucky and located in Mason county. James Pemberton came out he thinks to Kentucky in 1818 or 1819 and lived in Mason county. He married in Maysville, as he understood, about the year 1823 and some months afterwards he left for New Orleans where it is reputed he died. George C. Pemberton of Maysville, Kentucky, has always been reputed to be his son by that marriage and his only child and heir. Affiant is well acquainted with him and considers him a very worthy and correct young man. (Signed Rice Boulton.) Which is ordered to be certified.

### Page 263—March Court, 1853

This day Strothers B. Nicholson well known to the court to be a credible witness came into court and upon his solemn oath made the following statement which is duly certified on record, viz.:

Strothers B. Nicholson states he knew James Pemberton, the father of George C. Pemberton, well. He was married to Catherine Woodfield in the year 1823 on Second street in Maysville, Kentucky, immediately opposite where affiant then lived. He recollects the occasion of the marriage perfectly. He understood, and it was so reputed, that said James Pemberton was from Virginia. George C. Pemberton was born some 9 or 10 months after the said marriage and has always been reputed and recognized as the son of the said James Pemberton and Catherine Pemberton. He is now about 29 years of age. Some four months after the said marriage James Pemberton left Maysville and went as affiant understood to New Orleans and there died. Affiant has been acquainted with said mother of George both before and ever since her marriage with James Pemberton. She remained a widow some years and then married William R. Rowland, and they are now living in Portsmouth, Ohio. George C. Pemberton has lived in Maysville ever since his birth, and is a very discreet and worthy young man, and is, as far as ever he has heard and believes, the only heir at law of his father, James Pemberton, deceased.

### Page 307—June Court, 1853

Satisfactory proof by the oath of Conquest W. Owens and Nancy Mefford that Dominick McNeill, late of the town of Washington, Mason county, Kentucky, departed this life in said town on the 26th day of July, 1827, intestate, leaving a widow who is still living and the following named children:

Elizabeth McNeill, born 9-25-1816; Mary McNeill, born 11-11-1817; Martha McNeill, born 3-10-1819; John McNeill, born 9-11-1821; James McNeill, born 3-25-1825; Stanfield McNeill, born 2-14-1827.

Elizabeth, the eldest died in the fall of 1832 with cholera. Mary McNeill married Morgan Evans in the fall of 1835. Her husband died in the year 1846. She is still living and a widow. Martha married Thomas Poe on 9-25-1836 both of whom are living in the state of Indiana; John died unmarried and without children in the month of August, 1848. James died unmarried and childless on 2-14-1841. Stanfield is still living. The children above named who are living are the heirs at law of said Dominick McNeill; that the said Dominick McNeill at the time of his death was the legal owner of two quarter sections of land in the State of Illinois for which he held patent from the Government of the U. S.

That the said witnesses believe though they have not the patents present that said lands were the n.w. qr. of Section 12-14 N. 4 E. & N. E. qr. of Section 12-14 N. 4 E. they have been so informed and believe. It is further proved by the records of this court it being the probate court for the county of Mason that Stansfield Pinchard's administration upon the estate of the said Dominick McNeill, deceased, and settled his account as Admr. at November Term of said Court in the year 1830. It further appears from an examination of the records of this court that no administration has been granted to any one upon the estate of Elizabeth McNeill, James McNeill and John McNeill, the three deceased children of said Dominick McNeill, deceased.

### Page 329—Thursday Morning, August 11, 1853
#### Court met pursuant to adjournment
#### Present Lewis Collins, Presiding Judge:

Ordered that Mary McClelland be and she is hereby appointed guardian of Robert P. McClelland and Margaret C. McClelland, children and heirs at law of Robert P. McClelland, deceased, late a private in Captain Churchill's Co. Ohio Volunteers, for the special purpose of selling and conveying Military Bounty Land Warrant Certificate No. 78326 for 160 acres of land issued to said Mary McClelland, widow, and said minor heirs of said Robert P. McClelland, deceased. Whereupon the said Mary McClelland with John A. Keith as her surety entered into and acknowledged bond to the Commonwealth of Kentucky conditioned according to law, all of which is ordered to be certified.

### Page 360—December Court, 1853

Ordered that Henry R. Reeder be and he is hereby appointed guardian of Mary Ellen Holmes, child and heir at law of Peter W. Holmes, deceased, late a private in Captain Reed's (John Moore Reed) Company of Texas Mounted Volunteers, for the special purpose of selling, assigning and conveying Land Warrant No. 78599 for 160 acres of land issued to the said Mary Ellen Holmes, infant heir as aforesaid. Whereupon the said Henry R. Reeder with John A. Keith as his surety gave bond, all of which is ordered to be certified.

### Page 365—Monday, December 26, 1853

This day satisfactory proof was adduced to the court that Mary Ellen Holmes, infant child of Peter W. Holmes, deceased, is without any personal estate and that she is possessed of no productive real estate. That the only means that can be made available for her support and maintenance will be by the late Military Bounty Land Warrant No. 78599 for 160 acres, issued to his child and heir at law of Peter W. Holmes, deceased, late a private in Captain Reed's Company of Texas Mounted Volunteers, and that it is absolutely necessary that the said sale be made.

### Page 383—March Court, 1854

This day Christopher Cole came into court and being of lawful age and first duly sworn testified that his father, John H. Cole, to whom was issued Bounty Land Warrant No. 25322 for 60 acres on the 8th day of January, 1852, was dead previous to the issuing of said Warrant, that he died on the 15th day of November, 1851, leaving no widow, his wife having died on the 6th day of April, 1850, preceding; that he left only one minor child to-wit: Indiana T. Cole, the sister of affiant; that said Indiana T. Cole was born on the 27th day of July, 1835, and was therefore 18 years old on her last birthday, that the family record is lost and cannot be procured; that his brother, John H. Cole, on the 12th of September, 1853, qualified as guardian of their said minor sister in this court, and that this proof is made for the purpose of obtaining from the Department of the Interior (for the benefit of the said minor child, Indiana T. Cole) the Warrant for Bounty Land to which she is entitled under the Act of Congress passed September 28, 1850, and that affiant has no interest whatsoever in said Warrant when issued, which is ordered to be certified.

### Page 436—June Court, 1854

It appearing to the satisfaction of the court upon the oaths of Washington How, Robert A. Cochran and Richard H. Collins, credible witnesses of lawful age and well known to the court, that Joseph Best, Grandison Reynolds and Ellen Reynolds (late Ellen Best), Paul T. Best, and Edward M. Best, children of James Best, deceased, to whom was issued on the 20th of August, 1851, 40 acres Bounty Land Warrant No. 15771 and which children are sole devisees of said Warrant, as appears by Warrantee's Will of record in this court, had each attained the age of 21 years prior to the assignment of said Warrant on the 26th day of March, last, and that one of the said devisees is a femme covert, viz.: Ellen Reynolds and that her husband, Grandison V. Reynolds, has united with her in the assignment thereof, which is ordered to be certified.

### Page 483—November Court, 1854

Ordered that John A. Black be and he is hereby appointed guardian of Elizabeth E. Black, minor child of William Black, deceased, a private in Captain Norris' Co. 3rd Regiment Kentucky Mounted Volunteers,

War of 1812, for the special purpose of selling, conveying and assigning Military Bounty Land Warrant No. 53008 for 40 acres issued to said Elizabeth E. Black, minor as aforesaid, under the Act of Congress of September 28, 1834, which is ordered to be certified.

## Page 496—December Court, 1854

Ordered that David T. Mitchell be and he is hereby appointed guardian of Sarah Jane Gray, Robert K. Gray, Anna Maria Gray, Deborah Gray, and Mary Gray, minor heirs at law of Robert K. Gray, deceased, who was a Sergeant in Lieut. William Fatherstone's Company of the 17th Regiment of U. S. Infantry, War of 1812, for the purpose of selling Military Bounty Land Warrant No. 11558 for 160 acres issued in the name of said Robert K. Gray, deceased.

## MASON COUNTY TAXPAYERS, 1793

Mason county of 1790 was what is today area covered by Mason, Bracken, Fleming, Greenup, Lewis, Lawrence, Carter, Johnson, Rowan, Boyd, Elliott, Martin, Robertson, Campbell, and by parts of Floyd, Nicholas, Pike, Morgan, Magoffin, Pendleton and Harrison counties.

Mitchell Hall, in his History of Johnson County, Kentucky (apart of old Mason) vol. I, page 57, gives taxpayers in 1793 within the District of Wm. Lamb No. 2, Commisisoner in the County of Mason.

| | | |
|---|---|---|
| Aldridge, Christopher | Boone, Jacob | Carrol, Daniel |
| Aldridge, Henry | Boyard, Jacob | Casherwood, Sam |
| Allen, Jeremiah | Bradley, Moses | Chandler, Nathaniel |
| Arms, William | Bradrock, David | Chaney, Edward |
| Armstrong, James | Brannon, Patrick | Cockran, Henry |
| Arrowsmith, Sam | Branton, Thomas | Colgin, William |
| Atkins, John | Brion, John | Collins, Edward |
| Bailey, Jane | Briont, Benjamin | Collins, Thomas |
| Balding, John | Brooks, James | Conaway, Richard |
| Balla, George | Brooks, Thomas | Conway, Miloo |
| Baltimore, Phillip | Brooks, William | Conner, Peter |
| Bane, Richard | Bulger, James | Consaules, James |
| Banfield, Theodore | Bullock, Lewis | Consoles, John |
| Barr, John | Burk, Thomas | Cooper, John |
| Bearley, Charles | Burkhorn, Zephaniah | Cord, Jacob |
| Beck, Jeremiah | Byron, Peter | Cornick, Thomas |
| Beckley, William | Byron, William | Cox, Thomas |
| Bennett, Joel | Cain, John | Craig, John |
| Bennett, Moses | Calvin, William | Crawford, John |
| Bennett, Robert | Campbell, James | Criswell, James |
| Bennett, William | Campbell, Mathew | Cunningham, Thomas |
| Berry, George, Jr. | Campbell, Squire | Curtis, Isaiah |
| Berry, George, Sr. | Campbell, William | Dale, Lawrence |
| Berry, Ruben | Camron, Samuel | Dausom, Joseph |
| Berry, William | Cannon, Isaac | David, Zebaniah |
| Blanchard, David | Carewine, Richard | Davis, Beeson |

Davis, David
Davis, Phillip
Davis, Samuel
Davis, Sarah
Davy, John
Delap, William
Derrill, Richard
Day, John
Dobyns, Edward
Dobyns, James
Dobyns Thomas
Dougharty, Michiel
Doughty, Benjamin
Dragoo, Bell
Drugan, Abraham
Druzan, Peter
Dunavan, Daniel
Dunleavy, Anthony
Duncan, Daniel
Dunn, Henry
Evans, Daniel
Evans, Francis
Evans, W. Richard
Ferguson, Isaac
Flaugher, Adam
Flin, Pethias
Fowler, Jonas
Fowler, Moses
Fox, Arthur
Frazer, Moses
Giffard, Elisha
Graham, John
Grey, Robert
Grimes, David
Grymes, Noble
Guthridge, James
Guthridge, John
Hall, Andrew
Hall, Benjamin
Hall, Edward
Hall, Elijah
Hall, Thomas
Hancock, Joseph
Haner, James
Hanna, John
Hanum, Jonathan
Harris, Edward
Hatfield, Thomas
Haugham, Moses

Haughton, Aaron
Hempleman, Adam
Henry, James
Henson, John
Honsucker, Abraham
Honsucker, Joseph
Hopkins, Joseph
Hurst, Henry
Hurst, Michael
Hutton, Charles
Hutton, George
John, Thomas
Jones, Ignas
Judd, Joshua
Judd, William
Justus, John
Karr, Paul
Kenton, Simon
Kilgease, George
Killin, John
Killin, Patrick
Kirk, Thomas
Knary, Charles
Ladwick, John
Lashbrook, John
Leak, Harmon
Lee, Anne
Lee, Lewis
Lee, Henry
Leming, Joseph
Lewis, George
Lewis, James
Lewis, John
Lindy, Hezekiah
Lock, Andrew
Lucian, John
Lucust, Thomas
Makey, William
Mageveny, James
Mahan, Jawbin
Marney, Jonathan
Marshall, Thomas
Martin, Davis
Martin, Harry
Massey, Nathaniel
Master, William
Matslerr, Elizabeth
Mayhall, Timothy
McBride, John

McCannon, John
McCash, David
McClure, Francis
McCrackin, John
McDonald, William
McKay, James
McKenny, Daniel
McKenny, John
Medola, John
Mefford, George
Mesner, Coonrad
Metcalf, John
Middleton, Thomas
Mitchell, George
Mitchell, Ignas
Mitchell, John
Mizner, Henry
Moore, Hosea
Moore, Samuel
Moore, Thomas
Moore, William
Morgan, Abel
Neeley, Thomas
Nickels, John
Norris, Abraham
Orr, D. Alexander
Oursler, Charles
Owens, Amasa
Owens, Aaron
Owens, Bethall
Owens, John
Ozburn, Abraham
Pangburn, Sam
Parker, Richard
Parker, Winslow
Parkinson, William
Parks, Robert
Parrimore, Ellis
Parrimore, Gideon
Patterson, James
Patton, Eleanor
Patton, James
Patton, Thomas
Pelham, Charles
Pelham, John
Perry, Anne
Philips, Ann
Philips, Gable
Philips, John

Philips, Moses
Pollard, Benjamin
Preston, Bernard
Price, William
Prickett, Isaac
Reed, Enoch
Reed, Isaac
Regin, Thomas
Rich, Thomas
Riggs, John
Riley, James
Ritter, John
Ritter, Richard
Roberts, Thomas
Roe, William
Roebuck, Ben
Rogers, James
Rogers, John
Rubert, Isaac
Rubert, Samuel
Rust, Matthew
Sharp, Solomon
Shelby, Joshua
Shepherd, George
Shepherd, John, Jr.
Shepherd, John, Sr.
Shepherd, John W.
Shepherd, Solomon
Shepherd, William
Shields, William
Shilock, John
Sibbett, James
Simpson, Allen
Sites, Henry
Skimer, Jesse
Slack, John
Smart, Elizabeth
Smith, Ben

Smith, Christian
Smith, Moses
Southard, Hezekiah
Soward, Richard
Stafford, Sterling
Stansbury, Silas
Stansil, Henry
Staton, Joseph
Stevenson, James
Steward, William
Sticklet, Peter
Stout, Thomas
Strickland, David
Strode, Samuel
Stuart, Robert
Sutton, Benjamin
Swim, Jesse
Symonds, Henry
Talbert, Thomas
Taylor, Francis
Taylor, John
Templiss, James
Tevis, Peter
Thatcher, James
Thomas, David
Thomas, Ephriam
Thomas, John
Thomas, Levi
Thomas, Phineas
Thompson, George
Thompson, James
Thompson, John
Thompson, Zachariah
Thompson, William
Todd, Robert
Trebalds, Clem
Tups, Henry

Underwood, Isa
Utter, James, Jr.
Utter, James, Sr.
Walker, Alex, Sr.
Walker, Robert
Waller, Edmond
Walsh, James
Wamsley, Isaac
Ward, James
Ward, Joseph
Ward, William
Waring, Thomas
Warringford, Ben
Watkins, William
Watson, Aaron
Watson, Michael
Wauldron, David
Welch, George
Welch, James
Welch, John
Wells, Aaron
Wells, James, Jr.
Wells, Joseph, Sr.
Westbrook, Joseph
White, George
White, John
Williams, Charles
Williams, David
Williams, Francis
Williams, Jonathan
Williams, Pleasant
Willson, James
Willson, John
Wood, Moses
Wood, Nicholas
York, Joshua
Young, William

## LINCOLN COUNTY

(From original records copied by Mrs. Ila Earle Fowler and
Miss Gabriella Bradshaw, at Stanford.)

8/10/1789.—Will of *John Berry*, proved 7/20/179..(0). To two sons: James Berry and Wm. Berry, 300 acres on Lickin Creek, bought of Wm. McCrackin; movable estate to daughters: Betsey Berry; Polly Berry; Sally Berry; Hannah Berry; Peggy Berry; Jane Berry, to be delivered to them when of lawful age. To two sons: Joseph Berry and John Berry, tract the family lives on in Lincoln County, Virginia;

neither of them to make any demands until the marriage or death of Hannah, my wife. Wit.: James Piggott; James Kerr; Isaac Fallis.

3/10/1782.—Will of *James Berry*, proved 1/15/1782. To daughter Elizabeth 200 acres on Gilbert's creek, ½ of 400-acre tract; to wife Christiana, 200 acres of said tract for her lifetime, daughter Elizabeth after (if no other heir); mentions stepson John Wilson; exc. wife, Christiana Berry, Ebenezer Miller, John Smith. Wit. John Kearne; Sam'l Dennis; Thomas Denton.

Jan. court, 1781.—Order Book 1, p. 3, Thomas Denton, Lt.; Stephen Trigg, colonel; John Logan; Hugh McGary; Wm. McBride; John Cowan; Samuel Scott; John Allison, gentlemen, Captains. p. 9, same recommended for Captains, May 1781.

Order Book B. 2, p. 6.—Jesse Robards, assignee of Lewis Robards who was assignee of Wm. Conway, suit against Thomas Denton ordered discontinued.

B. 1, p. 70.—Thomas Denton against Daniel Chambers, for debt, ordered discontinued, June court, 1783.

B. 1, p. 236.—Thomas Denton against Wm. Casey, proceedings stayed until next court, Sept. court, 1784.

4/6/1800.—Will of *John Goode*, Book C, p. 23; To wife Jenny, for life, tract on which he lived, to pass to son Timothy; live stock to wife during widowhood. Names three children: son Timothy Goode; daughter Nancey Goode; daughter Ellender Goode. Mentions estate of his deceased father, Thomas Goode. Proved July 8, 1800. Exec. Maj. Joseph Gray of Washington County, Ky.; Thomas Hutchins of Lincoln county, Ky. and wife Jenny Goode. wit. Wm. Cosby; Joseph Ayre; John Cosby.

7/21/1812.—Will of Nicholas Hocker, proved 3/8/1813. Book E, p. 78. Wife, Sarah Hocker; sons, Philip Hocker; Alfred Hocker; Nicholas Hocker; George Hocker. Daughters Margaret Dunn, wife of Benj. Dunn; Mary Clements; Dorcas Hocker, wife of Philip Hocker. To wife three negroes, Frank, William and James. To Margaret Dunn, negro Chloe. To Alfred Hocker, negro Alexander. Mentions Benj. Logan. Mentions Rebecca Wilson.

12/6/1813.—will of Samuel Hocker, proved 1815, Book G, p. 17. Wife Nancy Hocker; sons Joseph Hocker; John Hocker; Richard Weaver Hocker; Philip Hocker; deceased son Jacob Hocker and his daughter Nancy Hocker. Daughters: Polly Hocker, Nancy Hocker, Betsey Helen Hocker. Negroes: Abram; Rachel; Beck; Celia; Chloe; Squire; Jenney; Richmond; Abba; Rose; Melissa; Cerelda; Caroline; Hennery; Maria; Mahala. exers. son Philip and Joseph Hocker. These extracts certified to by V. C. Gilliland, clerk, of Lincoln county 2/22/1933.

12/15/1865.—Will of Mary Goode, proved 2/4/1866, Book W, p. 184. Mentions House and lot in Milledgeville, Lincoln county; 5 youngest children: George A. Goode; Amanda F. Goode; Jane Goode; Sarah Goode; Bell Goode; and two oldest children: Alexander Goode; William Goode. Exc. J. E. Carter.

1/30/1879.—Will of Mildred A. Goode, proved 4/7/1886. Mentions deceased husband, Lorenzo D. Goode. Says children had received their part except daughter Maria Crow, so to her left the estate after debts were paid. Excepts bequests to three grandchildren: Lorenzo D. Anderson; Overton Anderson; Wm. Anderson. In 1866 had bought 11 acres in Henry county, Missouri and leaves life interest in this to Mrs. Nancy J. Morris for a home. Exec. friend, E. G. Hocker. Wit. L. G. Hocker; H. Brown; J. B. VanArsdell; and wit. to codicil: Dr. H. Brown; Robert M. Dodds.

12/4/1902.—Book 5, p. 335.—will of J. F. Goode, proved 2/10/1903. Mentions deceased wife. To daughters Lucy and Sally in addition to their equal share of the estate, house and kitchen furniture. Mentions Moses Coffey husband of daughter, Kate Coffey. exc. Edward Alcorn, A. M. Frye.

9/15/1897.—Will of Benjamin F. Goode, Book 6, p. 103, proved August 11, 1914. Beloved wife, Sarah Goode to have widow's share; residue to Gabriella Ward, Wilbur B. Goode and Mattie Bradshaw, equal shares. Son Wilbur and son-in-law W. T. Ward exec. without bond.

wit. J. D. Alcorn; J. D. Hocker; J. T. Martin. Codicil, April 18, 1918, appoints W. T. Ward sole executor; son to make good to sisters their share of the debt which he may owe at my death as shown by "my book or books."

Codical No. 2, July 27, 1909.—witnessed by J. W. Alcorn and Pattie Alcorn. Had collected indebtedness of son at $307.72, this to be discharged, but any such future debts to be made good to the sisters, "a charge upon the devise to him." Division, 10/10/1910. To daughter Gabriella Ward, part of farm on south side of Stanford and Hustonville Road, only prohibition not to sell off in lots. To daughter Mattie Bradshaw part on north side of this said road for life and at death to heirs of her body. Values to be set by three men and any difference to be made good. To son such other part of estate as will make him equal, residue to be divided by three. Wit. J. T. Martin, Talitha Root.

(Bible records of Lorenzo Dow Goode published in "Our Virginia Cousins" by B. G. Brown Good. Bible records of John Crow published in Ky. County Court and other records, v. 12, by Julia Ardery.)

1925, Book 6, p. 426.—Will of Maggie G. Good, proved 1/30/1911. Property to husband, Thomas J. Good; remainder to grand-daughter, Margaret McClure for her lifetime and after her death in fee simple to her issue. Failing that, niece Hattie H. Green. Husband to be executor, Wit. J. B. Paxton, W. B. Good.

Names from Deed Books, Stanford, Lincoln County: John Goode, 1800, C, p. 23; Mary Goode, 1866; W, p. 184; Mildred A. Goode, 1879, 5, p. 124; J. T. Goode, 1902, 5, p. 335; Sarah M. Goode, 1910, 6, p. 10; B. F. Goode, 1897, 6, p. 103; Thos. J. Goode, 1925, 6, p. 426; Bourne Goode, 1933, p. 123; James Berry, 1782, A, p. 9; John Berry, 1789, A, p. 189; Clifton Fowler, 1904, 6, p. 39; Elizabeth Hocker, 1918, 5, p. 174; James Warren, 1923, 6, p. 366; Annie Hocker Phelps, 1924, 6, p. 385; Margaret A. Hocker, 1924, 6, p. 402; Charlie Hocker, 1933, 7, p. 116; Maggie Hocker, 1907, 5, p. 439; S. G. Hocker, 1895, 5, 144; W. H. Hocker, 1888, 4, p. 471; Philip L. Hocker, 1857, T, p. 2; Philip S. Hocker, 1856, 5, p. 367; R. W. Hocker, 1855, S, p. 333; Joseph Hocker, 1851, R, p. 81; Catherine Hocker, 1846, Q, p. ....; John Hocker, 1848, Q, p. 21; Samuel Hocker, 1815, G, p. 17; Nicholas Hocker, E, p. 78.

## GOODE

Benjamin Goode was born in Amherst county, Va., in 1763 (ca), son of Daniel Goode and his wife who was Miss Campbell. Benjamin Goode married Elizabeth Camden; their children: 1. John Goode; 2. Joseph Goode; 3. William Goode; 4. Samuel Goode; 5. Micajah Goode; 6. Elizabeth Goode; 7. Amarilla Goode.

Joseph Hoskins Goode, son of Benjamin and Elizabeth Camden Goode, was b. 1788, md. Nancy Combs Dec. 2, 1807, both d. 1876, buried near Perryville Washington Co., Ky. (another record gives middle name as Hawkins). Their children: 1. Lorenzo Dow Goode, b. at head of Kentucky River; 2. Alexander Goode; 3. Daniel Goode; 4. Amarilla Goode; 5. Sallie Goode md. Henry Hafley; 7. Annie Goode md. Memos Miller; 8. Jane Goode md. Joseph Trowbridge; 9. Nancy Ann Goode md. Uriah Graves; their daughter Eliza Graves md. Daniel Cooley.

Lincoln county, Ky. marriage bond. Know ye by these presents that I, John Combs, of Lincoln county and state of Kentucky, do grant that Joseph Goode of said county and state and Nancy, my daughter, shall join in the bonds of matrimony. Given under my hand this second December, 1807. Test. Sanders Russell; Edward Russell. Sworn to by Sanders Russell on the second of December, 1807. Test. Thomas Montgomery, C.L.C.C.

\* \* \* \* \*

Tombstone record: In Memory of Elizabeth Good, died Dec. 26, 1816, in the 103 year of her age.

\* \* \* \* \*

Lincoln county Order Book, 1812-1815, p. 165, Nov. Term court. Order that it be certified to the Auditor of Public Accounts that it was this day proven to the satisfaction of the court by the oaths of Abraham Miller and Peter Carter, two disinterested persons, accredited witnesses, that Benjamin Goode is and was an actual settler upon the 150 acres of vacant land lying in Lincoln county.

Bible records of Lorenzo Dow Good's Bible, published in 1841 by Brattleboro Typographic Company, "Our Virginia Cousins," by B. G. Brown Good. Lorenzo Dow Good, son of Joseph Good and Nancy Combs, b. 8/26/1800, md. Milly Ann Stegall, 11/29/1826, died 6/23/1878; member of House of Representatives, 1869-1871.

Marriage Bond: Mr. Thomas Helm this is to authorize you to grant my son Lorenzy Goode marriage license to marry Milly Ann Stigall. Given under my hand this 27th day of November, 1826. Joseph Goode; sworn to by Samuel Givens, Nov. 29, 1826. witness Samuel Givens, Margis Helm. State of Kentucky, County of Lincoln. I, V. C. Gilliland, clerk of Lincoln county court do hereby certify that the foregoing is a true and correct copy of the order from Joseph Good authorizing his son Lorenzy Good to marry Milly Ann Stigall as appears of record in my office. Witness my hand this 30th day of November, 1937. V. C. Gilliland, clerk, by Jasper Gilliland, D.C.

Of the children of this couple, 1. Nancy Jane Good md. Thomas Morris; 2. Joseph Good md. (1) Mary Hocker, (2) Nancy Barned Hocker; 4. a girl not named; 5. Thomas Jefferson Good; 6. Mary Ann Good; 7. Elizabeth T. Good md. Isaac Anderson; 8. Martha Ann Good md. O. J. Crowe who after her death md. (2) her sister; 9. Maria Louise Good; 10. Mittie Good md. Richard Bibb; 11. Lorenzo Dow Good, Jr.

* * * * *

(Halifax Co., Va. Book 10, p. 248 for Philemon Green and William Stegall, May 6, 1776, 150 acres land bounty, Greene's wife Ann.   Also Book 11, Wm. Stegall and John Scoggin; Wm. Stegall, Feb. 1788, and Porter Stegall 100 acres land on Difficult creek.)

Stanford, Lincoln county Order Book 7, 9/7/1818: Order that Gabriel Hughes be appointed guardian of Clementine, Henry and Milly Ann Stegall, infants and orphans of Wm. Stegall, dec'd, whereupon said Gabriel Hughes with Wm. Gooch and Thomas Feland as security executed bond with penalty of 3,000, with proper condition.   Sworn to by V. C. Gilliland, clerk at same time as marriage bond of Lorenzo Good and Milly Ann Stegall.

## STEGALL-ATKINSON

William B. Stegall was married Aug. 3, 1808 to Judy Atkinson; their children: 1. Milly Ann Stegall; 2. Clementine Stegall; 3. Henry Stegall. Wm. B. Stegall d. before March 1814.

By marriage bond in Stanford, Lincoln county we see that his widow, Judy Atkinson Stegall, married Samuel Potter, license March 3, 1814. (From Order book of that county, No. 7, 1818.)

Joel Atkinson, father of Judy Atkinson, died before 1808 as the following will show:   Lincoln county order book 6, p. 436, March 1, 1808.   William Gooch appointed guardian to Elijah, Henry, Charles, John Jefferson, Nancy, Joel, Jeptha, orphans of Joel Atkinson, deceased, whereupon William Gooch, John Blain, Wm. D. and Nicholas made security; Henry Co., Va.   (Va. magazine, vol. 9, p. 139.)   In a memorandum of those who had taken the oath of allegiance, Sept. 3, 1777, the name of Joel Atkinson is found.

Montgomery C L C, Stanford, Ky. ord-er book 6, 1801-1808, March 1808, Judith Atkinson, daughter of Joel Atkinson, deceased, now here in court made choice of Wm. Gooch as her guardian, whereupon John Blain and Nathaniel Gooch as securities executed bond according to law— proper conditions.

* * * * *

(Order book, Stanford, Lincoln county, Ky., 6, p. 436)

I do certify that security has been taken in my office for the marriage intended between William Stegall and Julia Atkinson, daughter of Joel Atkinson, deceased, and that the consent of William Gooch her guardian, was personally given they are therefore licensed and permit any minister of the Gospel or Justice of the Peace legally authorized to solemnized the rights of matrimony to join together the said William and Judy in the holy estate of matrimony agreeable to the form and ceremony in his church or society.   I witness my hand as clerk of the court aforesaid this 3rd day of August, 1808.

Children of Wm. B. Stegall and Judy Atkinson Stegall: 1. Eliza Stegall; 2. Henry Stegall; 3. Charles Stegall; 4. John Stegall; 5. Jefferson Stegall; 6. Nancy Stegall; 7. Joel Stegall; 8. Jeptha Stegall; 9. Judy Stegall.

\* \* \* \* \*

(Bible records of James Crow published in Kentucky Court and other records by Julia Ardery, V. II.)

Oliver Jackson Crow, b. 1/28/1837, son of James Porter Crow and Parmelia T. Crow, nee Carter. Oliver Jackson Crow md. (1) Martha Ann Good 2/8/1856; their children: 1. Elizabeth T. Crow; 2. Permelia (Minnie) Crow; 3. James Porter Crow; 4. Martha Ann Crow (Mattie); O. J. Crow md. (2) Maria Louise Good; their children: 1. Mittie Crow; 2. Anna Crow.

## HOCKER

Joseph Hocker was b. in Maryland, near Elicot Mills, Oct. 29, 1786. Elizabeth Dunn was b. in Maryland, Sept. 3, 1794. Joseph Hocker and Elizabeth Dunn were married near Bryantsville, in Garrard county, Ky., Jan. 24, 1811. 13 children were born to bless their union:

1. Ben D. Hocker was born Feb. 12, 1812
2. Samuel Hocker was born April 8, 1814
3. Richard W. Hocker was born Jan. 15, 1816
4. Margareta Hocker was born April 8, 1818
5. Tilman Hocker was born July 18, 1820
6. James M. Hocker was born June 28, 1822
7. Dorcas Hocker was born May 24, 1824
8. Mary Hocker was born June 7, 1826
9. Sarah Myers Hocker was born May 31, 1828
10. Isaiah Dunn Hocker was born April 30, 1830
11. William Dunn Hocker was born Feb. 26, 1832
12. Nannie Barnes Hocker was born ....-...., 1834
13. Gabriella Hocker was born July 3, 1836.

State of Kentucky,
County of Lincoln,

I, Gabriella Ward Bradshaw, do hereby certify that the foregoing are true and exact copies found in the personal papers of Isaiah Dunn Hocker, and that the said papers were written in the handwriting of the said Isaiah Dunn Hocker, I being his great-niece, and being well acquainted with his handwriting. This Feb. 22, 1933.

(Signed) Gabriella Ward Bradshaw

Subscribed and sworn to before me by Gabriella Ward Bradshaw, this February 22, 1933.

(Signed) D. C. Guinin, Clerk
Lincoln county, Ky.

Tilman Hocker married Sarah Woods Morrison, June 19, 1843. To this union were born four sons and three daughters: 1. Jimmie Hocker; 2. Arthur Hocker; 3. Samuel Hocker; 4. Leslie Hocker.

Belle Hocker, a daughter married James K. Helm, Sr., son of Marcus Helm. She was living in Missouri at the time of her wedding. Their former home was near Hustonville, Lincoln county, Ky.

Laura Hocker, a daughter of Tilman and Sarah Hocker, married a Mr. Arnold, in Missouri.

Sophia Hocker was another daughter, I do not know whether she married, or if so, to whom.

Arthur Hocker visited Kentucky in 1901 or 1902. He was a practicing physician in Wyoming Territory.

## BRADSHAW

Col. Wm. Bradshaw, in Revolutionary War, member of Legislature from Adair County, Ky., md. Charlotte Williams, their children 5 boys and 5 girls, as follows: 1. Arthur Bradshaw md. Lucy Ann Williams; 2. Dolphus Bradshaw; 3. Asia Bradshaw, had a son, G. A. Bradshaw; 4. William Bradshaw d. in Texas; 5. Alban Bradshaw md. (1) Miss Robertson, (2) Polly Walker; 6. Patsy Bradshaw md. Wm. Todd; 7. Trecy Bradshaw md. Lu Rue Walker; 8. Charlotte Bradshaw md. Wm. Eperson; 9. Ann Bradshaw md. ........ Oaker, lived in Ala.; 10. Polly Bradshaw md. Frank Edington.

Alban Bradshaw (above) md. Miss Robertson; their children: Billy Bradshaw; Lewis Bradshaw; Mary Ann Bradshaw; Alban Bradshaw, Jr. killed at Battle of Shiloh. Alban Bradshaw, Sr. md. (2) Polly Walker, their daughter, Helena Bradshaw md. Isaac Nicholas Williams who had helped to bury her half-brother Alban Bradshaw, Jr. at Shiloh.

Polly Bradshaw md. (1) Frank Edington; md. (2) Perry Bryan, their daughter, Lottie Bryan Dunbar lives at Columbia, Adair county, Ky.

Wm. Preston Bradshaw, son of Arthur Bradshaw and Lucy Ann Williams, md. Mattie Goode, daughter of Benj. F. and Sarah Goode, their children: 1. Gabriella Ward Bradshaw, 217 S. Ashland, Lexington, 37, Ky.; 2. Joseph Bryan Bradshaw, in World War I, 52nd Infantry which was wiped out except for 5 men, including him, who were replaced in the 85th Division; he died 8/11/1940.

## MADISON COUNTY

### TRIBBLE

(Contributed by Mrs. Benjam in F. Buckley)

### Bible Record of Rev. Andrew Tribble

Andrew Tribble born March 22, 1741; Sallie Burroughs born Sept. 30, 1753. They married 1768.

## Children

1. Frances Tandy Tribble born Sept. 3, 1769
2. Samuel Tribble born December 30, 1771
3. Peter Tribble born Oct. 8, 1773
4. Thomas Tribble born June 13, 1776
5. Nancy Tribble born Nov. 6, 1778
6. Sally B. Tribble born Feb. 9, 1781
7. Silas Tribble born June 3, 1783
8. Andrew Tribble born Dec. 2, 1785
9. Mary Tribble born March 29, 1788
10. John Tribble (General) born Aug. 15, 1790
11. Patsey Tribble born March 7, 1794
12. Dudley Tribble born May 1, 1797

## Marriages

Frances T. Tribble married Michael Stoner, b. Sept. 30, 1753; d. Sept. 3, 1814.

Peter Tribble mar. Oct. 8, 1793 Polly Boone she died Sept. 14, 1831

Samuel Tribble mar P. Martin

Thos. Tribble mar Mary Phelps

Nancy Tribble mar. Mar. 3, 1794 David Chenault

Sally B. Tribble mar Mar 7, 1784 David Crews

Silas Tribble mar. Oct. 30, 1809 Jerusha White

Andrew Tribble mar. June 24, 1810 Lucy Boone

Mary Tribble mar. Dec. 23, 1806 Joseph Stephenson

John Tribble mar Mar. 1st Martha White. She died June 10, 1850 mar 2nd Sally Coffee. She died Jan. 3, 1865

Patsey Tribble mar Oct. 5, 1812 Jacob White

Dudley Tribble mar. Jan 1, 1819 Matilda H. Tevis

## Deaths

Rev. Andrew Tribble died Dec. 30, 1822

Sally Burrass Tribble died Dec. 15, 1830

Samuel Tribble died Sept 3, 1814

Peter Tribble died Sept. 14, 1831

Sally B. Tribble died Feb., 1810

Silas Tribble died Nov. 8, 1842

Andrew Tribble

Dudley Tribble died June 1877

## Family Record of Nancy Tribble and David Chenault

Nancy Tribble born Nov. 6, 1778

David Chenault born Sept. 30, 1771

Nancy Tribble and David Chenault married April 3, 1794

## Children

Cabell Chenault born July 25, 1795

Joyce Chenault married Capt. James Munday

Harvey Chenault 1802-1843 married March 30, 1826 Ann McCord Douglas. Ann M. Chenault mar. 2nd Dr. Wm. R. Lee

Sally Chenault 1804 married Duke Simpson
Wm. Tandy Chenault 1807 mar. Virginia Quisenberry.
Waller Chenault 1809-1843 mar. Berlinda McRoberts Nov. 17, 1835
No issue.
Anderson Chenault 1812-1884 mar. Margaret Kavanaugh Oldham
John Chenault 1815-1843—unmarried
Nancy Chenault 1819 married Alexander Tribble Oct. 26, 1843 mar.
2nd Clay Broaddus—no issue.

Children of Anderson Chenault and Margaret Kavanaugh Oldham

Nannie Chenault mar John T. Woodford
W. O. Chenault
Waller Chenault
Anderson Chenault
Mollie Chenault mar James S. Bogie
Margaret Chenault mar W. G. Denny
Lucy Chenault mar Bishop Clay.

### Family Record of Samuel Tribble

Samuel Tribble born Dec. 31, 1771
Polly Martin born Mch 13, 1772

#### Children

P. M. Tribble born Nov. 22, 1792
Andrew Tribble born March 31, 1794
Orson Tribble born July 4, 1795
Amelia Tribble born Oct. 1, 1796
Malinda Tribble born Jan. 11, 1798
Sam'l Tribble born Jan. 24, 1800
Mary Tribble born Aug. 1, 1801
John H. Tribble born Nov. 20, 1803
Rachel Tribble born Dec. 5, 1805
Sarah B. Tribble born Dec. 23, 1807
Alfred Tribble born Jan. 11, 1811
Thos. M. Tribble born April 14, 1813

Peter Tribble, born March 8, 1774; died Mar. 18, 1849; married Oct.
8, 1793 Mary Boone, born Apl. 2, 1776; died Sept. 4, 1831.

#### Children

Nancy Tribble born Aug. 20, 1794
Sally Ann born Aug. 15, 1796
Elizabeth born Aug. 1, 1798; died April 27, 1881
Mariah born June 9, 1800; died Nov. 1865
Frances born Dec. 9, 1802
Geo. W. born Jan. 1, 1804
Sam'l born Nov. 5, 1805; died May 3, 1831
Matilda born May 1, 1808; died June 27, 1867
Alex. born April 10, 1810

Peter born June 9, 1812; died in South about 1840
Wellington born April 21, 1814; died 1834
Minerva born Jan. 30, 1817

### Bible Record of Dudley Tribble, Sr.

Dudley Tribble, Sr., born May 1, 1797
Matilda Ann Tevis born Jan. 10, 1805; married Jan. 21, 1819.

#### Children

Robt. T. Tribble, born July 13, 1820
Mary Tribble, born Dec. 7, 1822
Amelia Tribble born Dec. 7, 1822
Napoleon T. Tribble, born April 17, 1825
Harriet Tribble born Jan. 15, 1827
Sallie Tribble born Oct. 26, 1828
Peter Tribble, born July 26, 1830
Pat Tribble, born May 4, 1832
Nannie Tribble, born Jan. 5, 1834
Alec Tribble born April 18, 1836
Lucy Tribble born Feb. 21, 1838
Robt. G. Tribble, born April 6, 1840
James P. Tribble, born Jan. 8, 1842
Dudley Tribble, born Oct. 3, 1843
Andrew Tribble, born June 18, 1848

#### Deaths

Matilda Tevis Tribble died 1861
Dudley Tribble, Sr., died June 1877

### Bible Record of James Polk Tribble as given by his daughter Mattie O. Tribble

James Polk Tribble, born January 8, 1842, and passed away Jan. 17, 1893.
Alice Phelps Tribble, born January 2, 1846.
James Polk Tribble and Alice Phelps Tribble married Feb. 27, 1872.

#### Children

Edwin Phelps Tribble, born August 28, 1873; died May 18, 1895.
Matilda Olive Tribble, born May 20, 1877.
Joel Dudley Tribble, born December 19, 1878
James Polk Tribble, Jr., born Jan. 19, 1884.
James Polk Tribble married Adele Cooper November 30, 1923.
The only child of James Polk and Adele C. Tribble, Alice Jane Tribble, born July 14, 1924.

### Bible Record of Dudley Tribble, Jr.

Dudley Tribble born Oct. 3, 1843.
Dudley Tribble died Dec. 6, 1911.

Fetnie A. Weathers born Nov. 3, 1851.
Fetnie W. Tribble died Jan. 14, 1912.
Dudley Tribble and Fetnie Weathers mar. Feb. 1, 1872.
Caswell W. Tribble born Nov. 6, 1872.
Caswell W. Tribble died March 25, 1911.
Matilda Tribble born Aug. 30, 1874.
Matilda Tribble married Dec. 12, 1912, John J. Williams.
John J. Williams died Dec. 24, 1930.
Mary Tribble, born Feb. 25, 1877 married Nov. 29, 1911, **James J. Neale.**
Margaret Neale, born Dec. 20, 1915.
James J. Neale, Jr., born March 12, 1917.
Lucile Tribble, born April 25, 1882.
Lucille Tribble, died April 25, 1883.
Florence Tribble, born Oct. 12, 1879.
Florence Tribble died Jan. 3, 1888.
Bessie Tribble, born June 2, 1885.
Bessie Tribble, married Vernon Leer June 30, 1914.
Bessie Tribble Leer, born Nov. 17, 1917.

----

Bessie Tribble Leer married Duncan Nave. One child, **Ann Duncan Nave.**

----

### (Contributed by Mrs. Vernon Leer)

Peter Tribble, born July 26, 1830.
Avie Miller, born Sept. 22, 1853.
Peter and Avie Miller Tribble married Feb. 14, 1877.

### Children
Pattie Mildred Tribble, born Feb. 11, 1878.
Felix Winfield Tribble, born Dec. 26, 1880.
Dudley Tribble, born Jan. 10, 1881; died May 20, 1905 (unmarried).

Pattie Tribble married Charles A. Chenault Feb. 24, 1904. No issue.
Felix W. Tribble married Dovie Davenport 1918.
They had one child, Helen Frances Tribble, born July 12, 1929.

Mary Jane Tribble, daughter of Dudley Tribble, Sr., and Matilda Tevis, married James Berry Turner on Sept. 28, 1841.

### Children
Bettie Ann, born 1842 and died 1900.
Matilda, born 1844 and died 1926.
Thomas, born 1848, died 1902.
Dudley, 1850, died in infancy.
Amelia, born 1852, died 1915.
Brown, 1853 and living in 1932.

## Marriages

Bettie Ann married Thomas Phelps Oct. 20, 1860, in Richmond, Mo.
Thomas married Ellen Duncan, 1876, in Missouri.
Matilda married Joseph Phelps, 1864, in Richmond, Ky.
Amelia married James Monroe Leer Oct. 29, 1894, in Madison County, Ky.
Brown married Emma McWilliams June 3, 1877 in Mo.

(Contributed by Mrs. Benjamin F. Buckley)

### Madison County Court House

Will Book No. 1, Page 89. Certified Copy

Leaves $8477.59 to each of his children. Have advanced to Mary Jane Turner, now deceased, that amount. Note for $2000 against my son-in-law J. F. Collier, husband of my daughter Nannie Collier. Leaves his estate to be equally divided between all his chidren and the descendants of any child which may be dead.

Appoints his son-in-law, Francis M. Smith and sons, James P. Tribble and Robt. G. Tribble Executors.

Will dated April 26, 1872.

Signed, Dudley Tribble Sen.

### Dudley Tribble—Executors Settlement—January 1, 1879

### Summary

The Executors are indebted to the heirs as follows:

| | |
|---|---:|
| Mrs. Amelia Thompson | $2522.92 |
| N. T. Tribble | 2522.92 |
| Peter Tribble | 2522.92 |
| Mrs. Harriet Mason | 2522.92 |
| Mrs. Sally Quisenberry | 2522.92 |
| Mrs. Pattie Chenault | 2522.92 |
| Mrs. Nannie Collier | 2522.92 |
| Mrs. Lucy Smith | 2522.92 |
| Robt. G. Tribble | 2522.92 |
| Jas. P. Tribble | 2522.92 |
| Dudley Tribble, Jr. | 2522.92 |

### Children of Mrs. Mary Jane Turner:

| | |
|---|---:|
| Bettie Phelps | 504.58 |
| Tilly Phelps | 504.58 |
| Thos. Turner | 504.58 |
| Jno. Brown Turner | 504.58 |
| Amelia Lear | 504.58 |

Mar. 7, 1879 Robt. G. Tribble, one of the Executors this day filed with this settlement, in open court final receipts for the amounts due all the respective heirs, as shown in this settlement, the same to be noted of record at foot of this settlement.

Att: James Tevis C.M.C.C.

Deed from Perry, Noble Co. Okla. Book DR, page 5
from Certified Copy.

This indenture made this the 3rd day of February in the year 1920 between, Corday Leer Buckley and her husband B. F. Buckley of Lexington, Kentucky: Vernon Leer and his wife Bessie T. Leer of Richmond, Kentucky: Tillie Leer Denton and her husband, John Will Denton of Lexington, Kentucky; Amelia Leer Caruthers and her husband Alfred Caruthers of Pineville, Kentucky; Loura Leer Early and her husband Roger Early of Lexington, Kentucky; J. Monroe Leer and his wife, George Leer, of Paris Kentucky, parties of the first part and Davereau Leer of Chicago, Illinois, party of the second part;

WITNESSETH: That the parties of the first part in consideration of the sum of One ($1.00) Dollar unto each of said parties of the first part duly paid, the receipt whereof is hereby confessed and acknowledged, and the further consideration that Corday Leer Buckley, daughter; Vernon Leer, son, Tillie Leer Denton, daughter, Amelia Leer Caruthers, daughter, Loura Leer Early, daughter, and J. Monroe Leer, son the grantors herein and the grantee Davereau Leer, are children of Amelia T. Leer, deceased and are the only children surviving her and in consideration of the fact that she was a widow at the time of her death, to-wit on 1st day of March 1915 and that there were no children or heirs of deceased children and that her said children herein enumerated were and are the only heirs and of the relationship herein described and as such did inherit all of her property real and personal and that said parties in the course of settling and adjusting the property mutually inherited by them by the law of descent, and distribution of the various states where such property was located have elected to and are exchanging and accepting benefits therefrom and this being the course of the adjustment and settlement of property interests between them the grantors above enumerated to by these presents, grant, bargain, sell unto said party of the second part, his heirs and assigns all of the following described property and premises situated in the County of Noble, State of Oklahoma:—

Lots One (1) Two (2) Three (3) Four (4) Five (5) Twelve (12) Thirteen (13) and Fourteen (14) in Block Seven (7) North and West Perry, in addition to the Original Townsite of the City of Perry.

\* \* \* \* \*

It is hereby covenanted that the said Amelia T. Leer was the mother of the above enumerated sons and daughters and that they are her sole and *exlusive* heirs and that there was no surviving husband nor other children, grandchildren, or issues than those herein enumerated and that the said Amelia T. Leer left no will, but that all of her property passed by law of descent and distribution under the law of succession of the states where same was located. That she departed this life on the 1 day of March 1915 at home in County of Bourbon State of Kentucky and that she was a resident of said Bourbon County, Kentucky, at the time of her death, covenants are covered by Warranty Deed of title here-inbefore set out.

In witness whereof, The said parties of the first part have hereunto set their hands the day and year first above written

| | |
|---|---|
| Amelia Leer Caruthers | Corday Leer Buckley |
| A. Caruthers | B. F. Buckley |
| Loura Leer Early | Vernon Leer |
| Roger Early | Bessie T. Leer |
| George Leer | Tillie Leer Denton |
| J. Monroe Leer | John Will Denton. |

## WORTHINGTON

Bible records contributed by Mrs. Walter B. Worthington, of "Hilltop," Mason county, Kentucky. Copied by Mrs. Lula Reed Boss.

Worthington Bible published by N. J. White, No. 108 Pearl street, New York, 1833.

### BIRTHS

Samuel Worthington born Jan. 25, 1807.

Elizabeth Worthington, wife of Samuel Worthington and daughter of Edward and Elizabeth Robertson, born Dec. 29, 1808.

Trolucia Stegar Worthington, 2nd wife of Samuel Worthington and daughter of Edward and Elizabeth Robertson, born Mar. 13, 1817.

Sarah M. Worthington, 3rd wife of Samuel Worthington and daughter of Daniel and Ruth Runyan, born Aug. 19, 1818.

Thomas E. Worthington, son of Samuel and Elizabeth Worthington, was born Sept. 11, 1830.

John Tolly Worthington, son of Samuel and Trolucia S. Worthington, born Aug. 29, 1835.

Elizabeth Airy Worthington, daughter of the same, born Mar. 4, 1838 at 2 o'clock A. M.

William Henry Worthington, son of the same, born Sept. 30, 1839 at 10 P. M.

Mary Ruth Worthington, daughter of Samuel and Sarah M. Worthington, born Feb. 24, 1844.

Elizabeth Worthington, daughter of Samuel and Sarah M. Worthington, born Nov. 27, 1845.

Sarah Ann Worthington, daughter of Samuel and Sarah M. Worthington, born Aug. 29, 1847.

Charles Daniel Worthington, son of Samuel and Sarah M. Worthington, born June 30, 1849.

Richard Runyan Worthington, son of Samuel and Sarah M. Worthington, born Aug. 14, 1851.

Walter V. Worthington, son of Samuel and Sarah M. Worthington, born Jan. 19, 1854.

Martha Love Worthington, daughter of Samuel and Sarah M. Worthington, born May 21, 1855.

Lydia Lenora Worthington, daughter of Samuel and Sarah M. Worthington, born Aug. 30, 1857.

Samuel Worthington was married to his beloved wife, Elizabeth Robertson, September 11, 1828.

Samuel Worthington was married to his beloved wife, Sarah M. Runyan, January 19, 1843.

## DEATHS

Elizabeth Worthington, consort of Samuel Worthington, departed this life Aug. 12, 1833, aged 24 years 7 months 13 days.

Trolucia Stegar Worthington, 2nd wife of Samuel Worthington, departed this life Oct. 26, 1840, aged 23 years 7 months 25 days.

Charles D. Worthington, son of Samuel and Sarah M. Worthington, departed this life Aug. 25, 1850, aged 1 year 1 month 25 days.

Eliza Jane Worthington, daughter of Samuel and Sarah M. Worthington, died Sept. 30, 1850, aged 4 years 10 months 3 days.

Walter Worthington, son of Samuel and Sarah M. Worthington, died Feb. 20, 1854, aged 1 month 1 day.

John Tolley Worthington, son of Samuel and Trolucia Worthington, died Feb. 22, 1854, aged 18 years 5 months 23 days.

Dr. Thomas E. Worthington, eldest son of Samuel and Elizabeth Worthington, died April 15, 1859, aged 28 years 6 months 24 days.

Gen. Sam Worthington died Oct. 3, 1862, aged 55 years 8 months 28 days.

Lydia Lenora Worthington died Jan. 23, 1863, aged 4 years 4 months.

Mary Ruth Worthington died Mar. 22, 1863, aged 19 years 27 days.

Sallie M. Worthington died Dec. 2, 1910, aged 93 years.

Martha Love Worthington Thompson died Mar. 12, 1939, aged 83 years 10 months.

Samuel Worthington born Nov. 17, 1734. Mary, daughter of Walter Tolley, wife of Samuel Worthington, born Mar. 12, 1740. They were married Jan. 29, 1758.

Sons and daughters of Samuel and Mary Tolley Worthington:

(1) John Tolley Worthington, born Sept. 29, 1760, intermarried with Mary, daughter of Drice Worthington. Died Sept. 3, 1834.

(2) Comfort Worthington, born Jan. 6, 1762, intermarried with John W. Dorsey. Died July 23, 1837.

(3) Ann Worthington, born Nov. 20, 1763, intermarried with William Rigoley (?) and Trueman Hawley. Died June 29, 1827.

(4) Walter Worthington, born Feb. 1765, intermarried with Sarah Hood, 1786.

(5) Vachel Worthington, born Feb. 8, 1767; died Oct. 22, 1832.

(6) Elizabeth Worthington, born July 14, 1768; died Aug. 15, 1768.

(7) Charles Worthington, born Sept. 22, 1770, intermarried with Sarah Johns, 1803. Died 1847.

(8) Thomas Tolley Worthington and (9) James Tolley Worthington, born Dec. 17, 1771; intermarried—Thomas, the Misses Whipps; James with Miss S. James died October, 1830. Thomas died July 30, .....

(10) Edward Worthington, born June 18, 1773, intermarried with Elizabeth L. Madison (Morrison?) 1798; died 1846.

(11) Martha Worthington, born April 9, 1775, intermarried with Ed Ripoley (?) 1793, who died in 1798, and Dr. Thomas Worthington, 1802. She died Jan. 23, 1846 at 72 years.

(12) Samuel Worthington, Jr., born Sept. 23, 1776; died Dec. .......
Mary, his wife, died Oct. 2, 1777 (This date seems inconsistent. More than likely the date of her birth. This added by L. R. B.)

Samuel Worthington, Sr., intermarried with Martha Garrison (2nd wife) cousin of first wife, September 1778, by whom he had the twelve children.

Samuel Worthington, Sr., died April 8, 1815. Martha, his 2nd wife, died Dec. 31, 1831, aged 78 years.

Abraham Worthington of Missouri, late of Fleming county, Kentucky, died in Missouri, December, 1820.

John Worthington - Lydia Worthington married March 19, 1851.

## CHILDREN

**Lydia Worthington, born Dec. 12, 1824; died Dec. 16, 1875 (or 95).
Julia Matt Worthington, born April 23, 1853.
William Walter Worthington, born Apr. 23, 1855.
Thomas Worthington, born Jan. 23, 1858.
John Henry Worthington, born Dec. 22, 1860.
Jacob Andrew Worthington, born Oct. 7, 1863.
Scott Worthington, born Dec. 1, 1867; drowned June 24, 1884.
John Henry Worthington, Sr., born July 26, 1825; died July, 1872.

**Perhaps this is the birth date of Lydia Worthington, wife of John Worthington. This added by L. R. B.

Records from the Bible of the late Mrs. Elizabeth Hildreth (Fristoe) Reed, and now in the possession of her son, Mr. Charles Franklin Reed, of Maysville, Kentucky.

The Bible was published in 1866 by William W. Harding, No. 326 Chestnut street, Philadelphia, Pennsylvania.

## MARRIAGES

Robert Fristoe and Lucinda Bartlett were married May 11, 1824.
Byram Harding and Elizabeth Hildreth Fristoe were married October 23, 1845.
Jacob Reed and Elizabeth H. Harding were married April 17, 1855.
J. C. A. King and Lucinda V. Harding were married March 13, 1864.
Charles F. Reed and Jennie Kehoe were married February 11, 1885.

## BIRTHS

Robert Fristoe was born April 4, 1801.
Lucinda Bartlett was born November 30, 1807.
Jacob Reed was born August 3, 1823.
Elizabeth H. Fristoe was born August 20, 1826.
Lucinda Virginia Harding was born July 29, 1846.

Robert Parker Reed was born October 27, 1858.
Charles Franklin Reed was born September 17, 1861.
James B. F. Reed was born February 9, 1868.
James Bailey Fristoe was born April 10, 1828.
Silas Franklin Fristoe was born April 30, 1833.

## DEATHS

Lucinda Fristoe died November 15, 1867.
Robert Fristoe died June 16, 1873.
James Bailey Fristoe Reed died November 3, 1888.
Robert Parker Reed died May 29, 1859.
Lucinda V. King died January 2, 1871.
Jacob Reed died November 26, 1913.
Elizabeth Hildreth Fristoe Reed died December 4, 1919.

---

Records copied from Bible published in 1817 by M. Carey and Son, No. 126 Chestnut Street, Philadelphia, Pennsylvania, and owned by Mrs. Harry M. Clark, 136 East Third Street, Maysville, Mason county, Kentucky.

## BIRTHS

John W. Clark was born August 25, 1792.
Jane Mitchell was born October 4, 1797.
William B. Clark was born February 3, 1816.
James M. Clark was born July 29, 1817.
Richard C. Clark was born July 5, 1819.
John W. Clark was born January 10, 1824.
Nancy E. Clark was born May 14, 1826.
Frances Marian Clark was born October 13, 1828.
James McNeeley was born June 15, 1848.
Jane Graham McNeeley was born June 17, 1849.
Mary Frances McNeeley was born June 11, 1851.
Robert McNeeley was born November 4, 1852.
Jeremiah McNeeley, Jr., was born March 19, 1854.
Ann Elizabeth McNeeley was born July 29, 1857.
Jerry McNeeley, Jr., was born May 26, 1861.
Ann Cooper McNeeley was born March 9, 1863.

## MARRIAGES

John W. Clark was married to Jane Mitchell, April 27, 1815.
James Clark was married to Jane Lynn, November 15, 1838.
Richard Clark was married to Eleanor Harris, April 30, 1840.
Jeremiah McNeeley was married to Ann Elizabeth Clark, June 30, 1847.
Jennie McNeeley was married to Joe Thompson, May 23, 1872.
Mary F. McNeeley was married to John J. Klipp, October 17, 1878.

## DEATHS

William B. Clark, 18 months old, departed this life July 27, 1817 of cholera morbus.

**Nancy Mitchell, mother-in-law, 46th year, died July 30, 1821.

William Clark, brother, died October 29, 1823.

John Mitchell, 70th year, departed this life December 4, 1830.

John W. Clark, 43rd year, departed this life June 5th in the year 1833.

John W. Clarke, Jr., departed this life September 25, 1826 in the 13th year of age.

Richard C. Clarke died May 25, 1862.

Jane Clark departed this life April 22, 1846.

James McNeeley, 8 days, departed this life June 22, 1848.

Jeremiah McNeeley, 16 months, departed this life July 27, 1855.

Ann Elizabeth McNeeley, 5 years, died June 7, 1862.

Jerry McNeeley, 17 months, died October 16, 1862.

Ann Elizabeth McNeeley, our mother, died April 8, 1871.

Ann Cooper McNeeley died January 1, 1875.

**Nancy Mitchell, wife of John Mitchell (1770-1830), born September 14, 1775; died Maysville, Kentucky, July 30, 1821, was the daughter of Jacob Boone (born Bucks county, Pa., August 15, 1754; died Maysville, May 4, 1827) and his wife, Mary DeHart (born October 10, 1753 in Pa.; died Maysville, July 30, 1828.) Jacob Boone was a soldier of the Revolution. See: Pennsylvania Archives, 3rd Series, Volume 6, page 314. Jacob Boone also signed the Oath of Allegiance in Bucks county, Pennsylvania, June 13, 1777. (This information added by LRB.)

---

## CHRISMAN

Contributed by Elizabeth Land Smith (Mrs. W. H. Smith)

Marriage bond between James Porter and Miss Rebecca Chrisman, found in Old File Box 8, Office of the Clerk of the County Court of Jessamine County, Kentucky

Know all men by these presents that we, James Porter and Joseph H. Chrisman, are held and firmly bound unto the Commonwealth of Kentucky, in the just and full sum of fifty pounds current money, for which payment well and truly to be made we bind ourselves jointly and severally firmly by these presents sealed with our seals and dated this 11th day of November, 1818.

The condition of this obligation is such that whereas there is a marriage shortly intended to be solemnized between the above bound James Porter and Miss Rebecca Chrisman of this County, now if there be no lawful cause to obstruct said marriage then the above obligation to be void, else to remain in full force and virtue.

James Porter (Seal)

Jos. H. Chrisman (Seal)

Dan. G. B. Price, Clk.

## WILL OF JAMES HITER, SR.
### Will Book B, page 137, Woodford County, Kentucky.

In the name of God, Amen. I, James Hiter, Sr., of Woodford County and State of Kentucky, being very sick and low in health but in no ways deranged in mind and knowing it is appointed for all men once to die, do make, ordain and constitute this to be my last Will and Testament.

And first my body I commit to the Earth, my soul to God that gave it, and all my Estate, both real and personal, I give and bequeath to my beloved wife, Betsy Hiter, during her life (all my just debts to be first paid) to be enjoyed by her fully during her life and at her death all my Estate both real and personal to be sold and divided into twelve and one-half equal parts, in order that my son, James Hiter, Jr., shall and may enjoy one and half portion in consideration of his services in building my dwellinghouse, the other eleven parts to be divided among the other eleven children.

I also give and bequeath to my two sons, Richard and Benjamin Hiter, one horse, mare or gelding, to be valued at least to forty dollars exclusive of their equal portion, to my youngest daughter, Polly, I do give and bequeath one bed and sufficient furniture, exclusive of her equal portion.

I do hereby constitute and ordain Charles Hiter and Betsy Hiter, my wife, my executor and executrix, and in order that no part of the within shall be misconstrued, I do most solemnly desire that no meaning shall be put on any part but that in which it reads.

In Witness Whereof I have hereunto put my hand and seal this 29th day of August, 1801.

Signed James Hiter, Sr.    (Seal)

Signed, sealed and
delivered in presence of
Samuel Woolfolk
Leroy Howard
William Lewis

At a Court held for Woodford County, the 5th day of October, 1801. This will was brought into Court, proved by the oath of Samuel Woolfork and Leroy Howard and ordered to be recorded.

Teste George Brook, C.W.C.C.

## WILL OF EDWARD WILLIS
### Will Book D, page 537, Garrard County, Kentucky.

The State of Kentucky, the 20th day of May, 1818. In the Name of God, Amen. I, Edward Willis, of Garrard County, being low of body but of sound and disposing mind, I do ordain this to be my last Will and Testament.

1. I wish to be buried in a decent manner.
2. I wish all my just debts paid.
3. I will and bequeath to my *beloving* wife, Ellender Willis, all my estate, real and personal, to dispose of as she thinks proper, for the use

of the family in during her life or widowhood. And if my wife, Ellender Willis, should marry, I wish my property to be sold and disposed of as the law directs.

Lastly I wish my children, as they come of age, to used to be made equal with the first.

Given under my hand and seal.

his

Edward x Willis    Seal

mark

Teste:
James Phillips
John Ham
Mourning Phillips

Garrard County Court.

I hereby certify this Last Will and Testament of Edward Willis, dec'd., was exhibited into Court at December County Court, 1818, and proven by the oaths of James Phillips and John Ham, two subscribing witnesses thereto, and ordered to be recorded, and the same is done. Admitted to record.

Teste, Ben Letcher, C.G.C.C.

Note: Estate papers of Edward Willis mention the following as his children: Sterling Willis; David Willis; Elizabeth Nicholson; Catherine Willis; William H. Willis; Mourning Willis.

## WILL OF WILLIAM WILLIS

Will Book D, page 447, Madison County, Kentucky.

Madison County, State of Kentucky, September, 1828. By these few lines I communicate my mind to paper as my last Will and Testament, by which the world and all it may concern may know that I, William Willis, first request that all my just debts be paid and after they are satisfied I give all that I have, both real and personal estate, to brother Samuel Willis, his heirs and assigns forever, which he is to hold as or for his own from henceforth and forever; as Witness Whereof I have subscribed my name.

William Willis    (Seal)

Teste: Henry Willis
       John Willis

Kentucky, Madison County, Sct.

I, David Irvine, Clerk of the Court for the County aforesaid, do hereby certify that at a County Court held for Madison County on Monday the 6th day of October, 1828, this instrument of writing was produced in open court and proven to be the last will and testament of William Willis, dec'd., by the oaths of Henry Willis and John Willis, two subscribing witnesses thereto and ordered to be recorded and the same has been done accordingly.

Att: David Irvine, M.C.C.C.

## WILL OF SHERROD WILLIS

Will Book A, page 160, Jessamine County, Kentucky.

In the name of God, Amen. Whereas I, Sherrod Willis, being at this time infirm in body but mental faculties sound, knowing that all men have to die, I wish to settle my worldly or personal property, as followeth, viz.:

To my beloved wife, Maryann, I leave during her widowhood all property I am possessed of, cash, notes, bonds, only the following exceptions: to my youngest son, Lewis, I leave my negro boy named Isaac; to my daughters Eliza and Jenny I leave to each bed and furniture and ten dollars in cash; at my wife's marriage or decease which comes first, all the remainder of my estate is to be equally divided among my children, each one to have their legal quota, and I do appoint the following persons my executors: My wife, Maryann, John Ellenbaugh and John Hunter, and this I maintain to be my last will and testament, given under my hand and seal this 3rd day of March, 1806.

his

Sherrod x Willis    Seal

mark

Signed, sealed and delivered
in presence of us
Jas. Hemphill
James Dickerson
Anna x (her mark) Jammieson.

Jessamine County, to-wit, June Court, 1806.

This last will and testament of Sherrod Willis, dec'd., was produced in Court and proven by James Hemphill and Anna Jammieson, two of the subscribing witnesses thereto, and ordered to be recorded.

Teste:  Sam'l. H. Woodson.

## WILL OF EDMOND SINGLETON

Will Book B, page 152, Jessamine County, Kentucky.

In the name of God, Amen. I, *Edmond* Singleton, of Jessamine County and State of Kentucky, being weak in body but of sound and perfect mind and memory, blessed be Almighty God for the same, do make this my last will and testament in manner and form following:

First I give and bequeath unto my beloved wife, Margaret Singleton, the house and land on which I now live with all the household and kitchen furniture and the plantation, tools and utensils of every kind, also all my stock of cattle, sheep and hogs, to her during her natural life or widowhood, for the support of herself and family; also a negro man, Humphrey, and a negro woman named Rachel, and Rachel's *child,* namely, Ham, Mariah, Jinny, and Jerry, to her, my beloved wife, during her natural life or widowhood, as the other property stated above.

I also have given and bequeathed unto my daughter, Elizabeth Mason, formerly to the amount of fifteen hundred dollars in land and a negro woman named Judith and her increase forever, which I estimate being worth five hundred dollars; also a beast and saddle, one feather-bed and furniture which I estimate to be worth $100, total amount that I have given and that the said Elizabeth Mason has received is twenty-one hundred dollars; and to my daughter, Martha Craig, I have given and bequeathed in the same kind of property and to the same amount of twenty-one hundred dollars which the said Martha Craig has received, being equal with her sister Mason.

And to my beloved children who have not had any of my estate, I will and bequeath to each of them after my just debts are paid off, namely, as followeth: To Daniel Singleton, twenty-one hundred dollars out of my estate when he, the said Daniel Singleton, comes of age; to Polly Singleton, I give twenty-one hundred dollars out of my estate to be paid to her when she, the said Polly Singleton, marries or comes of age; and to Sally Singleton I give twenty-one hundred dollars out of my estate to be paid to her when she, the said Sally, marries or comes of age; and to James Singleton, to John Singleton, to George Singleton, I give to each of them twenty-one hundred dollars out of my estate to be paid to each of them when they come of age.

But if any of my six last mentioned children should die, having no heir lawfully begotten of his own body or her own body, *there* estate shall be equally divided between those of the six that may be living, and none of my children is to be charged with raising, and if my loving wife and each of my children have all got their parts as above stated, if there should be yet a surplus of my personal estate it is to be divided equally amongst the six last mentioned, my first two children, namely, Elizabeth Mason and Martha Craig, I will and bequeath unto them an equal share of all my outlands with the other six children, and I hereby appoint my beloved wife Margaret Singleton and Elijah Carmell and Samuel Craig as my Executrix and Executors of this my last will and Testament, having revoked all former wills I ever made, signed, sealed and published this my last Will and Testament. In the presence of us the undersigned witnesses,

his<br>
*Edward* x Singleton    Seal<br>
mark

Thomas Davix
    his
Harvey X. Walker
    mark
Fielding Pilcher

Jessamine County, Sct., May, 1814.

This last will and testament of *Edmund* Singleton, dec'd., was this day produced in Court, proven by the subscribing witnesses thereto, and ordered to be recorded.

Teste:  G. H. Woodward, Clk.

## WILL OF MASON SINGLETON

Will Book D, page 410, Jessamine County, Kentucky.

I, Mason Singleton, of Jessamine County and State of Kentucky, do make this my last will and testament, and publish the same.

First, I will my wife, Fanny, and my son, Waller, the home place, a block house with one hundred and ten acres of land attached thereto. It is my wish that my wife, Fanny, have the following slaves: Nancy, Nan, Jane, Rachel, etc., given as per proportion of the slaves, with such stock as she may choose to the amount of one-fourth of every kind, and kitchen furniture, farming tools, etc.

I will that my son, Jeremiah, have the land where he now lives, also Suck with her increase, the land at twenty-five dollars per acre, and Suck and child at two hundred dollars, he having paid the balance of her price. My son, Moses, to have Sam and what I paid for the land he sold to Merit Singleton at twelve hundred dollars, and the balance of property agreeable to a list which I have recorded for each child as having received heretofore, and Merit to have Lewis with child as having been received heretofore, and with what I paid for his land at one thousand dollars; the other property as listed and also the balance of the Williams place at twenty dollars per acre; and also twenty acres of land adjoining Merit's place at twenty-five dollars per acre.

My daughter, Lucy, to have Mitty and Eve at six hundred dollars with the property as listed. My daughter Jane to have Winny at two hundred and fifty dollars and other property as listed heretofore. Mason to have May at two hundred dollars and one hundred for Ginny which he sold and property as listed.

I will Joel W. Singleton the stone house where Mother lives, with so much of the home place beginning in Lewis Singleton's line running near the spring northwestwardly, so as to give him one hundred ten acres, and I give to Joel, Lewis and Jerry, the land to be valued at twenty-five dollars per acre. I will unto Waller Singleton the land assigned in this will for him and his mother (?) as also Peter, the land to be valued at twenty-five dollars per acre.

It is my last will that Elizabeth Price be made equal in every respect with the rest to my children. It is my understanding of my above will that if the sale of the surplus property is not sufficient to make all my children equal, that those who have received the most shall respond (?) back until all have received an equal proportion of my estate.

Written by my request and sealed with my own seal this 27th day of July, 1833. I appoint as my executors my beloved friends, Hawkins Craig, Merit S. Singleton, Joel W. Singleton.

Mason Singleton    (Seal)

Teste: R. B. Berry
       W. E. Walton
       Hawkins Craig
       John Lafon.

August Court, 1833.

Jessamine County, Sct.

The foregoing last Will and Testament of Mason Singleton, dec'd., was this day produced in open Court and proven by the oaths of W. E. Walton, Hawkins Craig, and John Lafon, subscribing witnesses thereto, to be the last Will and Testament of said Mason Singleton and Whereupon the same was ordered by the Court to be recorded.

Teste: Dan'l. G. Price, Clk.
by I. C. Price, D. C.

## WILL OF JOSEPH CHRISMAN, SR.

### Will Book D, p. 79, Jessamine County, Kentucky

In the name of God, Amen. I, Joseph Chrisman of the County of Jessamine and State of Kentucky, being weak of body but of sound disposing mind and memory, do make, ordain and publish the following to be my last will and testament, for the distribution of the estate of which I am possessed.

First, it is my will and desire that all my just debts be paid as also all expenses attending my burial.

Item Second. It is my will and desire that my beloved wife, Jane Chrisman, take the third of the farm and plantation whereon I now live to be laid off to her on the east side of the Hickman Road in any way she may choose; that she have her choice of two of my negroes, a man and a woman, also a negro woman named Sally, and their increase, if any. I give to her also as many cows as she may think proper to keep for her support; she is further at liberty to retain as many hogs and sheep as she may think necessary for her support and the support of her family. She is also to have and retain her choice of three horses out of my stock, the wagon and as much of the gear as may be necessary, also as many of the farming utensils and as much of the household and kitchen furniture as she may think proper and necessary for the use and comfort of herself and family.

I furthermore give unto my beloved wife two hundred dollars in money for her own proper use and disposal. It is my will also that my wife have the use of the stock until her death at which time it is my will and desire that the whole of the property then remaining in her possession which I have given her (except the third of the land and the sum of money which I have given her) be sold by my executors hereinafter appointed and the proceeds of the sale be equally divided between my eight daughters. It is my wish that the three negroes and their increase be purchased by some of my family.

In the lifetime of my son, George Chrisman, I gave and conveyed to him by deed two hundred acres of my land which was laid off on the west side of the Hickman Road, which together with the other property which I had given to him agreeably to a Book account which I have kept of the distribution of property to my children, I deem a full portion and therefore give to his heirs nothing more.

Item 3. I give and bequeath to my son, Lewis H. Chrisman, one horse and a bridle, one negro boy named Patrick. I further give to my son Lewis, 250 acres of the tract of land and plantation on which I now live, to be laid off on the east side of the Hickman road, to have possession thereof when he shall marry or arrive to the age of twenty-one years, but not to have possession of the third part which is devised to his mother until after her death unless it is her good pleasure to give it to him sooner.

It is my will and wish that my son, Lewis, be raised and have a good English education given him and the expenses to be paid out of my estate. If my son Lewis should die without issue it is then my will and desire that the land and other property which I have devised to him be sold by my executors and the proceeds of the sale be equally divided between my eight daughters or the heirs of their bodies.

Item 4. It is my will and desire that the balance of the plantation, after my wife has taken her third part, be rented out by my executors to the best advantage. It is my will and my executors are hereby authorized to make sale of the one hundred acres of my land lying on the west side of the Hickman Road and fifty acres to be laid off on the east of the tract adjoining Martin Whip's land, my lots in and adjoining the town of Nicholasville, and all the rest of my estate, both real, personal, not herein particularly devised, or heretofore given to my children, and the proceeds of the sales, together with the money arising from the rent aforesaid, the money which may be coming to me from my father's estate, and the money which I may have on hand at my death, or which may be then due me (except the two hundred dollars given to my beloved wife), be placed by my Executors in one fund, and by them equally divided between my eight daughters or the heirs of their bodies, to-wit: Jinny Keller, wife of Joseph Keller, Polly McDowell, wife of Samuel McDowell, Peggy Hill, wife of James Hill, Betsy Bradshaw, wife of Smith Bradshaw, Rebecca Porter, wife of James Porter, Love Hogan, wife of William Hogan, Nancy Bradshaw, wife of John Bradshaw, and Hannah McCampbell, wife of John McCampbell.

And in as much as I have been unable in the gifts I have made to my daughters to make them all equal in value, one with another, which has always been my wish, I have kept a book of accounts in which I have charged each with the advances made to them; and it is according to the proportion which those advances bear to each other, that I wish them to receive each their portion of the estate embraced in this my will so that they may be made equal, taking into view what they have received and what they are to receive.

And to enable my Executors or such of them as may think proper to act to carry my intention (in this respect) into full effect, I most earnestly desire that they may take for their guide the account book aforesaid, and make division among my daughters of the estate devised for that purpose so that finally all shall be equal. It is furthermore my desire that the negroes which may be sold be purchased in by the family unless they shall choose to be sold to persons out of the family.

And lastly I do hereby appoint Samuel McDowell, William Hogan and Samuel Barkley Executors of this my last Will and Testament or such of them as may choose to qualify to carry the same into effect.

In Testimony whereof I have hereunto set my hand and seal, this eighth day of February, in the year of our Lord, 1826, hereby revoking all other wills by me heretofore written or signed.

Joe Chrisman (Seal)

Witnesses:

    Dan'l B. Price
    James Porter
    John G. McCampbell

### Jessamine County Court, February Court, 1828

The foregoing last will and testament of Joseph Chrisman was this day produced in court and proven by the oaths of Daniel B. Price, James Porter, John G. McCampbell, the subscribing witness thereto, to be the last will and testament of Joseph Chrisman and ordered to be entered of record.

    Att: Daniel B. Price, Clk.

## WILL OF JANE CHRISMAN

### Will Book E, p. 74, Jessamine County, Kentucky

In the name of God, Amen. I, Jane Chrisman, being of sound mind and disposing memory, do make, ordain and publish this to be my last will and testament in manner following:

I give and bequeath to my son, Lewis Chrisman, my negro woman slave named Mary and her future increase. Also his choice of three of my stock of horses, also three cows and calves, ten sheep, one bed, two bedsteads, six blankets, six sheets, five pairs of pillowcases, a coverled quilt, two white or two checked counterpanes, four tablecloths, four towels and the *Ballance* of the household and kitchen furniture which I have procured since my husband's death; also I give to him the farming utensils I have procured since my husband's death.

I also give to him all the benefits of the crops of produce remaining on the farm at my death of every description; I also give to my said son (now in his possession) fifteen two year old *stears* this spring, four yearling stears and three heifers, two *yearly* mare colts, one a bay, the other a sorrel, and a bay mare now five years old this spring; one small gray mare four years old this spring; one *sorrell* horse, baldface colt, three years old this spring, which last mentioned stock he is at liberty to dispose of then or at any time as he pleases.

It is my will that my negro named Perry, together with the balance of my property of every kind not otherwise disposed of in this will be sold by my executors and the proceeds be equally divided between my daughters, Jane Keller, Polly McDowell, Margaret Hill, Betsy Bradshaw, Rebecca Porter, Love Hogan and my grand-daughter, Jane Love Mc-

Campbell, daughter of my daughter, Hannah McCampbell, deceased, to be given to my said grand-daughter when she marries or becomes of age, but should she die before either event then her part to be equally divided between the above named daughters or their heirs.

It is further my will that my son, Lewis H. Chrisman, out of what I have given him, pay all my debts and funeral expenses.

Lastly, I do hereby nominate and appoint my son, Lewis H. Chrisman, and George Caldwell executors of this my last will and testament, hereby revoking all former wills by me made.

In Testimony whereof I have hereunto set my hand and seal this twenty-second day of February, 1834.

Jane Chrisman (Seal)

Published in
presence of
Dan'l. B. Price
George Caldwell

Codicil. I do hereby now revoke that portion of the will which directs the sale of my negro boy Perry. I now give and bequeath the said negro boy, Perry, to my son, Lewis H. Chrisman, upon the condition that he pay four hundred dollars to my above named daughters or their heirs if they be not living, to be equally divided among them, to be paid them if I should die before that time, on the 25th day of December, 1837. I hereby declare the foregoing in all other respects, together (illegible) to be my last will and testament as witness my hand this 16th December, 1834.

Jane Chrisman (Seal)

Pub. & Dec. in
presence of
George Caldwell
Dan'l. B. Price

Jessamine County, Sct.                                    March Court, 1835.

The foregoing writing, purporting to be the last will and testament of Jane Chrisman, dec'd., was this day produced in open Court and proven by the oath of George Caldwell and Daniel B. Price, subscribing witnesses thereto, to be the last will and testament of said decedent, whereupon the same was ordered to be recorded, which is done.

Teste, Dan'l. B. Price, Clk.

## MAYSVILLE, KENTUCKY CEMETERY RECORDS (Old)

(Contributed by Mrs. Ann Delia Yellman)

Lot 205—George Cox, Sr.; Lissant Cox, 1905; Ann Cox, 1853; George Cox, 1881; Mary C. Cox, 1895; Horatio Nelson, 1865; Jos. H. Cox, 1861; M. S. Dimmitt; E. L. Reedy, 1905; George W. Reedy, 1876.

Lot 206, Sec. 6—(Jos. T. Broderick)—Edw. Cox Broderick, 1850; Forman Broderick; Fannie Broderick, 1894; Jos. Broderick, 1905; Morris Broderick, 1874; Fannie Broderick, 1898; Lizzie Broderick, 1860; James Broderick, 1854; Phoebe Hitner, 1937; grave.

Lot 207, Sec. 6—Jacob Wormald, 1857; Frances Wormald, 1857; Frances Wormald, 1865; James Wormald, 1878; George Wormald, 1890; Margaret Wormald, 1900; Catherine Rose Rice, 1912; Mary Wormald Bray, 1921; 3 other graves.

Lot 208—Section 6—John B. McIlvan, Francis Cooper, 1838; 2 graves unmarked.

Lot 209, Section 6—5 graves unmarked; Thornton Taylor; Children of Frances Taylor; Frank Robinson, 1926; Lucretia Robinson, 1869; James B. Robinson, 1854; Fannie R. Glascock, 1918.

Lot 210, Section 6—Julia Ann Parker, 1864; Eliza Mary Parker, 1890.

Lot 211, Section 6—Henry Waller; John H. Langhorn, 1833; Mrs. J. H. (Elizabeth) Langhorn, 1872; John T. Langhorn, 1833; Thomas Young, 1837, Captain in Revolutionary War; Rev. Maurice Waller, 1916.

Lot 212, Section 6—Wm. S. Allen, Samuel Allen, 1844.

Lot 225, Section 7—Arthur B. Given; ......Harrison.

Lot 226, Section 7—Wm. H. Carnahan, 1898; Alonzo Kidder, 1907; Edith Williams, 1912.

Lot 227, Section 7—Edward Forman, 1906; Jack Meyars; J. A. Teagar, 1914; Matilda Teagar, 1940; Henry Willett, 1939; Wm. Spromberg; Charley Spromberg, 1892; Margaret Molen, 1900; Miranda Molen, 1890; Lucy Molen, 1907; Henry Molin.

Lot 228, Section 7—Wm. Holliday; Nancy Holliday; Genia Sparks; Mrs. ........ Sparks; Lesley Sparks; W. H. Sparks—10 Ky. Co. K.

Lot 229, Section 7—Eliza B. Clinger, 1926; George M. Clinger, 1906; Geo. A. Clinger, 1914; Lutie Clinger Jones, 1916; Earl Wo.

Lot 230, Section 7—Mary E. Warwick, 1895; Alfred Warwick, 1898; Lizzie B. Sadler, 1895; Weta Sadler, 1900; W. C. Sadler, 1915; George Wood, 1904; Andrew Wood, 1925; Mary E. Wood, 1902; Martha Dudley Sadler, 1917.

Lot 231, Section 7—Catherine Stallcup, 1901; W. E. Stallcup, 1915; Frances Stallcup, 1923; Fannie Stallcup, 1925; Charles Stallcup; B. F. Huff, 1909; Elizabeth Huff, 1897.

Single Rights, Lot 337, Section 7—Ira Norton; John Jones; Addison Pollitt, 1905; Nancy J. Anderson, 1911; John B. Anderson, 1907; Sarah McCall, 1907.

Lot 213, Section 6—Gertrude Hord; Elizabeth T. Hord, 1884; Francis T. Hord, 1869; Harry C. Hord, 1864; Elias R. Hord, 1923; Mary C. Gordon, 1889; John R. Clarke, 1865; Judith Grant, 1866; Josephine Noyes, 1919; James B. Noyes, 1913; Mary G. Clarke, 1915; Jennie O. Clarke, 1919.

Lot 214, Section 6—I. Payne, A. E. Payne, Elizabeth Ann Payne, 1881; Thomas Young Payne, 1857; Elizabeth Ann Payne, 1835.

Lot 215, Section 6—Mary C. Crawford, 1879; Thomas Crawford, 1882; Henry Crawford; Mary Crawford, 1876; Joseph Crawford.

Lot 216, Section 6—Matilda G. Ranson, 1905; Achsah L. Ranson, 1889; R. H. Ranson, 1858; F. B. Ranson, 1914; Cordelia Green, 1861; M. C. Green, 1881; Elizabeth R. Morgan, 1926; Edith Morgan Purden, 1941.

Lot 217, Section 6—Ann Green, 1875; John Green, 1851; Caroline B. Hickman, 1836; David B. Hickman, 1823; Achsah Green, 1834; John

Green, Sr., 1818; John Green, 1838; Sarah Green, 1862; Cornelius Beatty, 1847; Caroline and Sarah Beatty, 1845. (or 1843)

Lot 219, Section 6—John A. Blanchard, 1898; James P. Blanchard, 1886; John Blanchard, 1908; Jane Blanchard, 1916; Kate Blanchard, 1912; Thomas Blanchard, 1915; Henry Blanchard, 1937; Kate D. Jones, 1938.

Lot 336, Section 7—Chas. B. Day, owner; Henry P. Day, 1913; Chas. Day; Anna Day, 1921; Edwin Day, 1903; Flora Day, 1940; Alice Day, 1943.

Lot 338, Section 7—Duke W. Kirk, 1904; Harry Tolle Child; Robert Kirk, 1914; Eleanor Kirk, 1927.

Lot 331—Adaline Potter, 1877; George Potter, 1875; Mrs. George Potter; Henry G. Potter, 1876; Geo. R. Potter; Charles Potter; Winfield S. Potter; Thankful P. Potter; Steven E. Potter; Christian Altmeyer, 1889; Anna M. Altmeyer, 1873; Christian Jr. Altmeyer, 1910; Racel Altmeyer, 1929.

Lot 330, Section 7—Mary S. Payne, 1919; Mary A. Payne, 1894; Nannie E. Payne, 1912; J. Rudy Payne, 1901; Lizzie Payne; John G. Payne, 1895; Hannah Daulton, 1901; Delmar Daulton, 1907; Miss Anna Payne, 1908; Bertha Caywood, 1912; Alice Robinson, 1924; Thelma Robinson, 1928.

Lot 316, Section 7—Taylor Alexander, Margaret Alexander, J. Duncan; Mary E. Breeze, 1887; Lloyd Senteney, Carrie D. Cobb, Daniel Cobb, 1923.

Limestone Chapter D. A. R., of Maysville, Ky., dedicated D. A. R. markers placed at the graves of deceased members in Maysville Cemetery.

Mrs. John D. Keith wrote the following tribute to Mrs. Martha Elizabeth Moore Power which was read at the grave, Monday, May 31, 1948, by Miss Wilson.

Martha Elizabeth Moore, wife of Hugh Power, was born at "Sharon", the family home near Aberdeen, Ohio Aug. 13, 1841, and died in Rock Island, Ill., Nov. 15, 1921. After six years of invalidism in the home of her daughter, Mrs. Ann Delia Yellman.

She was the daughter of Dr. Thomas Miles Moore and his wife, Ann Delia Harris Moore, married in Baltimore, Md., Feb. 14, 1832.

Mrs. Power came to Maysville as a bride in 1869 (Oct.), was left early a widow, with two children to raise, which in that day was a pretty difficult task to accomplish.

After Mrs. Power's mother and sister, Ruth, had entered into eternal rest, she and the children moved from Maysville over to "Sharon," the old home, one mile north of Aberdeen, where she cared for her father, until he joined his wife and daughter on the other side in 1895. Mrs. Power and her children Ann Delia and Frederick Moore, then returned to Maysville.

To those who had the rare privilege of knowing Mrs. Power, knew they had come in contact with a refined genuine lady with a soft spoken voice.

My mother-in-law, Mrs. Annie Dudley Richardson Keith, who has been a life long close friend of the family, sums it up in a very few words. She said, "Mrs. Power was the finest woman I ever knew."

Martha E. M. Power was a member of Fort Armstrong Chapter DAR of Rock Island, Ill., a devout member of the Church of the Nativity Maysville and a member of a circle formed within the Episcopal Church, of the National Order of Kings Daughters.

In closing, I feel like saying, to have known her was to love and admire her.

Lot 317, 319, Section 7—Thomas Purnell; Mary Purnell; Frank Purnell, 1921; Lulie Purnell, 1843; Ed Esham; Elizabeth Stull, 1905; Gurtrude Stull, 1890; Catlett Stull, 1929; Mrs. Weber; John Breeze; Jas. Sears Child; Ivy Duke Graham, 1898; J. P. Graham, 1890; Sallie Graham, 1919.

Lot 307, Section 7—Samuel Forman, owner; Anna F. Forman, 1887; Samuel Forman, 1888; Hattie Forman, 1902; Fannie Reed, 1908; Dr. John A. Reed, 1908.

Lot 306, Section 7—W. B. Perkins, 1903; Mrs. W. B. Perkins, 1912; Miss Eliza Perkins, 1940; V. H. Perkins, 1929.

Lot 305, Section 7—Achsah Wood, 1871; Charles Wood, 1851; John T. Wood, 1871; Charlete Wood, 1922; Belle S. Wood, 1915; Anna G. Fletcher, 1904; Samuel W. Gill, 1940; E. Fletcher, 1892.

Lot 304, Section 7—Eugene E. Dodson, 1902; Jennie Williams Dodson, 1903; R. H. Dodson, 1927; Rosie Maize; Martha Maize; John Maize; Dr. Charley Wardle; Mrs. Charley Wardle; Lottie Dugan; Gurtrude King.

Lot 303, Section 7—Eliza Courtney, 1889; Albert L. Chisholm, 1879; Chassie Hall, 1892; Laura Hall, 1896.

Lot 232-3, Section 7—Mattie Trumbo, 1900; Wm. Shephard; Eliza Shephard, 1899; ........ Geiss; Wm. Alexander, 1881; Reuben Hunt; Mrs. Reuben Hunt; John Kinkaid; Sarah Hawkins; W. J. Harrison; Marion Nolen Garrett, 1903; Mary E. Walcott, 1902; Mary Clinger, 1896; Sabina Wells, 1910; Thomas Wells, 1903; Robt. Storer, 1894; Mary J. Kinkaid; John Henry Kinkaid; Sam Kinkaid; Wm. Gillespie; Jane Storer, 1903; David Storer, 1901; James Whitelaw, 1883; Mrs. Marian Garret, 1903; .......... Grigsby; Park Green; David Green; Jas. Kinkead; F. F. Kinkead, 1890; Elizabeth Workman.

Lot 235, Section 7—John Stephens, 1939; Mary F. Stephens, 1920; Wm. G. Bloom, 1895; Eliza J. Poth; John W. Stephens, 1916; Elias Bloom, 1930.

Lot 242, Section 7—Bert Holiday, Hannah J. Holiday, 1904; Wm. Holiday; Chas. McKibben; Mrs. Mary E. McKibben.

Lot 332, Section 7—Almer Dodson's lot; Mrs. Almer Dodson; Mrs. Dick Dodson.

Lot 335, Section 7—Mrs. Angeline Calvert; R. K. Stickley; Milton Bramel, 1902; Mrs. Mary Bramel, 1908.

Single Rights—George P. Beasley, 1903; Eliza F. Beasley, 1903; Clarence Stockdale; W. B. Stockdale; Mrs. W. B. Stockdale; Reub. Stockdale; Wm. and Jane Ginn; Anna Milly, 1904; Barbara Milly, 1899; Anna Clark, 1911; ........ Hise; ........ Hise; ........Miller; Mrs. Piper; Geo. McFee Bright; Anna E. Strode; Mrs. Ann Sharp; Wm. Brewington; Sarah Brown; Peter Brown; Lorena and Bertha H. ..........; Elizabeth

Bruce; Mrs. John Suns; James Storer; Alice D. Gill, 1853-1908; Jos. Handley; Samuel Brooks; John Kidder; J. Rankins; J. Rankins; Margaret Newman; Thomas Newman, 1892; Charles Brown; Samuel Baldwin; James Wroten; Sarah Hughbanks; W. H. Bradford; John A. Blair, 1853; Anna Blair, 1905; Pernell Bradford; John White; Tillie White; Mrs. John White; Eddie Blair, 1892; Wm. Price; Rev. J. B. Simons, 1907; Anna Case Wheeler, 1907; Carrie Hill; Ada Fletcher; R. T. Hampton; Barbour Luman; Charley Skinner; Melissa Skinner; Allie Sears; John Sears; Walter L. Skinner; Mrs. Lutie Hollie; Arthur B. Girvin.

Lot 200, Sec. 6.—Elijah Calvert; Sallie Bland; N. O. Bland, 1848; F. W. Cleary; 8 graves on lot.

Lot 201, Sec. 6.—Alexander Maddox, 1874; Robt. Maddox, 1868; Wm. Maddox, 1836; James Sinclair, 1848; Geo. Maddox, 1832; Elizabeth Maddox, 1848; Bailer H. Maddox, 1836; Eliza Johnson; Alexander Johnson; Phoebe Williams, 1913; G. M. Williams, 1919; Alice Williams.

Lot 202, Sec. 6.—D. F. Barker; Edward Mitchell, 1899; Mary Mitchell, 1929; Earnest Miles, 1842; T. Kemp Mitchell, 1843.

Lot 200, Sec. 6.—George Arthur; Thos. Harrison, 1885; Elizabeth Harrison, 1895; Stephen H. Harrison, 1923; Steve Harrison, 1892; Mable Harrison, 1893; Mary E. Harrison, 1904; John G. Rogers, 1865; Sallie A. Rogers, 1800; Amy A. Brooks, 1876; Ambrose Seaton, 1866; Mary W. Seaton, 1863; Sarah Seaton, 1848; Ann Martha Seaton, 1848.

Lot 204, Sec. 6.—Mrs. Ann Cox; Elizabeth Cox, 1835; John Cox, 1845; H. H. Cox, Jr.; Henry H. Cox, 1899; Eddie Cox, 1863; Lizzie Cox, 1884; Edward Cox, 1847; Anna M. Cox, 1867; Alfred Cox, 1861; George Cox, 1864; Orlando Cox, 1908; Mrs. Sarah Cox, 1912; Ann Kerr, 1849.

Lot 194, Section 6—Jacob Shafer, 1847; Geo. P. Shafer, 1847; Samuel Shafer, 1883; Daniel Shafer, 1892; Elizabeth Shafer, 1899; Daniel Shafer, 194-; Mary L. Golling, 1848; Helena Golling, 1854; Louis Golling, 1886; Mrs. Louis Golling, 1915; Frederick Yockey, 1854; Dorthey Yockey, 1854; E. S.; D. W. S.; AMS.

Lot 195, Section 6—Alice Taylor, 1860; Charlette Taylor, 1884; Harrison Taylor, 1876; Charlette J. Taylor, 1886; Harry Taylor; John Duke Taylor; Mrs. Henry Pelham; Bessie H. Gill, 1882; Henry Pelham.

Lot 196, Section 6—Sallie W. Armstrong, 1851; John Armstrong, 1851; Mary Armstrong, 1850; Mary W. Armstrong, 1849;

Lot 197, Section 6—Ebenezer Jenkins, 1849; Jessie Wood Jenkins, 1839; W. R. Jenkins, 1849; Ezekiel Jenkins, 1849; Hannah B. Wilson, 1871.

Lot 198, Section 6—John Armstrong; A. R. Armstrong; Mary S. Armstrong, 1830; Wm. Armstrong, 1833; Mary A. Dobyns, 1855; Emily A. Dobyns, 1905.

Lot 199, Section 6—Sarah Collins, 1890; Mary A. Collins, 1836; John A. Collins, 1850; Laura J. Collins, 1912; Samuel W. Owens, 1868; Willie Owens, 1868; Samuel Owens, 1868; Mrs. Julia A. Owens, 1907; Alice G. Owens, 1916; Sarah Owens Hartman, 1947.

Lot 190, Section 6—Emma Archdeacon, 1858; Ann Archdeacon; Sarah J. Mefford, 1870; Elizabeth H. Rice, 1872; James Rice, 1898; John Parrott, 1863; Henry Guthrie, 1839; Eliza Guthrie, 1845; John Burnside,

1846; Wm. Thompson; Margaret Thompson, 1852; Wm. Thompson, 1852; Henry Thompson, 1858.

Lot 191, Section 6—Anna Bell & John G. Crowell, 1858; G. W. Orr, 1890; Massie C. Orr, 1899; Lizzie Orr, 1880; Elizabeth A. Orr, 1906; Elizabeth Orr, 1860; Ada Bell Orr, 1849; Cassius Lowry; Ullmann Lowry, 1889; Theophitus Lowry, 1895; Cora Lowry, 1901; Lee Haucke, 1931.

Lot 192, Section 6—Dr. William Hays, 1869; Eliza A. Marshall, 1876; Garrett Worthington, 1857; Garrett Worthington, Jr., 1855; Harry Worthington, 1901; Laura Worthington, 1907; Alice Worthington, 1928; Wm. F. Hays, 1908; Mrs. Fannie Hays, 1919.

Lot 183, Section 6—Samuel Pearce, 1878; Emily Pearce, 1893; John Ballenger, 1902; Mrs. John (Allie Bascome) Ballenger, 1912; Florence P. Browning, 1879; Robert L. Browning, 1898; James S. Bascombe, 1874; Josephine Bascome, 1947; Allie C. Bascome, 1906; Samuel Pearce Browning 1944; James H. Bascome, 1878.

Lot 184, Section 6—M. A. Hutchins; John C. Hutchins, 1845; Eliza Hutchins, 1835; Amarita Hutchins, 1828; Mary E. Hutchins, 1867; Claudia Baker Hutchins, 1900; Cyrus Delong, 1837; Millie Johnson; Fannie D. Hutchins, 1900; M. A. Hutchins, 1873; Evaline Hutchins, 1895; Morris C. Hutchins, 1910.

Lot 185, Section 6—Newton Cooper, 1902; Milton Cooper, 1903; Chas. C. Tabb, 1904; Kate C. Tabb, 1931; Nat Pointz Cooper, 1872; Katherine Cooper, 1884; Marion B. Powell, 1917; Enoch B. Powell, 1916.

Lot 186, Section 6—Virginia Edmonds, 1866; Anna A. Edmonds, 1868; Adolphus Edmonds, 1872; Mollie T. Edmonds, 1936; Allen A. Edmonds, 1903; Mary J. Martin, 1873; John Duley, 1909; Ida Edmonds Duley, 1921; Thomas A. Davis, 1915; Levinia Davis (Mrs. T. A.) 1912.

Lot 187, Section 6—Virginia Kackley, 1888; Wm. McClanahan, 1886; Eliza McClanahan; Mary W. Ross, 1902; Olive C. Ross, 1895; other graves.

Lot 188, Section 6—Mary Morford, Ann C. Gilpin, 1852; Francis Gilpin; Jennie Bell Gilpin, 1856; Mary Ellen Morford, 1846.

Lot 189, Section 6—Martha Reed, 1832; Sarah Reed, 1859; Isabella Reed; Jimmie Morris, 1867; Emily Reed, 1861; John G. Reed, 1871; Eliza Cooper, 1869; Emily R. Harrison, 1890.

Lot 190, Section 6—Emma Archdeacon.

## MAYSVILLE, MASON COUNTY CEMETERY (New)
### (Letter grouped, but not alphabetically listed.)

1911—Heiser, John Jos.—2—ashes from Denver
    Holland, Chas.—5-2-
    Holton, Lidia Ellen—5-8-
    Hardyman, Mary Alice—5-12-
    Hamilton, Jonathan—5-24-
1912—Jacobs, Justina—7-22-
    Housh, Eva Alice—5-18-
1913—Hall, Margaret Duke—7-24-

1914—Helmer, Elizabeth—2-25-
  Hall, W. W.—10-14-
  Harrison, Chas. H.—11-15-
  Hill, Marie—12-29-
  Hunter, Steven D.—12-5-
1915—Hamilton, Rebecca M.—4-6-
  Hull, Thos.—7-27-
  Helmer, Albert N.—10-29-
1916—Hampton, Birtie—4-12-
  Hechinger, David—5-10-
  Harrison, W. H.—5-14-
  Housh, Robert—8-25-
  Herron, Thos.—11-23-
1917—Horrack, Mary—2-20-
  Hechinger, Jos.—5-25-
  Helmer, Mary—9-3-
  Holland, Ollie—12-30-
1918—Harding, Wm.—2-13-
  Hendrickson, J. P.—5-17-
  Holze, Jno. Raymond—7-15-
  Hull, Chas.—7-25-
  Hopper, C. C.—8-9-
  Henry, O. C.—10-16-
  Heiser, Anna—12-7-
  Helphenstine, Robt.—1-11-1919

1919—Heiser, George H.—2-10-
  Hunter, Perry Thomas—4-13-
  Hays, Henry—4-16-
  Huff, John—4-27-
  Heilbert, Harvey—6-10-
  Hooper, Chas.—11-22-
  Hutchins, Cecil Dunbar—11-5—from Indianapolis
  Helmer, Chas—12-26-

1920—Hall, Sallie—2-9-
  Hill, Elizabeth—2-9-
  Hicks, Ada Porter—2-12-
  Hechinger, Mrs. Louise—5-22-
  Helmer, Eva, Mrs. J.—6-8-
  Haggart, Anna W.—11-17-
  Hampton, Mrs. Mary—12-2-
  Hill, Perry—12-18-
1921—Humphers, Hilda—2-21-
  Hooper, Mrs. Lida—3-1-
  Hornback, Anna—3-17-
  Hamrick, Carter—3-12—from Rectorville
  Highfield, Paul A.—3-18-
  Houston, Jewell Lee—4-6-
  Humphries, Elsie May—6-15-
  Hutchison, Minnie A.—8-9-

Houston, Everett C.—9-19-
Hamilton, Clifford—10-11-
Hall, Eva—10-14-
Hull, Moses—11-11-
Heminger, Sherman—12-4-
Hampton, Virginia—12-5-
1922—Hunter, Emily Tolle Thomas—2-28-
Hamilton, Jacob—3-11-
Hiatt, Elizabeth—4-22-
Holton, Mrs. C. S.—7-3-
Hawley, Nannie—8-13—Cincinnati, O.
Hubbard, Murray—9-24—Atlanta, Ga.
Harrington, Cornelius—9-29-
Harding, Mary Dotson—11-11-
Hendrickson, Laura L.—12-7-
Halfhill, Mary F.—12-13-
1923—Holmes, Austin—1-17-
Hamrick, Francis—4-19—Tollesboro
Hall, S. M.—4-20-
Holland, Rosa M.—7-23-
Hunsicker, Frank C.—7-28-
Hull, Pauline—12-22-
1924—Hamilton, Amanda—1-1-
Holland, Chas. C.—2-18-
Holland, Charley—2-22-
Hancock, C. M.—3-19-
Hopgood, Jas.—4-10-
Helmer, Anna M.—9-3-
Hughes, Harold—8-18-
Hutton, George—12-21-
1925—Humphreys, James—2-3-
Hicks, W. H.—2-4-
Hamrick, John E.—3-14-
Hiatt, Laurel M.—3-29-
Horsley, Malvina—10-14-
Hiett, Dorothy—10-22-
Hoops, Edw.—10-30-
Holmes, Mary L.—11-13-
Holmes, Amia W.—11-13-
Heddleson, Luciele—11-14-
Harison, Mrs. R. M.—11-25-
Hankins, B.—11-25-
1926—Hunsicker, Chris.—1-18-
Hall, Bettie P.—4-28-
Hesler, Geo.—5-4-
Hord, G. N.—8-17-
Houston, Alberta—10-6-
Hubbard, Henry—7-13-1892
Heflin, James—9-17-1892

Hunsicker, Cora—1-17-1893
Hubbard, Edward—7-8-1893
Hill, Charles—10-2-1893
Hubbard, Miss Daisy—2-13-1894
Holliday, George—5-22-1894
Hiatt, Jemima—4-27-1895
Haulman, John Reed—7-2-1895
Hull, Robt.—4-15-1896
Hill, Margaret L.—4-16-1896
Haulman, Jos.—5-30-1896
Hains, Mrs.—2-12-1897
Holmes, Mrs. Austin—11-3-1897
Helmer, Mrs. Jacob—3-30-1898
Hamilton, Waldo—10-25-1898
Hill, Jas.—10-29-1898
Hall, Tom J.—1-9-1899
Hill, Littleton—4-30-1899
Helm, Mrs. Barbara—5-24-1899
Heiser, Geo. H.—0-22 1899
Howe, Miss Miley—8-23-1899
Hall, John H.—2-16-1900
Hall, Anna Bell—3-2-1900—Mrs.
Howe, W. U.—4-7-1900
Howard, John B.—6-18-1900
Helmer, Miss Minnie—8-30-1900
Hiatt, Mrs. Mary—1-31-1901
Hill, Chas.—5-1-1901
Hiatt, Ella—6-18-1901
Holliday, Wm. D. 11-14-1901
Hall, John H.—7-4-1902
Hiatt, Hester—9-15-1902
Henderson, C. T. L.—11-4-1902
Helmer, Mary—12-24-1902
Haines, Wm.—3-19-1903
Holmer, John—4-11 1903
Hunt, Jas—6-29-1904—G A R Lot
Helmer, Christian—12-26-1905
Hill, Edward—4-10-1906
Haley, Sherman—7-30-1906
Hildreth, James F.—9-12-1906
Hamilton, Mrs. Linda—9-30-1906
Hiatt, E. B.—1-29-1907
Hancock, Mrs. Sarah B.—8-14-1907
Hubbard, Mrs. Bettie—4-21-1907
Hall, James H., Sr.—1-11-1909
Helmer, Chas. H.—6-28-1909
Helmer, Jacob G.—12-12-1909
Heiser, Wm. G.—4-17-1910
Hazelrigg, Jeff—8-26-1910

Hughes, Mrs. Wm.—9-28-1910
Holland, George—10-19-1910
Haucke, Albert—12-15-1910
1926—Hamton. Wm.—11-10-
1927—Hensker, David—1-15—Columbus, Ohio.
Holland, Jas.—6-13—Washington, Ky.
Hame, Rose C.—7-14-
Holiday, Mary Jane—10-25-
Helpenstine, Oscar—12-2-
Helpenstine, Bessie—12-15-

## I

1892—Ireland, Wm.—7-12-
1893—Ireland, Mrs. Wm.—1-30-
1898—Ireland, Dr.—10-23-
1899—Irwin, Louis—5-21-
1919—Igo, Carl T.—8-4-

## J

1892—January, Douglas—5-13-
1893—January, Horace—3-10-
1894—Jenkins, Wm. G.—6-11-
1896—Jacobs, Miss Lucretia—7-12-
Johnson, Mrs. Elizabeth—12-11-
1899—Jenkins, R. P.—6-8-
January, W. II.—12-11-
1902—January, Mrs. Wilson—6-7-
1903—Johnson, Mrs. Geo. T.—12-13-
1904—January, Wilson—7-3-
1906—Jackson, Susan L.—1-12-
Judy, Warren Mc.—12-4-
1909—January, Mrs. H. J.—8-10-
1910—January, Mrs. Emma D.—3-8-
1912—Jacobs, Justina—7-22-
Johnston, Paul Hamilton—8-22-
1914—Jones, Wm. E.—1-23-
1915—James, Thos. R.—4-15-
1916—Johnson, Wm. D.—7-11-
1919—Jacobs, Ophelia—2-20-
1920—Johnson, Nancy—1-7-
1921—Johnson, Wm.—1-26-
Jacobs, Martin—1-28-
Johnson, Neal—11-22-
1922—Johnson, Jos.—8-17-
January, Andrew M.—10-10-
1923—Jenkins, Birdie—8-26-
1924—Jenkins, Geo.—12-23-

1925—Jones, Hazel L.—3-24-
    Jones, Geneva—3-25-
1926—Jones, Louis—6-7-
    Jenkins, Mary F.—7-19-
1927—Jasper, Pearl—1-11-
    Jones, Henry—5-10-
    Jefferson, Ollie 10-27—Covington, Ky.

### K

1892—Keefer, Mrs. Isabella—4-19-
    Krintz, Clara A.—5-1-
1893—Kirk, Richard—4-7-
1894—Keep, C. H.—2-10-
    Krintz, Charles—7-30-
1895—Krintz, Susana—3-5-
1899—Kirk, Mrs. Richard—5-28-
1900—King, Mrs. Hulda—6-22-
1901—Kincade, Mrs. Minnie—4-27-
    Knoveshaw, Katherine—7-26-
    Keefer, Will S.—12-28-
1903—King, W. W.—11-7-
1904—Keane, John E.—4-6-
    King, Nina B.—4-22-
1905—Kelly—1-19-
    Kirk, Wm.—4-28-
1906—Kirk, E. G.—9-29-
1907—Kreitz, Aug.—9-9-
1908—Keith, J. F.—1-28-
    Kreith, Adam—3-1-
    Kirk, Benjamin—10-16-
    Kellcy, Elmer—11-9-
    Keep, Mary M.—11-15-
1909—Kelly, Chas.—3-14-
1910—Keith, Elizabeth—12-5-
1911—Kennedy, Lillie F.—4-11-
1912—King, Wm. F.—3-13-
1913—King, Allen Rogers—8-20-
1914—Key, Sarah J.—3-5-
    Kirk, Morris C.—3-29-
1915—Key, Richard—11-6-
1917—Kennen, Mary L.—7-18-
    King, Minerva (Mrs. Wm. T.)—11-12-
1918—Keith, Lucy Cox—2-6-
    Kyle, Edith W.—2-10-
    Kelly, W. N.—4-29-
    Keeper, Mary Frame—12-10-
1919—Key, Louise—1-11-
    Key, John J.—7-24—(Lexington)

Kirk, Jas. N.—8-15-
Kirkland, Mrs. J. H.—12-5-
1920—Kehoe, Harold—1-7-
Kidder, Lewis D., Aberdeen, O.
1921—Kuhn, Chas.—9-4-
1922—Kerwin, Mrs. Thomas—1-9-
King, Wm. R.—2-3-
Kirk, Minerva Rees—3-29-
Kirwin, Thomas—4-26-
Kenneson, Louis—9-18-
Knight, Miss Maud—9-19—Salem, Va.
1923—Kidder, Mrs. Thelma—2-1-
Kirk, Elizabeth W.—6-20-
Kalb, Virginia—7-26-
1924—Kirkland, James—4-9-
Kennan, Ricd.—6-14-
1924—King, Wm. H.—12-26-
1925—Kuble, M. & L.—1-27-
King, Sarah—3-20-
1926—Kelleum, Charity L.—2-8-
Knoveshaw, Geo.—4-30-
Kinkade, Sarah—7-24-
Kenner, Elizabeth P.—10-1-
1927—Knight, Leslie—6-10-
Kennie, Jno. C.—6-15-
Klipp, Mary F.—11-14-

## L

1892—Lloyd, Elizah—6-27-
1893—Lane, Mrs. I. N.—5-3-
Long, Jas. C.—6-7-
Long, Chas.—7-15-
1894—Langcraft, Geo.—2-29-
Lang, Mrs.—10-28-
1895—Loughridge, Jon. A.—11-9-
1896—Long, Mrs. Ann H.—10-28-
1899—Loughridge, Maggie—3-8-
Leonard, Julia—3-13-
1900—Linns, Mrs. Henry—2-7-
Long, Elizabeth Hord—4-24-
Leonard, John Stella—
Layton, Mrs. L.          O.G. Layton—1902
1902—Linn, Jacob—3-14-
1903—Lawwill, Dr. W. H.—4-1-
Leach, Frank P.—11-19-
1904—Lynch, Mrs. Emily—6-17-
Long, L. H.—6-25-

1906—Langraft, 2-6—George
　　　Lindsay, R. A.—7-16-
　　　Lamden, E. L.—9-5-
1907—Lewis, Mrs. Chas.—9-23-
1909—Luttrell, Mrs. Nancy—2-3-
1910—Lloyd, Jas.
　　　Luttrell, Wm.—8-31-
　　　Laycock, Laurence R.—12-6-
1911—Lee, John Graham—3-11-
1912—Lloyd, Elizabeth—9-2-
　　　Louderback, Chas.—9-3-
1913—Latham, Edw.—12-22
1914—Leach, C. S.—3-23-
　　　Love—4-23—Wm.
1915—Landreth, D. G.—2-8-
　　　Landreth, Edgar Davis—5-26-
　　　Lindsay, Lyda C.—9-25-
　　　Linton, Bessie—12-4—Paducah, Ky.
　　　Love, Sallie Price—12-18-
1916—Lewis, C. E.—1-18-
　　　Luttrell, Thomas—3-24-
1917—Laycock, Bessie—2-9-
1918—Lee, Anna Ficklin—3-19-
1919—Lane, I. N.—2-2-
1920—Lacy, Benj.—1-16-
1920—Lynn, Catherine—3-3—Covington, Ky.
　　　Lane, Mrs. Lutie—7-4-
1921—Lowe, Carl—3-19-
　　　Locke, Allie T.—6-5-
　　　Locke, W. L.—10-26—& Locke, Lloyd Allen—11-22—Starrett, Va.
　　　Lindsay, Mary—12-3-
1922—Luttrell, Mrs. Thos.—7-11-
　　　Laytham, Andrew—11-14-
1923—Lewman, Carl—1-11-
　　　Leach, Sallie McCann—11-18-
1924—Lucas, Charles—7-9-
　　　Lee, Fannie Nelson—8-23-
　　　Langraft, Phoebe—11-12-
1925—Lyons, Mary E.—7-5-
1926—Lytle, Margaret—1-4-
1927—Lykins
　　　Lewis, Elizabeth—1-29-
　　　Loyd, Sallie Holton—12-17-


## Mc

1892—McCarthey, Miss May 10-20-
1893—McDaniel, Wm. T.—3-4-
1895—McIlvain, James—5-10-
　　　McCormick, Mrs. Mary—12-2-

1897—McCormick, John W.—1-24-
1898—McCormick, Alfred—12-28-
1899—McGregor, Dennis—4-18-
     McKinley, Mrs. A. J.—11-10-
1900—McIlvainy, Miss Anna—4-23-
1901—McDougle, Harry C.—4-23-
     McIlvain, I. L.—10-31-
1902—McDonald, Samuel—8-8-
1905—McCormick, Jas.—11-10-
1907—McMahan, Leslie—8-4-
     McKellup, Mary B.—8-17-
1912—McIlvainy, Catherine—11-15-
     McIlvainy, John—8-31-
1913—McGowan, Martha—3-9-
1914—McIlvain, Martha—12-9-
1918—McClanahan, C. W.—2-9-
     McClain, David—9-19-
     McGowan, Leslie B.—10-21-
1920—McCarthey, Geo. A.—11-2-
     McIntosh, Frank—11-3-
1921—McCord, Alta M.—2-14-
     McLaughlin, A. A.—10-6-
     McDougal, Mrs. Mary—10-16-
1922—McGill, Charles—4-10-—John—7-9-1912
     McNutt, John B.—12-4-
1924—McLung, Lucy—12-3-
1925—McCall, Elizabeth—3-30-
     McClain, Mary—5-23-
     McClanahan, Adna—6-21-
     McNutt, Rachel—10-25-
1927—McCarthey, Melvina M.—1-11-
     McCarthey, Eugene—3-17-
     McGill, Mary—6-12-
     McNutt, Owen—12-18-

## M

1891—Miller, Mrs. Charlette—12-19-
     Means, Edwin C.—12-28-
     Matthews, Jr.—John I.—3-5-
1892—Miner, C. S.—3-19-(removed)
1893—Martin, Mrs. Lida B.—1-17-
     Miller, Mrs. John—12-4-
1894—Mountjoy, Miss Anna—1-29-
     Morehead, Alfred—10-31-
1895—W. S. Moores—9-18-
1895—Moore, Dr. Thomas Miles—12-7—B. March 20-1809—Mercer Co.
     Pa.
     Moore, John Francis, died 1907
     Moore, Ann Delia Harris—4-7-1886—B Oct., 1809, Baltimore, Md.

Moore, Gwynne Harris—12-26-1890.
Moore, Ruth Tunstill—3-28-1890
Moore, Hannah Miles (wife of Wm. B. Dennis)—6-23-1890
Mountjoy, Anna Dimmitt—3-27-
1896—Maddox, Mrs. Elizabeth—4-30-
1897—Miller, Mrs. H. J.—4-25-
Morgan, Andrew W.—6-11-
1898—Mitchell, Mrs. Anna—1-2-
Mills, Mrs. Sophia—2-4-
Matthews, Margaret—6-24-
Miller, Wilson—9-5-
Morgan, Mrs. Julia S.—10-18-
1900—Morehead, Mrs. Lida—4-23-
Means, Mrs. Rebecca—5-7-
Mills, Pearce B.—6-12-
Martin, Mrs. D. C.—12-17-
1901—Martin, Miss Anna—2-28-
Martin, Infant
Matthews, Mrs. Margaret—10-23-
Molloy, Mrs. Nettie R.—12-11-
1903—Mills, Willa M.—5-27-
Miller, Mrs. Jacob—8-29-
1904—Matthews, John I.—1-23-
Moran, Katie—5-22-
Miller, Jacob Capt.—8-29-
1905—Marsh, M. F.—1-1-
Meyers, S. N.—1-4-
Miller, Mrs. L.—3-6-
Mustchelkraus, Violet—6-6-
1906—Miller, Chas. Owens—3-9-
Martin, Chas. V.—4-29-
Means, G. A.—5-4-
1007  Means, Wm.—7-1-
Mercer, Clemmie W.—9-9
1908—Morton, Louisa D.—2-27-
Mason, Henry—4-2-
Marshall, Mrs. Amelia—4-15-
Morris, J. W.—7-12-
Miller, Charlette—9-20-
Martin, J. F., Jr.—11-19-
Mason, Wm. H.—12-10-
1908—Mitchell, Richard B.—7-12-
Martin, Edna T.—9-16-
Miller, Henry A.—10-28-
1910—Mattingly, Jane—7-15-
1911—Meyers, Miss Amanda O.—9-7-
1912—Moody, Jas. Wallace—1-23-
Martin, Thomas—3-14-
Morehead, Katherine A.—5-15-

1913—Morris, Geneva—1-23-
    Mitchell, Nellie W.—2-6-
    Moran, Margaret—3-16-
1914—Mason, Elwood Lloyd—2-3-
    Moore, Austin Ellsworth—7-21-
    Matthews, Ollie—11-17-
    Myall, Edward—12-18-
1915—Mefford, Jennie B.—7-5-
1917—Mulschelknaus, Wm.—4-2-
    Matthews, W. B.—4-30-
    Morris, Margeret—8-17-
    Manchester, E. L.—10-12-
1918—Manchester, F. B.—2-9-
1919—Montgomery, Anna Morgan—8-3-
    Myall, Mrs. Lucy A.—11-25-
1920—Mallory, Emma—2-23-
    Marshall, Chas. P.—3-6-
    Mullikin, Mrs. M. E.—9-7-
    Mullikin, June—11-10-
    Martin, Louis—12-23-
1921—Mattingly, Virginia—4-15-
    Miller, Louis—8-1-
1922—Marshall, N. J. B.—3-30-
1923—Miller, John A.—5-24-    (Cloverport, N. Y.)
1924—Mason, Sarah—11-15-    Roy A. Mason—4-28-
    Mitchell, Geo. M.—7-22-
    Moody, Robt. P.—10-2-
    Meyers, H. C.—10-13-
    Matthews, Sarah—2-6-
1926—Martin, Chas. E.—2-24-
    Mitchell, Ida Irene—5-15-
    Mitchell, Rose—4-13-
    Mitchell, Margeret—3-14-
    Mattingly, Mrs. Robt.—7-11-
1927—Manning, Irma—3-4-    Vanceburg, Ky.
    Mitchell, Mirian—3-21-
    Means, Amanda W.—12-7-

## N

1896—Nolin, Stanley B.—4-26-
1898—Nolin, W. W.—11-4-
    Nolin, Maurice—11-4-
    Nelson, Jos.—12-6-
1900—Nolin, Mrs. J. M.—11-6-
1901—Nesbitt, Carlton M.—6-23-
1923—Newdigate, Edw. C.—5-15-
1925—Neal, Lucy N.—6-2-
1926—Nauman, Chas. E.—1-24-
    Nash, S. A.—7-12-

Nicholas, Frank—8-8-
Neal, W. J.—11-7-
1927—Noe, Thos. A.—11-8-
1927—Nichols, Donald—1-27-
1927—Nichols, Alice—3-1-
Nichols, James—11-20-
Nelson, Frank J.—4-17-
Nace, Chas., Jr.—5-7-
Nicholas, Ethel—12-24-

O

1892—Otto
1894—Oldham, Wm. G.—11-12-
Omens, F. S.—1-14-
Ort, Mrs. Geo.—7-17-
1896—Oldham, Sam'l—1-
1896—Owens, John U.—6-18-
1902—Oder, Mrs. Wooley—10-7-
1903—Owens, Mrs. Ann C.—2-13-
1905—Overly, Louis—8-28—(Soldiers Lot)
1907—Oldham, Mrs. Mollie—2-22-
1908—Oliver, Elizabeth A.—7-15-
1909—Osborn, John S.—1-3-
Owens, B. D.—8-29-
Oliver, Edw.—7-16-
1911—Oliver, Mary F.—1-22-
Oldham, John W.—2-2-
1912—Otto, Margaret J.—4-28-
Osborn, Mary E.—6-13-
1914—Osborn, Birdie—10-24-
1915—Oder, John Wesley—10-27-
Owens, Dr. C. C.—10-11-1916
Owens, Alice Forman—2-10-1923
Owens, Anna 1-20-1921
Owens, Janes C.—1-26-1921
Owens, R. B.—7-19-1926
1917—Oliver, Rebecca E.—8-2-
1918—Ormes, Albert—11-6-
1919—Otto A. Altmeyer—1-10-
1920—Outten, Wm. O.—2-1-
1924—Otto—9-29—Henry
1925—Outten, Mary F.—12-12-
1926—Outten, Anna M.—4-18-
1927—Otto, Henry—5-3-

P

1892—Payne, Mrs. Amelia—4-29-
1893—Poyntzs, Jr., John B.

1894—Poyntzs, Mrs. Vina S.—12-9-
1895—Pollitt, Adna—3-6-
      Pearce, E. E.—8-5-
      Poyntzs, Elizabeth Thompson—8-19-
      Parker, Mrs. P. P.—9-25-
1896—Perrine, Mrs. Mollie—5-30-
      Parker, Lillian Lee—6-30-
1913—Parker, Robt. E.—8-11-
      Pickett, Dr. Thos. E.—9-5-
      Porter, Mary Ann—10-6-
      Peers, Chas. E.—10-8-
1914—Price, Martha S.—1-4-
      Prather, Inez E.—7-8-
      Parry, Glenn—3-6
1915—Pearce, Bert L.—3-18-
      Poyntz, Fannie M.—6-26-
      Purcell, Clifford—9-10-
      Pugh, Viola—9-30-
1916—Porter, Sam O.—1-24-
      Poyntz, Katherin Shultz—4-10-
      Power, Mrs. Sarah—11-14-
1917—Poyntz, John—6-20-
1918—Peterson, Evelyn—10-21-
      Plumber, Wm.—1-19-
      Pettit, John—10-25-
1919—Pollitt, Arthur—1-19-
      Pyatt, Ricd.—1-29-
      Peterson, Sam'l.—2-21-
      Pogue, Henry E.—3-5-
      Pearce, C. D.—7-14-
      Piper, Edw. W.—8-20-
      Parker, P. P.—10-11-
      Pickett, J. C.—11-5-
      Phillips, Mrs. Samuel—11-15-
1920—Percy, Wm.—2-6-
      Purdon, James—3-21-
      Perrine, Wm. M.—4-26-
      Perrie, Frank R.—8-2—Washington, D. C.
      Perry, Waldo—4-23—Cincinnati, O.
      Pettit, Elizabeth B.—5-20-
      Pigg—L. F.—8-14-
      Pearce, Mrs. Anna Belle—9-14-
1921—Pollitt, Robt.—1-9-
      Pollitt, Lucy Johnson—4-1-
      Pollitt, Robert T.—4-1-
      Pollitt, Annie Howard—4-1—removed from Old Cemetery
      Payne, Fred D.—4-25-
      Perrie, Miss Porter—7-17-
      Poor, Wm.—8-5-

1922—Purdon, James—3-19-
    Perrine, Julia B.—6-28-
    Purden, Mrs. Jas.—11-22-
1923—Porter, Stanley—3-22—Pittsburgh, Pa.
    Payne, W. C.—7-26—Hillsboro, Ky.
    Peers, Julia, Owens—11-23-
1924—Proctor, T. K.—6-6-
    Pogue, Jennie B.—6-20-
    Peak, James—8-3-
1925—Pollitt, Ovil—4-7-
    Purden, Eva—4-13-
    Poyntz, C. B.—4-20-
    Piper, Loyd—8-5-
    Parker, F. C.—12-9-
1926—Pyatt, Minerva—7-27-
1896—Paul Henry Lee—6-30-
    Porter, Julia A.—9-12-
    Parks, Mrs. M. J.—11-7-
1897—Pearce, T. M.—1-12
    Pepper, Mrs. Apphia—7-6-
    Powell (Piper) S. A.—7-21-
1898—Perrie, Mrs. F. R. —4-7-
    Powell, Mrs. Margaret E.—4-15-
    Poyntz, Mrs. Mary Dewees—6-14-
    Peggs, Mrs. Mollie—11-8-
1899—Petry, C. F.—1-15-
    Poyntz, John B.—11-20-
    Pierce, J. W.—12-12-
1900—Pickett, Abbie Gray—2-22—Infant of Geo. and Abbee Barbour
    Pangburn, Dr. Samuel—10-5-
1901—Proctor, Miss Bettie—8-3-
    Porter, Juliet—10-5-
1902—Pickett, T. J.—10-27-
1903—Petry, Mrs. M. J.—4-27-
    Power, John W.—5-22-
    Proctor, Mr. T. K.—6-28-
    Pierce, Mrs. J. W.—9-22-
    Perrie, J. F.—11-7-
    Porter, Lee H.—12-10-
1904—Peters, J. B.—4-20-
    Payne, Jno. R—5-5-
    Payne, Henry—6-17-
    Pollitt, Lida Ruth—7-12-
    Peters, Mrs. Bettie—8-26-
1905—Pearce, C. B.—5-6-
    Payne, Emeline—8-14-
1906—Pickett, Margerett—6-6-
    Pickett, T. M. P.—7-31-
    Price, J. Freeman—12-8-

1907—Parry, Ben D.—2-6-
    Petry, J. Christian—8-8-
1908—Pogue, Mrs. Frances—7-13-
1909—Poth, Henry—1-30-
    Parker, Peter L.—2-25-
    Pendergast, Mrs. John—4-5-
    Powell, Mrs. S. A.—10-27-
1910—Porter, Hiram B.—3-16-
    Piper, Mrs. E. A.—3-16-
    Petry, Mrs. Anna M.—3-31-
    Power, Mary Wilson—7-13-
    Proctor, J. R.—10-10-
    Perry, Chas.—9-4-
    Pearce, H. T.—9-20-
    Pearce, C. Burgess—11-28-
    Pearce, Mrs. Barbara—12-10-
    Pugh, Earnest—12-15-
1911—Payne, Ella—6-24-
    Potts, Mary L.—7-31-
    Power, Wm. F.—10-3-
    Power, Ellen Marvin—10-19—Mrs. W. F.
    Parker, Ella D.—9-11-1926
1926—Perrine, Laura L.—10-1-
1927—Pearce, Mollie Fant—1-7-
    Perrine, J. J.—1-10-
    Presley, Mary—1-12-
    Poynter, Taylor—3-10-

## R

1892—Ross, Robt. C.—6-5-
    Russell, Mrs. J. L.—9-19-
1893—Roberts, Mrs. D. E.—1-22-
    Russell, Mrs. C. D.—8-9-
1894—Robinson, Brownie—10-25-
    Reynolds, Harvey—1-14-
1895—Roberts, Mrs. D. E.—1-23-
1896—Rogers, Thos. J.—4-20-
    Roberts, Chas.—10-27-
1897—Russell, Jr. M. C.—4-11-
    Russell, Addison P.—4-11-
    Rogers, Geo. W.—8-2-
1898—Redden, J. M.—9-14-
1899—Reed, Thos.—1-23-
    Robinson, Mrs. Laura—1-26-
    Riley, Geo. Myall—4-25-
    Robinson, Mrs. Sarah —10-30-
1900—Roper, Jesse B.—5-22-
    Ross, Mrs. R. C.—7-9-
    Rains, Virginia—7-15-

1901—Russell, Mrs. J. B.—3-4-
  Rumford, James—3-30-
1902—Russell, M. C.—7-24-
  Ross, Mrs. Mary—9-17-
1904—Raine, Jas. H.—1-9-
  Rees, Thos. T.—4-27-
  Ross, Herman—10-5-
  Roberts, Mrs. Emma S.—11-30-
1905—Roper, Mrs. Nellie—1-21-
  Rasp, Elizabeth—1-22-
  Rosser, G. S.—5-4-
  Ross, Mrs. Wm.—6-13-
  Reed, Margaret—12-29-
1906—Robertson, Leigh W.—5-16-
  Ross, Robert C.—6-23-
  Redden, Eliz. R.—11-10-
1907—Ross, G. W.—1-14-
  Ross, John W.—9-9-
  Russell, C. D.—10-17-
1908—Ross, Amanda—3-28-
  Rogers, W. C.—4-15-
1909—Rogers, Nelson—5-31-
  Rains, J. M.—11-3-
1910—Rice, J. H.—2-17-
  Rice, four Rice Graves removed from the county—4-8-
  Ross, Mrs. Wm.—8-30-
  Rogers, Mrs. E. A.—9-7-
1911—Rogers, Mrs. Lucinda H.—1-25-
  Reed, J. B.—10-18—removed from county
  Rogers, Mrs. Mary—1-27-
  Robinson, Mrs. Douglas—10-5-
1912—Rasp, Iola J.—8-20-
1913—Reed, Grace—2-10-
  Rogers, H. B.—9-29-
  Reed, Jacob
  Rosser, Wm. H.—12-17-
1914—Robinson, James F.—6-18-
1915—Rice, Margaret—4-19-
  Rosemham, C. L.—5-7-
  Robinson, Hazel G.—9-26-
  Robinson, Chas. Adams—10-2-
1917—Roden, B.—2-2-
  Ruggles, Robt. 8-10-
  Roads, Margt.—11-30-
1918—Reed, Mrs. J. C.—4-12-
  Rudy, Emma—8-13-
  Riggs, Lelia—10-20-
  Rogers, Myrtle—10-26-

Rice, Elizabeth—-10-29-
Ruggles, Wm.—11-28-
1919—Ruggles, Wm.—3-9-
Riley, J. B.—5-24-
Riley, Wm.—12-17-
Riley, Alice—1-25—1920
Reed, Mrs. Elizabeth—12-6-
1920—Rankins, Mary—1-13-
Rudy, Byron—2-29-
Riggs, Thos.—3-7-
Rowls—
Robb, Parthena—8-2-
Rice, Mrs. Judith A.—10-5-
Runyan, J. M.—12-29-
Rudy, Walter—12-29—Cincinnati, O.
1921—Rice, Mrs. J.—3-16—Cincinnati, O.
Robinson, E. A.—3-21-
Reed, Mary E.—5-27-
Rogers, Wm. B.—6-11-
Rosser, Robt. Lee—6-20-
1922—Rosser, Mrs. Wm.—1-10-
Rumford, Mattie—3-25-
Roberson, Florence C.—9-22-
Royse, Margt. C.—10-11-
Ross, Lucinda C.—11-22-
Riggs, Wm.—12-7-
Russell, M. C.—(Mrs.)—12-8-
1923—Rains, Frances Tarlton—8-13-
1924—Ruggles, Frances—5-19-
Rogers, Robert—7-18-
Rees, D. J.—9-19-
Redden, Anna H.—10-14-
1925—Rees, Ollie F.—1-4-
Rogers, John—1-17-
Russell, Thos. M.—1-20-
Royse, Geo. W.—2-23-
Robb, Wm.—5-3-
1925—Rosenmeirer, Henrietta—8-2—Sciotaville, O.
1926—Ritchie, Bulah—3-17-
Ramey, Fannie—12-6-
Reed, Claud—12-20—Newport, Ky.
1927—Roberts, Andrew—1-5-
Reitz, John—6-2-
Rees, Elizabeth B.—8-3-
Reed, Mary—12-3-

## S

1892—Stockton, Rebecca—3-14-
Spencer, Ricd.—11-1—G. A. R. lot

1893—Schnelle, Kate—7-18-
1895—Shephard, C. D.—3-4-
  Shackelford, Kittie Keith—6-1-
  Schnelle, Emma—8-1-
  Simmons, Lee—9-18-
  Stockton, Mrs. J. M.—12-6-
  Stockton, Jr. J. M.—12-6-
1896—Stewart, Clarence T.—3-24-
  Sullivan, Mrs. Alice—10-12-
1897—Stewart, Lucy Lee—4-10-
  Scott, Samuel Brooks—8-4-
  Shackleford, J. J.—8-25-
  Sidwell, J. M.—9-3-     to Flemingsburgh, Ky.
  Snedeker, Clara E.—11-20-
  Sousley, Thos.—12-12-
1898—Smoot, Chas. S.—4-6-
  Smith, Mrs. Geo. Ann—10-19-
  Seemens, Mrs. Frank—12-21-
1899—Shanklin—5-9—to Mayslick
1900—Schatzmann, Chris—2-6-
  Squires, Mrs. Eliz. C.—4-25-
  Seaton, Mrs. Alice—7-28-
1901—Sherwood, Mrs.—7-29-
  Sulser, Geo. W.—8-9-
  Stewart, Frank—8-15-
  Stough, Edward—9-18-
1902—Seymour, H. Porter—1-18-
  Stewart, Miss Emma—1-29-
  Seaton, T. H.—2-6-
  Shackelford, Fred—5-2-
  Smoot, Retta F.—12-13-
1904—Stransbaugh, Anna—10-30-
1905—Starrett, A. W.—2-11-
  Sweet, Juanita—3-6
  Schatzmann, W. F.—5 17
  Sharp, Elmer—8-30-
1906—Seddon, Mrs. Geo.—3-7-
  Stewart, St. Clair R.—5-16-
  Strode, Mrs. J. T.—10-16-
1907—Slemmons, Mrs. Lizzie—2-23-
  Starrett, Calvin—4-17-
  Starrett, Rebecca—4-17—from Stonelick Church.
  Strode, James N.—9-6-
1908—Smith, Mrs. Kate—8-28-
  Smith, Smith, Smith, removals
1909—Schatzmann, Mrs. Kate—2-6-
  Shepard, Wm.—3-29-
  Smoot, Wm. P.—5-29
1910—Schatzmann, W. A.—2-3-
  Simpson, James—7-24-

Snediker, John—10-2-
Smith, James A.—6-5-
1911—Soward, Rich.—5-1-
Saunders, Sarah G.—7-11-
Supplee, Wm.—11-27-
1912—S......, Augustus C.—8-6- (Simmons)?
Suit, Lawson B.—10-19-
1913—Shepard, Mary W.—1-27-
Stickley, Harriet A.—4-5-
Stevens, Archie—5-27-
1914—Sharp, Emanuiel—3-22-
Smart, Jas. H.—4-14-
Shackleford, W. C.—8-19-
1915—Sharp, Chas.—2-9-
Sharp, Bettie—3-9-
Schatzmann, Geo. 4-29-
Sharp, Daniel T.—8-3-
1916—Sims, Sallie—2-9-
Stoker, Lou Ann—4-24-
Starrett, Campbell—6-1-
Sharp, Belle G.—7-18-
Seddon, Hecubia—12-23-
1917—Smith, John T.—3-4-
Sharp, Eliza—3-16-
Smith, Mollie—5-28-
Shelton, Samuel—11-30-
Smoot, Bettie Bacon—12-17-
1918—Slack, E. C.—3-5-
Stoughton, Gladys—3-31-
Stephens, Mrs. T. F.—4-29-
Stephens, F. F.—4-30-
Sweetzer, Anthony—5-24-
Stevens, Robert—6-11-
Spencer, Martin—6-23-
Schwartz, Pauline L.—9-25-
Strode, Ella Case—11-19-
Snapp, Edith E. A.—12-8-
1919—Sargert, Marg.—1-4-
Spahr, Eliza Clark—5-4-
Sapp, Samuel—5-20-
Sidell, Ellen—10-13-
Shoemaker, Ben. A.—12-10-
Strode, Dr. J. T.—12-26-
1920—Slack, Wm.—3-3-
Schnelle, Mrs. Emily—5-13-
Sphar, A. C.—9-13-
1921—Sulser, Anna Harrison—4-4-
Snapp, Bonnie J.—7-14-
Smith, Louise (Mrs. Ben)—7-25-

Slye, Leslie—9-1
Schuh, Clarence, Jr.—10-25-
Sellers, Wm.—12-23-1921
1922—Shelton, Mrs. Nard—10-14-
1923—Shephard, Emmitt—1-27-
Schnelle, Fred—10-25-
Smith, Ben T.—11-24-
Smoot, H. Wall—12-24-
Strode, Mrs. Marg.—12-29-

1924—Simpson, La Fayette—2-21-
Smoot, Mary K.—10-4-
Simpson, Hattie M.—12-31-

1925—Smith, Edw.—5-30-
Shanklin, S. A.—8-2-
Shephard, L. W.—9-5-

1926—Sidell, Jas. R.—3-9-
Simpson, Dorris—4-11-
Sherwood, Walter—7-2-
Schaeffer, Henry—8-27-
Sidwell, Alice—10-4—Minerva, Ky.
Sharpe, H. C.—10-4-
Swanson, John B.—12-11-

1927—Schwartz, Geo.—4-18-
Smith, Wm.—5-25-
Stevenson, Emma C.—6-17-
Saulisbury, John—8-13-
Schwartz, Margaret—9-22-
Stoker, Jno.—11-27-
Shelton, Noah—12-31—Newport, Ky.

## T

1891—Thomas Staley—12-21-
1892—Teetens, Scott—11-21-
1893—Thompson, Jr. A. H. 12-20-
1899—Taylor, Mrs. Katie D.—4-30-
1900—Thacher, John—8-8-
1902—Thomas, O. H. P.—3-28-
Toup, R. A.—5-7-
1903—Thomas, Hayes—7-3-
1905—Tolle, Dorothy Ludor—8-6-
1906—Tolle, Mrs. Jno.—3-28-
1909—Theademan, Ray—3-23-
1911—Taylor, Bessie—4-5-
Thomas, Geo. Bruce—4-10-
Thomas, O. A.—5-25-
1913—Teager, Nannie Hord.—7-7-
1914—Thomas Eliz. Hall—1-25-
Thomas, Ben F.—6-27-

1915—Tucker, C. A.—7-3-
      Toup, Sarah J.—12-28-
1917—Thomas, J. H.—7-7-
1918—Tolle, Wm. A.—1-11-
      Threlkeld, Lewis Bell—9-16-
1919—Tolle, Helen J.—3-26-
      Turnipseed, Thos. H.—4-19-
      Tucker, Mrs. C. A.—9-14-
1920—Trouts, Wm., Sr.—1-17-
      Threlkeld, Jas. E.—1-21-
      Thomas, Mary—2-6-
      Thompson, J. J. Jr.—2-9-

## W

1894—Wilson, Eliz. P.—5-14-
1895—Wood, Miss Phoebe—1-16-
      Wells, Thomas—3-22-
      Williams, Mrs. Eliz.—3-26-
1896—Wright, J. H.—5-26-G. A. R. Lot
1897—Wheatley, Miss Martha—3-29-
      Walker, F. M.—11-6-
1898—White, David S.—1-17-
      Wall, Mrs. A. H.—4-16-
      Willison, W. M.—7-27-
1900—Watkins, Gertrude—6-8-
      Winter, Dr. R. E.—7-23-
      Wall, Mrs. G. S.—4-11-
      Watkins, W. W.—8-23-
      Watkins, Mrs. H. D.—12-27-
1901—Wells, John—3-2-
      Wells, George R.—3-23-
      Wise, Mrs. Amanda—4-22-
      Wood, Mrs. Nannie H.—10-18-
1902—Watkins, Mrs. Lida—7-8-
      Wood Randolph—9-16-
1904—Wirtz, Miss Ann—1-8-
      White, Charles H.—2-24-
1905—Wood, Mrs. Marg.—3-11-
      Williams, Mrs. Bettie—4-12-
      Williams, Mrs. Marg.—8-4-
      Walther, Emma—8-6-
      Wilson, Mrs. 11-23-
1906—Wall, A. H.—2-24-
1907—Wood, Jas Lindon—1-30-
      Wheeler, Peyton—2-3-
      Wells, Mrs. Melissa—2-25
      Wood, T. M.—3-9-
      Writt, E. M.—3-10-
      Writt, Ruth R.—6-27—from Minerva, Ky.

White, Dr. Russell A.—3-13-
Wells, Wm. E.—11-15-
1908—Wills, Wm.—1-30-
Wilson, Mrs. Mary C. —2-2-
Whipps, Mrs. Robt.—5-24-
Wheeler, Emma—7-15—Removed from Old Cemetery
1909—Watson, Thos.—2-12—GAR Lot
Williamson, Curtis—9-10-
1910—Williams, Sarah—1-4-
Wells, Mrs. Mary R.—1-29-
Weis, D. K.—4-17-
Wood, Mrs. Pickett—9-17-
1911—Walker, Monroe M.—1-18-
Winter, Mrs. Rebecca R.—2-11-
White, Laura Russell—5-6-
Winter, George F.—5-12-
1912—Wells, Virginia—7-7-
Woodward, Isaac—9-10-
1913—Worthington, Judith Cook—7-19-
Walker, J. J.—8-19-
Wells, Lida G.—12-5-
1914—Winter, J. J.—10-6-
1914—Watson, Emma—10-21-
1915—Watson, Isaac N.—6-3-
Wilson, Clark Hart—5-28-
Wood, Wm. E.—10-3-
1916—Wood, Marian—4-4-
White, D. Sam—9-22-
Wheat, Marg. Lessant? (Lessast) 11-18-
1917—Watkins, Wm.—2-13-
Walker, Belle Newell—2-17-
Winter, Mary Ellen—3-9-
Walker, Lou Ella—3-25-
Ward, Rebecca—9-28-
Watkins, Dorothy Duke— 9-30-
Woods, Jos. D.—10-8-
1918—Werline, Carrie—1-23-
Williams, Frank H.—10-18-
Woods, Morris T.—10-28-
Ward, Jas.—11-14-
1919—Webb, Albert—1-19-
Whipps, Robt.—3-10-
Williams, Mrs. Howard (Edith)—3-13-
Walker, Mrs. Hattie—6-29-
Winter, T. J.—8-24-
Williams, Fred—12-15-
Wheeler, Philipp W.—12-21-
1920—Wilson, Herbert—2-22-
Weaver, Clyde—3-26-

Weaver, Mrs. Lottie—4-11-
Weeks, Clifford, Sr.,—6-29-
Word, Jas. R.—9-28-
Walker, Jessie—12-20-
1921—Wilson, Beatrice H.—4-1-
Weber, Althea—5-30-
Walsh, Ira Russell—6-30-
Watson, Henry—7-31-
Watkins, Elmer—8-22-
White, Kenneth—8-25-
Warder, Susan M.—11-12
Wise, W. O.—12-6-
Writt, Mrs. Mary—12-8-
1922—Winter, G. K.—2-5—Minerva, Ky.
Wood, Elizabeth—3-16-
Watkins, Eliza Foster—3-18-
Williams, Anna—3-25-
Wood, Sophia C.—4-9-
Watkins, Dorothy Duke—5-17-
Williams, Mrs. Robt.—9-8-
Wilson, Amos—10-18-(Springdale, Ky.)
1923—Williams, Lorenzo Warder—4-14-
Wolfe, Mary L.—6-17-
1924—Watkins, Wm. C.—1-17-
Winter, Alice McClanahan—3-20-
Wood, Mrs. Eliza—4-10-
Wood, Jas. M—8-2-
Ward, J. C.—8-18-
Willitt, Ira—10-22-

## BRACKEN ASS'N BAPTIST CHURCH

### Year 1804, at Richland Creek, Saturday, September 1st

Churches                        Messengers' Names

Washington—Wm. Payne, Miles W. Conway, Amos Corwine, Henry Putman.

Mays Lick—Jacob Grigg, Nat'l Hixon, Laurence Crail, John Johnston, Wm. Alben.

Bracken—Lewis Craig, Wm. Holton, Sen., Samuel Frazer, Wm. Holton, Jr.

Stone Lick—Thos. Elrod, Aaron Houghton (or Houghtois), Wm. Bean, Wm. Byram.

Lees Creek—Philip Drake, Chas. Anderson, Griffin Evans, Richard Robinson.

Ohio Locust—James Thompson, Amos Miller.

Rich'd Creek—Joshua Singleton, Stephen Lee, John Owens, Aaron Owens.

Licking C/—Jonathan Jackson, Henry Man.

Foxes Creek—James (or Jovs) Wright, Joel Havens, Jas. Jos. Foster.

Salt Lick—Wm. Harper, Wm. Davis, Sam'l Cox.

Cedar Hill—James Lawson, John Gutteridge.
Johnston—Charles Metcalf, George Fauguker.
Indian Run—John King.
Wilson Run—Jas. Johnston, John Williams, Joseph Power, John Debell.
Three Mile—Eli Oxley, Wm. Stephenson.
Clover—David Beale, Castor Shrout.
Soldier Run—Bart's Anderson, Jas. Corson, David Thomas.
South Fleming—John Passons, Ishmael Davis.
Licking Locust—James Sanders, Laurence Triplett, Henry Hust.

1805 Bracken Ass'n held at Ohio, Sept. 7, 8, 9, at Ohio Locust

Washington—Wm. Payne, Miles W. Conway, Thos. Sloo, Wm. Cheesman, Henry Putman.
Mays Lick—Cornelius Drake, Tho. Young, James Morris.
Bracken—Philimon Thomas, David Chiles (Chilis?), Abraham Sally (Sallee?).
Stone Lick—Aaron Houghton, Wm. Been, Wm. Byram, Rawleigh Chinn.
Lees Cr.—Phillip Drake, Chas. Anderson, Griffin Evans, Rich'd Robinson.
Ohio Locust—Jas. Thompson, Zacharah Thompson, Wm. Thompson.
Richland Cr.—Joshua Singleton, Stephen Lee, Aaron Owens, John Owens.
Licking—Robt. Duffy, Henry Man.
Foxes Cr.—Nathaniel Foster, Joel Havens, James Wright.
Salt Lick—Wm. Harper, Landon Calvert, Wm. Hance.
Cedar Hill—Abraham Evans, Jas. Lawson.
Johnson—Caleb Fenton, Geo. Asbery?, John King.
Indian Run—John Hurst.
Wilsons Run—Jursham Hull, John Williams, Jas. Johnson, John Debell.
Three Mile—John Mozea, Wm. Morgan.
Clover—Jer. Foster, Jasper Shrout, David Beale (Beaale).
Soldier Run—Hampton Pangburn, Jas. Parsons.
Mouth Fleming—John Parsons, Garrard Morgan, Nely Roborts.
Licking Locust—Laurence Triplett, Jas. Sanders, Truman Day.

Just here CHARGES against certain members declaring against slavery were made   No meeting is recorded in this book for 1806.

A sermon "Is slavery a sin against the Lord, or is it not?"  The Minutes say: "It is our Opinion that as An Ass'n we have nothing to do with Slavery, seeing that it involves political questions, but do advise every soul to be subject to the higher powers.  Rom. 13 chapter.

1807—Bracken Ass'n of Baptists held at Washington, Ky., Sept. 5, 6, 7.

Churches                          Messengers

Washington—Wm. Payne, Miles W. Conway, Henry Putman, Amos Corwine, Lewis Gorden.
Mays Lick—Wm. Allen, Thos. Young, Jno. Shotwell.
Bracken—Lewis Craig, Wm. Holton, Jr., Jas. Blasinggin, Samuel Frayser.
Stone Lick—Aaron Houghton, Wm. Been, Rawleigh Chinn, Wm. Byram.

Lees Cr.—Philip Drake, Chas. Anderson, Griffin Evans.
Ohio Locust—Wm. Holton, Sen., Thos. Powers.
Richland Cr.—Josh. Singleton, Stephen Lee, John Owens.
Licking—Jer. Devore, Henry Man.
Foxes Cr.—Joel Havens, Samuel Cox, Wm. Markwell.
Salt Lick—Wm. Harper, Sam'l Cox, Landan Calvert, Roland Parker.
Cedar Hill—Carlile Evans, James Lawson.
Johnson—Eli Davis.
Wilsons Run—John Thompson, John Williams, Wm. Scott, Jos. Powers.
Three Mile—John Mousea, Wm. Morgan.
Soldiers Run—David Thomas, Joshua Robinson, Bar. Anderson.
Clover—Jasper Srout?, Samuel Nailer.
Mouth Fleming—John Parsons, Garrard Morgan, Henry Roberts.
Licking Locust—Henry Hurst, Wm. Cannon, Ailos Sanders.

### Bracken Ass'n Baptists, Mason Co.—1808

| Churches | Messengers |
| --- | --- |

Washington—Wm. Payne, Henry Putnam, Lewis Gorden, Amos Corwine.
Mays Lick—Baldwin Clifton, Wm. Allen, Thos. Young.
Bracken—John King, Samuel Frayzer.
Stone Lick—A. Houghton, R. Chen, W. Been, W. Byram.
Lees Cr.—Chas. Anderson, G. Evans, John Holton.
Ohio Locust—Thos. Power, Wm. Holton, Z. Thompson.
Richland Cr.—Joshua Singleton, Stephen Lee, John Owens.
Licking—John Routt.
Foxes Cr.—Joel Havens, Chas. Harper, Wm. Markwell.
Salt Lick—Sam'l Cox, Landen Calvert.
Johnson—Jelson Hambruk, Eli Davis.
Wilson Run—Jas. Johnson, Jno. Williams, Jno. Debell.
Three Mile—Henry Roach, (Pecock?) Wm. Morgan.
Clover—Jasper Shrout, Jeremiah Foster.
Mouth Fleming Cr.—John Parsons, Garrard Morgan. .
Licking Lower—Laurence Triplett, Wm. Kennan, F. Day.

### TOMBSTONES AND RECORDS OF KNIGHT FAMILY IN FLEMINGSBURG, KY.

Wesley Knight, born Aug. 14, 1803, d. Jan. 9, 1885.

Sarah, wife of Wesley Knight, b. May 17, 1802, d. May 8, 1876.

Wm. Rufus Knight, b. Jan. 15, 1840, d. May 6, 1872.

James W. Knight, b. Aug. 29, 1831, d. Oct. 1, 1869.

Lucy Knight, Oct., 1841.

Thomas Jefferson Knight, b. May 3, 1846, d. Dec. 28, 1885. Tombstone in Sharpsburg Cemetery.

Thomas Jefferson Knight died in Bath Co., Ky., 1885 (wife Eva Matthews living in 1931.) Married Nov. 16, 1875.

Mrs. Eva Knight, in will book 19, page 269, is named guardian to her infant children Jan. 29, 1886, namely Florence, Rufus, Oliver, Eda, Thos. Charles.

Thomas J. Knight, son of Wesley Knight (aged 47 in 1850 census) of Fleming Co.

Wife, Sarah Gallaghar Knight (Fleming County marriages), Dec. 16, 1826, age 47 in 1850 Census. Wesley Knight's Will (in book N., page 613, Fleming Co., Ky. wills) names sons Charles Henry Knight, John W. Knight, Thomas J. Knight, daughter Lucy A. Knight, Oct. 1, 1876; Jan. 26, 1885.

Sarah Gallagher Knight, dau. of John Gallagher, (gave his consent in Fleming Co.) Marriage bond Dec. 16, 1826.

John Gallagher's will (in book H., page 98, Fleming Co., Ky., (names daughter Elizabeth Gallagher, Sarah Knight, Mary Dewey, Gr. dau. Lucinda Jane Gallagher, Grandson John Henry Gallagher), Aug. 2, 1845; Nov. 24, 1845.

John Gallagher married April 19, 1798 to Elizabeth Beard, dau. of David Beard, who gave consent in note marriage recorded in Fleming Co. Book I., but the bond is filed in Mason Co. Box labeled 1798 bonds.

David Beard and wife Eleanor execute deeds in Mason Co. Deed book K, page 328, June 1, 1808.

## MAYS LICK, KY. DISCIPLES OF CHRIST

Some quotes from the book of Mrs. Robert M. Yancey, "commemorating the Centennial of their meeting house and the one hundred eleventh year of their life as a church."

### 1941

"When the first settlers came to this section, the years immediately following the Revolution, Kentucky was still part of Virginia. The town of Washington, laid off in 1785, was the oldest settlement in northeastern Kentucky; Maysville was a small collection of pioneer homes called Limestone, and the county of Mason had just been established by the Virginia Legislature."

——"the year 1788 is notable for two widely separated events; at Ballymena, north of Ireland, a child was born in a Presbyterian family of Scotch-Irish lineage, and they named him Alexander Campbell; while on the other side of the Atlantic, over in the new union of North American states, a little Kentucky village had its birth—Mays Lick. In time to come, the two were to know each other well."

In that year 1788 a band of sturdy pioneers set out from the Scotch Plains in New Jersey, 400 miles, with all their possessions in Jersey wagons, across the Allegheny mountains, down the Ohio river—the five families of Abraham, Cornelius, and Isaac Drake, and David Morris, and John Shotwell—to found a new home in Kentucky wilderness of which they heard such glowing accounts.

Landing at Limestone, resting at Washington, they chose a location twelve miles south of the Ohio river, buying Fourteen hundred acres from a man named May. The five families divided their property so that each had a corner in the salt lick or spring, where the deer and buffalo were in the habit of licking the surrounding earth. Thus logically the name Mays Lick.

Dr. Daniel Drake (son of Isaac Drake) was less than three years old when he reached Mays Lick with the five families. He became a great scholar, a great naturalist, a great doctor, and a teacher of pioneer doctors west of the Alleghenies, and deserved the undying gratitude of doctors and patients in those isolated settlements.

Four of the pioneers, David Morris, Cornelius Drake, Anna Shotwell, and Lidia Drake had brought with them "Letters of Dismission from a church at Scots Plains, Essex County, New Jersey." A community of devout Welsh Baptists. These were the first members of May's Lick's first church, constituted on Nov. 28, 1789 "a church of Jesus Christ according to the regular order of First Day Baptists."

With Immigration into Kentucky increasing rapidly at that time and many travelers from the North to the South passing over the highway, which is now The Maysville-Lexington road, it was not long before several hundred New Jersey and Virginia families were settled in the surrounding country."

The Division of the Baptist and Christian Churches in 1830 was made but few records were kept, till 1846, when the names of some of the members appear. Among those first members were Elias Anderson and his wife, Sallie M., Aaron Mitchell and his wife, Elizabeth, Francis W. Wheatly and his young wife, Mary Ann, Thomas Wheatly, Augustus, H. F. Payne, and his wife, Mary Morris;

Early Members: Mason Summers, Asa R. Runyon, James Morris, Leroy Dobyns, Waller Small, Elijah Groves, Lucinda Groves, Edward Groves and his wife, Francis J. Kerchival Groves, John T. Johnson, John Allen Gano.

Augustus H. F. Payne, in 1834 was chosen to the work of the ministry in the Old Stone Schoolhouse. T. P. Haley records that he preached regularly in Mason and surrounding counties till 1836, when he moved with his little family, and settled near Liberty in Clay County, Missouri. He married in 1828 Mary, daughter of Judge James Morris of Mason County. He became a member of the Baptist Church that same year at Mays Lick, immersed by Elder John Smith and was one of those who became "Diciples" after the division in 1830.

Richard C. Ricketts, a young man, had shown a talent for public speaking in the Lawrence Creek Church—ordained in 1833; in 1835 he married Miss Cornelia Pickett Desha, formerly of the Mays Lick Church of Christ—they moved to Maysville, Mason Co. R. C. Ricketts did evangelistic work in Mason and adjoining counties between 1845-65. A Millersburg lady remembered him as he looked in 1865, wearing the tall silk hat and the high heeled boots of the period; two sons became preachers, R. C., Jr., and Ben. For some years he lived near Midway, a trustee of the Orphan School from 1852 till his death in 1892. Still distinguished looking, in his frail old age, when he again lived in Maysville.

## List of Mays Lick Ministers

| | | | |
|---|---|---|---|
| 1836 | R. C. Ricketts | 1867 | Harry Turner |
| 1845 | County Cooperation | 1871 | W. J. Loos |
| 1848 | John M. Holton | 1883 | Wm. H. Tiller |
| 1850 | Walter Scott | 1884 | Lewis N. Early |
| 1852 | J. Young | 1886 | Wm. A. Gibson |
| 1854 | J. N. Payne | 1889 | Frank M. Tinder |
| 1854 | Jas. Henshall | 1898 | George P. Taubman |
| 1858 | John Shackleford | 1900 | Jos. A. Severance |
| 1859 | Henry Pangburn | 1903 | Robt. M. Giddens |
| 1860 | J. P. Streater | 1909 | D. R. Matthews |
| 1861 | R. C. Ricketts, Jr. | 1911 | C. A. Coakwell |
| 1862 | O. P. Miller | 1913 | W. J. Loos |
| 1863 | J. W. Cox | 1925 | Chas. S. Van Winkle |
| 1864 | Milton Pyles | 1929 | Herbert D. Woodruff |
| 1866 | Jos. D. Pickett | 1935 | Geo. J. Darsie |

## BIBLE RECORDS, MASON COUNTY, KY.

From the Bible of Captain James Ward II (published 1802) given by his greatgranddaughter, Margeret Holton Cunning, of Mason County, Kentucky.

James Ward, born Sept. 19, 1763—died Feb. 27, 1849—married 11 of June 1795 to Margeret Machin, born Oct. 1771, died Sept. 3rd, 1831.

John Henry Ward, b. March 30, 1796—died July 18, 1799.

Matilda Ward, b. July 2d, 1798—died 1822?

Sally Ward, b. July 29, 1800—d. July 23, 1845.

Wm. Ward, b. Oct. 23, 1802—d. Aug. 27, 1852.

Mary Ann Ward, b. Feb. 4th, 1805—d. Oct. 2nd, 1823.

James Ward, b. July 29, 1807—d. March 2nd, 1859.

Elizabeth Ward, b. Aug. 12, 1810—d. March 22, 1832.

Charles Ward, b. May 8, 1815—d. Sept. 24, 1859.

Mary Bell Ward, b. March 31st, 1856—d. April 26, 1929.

Sally Ward, b. May 9th, 1858

Charles Ward, Sr., b. Jan. 30, 1769—d. Jan. 20, 1830.

## TOMBSTONES IN OLD MAYSVILLE CEMETERY

Maysville City Hall, on site of First Ky. Central Depot, which was originally an old Cemetery. The graves were moved to Maysville Cemetery. These are names on the old tombstones that are standing:

B. F. Reynolds, died Dec. 7, 1845, aged 22 years. Erected by his brother, Newton.

Daniel McClaughlin, a native of Ireland, Parish of Glenn, County Donegall, d. Aug. 5, 1838; aged 32 years.

Cormick Breslin, native of Ireland, town of Glentel Parish, Co. of Donegall; died July 28, 1838.

Waldarmard Mentell, son of Wm. H. and Elizabeth B. Moss, died Dec. 1833.

Eugene John Murphey, died Oct. 28, 1847, in 56th year of his age.

Henry Krimmel, d. June 6, 1832. Coming among us a stranger, the blandness of his manners and the kindness of his heart soon made for him many friends who loved him affectionately, while living among us.

Albert Bowman, d. June 26, 1849, aged 18 years.

Margeret Jones, a native of Wales, d. May, 1839.

Elizabeth, consort of Thomas Hammer, d. Feb. 11, 1833.

James, son of George & Jane Montague, d. Aug. 1838.—George d. Aug. 1838.

Ellis Higgins, d. May, 1841, aged 26 years.

Eliza, consort of Jesse Martin, d. Jan. 1837, age 28.

Calvin Crowell, died Apr. 1837, aged 65 years.

Zipparah, wife of J. W. Wroten, b. Feb. 13, 1816.

Joseph Edwards, d. Nov. 11, 1842.

Mary Trevor, d. Feb. 2, 1837, aged 16.

Blanch, daughter of G. W. & Sarah Hall, d. Sept. 1836, 6 years old.

Julia Ann, daughter of D. & E. M. Cook, 6 years old.

Henry Jacoby, b. Apr. 9, 1842, d. 1844.

Oliver Moss, d. Nov. 19, 1938, 7 days.

Sarah C., consort of George W. Dunbaugh, and youngest daughter of L. & S. Chowning, aged 25 years, d. 1840.

Susanna, dau. of Jas. & Mary Phillips, d. Nov. 1836.

James Phillips, d. Apr. 15, 1845, age 55.

Elizabeth Phillips (marker buried too deep to see dates.)

Cynthia Amanda, dau. of J. W. & E. C. Johnston, d. Oct. 2, 1845, 3 years.

Charlette Hull, d. in Maysville, 1833.

James Chowning, d. Sept. 5, 1857. Sarah, his wife, d. Dec. 1836.

John Rasp, d. 1849.

John Burns, d. Feb. 1839, aged 22 years.

Frances Elizabeth Skidmore, dau. of Wm. & Rachel, d. Apr. 2, 1838, 6 mos.

William H. Blaine, native of Washington Co., Pa., d. Apr. 1840, age 36.

Mary, consort of Howkins Hand, d. 1836.

John Daniel, d. 1852.

James Ross, d. June 30, 1843, age 45.

John Thomas, d. Dec. 3, 1856, age 25.

William Brown, one of the Polish brothers, who departed this life Sept. 1838, age 22.

Henry C. Wilson, d. Nov. 29, 1834.

## Some Old Ones Nearby

Wm. C., son of Wm. & Violet Ballenger, b. June 6, 1822, d. Aug. 6, 1832.

Peter Curran, son of John F. & Mary Ballenger, d. Sept. 9, 1839.

Wm. Ballenger, b. Aug. 4, 1781, d. Aug. 1864.

Margeret W. Ballenger, Apr. 7, 1816, d. Mar. 24, 1844.

John F. Ballenger, 1810, June 20, 1889.

Sarah C. Taylor, wife of John D. Taylor, daughter of Wm. & V. Ballenger, b. Aug. 29, 1819, d. 1844.

Elizabeth M., wife of Moses Bratt, b. Dec. 22, 1835, d. July 19, 1887.
George Hancock, born in Virginia, Jan. 24, 1824.
Mary, wife of John W. Hancock, b. Mar. 3, 1801, d. July 6, 1866.
Wm. Erb, b. June 30, 1810, d. May 21, 1867.
Nannie Wilkenson, wife of George S. Hancock, b. Feb. 10, 1829, d. Jan. 9, 1885.
Mrs. Lida Watkins, 1902.
Wm. P. Watkins, b. Jan. 28, 1814, d. Feb. 9, 1878.
Amelia Earle Watkins, 1869-1886.
Nannie Anderson Watkins, 1871-1880.
George Nicholas Watkins, 1877-1881.
H. H. & H. J. Lawell lost two children, Geo. & Henry, 1864, 1868.
George W. Wells, b. May 26, 1809, d. July 22, 1876.
Mildred Wells, b. Aug. 24, 1844, d. Oct. 22, 1872.
Wm. N. Franklin, Dec. 8, 1849, May 19, 1888.
John L. Franklin, July 31, 1851—June, 1853
Alvin L. Franklin, Feb. 9, 1853—Jan. 4, 1888.
Staley Thomas, Feb. 7, 1807—Nov. 1881.
Caropta, wife of Staley Thomas, b. Feb. 1, 1807—d. Apr. 13, 1890.

## All on One Monument.

Emily S. Hunter, nee Thomas, July 13, 1888, age 44 years.
Daisy Thomas, 1877-1891.
James B. Tucker, Nov. 27, 1870, age 17 years.

## Smith Monument.

Jane Smith, wife of George Clarkson, b. in Preston, Eng.; b. Dec. 18, 1817; d. in Maysville, Ky., Apr. 3, 1896.
John D. Tash, Aug. 2, 1861—May 4, 1935.
Lillie B. Smith, wife of J. D. Tash, March 1862—Oct. 28, 1921.
Alex Rogers, 1850—1890.
Episcopal Church Lot: Child Kate Rutledge.
Kate, wife of Rev. W. D. Harlowe, d. Jan. 13, 1855.
Fannie, dau. of Rev. F. B. Nash & E. M. Nash, Nov. 15, 1845, d. Oct. 22, 1860.

---

Alonzo H. Denning, b. Feb. 7, 1826, d. Aug. 3, 1849.
Ravenscraft lot: Alice D. Gill, 1853—1908.
Wm. Newell, b. in Belfast, Ireland March, 1792, d. Maysville 5-11-1849.
Michael Ryan, b. Apr. 9, 1816, d. May 16, 1879.
Martha Louise Ryan, dau. of John B. & Mildred Richeson & relict of Michael Ryan, b. July 11, 1821—Jan. 25, 1890.
William, son of W. & J. Morris—July 2, 1849—July 18, 1864.
Judith A. Browning.
(Mother) Mary J. Browning, 1831-1913.
Charles P. Adams, 1849—1934.

Robert H. Baldwin—Jan. 25, 1821—Apr. 9, 1863.

Sallie T., wife of Robt. H. Baldwin Apr. 11, 1828—May 15, 1862.

John G. Avery died of Cholera Sept. 29, 1849.

Dr. J. D. Collins July 11, 1828; Jan. 17, 1890.

Sadie, wife of Dr. J. D. Collins, Jan. 12, 1848; Sept. 21, 1890.

James McMillin, b. July 26, 1806, was murdered in the City of Memphis by Isaac L. Bolton, May 23, 1857, age 50 years.

Thomas M. McMillin, M. D., U. S. Army, d. at Lake Califorinia April 6, 1873, age 32 years.

On same monument: Elizabeth Webb Yancy, b. Jan. 8, 1817; Nov. 29, 1889.

J. G. Baldwin, b. March 28, 1796; d. March 11, 1831.

Nancy M. Baldwin Sept. 11, 1796; d. July 28, 1849.

John A. Baldwin, b. April, 1825; d. Dec. 6, 1845.

Laura Belle, dau. of Capt. Wm. T. and Laura Wood, died in Memphis, Tenn., April 8, 1857, age 6 years.

Milton Culbertson b. in Maysville, Ky., Aug. 27, 1808; d. Oct. 26, 1874.

"Our Sister" Miss Jane M. Byrne of Philadelphia d. in Maysville, Ky., May 3, 1851.

Tillie, dau. of F. & E. F. Weedon; b. July 17, 1848; d. May 12, 1872.

Frederick M. Weedon, b. Feb. 19, 1817; d. Octo. 26, 1872.

Elizabeth, wife of F. M. Weedon, b. May 15, 1822; d. Feb. 14, 1856.

Names on old undated tombstones:

John B. Richeson

Elizabeth Clark Triplett

Sarah Jones Triplett

Lizzie C. Triplett

Preston B. Vanden, b. Feb. 17, 1815; d. May 7, 1883.

Adelia S., wife of P. B. Vanden, b. March 11, 1820; d. Jan. 2, 1910.

Ann, wife of James Smith, born in Preston England, July, 1823; died in Maysville, Ky., Jan. 11, 1895.

James Smith, b. in Preston, Eng., Feb. 28, 1823; d. Maysville, Ky., April 5, 1897.

Thomas Smith, b. in Liverpool, Eng., Mar. 6, 1799; d. in Maysville Jan. 14, 1849. Ann, relict of Thomas Smith, b. in Liverpool, Eng. Nov. 15, 1787; d. in Mason County Aug. 31, 1859.

Henry Smith, b. in Preston, Eng., June 24, 1829; d. in Maysville, Ky., Feb. 19, 1896.

Richard Smith Jones, b. Oct. 13, 1832; d. Nov. 20, 1849.

Elizabeth Smith, wife of Hugh Topping b. Jan. 13, 1816; April 30, 1857.

## NEW PART OF MAYSVILLE CEMETERY

B. Dale Bryant, 1864, 19—, Ora Wallingford Bryant, 1868-1940; married, 1887.

Dale Bryant Rose, 1907—On the monument is the following, "The Bryants settled at Bryants Station in Fayette Co., Ky. On the south bank

of the North Elkhorn in 1779—William Bryant married **Mary Boone.**
Daniel Boone married Rebecca Bryant.

1924—Wise, Flora—11-13-
1925—Worthington, Anna K.—2-20-
    Wilson, Rebecca Cady—2-21-
    Wheatley, Mary 3-5-
    Washburn, Harold B.—3-12-
    Washburn, Cynthia—1-11-
    Wells, L. 5-14-
1926—Willett, Anna White Lee—1-10-
    Wheeler, Alwila O.—2-4-
    Wright, Wm.—3-20-
    Washburn, Marlin—3-28-
    Williams, Kate—4-14-
    Williams, Chas. R.—4-23-
    Winter, Lula—11-1-
    Williams, Wm.—12-22-
1927—Wood, Alice—2-12-
    Wilson—3-7—Nannie
    Williams, Henry—5-11-
    Wood, Wm.—10-4-
    Wallingford, John A.—7-22-1878
    Augusta Byron, wife of John A. Wallingford
    Landy R., son of M. P. and M. L. Wallingford, died 1869, aged 19.
    Wallingford, M. P., born Nov. 8, 1814, died Feb. 22, 1865.
    Wallingford, George, son of M. P. and M. L., died 1869, aged 27
    Wallingford, M. G., died—2-28-1892
    Wallingford, Mrs. Joel—5-10-1893
    Wallingford, Mrs. Joseph—1-24-1893.
    Wallingford, Joseph—2-3-1895
    Wallingford, Joseph—1-11-1898
    Wallingford, Joel M.—2-14-1812
    Wallingford, M. A.—6-6-1916
    Wallingford, Buckner A.—3-7-1917
    Wallingford, Amanda—1-11-1921
    Wallingford, Girtie M.—2-19-1926
    Wallingford, Kate, Mrs.—7-28-1921
    Wallingford, Nellie—12-8-1918—of Cincinnati, O.
    Wallingford, George W.—6-28-1915
    Wallingford, W. Loebzer, b. 1844-1892
    Wallingford, Ora—b. 1869
1920—Thompson, Hugh—10-28-
1921—Turner, B. C.—9-13-
    Turnipseed, Mrs. Hattie—1-22-
    Tully, Alma—1-25-
    Toliver, James—9-7-
1922—Thomas, Lee—4-27-
    Tuggle, Wm. L.—12-11-
    Therkeld, Mrs. Albert—12-20—Harrodsburg, Ky.

1923—Toncray, Bessie L.—3-2—Tolesboro, Ky.
    Trussell, Nannie Rhoads—3-29—Tolesboro, Ky.
    Trumbo, Lee C.—Tolesboro, Ky.
    Triplett, Eulah—10-8-
    Tolle, Rachel—11-21—Huntington, W. Va.
1924—Tully, Elwood—4-23
    Tully, S. B.—4-11-
    Toncray, Lula M.—4-24-
    Thompson, Mrs. Hattie—5-1-
    Taylor, Mrs. Martha—8-20-
    Tully Wm. Boyd, Sr.—9-17-
    Taulbee, Woodson H.—9-21-
1925—Trouts, Eliz.—4-6-
    Tolle, Mrs. Elwood—5-25-
1926—Tully, Geneva—6-6-
    Tolle, Helen V.—6-21-
1927—Taylor, Chas.—9-3-
    Thomas, Margaret—10-15-
    Thomas, Wm.—10-18-
    Tuggle, Birdie B.—10-30-

## V

1898—Varian, Jos.—12-3-
1913—Valentine, Marg, E.—4-5-
1916—Valentine, J. W.—6-8-
1917—Valentine, Heltie—6-28-
    Valentine, Henry—7-19-
1921—Vogal, Mrs. Etta—10-17-
1925—Valentine, W. H.—2-18-

## W

1892—Wallingford, Mrs. M. J.—2-28-
    Wheatley, T. W.—12-17-
1893—Wallingford, Mrs. Jos.—1-24-
    Wilson, Josia—9-12-
1913—Young, Geo.—6-12-
1916—Yancy, Rebecca B.—3-3-
1917—Yancy, W. H.—5-21
1918—Yazell, Jane—10-25-

## MAYSVILLE, KY. CEMETERY (OLD)—SINGLE RIGHTS

Lot 35- Section 8—Jonnie Wise; Violet Wise; Mrs. Anna Gilbert; Mary Hilton, 1912; Wm. McNutt; John Sons; Cyntha Sons; ...... Owens; Nannie Beadley, 1901; John Hood, 1910; Anna C. Green, 1916; Ellena M. Jenkins, 19...; Darius Jenkins, 1939.

Lot 9, Section 9—Harry Dressell, 1894; John Hill, 1910; Fred Dressell, 1925; Mary J. Dressell, 1928; Bettie Hill, 1933; George Dressell, 1935.

Lot 11, Section 8—Frank Ryder, 1929; Geo. A. Ryder, 1896; Mrs. W. H. Ryder, 1907; W. H. Ryder, 1908; Mrs. Lee Ryder, 1935; Lee Ryder, 1945; Mary E. Ryder, 1943.

Lot 15, Section 8—Dr. Brough, owner.

Lot 16, Section 8—Arthur C. Donovan, 1906; Arthur J. Donovan.

Lot 19, Section 8—Thomas J. Nolin, 1898; Daniel Perrine, 1912; Edith Mooty, 1926; Effie N. Perrine, 1932; Daniel Perrine, 1932; Amanda Nolin, 1913; Emily C. Nolin, 1932; Mary V. Nolin, 1934.

Lot 220, Section 7—Geo. W. Schlitz, owner of lot. Anna Belle Hooper, 1871; Augustus Sullivan, Mrs. Augustus Sullivan; Eugene Crowell; Martin Crowell, 1910; Mattie Crowell, 1909; Louis Naden, 1923; 27 graves on this divided lot.

Lot 221, Section 7—J. B. Shockey, original owner; J. B. (or D.) Shockey, 10th Ky. Cavalry, Civil War; I. M. Shockey, 10th Ky. Cal.; Katie King, 1940; Martin Schlitz, 1943; Martin King, 1905; Wm. Coburn; Henry Wm. Coburn, 1829; Frances Coburn, 1840; John James Coburn, 1832; John Coburn, 1932; John Coburn; Mary Coburn, 1835; John Coburn; Ann Adams, 1831.

Lot 223, Section 7—Single Rights—Bennie Fristoe; Alice May Tolle, 1876; George W. Austin; Adie, Daisy, Lillie Puul; Dickey Mefford.

Lot 224, Section 7—Jas. Holliday, owner; 15 graves on lot; J. T. Garrison; Valeria Dryden, 1902.

Lot 1, Section 8—George Smith; Ada B. Smith; Emily Smith; Elizabeth Smith; Maggie Hoffman, 1892; Sallie, 1889; Mattie, 1888; Hoffman; Almira Hoffman, 1924; Isaac Hoffman, 1927.

Lot 3, Section 8—Mrs. Angie Bramel; Alice Yazell, 1918; James Yazell, 1898; Mary Ann Wilburn; Effie Jackson, 1914.

Lots 2 & 4, 5, 6, 7, 8, 10, 12, 13, 14, 17, 18, 20, 22, 24, 26, 27, 28, 29, 30, 32, 33, 34, 35—Lutie C. Daniels; Esteline Williams, 1887; Maria Williams, 1896; Marcus Williams, 1899;

Chas. Gilling; Anna D. Gray, 1900; Mary Frances Williams, 1888; Lucie McLane; Benjamin Duncle; Grace Kidder, 1896; Amanda Jackson, 1895; Di. Bratt; David Clarke (or Clarks) child; Jorden Clark, 1916; Andy W. Swice, 1901; Josie Davenport, 1919; J. T. Hoops; Wm. R. Meyers; Martin S. Minton; Dorothy Breeze; Morris Breeze; Lillie Crosby East, 1890; Elizabeth Barnes, 1900; Moses Liggett; Willie Reece; H. Yarnell; Mrs. Harding, 1902; Dave Harding; Robert Adams; Lorena Gilbert; Oscar Reed's Child; Wm. Crawford; Mrs. B. F. Jones; B. F. Jones, 1913; John Brown; Wm. H. Daulton; George R. Daulton, 1905; Annie Daulton, 1896; Andrew Daulton, 1901; Mrs. B. F. Burriss; Sarah M. Austin; Nannie Bradley; Mrs. W. N. Ryan; Geo. White; Clarence White; Robert Vane Sininger, 1939; Alberta Vane Johnson; Elizabeth Jane Boughner;

Leslie Downing; Thomas Downing; Frances Downing, 1937; Emma Wedding, 1922; Ola Haley, 1905; Clyde Haley, 1906; Alonzo Williams; James Haley, 1906; Louisa Haley, 1925; James Haley, 1906; James Alley, 1906; Elizabeth Jones, 1906; Josephine Sunier, 1928; Augustus Sunier, 1940; Walter Sunier, 1906; Fannie Edgington; Frank Edgington; Levi Pugh, 1939; Maslack Stacy; Alvin Wallingford's child; Andrew Swice;

Henry S. Valentine; Noble Earle Gilkerson, 1946; Fannie Trisler, 1894; Mrs. Joseph Trisler, 1906; Joseph Trisler, 1912; Robert Frost, 1907; Randolph Frost, 1909; Mrs. Isobel Frost; Edna McDonald, 1908; Edwin McDonald, 1918; Cynthia A. Dodson, 1924; W. T. Dodson, 1909; W. T. Elliott, 1909; Robert Clayton; Mrs. Arvil Damick, 1910; Frank Bradford (small pox); Mrs. Z. T. Fristoe, 1902; Z. T. Fristoe, 1906; Mrs. Wm. Parker; Leslie Forman, 1909; Bertha Walker, 1918; Mrs. Charles Walker; Anna A. Dickson; Mrs. Henry Kidder; Jos. H. Hoops, 1909; Noah Flaugher; Miss Laura Hayes; Myrtle Harover; John J. Dickson; Mrs. John J. (Sudie) Dickson, 1913; Minie Dickson, 1909; George T. McLaughlin, 1915; Virginia McLaughlin, 1936; Joseph Harney, 1910; Mrs. O. H. Morford; O. H. Morford; Hugh Warren, 1911; Lee Hayes; John H. Bohannoy.

## CALDWELL COUNTY MARRIAGES—INDEX

Early Marriage Bonds, Caldwell County, Ky., copied Aug. 14, 1940, by Mrs. W. T. Fowler and Miss Mary Prince Fowler, at Princeton, Kentucky.

First Page of Index—

Nov. 22, 1809—Jacob Holman to Nancy French, married Oct. (?) 26, 1809 by I. Browne.
June 5, 1809—James Wallace to...... I certify that I have joined June, 1809, Henry Darnal, M.
June 5, 1809—Lewis Duncan to Hannah Holcomb.
June 5, 1809—John McElroy to Sally Dunklin—6th July. J. Mercer.
July 3, 1809—Nicholas Lacey to Mary Bates—July 6, 1809, Henry Darnal, min.
July 8, 1809—Wm. Campbell to Mary Holman.
July 27, 1809—John Eison to Ann Jones—by Daniel Brown, M. G.
Aug. 8, 1809—Daniel Ford to Polly Gregory—Aug. 17, 1809, by Bennett Langston, J. P.
Aug. 5, 1809—Isaac Gray to Jane Martin.
Aug. 26, 1809—Wm. Osborn to Rachel Wadlington.
Aug. 29, 1809—Wm. Shoemaker to Polly Adams—Aug. 29, 1809, married by B. Langston.
Sept. 23, 1809—Joshua Dillingham to Ritty Smith.

2nd Page—

Oct. 3,1809—Wm. Dillingham to Mourning Smith.
Oct. 6, 1809—Stephen Bennett to Sally Cruise—Oct. 10, 1809, Ben Langston, J. P.
Oct. 14, 1809—Reuben Campbell to Polly Anderson—Oct. 15, J. Browne, J. P.
Nov. 11, 1809—John Brice to Jane Vaughn—Nov. 12, 1809, D. James, J. P.
Noc. 17, 1809—Wm. Frick to Polly Roberts.
Dec. 7, 1809—James Stevenson to Peggy Clinton—Dec. 19, 1809, Joseph Miller, J. P.
Dec. 17, 1809—Henry Skinner to Amelia Lyon.

Dec. 18, 1809—Elisha Rhoads to Reamy Carter.

Nov. 21, 1809—Thomas Crabtree to Fanny Black.

Jan. 4, 1810—John Gray to Betsey Roberts, Jan. 7, Wm. Gillihan, J. P.

Jan. 9, 1810—Charles Sullivant to Ruth Hammack, Jan. 9, 1810—B. Langston, J. P.

Jan. 10, 1810—James E. Castleberry to Agatha Smith, Jan. 16, Edwin C. Bearden.

Jan. 15, 1810—John W. Ford to Lucretia Satterfield, Jan. 18, Wm. Mitchuson.

Jan. 16, 1810—Andrew Lepley (Leeper?) to Nancy Dryer, Jan. 18, B. Langston, J. P.

Jan. 29, 1810—Isaac B. McElroy to Elizabeth Bennett, Feb. 4, B. Langston, J. P.

Feb. 5, 1810—Winfrey Bond to Nancey Easley, Feb. 13, Edmund Bearden.

Feb. 5, 1810—Theophilus Vickers to Judith Taylor, Feb. 7, Henry Darnal, minister.

Feb. 12, 1810—Elijah Brooks to Betsey Young, Feb. 15, Wm. Mitchuson.

Feb. 23, 1810—John Doom to Polley Kelley, Feb. 25, Bennett Langston, J. P.

Feb. 27, 1810—John Hancock to Barbary Purtle, July 25, Bennett Langston, J. P.

Feb. 24, 1810—James Stewart to Jane Smith, Feb. 25, D. James, J. P.

Feb. 26, 1810—William Elder to Ann Armstrong.

Mar. 7, 1810—Thomas Franklin to Patsey Harrell.

Mar. 13, 1810—Alfred Moore to Jane N. Love, 19th Mch., J. Brown, J. P.

Mar. 20, 1810—John Stormatt to Polly Perkins, Mar. 20, J. Browne, J. P.

Mar. 20, 1810—Thomas Campbell to Betsey Robertson.

Mar. 25, 1810—Thomas Newcomb to Ruth Carroll, Mar. 25, Bennett Langston, J. P.

April 4, 1810—Jacob Langston to Nancey Chandler.

April 6, 1810—William Cowan to Jane Williams.

April 4, 1810—William Willoby to Jane Overly, April 5, David James, J. P.

April 8, 1810—Hugh McWaters to Lucretia Shelby, Ap. 8, Wm. Gillihen, J. P.

April 19, 1810—Arthur Jenkins to Polly Gillehen, Ap. 9, D. James, J. P.

April 29, 1810—Joshua G. Church to Margaret E. Beck.

May 19, 1810—Samuel Barnett to Sarah Gehen.

May 19, 1810—Wm. Lazell to Nancy Adams, May 24, B. Langston, J. P.

May 19, 1810—Philip Henson to Matilda McKinney, Henry Darnall, min, of Gos.

May 21, 1810—John Mitchell to Sally Sullivant.

May 28, 1810—David Doom to Charlotte Sullivant, May 29, Sam Glenn, J. P.

June 15, 1810—James Sullivant to Lucinda Brown, June 21, Edmund Bearden.

July 9, 1810—Williamson Boyakin to Elizabeth Baynes, July 17, by Edmund Bearden.

July 25, 1810—Thomas Bean to Elizabeth Martin.

Aug. 2, 1810—Wm. Stone to Lavina Birdsong, Aug. 4, Wm. Mitchuson.

Aug. 28, 1810—Josiah Greer to Jenny McClure, Aug. 28, Wm. Gillihen, J. P.

Aug. 7, 1810—Benjamin Smith to Nancy Easley, Aug. 16, Edmund Bearden.

Aug. 31, 1810—Wm. Harris to Anna Ridge, Sept. 4, Alexr. Stevenson, J. P.

Sept. 14, 1810—Wm. Scott to Julia Rush, Sept. 18, Danl. Brown, M. G.

Sept. 3, 1810—James Farmer to Peggy Lamb, Sept. 11, Edmund Bearden.

Aug. 20, 1810—Samuel Stevens to Rebecca Kevil, Aug. 23, Wm. Mitchuson.

Oct. 9, 1810—George Davenport to Sally Thornton.

Oct. 11, 1810—Malachi Hafford to Susan Martin, Oct. 11, John Bradley.

Oct. 11, 1810—Eli Ingram to Nancy Banister, Oct. 21, W. Gillehen, J. P.

Dec. 3, 1810—Rufus Beech to Elizabeth Stevenson, Dec. 6, J. Brown, J. P.

Dec. 9, 1810—Matthew P. Dunn to Charlotte Mercer, Jan. 30, Wm. Mitchuson.

Dec. 9, 1810—John Kellion to Elizabeth Elliott, Dec. 25, Wm. Gillihen, J. P.

Dec. 19, 1810—Coleman Barnett to Ann Scott, Dec. 20, date of marriage ret. Jan. 7, Sam Glenn.

Dec. 24, 1810—Wm. Woods to June Framan (Freeman?)

Dec. 27, 1810—Jonah Robinson to Mahaley Vaughn.

Dec. 29, 1810—Thomas Clayton to Candy Bradshaw.

Dec. 30, 1810—Sylvanus Palmer to Elizabeth Gillispie, Dec. 30, John Bradley.

1811:

Jan. 23, 1811—Stephen Cruce to Nancey Duff.

Feb. 2, 1811—James Bainston (Banister?) to Rebecca Shelford.

Feb. 4, 1811—Peter Fuller to Catherine Conway.

Feb. 11, 1811—James Woodside to Ann Brown, Feb. 14, "rites of our church," Samuel Brown, V. D. M.

Feb. 12, 1811—James Balsengam to Milly Brown.

Feb. 20, 1811—Lewis Kuykendall to Peggy Richey, Feb. 21, D. James, J. P.

May 28, 1811—Reddick Nichols to Celia Jenkins.

May 29, 1811—John Miller to Polly Hamilton, May 30, Terah Templin.

June 20, 1811—Andrew Anderson to Rebecca Stephens, June 20, John Bradley.

June 26, 1811—Alfred Wolf to Polly Bond, June 27, E. Bearden.

July 1, 1811—Obadiah Moss to Susan Stone, July 25, J. Browne, J. P.

July 6, 1811—John Kelly to Sally George.

July 7, 1811—Isaac Johnson to Charlotte Baker.

July 10, 1811—Daniel Holcomb to Malinda McKinney, July 10, B. James, J. P.

July 27, 1811—David Davenport to Jane Elliott.

July 30, 1811—James Bug to Elizabeth McDowell, Aug. 1, Alec. Stevenson, J. P.

Aug. 8, 1811—Jesse Ford to Nancy Ford.

Aug. 21, 1811—James M. Russell to Nancy Bailey, Aug. 22, Edmund Bearden.

Feb. 23, 1810—(so copied)—Wm. White to Phoebe Arnold, Feb. 24, Thos. Ezell.

Feb. 22, 1811—Ennis Leeper (Hooper) to Elizabeth Wood, Feb. 24, Edm. Bearden.

Feb. 22, 1811—John Grider to Elizabeth Son, Feb. 25, Alexr. Stevenson, J. P.

Feb. 25, 1811—Henry Lewis to Jane Neely, Feb. 24, D. James, J. P.

Mar. 4, 1811—George H. Owens to Martha Story, Mar. 6, James Rucker, Sen.

Mar. 5, 1811—Henry Dodds to Clary Perkins, Mch. 7, Alexr. Stevenson, J. P.

Mar. 13, 1811—John E. Stone to Nancy Pennington, Mch. 14, Alexr. Stevenson, J. P.

Apr. 11, 1811—Stephens Perkins to Lizza Stone, Apr. 12, 1811, J. Browne, J. P.

May 6, 1811—Andrew Dunn to Betsey Jenkins.

Mch. 21, 1811—Alexr. George to Jane Robinson.

May 14, 1811—John Lewis Laughlin to Charlotte Durley, May 16, Alexr Stevenson, J. P.

**(Some of these inserted not in consecutive order).

Sept. 29, 1811—James Baker to Sophia Philly, Oct. 3, Sam'l. Glenn, J. P.

Oct. 8, 1811—Jesse Clayton to Jane Lamb.

Oct. 28, 1811—Jacob Bradbury to Caty Thedford, Oct. 24, D. James, J. P.

Nov. 4, 1811—Joseph Bowman to Jane Hobert.

Dec. 2, 1811—Thos. D. Clark to Jane Cunningham, Dec. 3, J. Browne, J. P.

Nov. 25, 1811—Dunning Baker to Mourning Bearden.

Dec. 12, 1811—Owen Franklin to Hannah Pratt.

Dec. 23, 1811—John Cross to Peggy Smith.

Dec. 23, 1811—Isaiah Ross (or Ron or Rou) to Nancy Bridges.

Dec. 13, 1811—Garrett Gray, Jr., to Nancey Hall.

Nov. 17, 1811—Samuel Underwood to Polly Robertson, Nov. 29, D. James, J. P.

1812:

Jan. 6, 1812—Thomas Hammond to Betsey Jones.

Jan. 7, 1812—James Crider to Rebecca Holman.

Jan. 7, 1812—James Maxwell to Betsey Smith, Jan. 9, Terah Templin.

Jan. 7, 1812—Joseph Gregory to Minney Hammack.

Jan. 20, 1812—Brandon Armstrong to Massa Kilgore.

Jan. 23, 1812—Andrew Dunn to Penniah Freeman.

Jan. 27, 1812—Richard Bonds to Elizabeth Hughes.

Jan. 30, 1812—James Harrell to Jane Rush, Feb. 3, Arther H. Davis, J. P.

Feb. 1, 1812—Mahala Ingram to Rebecca Randolph, Feb. 6, M. Thompson.

Feb. 1, 1812—Thos. Gilleland to Patsey Armstrong, Feb. 4, Terah Templin.

Feb. 4, 1812—Thos. Malone to Matilda Ingram, Feb. 6, M. Thompson.

Feb. 5, 1812—Wm. Alturn to Esther Kuykendall.

Feb. 10, 1812—Dennis Davis to Anna Thomas, Feb. 13, A. Cravens.

Feb. 15, 1812—Basil George to Mary Randolph, Feb. 10, M. Thompson.

Feb. 22, 1812—James Curry to Peggy Magill, Feb. 26, David Brown, M. G.

Mch. 2, 1812—Edwd. Cantwell to Susannah Cames (or Comes).

Mar. 7, 1812—Ewin Kelly to Elizabeth Roach.

Mch. 16, 1812—Henry Clark to Jane Ross, Mch. 19, Arthur H. Davis, J. P.

Mch. 16, 1812—Abraham Howton to Darcas Castleberry, Mch. 23, Alexr. Stevenson, J. P.

Mch. 16, 1812—David Howton to Elizabeth Castleberry, Mch. 19, Alexr. Stevenson, J. P.

April 14, 1812—John Gregory to Rohena Hail, Ap. 16, Sam Glenn, J. P.

April 23, 1812—James Mitchell to Palatine Trailer. "According to the customs and usages of the church of which I am a member," Ap. 28, John Travis.

April 24, 1812—Cyrus Woods to Polly Trailer, Ap. 28, John Travis.

April 25, 1812—William Joiner to Sally Allen, Ap. 26, A. H. Davis, J. P.

April 27, 1812—William Goodacre to Elizabeth Bryants May 1, Daniel Brown, M. G.

April 27, 1812—John Thetford to Nancey Thetford.

April 29, 1812—Thos. Gordon to Eliza Brooks.

May 28, 1812—Wm. Hughes to Sarah Stevens, May 28, D. James, J. P.

June 9, 1812—Luke Devore to Elizabeth Brown.

June 15, 1812—Wm. Bond to Sally R. Birdsong.

June 22, 1812—Brooks Perkins to Vashti Moore, July 2, George Robinson, J. P.

June 22, 1812—John Shelley to Jane Smith.

June 23, 1812—James Gray to Rosanna Cannon, June 25, Henry Darnall.

June 29, 1812—Hugh Stevenson to Mary Bird, June 30, Sam B. Brown, V. D. M.

July 7, 1812—Aaron Smith to Sally Gately.

July 13, 1812—Isaac Green to Elizabeth Ross.

July 20, 1812—Thos. Bennett to Peggy Son, July 23, George Robinson, J. P.

July 26, 1812—Robert Lyon to Elizabeth East, July 26, W. Thompson.

July 6, 1812—John Kelly to Sally George, July 7, M. Thompson.

Aug. 3, 1812—Larkin Colley to Rhoda Fulks, Aug. 13, D. James, J. P.

Aug. 8, 1812—John Thomas to Nancey Smith.

Aug. 22, 1812—Jacob Pennington to Pamela F. Mitchuson.

Sept. 2, 1812—John Algea to Sally Greer.

Sept. 5, 1812—Michael Son to Sally Kenady, Sept. 6, J. Brown, J. P.

Sept. 6, 1812—John W. Throop to Elizabeth Hannah, N. Cravens.

Sept. 19, 1812—John McKnight to Betsey Dillingham.

Sept. 25, 1812—Thomas James to Mary James.

Sept. 30, 1812—Elisha Lacey to Caroline Walker, Oct. 8, Henry Darnall.

Nov. 9, 1812—John Hammond to Martha Lamb, Nov. 10, A. H. Davis, J. P.

Nov. 17, 1812—Samuel Hewlett to Rebecca Frazier.

Nov. 18, 1812—David Magee to Polly Curlew, Nov. 19, W. Thompson.

Nov. 28, 1812—Absolem Bennett to Elizabeth Groves, Dec. 1, Terah Templin.

Dec. 13, 1812—Garrett Gray, Jr., to Nancey Hall, Dec. 23, W. Thompson.

Nov. 17, 1812—James Robinson to Betsey Purth.

Nov. 28, 1812—Joseph Vaughn to Betsey Reeves, Dec. 30, A. H. **Davis,** J. P.

Nov. 23, 1812—Lewis Grubbs to Polly McCaa.

1813:

Jan. 28, 1813—Thos. Hancock to Patsy Byrd, Jan. 28, Saml. Glenn, J. P.

Feb. 7, 1813—Redding Wolf to Elizabeth Matlock, Feb. 11, Fielding Wolf.

Feb. 10, 1813—Solomon Silkwood to Matilda Simmons, Feb. 11, N. Cravens, J. P.

Feb. 15, 1813—John Roach to Catherine Ingram, Feb. 28, W. Thompson, J. P.

Feb. 18, 1813—Larkin Bennett to Rebecca Smith, Feb. 25, Geo. Robinson, J. P.

Feb. 27, 1813—John W. McNab to Mary Hays.

Mar. 2, 1813—Jacob Furman to Susan Rawlins, Dec. 25, P. Cartwright, M. G.

Mar. 13, 1813—Crawford Anderson to Jinsey Cunningham, Mch. 17, Wm. Anderson, J. P.

Mar. 16, 1813—John Thomas to Hannah Flint, Mch. 18, Geo. Robinson, J. P.

Mar. 19, 1813—Geo. Robinson to Alcey Poor, Mch. 23, Saml. Glenn, J. P.

Mar. 20, 1813—John McCarty to Mary Harris.

Mch. 29, 1813—John Stevens to Lucretia Calhoun.

Mch. 30, 1813—Hugh Banister to Susan Briges, Ap. 4, Washington Thompson.

April 12, 1813—John Wilson to Cassey Killion, Ap. 12, Saml. Glenn, J. P.

April 10, 1813—Nicholas Keating to Ann Sanders, Ap. 11, Washington Thompson.

April 12, Martin Lacey to Dolley Young, Ap. 22, Wm. Anderson, J. P.

April 12, 1813—Joshua Henson to Nancey McClure, Ap. 15, Wm. Anderson, J. P.

April 17, 1813—Charles Partin to Isabella Goff, Ap. 17, N. Cravens, J. P.

April 21, 1813—John K. Brown to Sally R. Bush.

Sept. 15, 1813—Abner W. Smith to Margaret Kemp, Ap. 17, J. Browne, J. P.

Sept. 27, 1813—John Dobbins to Drucilla Smith, Sept. 24, N. Cravens, J. P.

Oct. 4, 1813—Wm. D. Stuart to Sarah Pennington, Oct. 7, Geo. Robinson, J. P.

Oct. 18, 1813—John Robb to Barbary Robinson, Oct. 19, Saml. Gleen, J. P.

Nov. 16, 1813—Jacob King to Jane Miller, Nov. 16, Geo. Robinson, J. P.

Dec. 27, 1813—James Anderson to Polly Briges.

Dec. 28, 1813—Elisha Reynolds to Sally Elliott, Dec. 30, Wm. Duncan, J. P.

Dec. 29, 1813—John Dickey to Martha Stevenson.

Oct. 27, 1813—James Carlisle to Mary McDowell, Oct. 27, N. **Cravens,** J. P.

Nov. 24, 1813—John Mangrove to Nancey Wafer (Waler or Walmen) Dec. 2.

1810:

Oct. 26, 1810—Thos. Shelby to Polly Love, Nov. 29, D. Brown, M. G.

1811 again: Feb. 13, 1811—Thos. Cochran to Lydia Feb. 25, D. Brown, M. G.

1814:

Jan. 5, 1814—Martin Hammond to Margaret Lamb, John Bradley.

Jan. 14, 1814—John T. White to Polley Williams, Jan. 17, D. Brown, M. G.

Jan. 24, 1814—William Bennett to Sally Dennis, Jan. 27, Geo. Robinson, J. P.

Feb. 28, 1814—Alexr. Stevenson to Margaret Bingham, Mch. 1, "by me." Alexr. Stevenson, J. P. (returned by him, wonder if he married himself to his bride!)

Mch. 7, 1814—Obadiah Fulks to Ellen Colley, Mch. 10, Wm. Duncan, J. P.

Mch. 7, 1814—Thos. Williams to Margaret Brown, Mch. 2, Saml. Glenn, J. P.

Mch. 21, 1814—Lewis Holmes to Mary T. Freer, Mch. 24, Saml. Glenn, J. P.

April 15, 1814—Frederick Graves to Sophia Towray, Ap. 17, Alex. Stevenson.

May 19, 1814—James Rutter to Sally Farmer, June 13, James Rucker, Sr.

May 30, 1814—Robert Smith to Mary Denson.

May 30, 1814—Jesse Gray to Effy Congon.

May 30, 1814—James Rucker, Sr., to Susannah Sampson, May 30, Daniel Browne.

June 8, 1814—William Coats to Sally Story, June 9, Saml. Glenn, J. P.

June 21, 1814—Anthony Mangrove to Ruth Simpson, June 23, Alex. Stevenson.

July 5, 1814—John W. Briges to Polly Hall, July 14, Fielding Wolf.

July 12, 1814—John S. Smart to Anna Tyler, July 14, Jas. Rucker, Min.

July 27, 1814—Wm. Armstrong to Ann Hamilton, July 26, Terah Templin.

July 29, 1814—John H. Ball to Sarah Edwards, J. Bradley.

Aug. 3, 1814—James Barnett to Elizabeth M. Ledbetter.

Aug. 10, 1814—John Johnson to Susan Brooks, Aug. 10, Edm. C. Wilcox.

Aug. 11, 1814—Thos. Moore to Betsey Reed, Aug. 11, James Rucker, Sr.

Aug. 16, 1814—Robert Hardin to Sarah Simpson, Aug. 22, Alexr. Stevenson.

Aug. 20, 1814—James Byrd to Betsey Simpson, Aug. 20, Alexr. Stevenson.

Sept. 6, 1814—Thruston Grubbs to Betsey Bowland.

Sept. 7, 1814—Stith Cosby to Alsey Henson, Sept. 7, John Bradley.

Sept. 17, 1814—Walter Robinson to Charlotte Bates, Sept. 22, Wm. Duncan, J. P.

Sept. 22, 1814—Shadrack Oliver to Jemima Easley.

Sept. 26, 1814—James Bell to Elizabeth Smith, Oct. 2, W. Thompson, J. P.

Sept. 30, 1814—Thos. Frazier to Elizabeth Prince, Oct. 3, Saml. Brown.

Oct. 18, 1814—Wm. C. Young to Betsey Rutherford, Oct. 21, Wm. Anderson.

Oct. 22, 1814—Edward Owens to Ruth Strong, Oct. 25, D. James, J. P.

Oct. 24, 1814—Isaac Gray to Nancy Duncan, Oct. 26, Fielding Wolf.

Nov. 3, 1814—Jesse Jenkins to Elizabeth Kilgore, Nov. 3, D. James, J. P.

Nov. 12, 1814—Jeremiah Cook to Polly Patterson.

Nov. 23, 1814—Wiley Babb to Sarah Hart, Nov. 24, J. Browne, J. P.

Dec. 4, 1814—John Hartwick to Caroline Brice, Dec. 4, John Bradley.

1815:

Jan. 5, 1815—John Flint to Elizabeth Hamilton, Jan. 5, Geo. Robinson, J. P.

Jan. 11, 1815—Lemuel Hopson to Nancey Davis, Jan. 12, Henry Darnall.

Jan. 23, 1815—John Burton to Nancey Lacey.

Feb. 9, 1815—Joseph McMahen to Jane Martin, Feb. 9, Saml. Glenn, J. P.

Feb. 27, 1815—James Walen (Wafen, Waler) to Sally Eldin (Elder) Mar. 2, Marham Easley, J. P.

Mar. 6, 1815—Josiah Langston to Betsey Chandler, Mar. 7, Saml. Glenn, J. P.

April 10, 1815—James Young to Sarah Roach, Ap. 23, Henry Darnall.

April 13, 1815—John Brown to Polly Sullivant, Ap. 20, Saml. Glenn, J. P.

Mar. 22, 1815—Charles Carter to Sally Montgomery, Mar. 23, D. James, J. P.

April 18, 1815—Wm. Smith to Rebecca Maxwell, Ap. 20, Terah Templin.

June 9, 1815—Noah Davis to Christiannia Sparrow, June 11, D. James, J. P.

June 28, 1815—John G. Clayton to Sarah A. Hinton, June 29, D. Brown, M. G.

July 18, 1815—Wm. Saterfield to Polley Williams, July 20, B. Langston, J. P.

May 28, 1815—Henry Rowland to Rachel Gray, May 29, D. James.

Aug. 24, 1815—Meredith Gibson to Hannah Moore.

Aug. 26, 1815—Robert Wadley to Comfort Paynes, Aug. 28, W. Easley, J. P.

Aug. 5, 1815—Moses Stallins to Nancey Jenkins, Aug. 6, Edmond Wilcox.

Sept. 2, 1815—Robertus Love to Sally Morse, Sep. 7, D. Browne.

Aug. 30, 1815—Zebulon Blackburn to Lois Ashurst.

May 22, 1815—Dederick Yons (or Yous) to Deborah Moore, May 22, D. James, J. P.

Sept. 19, 1815—John Travis to Cynthia Trailer, Sep. 23, "ceremonies of the Methodist Church." Edmund Wilcox.

Sept. 21, 1815—Elias Calvert to Eleanor Morse.

Sept. 27, 1815—Mark M. Sullivant to Fanny Hughes, Sept. 28, A. H. Davis, J. P.

Sept. 30, 1815—Moses Stevens to Polly Anderson, 1st Oct. "at house of Ambrose Anderson." A. H. Davis, J. P.

Oct. 7, 1815—Gilbert Dodds to Polly Clinton, Oct. 12, Geo. Robinson.

Oct. 10, 1815—Jesse Pemberton to Betsey Rucker, Oct. 11, Jas. Rucker, Sr.

Oct. 14, 1815—Jarrett Wofford to Mimey Higgins, Oct. 20, Edm. Wilcox.

Oct. 14, 1815—James W. Thompson to Gracey Calhoun, Oct. 19, Josiah Whitnal, Z. C. C.

Oct. 17, 1815—Wm. Ford to Nancey Mitchel, Oct. 23, Edm. Wilcox.

Oct. 23, 1815—Zadock Thomas to Sally Rutter, Oct. 26, D. Brown.

Nov. 7, 1815—John Baynes to Elizabeth Bamer (or. Barner or Barns or Bains) Nov. 8, Marham Easley, J. P.

Nov. 18, 1815—Cyrus Philley to Lucy Gregory, Nov. 19, Saml. Glenn, J. P.

Nov. 20, 1815—David Barns to Folly Egbert, Nov. 21, "ceremony of Methodist Church." Edm. Wilcox.

Dec. 2, 1815—James Dorough (or Downgh) to Elizabeth Sullivant Dec. 7, 1815, Saml. Glenn.

Dec. 5, 1815—John Mercer, Jr., to Matilda Freeman, Dec. 5, Hen. Darnall.

Dec. 5, 1815—Thomas Grubby to Caty Roach, Dec. 7, W. Thompson, J. P.

Dec. 21, 1815—Henry Cherry to Ann Rogers, Dec. 24, W. Thompson.

Dec. 25, 1815—Wm. Holcomb to Ann Lyon, Dec. 27, H. Darnall.

1816:

Jan. 19, 1816—Samuel Jenkins to Margaret Gary, Jan. 17, Jas. Rucker, Sr.

Jan. 16, 1816—John Neely to Mary Thompson, Jan. 16, John Travis.

Jan. 17, 1816—Jarrett Cherry to Sally Holland, Jan. 21, W. Thompson.

Jan. 18, 1816—Moses Perkins to Ann Burton, Geo. Robinson, J. P.

Feb. 10, 1816—Elijah Bennett to Ann Brown, Feb. 16, Geo. Robinson, J. P.

Feb. 17, 1816—Armiel Vincher to Sally George, Feb. 18, A. H. Davis, J. P.

Feb. 26, 1816—Geo. Gracey to Mary McDoo, Feb. 26, Saml. Glenn, J. P.

Mar. 1, 1816—Robert Patterson to Lavinia Morse, Mch. 7, "Meth. Ch." Edm. Wilcox.

Jan. 2, 1816—Shadrack Oliver to Sarah Vaughn, Jan. 4, Danl. Browne.

Mch. 4, 1816—Arrington C. Potts to Polly Matlock, Mch. 5, D. Browne.

Aug. 24, 1816—David Grace to Jane Fowler.

Sept. 3, 1816—Burrell Anderson to Priscilla Jones.

Sept. 9, 1816—Johnah Bigham to Eliza B. Freeman.

Sept. 10, 1816—James H. Bigham to Elizabeth B. Algea.

Sept. 10, 1816—Hugh Jackson to Jemima Cannon, Sept. 19, Geo. Robininson, J. P.

Sept. 17, 1816—Wm. Clayton to Betsey Woods, Sept. 19, A. H. Davis, J. P.

Sept. 18, 1816—Aleexander Dunn to Betsey Saterfield, James Rucker, Sr.

Sept. 19, 1816—Hiram Pinnell to Phebe Boland, Sept. 24, Henry Darnall.

Sept. 20, 1816—Wm. Chambers to Sally Ingram, Sept. 26, Henry Darnall.

Sept. 28, 1816—Edmund Morse to Nancey Ashur.

Oct. 2, 1816—Stephen Sullivant to Darcas Pinnell.

Oct. 10, 1816—Wm. Goff to Margaret McClure, Oct. 11, Saml. Glenn, J. P.

............—James Clayton to Sally Crow, Oct. 24, A. H. Davis.

Oct. 28, 1816—Moses Lamb to Lucinda Smith, Oct. 31, W. Easley, J. P.

Oct. 28, 1816—Henry Jones to Lavina Duncan.

Oct. 31, 1816—Thos. Ritch to Rebecca Harrell, Nov. 5, W. Easley, J. P.

Oct. 31, 1816—Hugh McCastlin to Nancey Brazzle, Nov. 5, W. Easley, J. P.

Nov. 2, 1816—John Price to Jane Cochran, Meth. Ch., Edm. Wilcox.

Nov. 2, 1816—Stephen Roach to Mourning Gillehen, Nov. 5, H. Darnall.
Oct. 31, 1816—Isaac Jones to Polly Purtle, Dec. 21, Saml. Glenn, J. P.
Dec. 21, 1816—Wm. Jenkins to Honor Hark, Dec. 21, A. H. Davis, J. P.
Dec. 21, 1816—Joseph Cook to Pamela Morse.
Dec. 10, 1816—Tyre Kelly to Lucy Davis, Nov. 15, V. W. Thompson, J. P.
Dec. 31, 1816—Wm. Dillerline to Louisa Cook, Jan. 2, Geo. Robinson, J. P.

1817:

Jan. 18, 1817—Wm. Gore to Betsey V. Throup, John Bradley.
Jan. 4, 1817—John Ovey to Maria Simpson, John Bradley.
Jan. 4, 1817—John Walpert to Delphia Green, Jan. 5, John Bradley.
Feb. 14, 1817—Wm. Stevens to Emiranda Cakhoun.
Feb. 18, 1817—Whitwell Jenkins to Mourning Phelps, Feb. 23, Marham
    Easley.
Feb. 24, 1817—Perkins Pool to Nancey Sullivant, Mar. 1, Saml. Glenn,
    J. P.
Feb. 4, 1817—Abner Leach to Frances White, Mch. 6, A. H. Davis, J. P.
Feb. 4, 1817—Francis Prince to Polley C. Ford, Mch. 6, Daniel Brown, M.
    G.
March 6, 1817—Marcus Molley to Ann Beck, Mch. 9, James Rucker, Sen.
March 6, 1817— Benjamin W. Flint to Nancy Ford, Mch. 0, Saml. Glenn,
    J. P.
March 21, 1817—Benj. A. Darnell to Mary Cannon.
Mch. 21, 1817—John Corleu to Deborah Gore.
Mch. 31, 1817—Elijah Bennett to Polly Fesiale (Fesiate) Mach. 27, Saml.
    Glenn, J. P.
Mch. 24, 1817—Miles Dunning to Patsey Pettit, "church to which they
    belong," A. H. Davis, J. P.
April 3, 1817—Wm. Robinson to Elizabeth Gallway.
April 6, 1817—Chittenden Lyon to Nancey Vaughn.
April 15, 1817—Wm. Shanmose to Ally Ghren (Thren) Smith.
April 16, 1817—James Elden (or Elder) to Peggy Hamilton, Ap. 17,
    Samuel Brown, she of Livingston Co.
April 16, 1917 John Penington to Ruth Green, Ap. 22, Geo. Robinson.
April 23, 1817—John Bush to Patsey Roach, Ap. 27, Henry Darnall.
May 6, 1817—Robt. Gray to Charlotte Coleman, May 8, W. Thompson,
    J. P.
May 13, 1817—John Cunningham to Mahala Anderson, May 25, Wm.
    Duncan, J. P.
June 25, 1817—Vincent Anderson to Joanah Langsdon.
June 24, 1817—Charlton Ingram to Elizabeth Flemmin.
June 9, 1817—Eli Cochran to Betsey Catha.
July 14, 1817—John Palmer to Darcas Terel, John Bradley.
June 3, 1817—James Hix to Lavina Kelly.
June 25, 1817—Elisha Bams (or Banis) to Polley Harison, June 20, Geo.
    Robinson.
July 21, 1817—Alex Anderson to Leah Gillenen.
July 21, 1817—Wm. Love to Honor Tiron, July 24. "Meth. church of which
    I am a member." Francis Travis, M. E.

July 24, 1817—Henry Young to Polley Christman, John Bradley.

Aug. 7, 1817—Wm. B. Bond to Lucy Rucker.

Aug. 13, 1817—Drury Mercer to Susy Clark.

Aug. 19, 1817—Saml. Bell to Kindness Bearden, Aug. 22, Daniel Browne.

Sept. 16, 1817—Jonathan Stevens to Elizabeth Rushing.

Sept. 8, 1817—Thos. Shelly to Malinda Bradburn, Sep. 11, Saml. Brown.

Sept. 9, 1817—John Steptdon to Racel Weeks, Oct. 26, Edm. Wilcox.

Sept. 25, 1817—Thomas Patterson to Luana Smart, form of Presbyterian church, Sep. 25, John Barnett.

Sept. 20, 1817—James Edwards to Rebecca Henderson, John Bradley.

Sept. 30, 1817—Hugh Kincade to Eliza Green, Oct. 2, John Barnett.

Oct. 2, 1817—Alexander Ritchey to Rachel Drennan, Oct. 8, A. H. Davis, J. P.

Oct. 6, 1817—Israel Cannon to Lucinda Lowry, Oct. 9, Geo. Robinson, J. P.

Oct. 8, 1817—Wm. Kebly to Catherine Darnall, Oct. 12, H. Darnall.

Oct. 8, 1817—Samuel Glenn to Nancey Langston, John Bradley.

Oct. 11, 1817—David B. Freeman to Pelina Kuykendall, by H. Darnall.

Oct. 19, 1817—James Boland to Margaret Jones, Oct. 23, A. H. Davis, J. P.

Oct. 21, 1817—Zachariah Chandler to Elizabeth Boyd, John Bradley.

Oct. 24, 1817—Howard Husbands to Edith Pyle, Oct. 24, 1817, S. Brown.

Oct. 24, 1817—Drury Compton to Jane Cheek, Oct. 26, A. H. Davis.

May 9, 1817—James Rush to Milly Spurlock, May 11, A. H. Davis, J. P.

May 9, 1817—Othoa Hays to Elizabeth Haworth, Oct. 30, A. H. Davis, J. P.

Nov. 13, 1817—Wm. Ford to Ann Edmundson.

Nov. 3, 1817—John Boland to Susan Gray, Nov. 6, H. Darnall.

Nov. 4, 1817—Aaron George to Jinney Ramey, Nov. 6, Henry....

Nov. 5, 1817—Wm. Jefford to Eliza Gregory.

Dec. 3, 1817—Wm. Jennings to Polley Boland, Dec. 4, Henry Darnall.

Dec. 8, 1817—Reuben Smyth to Elizabeth Langston, Dec. 11, Saml. Glenn.

Dec. 10, 1817—Joseph Dunklin to Satret Perkins, Dec. 11, "form of Presbyterian church," John Barnett.

Dec. 14, 1817—Nathaniel Thompson to Susannah Stow, Dec. 14, A. H. Davis.

Dec. 3, 1817—Coleman Brown to Pricey Kemp.

Nov. 26, 1817—Josiah C. Hayle to Rhodia Gregory.

Dec. 13, 1817—Charles Chandless to Mancey Langston, Dec. 14, S. Glenn.

Dec. 23, 1817—Standrock to Elizabeth Rogers, Dec. 25, H. Darnall.

1817—Samuel Smith to Betsey Thornton.

1818:

Jan. 5, 1818—John Ford to Edney Petty, Jan. 5, Jas. Rucker, Sr.

Jan. 14, 1818—Isham Kilgore to Cassey Kilgore, H. Darnall.

Jan. 7, 1818—James Mercer to Polly Brooks, Jan. 11, John Barnett, rites of Presbyterian church.

Jan. 15, 1818—George Lovegrove to Susan Dunbar, Jan. 16, A. H. Davis.

Jan. 26, 1818—John Bams (or Barnes) to Nancey Word.

Jan. 31, 1818—Hardin Bennett to Lavinia Crop (Cross?)

Jan. 31, 1818—Lard Johnson to Betsey Robinson, Feb. 1, W. B. Duncan, J. P.

Feb. 19, 1818—John F. Son to Jane Reed, Mar. 3, Geo. Robinson, J. P.

Feb. 20, 1818—John Pugh to Delilah French, Feb. 22, A. H. Davis, J. P.

Feb. 21, 1818—Tolly C. Gholson to Phoebe Dyer, Feb. 3, A. H. Davis.

March 2, 1818—John Adair to Polley Bearden, H. Darnall.

March 4, 1818—Bryan W. Bennett to Judah Burton, March 5, Saml. Glenn, J. P.

March 10, 1818—John Elder to Martha M. Alexander, March 12, John H. Chelyn, Samuel Brown.

March 14, 1818—Thomas Margrove to Celia Simpson, March 19, A. H. Davis.

March 12, 1818—Bartholomew Jenkins to Matilda Scott.

March 9, 1818—Wm. Dorough to Polley Stone, Mch. 12, Saml. Glenn.

1818—Chas. Kelly to Lily Ann Holmes, Mch. 12, John Barnett "Presbyterian church."

April 1, 1818—Edmund C. Bearden to Polley B. Mitchuson

March 26, 1818—Simon Dunn to Polly Dobbins, John Barnett, Pres. Church.

April 6, 1818—Robt. Paterson to Mary Ann Kincade, Mch. 6, 1819, M. E. Church, Edmund Wilcox.

April 9, 1818—Wm. Perkins to Presia George, Ap. 9, A. H. Davis, J. P.

April 22, 1818—John Miller to Jinsey Ross.

April 28, 1818—Robt. Hooker to Frances Guess.

May 10, 1818—John Godfrey Butler to Kesiah Terrell.

May 17, 1818—Rowland Jennings to Rhoda Roberts, H. Darnall.

May 27, 1818—Asahel Leach to Polley Fry.

June 18, 1818—Matthew Stevenson to Delilah Freeman.

June 27, 1818—Mason Foley to Virginia Anderson, July 2, W. B. Duncan.

July 4, 1818—Jesse Midyett to Sarah Collie, July 9, W. B. Duncan, J. P.

July 29, 1818—Nathan O. Gray to Elizabeth Fowler, July 29, H. Darnall.

Aug. 13, 1818—Matthew Ledbetter to Rachel Wood, Aug., A. H. Davis, J. P.

Aug. 13, 1818—Greenberry Brown to Kesiah Chandler.

Aug. 15, 1818—Miles Tilley to Caroline Baker, Aug. 16, W. B. Duncan, J. P.

Aug. 17, 1818—Joseph Robinson to Anna Cooke.

Aug. 19, 1818—Edw. C. Jenkins to Sally Parrent.

Aug. 27, 1818—James Holderby to Rutha Robinson, Sept. 3, Micajah Rowland.

Sept. 4, 1818—Jas. Easley to Rebecca George, Sept. 6, H. Darnall.

Sept. 9, 1818—Wm. Oliver to Charlotte Winn, Sep. 10, Henry Darnal.

Sept. 10, 1818—Harbard Wallis to Anna Dallas.

Sept. 11, 1818—Garrison Anderson to Sarah Cates, Sept. 13, H. Darnall.

Sept. 15, 1818—John Williams to Sarah Rowland, Sep. 18, Sam Glen, J. P.

Sept. 19, 1818—Oliver Scott to Rutha Clayton, Sep. 24, A. H. Davis, J. P.

Sept. 21, 1818—Hobert Quarles to Elizabeth Cates, Sep. 21, H. Darnall.

Sept. 23, 1818—John Holland to Catherine Parent, Sep. 23, H. Darnall.

Sept. 29, 1818—Jas. Patterson to Polley Henry, Oct. 1, Geo. Robinson, J. P.

Oct. 3, 1818—Wm. Shelly to Peggy Orr.

Oct. 5, 1818—Robt. T. Leeper to Elizabeth Saxon, "Cumberland Pres. Ch. to which I belong." John Barnett.

Oct. 13, 1818—Joseph Brown to Catherine Steel, Oct. 13, Dec. 14, John H. Phelps.

Oct. 20, 1818—Anderson Walker to Frances Guess.

Oct. 25, 1818—John Vaughn, Jr., to Mary George, H. Darnall.

Dec. 2, 1818—John C. Smith to Dorothy Gates, John Barnett, C. P. Ch.

Dec. 7, 1818—Caleb Quinton to Clara Kelly.

Dec. 10, 1818—Wm. Laughlin to Winefred Prescott, Dec. 13—

Dec. 15, 1818—Joseph Jones to Sally Smith.

Dec. 21, 1818—John McClusky to Polly Carrick, Dec. 31, Geo. Robinson, J. P.

Nov. 28, 1818—John Collie to Polly Gregory.

Dec. 24, 1818—Jas. Grace to Kitty White, Dec. 24, A. H. Davis, J. P.

Dec. 30, 1818—Johnson Laughton to Louria Cook, Dec. 21, John Travis, J. P.

### 1819:

Jan. 6, 1919—Frances Clayton to Lucy Scott, Jan. 6, A. H. Davis, J. P.

Jan. 9, 1919—David Brown to Honor Barron, Jan. 12, A. H. Davis.

Jan. 24, 1819—Hardeman Wadlington to Medis Saxon.

Dec. 1, 1818—Jas. Stevenson, Jr., to Peggy Williams (omitted above).

Dec. 21, 1818—James Williams to Peggy Stevens.

Jan. 7, 1819—Thos. Jones to Polley Dillingham, Jan. 14, John Chapel.

Jan. 25, 1819—Tarleton Cannon to Elizabeth Darnall.

Jan. 26, 1819—Absolem Duckworth to Kezia Williams, Jan. 24, Edm. Wilcox.

Jan. 30, 1819—Thomas Long to Anne Hamby.

Feb. 8, 1819—James Hill Jones (or Janes or Juns) to Eliza Tarrett.

Feb. 27, 1819—Robert Armstrong to Elizabeth Barton.

Feb. 24, 1819—James Watson to Sally Spinks.

Feb. 2, 1819—John Prince to Nancy Mattock, A. H. Davis, J. P.

Mar. 17, 1819—Joseph Bigham to Sally Brown, Joel Smith, J. P.

Mar. 27, 1819—Preston Grace to Jane Kilgore.

March 20, 1819—Robert Dobbins to Jane Willaby.

Mar. 30, 1819—Zachariah Chandler to Hope Bennett.

Mar. 30, 1819—Edward Ashley to Elizabeth Hayle, 30th Mch. Methodist E. P. C., Given Jan. 21, 1820. Edm. Wilcox.

Ap. 3, 1819—Lawson Cook (?) to Maria Beck, 15 Ap. Meth. Ch. E. P. C., Given 21st Jan., 1820. Edm. Wilcox.

Ap. 15, 1819—Marshall Grasty to Lucinda Burk.

Mar. 23, 1819—Phillip Davis to Nicey Wofford.

Ap. 26, 1819—Amos Sigler to Elizabeth Holeman, 27 Ap. Meth. E. P. C. Given. Edm. Wilcox.

Ap. 11, 1819—Hezekiah Jones to Elizabeth Perkins, 29 Ap., 1819, A. H. Davis, J. P.

May 5, 1819—Jas. Scott to Polly Wood, 6 May, A. H. Davis.

May 3, 1819—Jonas Sikes to Obedience Fulks, May 6, 1819. W. D. Duncan, J. P.

May 26, 1819—John Boerington (Brerington?) to Kitty Sparrow.

July 8, 1819—Jeremiah Hamby to Sally Brayer.

July 20, 1819—Samuel Bradshaw to Jemima Gately.

Aug. 5, 1819—Johnson W. Dunn to Ann Cherry.

Aug. 5, 1819—John Wylie to Elizabeth Whitney, Methodist Epis., Edmund Wilcox.

Aug. 10, 1819—Saml. Duncan to Elizabeth Duncan.

Aug. 12, 1819—Jepe Henson, Jr., to Polly McKinney.

Aug. 24, 1819—Bowen Tison to Fanny Ray.

Aug. 25, 1819—John Brown to Ann Yates, Aug. 26, A. H. Davis.

Aug. 25, 1819—John Story to Elizabeth Lenox.

Sep. 26, 1819—Edm. M. Stevens to Sophia A. G. S. M. L. Stromat 9 Sept., Edm. Wilcox.

Sep. 9, 1819—John Grubbs to Jane Duncan.

Oct. 1, 1819—Martin Newman to Letty Bearden.

Oct. 5, 1819—Samuel Brown to Ellen Steel, Oct. 5-Oct. 7, Samuel Brown.

Oct. 6, 1819—Wm. Brown, Jr., to Jennett Smith, (John H. Phelps) Oct. 7, Samuel Brown.

Oct. 6, 1819—Robert Whitnel to Elizabeth Moore, Oct. 7, Edm. Wilcox, ret. Jan. 8, 1820.

Oct. 8, 1819—Spencer M. Calvert to Mary Morse.

Oct. 14, 1819—Moses Tindel to Pamela Dudley.

Oct. 20, 1819—Thos. H. Garner to Cynthia B. Wadlington.

Oct. 20, 1819—Enoch Howard to Jane Cain.

Oct. 18, 1819—William Larkin to Penelope Holawell, Thos. Humphries.

Oct. 21, 1819—Richard Johnson to Ann Wethers.

Oct. 27, 1819—George Bell to Cynthia Piler (Pily?)

Oct. 28, 1819—Joseph Rucker to Eliza Draper.

Oct. 3, 1819—Sampson Harper to Malinda Berry, 4th Oct. Joel Smith, J. P.

Nov. 9, 1819—James Wade to Polly Bains, 11 Nov. Edm. Wilcox, 8th Jan., 1820.

Nov. 23, 1819—Theophilus Killion to Malinda Owens.

Nov. 28, 1819—Naum Dunning to Polley Hughes.

Dec. 3, 1819—Richard Swan to Fanny Midgett.

Dec. 13, 1819—Robert Pindergrass to Rhoda Hammond.

Dec. 21, 1819—John Whitnel to Mary R. Ladd, 21 Dec. Edm. Wilcox, 21st Jan. 1820.

Dec. 21, 1819—Wm. Bumpass to Sally Stromart, Dec. 24, Jas. Morse, J. P.

Dec. 22, 1819—Dabney Pentecost to Rebecca Reynolds.

Dec. 27 1819—John Cannon to Rachel Wooten.

Dec. 27, 1819—Joshua Hammond to Anna Killion.

1820:

Jan. 2, 1820—John Staten to Flora Philley.

Jan. 3, 1820—Aaron Woodruff to Sally Davenport.

Jan. 6, 1820—Edward Touray to Peggy McDowell.

Jan. 7, 1820—Joseph Brown to Judith Johnson.

Jan. 19, 1820—Elias Rankin to Matilda Hernny (or Klernny?).

Feb. 2, 1820—Beverley Lester to Nancey Henson.

Feb. 2, 1820—Austin Williams to Polley Slater.

Feb. 12, 1820—John S. Ball to Caroline Hill.

Feb. 15, 1820—John Matlock to Sabrina Robinson, Feb. 17, 1820, Jas. Payne.

Feb. 15, 1820—David Purtle to Delilah Kelly, Cumb. Pres. Ch., 16 Feb., 1820, John Barnett.

Feb. 22, 1820—Wm. Price to Rachel Cochran, 22 Feb. Edm. Wilcox (he returned a bunch Jan. 8, 1820 and Jan. 21, 1820 and this one Jan. 2, 1821).

Feb. 22, 1820—Robert Huggins to Jane Cook, 22 Feb., 1820, 27 Jan., 1821, Edm. Wilcox.

Feb. 28, 1820—John Fulks to Phoebe Colley.

Feb. 29, 1820—Jacob Crider, Jr., to Harpy Bivens.

Mch. 2, 1820—Thos. Roach to Fanney Hobert, 7th Mch. Jas. Rucker, Sr.

Mar. 5, 1820—Alterson Russell to Sally Dudley.

Apr. 3, 1820—John Russell to Nancey Campbell.

Apr. 4, 1820—John Burnett to Martha Barnes.

Apr. 24, 1820—Robert Hooper to Peggy Garner.

May 24, 1820—William Trayler to Ann Duckworth.

June 12, 1820—Stephen Barnes to Penelope Cowan, Meth. Espec. Edmond Wilcox.

June 20, 1820—William Owens to Martha Bell.

July 3, 1820—Ambrose Dudley to Minerva Miller, Meth. Epis. Edmond Wilcox.

June 26, 1820—James Duvall to Mary Ann Owens.

July 5, 1820—Thomas Flint to Nancey Statton.

July 7, 1820—Asa Clother to Minerva McWerthy.

July 12, 1820—Caleb Stone to Anna Duncan, 12th Feb. Jas. Rucker, Sr.

July 21, 1820—Wm. Kilgore to Nerissa Cook.

July 22, 1820—Hugh Bratton to Zilpha Midgett, 27th July, Edm. Wilcox, 18 Jan., 1821.

July 24, 1820—John Hall to Polley Gray, 27 July, Jas. Payne.

July 24, 1820—Jacob Z. Jennings to Rhoda Prewitt (Preiatt) July 28, Joel Smith, J. P.

July 25, 1820—Jas. Scullion to Pally Stone, 27 July, Jas. Rucker, J. P.

Aug. 8, 1820—John D. McMahen to Sally Watson.

Aug. 1, 1820—John Cobb to Sally S. Cresap, Ap. 26, 1821, John Bradley.

Aug. 9, 1820—George Wales to Jane Asher, Aug. 10, Edm. Wilcox.

Aug. 12, 1820—Bennett Sory or Sorg to Malinda Cook, 13th Aug., 1820; ret. 17 Jan., 1821,

Aug. 22, 1820—Isham C. Baynes to Rhoda Johnson.

Aug. 24, 1820—John T. Culvert to Fanny Morse.

Aug. 26, 1820—Lewis Vaughan to Hetty Baker.

Aug. 28, 1820—John Salyers to Lucinda Wofford.

Aug. 30, 1820—Alexander Trayler to Elmina Kenady.

Aug. 30, 1820—Alfred Reno to Elizabeth Wilcox, John S. Payne.

Sept. 5, 1820—Henry H. Hanks to Catherine Prichett.
Sept. 14, 1820—William D. Christopher to Polly Williams.
(Omitted above.)
June 3, 1819—John Denson (or Duncan?) to Matilda Thelford.
Sept. 25, 1820—Wm. Roberts to Betsey East.
Sept. 28, 1820—Allen Travsi to Peggy Campbell.
Sept. 29, 1820—Peter Kennady to Phoebe Cay.
Oct. 3, 1820—Burt G. Moore to Polly French, Oct. 3, Mercer Wadlington.
Oct. 7, 1820—Wm. Duncan to Susan Bennett.
Oct. 11, 1820—Wm. Barns, Jr., to Tabitha P. Burton, Oct. 12, M. Wadlington.
Oct. 20, 1820—Lewis M. Harper to Hander Bowland, 21 Sept., Joel Smith, J. P.
Oct. 12, 1820—Geo. Nall to Margaret Holeman, 12 Edm. Wilcox, ret. Jan. 18, 1821.
Oct. 17, 1820—Archibald Sperry to Louisa Walston, Oct. 19, James Rucker, Sr.
Oct. 25, 1820—Robt. Draper to Frances A. Tandy, Will Tandy
Noc. 13, 1820—Wm. Laughlin to Isabella Holland.
Nov. 24, 1820—Thomas Duncan to Polly Owens.
Dec. 0, 1820  Alexander Erwin to Patsy Orr.
Dec. 11, 1820—Henry J. Martin to Sarah Bush.
Dec. 15, 1820—John Kilgore to Phebe Task (Tart).
Dec. 23, 1820—Drury C. Champion to Martha Rucker, Jeremiah Rucker, J. P.
Dec. 24, 1820—William Ray to Phebe McElyia (?)
Nov. 27, 1820—Reuben Hanell to Rachel Wolf, Fielding Woolf.

1821:

Jan. 6, 1821—Benjamin Johnston to Sally Hall.
Jan. 3, 1821—Alexander McManes to Patsey Copeland, 8 Jan., H. Darnall.
Jan. 9, 1821—Milton C. Ingram to Cynthia Harris, 14 Jan., Joel Smith.
Jan. 10, 1821—Elijah Stevens, Jr., to Elinor Cook, 11 Jan. Abner W. Smith.
Jan. 11, 1821  Matthew Lyon, Jr., to Elizabeth M. Martin, 15 Jan. Edm. Wilcox.
Jan. 20, 1821—Spencer Wood to Rhoda Smith, 21, Jan., M. Wadlington, J. P.
Jan. 22, 1821—Israel Cannon to Fanny Clinton, 1st Feb., Abner Smith.
Jan. 27, 1821—Jas. Durley to Sally Harper, 1st Feb. ret. Dec. 26th, 1821, Edm. Wilcox.
Jan. 29, 1821—John B. Groom to Nancy Draper.
Feb. 3, 1821—John Kenady to Elizabeth Jones, 6th Feb., H. Darnall.
Feb. 5, 1821—Fleming Gatewood to Lucy M. Dillingham, 6th Feb. (Mercer) M. Wadlington, J. P.
Feb. 5, 1821—Charles Jones to Ann Rowland.
Feb. 6, 1821—John Robinson to Elizabeth Powell.
Feb. 7, 1821—Thomas Dunagin (?) to Polly Ann Mitchell.
Feb. 8, 1821—Michael M. Cravins (Cravens) Elizabeth Towery, Meth. Epis. Edm. Wilcox.

Feb. 11, 1821—Irvin Duning to Susan Purdy.

Feb. 12, 1821—Joseph Bergher to Anna Burnett (?)

Feb. 13, 1821—Richard Carnes (?) Cames (?) to Sally Powell.

Feb. 26, 1821—James Cunningham to Polly Smith.

Feb...., 1921—James Tull (Full) to Ruth Atkinson.

Feb. 26, 1821—Walter Oliver to Fanny Riddle.

Feb. 27, 1821—Walter Scott to Priscilla Pirtle.

Feb. 28, 1821—Anderson Jesse to Rhoda Ellis, 1st Mch., 26 Dec., Edm. Wilcox.

Mch. 10, 1821—Nehemiah Williams to Sally Bonde, 15 Mch., H. Darnall.

Mch. 10, 1821—Daniel I. Herkless to Ann C. Gholson.

Mch. 10, 1821—Jeptha Griffith to Nancy Hewett or Hewell, 15 Mch., H. Darnall.

Mch. 13, 1821—James Hunter to Hannah Rogers, Mch. 18, Fielding Woolf.

Mch. 13, 1821—Wm. Coy, Jr., to Polly Hutchison, Mch. 15, Fielding Woolf.

Mch. 14, 1821—Hiram Bowland to Sally Armstrong.

Mch. 16, 1821—Thomas Brown to Patsy Nichols.

Mch. 24, 1821—William Nichols to Nancy Green.

Mch. 24, 1821—John Sample (Tample) to Aseneth Dyer.

Mch. 26, 1821—(?) Therill Tisdale to Lucy Bennett.

Mch. 29, 1821—Elisha Johnston to Lutilda Baker.

Mch. 31, 1821—Archabald Duvall to Elnor White.

Apr. 10, 1821—Hollaway Collie to Jenny Hollaway.

Apr. 11, 1821—Adam Perkins to Matilda Goldsby.

Apr. 11, 1821—John Goldsby to Nancey McElroy.

Apr. 13, 1821—Cornelius Dilly to Ann Dobbins.

Apr. 16, 1821—John B. Haris to Elizabeth Oliver.

Apr. 17, 1821—Isaac Witherspoon to Louvena Clinton.

Apr. 19, 1821—Wyman Groves to Elizabeth G. McGough.

Apr. 23, 1821—Wm. Malony to Lucinda Draper.

May 5, 1821—Isaac A. Lockhart to Vina Cook.

May 16, 1821—John B. Gholson to Judith W. Ford, April 17, 1821, ret. 26 Dec., 1821, Edm. Wilcox.

May 24, 1821—Jas. McCaslin to Polly Herrold, 24 May, 26 Dec., Edm. Wilcox.

May 28, 1821—Wm. F. Grubbs to Jane Collie, 31 May, A. H. Davis, J. P.

June 1, 1821—Arch L. Lackman to Matilda Long.

June 2, 1821—Johnathan C. Lungston to Susana Layton.

June 12, 1821—Thos. W. Cochran to Virginia B. Wade.

June 13, 1821—Theophilus Cooksy to Narcissa L. Harris.

June 18, 1821—Charles Jones to Tamsey Ingram.

June 23, 1821—Land Ladyman to Elizabeth Arbridge.
William McDowell to Rachel Smith.

July 11, 1821—Rich (Riche) Covington to Polly Pen.

July 24, 1821—William Harper to Naoma Cannon.

July 27, 1821—Jarvis Starkey (Harky) to Ruthy Davis.

Aug. 2, 1821—James Garrett to Polly Cheek, 2nd Aug. Jeremiah Rucker, J. P.

Aug. 7, 1821—Wiley Pinnell to Peggy Easley.

Aug. 19, 1821—John Cleaveland to Susannah Walston.

Aug. 21, 1821—John Moore to Susannah Nowlin, dau. Rich. Nowlin Wm.
Buckley, M. G. ret. Aug. 1, 1822.

Aug. 27, 1821—Wm. B. Harper to Rosa Whitnel, 28 Aug. ret. Dec. 26, Edm.
Wilcox.

Aug. 28, 1821—John McAtee to Phoebe Coy (or Cay).

Aug. 29, 1821—James Carter to Maria Clayton, Aug. 30, Edm. Wilcox.

Aug. 30, 1821—Howard Cassidy to Pally Haworth, 30 Aug., Edm. Wilcox.

Sept. 3, 1821—Isaiah Goldsby to Lucy W. Nolin, dau. Rich. Nolin, 6th
Sep. Wm. Buckley, M. G.

Sept. 19, 1821—William Robison to Peggy Foley.

Oct. 2, 1821—James Harper to Lavinia Stevenson, Samuel Brown.

Oct. 20, 1821—Stephen Ford to Bilny Avirell (Averill ?).

Oct. 26, 1821—Geo. H. Young to Nancy Wofford.

Oct. 22, 1821—Darling Reynolds to Nancy Henson.

Oct. 30, 1821—William Ingram to Nancey Lowry.

Oct. 30, 1821—James Dillingham to Jane Galoway.

Oct. 31, 1821—John Weeks to Betsey Wafer.

Nov. 6, 1821—William Wood (?) to Nancy Dunbar.

Nov. 6, 1821—Daniel Chambers to Nancy Gray.

Nov. 10, 1821—John Roe to Elizabeth Arrington, 11 Nov., 26 Dec.

Nov. 11, 1821—John Godand or (Godard) to Malinda Moseley, 12 Nov.,
ret. 3rd July, 1822, Jas. Rucker, Sr.

Nov. 12, 1821—George Ball to Elcy H. Guinton, 14th Nov., A. H. Davis.

Nov. 17, 1821—Stephen Hogg to Elizabeth Allin, C. P. Ch., Nov. 18, John
Barnett.

Nov. 19, 1821—Thos. H. Flournoy to Jordena Harris, C. P. Ch., Nov. 20,
John Barnett.

Dec. 1, 1821—Wm. Dixon to Sarah Hicks, 4 Dec. Saml. Glenn, J. P.

Dec. 1, 1821—Henry L. Cartwright to Catherine Cash, 2 Dec., ret. 26 Dec.,
Edm. Wilcox.

Nov. 28, 1821—Peter Sparrow to Cecila Chandler.

Dec. 4, 1821—John Cotton to Patsy Faughn (or Vaughn).

Dec. 11, 1921—James McClure to Nancy Green.

Dec. 12, 1821—William Birdsong, Jr., to Susan Stone.

Dec. 12, 1821—Joseph Doubty to Rebecca Chandler.

Dec. 17, 1821—Isaac Parker to Joicey Dudley.

Dec. 18, 1821—Isaac Rumey to Ann Cotton.

Dec. 24, 1821—Samuel Baker to Patsy Groom, Fielding Wolf.

Dec. 28, 1821—Andrew Trayler to Jane Roberts.

Dec. 28, 1821—Thomas B. Sheffield to Charlotta Parrant.

Dec. 25, 1821—Cadar Mitchell to Patsy Nichols, 1st day Jan., 1822, Micajah Rowland.

Dec. 29, 1821—Allen Stephens to Sally Reade, 2 Jan. 1822, ret. 30 Dec.
1822, Edm. Wilcox.

Jan. 29, 1821—James Reade to Nancy Adamson, Jan. 1822 ret. 30 Dec.
1822, Edm. Wilcox.

Dec. 29, 1821—John Warren to Susan Chandler.

1822:

Jan. 5, 1822—Danl. Bineson to Nancy Loughborough.

Jan. 7, 1822—Wm. Story to Peggy Tisdale, Jan. 7, Saml. Glenn.

Jan. 21, 1822—Henry Thompson to Elizabeth Roach, Jan. 30, A. H. **Davis.**

Jan. 22, 1822—Geo. J. B. Caldwell to Martha W. Simpson, Jan. 22, 1822, Edm. Wilcox.

Jan. 24, 1822—John Parker to Catherine Howard, Jan. 24, Joel Smith, J. P.

Jan. 28, 1822—Hiram C. Smith to Gately Davis, 31 Jan. H. Darnall.

Jan. 31, 1822—Live Sigler to Patsey Rind (?).

Feb. 1, 1822—Cirylant (?) Simons (?) to Cynthia Rogers.

Feb. 4, 1822—John Gray to Nancy Tandy.

Feb. 8, 1822—James G. Glenn to Nancy McElroy.

Feb. 11, 1822—James Hollaway to Nancy Collie.

Feb. 18, 1822—Robert Harper to Elsy Fowler.

Feb. 20, 1822—James B. Black to Rebecca Brazil.

Feb. 26, 1822—Daniel Price to Martha Cochran.

Feb. 28, 1822—Walen (or Malen) Wadlington to Elizabeth Perry, **Mercer** Wadlington, J. P.

Mch. 2, 1822—Otis Hinkley to Elizabeth Henderson, 5 Feb., 1822, **M.** Wadlington.

Mch. 11, 1822—Solomon Williams to Mariah Williams, 14th Mch., Joel Smith, J. P.

Mch. 14, 1822—Charles Johnson to Betsey Meals (Neals), 14th Mch. Micajah B. Rowland.

Mch. 26, 1822—Saml. Collie to Lydia Holloway.

Ap. 1, 1822—Geo. W. Grubbs to Lizza Stone, 4 Ap. Fielding Wolf.

Ap. 3, 1822—Nutter Scott to Jersey Freeman, Ap. 4, John Travis.

Ap. 6, 1822—Joel Motley to Sarah Ann Oliver.

Ap. 8, 1822—Daniel Carbone to Nancy Manns.

Ap. 15, 1822—Leesil Stone to Miriam Grubbs, 13 Ap., 1822. Fielding Wolf, M. G.

Ap. 17, 1822—David Jones to Polly Pound.

May 8, 1822—Drury Sanders to Eliza Wilson.

May 13, 1822—John B. Crow to Sally Crow.

May 23, 1822—Thomas W. Chambers to Pamelia Saterfield, Edmond Wilcox.

June 6, 1822—James B. Perry to Mary Tandy, Balsam Ezill, Esq.

June 19, 1822—Peter Fate to Mary Williamson, Cumberland Pres. Ch., Jno. Barnett.

June 29, 1822—John F. Bennett to Permalia Ball.

July 3, 1822—Walter Towery to Sarah Reed.

July 4, 1822—Aaron Holmes to Sally Terrill.

July 15, 1822—Elihu P. Calvert to Malinder Kuykendall, 16 July, John Barnett, C. P.

July 15, 1822—Robt. Rodgers to Dicey Baker, 18 July, Micajah, B. Rowland.

July 19, 1822—John Anderson to Catherine Parker.

July 29, 1822—John Murphy to Mary B. Robertson.
Aug. 9, 1822—Wm. Sanders to Polly Salyers, Aug. 15, Joel Smith, J. P.
Aug. 13, 1822—Perryman Cannon to Polly Freeman.
Aug. 13, 1822—Robt. Wood to Fanny Bearden, Aug. 13, M. Wadlington.
Aug. 19, 1822—Daniel Dennis to Polly Pound, 28 Aug. M. Lyon, Jr., J. P.
Aug. 1, 1822—Thomas Vaughn to Rachel Davis.
Aug. 1, 1822—George Marshall to Clary Fowler, Edmond Wilcox.
Aug. 23, 1822—Christo Creekmier to Rutha Ellip.
Aug. 26, 1822—James D. (or P) Dobins to Martha Bean.
Aug. 27, 1822—Thomas Price to Delany (?) Nichols.
Aug. 27, 1822—Samuel Tayler to Elizabeth Henderson.
Sept. 17, 1822—Joseph McNeely to Nancey Roberts.
Sep. 28, 1822—Dan'l Vaughn to Nancey (?) Cooper.
Oct. 11, 1822—Jacob E. Faller to Rebecca Patterson.
Oct. 14, 1822—Danl. Bond to Rachel Johnson, 14 Oct. Jeremiah Rucker,
    J. P.
Oct. 14, 1822—Saul L. Jones to Terecy Campbell, 14 Oct. Abner W. Smith.
Oct. 24, 1822—Jacob Childress to Priscilla Armstrong, 24 Oct. M. Wad-
    lington.
Oct. 26, 1822—John Haggard to Ann Snelling, 1st Nov. Micajah B. Row-
    land.
Oct. 31, 1822—Reuben Rowland to Maria Simpson, 31 Oct. Edm. Wilcox,
    30 Dec.
Nov. 11, 1822—Joseph Read to Jemima Easley, 14 Nov. Edm. Wilcox.
Nov. 14, 1822—Joshua Stallions to Delilah Carter, 17 Nov., Edm. Wilcox.
Nov. 4, 1822—George Guess to Malinda Morse, 14 Nov. M. Wadlington.
Nov. 12, 1822—Beny I. Osbourn to Sarah Cunningham.
Nov. 16, 1822—Joel Carnes to Nancy Peigler (?), Edmund Wilcox.
Nov. 23, 1822—Albertes Prince to Mary Wadlington.
Nov. 23, 1822—William Marshall to Hannah Gragg.
Dec. 2, 1822—Caleb C. Cobb to Mary W. Machen.
Dec. 5, 1822—John W. Marshall to Martha Gracey.
Dec. 7, 1822—Henry Roberts to Nancy McNeeley.
Dec. 16, 1822—Darlington Reynolds to Betsy Henley.
Dec. 18, 1822—Wm. Whitesides to Nancy Ford.
Dec. 18, 1822—John W. Barnett to Peggy Smith.
Dec. 28, 1822—Henry Banister to Elizabeth Tharp, Dec. 29, Joel Smith,
    J. P.

    1823:

Jan. 16, 1823—Wm. Baynes to Gatsy Allen, 16 Jan. M. Wadlington.
Jan. 18, 1823—Geo. Hall to Prudence Thompson.
Jan. 21, 1823—Charles Hues to Sarah Salyers.
Feb. 5, 1823—Wm. Sanders to Marguriet (?) Drish or Irish, John Bar-
    nett, (M. G.)
Feb. 11, 1823—Seth Parker to Rhody Wood, 13 Feb., M. Wadlington, J. P.
Feb. 11, 1823—Pennington Morse to Frances Guess, 11 Feb. Jas. Morse.
Feb. 17, 1823—James Armstrong to Susannah Hall, 18th Feb. ret. Nov. 18,
    Joel Smith, J. P.

Feb. 17, 1823—John D. McConnell to Sally Miller, 20th Feb. ret. Dec. 7, 1823 and Oct. 5, 1824.
Feb. 17, 1823—John Laughlin to Mary Smith, Edmund Wilcox.
Feb. 25, 1823—Arch N. Darly to Leodisha Belton.
Feb. 25, 1823—Joel Leach to Eliz. G. Lear.
Feb. 25, 1823—Robert Smith to Sarah Armstrong.
Apr. 3, 1823—William Gragg to Dorcus Clayton, Samuel Brown, V. D. M.
Apr. 13, 1823—Gabriel Thelford to Betsy Knight, Minister, Fielding Wolf.
Apr. 15, 1823—Jas. Olliver to Susannah Armstrong.
Apr. 21, 1823—Jas. Wadlington to Milly Warner.
Apr. 23, 1823—Henry B. Cowles to Rebecca Hall, 24 Ap., Jas Rucker, Sr.
Apr. 24, 1823—Joseph Grindle to Peggy Smith.
Apr. 26, 1823—John Hankins to Nancy Sigler, 26 Ap., 3rd Jan., 1824, Edmund Wilcox.
May 5, 1823—Mordecai Fowler to Jane Ramey, May 24, Jas. Payne.
May 14, 1823—Robert A. Lapsley to Catharine Milker.
May 14, 1823—Zephaniah Gilkey to Jane F. Jenkins.
May 20, 1823—Martin McKenney to Sarah Fowler.
June 7, 1823—Aaron Perdey to Elizabeth Nalls (?)
June 9, 1823—James B. Waddile to Louisa A. Jackson.
July 30, 1823—William Cash to Mariah Gates.
July 30, 1823—Joel Cash to Nancy Reed, 31 July, 2 Dec., 5 Jan., 1824, Edm. Wilcox.
Aug. 8, 1823—John Durning to Jane Maxwell, Aug. Pres. Ch., Robt. A. Lapsley.
Aug. 13, 1823—Lesil Stone to Nancy Killion.
Sep. 15, 1823—Hampton Towney (?) to Nancy Groves.
Sep. 18, 1823—Chas. Hughes to Dorcas Onielle.
Sept. 29, 1823—Jas. C. Luck to Malinda Glenn.
Oct. 1, 1823—Joseph Grovin to Nansey Hutchinson.
Oct. 7, 1823—Alfred Clayton to Edaline M. Lewis, Jan. 5, Edmund Wilcox.
Oct. 15, 1823—John East to Nancey Hefton.
Oct. 30, 1823—Greenbury George to Lucinthey Parks.
Nov. 5, 1823—Jeremiah Russell to Jemima Gilkey.
Nov. 5, 1823—George Laughlin to Frances Harris, Edmund Wilcox.
Nov. 18, 1823—Thos. Reed to Ann Adamson, 20 Nov., 24 Dec., 1824, Edmund Wilcox.
Nov. 16, 1823—Nathan Gates, Jr., to Caroline Davidson, Nov., Pres. Ch., Robt. A. Lapsley.
Nov. 27, 1823—Wright Nichols to Sally Louisa Rhodes, 27 Nov., 26 Dec., 1823, Jan. 5, 1824, E. Wilcox.
Dec. 16, 1823—Hiram Cook to Sarah Sigler, 15 Dec., Abner W. Smith.
Dec. 31, 1823—Westley Adams to Margaret H. Dillingham, 1st Jan., 1824, ret. Feb. 6, 1824, M. Wadlington, J. P.

1824:

Jan. 7, 1824—Wm. P. George to Hester Lamb.
Jan. 13, 1824—Wm. McGowin to Caroline Simpson, Pres. Robt. A. Lapsley.

Jan. 20, 1824—Grover L. Howard to Judith Thorp.

Jan. 21, 1824—James Vaughn to Sarah Cotton.

Jan. 21, 1824—Delany W. Hall to Rachel Thompson.

Feb. 4, 1824—William Lowrey to Elizabeth Ordway.

Feb. 13, 1824—Henry D. Lane to Nancey Dobbins.

Feb. 14, 1824—Bartholomew Jenkins to Polly Leman, 11 July, Jas. Mooser (?)

Feb. 19, 1824—Sam'l Lester to Sindrinley Wolf, 19 Feb. Fielding Wolf, M. G.

Feb. 19, 1824—Cullin Cook to Matilda Howard, 22 Feb., Micajah B. Rowland.

Feb. 23, 1824—Jared Bellamy to Susannah Lear, 27 Feb., Jas. Rucker, Sr.

Feb. 23, 1824—Isaac Rucker to Edna King, Harris, 25 Feb., Jas. Rucker, Sr.

Mar. 2, 1824—Sampson Deas (Dear) to Selina Cartwright.

Mar. 6, 1824—Robert Adams to Ann Owens.

Mar. 6, 1824—Isaac Barnett to Pamela Smith.

Mar. 10, 1824—Wm. Hooper to Mary Campbell.

Mar. 25, 1824—Charles Garner to Bulah Wadlington.

Mar. 30, 1824—Edward Franklin to Elizabeth Armstrong.

Ap. 7, 1824—Abraham Duning to Nancy Moore, 10 Ap. M B. Rowland.

Ap. 12, 1824—Henry A. Harman to Parmelia Bennett.

Ap. 15, 1824—Jas. Clark to Ann F. Byrne.

Ap. 23, 1824—Daniel Davis to Mary Doles, 23 Ap. F. Wolf, M. G.

Ap. 22, 1824—Leonard Martin to Darky Smith, 22 Ap. F. Wolf.

Ap. 28, 1824—James B. Black to Mary G. McCaslin.

May 11, 1824—Aquilla Martin to Kitty Joiner.

June 2, 1824—David Smith to Mariah Hamby.

June 12, 1824—Abner Hollowell to Polly Dunning.

July 19, 1824—Michael W. Freeman to Tabbithy Cash.

July 20, 1824—Spencer Calvert to Ann Cox, 22 July, Jas. Rucker, Sr.

Aug. 3, 1824—Orvan Duncan to Nancy Lear, 5 Aug., Jas. Rucker, Sr.

Aug. 26, 1824—Aaron Smith to Mary Laughlin, 26 Aug. ret. Jan. 4, 1825, Edm. Wilcox.

Aug. 30, 1824—Saml. Cobb to Nancy H. Cobb, 2 Sept. 1824, Jas. Rucker, Sr.

Sept. 7, 1824—Henry Freeman to Nancy W. Thompson, Sept. 13, Abner W. Smith.

Sept. 29, 1824—Joseph Barton to Katharine Lofton, Fielding Wolf.

Oct. 11, 1824—James Grace to Nancy Gehin (Gehn), Oct. 21.

Oct. 12, 1824—Alfred Boyd to Lucy A. Harrison, Edm. Wilcox.

Oct. 21, 1824—William McCarty to Sally Mitchison.

Nov. 1, 1824—Philipe Coleman to Elizabeth Gray.

Nov. 13, 1824—Chis. (?) Galloway to Lettice Smith.

Nov. 15, 1824—John Wilson to Jane Hunter.

1824—Buford Lewis to Polly (Mary) McCarty. M. E. Ch., 25 Nov., B. Ogdon.

Dec. 4, 1824—David Gossett to Deborah Wynn, C. P., Dec. 9, David Lowery.

Dec. 6, 1824—Abram H. Brelsford to Selestine L. Black, 9 Dec., Edm. Wilcox.

Dec. 7, 1824—John Higgs to Elizabeth Allen, 7 Dec., F. Wolf.

Dec. 13, 1824—Felix Wadlington to Mariah Wadlington.

Dec. 28, 1824—Wm. Craig to Jennett Steele, Dec. 30, Saml. Brown.

1825:

Jan. 5, 1825—Alexander Lowry to Nicy Morse, Edm. Wilcox.

Jan. 12, 1825—Frances Gardner to Margaret Hollins (?) C. P., J. W. B. Arnett.

Jan. 15, 1825—Thompson Hilyard to Polly Anderson, Edm. Wilcox.

Jan. 15, 1825—Francis Ladd to Sarah F. Bigham, James Rucker, Sen.

Jan. 31, 1825—Thos. McNabb to Mary Ross, Pres. Ch., David Lowry.

Feb. 3, 1825—Shelton Jones to Dolly I. Harris, Presby. Ch., David Lowry.

Feb. 7, 1825—Stephen Grove to Ann Wyatt, Cumb. Pres. Ch., John Barnett.

Feb. 10, 1825—Cynes Colley to Betsy Bernard.

Feb. 12, 1825—John I. Satterfield to Polly Satterfield.

No date—Thos. B. Wilson to Polly Sue Forbes.

Feb. 12, 1825—Jeptha Griffith to Esenath Griffith.

July 29, 1824—John D. Kelly to Mary Jane Wacher (?), Robt. A. Lapsley.

Mch. 15, 1825—Andrew R. Boland to Medis Jones.

Mch. 21, 1825—Henry Fulks to Polly Newby.

Ap. 6, 1825—Daniel Freer to Elizabeth Marbury, Edm. Wilcox.

Ap. 6, 1825—Jas. Nichols to Betty Holloway.

Ap. 7, 1825—Wm. McElroy to Elizabeth Hopper, Fielding Wolf.

Ap. 8, 1825—John McCain to Ailcy McDowell.

Ap. 26, 1825—Andrew Stevenson to Margaret Carrick, Robt. A. Lapsley, Pres. Ch.

May 7, 1825—Andrew Ross to Sarah H. Walker.

May 16, 1825—Cynes Broadwell to Virginia Goodall.

May 17, 1825—John Worman to Sarah Salyers.

May 28, 1825—Benj. A. Evans to Ann Adams.

June 17, 1825—Thos. Jackson to Wineford Greekmur, Abner W. Smith.

June 20, 1825—Edward Lawton to Jane Young, Cumb. Pres. Ch., John Barnett.

June 28, 1825—Michael H. Freeman to Polly Crow, C. P. David Lowry.

July 13, 1825—John M. Franklin to Betsy Eggbert, Meth., Edm. Wilcox.

July 15, 1825—Jas. Clark to Normy Harper, Edm. Wilcox.

July 19, 1825—Isaac Bowman to Ann Garrett.

July 25, 1825—John Hubbard to Sarah Trayler, John Travis.

July 27, 1825—Jesse F. Lamb to Isabella Adamson, Edm. Wilcox.

July 28, 1825—Jas. Bowland to Susan Osborn.

Aug. 1, 1825—Lind Hubbard to Patsy Couser.

Aug. 3, 1825—Francis Prince to Mary Lewis, Edm. Wilcox.

Aug. 22, 1825—French Winn (Mun or Mirn) to Elizabeth Oliver.

Sept. 8, 1825—Jo. W. Fowler to Giney Gray, Edmund Wilcox.

Sept. 8, 1825—Allen Pearce to Polly W. Morse, M. Wadlington, J. P.

Sept. 16, 1825—James W. Sivels to Hannah Marsh, Methodist Eps., Edm. Wilcox.

Sept. 17, 1825—James Freer to Perminday Sulivant.

Sept. 19, 1825—John Lowry to Gracy Ordway, Edm. Wilcox.

Sept. 20, 1825—Hosea Morgan to Julietta Reynolds, Chittenden Lyen, J. P.

Sept. 20, 1825—Saml. Musgrove to Elizabeth Kenny, Edm. Wilcox.

Sept. 21, 1825—Wm. Moore to Jane McCastlin, Edm. Wilcox.

Sept. 22, 1825—Jas. Ross to Sophia Shurrad, Holloway Collie, J. P.

Sept. 29, 1825—Wm. R. Thompson to Eliza Rickett.

Sept. 10, 1825—Tho. Sheridan to Hannah Moore.

Oct. 1, 1825—Elihu C. Duncan to Susannah Riley, Jas. Rucker.

Oct. 10, 1825—Eli Ingram to Nancy Thetford, Holloway Collie, J. P.

Oct. 17, 1825—Jonathan McElroy to Polly Cooper.

Oct. 26, 1825—Christopher H. Jones to Sarah F. Freer.

Oct. 29, 1825—Larkin Collie to Jenny Cradock, Holloway Collie, J. P.

Oct. 29, 1825—West Fowler to Margaret Hall.

Nov. 1, 1825—Lewis Pinnell to Margaret Sigler, Meth. Eps. Edmund Wilcox.

Nov. 8, 1825—Thos. Fowler to Jane Hall.

Nov. 13, 1825—Benj. Hart to Jane Harper, Abner W. Smith, J. P.

Nov. 14, 1825—Eli Drennon to Peggy McDowell, Abner Wilson Smith, J. P.

Nov. 14, 1025—Peter Leroy to Jane L. Smart, John Barnett, C. P.

Nov. 30, 1825—John Arnold to Tabitha Killen.

Dec. 8, 1825—Enoch Bolling to Martha Hays, W. A. Rucker, J. P.

Dec. 23, 1825—Winfrey Cotton to Sarah Davis.

Dec. 24, 1825—Ephrain Hill to N. Brown.

Dec. 24, 1825—Alexr. Craig, Jr., to Letitia Brown.

1826:

Jan. 11, 1826—Malachi Landingham to Joanna Anderson.

Jan. 16, 1826—David B. Glen to Matilda Gray.

Jan. 25, 1826—Levi Jones to Ailsey Kilgore.

Jan. 25, 1826—Francis W. Urey to Pernecia Bond, Robt. A. Lapsley.

Feb. 1, 1826—Athel Woolf to Elizabeth Kennedy, Minister of Gospel Fielding Woolf.

Feb. 7, 1826—Jacob Brown to Anna Layton.

Feb. 20, 1826—William Woods to Isabel Kilgore.

Mch. 16, 1826—Owen Hays to Martha Hunter, Jas. Rucker, Sr.

Mch. 27, 1826—Moses Stubbs to Elizabeth Faris, Saml. Glenn, J. C. C.

Mch. 25, 1826—John Armstrong to Nancy Orr, C. P. John Barnett.

Ap. 18, 1826—Jas. Armstrong to Eleanor Maxwell, John Barnett.

Ap. 12, 1826—Thos. Bennett to Mary Sullivant, Saml. Glenn, J. C. C.

Ap. 13, 1826—Wm. Owens to Mary Orr.

Ap. 20, 1826—Wm. P. Wadlington to Martha B. Ford.

May 23, 1826—William Parker to Sally Marsh, Fielding Woolf, Minister.

June 7, 1826—John McIntosh to Lavinia Watkins, C. Lyon, J. P.

June 26, 1826—William Atkinson to Malinda Hildreth, C. Lyon.

July 19, 1826—Joshua Hightower to Martha Watkins, C. Lyon.

July 20, 1826—Bayliss Phelps to Mahana Jones, Edm. Wilcox.

July 25, 1826—Isaac Wilson to Sally Wadlington.

July 26, 1826—Mason G. Pemberton to America Rucker.
July 31, 1826—Peter Baker to Rhoda Woolf, Fielding Woolf, M. G.
Aug. 2, 1826—John Lester to Elizabeth Kesteyon, F. Woolf.
Aug. 21, 1826—Orestes Cook to Nancy Strawmat, Abner W. Smith, J. P.
Aug. 24, 1826—John Prince to Celia Brooks, M. Lyon, J. P.
Aug. 28, 1826—Giles Barrett to Margaret Bean, M. Lyon, J. P.
Sept. 23, 1826—Thos. W. Nichols to Barbary Gregory, Holloway Collie,
        J. P.
Sept. 30, 1826—Urias Rountree to Lena (?) Moore.
Oct. 5, 1826—Wm. Weathers to Sarah Sterns, Isaac Grubby, J. P.
Oct. 7, 1826—Joshua Orr to Malinda Lowry, Abner W. Smith, J. P.
Oct. 14, 1826—Edw. Satterfield to Nancy McCarty, Wm. Lander, J. P.
Oct. 17, 1826—Alsup Y. Daniel to Mary Harris.
Oct. 30, 1826—William W. Howard to Susannah Thorp, Fielding Woolf.
Oct. 31, 1826—Francis Goff to Tabitha Perrin, Isa Rucker, Sen.
Oct. 31, 1826—Alexander Dean to Anna Gates, John Barnett.
Oct. 31, 1826—Benj. Easley to Pernecia Nichols, Will Lander, J. C. C.
Nov. 14, 1826—Wm. L. Harris to Frances Coyle.
Dec. 4, 1826—Danl. H. McCoy to Sarah Cherry.
Dec. 5, 1826—Robt. A. Patterson to Elvira E. Jacob, Robt. A. Lapsley.
Dec. 9, 1826—Matthew Clinton to Jane Guess, John Travis.
Dec. 9, 1826—Joseph Howton to Jemima Smith, Wm. Lander, J. P. C. C.
Dec. 11, 1826—Roger Tandy to Virginia Draper, Fielding Woolf.
Dec. 19, 1826—Tho. Waddlington to Fewey Baker, Wm. Mitchisson, J. P.
Dec. 23, 1826—Daniel Young to Hannah Smiley, Fielding Woolf.
Dec. 25, 1826—Eddin Lewis to Wineford Easley, Edm. Wilcox.

        1827:
Jan. 2, 1827—Elisha Smith to Mary Steven.
Jan. 3, 1827—Robertson Ramey to Nancy Sanders.
        Tubal Carner to Priscilla Creakmur (no date).
Jan. 6, 1827—Wm. Roach to Sally Williams, Holloway Collie, J. P.
Jan. 8, 1827—Wm. Jackson to Polly Cook.
Jan. 15, 1827—James Lawrence to Theresa Sparrow.
Jan. 24, 1827—Wiley Baker to Nancy Howard, F. Woolf.
Jan. 27, 1827—Spencer G. Metcalf to Mary Wilson.
Jan. 29, 1827—Wiley P. Stallions to Mary Armstrong, Will Lander, J. P.
Feb. 8, 1827—John Masden to Anna Williams, Saml. Glenn, J. P.
Feb. 27, 1827—Thomas Hughes to Isabella McVay, Robt. A. Lapsley.
Mar. 1, 1827—William Cleaves to Sarah Cook, Abner W. Smith, J. P.
Mar. 13, 1827—George L. Dillingham to Jane Young, Will Lander, J. P.
Mar. 15, 1827—Thomas Smith to Sarah Hall, Fielding Woolf, Minister.
Mar. 19, 1827—Absalom Landers to Rebecca Crow.
Mar. 19, 1827—Owen W. Oliver to Elizabeth Oliver.
Mar. 31, 1827—David W. McGoodwin to Susan C. P. D. Wigginton,
        Methodist Ch., John Johnston.
Ap. 7, 1827—Comely Elliott to Margaret Carter, Will Lander, J. P.
Ap. 12, 1827—Pulaski J. Hughes to Rachael Ellis, Will Lander, J. P.
May 12, 1827—Charles Allen to Elizabeth Russell.
May 18, 1827—Josiah Lester to Polly Purdy, Isaac Grubbs, J. P.

May 23, 1827—Wm. D. McCoy to Huldy Kilgore, Wm. Mitchison, J. P.
June 2, 1827—John Long to Maria Goodall.
June 14, 1827—Alfred Brock to Nancy Haworth, D. Lowry, minister.
July 5, 1827—Benjamin Wilson to Polly Rupert, Timothy Sisk.
July 7, 1827—Benj. D. Cobb to Mary Tucker.
July 26, 1827—Arthur Colley to Edey Griffith, Fielding Woolf, min.
Aug. 19, 1827—Spencer Calvert to Mrs. Lydia Shellhouse.
Aug. 23, 1827—Aaron Brown to Jane Holbert, Holloway Collie, J. P.
Sept. 4, 1827—Abraham Dudley to Elizabeth Vaughn.
Sept. 7, 1827—Freak L. Jarrett to Jane Harman.
Sept. 12, 1827—Clement L. Clifton to Lucinda Watkins, Meth. E. Ch., John
    Johnson.
Sept. 27, 1827—James Brown to Martha Forbes.
Sept. 27,1827—Saml. Reese to Susan Matlock.
Oct. 1, 1827—David Rowland to Frances Layton, Saml. Glenn.
Oct. 1, 1827—Wm. Stubbs to Minerva Layton, S. Glenn.
Oct. 1, 1827—John Hays to Alcey H. Kivel, D. Lowry, C. P. Ch.
Oct. 22, 1827—Wm. Layton to Elizabeth McElroy, J. W. Manfield, Bap.
Oct. 22, 1827—John Sheridan (?) to Catherine Huey, Isaac Grubbs, J. P.
Oct. 23, 1827—Noah Fulks to Rachel Nichols.
Oct. 24, 1827—Alexr. Glass to Nancy Russell or Rupert, F. Wolf.
Nov. 8, 1827—John Wells to Nancy Miller, Wm. Duckley, M. G.
Nov. 12, 1827—Joseph White to Mary Moore, Meth. E. Ch., John Johnson.
Nov. 13, 1827—John Davis to Elizabeth Grubby, Fielding Woolf.
Nov. 26, 1827—John Howard to Elizabeth Ann Lofton.
Nov. 26, 1827—James R. Cole to Mary A. Bennett.
Nov. 30, 1827—Peter Purtle to Ruth Creekmur, J. W. Mansfield, Baptist
    Ch.
Nov. 30, 1827—John W. Swills (Twills) to Marilla T. Boyle.
Dec. 6, 1827—John Adamson to Mary Reed.
Dec. 11, 1827—Jas. McDowell to Polly Parish.
Dec. 17, 1827—Howard Moore to Maria Pugh, Will Lander.
Dec. 17, 1827—Wm. Stevens to Rachael Walling.
Dec. 17, 1827—Greenlee Colley to Frances Innes, Isaac Grubbs.
Dec. 20, 1827—Saml. S. Smiley to Isabel Gillespie.
Dec. 25, 1827—Wm. H. Oliver to Jane Catherine Oliver.

    1828:

Jan. 1, 1828—John George to Nancy Coleman.
Jan. 7, 1828—Nathan Langeton to Sally Glen, Saml. Glenn, J. P.
Jan. 23, 1828—Sherwood Savage to Jane Sparks, Isaac Grubbs, J. P.
Jan. 12, 1828—Harvey Ladd to Susan Garrett.
Jan. 30, 1828—John Jackson to (?) Delah Hart.
Feb. 4, 1828—James Orr to Jimmy Young, A. C. Collie, J. P.
Feb. 6, 1828—Wm. French to Nancy Lamb, Isaac Grubbs, J. P.
Feb. 7, 1828—Thos. L. Oliver to Jane McMahan, Will Lander.
Feb. 10, 1828—John Smith to Narcissa Johnson.
Feb. 10, 1828—John Garrett to Pally Cotton.
Feb. 18, 1828—Wm. Mathis to Polly Stinnett, Wm. Mitchuson, J. P.
Feb. 20, 1828—Noah H. Cummins to Delila G. Crow.

Feb. 22, 1828—Henry F. Carr to M. A. Throop, G. H. Cobb, J. P.

Mch. 13, 1828—Jas. Cook, Jr., to Sally Darnall, Isaac Grubbs, J. P.

Mch 20, 1828—Edward Pearson to Louisiana Rucker, Wm. Buckley, M. G.

Mch. 26, 1828—China Wilder to Ann Salliers, Will Landers, J. P.

Mar. 26, 1828—Jesse Nichols to Elizabeth Wadlington, Isaac Grubbs.

Mar. 26, 1828—James Keeny to Elizabeth Leech, Edmund Wilcox.

Apr. 1, 1828—Isaac Coy to Elizabeth Lamb, Fielding Woolf.

Apr. 3, 1828—Morgan Holeman to Nancy Holeman, Edm. Wilcox.

Apr. 7, 1828—Enoch Billing to Abey Satterfield, Wm. Mitchisson, J. P.

Apr. 7, 1828—Caswell Shelhouse to Elizabeth Laughlin, Edm. Wilcox.

Apr. 7, 1828—Joseph Laughlin to Rebecca Shelhouse.

Apr. 16, 1828—Thos. Henson to Lucy Ann Cooke.

Apr. 18, 1828—Thos. Jones to Delilah Walker.

Apr. 28, 1828—Josiah Barnet to Fanny Holloway.

Apr. 27, 1828—John Grissam to Synthy Roach, H. Collie, J. P.

Apr. 29, 1828—Hardin West to Catherine Milholland, Jas. C. Weller, J. P.

June 2, 1828—Ira Hewett to Sally East.

June 9, 1828—Wm. Dudley Calloway to Inez B. Barnard, John Johnson, minister.

May 5, 1828—John S. Jackson to Cyntha Gosset, John Travis.

May 28, 1828—John Hutchison to Theodocia Snelling.

May 30, 1828—Berryman Timons to Sienrayma (Na) Olliver.

June, 1828—William Reymes to Elizabeth Anderson.

July 8, 1828—William T. Coward to Wm. Sarah Rupert (a widow) Wm. Buckley.

Aug. 19, 1828—Singleton Asher to Jane Davidson, Presby. Ch., D. Lowry.

Aug. 21, 1828—Simpkins Young to Rebecca Grubb, Isaac Grubbs.

Aug. 27, 1828—Nathan Oliver to Barbary Gilkey.

Sept. 4, 1828—Wm. Kesterson to Sally Nichols, Isaac Grubbs, J. P.

Sept. 18, 1828—Denny Cook to Isabella Glass, F. Woolf.

Oct. 8, 1828—Wm. H. Boyd to Nancy Huey, H. Collie, J. P.

Oct. 9, 1828—Thos. H. Basham (?) to Polly Darnall, Isaac Grubbs, J. P.

Oct. 13, 1828—Moses Crow to Nancy Harris.

Nov. 18, 1828—Jacob Lawrence to Ila Orr, D. Lowry.

Oct. 18, 1828—John P. Gray to Betsey Hall.

Nov. 10, 1828—John More to Susan Ann Morrow, F. R. Cassill.

Nov. 11, 1828—Lemuel Duning to Eliza T. Currey.

Nov. 17, 1828—Alexander B. Gilliland (?) to Betsey Armstrong, Robt. A. Lapsley, Min.

Nov. 20, 1828—Nicholas Copland to Sarah Rilley, James W. Mansfield.

Oct. 24, 1828—David L. Bridges to Malinda Bridges, Holloway Collie, J. P.

Oct. 25, 1828—Ira Sake to Barbara Dooms, M. Lyons, J. P.

Oct. 27, 1828—Rich. S. Hardy to Amanda Simpson, G. D. Cobb, J. P.

Oct. 29, 1828—Jos. Anderson to Maria Williamson, M. Lyon, J. P.

Nov. 24, 1828—Geo. L. Weeks to Nancy Smith, Edm. Wilcox.

Dec. 5, 1828—Ambrose Wheeler to Ruth Tabb, J. W. Mansfield.

Dec. 7, 1828—Wm. W. Franklin to Elizabeth Goodman, Will Lander, J. C.

Dec. 18, 1828—Henry Cartwright to Polly Carner, Abner W. Smith, J. P.

Dec. 29, 1828—John W. Davidson to Polly Smith, Jas. Mansfield.
Nov. 29, 1828—John Cannon to Elizabeth Lofton.
Dec. 30, 1828—W. I. Fowler to Nancy Holloway.

    1829:

Jan. 1, 1829—Wm. Morse to Ann Guess, Jno. Mansfield.
Jan. 26, 1929—Larkin Teer to Elizabeth Witherspoon, Isaac Grubbs.
Feb. 4, 1829—Dempsey Holderby to Sarah Robinson, Timothy Ash.
Feb. 16, 1829—John S. Drennan to Patsey Roberts.
Feb. 5, 1829—Ebenezer Morse to Paulina B. Morse, Jas. C. Weller, J. P.
Feb. 6, 1829—Wm. Parker to Aby V. Cherry.
Feb. 24, 1829—Lin Sigler to Adah Beck, Rev. Edm. Wilcox.
Feb. 25, 1829—William Johnston to Frances Rogers (a widow), J. W.
    Mansfield .
Mar. 4, 1829—Thomas H. Wilson to Lucinda B. Smith.
Mar. 7, 1829—William Wafer to Perney Smith, Edm. Wilcox.
Mar. 9, 1829—John Armstrong to Matilda Smith, Will Lander.
Mar. 11, 1829—James Wilson to Amanda Wyatt, D. Lowery, Pres. Ch.
March 12, 1829—Hardy Perry to Sarah Cooke, Isaac Grubbs, J. P.
Mar. 16, 1829—John Leech to Cyntha Crowder.
Ap. 17, 1829—John Jarrett (?) to Miss Joanna Marshall, M. Lyon, J. P.
Ap. 20, 1829—Saml. McCollum to Betsy Holloway.
Ap. 20, 1829—Wm. Grasty to Tabitha Harkins (Hankins).
May 12, 1829—Shadrack Dunning to Mrs. Peggy McCord (widow), F.
    Woolf.
May 16, 1828—Eleazer Smith to Cyntha Clinton, R. A. Lapsley.
May 16, 1829—Bennett Crouch to Esther Wilson.
Feb. 7, 1829—Wm. Martin to Caroline Walker, G. D. Cobb, J. P.
May 9, 1829—John Craig to Rachel Brown, R. A. Lapsley.
May 18, 1829—Lewis Blackburn to Rosanna Laughlin, J. W. Mansfield.
June 28, 1829—William Cannon to Jane Stevens, Abner W. Smith, J. P.
July 4, 1829—James Chapel to Rosanna Franklin, Will Lander, J. P.
July 10, 1829—David Walker to Anna Purkel, R. A. Lapsley.
July 12 (?) 1829—James Gordon to Tinsie Harrows (?) G. D. Cobb, J. P.
July 15, 1829—John Yates to Martha Henson, G. D. Cobb.
July 27, 1829—Lin Peal to Queen Lester.
Aug. 1, 1829—Wm. T. Dillingham to Mary Robinson, J. C. Wells, J. P.
Aug. 17, 1829—Wm. T. Draper to Mary Jane Thomson.
July 23, 1829—John S. (or T.) Edmunds to Fanny Cecil (or Ceed) J. T.
    Dallam, D. C.
Aug. 19, 1829—Spencer Calvert to Mrs. Lydia Shellhouse (widow) ind
    20th, Edm. Wilcox, ret. Mar. 16, 1830.
Aug. 22, 1829—Ransford Smith to Katherine Ann Parker (widow).
Sept. 4, 1829—Henry McCardy to Charlotte Conway, M. Lyon, J. P.
Sept. 12, 1829—Wm. H. Neely to Eleanor Boyd.
Sept. 21, 1829—Wm. Roberts to Malinda Campbell, J. S. Dalland.
Sept. 28, 1829—Hugh M. Crowel to Eliza Ann Kemp.
Sept. 29, 1829—Tinsley Harris to Lucresa Kilgore, Meth. Eps. Ch.
Sept. 29, 1829—Allen Gary to Louisa Wadlington, C. Waller.
Oct. 14, 1829—Moses Cantrell to Fanny Carner.

Oct. 14, 1829—Ellis H. Gardner to Pemeca Johnson, Jno. Mansfield.

Sept. 10, 1829—Jas. Clark to Mary W. Cobb, Robt. A. Lapsley.

Sept. 10, 1829—Soloman Martin to Allezera Harman, M. Lyon.

Sept. 16, 1829—Crittenden Lyon to Frances B. Jones, M. E. Ch., Jno. Johnson.

Oct. 19, 1829—David T. Whitlock to Amy Gatewood, J. C. Weller, J. P.

Oct. 29, 1829—Irwin Hollowell to Mary Parker, Coleman Rathfield.

Nov. 2, 1829—Stephen W. Herring to Rhoda Stafford, Wm. Mitchum, J. P.

Nov. 2, 1829—Jeremiah Buckley to Milinda Currey.

Nov. 16, 1829—Wm. D. Miller to Mary Black, Edm. Wilcox.

Nov. 24, 1829—Jno. S. Elder to Phoebe A. Hallowell.

Dec. 16, 1829—John E. Prince to Elizabeth Tandy.

Dec. 21, 1829—John R. Boyd to Louisa A. Jones, James Morse, J. P.

Dec. 24, 1829—Wm. Nana to Eliz. Atkinson, Saml. Glenn, J. P.

Dec. 28, 1829—Robt. Priddy to Pennecy Evans, Saml. Glenn.

1830:

Jan. 5, 1830—Jno. D. Tyler to Mildred D. Waller, F. R. Capitt, M. G. (?)

Jan. 22, 1830—Geo. W. Thompson to Eliza W. Bowyer, Wm. Mitcherson, J. P.

Jan. 27, 1830—Jesse Stevens to Harriet E. Herrell.

Jan. 30, 1830—Thos. Neel to Arminda Son.

Feb. 3, 1830—Jno. W. Davis to Malissa Jones, Edm. Wilcox.

Feb. 4, 1830—Jas. N. Gracey to Youlda O'Hara, Cumb. Presby. Ch. D. Lowey.

Feb. 20, 1830—Cullen Carter to Rhoda Nichol, Edm. Wilcox.

Mar. 4, 1830—Wm. Thetford to Abigail Johnson, Coleman Ratliff, J. P.

Mar. 16, 1830—Jak M. Bumpuss to Elvira D. Morse, J. C. Weller.

Mar. 23, 1830—Nathan Smith to Polly S. Wofford.

Mar. 9, 1830—Jno. Etheridge to Cecily Newby, H. Collie, J. P.

Mar. 25, 1830—Geo. Holesapple to Modena Killion, Saml. Glenn, J. P.

Mar. 31, 1820—Briant Nichols to Mrs. Rhoda Jessee (widow).

Apr. 12, 1830—Moses Brown to Nancy Parks, T. N........, J. P.

Apr. 15, 1830—W. B. Greer to Evolina Caldwell, Robt. Lapsley.

Apr. 15, 1830—Jno. McCarty to Mary Johnson, M. Lyons, J. P.

Apr. 27, 1830—Geo. Sikes to Mary E. Davenport, M. Lyon, J. P.

Apr. 27, 1830—Wm. Cloud to Patience LeMarr.

May 6, 1830—Wm. Mosley to Eliza M. Dunn, J. W. Mansfield.

May 17, 1830—Caleb Munner to Elizabeth Reed.

June 7, 1830—Moore Womberley to Emily Rucker.

June 10, 1830—Geo. W. Collins to M. A. Groom.

June 14, 1830—Augustus F. Jacob to Lucy L. White, D. Loury, Presby.

June 15, 1830—D. P. Herring to Arim Stafford, Wm. Mitcherson, J. P.

June 21, 1830—Peter Kesteron to Betsy Cherry, F. Woolf.

June 26, 1830—Chasteen Hord to Charity Land.

July 22, 1830—John Eson to Martha Mason.

Aug. 2, 1830—Peter Smith to Catherine B. Sigler, Jas. C. Weller, J. P.

Aug. 2, 1830—Jas. Wilson to Nancy Lewis, J. C. Weller, J. P.

Aug. 12, 1830—Thos. G. Pettit to Polly Gray, D. Loury.
May 6, 1830—Matthew Gracey to Maria Tilford, John Johnson, Meth. Eps.
May, 1830—Thos. Jones to Rachel Walker.
May 10, 1830—Robt. G. Tricker to Sally Langstone, G. D. Cobb, J. P.
May 25, 1830—James Parks to Nancy D. Davenport, M. Lyon, J. P.
June 12, 1830—Wm. Jones to Lucinda Rowland, H. Collie, J. P.
Sept. 8, 1830—John Hallick to Hannah Cobb, R. A. Lapsley.
Sept. 11, 1830—Harison Blackburn to Mrs. Jane E. Waters, widow.
Sept. 11, 1830—Thos. Sloan to Mrs. Sarah Wilkes (widow) Will Lander,
    J. P.
Sept. 11, 1830—Drury M. Kivell to Lucretia Mitcherson, Wm. Mitcherson.
Sept. 20, 1830—Henry Wolf to Julia A. Harman, Saml. Glenn, J. P.
Sept. 28, 1830—Thos. Flournoy to Mana A. Dallam, C. P. Ch., D. Lowry.
Oct. 9, 1830—Geo. Drennon to Eliza Wimbleduff, T. W. Mansfield.
Oct. 11, 1830—Jas. Cook to Peggy N. Shirley.
Oct. 18, 1830—Jno. Elder to Edah Carner, T. B. Mansfield.
Oct. 23, 1830—Wm. Meakwell to Nancy T. Guess, D. Loury.
Oct. 21, 1830—Sharp D. Baldwin to Mary B. Prince, Wm. Mitcherson.
Oct. 30, 1830—Justinian Cartright to Mrs. Mary Harris (widow).
Nov. 2, 1830—Whitmiel Slattins to Nancy Armstrong, J. C. Weller, J. P.
Nov. 3, 1830—Robt. Black to Elizabeth McCreary, J. C. Weller.
Nov. 6, 1830—Thos. Anderson to Nancy Laughlin.
Nov. 8, 1830—Wm. Lewis to Jemima Easley, J. C. Weller.
Nov. 23, 1830—Jno. W. Harper to Elmira Stevenson, D. Lowry.
Nov. 24, 1830—Wiley B. Stallins to Hannah Armstrong, J. C. Weller.
July 20, 1830—Bartlett Cash to Letitia Owens.
Nov. 2, 1830—Jas Hall to Susannah Lafton, C. Ratliff.
Nov. 29, 1830—Thos. White to Mary Ann Johnson, Saml. Glenn.
Dec. 1, 1830—Dans Pigg to Lucinda Gilley, Will Lauder.
Dec. 2, 1830—Thos. D. Wilson to Polly Ann Towles, M. E. Ch. John John-
    son.
Dec. 9, 1830—Jas L. Priest to Deborah M. Byrne, C. Ratliff.
Dec. 15, 1830—Jas. L. Dallam to Elisabeth M, Flournoy, C. P. C., D.
    Lowry
Dec. 20, 1830—David Roberts to Melissa A. M. Jones.
Dec. 27, 1830—Jordan Cash to Frances Savage.

    1831:
Jan. 4, 1831—Wm. Glass to Brummetty Woolf.
Jan. 4, 1831—Johnson Laughlin to Mildred Waller, J. C. Weller.
Jan. 20, 1831—Powell Rick to Mary G. Jones, J. W. Mansfield.
Feb. 4, 1831—Jno. W. Simpson to Eliza B. Ford, Jon Johnson.
Feb. 8, 1831—Jas. Paterson to Nancy L. Grant.
Feb. 8, 1931—Jas F. Ballard to Sarah M. Hawkins.
Feb. 8, 1831—Sir James Marthnelle to Elizabeth Baher.
Feb. 12, 1831—Robt. Halloway to Catherine Boyd, John Johnson.
Mar. 1, 1831—Norman Land to Lucy Le Marr (widow) Geo. McNelly, N.
    G.
Jan. 18, 1831—Jere Hammock to Polly Sullivant, M. Lyon, J. P.
Jan. 19, 1831—Enoch George to Pernecy Gray—John Johnson.

Mar. 1, 1831—Jno. Crider to Elizabeth Holeman, J. W. Mansfield.

Mar. 2, 1831—Milton H. Carson to Sinai Mitcherson, Wm. Mitcherson, J. P.

Mar. 3, 1831—Henry Garner to Elizabeth Short.

Mar. 5, 1831—Logan Howard to Mary King.

Apr. 2, 1831—Jno. Holmes to Nancy Matthews, J. C. Ratliff.

Apr. 6, 1831—Drury C. Mitcherson to Clarinda S. Mitcheson, D. Lowry.

Apr. 12, 1831—Meredith Archer to Adaline Goodall, John Johnson.

Mar. 20, 1831—Thos. Tamerlin to Polly Layton, Saml. Glenn, J. P.

Mar. 1, 1831—Wm. Ashbridge to Elizabeth Hewitt, M. Lyon, J. P.

Apr. 20, 1831—Jno. Sigler to Catherine Nall.

May 6, 1831—Robt. Martin to Rebecca Carner, Robt. T. McReynolds.

May 23, 1831—Henry T. Mason to Polly Jones, J. C. Weller.

June 23, 1831—Jas. Salyer to Orilly Hays.

June 23, 1831—Jno. Neely to Mary Ann Boyd, Jno. Trans.

June 14, 1831—Jas. East to Hanah Lafton.

Feb. 23, 1831—Wm. Halcomb to Elizabeth Faugher, C. Ratliff.

May 31, 1831—Henry Pearcy to Nancy Flawn, Ratliff.

July 17, 1831—Jno. Vead to Louisa Johnson, M. Lyon.

Aug. 10, 1831—Thos. Pruit to Cynthia George, J. C. Weller.

May 7, 1831—Chas. Atkinson to Elizabeth Chandler.

May 23, 1831—Samuel Hill to Lucinda Emily Williamson, M. Lyon.

July 17, 1831—John Dead to Louisa Johnson.

July 20, 1831—Jno. F. Bennett to Lauran W. Brooks, J. W. Mansfield.

July 30, 1831—Jno. N. Stevens to Elizabeth K. Stephens, Robt. T. McReynolds.

July 22, 1831—Jas. Wood to Sally Draper.

July 30, 1831—P. B. McGoodwin to G. Machen.

July 30, 1831—Jerome B. Cash to Nancy Travis, Jno. Johnson.

Aug. 30, 1831—Mordecai Oldham to Catherine Eison, Jas. C. Waller, J. P.

Sept. 1, 1831—Jas. Wadlington, Jr., to Maria Young, J. W. Mansfield.

Sept. 3, 1831—Matias Bagwell to Mrs. Ann Phillips, Isaac Grubbs, J. P.

Sept. 13, 1831—Zack Dunning to Nancy Will.

Sept. 14, 1831—Geo. W. Rieger to Ann Robinson, Jno. Johnson.

Sept. 16, 1831—Alexander Purdy to Charity Woolfe.

Sept. 17, 1831—Jno. Wells to Mrs. Elizabeth Sleesing, Isaac Grubbs, J. P.

Aug. 31, 1831—Lorenza Parks to Elizabeth Rily, J. W. Mansfield.

Sept. 24, 1831—Samuel Campbell to Louisiana Wilcox, D. Lowry.

Sept. 26, 1831—Jacob Eison to Sally C. Mason, J. C. Weller.

Sept. 29, 1831—Gabrill R. Marshall to Lucinda Stafford, Wm. Mitchisson, J. P.

Sept. 29, 1831—Jno. Baker to Nancy Davis, Isaac Grubby, J. P.

Oct. 13, 1831—Robt. C. Dunn to Martha Craig, J. W. Mansfield.

Sept. 26, 1831—A. N. Hunter to Sharlett Bennett, John Johnson, M. E. Ch.

Oct. 1, 1831—John Ray to Caroline Timmond.

Oct. 4, 1831—John H. Mims to C. Cresap, John Johnson, M. E. Ch.

Oct. 11, 1831—Wilson Parent to Cynthia Galush, John Johnson.

Oct. 25, 1831—Geo. Draper to Amelia Tandy, C. Ratliff.

Oct. 26, 1831—Hiram Fowler to Pernisea Hall, C. Ratliff.

Nov. 1, 1831—Robt. Lowry to Fanny Stevens, J. C. Weller.
Nov. 2, 1831—Henry T. Cossitt to Lucinda M. Greer, C. P., Richard Beard, M. G.
Nov. 8, 1831—Ebenezer Morse to Delilah Hobby, J. C. Weller.
Nov. 14, 1831—Porter Jones to Elizabeth Pendleton, Isaac Grubbs, J. P.
Nov. 21, 1831—Jeremiah Farley to Melissa F. Smith.
Nov. 30, 1831—Wm. Gray to Mildred Gray, Ratliff.
Dec. 11, 1831—Geo. F. Darly to Mary Wyatt, J. W. Mansfield.
Dec. 11, 1831—David Leech to Malica Lowry, D. Lowry.
Dec. 20, 1831—Will Davenport to Lucinda Draper, J. C. Ratliff.
Oct. 25, 1831—Wm. Risdon to Elen Fulks, Jas. Morse.
Oct. 31, 1831—Henry A. Harman to Elizabeth Luper.
Nov. 1, 1831—Isaac D. Carter to Margaret Martin, M. Lyon.
Dec. 2, 1831—Geo. F. Howard to Isabella Tharp, M. Lyon.
Dec. 23, 1831—John Sigler to Peggy Sigler, Jno. Weeks.
Dec. 29, 1831—Thos. Dare to Minerva Martin, Jno. Travis.
Dec. 31, 1831—Mathew Pettigrew to Dicy Dunning, Isaac Grubbs, J. P.
Jan. 4, 1832—Wm. P. Calowell to Jane Jackson, J. W. Mansfield.
Dec. 23, 1831—Nathan Veatch to Caroline Thrift, J. S. Brown, J. P.
Jan. 10, 1832—David D. Marshall to Polly Stubbs, J. C. Langston, J. P.
Jan. 30, 1831—Washington Johnson to Polly Hall, C. Ratliff, J. P.

1832:

Jan. 31, 1832—Wm. A. Stewart to Keziah Wilson, J. W. Mansfield.
Feb. 14, 1832—Wm. Ford to Martha Cooper, Will Landon.
Feb. 21, 1832—Geo. Dunning to Sarah Ashby, Isaac Grubbs, J. P.
Mar. 3, 1932—Jas. Wallace to Keziah Duckworth, J. W. Mansfield.
Mar. 6, 1832—Alexr. Mc ame (?) to Esther Boyd, Wm. Mitcherson.
Mar. 8, 1832—Cedar Hallall to Mrs. Elizabeth Ritchey, Jas. Weller.
Mar. 14, 1832—John J. Hayden to Mary R. Miller.
Mar. 19, 1832—Starling Z. Morse to Helen A. Lowrey, Sam Waller, J. P.
Mar. 22, 1832—Daniel Walling to Mary Hammonds, Will Lowry, J. P.
Apr. 3, 1832—Jesse A. Smith to Martha K. Barnett.
Feb. 6, 1832—Nathan W. Bridges to Matilda Gregory.
Apr. 13, 1832—Lewis Duvall to Mary McElroy, Saml. Glenn, J. P.
Apr. 18, 1832—Jno. Glass to Jane French.
Sept. 17, 1832—Wm. F. Holeman to Nancy Holeman, Jno. Weeks, J. P.
Sept. 17, 1832—Isum Wyatt to Mary Young, J. W. Weller, J. P.
Sept. 18, 1832—Robt. A. Lapsley to Sarah Cooper, J. W. Mansfield.
Sept. 3, 1832—Alex. Randolph to Malinda Watkins, C. B. Clifton.
Sept. 30, 1832—Wm. Wadlington to Eliza H. Holmes, J. C. Weller.
Oct. 6, 1832—John F. Morse to Jane E. Fryer, J. C. Weller.
Oct. 13, 1832—Jas. Clinton to Margaret B. Caldwell.
Apr 18, 1832—Jas. Kirkpatrick to Maria P. Flournoy.
Apr. 21, 1832—Lee C. Martin to Minerva Dean.
May 1, 1832—Jas. D. Morse to Catherine Holman, Jno. Weeks.
May 14, 1832—Jas. H. H. Dunn to Lucinda Bigham, B. O. G. D. E. N.
Apr. 26, 1832—Andrew Craven to Louise Gordon, S. Glenn.
June 2, 1832—Edwd. J. Smith to Mary Bembray, M. Lyon.
July 3, 1832—John George to Miss Chris Wilcox.

July 3, 1832—Truman C. Martin to Margaret Evans, M. Lyon, J. P.

July 20, 1832—James Slone to Mrs. Edy Canidy, J. C. Willer, J. P.

Aug. 20, 1832—Seth B. Wigginton to Sarah M. Gates, Cumb. Presby. Ch. F. R. Copitt.

Sept. 1, 1832—Harison A. Johnson to E. Mitchisson, Wm. Mitchission, J. P.

Sept. 4, 1832—Jas. M. Kelly to Harriet Branch, Jno. Johnson.

Sept. 10, 1832—Levi Baker to Parmilia Crider, Jno. Weeks, J. P.

Sept. 13, 1832—Jas B. Sassen to Elizabeth Bright, Jno. Johnson.

Oct. 4, 1832—Daniel Crider to Mary McElroy, Saml. Glenn.

Nov. 10, 1832—Jno. B. Craig to Helen M. Caldwell, M. Lyon.

Nov. 19, 1832—Jno. S. Downer to Elizabeth Cabaness, Robt. A. Lapsley.

Dec. 10, 1832—Wm. H. Boyd to Polly A. Hanm, Jno. Weeks, J. P.

Nov. 11, 1832—Jas. Ramey to Irena E. Cummins, Coleman Ratliff.

Nov. 12, 1832—Jas. H. Roberts to Sarah D. Kemp, J. Weeks, J. P.

Oct. 15, 1832—David S. Dodds to Elizabeth Brown.

Oct. 18, 1932—Deson McGregor to Margaret Goodacre, Timothy Sisk.

Oct. 22, 1832—Harry F. Freeman to Ruth A. Son, J. W. Mansfield.

Oct. 25, 1832—John Nashbitt to Polly Shirley, Jno. Weeks, J. P.

Oct. 27, 1832—Isaac Holman to Cynthia Campbell.

Oct. 31, 1832—Reuben Harris to Malinda Thomas, John Johnson.

Nov. 10, 1832—Wm. Bruster to Pamela Duncan, Jno. Barnett, Presby. Ch.

Jan. 16, 1833—Geo. W. Carter to Malissa Grubbs, Sam Glenn.

Jan. 17, 1833—Daniel Bagwell to Margott Ticker (?)

Jan. 22, 1833—Wm. R. Hayle to Rebecca Corder, J. Weeks.

Jan. 22, 1833—Anderson Wade to Caroline Simmerman, F. R. Cassell, M. G.

Jan. 21, 1833—William Moore to Polly McDaniel.

Jan. 14, 1833—Wm. L. Rowland to Nancy Halloway, J. S. Brown, J. C. C.

Jan. 3, 1833—Wm. Erwin to Mary Ann Sparks, Coleman Radcliff.

Jan. 9, 1833—Alfred Guess to Mary L. Johnson, J. W. Mansfield.

Jan. 21, 1835—William Moore to Polly McDaniel.

Dec. 19, 1832—Wm. W. Gregory to Alzaday Berman (Beman).

. . . . . . . . . . . .Christopher Jones to Rachel J. Grubbs, Moses . . . . . . . . . .

Nov. 20, 1832—Blake Cooper to Elizabeth King.

Dec. 27, 1832—Allen Howard to Caroline Thorp.

Apr. 17, 1833—Wm. R. Mott to Polly Davidson, Jno. Barnett.

Apr. 22, 1835—Daniel Ordmay (?) to Eliza Smith, Jas. W. Mansfield.

Apr. 23, 1833—Wm. Hawkins to Elizabeth Winn.

. . . . . . . . . . . .Jas. N. Wells to Barbery McGuire, Will Lander, J. P.

May 16, 1833—Thos. L. McNary to Maria L. Flournoy.

May 20, 1833—Wm. H. Sigler to Elizabeth Holeman, J. Weeks.

Apr. 18, 1833—Jas. N. Wells to Barbery McGyer.

May 10, 1833—Saml. F. Dennis to Sally Dunton, J. C. Langston.

Mar. 12, 1833—A. Worthington to Malinda Hensley Radcliff.

Mar. 15, 1833—Gaimim (?) Dodson to Nancy Thompson, Will Sander, J. P.

Mar. 18, 1833—Lewis Hammonds to Winney Baidger (?)

Mar. 19, 1833—John J. Hillyard to Margaret Watson, Jno. Barnett.

Mar. 23, 1833—Francis Martin to Eliza Ann Woolf.

Mar. 26, 1833—Mathew McNeily to Louisa M. Walker, Jno. Weeks, J. P.
Mar. 27, 1833—Solomon Benson to Harriet E. Martin, Jno. Weeks.
Apr. 18, 1833—Franklin N. Smith to Susan Hollowell, M. Lyon, J. P.
July 8, 1833—Jas. A. Moore to Nancy Mitcheson, Wm. Mitcherson, J. P.
Aug. 1, 1833—Lewis Franklin to Mrs. Susan Hart, Archibald Browland.
Sept. 2, 1833—Frederick A. Croft to Sarah A. Menseer, A. Bourland.
June 29, 1833—Stephen Roach to Sarah Osborn.
Aug. 13, 1833—John Lovell to Nancy Hammond, J. C. Langston, P. C. C.
Aug. 31, 1833—Alexr. M. Hodges to Ann Eliza Rucker, F. R. Cassill, M. G.
Apr. 25, 1833—Reuben R. O'Hara to Mary Ann Lyon, John Johnson.
May 23, 1833—William P. Robison to Nancy Leech, Jno. Weeks, J. P.
June 8, 1833—Wm. Y. McCreery to Polly Ann Campbell, Jas. C. Miller, J. P.
July 1, 1833—Jeremiah Boucher to Mary Atkinson, T. C. Langston, J. P.
July 17, 1833—Nath'l. Rochister to Judy Martin.
July 20, 1833—John Cannon to Mary Carlisle, Jno. Weeks.
Sept. 30, 1833—Jas. Simpson to Sopha McDowell, Jno. Kirkpatrick.
Oct. 15, 1833—Robt. Rogers to Martha Baker.
Oct. 20, 1833—Jos. N. B. Harrell to Hannah Trim, John Johnson V. D. M.
Oct. 21, 1833—Angerean Franklin to Lucinda Stephens, Saml. Glenn.
Oct. 29, 1033—Wm. Smith to Henrietta Robertson, Jno. Hamilton, M. G.
Nov. 4, 1833—Aaron Threlkeld to Sarah Louise Dunn.
Sept. 10, 1833—Jos. Drennan to Hilda Leech, Jno. T. . . . . . . . . .
Sept. 12, 1833—Wm. Boyd to Catherine Cooksey, Saml. Willer, J. P.
Sept. 12, 1833—Leonard Oliver to Elizabeth Smith.
Sept. 24, 1833—John Ausenbaugh to Aurorah Eison, Saml. Willer.
Sept. 14, 1833—Geo. W. Carter to Belinda Young, Isaac Grubbs, J. P.
Aug. 21, 1833—Josiah Rice to Margarette Rice.
Nov. 23, 1833—John Dunning to Sarah Smith, Jas. Willer.
Nov. 27, 1833—John H. Dyer to Ellen Talbott, Jno. Johnson.
Nov. 27, 1833—Chas. J. White to Mrs. Emily Woolf, Jas. C. Weller.
Nov. 28, 1833—Eli Nichols to Mrs. Sarah Salyer.
Nov. 28, 1833—Elijah Terrell to Elizabeth Tranks, B. Ogden.
Dec. 12, 1833—Wiley Nichols to Eliza Hopper, J. C. Welles.
Dec. 16, 1833—Henry Enders to Adela J. Jacobs, F. R. Cassill, M. G.
Nov. 4, 1833—Coleman Dunning to Elizabeth Wells, C. Ratliff, J. P.
Nov. 5, 1833—Nathan C. Byod (?) to Elizabeth A. Pollard, F. R. Copett.
Nov. 7, 1833—Jas. H. McAllister to Elizabeth Weathers.
Nov. 7, 1833—Jos. French to Lucy Scott.
Nov. 11, 1833—Jno. W. McNeily to Nancy Hobby, Jas. C. Miller, J. P.
Nov. 21, 1833—Butler Hubbard to Betsy Perry.

1834:

Jan. 18, 1834—Geo. Clark to Elizabeth Nichols.
Jan. 14, 1834—Saml. Wilson to Laura Gregan, Isaac Grubbs.
Jan. 22, 1834—Jas. Wood to Sally Curry.
Jan. 22, 1834—Nathaniel David to Sarah Kesleton (?) J. A. Cartright, J. P.
Feb. 4, 1834—Geo. W. Guess to Mrs. Jane Clinton, Jas. W. Mansfield.

Feb. 11, 1834—Geo. M. Marshall to Persis Cobb, Jno. Johnson.

Dec. 5, 1833—Roling Langston to Catherine Ceider, Saml. Glenn, J. P.

Dec. 7, 1833—Thos. H. Poor to Elizabeth C. East, C. L. Clifton, Elder, M. E. Ch.

Dec. 24, 1833—Everard P. Jacob to Emma White, Jno. Johnson.

Dec. 28, 1833—Jesse Williams to Rebecca Morse, Jas. Morse, J. P.

Jan. 7, 1834—Morton A. Rucker to Salina D. Boyd, Jas. C. Waller, J. P.

Jan. 8, 1834—Wm. A. McChesney to Sarah Nash, Jas. Morse.

Jan. 20, 1834—Owen Cooper to Sarah Sandy, C. Ratliff, J. P.

Dec. 26, 1833—Jno. Carney to Lucinda King, Moses Stubly.

Mar. 13, 1834—Wm. H. Goodacre to Margaret R. Campbell, J. C. Waller.

Feb. 19, 1834—Thos. Wilson to Ruth H. Hammond, Saml. Glenn.

Jan. 17, 1834—Jos. Groses to E. Williams, Saml. Glenn.

Mar. 18, 1834—Liny Watson to Maria Jane Church, Jno. Johnson.

Mar. 24, 1834—Spartan Goodlett to Elizabeth Laugham, J. A. Cartright.

Mar. 27, 1834—Ennis Hooper to Elizabeth Stafford, J. C. Weller.

Feb. 17, 1834—Andrew Smith to Elizabeth Glass, Jas. C. Weller, J. P.

Feb. 22, 1834—Thos. Hunter to Susy Ann Rochester, Jno. Johnson.

Feb. 17, 1834—Elijah Stevens, Jr., to Martha McCrary, Jas. C. Waller.

Mar. 3, 1834—Edward M. Davidson to Malinda C. Barnett, Collins J. Bradley.

Mar. 4, 1834—C. C. Williamson to Caroline Jenkins, M. Lyon, J. P.

Mar. 11, 1834—Isiah E. Simpson to Eliza Rice, Jno. Johnson.

Mar. 12, 1834—Jacob M. Merritt to Lincy T. Kesterson.

Mar. 13, 1834—Wm. H. Goodacre to Margaret R. Campbell, Jas. C. Weller.

Feb. 19, 1834—Thos. Wilson to Ruth C. Hammond, Saml. Glenn.

Jan. 12, 1834—Jos. Groves to E. Williams, Saml. Glenn.

Mar. 18, 1834—Lerry Watson to Maria Jane Church, Jno. Johnson.

Mar. 24, 1834—Spartan Goodlet to Elizabeth Laugham, J. A. Cartright.

Mar. 27, 1834—Ennis Hooper to Elizabeth Stafford, J. C. Weller.

Mar. 31, 1834—Jno. A. Hopson to Pamelia S. Mitcherson, Wm. Mitcherson.

Mar. 31, 1834—Jno. P. Boyd to Sarah Rucher, Jno. Johnson.

Apr. 1, 1834—Henry W. Baker to Cassandra F. Stone, Jas. W. Mansfield.

Apr. 2, 1834—Jas. Hall to Hannah Kasinger, Coleman Radcliff.

Apr. 8, 1834—Jos. Boyd to Mrs. Permica Leeper.

Apr. 16, 1834—Lozarm Nichols to M. J. Harper, J. C. Weller.

Feb. 4, 1834—Geo. Fowler to Polly Gray.

Apr. 30, 1834—Jas. Craig to Margaret Miller, R. H. Lilly.

May 12, 1834—Conrad Crane to Polly Deboe, J. W. Mansfield.

Apr. 26, 1834—Caswell Biggs to Louisiana Bunton, J. C. Langston, J. P.

May 9, 1834—Jas. B. Fairbanks to Holly Doone, Saml. Glenn, J. P.

May 5, 1834—Wm. Tinsley to Elizabeth Galasper.

May 26, 1834—Wm. H. Heath to Nancy P. Duncan, B. Ogdon.

May 14, 1834—Thos. Holder to Lucinda Hildrith, J. C. Langston, J. P.

June 4, 1834—Albert Matlock to Mary Ann Chandler, J. C. Langston.

July 1, 1834—Jacob Morse to Lavantha Stone.

Sept. 2, 1834—Thos. J. Johnson to Eliza Ann Baniard.

Sept. 3, 1834—Benj. P. Dunn to Mrs. Matilda Armstrong.

Sept. 8, 1834—Howell Johnson to Mrs. Frances Marshall, Wm. Mitcherson, J. P.

Sept. 11, 1834—Chas. Brownwell to Elizabeth Young, Robt. Cobb, J. P.

Oct. 6, 1834—Jas. P. Furnall to Phoebe Haworth.

Oct. 8, 1834—Hiram B. Pearce to Henrietta Morse.

Mar. 21, 1832—Jas. Blen to Isabella Biles.

June 22, 1834—Morgan Smith to Sarah Holder, Saml. Glenn.

Aug. 3, 1834—Geo. L. Vicel to Lucey Hammond, Saml. Glenn.

Aug. 3, 1834—Chas. G. Graves to Elizabeth Henderson, M. Lyon.

Aug. 13, 1834—Benj. F. Holmes to Sarah Grubbs, Isaac Grubbs, J. P.

Sept. 8, 1834—Ben H. Stevins to Patsey Wilson.

Sept. 11, 1834—Chas. Brownwell to Elizabeth Young.

Sept. 16, 1834—Wm. Smart to Alsa Jane Powell, Isaac Grubbs.

Sept. 23,, 1834—Reuben R. Bush to Louisa Williams, Robt. S. Cobb.

Oct. 7, 1834—Jas. Hanley to Sarah Martin, M. Lyon.

Oct. 29, 1834—Eleazer Smith to Nancy Caldwell, John Barnett.

Nov. 3, 1834—Robert Barr to Junah Simpson, J. C. Weller.

Nov. 4, 1834—Robt. Craig to Nancy Cooper.

Oct. 3, 1834—Doctor W. Duncan to Martha Riley, J. W. Mansfield.

Oct. 28, 1834—Abraham Jourdan to Malinda Godard, J. C. Weller.

Nov. 24, 1834—Franklin Wadlington to Eliza J. Dobyns, R. Beard, M. G.

Nov. 25, 1834—Edward Martin to Rhoda T. Harris, Wm. Matcherson, J. P.

Nov. 29, 1834—Maxwell P. Phillips to Dorcas Black, Jno. Barnett.

Dec. 1, 1834—Jno. B. Hoyl to Elizabeth Hilyard, J. Barnett.

Dec. 1, 1834—Jno. P. Black to Anner H. Stevenson.

Dec. 2, 1834—Elias S. Jones to A. Armstrong, J. A. Cartright.

Dec. 16, 1834—Thos. W. Matlock to Jane E. White, Dudley Williams.

Oct. 22, 1834—Henry McElroy to Malinda Glenn, J. C. Langston.

Nov. 8, 1834—Thos. Norris to Polly Davis, J. C. Langston.

Dec. 7, 1834—Robt. Hodges to Martha Brown, Jno. Barnett.

Dec. 24, 1834—Wm. T. Perkins to Louisa S. Calvert.

Dec. 27, 1834—Andrew Jackson to Talitha Dunn, R. Black, M. G.

Dec. 28, 1834—Samuel A. Keel to Lucinda Langston, Robt. Cobb.

Dec. 31, 1834—David Unsell to Mary Ann Hughes, J. C. Weller.

1835:

Jan. 1, 1835—Lorenzo Brewer to Margaret Jane Spratt, Stephen Ogden.

Jan. 1, 1835—Samuel A. McChesney to Nancy F. Fryer, J. C. Weller.

Jan. 7, 1835—John Ray to Z. Caldwell, R. Beard, M. G.

Jan. 12, 1835—Jesse Stevens, Jr., to Jane Leech, J. C. Weller.

Jan. 14, 1835—Henry W. Champion to S. A. Wigginton.

Jan. 19, 1835—Wm. D. S. Taylor to Ann Owen.

Dec. 16, 1834—James Minks to Mrs. Eland Fulks, J. S. Brown, J. P.

Jan. 12, 1835—Isaac Martin to Mary Ann Black, Robt. S. Cobb.

Jan. 12, 1835—M. B. G. Kinsolving to Harriet Black, Robt. S. Cobb.

Jan. 2, 1835—Alexr. Cooper to Emily Reed, Stephen F. Ogden.

Jan. 12, 1835—Wm. Layton to Eleanor Hunter, Saml. Glenn.

Feb. 2, 1835—Jno. McCormick to Mrs. Nancy Tyson.

Feb. 2, 1835—Jno. Satterfield to Lucretia Martin, Stephen F. Ogden, M. E.

Feb. 9, 1835—Francis M. Cooper to Mary Barnard.

Feb. 12, 1835—Milton Dudley to Ann Eliza Harpending.

Feb. 19, 1835—Samuel Holeman to Mary Holeman, Isaac Harper, J. P.

Feb. 21, 1835—Wm. Sharp to Joanah Sevils, Stephen S. Ogden

Mar. 9, 1835—Garner G. Parmly to Elizabeth N. Morse, Isaac Grubbs.

Mar. 17, 1835—Geo. W. Guess to Margard Guess, Jno. Barnett.

Mar. 23, 1835—Arthur Love to Ann M. Stevens.

Mar. 23, 1835—Chas. F. Wall to Lucinda Gray, Dudley Williams.

Jan. 19, 1835—Hugh Hammock to Rebecca Patterson Marshall.

Feb. 2, 1835—Jas. J. Armstrong to Nancy Wilson.

Feb. 7, 1835—Elias Fomartin to Martha King.

Feb. 28, 1835—Wm. Hobert to Eliza Higgins, J. S. Brown.

Mar. 28, 1835—Robt. T. Phillips to Jane Johnson, Jas. W. Mansfield.

Mar. 30, 1835—Enoch Hooper to Margaret A. Gordlet.

Mar. 31, 1835—Jesse Garnett to Emily Colton.

Apr. 8, 1835—Jos. A. Mott to Lucinda Miller, R. A. Lilly.

Apr. 9, 1835—John Nichols to Nancy Nichols, J. C. Weller.

Apr. 12, 1835—Urial Smith to Marian Lewis.

Apr. 14, 1835—Jeremiah Rucker to Mrs. Mildred Rucker.

Mar. 11, 1835—Jas. Faughn to Mrs. Huldy McCoy.

Mar. 23, 1835—John H. Campbell to Jemima Pritchett.

Apr. 27, 1835—Wm. James to Mrs. Elizabeth Husk, Isaac Harper.

May 5, 1835—Wm. O. Wash to Frances B. Goodlett.

May 13, 1835—Robt. S. Cobb to Cornelia Mims, Jas. W. Mansfield.

June 23, 1835—Enoch B. Prince to Alcy Stevens, Wm. Mitcherson, J. P.

July 15, 1835—Jas. C. Jennings to Mrs. Mary Crouse, J. A. Cartright.

Aug. 25, 1835—Alexr. Hilyard to Rachel Drennon.

Aug. 29, 1835—David J. Drennan to Margaret Brown, J. W. Mansfield.

Sept. 10, 1835—Jas. A. Asher to Sarah P. Stone, J. C. Weller.

June 23, 1835—Joshua Cobb to Julia Mims, J. W. Mansfield.

July 7, 1835—Winchester Marman to Elizabeth Williams, J. C. Langston.

Aug. 12, 1835—Philip Woodward to Rutha Irwin, J. C. Langston.

Aug. 31, 1835—Jas. W. Farmer to S. Goins, J. C. Langston.

Sept. 5, 1835—Green B. Stephens to Polly Rich.

Oct. 6, 1835—Simpson W. Lunsford to Cerena E. McConnell.

Oct. 6, 1835—Jas. Darnall to Polly Copeland, J. A. Cartright.

Oct. 14, 1835—Wm. Wyat to Jane E. Johnson.

Oct. 14, 1835—John S. Son to Rebecca Palmer, J. C. Langston.

Oct. 14, 1835—Isaac N. Wilcox to Nancy L. Love, Jas. Morse, J. P.

Oct. 20, 1835—Jeremiah Wilhite to Jane Hunter.

Oct. 29, 1835—Jas. Henson to Mrs. Elizabeth Weeks.

Nov. 12, 1835—Wm. N. Sigler to Nancy Brooks, J. C. Weller.

Nov. 16, 1835—Henry Tandy to Serilda Gray, J. C. Weller.

Nov. 26, 1835—Robt. C. Boyd to Edith A. R. Hornin, J. C. Weller.

Nov. 26, 1835—Lindsey Shoemaker to Martha Derrington, J. C. Weller.

Dec. 12, 1835—Solomon Sivils to Marinda Bauch, Dudley Williams.

Dec. 12, 1835—Coleman Dunning to Ruth Adams, J. A. Cartright.

Dec. 17, 1835—Wm. W. Franklin to Mary Chapel.

Dec. 22, 1835—Groves Howard to Nancy Barnett, Clement T. F. Clifford, Elder in M. E. Ch.

Dec. 26, 1835—Chas. M. Jackson to Martha Jane Mansfield, Dudley Williams.
Dec. 26, 1835—Geo. T. Smith to Martha Jane Crowder.
Dec. 28, 1835—Willis B. Machen to Margaret A. Lyon.
Dec. 29, 1835—Willis L. Hobby to Easther Lowery, J. C. Weller.
Oct. 25, 1836—Wm. A. Crowder to Mary Ann Roberts, Jno. Harris.

1836:

......1836—Goodlet, John to Sarah A. Greer, by Jno. O'Hara.

1837:

Jan. 4, 1837—Jenkins, Chas. F. to Williams, Atha P.
Jan. 11, 1837—Pearcy, John to Ethridge, Elizabeth.
Jan. 21, 1837—Lacy, James M. to Black, Mary Jane.
Feb. 20, 1837—Jones, James S. to Crider, Martha M.
Feb. 27, 1837—Crider, Samuel to Brewer, Mary.
Mar. 4, 1837—Sims, Wm. R. to Robertson, Caroline by Jas. C. Weller.
Mar. 11, 1837—Ramsey, John S. to Wilcox, Eliza by H. Cassidy.
Mar. 13, 1837—Stone, Jonathan to Cooper, Margaret by Peyton S. Nance.
Mar. 13, 1837—Stevenson, Thos. K. to Stone, Rebecca by Jas. W. Mansfield.
Mar. 23, 1837—Walker, Samuel to Grace, Elvira by Robt. L. Cobb.
Mar. 26, 1837—Pettit, James to Dunning, Nancy by Jas. W. Munsfield.
Mar. 31, 1837—Lofton, Ezekiel to Pearcy, Elizabeth.
Apr. 9, 1837—Watson, Hugh to Duncan, Riller Pernetta.
Apr. 17, 1837—Carter, Lewis J. to Davis, Eleanor by Jesse Haile.
Apr. 17, 1837—Craig, Hugh to Meek, Sarah by R. H. Lilly.
Apr. 17, 1837—Knoth, Leontrart to Funcannon, Lovey (?) by R. H. Cobb, J. P.
Apr. 25, 1837—Wilson, James to Rogers, Prusey.
May 1, 1837—Mims, Davis N. to Cresap, Elizabeth by R. L. Lilly.
May 11, 1837—Smith, James to Lester (Mrs.) Elizabeth.
May 12, 1837—Roach, Wm. F. to Hubbard, Laurena by Bailey Adams.
May 13, 1837 Reynolds, Samuel to Bowles, Cassey by I. N. Kilpatrick.
May 25, 1837—Payne, Cuthbert C. to Rowland, Mary B. by Jno. S. Brown, J. P.
May 27, 1837—Dyer, Finis to Tolbert, Mahala by H. Casidy, J. P.
June 2, 1837—Samsford, Perleeman B. to Lowry, Eliz. by Jas. C. Weller.
June 3, 1837—Atkinson, John to Henson, Mary, by N. H. Cash.
June 6, 1837—Duncan, Ashall to Collie, Katherine by J. S. Brown, J. P.
June 12, 1837—Kemp, James to Phebe Campbell, by J. N. Kilpatrick.
June 20, 1837—Anderson, Wm. R. to Guess, Nancy by R. H. Lilly.
July 7, 1837—Goodacre, Lewis to Townsend, Nancy by H. Casidy.
July 10, 1837—Hubbard, Archibald N. to Parks, Mary by Robt. H. Cobb.
July 24, 1837—Chapel, John to Young, Nancy by H. Casidy.
July 31, 1837—Campbell, John M. to Turley, Catherine by Jas. W. Mansfield.
July 31, 1837—Sanders, Julius to Cummings, Louisa N.
Aug. 3, 1837—Holstead, Charles G. to Barnes, Martha Ann.
Aug. 3, 1837—Holloway, James H. to Bigham, Susan Jane.

Aug. 7, 1837—Howard, Samuel to Kelly (Mrs.) Harritt by Coleman Ratliff, J. C. C.

Aug. 7, 1837—Terry, George to Crowder, Mary Ann by Jno. Travis.

Aug. 19, 1837—Walker, Geo. S. to Varnell, Paulina by J. C. Langston, J. C. C.

Aug. 22, 1837—Scott, James to George, Sarah L.

Aug. 23, 1837—Guess, John R. to Son, Angeline by Jas. W. Mansfield.

Aug. 31, 1837—Withers, Littleberry to Ritchey, Ann by Jas. C. Weller.

Sept. 9, 1837—Kilgore, Pleasant R. to Pew, Susannah by Jas. C. Weller.

Sept. 30, 1837—Doom, Jacob H. to Martin, Elizabeth by Saml. Glenn.

Oct. 10, 1837—Hays, Wm. H. to Chandler, Mary by J. C. Langston.

Oct. 10, 1837—Houston, Fleming to Dunning, Sylva by Bailey Adams, C. C.

Oct. 12, 1837—O'Hara, Wm. to Cartwright, Mary Frances by Jno. Barnett.

Oct. 19, 1837—Carner, Jno. C. to Pew, Mary, by J. H. Cartwright.

Oct. 19, 1837—Jenkins, Presley O. B. to Shirley Eleanor R. by Jas. C. Weller.

Oct. 21, 1837—Drennon, Geo. to Lunsford, Eliza G. by J. N. Kilpatrick.

Nov. 1, 1837—Martin, Wilson to Peak, Mary Ann by Jas. W. Mansfield.

Nov. 2, 1837—Carner, Wm. to Carter, Sarah E. by Jas. C. Weller.

Nov. 10, 1837—Elder, Wm. S. to Gilliland, Margt. by R. H. Lilly.

Nov. 15, 1837—Harris, Aaron to Pickering, Permelia by J. A. Cartwright.

Nov. 16, 1837—Sanders, Henry to Wimberly, (Mrs.) Emily.

Nov. 24, 1837—Butler, Jno. W. to Starling, Mary by Jas. C. Weller.

Nov. 27, 1837—Lochar, John to Freer, Eliza by Robt. L. Cobb.

Dec. 1, 1837—Higgins, Jackson to Hubert, Rachel.

Dec. 11, 1837—Spence, John to Lunsford, Serilda Jane by Jno. Travis.

Dec. 13, 1837—Gilkey, John to Woodall, (Mrs.) Harritt Adaline by Coleman Ratliff.

Dec. 18, 1837—Madeira, John to Dicken, Mary by J. C. Langston.

Dec. 19, 1837—Duncan, Charles H. to Dallam, Mary F., by R. H. Lilly.

Dec. 28, 1837—Brindley, Benj. F. to Lockett, Sally B. by R. H. Lilly.

Dec. 30, 1837—Ervin, Presley to Pendegrass, Mary, by J. C. Langston.

Dec. 30, 1837—George, Washington S., to Jones, Lucinda.

1838:—

Jan. 5, 1838—Bridges, Jesse J. to Bowman, Elizabeth.

Jan. 11, 1838—Given, Dickson A. to Goodall, Clarissa H.

Jan. 15, 1838—Grubbs, Isaac to Roberts (Mrs.) Polly, by Robt. L. Cobb.

Jan. 15, 1838—McLin, John J. to Hockersmith, Florinda J., by Rich. Beard.

Jan. 18, 1838—Byrd, Nathan C. to Leeper, Sarah Jane by R. H. Lilly.

Jan. 23, 1838—Eison, David J., to Nichols, Mary Ann, by Jno. O'Hara.

Jan. 24, 1838—Moore, James J. to Love, Polly S., by Jas. Morse, J. P.

Jan. 27, 1838—Nickell, Coleman to Nickell, Eliza, by Jas. Morse, J. P.

Feb. 5, 1838—Pool, Henry H. T. to Newson, Sarah Susan F.

Feb. 9, 1838—Dunnaway, John W. to Murphy, Susan.

Feb. 20, 1838—McDowell, Shelton to Cannon, Polly Ann by J. N. Kilpatrick.

Feb. 26, 1838—Ervin, Jas. M. to Davis, Rosannah, by Jno. O'Hara, J. P.

Mar. 9, 1838—Wilson, Thomas to Rorer, Permelia.

Mar. 12, 1838—Duncan, Wilford N., to Shoemaker, Sarah, by W. Cash, J. P. C. C.

Mar. 12, 1838—Woolf, Jno. C., to Biggs, Sarah Elender, by Jno. O'Hara.

Mar. 19, 1838—Herring, Drury P., to Martin, Polly, by J. C. Langston.

Mar. 21, 1838—Pace, Turtley R., to Fox, Judith, by J. C. Langston.

Mar. 24, 1838—Hill, Daniel N., to Whalend, Mary, by Jno. A. Brown.

Mar. 26, 1838—McElroy, Stephen B., to Hughey, Eliz. L., by Saml. Glenn.

Mar. 27, 1838—Osborn, Charles E., to Been, Jane, by Jno. Barnett.

Mar. 31, 1838—Hill, Wm. Washington to Bennett, Mary Ann by Saml. Glenn.

Apr. 7, 1838—Baynes, James to Hill, (Mrs.) Nancy by Isaac Harper, J. C. C.

Apr. 7, 1838—Reed, James M. to Guess, Obedience by Jas. W. Mansfield.

Apr. 10, 1838—Hawkins, James to Watkins, Martha Jane, by R. H. Lilly.

Apr. 11, 1838—Perry, James R., to Hays, Adaline B., by Dudley Williams.

Apr. 13, 1838—McClure, Andrew to Williams, Sarah, by J. C. Langston.

Apr. 15, 1838—Nichols, Needum, to Marshall, (Mrs.) Polly, by J. C. Langston.

Apr. 17, 1838—Biddle, John G., to Phelps, Elvira D., by Rich. Beard.

Apr. 18, 1838—Scott, Wm. D., to Hildrith, Nancy V., by J. C. Langston.

Apr. 23, 1838—Winks, James, to Henson, (Mrs.) Mary, by J. C. Langston.

Apr. 24, 1838—Steel, Andrew, to Martin, Jane, by Jos. N. Kilpatrick.

Apr. 27, 1838—Rogers, Jno. D., to Hodge, Martha, by Coleman Ratliff.

Apr. 31, 1838—Ford, Allsbury, to Menser, Martha.

Apr. 31, 1838—Hamilton, Richard, to Menser, Lucinda.

May 14, 1838—Campbell, John H., to McConnell, Jane A.

May 18, 1838—Armstrong, James H., to Gilliland, Mary, by R. H. Lilly.

May 20, 1838—Dunning, Geo. M., to Parker, Vincy, by Jas. C. Weller.

May 26, 1838—Black, Jno. C., to Caldwell, Martha P., by R. H. Lilly.

June 4, 1838—Haydon, Joel to Elder, Martha Jane, by Jno. Bennett.

June 4, 1838—Jones, John R., to Groom, Julia A.

June 6, 1838—Edwards, Wm. H., to Henderson, Sarah, by M. Lyon, P. C. C.

June 21, 1838—Watkins, John W., to Bunton, Nancy, by J. C. Langston.

June 27, 1838—Ashridge, Charles, to Standard, Candie, by M. Lyons.

July 16, 1838—Rawls, Silas M., to Barnett, Mary Jane, by Rich. Beard.

Aug. 4, 1838—Baughter, Joseph, to Doorn, Nancy, by Saml. Glenn.

Aug. 4, 1838—Black, John to Doorn, Hannah by Saml. Glenn.

Aug. 7, 1838—Stone, Wm., to Gray, Susannah P., by Coleman Ratliff.

Aug. 8, 1838—O'Connell, Charlie J. to Quisenberry, Sally Ellen.

Aug. 13, 1838—Martin, Wm., to Darrok, Rebecca.

Aug. 14, 1838—Whyte, George to Martin, Catherine, by R. L. Cobb.

Aug. 15, 1838—Sills, David, to Hawley, Malvina, by Robt. L. Cobb.

Aug. 22, 1838—Church, Lafayette to Leigh, Parthenia, by Jno. Nevius, Meth. Epis. Ch.

Aug. 23, 1838—Adams, Richard S., to Gray, Lydra G., by Jno. Nevius.

Aug. 27, 1838—Decker, John, to Marshall, Mary Ann.

Aug. 27, 1838—Rogers, Jno. D., to Maratha Hodge, by Coleman Ratliff.

Aug. 28, 1838—Rogers, Darvin, to Bennett, Martha L., by Robt. L. Cobb.

Sept. 3, 1838—Maxwell, Edward, to Armstrong, Tabitha, by Rich. Beard.

Sept. 5, 1838—Everett, Jesse, to Rowland, Euphamy, by Jno. S. Brown.

Sept. 6, 1838—Hughey, Michael D., to Thompson, Mahuldah, by W. Cash.

Sept. 10, 1838—McDaneil, Samuel, to Corliew, Nancy.

Sept. 15, 1838—Murray, Randolph, to Jenkins, Narcissa, by J. C. Langston.

Sept. 20, 1838—Jackson, James, to Dunbar, Eliz., by Isaac Harper, J. C. C.

Sept. 29, 1838—Hill, James W., to Williamson, Margt. Jane, by Clement W. Clifton, M. E. Ch.

Oct. 3, 1838—Johnson, Wm. W., to Langston, Pernecey, by J. C. Langston.

Oct. 8, 1838—Garner, Wm., to Davidson, Nancy E., by Jno. Barnett.

Oct. 8, 1838—McWaters, Wyatt, to Gray, Martha Amanda, by Isaac Harper, P. C. C.

Oct. 15, 1838—Wharton, Wm. E., to Armstrong, Polly Ann, by Herrington Stevens.

Oct. 22, 1838—Cresap, Hanson B., to Marshall, Mary Ann, by Thos. E. Paine, Protestant Episcopal.

Oct. 24, 1838—Wright, Alfred, to Dunn, Margaret, by Clement L. Clifton.

Oct. 25, 1838—Townsend, Elcanah, to Wheatley, Elizabeth, by Jas. C. Weller.

Nov. 17, 1838—Moore, James B. to Carter, (Mrs.) Belinda, by Jas. C. Weller.

Nov. 20, 1838—Hughey, Wm., to Ann Fraley, by J. W. Mansfield.

Nov. 27, 1838—Rucker, Young, to Bryan, Maria M.

Nov. 28, 1838—Wilcox, Alonzo to Hudson, Maranda.

Dec. 4, 1838—Mason, Philip D., to Holeman, Margt., by Isaac Harper.

Dec. 11, 1838—Hopper, John, to Glass, Sarah, by Jas. O'Hara, P. C. C.

Dec. 13, 1838—Hooker, Benj. F., to Read, Christian E., by B. G. Rice.

Dec. 17, 1838—Fox, Daniel, to Sikes, Nancy, by Jno. S. Brown.

Dec. 25, 1838—Brindley, Young E., to Reynolds, Eliza Ann, by H. Casidy, P. C. C.

Dec. 31, 1838—Oliver, Walter, to Davis, Jane, by Ch. B. Dallam, Clrk.

1839:

Jan. 3, 1839—Witherspoon, Hiram M., to Armstrong, Jane M., by R. H. Lilly.

Jan. 6, 1839—Machen, Francis, to Jackson, Adelia F., by J. W. Mansfield.

Jan. 9, 1839—Borah, Chesterfield G., to Perkins, Samerrimus, by Jas. W. Mansfield.

Jan. 15, 1839—Bowling, Jesse, to Lorida Kesterson, by Jno. O'Hara.

Jan. 15, 1839—Morris, Jos., to Carlew, Betsey.

Jan. 21, 1839—Smith, Coleman, to Cosby, Mary.

Feb. 4, 1839—Atkinson, Charles P., to Moreland, Mary E., by Geo. Switzer, A. P.

Feb. 6, 1839—Jones, Thos., to Blackburn, by Isaac Harper.

Feb. 11, 1839—Ethridge, Carey, to Gray, Susan, by Dudley Williams.

Feb. 18, 1839—Berry, Wm., to Hubbard, Irena, by Jno. O'Hara.

Feb. 18, 1839—Gore, Wm. H., to George, Maria, by Coleman Ratliff.

Feb. 23, 1839—Cook, James, to Patterson, Elizabeth, by Jas. W. Mansfield.

Mar. 13, 1839—Coon, Thos., to Walker, Mary Ann, by Jno. O'Hara.

Mar. 19, 1839—Lam, John, to Scott, Nancy, by Jno. O'Hara.

Mar. 20, 1839—Langley, Robt. A., to Stafford, Margt. E. C.

Mar. 29, 1839—Black, James S., to Peden, Jannet D., by Jno. Barnett.

Apr. 1, 1839—Greer, Greenberry M., to Bigham, Laurene J., by Jas. C. Weller.

Apr. 6, 1839—Gresham, Drury, to Barnett, Lucinda, by Clement L. Clifton.

Apr. 8, 1839—Walls, Chas. F., to Snelling, Margt. M. A.

Apr. 9, 1839—Dallam, Francis Hy, to Barbour, Camilla J., by Thos. E. Paine, Pro. Epis. Ch.

Apr. 13, 1839—Moore, Wm. H., to Childs, Eliz., by Wm. Cash.

Apr. 15, 1839—Gilkey, Isaac to Dunn, Lucinda E., by Coleman Ratliff.

May 9, 1839—Thompson, Wm., to James, Elizabeth L., by Benj. F. Hawkins, Meth. Ch.

May 14, 1839—Butler, John W., to Oliver, Sarah.

May 20, 1839—Hillyard, Wm. L., to Spence, Mary, by Jno. Travis.

May 28, 1839—Bridges, Andrew, to Stevens, Rebecca, by H. Casidy.

May 28, 1839—Oliver, Andrew W., to Oliver, Elizabeth.

May 29, 1839—Ashridge, Jesse, to Moneymaker, Eliz., by Bailey Adams.

June 4, 1839—Gray, Garret, to Foley, Margt. Jane.

June 26, 1839—McLane, John, to Cash, (Mrs.) Nancy.

June 29, 1839—Larens, James, to Fox, Catherine C.

July 4, 1839—Carr, Edward, to Campbell, Sarah Ann, by Jas. C. Weller.

July 6, 1839—Adams, John, to Dunning, Cerena, by J. A. Cartwright.

July 9, 1839—Bazet, John, to Evans, (Mrs.) Eliz., by Jas. C. Weller.

July 9, 1839—Smith, Coalby, to Armstrong, Eliza Ann, by S. G. Brown.

July 17, 1839—Nance, R. L., to Coffey, Nancy, by W. C. Love, M. G.

July 22, 1839—Haile, Thos. J., to Cannon, Eliz., by W. C. Love, M. G.

Aug. 1, 1839—Holland, John, to Wilcox, (Mrs.) Sarah, by F. C. Usher.

Aug. 6, 1839—Rogers, John W., to Rowland, Helen, by R. H. Lilly.

Aug. 7, 1839—Starnes, James, to Watson, Aurelia P., by Bailey Adams.

Aug. 12, 1839—Smith, John, to Armstrong, Eliz. T.

Aug. 23, 1839—Collie, Isaiah, to Borland, Elizabeth.

Aug. 25, 1839—Tudor, Robertson, to Brown, Sarah, by J. N. Kilpatrick.

Aug. 28, 1839—Louvarn, James L., to Land, Mary Ann, by J. N. Kilpatrick.

Sept. 2, 1839—Leverett, Samuel, to Wells, Eliz., by Jno. S. Brown.

Sept. 2, 1839—Osborn, Benjamin to Eliza L. Wood.

Sept. 6, 1839—Hackney, Wm. J., to Franks, Nancy.

Sept. 12, 1939—Hotten, Isaac J., to Faughn, Sarah, by Coleman Ratliff.

Sept. 14, 1839—Webb, John S., to St. Aubin, Mahala E., by Jno. Barnett.

Oct. 3, 1839—James, Wm., to Mason, (Mrs.) Polly by Jas. C. Weller.

Oct. 7, 1839—Smith, Jas. B. to Gunter, Ruth, by Jas. C. Weller.

Oct. 8, 1839—Crider, Abram S., to Hail, Sarah T., by Jno. Travis.

Oct. 12, 1839—Clark, Joseph, to Walker, Aurenia, by Jas. C. Weller.

Oct. 12, 1839—Moulton, Darius, to Clark, Sarah, by Jno. Barnett.

Oct. 15, 1839—Parsons, Jos., to Ritch, Cynthia.

Oct. 16, 1839—Smith, Jas. W., to Clayton, Mary Ann, by Jno. O'Hara.

Oct. 17, 1839—Smith, James, to Pipkins, Lucinda.

Oct. 17, 1839—Yarborrough, Samuel W., to Howard, Sally, by J. A. Cartwright.

Oct. 18, 1839—Bennett, Bryan B., to Wilson, Nancy, by B. G. Rice, P. C. C.

Oct. 21, 1839—Been, John, to Holloway, Lucy Ann, by Jno. S. Bryan.

Oct. 21, 1839—Wood, Edmund M., to Osborn, Mary J., by Jas. W. Mansfield.

Oct. 23, 1839—Cochran, Crittenden, to Henson, Eliz. Jane, by H. Casidy.

Oct. 23, 1839—Gray, James, to Martin, Jane, by Coleman Ratliff.

Oct. 4, 1839—Butler, John, to Carroll, (Mrs.) Eliz.

Oct. 28, 1839—Deboe, John, to Smith, Maria Burton, by Jas. W. Mansfield.

Oct. 30, 1839—Morse, Wm., Sr., to Borders, (Mrs.) Susannah, by Jas. C. Weller.

Nov. 7, 1839—Cannon, Wm., to East, Rhoda.

Nov. 8, 1839—Maxwell, Alex. N., to Armstrong, Isabella, by Jos. B. Hadden, Presby. Ch.

Nov. 12, 1839—Guess, Alfred, to Smith, Elretta Jane, by F. C. Usher.

Nov. 18, 1839—Gray, James to Holsapple, Mary Ann, by Robt. L. Cobb.

Nov. 18, 1839—Love, Robert, to Machen, Margt. E., by S. G. Burney.

Nov. 26, 1839—Pennington, Wade H., to Dyer, (Mrs.) Jane, by J. A. Cartwright.

Nov. 28, 1839—Armstrong, James H., to Hewit, Sarah, by Jno. Barnett.

Dec. 2, 1839—Hardin, Benony, to Moore, Eliza Ann, by Jas. W. Mansfield.

Dec. 4, 1839—McConnell, Jos. A., to McConnell, Rosannah K.

Dec. 12, 1839—Rankin, Thos. M., to Groves, (Mrs.) Ann, by S. G. Burney, Presby. Ch.

Dec. 14, 1839—Howard, Calvin G., to Carter, Sarah T., by Jno. Barnett.

Dec. 18, 1839—Dawson, Joseph, to Eison, Almira Ann, by Foster Mason.

Dec. 18, 1839—Garrett, Jonas, to Jewell, Alcey, by Jno. O'Hara.

Dec. 18, 1939—Wilcox, Josephus, to Holland, Emily, by F. G. Usher.

Dec. 23, 1839—Gregory, Wm. H., to Matthews, Rebecca, by R. S. Cobb.

Dec. 28, 1839—Eison, Alexander, to Ausenbaugh, Mary Ann, by Foster Mason.

1840:

Jan. 2, 1840—Littlefield, Ezekiel, to Cotton, Sally Ann, by C. Ratliffe.

Jan. 9, 1840—Dukes, Albert, to Brindley, Angelina C.

Jan. 11, 1849—Phillips, Maxwell P., to Shaw, Evelina T., by F. C. Usher.

Jan. 15, 1840—James Childress to Elizabeth Julia Owens, by John O'Hara.

Jan. 15, 1840—Francis W. Dodd, to Dorcas A. Shaw, by F. C. Usher.

Jan. 16, 1840—James Drennan to Frances C. Lunsford, by H. ........

Jan. 20, 1840—Wm. C. B. Ray to Mary M. Wills, by Isaac Harper, P. C. C.

Jan. 25, 1840—Michael F. Wods to Sarah M. Williamson, by R. S. Reeves.

Jan. 25, 1840—Answell W. Ford to Lydia Jones.

Jan. 25, 1840—Thales D. Morrison to Mrs. Pernecey Fowler, by C. Ratliff, P. C. C.

Jan. 29, 1840—John N. Schinchart to Catherine Young, by Foster Mason.

Feb. 3, 1840—Sandford Adams to Sarah Elizabeth Groom.

Feb. 4, 1840—Jacob Storm to Harriet Dunning by John O'Hara.

Feb. 6, 1840—Thomas S. C. Asher to Sarah Ann Asher by W. C. Love, M. G.

Feb. 12, 1840—Clement M. Salzer to Elizabeth Copelane by John O'Hara.

Feb. 15, 1840—Finis E. Crider to Sarah Lowrey, by John Travis.

Feb. 22, 1840—Bartholomew Creekmur to Margaret Dunbar by Isaac Harper.

Mch. 2, 1840—Moses Stone to Lucinda Jane Ingram by Jas. W. Mansfield.

Mch. 2, 1840—John W. Jackson to Jane Ann Adamson, by L. G. Burney.

Mch. 5, 1840—Anthony P. Hardin to Mrs. Lucinda Gallaher, by B. G. Rice, J. P.

Mch. 7, 1840—Caleb W. Stone to Jane Cooper, by Jas. W. Mansfield.

Mch. 9, 1840—Alvis A. Howard to Jane M. Howard, by John Barnett.

Mch. 14, 1840—John Greenup Wheatley to Nancy Palmer, by Jas. C. Weller, J. P.

Mch. 17, 1840—Thomas McNabb to Sarah Roach.

Mch. 23, 1840—Wm. B. Meers to Nancy C. Campbell, by J. A. Cartwright, J. P.

Apl. 1, 1840—Loney Johnson to Elizabeth Petitt.

Apl. 1, 1840—Samuel Stevens to Bulah M. Galusha, by Herington Stevens.

Apl. 2, 1840—Jas. A. Stevens to Myrtilla Browning, by H. Casidy, P. C. C.

Apl. 6, 1840—George W. Sigler to Nancy N. Calvert, by Isaac Harper.

Apl. 8, 1840—Adam Reed to Louisa Smith, by John Taraven.

Apl. 14, 1840—Charles J. Miles to Arcena Ann Rorer by Jas. W. Mansfield.

Apl. 20, 1840—Wheatley, James to Palmer, Armenia.

Apl. 21, 1840—Pendleton, Wm. to Mrs. Anney Pettit, by J. A. Cartwright.

Apl. 27, 1840—Crider, Jacob to Stokes, Araminda, by Jas. W. Mansfield.

May 14, 1840—Quinn, James C. to Wheatley, Mary Jane.

May 18, 1840—Town, Millard C. to Jones, Elizabeth N., by Bailey Adams.

May 27, 1840—Saunders, Absalom to Standrod, Lucinda.

June 10, 1840—James, Harper, to Leech, Minerva, by W. Cash, P. C. C.

June 16, 1840—Davis, Caswell, to Lewis, Mary Jane, by Jas. C. Weller.

June 17, 1840—Young, Benj. F., to Harris, Alcey Ann, by R. S. Cobb.

June 29, 1840—Vickery, John to Kelly, Mrs. Ann, by H. Cassidy.

July 5, 1840—Hughey, Michael D., to Fralie, Sarah, by W. C. Love, M. G.

July 8, 1840—Ratcliffe, Richard S., to Kirkpatrick, Mary, by S. G. Burney.

July 11, 1840—Dunbar, James to Young, Frances, by Isaac Harper.

July 14, 1840—Jones, Thos. P., to Dunning, Sylvia, by B. F. Hawkins.

July 21, 1840—Davis, Thomas G., to Dunbar, Mary, by Isaac Harper, P. C. C.

July 23, 1840—Fletcher, James A., to Asher, Emily, by Isaac Harper.

Aug. 20, 1840—Robertson, John, to Jones, Mary Ann H.

Aug. 22, 1840—Walker, Chittenden D., to Marshall, Nancy Elizabeth, by Saint Turney.

Aug. 31, 1840—Hewitt, James E., to Banister, Sarah, by Robt. L. Cobb, P. C. C.

Aug. 10, 1840—Grubbs, Isaac J., to Ashley, Minerva Ann, by Saml. Turner.

Sept. 10, 1840—Redd, John, to Cartwright, Eliza Ann, by Thos. E. Paine.

Sept. 12, 1840—Dodds, William, to Watkins, Mary, by I. C. Langston.

Sept. 21, 1840—Wells, Abel S., to Dunning, Sally by J. A. Cartwright, P. C. C.

Sept. 28, 1840—Wadlington, Spencer F., to Cooksey, Eliza D.

Sept. 28, 1840—Clark, Matthew M., to Mason, Rebecca S., by Jas. C. Weller.

Sept. 28, 1840—McCaslin, James, Jr., to Bailey, Mrs. Elizabeth, by Jas. C. Weller.

Sept. 30, 1840—Duncan, Harbord, to Chandler, Miss Sally Ann, by Baley Adams.

Oct. 3, 1840—Blackburn, Harrison to Campbell, Mahala, by Jas. W. Mansfield.

Oct. 12, 1840—Early, Thomas J., to Pasher, Miss Mary G., by John Barnett.

Oct. 13, 1840—Franks, Richard, to Boyd, Cynthia, by W. C. Love.

Oct. 21, 1840—Patterson, Robt. B. to Blackburn, Adelia Jane, by Isaac Harper.

Oct. 23, 1840—Bennett, Coleman H. to Brooks, Mary Jane.

Oct. 24, 1840—Holeman, Gideon J., to Holeman, Elizabeth W., by Jacob Holeman, Baptist.

Oct. 28, 1840—Curry, Isaac S. to Riggin, Edna H., by James W. Weller.

Nov. 2, 1840—Peak, John W. to Walker, Emeline, by R. R. Marshall.

Nov. 3, 1840—Walling, Abraham to Ashley, Mary Jane.

Nov. 4, 1840—Hutchinson, Harrison to Brooks, Martha, by H. Hopson.

Nov. 4, 1840—Lee, William R., to Fulks, Nancy, by Robt. S. Cobb.

Nov. 10, 1840—Lumpkin, Charles A., to Baker, Sally, by J. A. Cartwright.

Nov. 13, 1840—Stevenson, David S., to Stevenson, Hannah S., by S. G. Biddle.

Nov. 14, 1840—Parker, Thomas to Earley, Pernecey, by John Barnett.

Nov. 17, 1840—Locker, Laban S., to Goodall, Judith S., by Drury C. Stevens.

Nov. 23, 1840—George, Thomas, to Hobby, Mary.

Nov. 24, 1840—Harris, James T., to Tuke, Pernesey.

Nov. 30, 1840—Johnson, Washington, to Salyer, Elizabeth.

Dec. 2, 1840—Kelly, Philip to Ashbridge, Eliza, by John Barnett.

Dec. 8, 1840—Castleberry, Elijah F. to Gates, Emily, by J. C. Lampton.

Dec. 14, 1840—Hill, Nathaniel B., to Tysone, Honor, by M. Ledbetter.

Dec. 17, 1840—Edwards, Henry M., to Brown, Anne R., by M. Ledbetter.

Dec. 21, 1840—Wyatt, John T., to Crider, Mary Jane, by S. G. Gurney.

Dec. 28, 1840—Dodd, John, to Decker, Frances, by R. G. Gardener.

Dec. 29, 1840—Given, Thomas, to Hunter, Margaretta M., by Joseph Board, M. V.

Dec. 29, 1840—Dawlin, Thomas, to Atkinson, Nancy, by J. C. Langston.

1841:

Jan. 2, 1841—Rhodes, Wm. to Perry, Mrs. Penelope, by Samuel Turner.

Jan. 2, 1841—Jones, John to Roberts, Lucinda, by Isaac Harper.

. . . . . . . . . .1841—Asher, Jefferson C., to Morse, Mary Jane, by W. Cash, P. C. C.

Jan. 4, 1841—Jones, Wm. to Holmes, Malinda by Drury C. Stevens.

Jan. 12, 1841—Owen, Evan to Green, Ruth H., by John O'Hara.

Jan. 19, 1841—Kesterson, George M., to Green, Martha, by John O'Hara.

Jan. 20, 1841—Kilgore, Samuel S., to Brown, Mary Jane, by J. G. Biddle.

Jan. 21, 1841—Scott, John, to Lamb, Sarah, by John O'Hara.

Jan. 23, 1841—Harly, Thomas, to Campbell, Elizabeth J., by J. G. Burney.

Jan. 28, 1841—Hunter, Andrew J., to Cantrell, Sabra B.

Feb. 4, 1841—Bebout, John, to Shoemaker, Sarah Ann, by W. Cash.

Feb. 8, 1841—Marman, Joshua, to Boyd, Elizabeth Ann, by W. C. Love, M. G.

Feb. 9, 1841—Armstrong, David S., to Ford, Jane.

Feb. 9, 1841—Phelps, Thomas Johnson, to Bryan, Nancy W., by J. G. Biddle.

Feb. 18, 1841—Palmer, Sam'l C. to Ritchey, Elizabeth R. by Samuel Turner.

Feb. 22, 1841—Darrah, John W. to Glenn, Catherine, by Jas. W. Mansfield.

Feb. 24, 1841—Glenn, Samuel P., to Brown, Mary G., by Samuel Turner.

Mch. 1, 1841—Bourland, Baylis E. to Donakey, Nanny S., by R. G. Gardner.

Mch. 3, 1841—Leigh, Henry, to White, Elizabeth, by James W. Mansfield.

Mch. 6, 1841—Cassidy, Henry, to Boyd, Maria, by James C. Weller.

Mch. 9, 1841—Stallion (?), Ephraim A., to Harris, Anna Josephine.

Mch. 11, 1841—Hopper, James, to Johnson, Lucinda, by John Barrett.

Mch. 15, 1841—Groom, Richard C., to White, Agnes Anna, by Jas. W. Mansfield.

Mch. 15, 1841—Pendergrass, Robt., to Winks, Mrs. Mary, by J. C. Langston.

Apl. 5, 1841—Groom, Wm. G., to Wall, Margaret, M. A.

Apl. 15, 1841—George, Jesse, to Perkins, Sarah, by James C. Weller.

Apl. 19, 1841—Ashbridge, Joseph, to Harris, Martha.

Apl. 19, 1841—Dodd, Sneed D., to Poor, Sarah Ann, by Samuel Turner.

Apl. 19, 1841—Graham, John C., to Todd, Sarah, by Samuel Turner.

Apl. 20, 1841—McPherson, Cornelius G., to Gorin, Maria E.

Apl. 20, 1841—Murphy, Beverly, to Hewett, Elenor, by John Barnett.

Apl. 26, 1841—Lewis, Braxton B., to James, Sarah, by James C. Weller.

Apl. 27, 1841—Redd, Curtis F. to Oliver, Mary, by J. G. Biddle.

May 17, 1841—Jackson, David to Ladyman, Sarah.

May 20, 1841—Kelly, Daniel to Asbridge, Mrs. Candace, by Janus (?) Mitchell.

May 31, 1841—Matthews, James to Arnold, Temperance, by Robt. L. Cobb.

May 31, 1841—Parker, William to Adams, Aramena.

June 5, 1841—Reice, Presley A., to Mansfield, Susanna M., by J. E. Grace.

June 8, 1841—Oats, Wm. R. to Hillyard, Elizabeth, by John Travis.

June 8, 1841—Hill, Marville, to Banister, Elizabeth, by Baily Adams.

June 19, 1841—Smith, Simon to Darnall, Caroline, by John O'Hara.

June 24, 1841—Slattins, James B., to Dorris, Norma, by Foster Mason.

July 5, 1841—Going, Alfred E., to Wigginton, Marion A.

July 13, 1841—Henny, Robert to Prince, Elizabeth.

July 13, 1841—Braswell, Nicholas to Dobbins, Mrs. Napler, by H. Cassidy.

July 17, 1841—Perkins, James M., to Ray, Mrs. Georgian H. W., by W. Calk, P. C. C.

July 19, 1841—Stone, Sandford to Rowland, Mary, by Robt. L. Cobb,

July 23, 1841—Wynn, Gabriel F., to Lofton, Elender, by Jas. W. Mansfield.

July 27, 1841—Gatewood, Henry, to Lewis, Martha D., by Jas. C. Weller.

July 29, 1841—Scott, James, to Nichols, Nancy, by John O'Hara.

July 27, 1841—Martin, Jefferson, to Driver, Mrs. Elizabeth, by H. Cassidy.

July 30, 1841—Carter, David W., to Bennett, Nancy Jane, by Jas. W. Mansfield.

Aug. 9, 1841—Wells, Jesse to Cherry, Nancy, by J. A. Cartwright.

Aug. 11, 1841—Birner, Stanford G., to Gray, Susan.

Aug. 14, 1841—Smith, Pexton, to Lamb, Polly, by J. A. Cartwright.

Aug. 17, 1841—Doyle, Thomas, to Jones, Mrs. Dowatha T.

Aug. 19, 1841—Franks, Joshua, to Guess, Elizabeth, by Jas. C. Weller.

Aug. 21, 1841—Dunn, Madison F., to Dunn, Mrs. Lucinda F., by H. Cassidy.

Aug. 31, 1841—Armstrong, Chittenden, to Howard, Mrs. Mary.

Sept. 7, 1841—Hyde, Daniel N., to Reed, Louisa, by Samuel Turner.

Sep. 11, 1841—King, Terry D., to Brooks, Mrs. Eleanor, by Joel E. Grace.

Sept. 14, 1841—Hexton, William, to Dobbins, Margaret Ann, by John Barnett.

Sept. 16, 1841—Pearce, Robert, to Rogers, Martha A., by John Barnett.

Sept. 23, 1841—Brown, Thomas P., to Drennen, Lucinda, by Ezekiel Hancock.

Sept. 23, 1841—Parks, Wm., to Browning, Martha, by Robt. L. Cobb.

Oct. 2, 1841—Brown, Hugh M., to Stafford, Providence, by J. C. Langston.

Oct. 2, 1841—Henson, Jas. J., to Peak, Sarah, by J. C. Langston

Oct. 13, 1841—Cotton, Jonathan, to Hepton, Mary Lucinda, by John Barnett.

Oct. 14, 1841—Cook, Cordy, to Hooper, Mary Ann.

Oct. 23, 1841—Starnes, Solomon, to Kelly, Sarah, by Robt. L. Cobb.

Oct. 25, 1841—Quisenberry, Wm., to McConnell, Lucy A.

Oct. 27, 1841—Calvert, Spencer W., to Wales, Elvira A., by Isaac Harper.

Oct. 26, 1841—Lamb, John W., to Glass, Mrs. Jane, by S. Scott.

Nov. 2, 1841—Wyatt, Alfred M., to Johnson, Martha S., by J. G. Riddle.

Nov. 4, 1841—Taylor, Rhesa, to Glass, Rhoda Jane, by J. A. Cartwright.

Nov. 13, 1841—Stout, Solomon, to Scott, Nancy.

Nov. 15, 1841—Oliver, Cornelius J., to Etheridge, Arsena.

Nov. 15, 1841—Gray, John, to Dunn, Lucretia M., by J. C. Grace.

Nov. 17, 1841—Fralick, John, to Bugg, Sintha Ann, by John Irwin.

Nov. 22, 1841—Prescott, Davis, to Sanders, Sarah, by Coleman Ratcliff.

Nov. 23, 1841—Chunk (?), James B., to Haile, Mrs. Mary W., by Herrington Stevens.

Nov. 25, 1841—Pickering, William C., to Pickering, Miss Pernecy, by John O'Hara.

Nov. 27, 1841—Rucker, John H. to Bembray, Miss Nancy, by Robt. L. Cobb.

Nov. 29, 1841—Koon, Kinson, to Glenn, Miss Elizabeth, by James W. Mansfield.

Nov. 30, 1841—Morris, John G., to Brooks, Miss Mary Ann, by Baily Adams.

Dec. 7, 1841—Clark, Reuben, to Weller, Miss Susan C., by J. G. Biddle.

Dec. 14, 1841—Bush, Tom, to Clark, Miss Lydia, by Barnett, John.

Dec. 18, 1841—Gray, Nathan O., to Hall, Mildred W., by John Barnett.

Dec. 20, 1841—Lamb, Andrew Jackson, to Nichols, Sarah, by James C. Weller.

Dec. 20, 1841—Beck, Thomas J., to Leigh, Mary Jane, by Herrington Stevens.

Dec. 20, 1841—White, Wm., to Camer, Sarah, by Eznca Hancock.

Dec. 21, 1841—Dunbar, Wm., to Young, Sarah, by Isaac Harper.

1842:

Jan. 4, 1842—Green, Wm. H., to Butcher (Mrs.) Mary, by J. C. Langston.

Jan. 13, 1842—Kilgore, Jonathan W., to Gray, Jinsey, by Joel E. Grace.

Jan. 18, 1842—Ingram, Eli B., to Fulks, Marthew, by John Barrett.

Feb. 2, 1842—Childers, Richard, to Cherry, Malinda, by John O'Hara.

Feb. 3, 1842—Holder, Shadrack, to Dicken, Elspy, by J. C. Langston.

Feb. 5, 1842—Thelford, King, to Wilson, Jane, by Robt. S. Cobb.

Feb. 21, 1842—Shoemaker, Wm., to Riggs, L. ........., by J. G. Biddle.

Feb. 7, 1842—McCormack, Wm., to Oliver, Melicia Jane.

Feb. 7, 1842—Joyner, Carroll, to Sheridan, by J. A. Cartwright.

Feb. 7, 1842—Halstead, Chas. G., to Boyd, Sarah, J. M., by S. Scott.

Feb. 8, 1842—Blalock, David II., to Creekmur, Nancy, by J. W. Temple.

Feb. 9, 1842—McCrory, Hugh, to Mills, Elizabeth, by J. C. Langston.

Feb. 14, 1842—Johnson, Thomas S., to Quisenberry, Eliza Ann, by J. G. Biddle.

Feb. 21, 1842—Dunning, John, to Young, (Mrs.) Sarah, by J. A. Cartwright.

Feb 24, 1842—Creekmur, Timothy, to Nichols, Elizabeth, by Jas. C. Weller.

Feb. 24, 1842—Easley, Benj. H., to Scott, (Mrs.) Mary, by J. N. Temple, M. G.

Feb. 26, 1842—Williams, Saml. P., to Doom, Harriet, by Robt. L. Cobb.

Feb. 26, 1842—Craxton, Thomas, to Martin, Eliz., by J. C. Langston.

Feb. 28, 1842—Farris, Robt. R., to Turley, Eliz., by J. W. Mansfield.

Mar. 1, 1842—Howard, Logan L., to Howard, Patsey, by John Barnett.

Mar. 21, 1842—Anderson, Shelby G., to Steely, Mary M. C., by Rev. S. Scott.

Mar. 22, 1842—Beardon, Madison, to Nichols, Eliz., by R. F. Hawk, M. E. Ch.

Mar. 23, 1842—Ellis, Matthew, to Timmons, Eliz. A., by John Barnett.

Apr. 6, 1842—Wadley, Jackson, to Williams, Margt., by J. N. Temple, M. G.

Apr. 12, 1842—Maxwell, Washington P., to Adamson, Isabella, by W. Love, M. G.

Apr. 14, 1842—Helms, Greenberry, to Crowell, Patsey, by I. Harper.

Apr. 29, 1842—Rucker, Joshua, to Crow, Zerilda M., by Stallard Scott.

Apr. 30, 1842—Doom, John D., to Love, Sarah M., by Ch. B. Dallam.

May 4, 1842—McElhany, Yancy, to Marshall, Joanna, by R. R. Marshall.

May 7, 1842—Stone, Imander P., to Johnson, Isabella Jane, by Foster Mason.

May 12, 1842—Cato, Miles C., to Nicholas, Caroline, by F. Hawkins.

May 16, 1842—Oliver, Levin T., to Sunnen, Delitha.

May 25, 1842—Coleman, James, to Right, Orpha, by J. G. Biddle.

May 25, 1842—Tyler, Marcus M., to Mims, Sarah Jane, by J. G. Biddle.

May 27, 1842—Hall, James, to Tolley, Jane, by J. G. Biddle.

May 27, 1842—Doom, Harvey, to Hildreth, Mary E., by J. C. Langston.

June 6, 1842—Dawson, David P., to Woodside, (Mrs.) Eliz., by W. C. Love, M. G.

June 6, 1842—Wall, John B., to Cartwright, Arabella, by J. G. Biddle.

June 7, 1842—Wilkinson, Wm., to Layton, Nina S., by J. N. Temple, M. E. Ch.

June 16, 1842—Cannon, Joseph, to East, Eliz., by John Barnett.

June 20, 1842—Chandler, Solomon King, to Brown, Sarah L., by J. C. Langston.

June 28, 1842—Jourdan, Abraham, to Ford, (Mrs.) Martha, by Jas. C. Weller.

June 29, 1842—Norman, Solomon, to Brooks, (Mrs.) Mahala, by Jas. C. Weller.

July 14, 1842—Littlefield, David, to Barnes, Maria S., by Stallard Scott.

July 16, 1842—Johnson, Wm. W., to Fraley, Seeny, by W. Cash.

July 18, 1842—Bass, Michael, to Lucas, Eliz., by J. N. Temple, M. G.

July 18, 1842—Riggs, Allen M., to Irwin, Harriet, by J. C. Langston.

July 19, 1842—Cummings, Elijah W., to Oliver, Lydia G.

July 28, 1842—Massey, Geo. S., to Mitchusson, Eliza Ann, by J. G. Biddle.

Aug. 2, 1842—Fraley, James, to Robertson, Margt., by Jas. C. Weller.

Aug. 2, 1842—Blalock, Henry J., to Scott, Nancy, by E. S. Scott.

Aug. 4, 1842—Smiley, Alex, Jr., to Gallaspie, Susan, by Jno. Barnett.

Aug. 8, 1842—Stone, John P., to Jones, Minerva, by J. C. Weller.

Aug. 9, 1842—Johnson, Daniel, to Dunning, Katherine, by J. A. Cartwright.

Aug. 10, 1842—Atkins, Jas. R., to Oliver, Ann Martha, by Ch. B. Dallam.

Aug. 17, 1842—Chandler, King Solomon, to Stephens, Jane, by Baley Adams.

Aug. 20, 1842—Stevens, Elijah, to Dunn, Elizabeth, by Elijah Hawes.

Aug. 24, 1842—Machen, Melzer B., to Stevens, Lucretia, by Herrington Stevens.

Aug. 25, 1842—Cooper, Archibald S., to Murray, (Mrs.) Eliza, by John Barnett.

Aug. 27, 1842—Bishop, Daniel to Ashley, (Mrs.) Betsy, by E. S. Scott.

Sept. 2, 1842—Nichols, Wm., Sr., to Price, (Mrs.) Lavina, by H. Stevens.

Sept. 7, 1842—Rodgers, Robert, to Pettit, Perlenia, by C. Scott.

Sept. 11, 1842—Shelby, Jacob, to Frazee, Sally, by Foster Mason.

Sept. 19, 1842—Reynolds, James, to Moore, Cyndaella, by Isaac Harper.

Oct. 3, 1842—Brasher, Andrew J., to Stone, Temperance G., by Joel E. Grace.

Oct. 6, 1842—Smith, Daniel W., to Hawkins, Matilda, by James Mitchell.

Oct. 7, 1842—Travis, Wm. B., to Bugg, Mary Catharine by W. C. Love, M. G.

Oct. 10, 1842—Morehead, James, to Sigler, Patience.

Oct. 10, 1842—Francis, Alfred, to Cherry, Mahala, by John O'Hara.

Oct. 20, 1842—Littlefield, Solomon, to Barnes, Nancy, by S. Scott.

Oct. 24, 1842—Hall, James P., to Davis, Hannah E., by Jas. S. Mitchell.

Oct. 29, 1842—Cochran, Thos., Jr., to Stevens, Lucinda, by J. C. Langston.

Oct. 31, 1842—Collie, Wm. C., to Duncan, Elizabeth, by John Barnett.

Nov. 1, 1842—Childers, Thomas, to Ezell, Zilpha, by E. S. Scott.

Nov. 1, 1842—Yates, James R., to Chandler, Nancy G., by J. C. Langston.

Nov. 5, 1842—Crin, Wm. N., to Gray, Lucretia, by E. S. Scott.

Nov. 8, 1842—Bond, Wm. B., to Kivel, Macey N.

Nov. 9, 1842—Ramey, Wm., to Satterfield, Eliza, by Jas. C. Weller.

Nov. 15, 1842—Satterfield, Jesse, to Martin, Eliz., by Jas. C. Weller.

Nov. 21, 1842—Barnes, Geo. W., to Littlefield, Eliz., by S. Scott.

Nov. 21, 1842—Fox, Azel T., to Young, Ann F., by F. Mason.

Nov. 21, 1842—McChesney, A. W., to Fryer, Sarah S., by Jas. C. Weller.

Nov. 21, 1842—Benice, Jonathan, to Grubbs, Polly E., by Jas. W. Mansfield.

Nov. 26, 1842—Freeman, M. S., to Dorroh, Eliz. A., by Jas. W. Mansfield.

Nov. 28, 1842—Stone, W. J., to Midgett, Pensy, by H. Casidy.

Nov. 29, 1842—Dennington, Jas. H., to Crowe, Milly Ann, by J. C. Langston.

Nov. 29, 1842—Kilgore, Jonathan S., to Tisen, Naoma S., by Jas. C. Weller.

Dec. 2, 1842—Bradford, A. E., to McKeeny, (Mrs.) Nancy B., by John S. Brown.

Dec. 3, 1842—Maxwell, A. N., to Parr, Agnes A., by W. C. Love.

Dec. 10, 1842—Mallory, Stephen A., to Rucker, (Mrs.) Eliza by Joel T. Grace.

Dec. 19, 1842—Cain, Stephen, to Rodgers, Emily, by Jas. C. Weller.

Dec. 24, 1842—Ashridge, Joseph, to Jackson, (Mrs.) Polly, by John Barnett.

Dec. 26, 1842—Elder, Samuel B., to Smith, Sarah Elizabeth, by W. C. Love, M. G.

Dec. 26, 1842—Johnson, Jesse W., to Wilcox, Maria L., by H. Stevens.

Dec. 26, 1842—Hughey, Coleman, to Moreland, Eliz., by J. N. Temple.

Dec. 31, 1842—Houghton, Henry, to Smith, Mary Ann, by Jas. C. Weller.

Dec. 31, 1842—Costilow, James, to Conn, Eliza Ann, by H. Stevens.

1843:

Jan. 2, 1843—Harris, Wm. G., to Bond, Sarah Frances.

Jan. 2, 1843—Taylor, Samuel, to Martin, Louisa T., by Ch. B. Dallam.

Jan. 4, 1843—Cox, Willoby, to Walston, Angeline.

Jan. 7, 1843—Lamb, William, to McElroy, Laetitia, by E. S. Scott.

Jan. 16, 1843—Vincent, Coleman C., to Johnson, Permelia, by Ch. B. Dallam.

Jan. 16, 1843—Hawkins, John H., to Armstrong, Malinda, by Jos. B. Hadden.

Jan. 16, 1843—Ryne, Michael, to Rodgers, Rhoda, by Jas. C. Weller.

Jan. 17, 1843—Taylor, Wm., to Cochran, Margaret, by J. C. Langston.

Jan. 18, 1843—Bugg, Wm. M., to Draper, Angeline, by Joel E. Grace.

Jan. 31, 1843—George, Jas. Ford, to Dycus, Laureny Ann, by Jas. C. Weller.

Jan. 31, 1843—Ballard, J. C., to Conway, Susan, by Robt. Fish, M. G.

Feb. 4, 1843—McQuigg, Wesley, to Colt, (Mrs.) Drusilla, by Robt. L. Cobb.

Feb. 6, 1843—Rodgers, John, to Pettit, Sally, by Walthum, J. C. Caldwell.

Feb. 6, 1843—Pettit, Jonas, to Hunter, Elvira Jane, by E. S. Scott.

Feb. 7, 1843—Steel, Young E., to Moore, Melinda Jane, by W. C. Love.

Feb. 8, 1843—German, Asa, to Mercer, Helen R.

Feb. 9, 1843—Faulkner, Chas G., to Blanks, Eddy, by John O'Hara.

Mar. 15, 1843—Rascal, John P., to Holmes, Dorcas Ann, by J. G. Biddle.

Mar. 16, 1843—Knight, Burrell, to Cherry, (Mrs.) Mary Ann, by Wm. P. C. Caldwell.

Mar. 16, 1843—Knight, Warren, to Knight, Margt. Jane, by Wm. P. C. Caldwell.

Mar. 27, 1843—Haden, Richard A., to Armstrong, Eliz., by Jos. B. Hadden.

Mar. 28, 1843—Rohabach, Conrad, to Moneymaker, Sarah, by Bailey Adams.

Mar. 30, 1843—Brown, Alex. C., to Radcliffe, Martha A., by Joel E. Grace.

Apr. 1, 1845—Timmons, Thomas, to Head, (Mrs.) Mary, by John Barnett.

Apr. 1, 1843—Starling, Israel, to Franklin, Idelia, by Jas. C. Weller.

Apr. 3, 1843—Satterfield, Jas. F., to Weller, Henry Ann, by J. G. Biddle.

Apr. 4, 1843—Young, Lewis, to Jones, Orleany, by Foster Mason.

Apr. 8, 1843—Whitney, Silas, to Cudd, Charlotte, by J. G. Biddle.

Apr. 10, 1843—Davis, Wm. B., to Bebbett, Eliza A., by R. L. Cobb.

Apr. 11, 1843—Stevenson, Jas., to Kendrick, Lucinda, by Wm. L. Langston.

Apr. 14, 1843—Dexter, Silas, Jr., to Bright, (Mrs.) Priscilla, by Wm. Cash, J. P.

Apr. 15, 1843—Snelling, Roger B., to Fowler, Elvira, by Wm. P. C. Caldwell.

Apr. 21, 1843—Glass, Geo. R., to Storm, Nancy, by John O'Hara.

May 6, 1843—Gregory, James, to Holeman, Margt. M.

May 10, 1843—Coon, Lewis, to Reynolds, Mary Jane, by R. L. Cobb.

May 13, 1843—Owen, E. N., to Young, Sarah Ann, by J. G. Biddle.

May 23, 1843—Henry, Wm., to Frazer, Henrietta, by S. S. Young.

June 3, 1843—Dobbins, Jas. W., to Golliher, Eliza, by J. G. Biddle.

June 6, 1843—Sills, John, to Lamb, Catherine, by H. Cassidy.

June 19, 1843—Barnes, Cullen, to Littlefield, Rebecca, by C. Scott.

June 19, 1843—Snelling, Reubin, to Draper, Ann Eliza, by Jas. W. Mansfield.

July 3, 1843—Davis, Thomas M., to Roach, Emily, by Robt. Fish.

July 4, 1843—Poe, Thomas, to Ashby, (Mrs.) Polly, by John O'Hara.

July 5, 1843—Lucky, Richard H., to Weller, Emily S., by Robt. Fish.

July 12, 1843—Kevil, Wm. H., to Bass, Mary Thomas, by Elijah Stevens.
July 19, 1843—Harris, Wm. H., to Lofton, Mary.
July 26, 1843—Skinner, Frederick H., to Catlett, Helen M., by S. C. Templeton.
July 31, 1843—Weeks, Francis A., to Martin, Eliz. P., by Isaac Harper.
Aug. 10, 1843—Bennett, Bryant W., to White, (Mrs.) Nancy, by Jas. W. Mansfield.
Aug. 28, 1843—Jarrett, Daniel B., to Peck, Nancy Eliz., by H. Cassidy.
Aug. 28, 1843—Bashears, Wilson, to More, Susan, by Jas. C. Weller.
Aug. 29, 1843—Cooksey, Jesse, to Meade, Eliz., by Elder S. Scott.
Aug. 29, 1843—Avey, Wilfred, to Hammond, Tymandra, by Robt. L. Cobb.
July 5, 1843—Martin, Richard, to Bennett, Ruth Ann, by R. L. Cobb.
Sept. 7, 1843—Moneymaker, William, to Holloway, Lucy M.
Sept. 7, 1843—Meek, John D., to Champion, Martha T.
Sept. 8, 1843—Rodgers, Absolem, to Saunders, Mary.
Sept. 9, 1843—Simpson, James, to Franklin (Mrs.), Susanna, by Foster Mason.
Sept. 11, 1843—Ramsey, John J., to Walker, Maria, by W. C. Love, M. G.
Sept. 12, 1843—Stafford, Enoch P., to Martin, Susan Ann, by J. C. Langston.
Sept. 18, 1843—Saunders, John, to Standard, Melvina.
Nov. 14, 1843—Brown, Benj. F., to Woolf, Mary Ann, by W. P. C. Caldwell.
Nov. 15, 1843—Acres, Joseph, to Hays, Mary, by Eld. S. Scott.
Nov. 20, 1843—McDowell, Robt., to McDowell, Martha Ann, by R. R. Marshall.
Nov. 27, 1843—Lowry, David, to McDowell, Frances, by W. C. Love, M. G.
Nov. 30, 1843—Carr, James R., to Dallam, Jane M., by F. B. Nash.
Dec. 2, 1843—Crickmur, Ansey, to Howard, Nancy.
Dec. 7, 1843—Williams, Stephen, to Hale, Rachel E. J., by T. J. Hale.
Dec. 14, 1843—Hogan, Jas. P., to Rowland, Nancy, by Eld. S. Scott.
Dec. 19, 1843—Brooks, John G. W., to Bennett, Harriett, by H. Cassidy.
Dec. 18, 1843—Ritch, Jas., to Edwards, (Mrs.) Sarah Ann, by Baily Adams.
Dec. 21, 1843—Holleman, Edmund, to Grubbs, Rebecca Ann, by R. L. Cobb.
Dec. 22, 1843—Wadley, James, to Creekmur, Phebe, by J. C. Hale, M. G.
Dec. 27, 1843—Landrum, Hubbard B., to Felker, Judith Ann, by W. C. Love, M. G.

1844:

Jan. 5, 1844—Snoden (Soden), Wm., to Long, Casander, by R. L. Cobb.
Jan. 5, 1814—Nickels, Wilbern, to Orr, Julia Ann, by H. Cassidy.
Jan. 11, 1844—Dabney, Cornelius T., to Wylie, Maria L., by Saml. C. Baldwin.
Jan. 16, 1844—Hanberry, Thos. W., to George, Rebecca.
Jan. 18, 1944—Gray, Garret, to Cooper, Elizabeth, by W. P. C. Caldwell.
Jan. 19, 1844—Pool, Jas. A. P., to Childress, Mary, by Wm. C. P. Caldwell.
Jan. 19, 1844—White, Abraham, to Carner, Alice, by Ezma Hancock.
Jan. 20, 1844—Stevens, John, to Hewitt, Melste, by S. S. Templeton.
Jan. 22, 1844—Lang, Patrick H., to White, Lucinda, by W. P. C. Caldwell.

Jan. 23, 1844—Clark, John B., to Hogan, Martha, by Eld. S. Scott.

Jan. 24, 1844—Smith, Hezekiah, to Jordan, Ann Eliz., by Jae. W. Mansfield.

Jan. 24, 1844—Wadlington, Wm. B., to Holmes, Margt., Jane, by F. E. Roberts.

Jan. 30, 1844—West, Wm. R. to Dunning, (Mrs.) Mary, by Jas. C. Weller.

Jan. 31, 1844—Wynn, Nathan O., to Wilburn, Keziah.

Feb. 1, 1844—Lacey, Earl to Gore, Permelia H., by Saml. G. Babom.

Feb. 7, 1844—Ennis, Wm. B., to Gregory, Eliza, by R. L. Cobb.

Feb. 14, 1844—Jones, Wm. M., to Langston, Sarah J., by R. Lancaster.

Feb. 14, 1844—Low, Abraham H., to Guess, Trecia Ann, by J. W. Mansfield.

Feb. 22, 1844—Jones, Jordan D., to Layton, Mary, by R. L. Cobb.

Feb. 22, 1844—Baldwin, Aquilla, to Layton, Martha, by R. L. Cobb

Feb. 27, 1844—Lamb, Allan P., to Phelps, Elvira, by Foster Mason.

Feb. 27, 1844—Morgan, Jas. Q. C., to Ford, Frances, by Wm. C. P. Caldwell.

March 5, 1844—Wyatt, Benj. B. Mansfield, Sarah Ann, by Joel E. Grace.

March 8, 1844—Craig, James, to Maxwell, Mary by Joseph Hadden.

March 20, 1844—Brigham, Alfred W., to Soden, Ann E., by H. Cassidy.

March 22, 1844—Hubert, Zebulon B., to Ellis, Rhoda.

March 28, 1844—Rogers, Wm. I., to Rogers, Charity E.

April 3, 1844—Holder, Aaron to McFurson, Sarah, by J. C. Langston.

April 9, 1844—Bibb, David M., to Grubbs, Susannah J., by R. L. Cobb.

April 17, 1844—Herrald, Wm., to Wright, Aphey.

April 28, 1844—Powers, James M., to Boyd, Eliza Ann, by John A. Brown.

May 1, 1844—Henson, Thomas, to Layton, Jane, by R. R. Marshall.

May 21, 1844—Krone, John W., to Hildreth, Charlotte, by R. L. Cobb.

May 25, 1844—Rucker, Wm. M., to Rascoe, Martha, by Jas. C. Weller.

June 15, 1844—Nichols, Wm. to Price, Mary, by Jas. C. Weller.

June 18, 1844—Satterfield, Jesse, to Beardon, Frances, by Elijah Stevens.

June 20, 1844—Wallice, John V., to Perkins, Malinda P., by Jas. C. Weller.

July 13, 1844—Luch, John W., to Stromatt, Adah B., by Isaac Harper.

July 13, 1844—Cook, Wm., to Cobb, Sophia M.

July 23, 1844—Brown, George G., to Mercer, Caroline, by T. E. Roberts.

July 24, 1844—Young, Hiram, to Jones, Nancy, by Foster Mason.

July 29, 1844—Rascoe, James E. B., to Brewer, Minerva T., by Jas. C. Weller.

Aug. 1, 1844—Guess, Thos. C., to Guess, Nancy, by J. C. Weller.

Aug. 1, 1844—Johnson, Galey, to Dillingham, Francis, by J. C. Weller.

Aug. 12, 1844—McQuigg, Henry, to Holloway, Mildred, by R. L. Cobb.

July 13, 1844—Sullivan, Elijah C., to Lowry, Martha—Never married (C. B. D.) (Dallam)

Sept. 4, 1844—McCormack, Wesley, to McFarland, Phebe, by Wm. Cash.

Sept. 7, 1844—Carner, Daniel, to Hail, Elizabeth E., by Isaac Harper.

Sept. 18, 1844—Lowry, James S., to Carner, Mary A., by F. Wurey (Caldwell Co. Sct.)

Sept. 20, 1844—Cruce, Ewell, to Dobbins, Elizabeth A., by Joseph B. Hadden, C. M. Pres Ch.

Sept. 23, 1844—Ritch, Obadiah, to Duncan, Mary.

Oct. 5, 1844—Nichols, Josiah, to Creekmur, Margaret, by Jas. C. Weller.

Oct. 7, 1844—Asbury, James S. to Harris, Pernecy.

Oct. 10, 1844—Robertson, Elder, to Elvira Ann, by W. C. Love, M. G.

Oct. 11, 1844—Connell, Cornelius to Smith, Mrs. Elizabeth, by F. W. Wren.

Oct. 19, 1844—George, Enoch P., to Rucker, Laura.

Oct. 22, 1844—Dunning, George W., to Lester, Sarah Ann, by Eld. S. Scott.

Oct. 29, 1844—Krone, James to Lakman, Jane, by R. L. Cobb.

Nov. 4, 1844—Evans, Enoch P., to Stone, Nancy E., by Jas. W. Mansfield.

Nov. 13, 1844—Wimbleduff, Henry, to Quisenberry, Nancy, by Wm. P. C. Caldwell.

Nov. 14, 1844—Scott, Aaron G., to Pickering, Martha W., by Foster Mason.

Nov. 15, 1844—Perry, Wm. H., to Lacey, Pernecy, by F. W. Wrey, P. C. C.

Nov. 21, 1844—McGough, John S., to Harper, Dicey Terrissa, by W. C. Love, M. G.

Nov. 26, 1844—Champion, Alfred H., to Scott, Mary L., by J. G. Biddle.

Nov. 30, 1844—Baker, Larkin, to James, Rebecca, by Jas. C. Weller.

Dec. 4, 1844—Sherley, Samuel F., to Sigler, Clarissa, by F. W. Urey.

Dec. 7, 1844—Prince, John Clark, to White, Merlissa, by Wm. P. C. Caldwell.

Dec. 11, 1844—Sumner, Nazworthy, to Brewer, Mary Elizabeth, by Jas. C. Weller.

Dec. 16, 1844—Campbell, Thomas, to Dunlan, Mrs. Mary F., by Geo. Beckett.

Dec. 16, 1844—Hiatt, James W., to Layton, Martha, by F. W. Urey.

Dec. 21, 1844—Cotton, Wm., to Faughn, Francis.

Dec. 21, 1844—May, August, to Kohn, Fanny, by Jas. C. Weller.

Dec. 23, 1844—Simpson, Saml. M., to Stone, Sarah, by Wm. Cash, (Caldwell Co., Sct.)

Dec. 26, 1844—Holeman, Beverly, to Ashridge, Catherine, by Elder S. Scott.

1845:

Jan. 1, 1845—Butler, John W., to Veatch, Jane, by John Barnett.

Jan. 2, 1845—Gore, Mastin, to McCoy, Pembrock.

Jan. 6, 1845—Bishop, James to Ratliff, Mrs. Margaret, by F. W. Urey.

Jan. 9, 1845—Stills, Lawson, to Gray, Rosanna A.

Jan. 14, 1845—Kilgore, John M., to Gray, Mary, by F. W. Urey, P. C. C.

Jan. 14, 1845—Coon, Benj. A., to Boyd, Laura, by Jas. C. Weller.

Jan. 15, 1845—Gresham, Lawson S., to Carter, Martha Ann, by John Barnet.

Jan. 16, 1845—Morse, Allen, to Cooksey, Celia Ann, by Eld. S. Scott.

Jan. 18, 1845—Miller, Wm., to Glenn, Mary Elizabeth, by Willis Champion, Caldwell Co., Sct.

Jan. 18, 1845—Stewart, Wm. R., to Guess, Constance by Thos. I. C. Hale, Caldwell Co., Sct.

Jan. 20, 1845—Ford, H. G., to Reese, Mrs. Susannah M., by Wm. P. C. Caldwell.

Jan. 20, 1845—Learen, Oliver, Jr., to Hall, Pernecy P.

Jan. 25, 1845—Lewis, John, to Pennington, Mary Louisa, by Wm. Cash.

Jan. 25, 1845—Wheatley, Isaac H., to Palmer, Mary Ann, by Jas. C. Weller.

Jan. 27, 1845—Hall, John G., to Hall, Nancy T.

Jan. 31, 1845—Gaines, Daniel W., to Smith, Mary.

Feb. 8, 1845—Clinton, John E., to Campbell, Elizabeth, by Gabriel Sisk.

Feb. 10, 1845—Young, Isaac, to Franklin, Mary, by Foster Mason.

Feb. 12, 1845—Hodge, Darien, to Gray, Elizabeth.

Feb. 17, 1845—Duvall, Thos. M., to Holmes, Mary H., by F. W. Urey.

Feb. 24, 1845—Haley, Samuel B. (Mor) to Reed, Maria Jane, by W. Cash.

Feb. 22, 1845—Gray, Needham C., to Freeman, Eliza Jane.

Feb. 23, 1845—Pearcey, Allen C., to Pearcey, Arreney.

Feb. 27, 1845—Lane, Wm. H., to Carner, Elizabeth, by Mitchell Jenkins.

Mar. 5, 1845—Griffith, Wm. H., to Greer, Permelia, by Eldr. S. Scott.

Mar. 5, 1845—Blackburn, Harrison H., to Shirley, Hester Ann, by F. W. Urey.

Mar. 11, 1845—Crow, James M., to Kilgore, Mary M., by F. E. Roberts.

Mar. 12, 1845—Morris, Thomas, to Veatch, Mrs. Elizabeth Jane, by John Barnett.

Mar. 20, 1845—Wagner, Jacob, to Johnson, Sarah J., by J. G. Biddle, Caldwell Co. Sct.

Apl. 7, 1845—Ritch, Jesse, to Holesapple, Julia Ann, by Robt. L. Cobb.

Apl. 7, 1845—Sauvage, Valentine, to Lake, Barbara, by Robt. L. Cobb.

Apl. 7, 1845—Duncan, Stephen, to Burnett, Sophia, by Collins Hoose, Caldwell Co., Sct.

Apl. 8, 1845—Darnall, Elijah to Dunn, Mrs. Matilda, by Jas. C. Weller.

Apl. 16, 1845—McConnell, Wm. B., to Brown, Temperance Ann, by Jacob Holeman.

Apl. 24, 1845—Crowell, Sanders to Laughlin, Sarah Jane, by Jas. C. Weller.

Apl. 30, 1845—Morehead, Wm. H., to Jones, Nancy M., by Jas. C. Weller.

May 1, 1845—Thompson, Spencer, to West, Elizabeth E., by J. A. Cartwright.

May 10, 1845—Hubbard, Nathaniel, to Penny, Sarah, by Jas. C. Weller.

May 12, 1845—Cook, James S., to Lester, Amarilla, by Eld. S. Scott.

May 12, 1845—Matthews, John to Gregory, Sarah, by John S. Brown, J. C. C.

May 14, 1845—McKenney, Warner W., to Campbell, Lavina S.

May 17, 1845—Dandge, Rezin H. J., to Wigginton, Miss Cornelia Ann, by J. G. Biddle (Davidge?).

May 22, 1845—Brown, Timothy E., to Ennis, Mrs. Maria Ann, by Wm. Cash.

May 23, 1845—Ellis, John to Timmons, Minerva.

May 28, 1845—Groom, James Bevin, to Snelling, Elizabeth E., by W. P. C. Caldwell.

June 11, 1845—Rice, Henry J., to Tally, Maria, by R. L. Cobb.

June 14, 1845—Hollman, Wm. W., to Cash, Jane S.

June 14, 1845—Cash, Littleton F., to Harris, Edney S.

June 20, 1845—Bradshaw, Isuns, to Caldwell, Jane, by J. G. Biddle.

July 2, 1845—Johnson, Washington, to Hodges, Ann.

July 7, 1845—Boaz, Wm. S., to Trimmons, (?), Sarah, by John Barnett.

July 7, 1845—Davis, Thomas G., to Young, Polly Ann, by Whitnell Jenkins.

July 10, 1845—Carver, John Jr., to Cartwright, Sarah Frances, by J. A. Cartwright.

July 12, 1845—Wells, Thomas, to Young, Lucretia E., by Howard Cassidy. J. P. C.

July 14, 1845—Radcliffe, Wm. S., to Walker, Margaret, by W. C. Love, M. G.

July 24, 1845—Ashridge, John Henry, to Powell, Sarah, by Wm. Cash, J. C. C.

July 26, 1845—Walling, Geo. M. to Menick, Elizabeth, by H. Cassidy.

July 28, 1845—Sterritt, John, to Smith, Luvenia, by H. Cassidy.

July 29, 1845—Perkins, Jefferson G., to Lady, Martha Ama, by Isaac N. Wilcox, J. C. C.

Aug. 6, 1845—Mackey, Robert to Dunn, Adelisa M.

Aug. 7, 1845—Stovall, David, to Anderson, Eliza, by M. A. Rucker, J. C. C.

Aug. 12, 1845—Jones, Elijah, to Fitts, Sally, by John Browne.

Aug. 16, 1845—Woodard, Wm., to Adams, Esther Jane, by J. N. Wilcox, J. C. C.

Aug. 18, 1845—Gore, Notley D., to Boyd, Adaline.

Aug. 19, 1845—Freman, Wm. H., to Coon, Martha Jane.

Aug. 20, 1845—Hitchcock, John V., to Fleming, Mary, by R. R. Marshall.

Aug. 25, 1845—Hopper, David, to Crow, Minerva J.

Sep. 1, 1845—Campbell, Edward Green to Ballard, Mary E., by F. W. Urey.

Sep. 3, 1845—Davis, Jeremiah S. to Harris, Martha Jane, by Jas. C. Weller.

Sep. 8, 1845—Crayne, James to Guess, Mary, by Claiborne Wilson.

Sep. 15, 1845—Travis, Wiley, to Cherry, Henrietta, by J. A. Cartwright.

Sep. 15, 1845—Cash, Marcus L., to Glenn, Dulcenea by Wm. Cash.

Sep. 17, 1845—Rodgers, Arthur B., to Rodgers, Mariah.

Oct. 1, 1845—Jones, Wm. W., to Dillingham, Lucinda, by J. A. Cartwright.

Oct. 1, 1845—Stevens, James D., to Baley, Nancy Caroline, by Isaac N. Wilcox.

Oct. 6, 1845—Purdy, Aaron, to Ivey Chapell, by F. W. Urey.

Oct. 7, 1845—Chandler, Wm. Bennett, to Molloy, Ann, by F. W. Urey.

Oct. 11, 1845—Stevenson, Melzar, to Litchfield, Susan, by W. C. Love.

Oct. 13, 1845—Adams, John W., to Bridges, Nancy, by Isaac N. Wilcox.

Oct. 14, 1845—Sigler, Daniel E., to Holeman, Pauline, by F. W. Urey.

Oct. 29, 1845—Patterson, Robt. S., to Hamilton, Polina E.

Nov. 8, 1845—Ramsey, Wm. R., to Mitchell, Louisa A., by Elijah Stevens.

Nov. 9, 1845—Eley, Thomas James, to Farmer, Nancy, by F. W. Urey.

Nov. 10, 1845—Lovegrove, Ulisses, to Jackson, Nancy, by Jas. C. Weller.

Nov. 15, 1845—Sollinger, John Adam, to Fairbanks, Mrs. Holly, by Robt. L. Cobb.

Nov. 17, 1845—Shoemaker, Alfred J., to Cole, Lucy Jane, by Wm. Cash.

Nov. 17, 1845—Stevenson, Jesse, to Thomas, Mrs. Sally, by Elijah Stevens.

Nov. 19, 1845—Cash, Geo. G., to Church, Mrs. Margaret E.

Nov. 26, 1845—Smith, Samuel K., to Miller, Eliza Amanda, by J. G. Biddle.

Dec. 3, 1845—Wright, Taylor, to Edrington, Mrs. Nancy.

Dec. 4, 1845—Hill, Jeremiah, to Marshall, Margaret, by N. H. Leet.

Dec. 9, 1845—Darroh (?), Clark C., to Dyson, Nancy, by Jas. W. Mansfield.

Dec. 13, 1845—Satterfield, Jesse, to Ramsey, Mary A. E., by Elijah Stevens.

Dec. 13, 1845—Trayler, John T. to Blackburn, Nancy Jane, by Thos. M. McGough, J. P.

Dec. 15, 1845—Harris, Frederick, to Jones, Sarah A.

Dec. 16, 1845—Deckman, Morris, to Clinton, Mrs. Elizabeth, by Jas. C. Weller.

Dec. 16, 1845—Duncan, Sandford, Jr., to Webb, Mary Susan, by Geo. Beckett, C. C. Sct.

Dec. 17, 1845—Howton, Harry, to Galloway, Mary W., by Eld. S. Scott.

Nov. 24, 1845—Black, David, to Trotter, Maria E., by F. C. Usher.

Dec. 22, 1845—Brown, Jas. M., to Pentgrass, Margaret, by John S. Brown, J. P.

Dec. 27, 1845—Calvert, Wiley C., to Blackburn, Mary M., by Jas. C. Weller.

Dec. 29, 1845—Smith, Wm. Jefferson, to Davenport, Jane, by H. Cassidy, J. P.

Dec. 29, 1845—Oliver, Levin C., to Oliver, Lydia G., by Jas. Mitchell.

Dec. 29, 1845—Cochran, Thos., to Jones, Mrs. Lucinda, by H. Cassidy.

Dec. 30, 1845—Lady, Henry, to Veid, Arrenia, by H. Cassidy.

1846:

Jan. 3, 1846—Moore, John F., Jr., to Jasker, Zenilda, by F. W. Urey.

Jan. 12, 1846—Brasier, Mitchell, to Gaines, Elizabeth, by Jas. W. Mansfield.

Jan. 14, 1846—Coleman, Archibald, to Powell, Mary, by R. L. Cobb.

Jan. 16, 1846—Bleek, John, to Corliew, Clarinda, by Jas. Mitchell.

Jan. 20, 1846—Miller, Samuel H., to Wigginton, Francis, by J. G. Biddle.

Jan. 24, 1846—Fryer, Wm. Sandf., to Stone, Malinda Louise, by Thos. M. McGough.

Jan. 26, 1846—Martin, Nathaniel, to Nelson, Rebecca, by Joseph B. Hadden, Caldwell Co. Sct. Mem. Pres. Church.

Jan. 29, 1846—White, Wm. T., to Stone, Mary M., by J. G. Biddle.

Feb. 3, 1846—Bozarth, A. M., to Dunn, Mary D.

Feb. 4, 1846—Coleman, James, to Fry, Catherine.

Feb. 11, 1846—Campbell, Wm. W., to Ritchey, Nancy Jane, by Jas. C. Weller.

Feb. 11, 1846—Cochran, Morris W., to Fulks, Pernecy, by I. W. Wilcox.

Feb. 11, 1846—Wadlington, Wm. B., to Jones, Sarah Elizabeth, by Eld. S. Scott.

Feb. 12, 1846—Campline, Henry, to Pendleton, Polly, by Foster Mason.

Feb. 18, 1846—Barrett, Giles, to Wilson, Mrs. Prisciller S., by H. C. Cassidy.

Feb. 18, 1846—Woodruff, Wm. P. to Hutchinson, Mrs. Martha, by O. N. Collins, C. C. Sct.

Feb. 25, 1846—Joiner, John R., to Hanks, Mary, by E. McOwn.

Feb. 25, 1846—Bryant, Wm. to Hanks, Jane, by E. McOwn, M. C. Caldwell, C. Sct.

Feb. 25, 1846—Gray, John P., Jr., to Coleman, Peach Ann.

Mch. 3, 1846—Axley, Jackson, to Gray, Susan, by R. L. Cobb.

Mch. 4, 1846—Borer, Richard, to Thompson, Sarah, by Jas. W. Mansfield.

Mch. 9, 1846—Blue, John R., to Glenn, Pernecy, by M. C. Love.

Mch. 9, 1846—Anderson, Shelley G., to Newsom, Caroline, by Mitchell Land.

Mch. 16, 1846—Duvall, Wm. S. to Tull, Elizabeth, by Collins Hodge, Caldwell Co., Sct.

Mch. 16, 1846—Wadlington, Felix G., to Riger, Mrs. Jennett Ann, by Warren M. Pittson, C. C. Sct.

Mch. 21, 1846—Sikes, Asa, to Bloodworth, Mary Ann, by H. Cassidy.

Mch. 23, 1846—Baker, Peter P., to Mansfield, Nancy E., by J. E. Grace.

Mch. 30, 1846—Jones, Samuel E., to Trayler, Peggy J., by F. W. Urey.

Apl. 13, 1846—Lovoons (Loomis), James J., to Land, Mrs. Letitia S., by Thos. J. C. Hill, C. C. Sct.

Apl. 13, 1846—Lee, Wm. R., to Collie, Happy, by I. N. Wilcox.

Apl....., 1846—Cone, George W., to Allison, Margaret R. L., by Joseph B. Hadden.

Apl. 18, 1846—Baker, James, to Barry, Matilda Ann, by J. G. Biddle.

Apl. 20, 1846—Jones, James H., to Whalen, Elizabeth, by Isaac N. Wilcox.

Apl. 21, 1846—Lamb, Robertson, to Robinson, Matilda, by L. H. Wilson.

Apl. 24, 1846—Crow, Moses, to Sanders, Margaret.

Apl. 25, 1846—Boemer, Matthias, to Mitchell, Susannah W., by Jas. C. Weller.

Apl. 30, 1846—Morse, Jefferson G., to McChesney, Elizabeth A., by Thos. M. McGough, Jr., C. C. Sct.

Apl. 30, 1846—Glass, Alexander, to Rupert, Elizabeth, by Wm. Cash, J. C. C.

May 1, 1846 Woolf, Wm H., to Baker, Matilda Louisa, by Eld. S. Scott.

May 11, 1846—Gray, John, to Morse, Mrs. Paulina B. by Wm. Cash.

May 12, 1846—Noel, Wm. C. to Greenfield, Stoney A., by Jas. H. Bristow.

May 14, 1846—Griffin, Jas. W., to Foley, Polly C., by J. Barnett.

May 17, 1846—Nash, Robert, to Calvert, Easter, by Thos. M. McGough.

May 17, 1846—Beck, Lewis J., to Cash, Mrs. Francis F.

May 21, 1846—Martin, Isaiah H., to Williams, Winnefred G., by Thos. J. C. Hale, C. C. Sct.

May 21, 1846—Sell, Wm., to Ritch, Elvira, by R. L. Cobb.

May 22, 1846—Hill, John, to Miozette, Matilda, by I. N. Wilcox.

May 22, 1846—Greer, Solomon, to Woolf, Lucy A., by Jas. W. Mansfield.

June 1, 1846—Wilds, Decatur, to Trayler, Sarah L., by Warren M. Pitts M. G., C. C. Sct.

June 1, 1846—Felker, Isaac, to Morse, Henrietta D., by W. C. Love, M. G.

June 4, 1846—Holloway, Jas. H., to Kilgore, Mrs. Ginsey.

June 8, 1846—Wilds, Alfred T., to Miller, Nancy Jane, by Warren M. Pitts.

June 8, 1946—Moore, Jno. P., to Morse, Nicey L., by Warren M. Pitts.

June 11, 1846—Parker, Robt. P., to Parker, Lizetta C.

June 13, 1846—Satterfield, Robertus, to Holloman, Mrs. Eliza, by Warren M. Pitts.

June 22, 1846—Herrald, Samuel G., to Ramey, Eliza.

July 1, 1846—Bembray, Jas. M., to Mitchell, Sarah, by Alex McOwn.

July 7, 1846—Carter, Turner, to Barnes, Mrs. Penelope, by J. A. Cartwright.

July 16, 1846—White, Joshua, to Cook, Zeritoa, by Eld. S. Scott.

July 17, 1846—Parker, Hiram, to Eli, Nancy, A. E., by Jas. C. Weller.

July 20, 1846—Harper, Rufus L., to Morse, Elvira D., by Jas. C. Weller.

July 25, 1846—Hays, Jonathan, to Sloan, Elizabeth, by Eld. S. Scott.

Aug. 3, 1846—Crow, Jno. M., to Harris, Louisa, by Eld. S. Scott.

Aug. 12, 1846—Butrum, Jas. L., to Martin, Sarah Jane, by Thomas M. McGough.

Aug. 18, 1846—Taylor, John M., to Copeland, Polly, by Jas. C. Weller.

Aug. 31, 1846—Adams, Isaac N. to Bannister, Elizabeth, by John Barnett.

Sep. 2, 1846—Slaton, Henry, to Shoemaker, Mary Louise, by Thos. M. McGough.

Sep. 19, 1846—Rodgers, Wm. T., to Mosley, Nancy B., by J. A. Cartwright.

Sep. 19, 1846—Wyatt, Robert, to Parker, Elizabeth A., by J. C. Weller.

Sept. 26, 1846—Yeats, Geo. W., to Herrmin, Martha, by B. B. Marshall.

Sept. 29, 1846—Stallings, Joshua B., to Nichols, Louisa, by J. C. Weller.

Sept. 29, 1846—Perry, Littleton, to Nichols, Eliza, by J. C. Weller.

Sept. 30, 1846—Blanks, Hardy, to Freeman, Martha.

Oct. 7, 1846—Pendleton, John, to Colley, Elizabeth, by Benj. F. Hawking.

Oct. 8, 1846—McDaniel, Samuel, to Dunn, Louisa C.

Oct. 14, 1846—Timmons, Thomas, to Chapman, Mrs. Nancy, by I. N. Wilcox.

Oct. 15, 1846—Jones, Wm. J., to Dodds, Celestine, by R. Beard.

Oct. 19, 1846—Jennings, Jas. E., to Duning, Malinda, by Eld. S. Scott.

Oct. 24, 1846—Conway, Chittenden, to Wilson, Adaline, by H. Cassidy.

Oct. 26, 1846—Roberts, Jas. H., to Crowder, Rejoina, by Thos. M. McGough.

Nov. 5, 1846—Ball, James, to Murphy, Ancey, by W. Cash.

Nov. 7, 1846—Wyatt, Franklin D., to Rice, Elizabeth C., by Joseph Hadden.

Nov. 21, 1846—Prewett, Jas. H., to Turley, Mary Ann, by Jas. W. Mansfield.

Nov. 21, 1846—Parker, Joseph, to Dunning, Melinda, S. J., by Wm. Cash.

Nov. 21, 1846—Trayler, John C., to Jones, Martha, by Warren M. Pitts, M. G.

Nov. 23, 1846—Lyon, Jas. G., to Archer, Catherine E., by W. W. Pitts.

Nov. 25, 1846—Ramey, John, to Etheridge, Susan.

Nov. 28, 1846—Wilkerson, David, to Blanks, Sally Ann.

Dec. 1, 1846—McLean, Geo. D., to Meek, Mrs. Martha I., by Richard Beard.

Dec. 3, 1846—Kelly, Wm., to Gracey, Mildred A., by E. J. Durbin, R. C. P.

Dec. 5, 1846—McChesney, Samuel A., to Mason, Elizabeth, by Thos. M. McGough.

Dec. 8, 1846—Ross, Bartholomew, to Hammond, Sarah, by W. W. Pitts.

Dec. 23, 1846—Jones, Shelton, to Jackson, Jerusha, by I. N. Wilcox.

Dec. 24, 1846—Baker, Bailey, Jr., to Nichols, Polly Ann, by J. C. Weller.

1847:

Jan. 2, 1847—Oliver, Washington W., to Oliver, Hannah.

Jan. 2, 1847—Biddle, John G., to Young, Isabella Jane, by R. Beard.

Jan. 4, 1847—Green, David S., to Crayne, Clarinda, by Claiborne Wilson.

Jan. 12, 1847—Galloway, Thos., to Littlefield, Mary, by Eld. S. Scott.

Jan. 18, 1847—Coon, Hinson, to Glenn, Margaret S., by Collis Hodge.

Jan. 18, 1847—Whalen, John, to Mitchell, Kitty, by I. N. Wilcox.

Jan. 18, 1847—Rees, Joseph, to Morgan, Charlotte, by W. M. Pitts.

Jan. 18, 1847—Childress, Beverly, to Beard, Sally, by Benj. F. Hawkins, M. E. Church.

Jan. 21, 1847—Hayles, John B., to Dawson, Mrs. Jane, by T. M. McGough.

Jan. 25, 1847—Coon, Wm., to Neel, Serena, by John S. Brown, P. C. C.

Jan. 28, 1847—Creekmur, Christopher, to Townsend, Mrs. Lucinda, by Whitnell Jenkins.

Feb. 3, 1847—Harker, Jacob, to West, Mrs. Sally, by I. N. Wilcox.

Feb. 4, 1847—Smith, Wm. W., to Littlefield, Rebecca, by J. C. Weller.

Feb. 5, 1847—Moore, Jas. A., to Martin, Mrs. Mary Ann.

Feb. 6, 1847—Holeman, Jas. A., to Hughes, Sarah A., by T. M. McGough.

Feb. 6, 1847—Hillyard, Wm. S. to Hayle, Miss Jane, by T. M. McGough.

Feb. 6, 1847—Fryer, Wm. S., to McDowell, Nancy Jane, by T. M. McGough.

Feb. 11, 1847—Martin, Isaac F., to Hughes, Salina, by J. W. Mansfield.

Feb. 15, 1847—Dees, Wm. S., to Moore, Mary Jane, by J. W. Mansfield.

Feb. 15, 1847—Ingram, Morris R., to Hanks, Elizabeth C., by H. Cassidy.

Feb. 15, 1847—Gardner, Francis, to McElwain, Mrs. Amanda, by Jas. Hawthorn.

Feb. 18, 1847—Cannon, Jesse D., to East, Mary, by John Barnett.

Feb. 20, 1847—Cato, Martin D., to Ashley, Melcina A., by B. F. Hawkins.

Feb. 22, 1847—Jennings, Elias B., to Mason, Tabitha Jane, by J. C. Weller.

Feb. 24, 1847—Lamb, Willis, to Talley, Rebecca Ann, by John Brown, P. C.

March 5, 1847—Owsley, Henry, to Mansfield, Louisa Anne, by Collin Hodge.

March 8, 1847—McConnell, John N., to Brown, Miss Eliza Jane.

March 13, 1847—Creekmure, Bartlett, to Smith, Miss Elener, by John Barnett.

March 17, 1847—Virdell, John T., to Chandler, Lucinda S., by R. R. Marshall.

March 19, 1847—Reece, James, to Wooding, Mrs. Mary, by J. W. Mansfield.

March 25, 1847—Bail, Richard J., to Lackman, Elizabeth, by H. Cassidy.

March 27, 1847—Wadlington, Jas., to Rodgers, Mrs. Hellen, by Eld. S. Scott.

March 29, 1847—Robinson, Joseph L., to Brelsford, Mary Jane, by Edward Graves.

March 29, 1847—Soden, John, to Blick, Sarah, by H. Cassidy.

April 2, 1847—Blackburn, Lewis, to Street, Elizabeth, by J. C. Weller.

April 5, 1847—Sparkman, Jas. W., to Wiley, Sarah, by J. C. Weller.

April 6, 1847—Glass, Greenberry, to Nichols, Rebecca, by J. C. Weller.

April 10, 1847—Spears, Nicholas, to Bunch, Nancy, by H. Cassidy.

April 12, 1847—Hayden, Nathan O. (?) to Miller, Martha Jane, by S. C. Phillips, M. C. B. Ch.

April 13, 1847—Caldwell, Robt. L., to Gomez, Myram G. F., by J. W. Mansfield.

April 19, 1847—Glenn, Jas. G., to Davis, Mrs. Eliza Ann, by J. W. Mansfield.

April 20, 1847—Archey, Joshua B., to Hale, Mrs. Sarah, by J. C. Weller.

April 22, 1847—Egbert, Willis C., to Stallions, Elizabeth, by J. C. Weller.

April 28, 1847—Lucas, George C., to Jenkins, Mary Ann, by Wm. Randolph, M. G.

May 5, 1847—Stafford, Enoch, to Atkinson, Zemilda, by R. R. Marshall.

May 11, 1847—Tyler, John D., to Harpending, Hellen Mary, by R. Beard.

May 11, 1847—Kuykendall, Isaac S., to Harpending, Ellen Cornelia, by R. Beard.

May 13, Litchfield, John, to Litchfield, Mrs. Sarah Ann, by F. W. Urey.

May 13, 1847—Lowry, Alexander C., to Cannon, Rachel, by Elijah Stevens, M. G.

May 18, 1847—Collie, Holland E., to Adams, Lydia E., by I. N. Wilcox.

May 20, 1847—Brantley, Holden to Crowell, Nancy A. by Whitnell Jenkins.

May 20, 1847—Powell, Williamson, to Wheatley, Mary Ann, by J. C. Weller.

June 9, 1847—Shirrin, Moses, to Sanders, Sarah Jane.

June 12, 1847—Arman, Frederick to Sherrin, Mrs. Polly, by I. N. Wilcox.

June 17, 1847—Lewis, Geo., to Cartwright, Helen A.

June 21, 1847—Dodds, Finis E. to Wadlington, Minerva J.

June 28, 1847—Caton, Francis M., to Johnston, Clitha M.

June 28, 1847—Leek, Mask to Brown, Elizabeth, by I. N. Wilcox.

June 30, 1847—Darnall, Willis, to Lamb, Miss Arthy Jane, by J. C. Weller.

July 15, 1847—Lady, Robt. C., to Bembray, Lavadia Catharine, by H. Cassidy.

July 19, 1847—Cox, John, to Cartwright, Nancy.

July 20, 1847—Veid, Henry, to Veid, Linea, by J. C. Weller.

July 21, 1847—Clinton, Victor, to Tyler, Harriet, by John S. Browne.

July 23, 1847—Glover, George, to Leonard, Mary Jane, by C. J. Crandall, M. G.

Aug. 4, 1847—Bail, Pierce F., to Coll, Mary, by H. Cassidy.

Aug. 7, 1847—McQuig, Henry D., to Holloway, Elizabeth, by John S. Brown.

Aug. 9, 1847—Harris, Nathan J., to Rogers, Martha (Mrs.).

Aug. 16, 1847—Walker, Freeman C., to Winter, Eliza, by R. R. Marshall.

Aug. 16, 1847—Crider, John, to James, Elizabeth.

Aug. 17, 1847—Crisp, Alfred, to Laughlin, Mary S., by J. C. Weller.

Aug. 23, 1847—Bond, Jeremiah R., to Massey, Emily M.

Aug. 26, 1847—Rogers, Finis, to Pettit, Julian, by J. C. Weller.

Aug. 27, 1847—Hobby, Wm., to Calvert, Nancy Jane, by J. W. Mansfield.

Sept. 13, 1847—Davis, Thos. I., to Lovan, Josephine, S. C., by J. C. Weller.

Sept. 16, 1847—Ford, Daniel, to Parker, Teeny, by F. W. Urey.

Sept. 20, 1847—Jones, William, to Trayler, Mary Emeline.

Sept. 20, 1847—Hildreth, Wm. W., to Fleming, Catherine, by J. C. Weller.

Sept. 27, 1847—Morse, Ebenezer S., to Crow, Nancy C., by J. W. Mansfield.

Sept. 27, 1847—Lawrence, Jas. M., to Crow, Mary Jane, by J. W. Mansfield.'

Sept. 30, 1847—Oliver, John, to Oliver, Elizabeth.

Oct. 2, 1847—Gray, Nathan, to Hall, Elizabeth.

Oct. 6, 1847—Hood, Chasteen, to Land, (Mrs.) Lucy.

Oct. 6, 1847—Hubbard, John, to Brasill, (Mrs.) Pernery, by J. A. Cartwright.

Oct. 13, 1847—Gray, Wm. R., to Barnes, Emerine W.

Oct. 14, 1847—Dobbins, Robt. B., to Stanfield, Mary J., by John Barnett.

Oct. 18, 1847—Towry, John W., to Davis, Ellvina, by G. Sisk, M. G.

Oct. 21, 1847—Brown, Wm. K., to Towry, Elizabeth Jane, by F. W. Urey.

Oct. 27, 1847—Hicks, Wm., to Morris, Rebecca, by F. W. Urey.

Oct. 27, 1847—Stevens, Edmund W., to Kilgore, Lucinda, by G. Sisk, M. G.

Nov. 3, 1847—Throckmorton, Wm. W., to Shepardson, Ann Mary, by Jas. Hawthorne.

Nov. 6, 1847—Wallace, Wm. R. to Scott, Wilmoth S., by H. Cassidy.

Nov. 10, 1847—Cranfield, Eaton, to Galloway, Martha J., by Eld. S. Scott.

Nov. 11, 1847—Goodwin, Jesse S., to Purdey, Julia Ann, by F. W. Urey.

Nov. 17, 1847—Stevenson, Jas., to Sanders, Nancy, by J. G. Biddle.

Nov. 18, 1847—Bland, Joshua, to Scott, Mary Ann, by Eld. S. Scott.

Nov. 19, 1847—Boyd, Joseph, to Chandler, Malinda, by R. R. Marshall.

Nov. 20, 1847—Travis, Francis L., to Briggs, Fanny E., by L. N. Wilson, M. G.

Nov. 24, 1847—Oliver, Levin Tho. to Hall, Mary Jane.

Nov. 25, 1847—Foley, Jesse, to Martin, (Mrs.) Elizabeth, by Jno. N. Rucker, J. P.

Dec. 6, 1847—Jenkins, Ambrose M., to Dennis, Eliz. M., by H. Cassidy.

Dec. 6, 1847—Early, Wm. C., to Keeny, Susan.

Dec. 8, 1847—Dunn, Wm. to Bumpass, Sarah Jane, by Elijah Stevens, M. G.

Dec. 13, 1847—Burrell, Cash, to Prince, Helen C., by F. M. English.

Dec. 13, 1847—Turley, John H., to Gomez, Sarah Ann, by J. W. Mansfield.

Dec. 17, 1847—Moore, Collin, to Hays, Eliz. S.

Dec. 18, 1847—Mims, Rufus K., to Jacob, Geroldine L., by Geo. Beckett.

Dec. 23, 1847—Hicks, John H. W., to Thompson, Eliz., by J. A. Cartwright.

1848:

Jan. 17, 1848—Johnson, W. A., to Groves, E. A., by J. G. Biddle.

Jan. 17, 1848—Calvert, Elihu P., to McDowell, Mary Jane, by Robertson S. Tudor.

Jan. 17, 1848—Jones, Dawson W., to Cherry, Martha C.

Jan. 18, 1848—Eison, Jacob, to McElroy, Agnes, by Eld. S/Scott.

Jan. 18, 1848—Gray, Isaac, to Howard, Martha.

Jan. 20, 1848—Castleberry, Wm. R., to Holeman, A. E. M., by Caswell Mason.

Jan. 22, 1848—Smith, Irby H., to Mason, Caroline.

Jan. 24, 1848—Lowry, Leonidas M. to Kemp. Sarah Ann, by F. W. Urey.

Jan. 27, 1848—Timmons, Thos. D., to Bloodworth, Elmira, by H. Cassidy.

Jan. 29, 1848—Pugh, Jesse D., to Lewis, Sarah, by Foster Mason.

Feb. 4, 1848—Coon, Thos., to Martin, Margaret, by Wm. Randolph, M. G.

Feb. 4, 1848—Perry, John B., to Ingram, Ann S., by F. M. English.

Feb. 7, 1848—Axly, Robert, to Blodworth, (Mrs.) Mary, by A. H. Cooper.

Feb. 7, 1848—Montgomery, R. K., to Laughlin, Sarah, by T. M. McGough.

Feb. 8, 1848—Freeman, Jas. M., to Morris, Sarah Catherine.

Feb. 9, 1848—Stevens, Milton, to Miller, Susannah M., by John S. Brown.

Feb. 14, 1848—Shelby, C. M., to Lyon, Helen M., by Geo. Beckett.

Feb. 14, 1848—Holloway, Edward, to Mitcherson, Nancy G.

Feb. 17, 1848—Allison, R. C., to McCarty, Eliza, by Jas. Hawthorne.

Feb. 17, 1848—Winn, Hez. G., to Cannon, Julia Ann.

Feb. 17, 1848—Neil, Jas. S., to Sigler, Mary J.

Mar. 2, 1848—Sparkman, Hugh, to Shadowen, (Mrs.) Eliz., by H. Cassidy.

Mar. 2, 1848—Cookley, Timothy, to Kelley, Rosanna, by R. R. Marshall.

Mar. 5, 1848—Allen, Joseph H., to Farmer, Sarah, by Wm. Cash.

Mar. 7, 1848—Lamb, Shelton, to Nichols, Levina, by Wm. Cash, J. P.

Mar. 8, 1848—Leech, David, to Nichols, Sarah, by T. M. McGough, J. P.

Mar. 9, 1848—Ward, Pleasant F., to Scott (marked out) Sinah, by H. Cassidy.

Mar. 10, 1848—Calvert, Silas W., to Mason, Mary C., by F. W. Urey.

Mar. 15, 1848—Barnett, Wm. H., to Gray, Nancy.

Mar. 22, 1848—Allen, Thos. J., to Martin, E. J., by J. W. Wilcox, J. P.

Mar. 22, 1848—Weeks, Zachariah, to Hobby, Elzy, by F. W. Urey.

Mar. 22, 1848—Beshers, Starling S., to Dunning, Eliza Jane, by Foster Mason.

Mar. 29, 1848—Fowler, Wm., to Hall, Susan.

Apr. 1, 1848—Hill, James, to Gregory, Mary Jane, by H. Cassidy.

Apr. 3, 1848—McElroy, Wm. B., to Young, D. H. D., by J. W. Mansfield.

Apr. 4, 1848—Lamb, Wm., to Tally, Martha, by J. A. Cartwright.

Apr. 4, 1848—Gillespie, Thos., to Sanders, Louisa.

Apr. 6, 1848—Nelson, Clark, to Riggs, Catherine by T. M. McGough.

Ap. 12, 1848—Holeman, Jacob to Liggins, Rebecca by Caswell Mason.

May 1, 1848—Martin, Jacob to Knox, Rebecca, by L. M. Beckett, M. G.

May 10, 1848—Parker, James M., to Allen, Mary.

May 16, 1848—Jones, W. D., to Satterfield, (Mrs.) M. A., by J. Hawthorne.

May 17, 1848—Spratt, B. J., to Chambers, Mary J., by J. Hawthorne.

May 24, 1848—Cobb, Thos. J., to Glenn, Almeida.

May 24, 1848—Wells, Peter F., to Murphy, Martha, by F. W. Urey.

May 23, 1848—Clark, David, to Easley, May P.

June 6, 1848—Pickering, R. W., to Scott, Julia A., by M. A. Rucker, J. P.

June 6, 1848—Clark, Jas. C., to Johnson, Tyressa, by T. M. McGough.

June 27, 1848—Whalen, Davis B., to Nickell, Mary E., by I. N. Wilcox, P. C. C.

July 6, 1848—Conyers, Jas. H., to Young, Mary J., by I. N. Wilcox.

July 13, 1848—Fraley, Wesley, to Nelson, Juliann, by T. M. McGough.

July 17, 1848—Holmas, John, to Leigh, Juliet A., by W. C. Love.

July 24, 1848—Hawkins, Wm., to Litchfield, Nancy, by John Barnett.

July 25, 1848—Riley, Philip, to Frazer, Rosanna.

July 31, 1848—Campbell, Thos. J., to Darnell, (Mrs.) Mary, by F. W. Urey.

Aug. 12, 1848—Rogers, Wm., to Stevens, Mahala, by I. N. Wilcox.

Aug. 15, 1848—Brown, A. C., to Langston, Matilda, by Wm. Randolph, M. E. C. SO.

Aug. 21, 1848—Smith, Harrison T., to Love, Elmira L., by H. Cassidy.

Aug. 21, 1848—McDowell, Jas. G., to Jones, Rachel, by T. M. McGough.

Aug. 29, 1848—Dunning, Doctor W., to Walling, (Mrs.) Eliz., by J. H. Rucker.

Sept. 5, 1848—Purdy, David, to Bradshaw, Ruth, by Whitnell Jenkins.

Sept. 6, 1848—Duncan, Isaac R., to Shoemaker, C. J., by Joshua Brown, J. P.

Sept. 6, 1848—Asherst, W. W., to Nichols, N. P., by F. W. Urey.

Sept. 7, 1848—Dawson, John, to Young, Louisa, by Foster Mason.

Sept. 14, 1848—Harris, Wm. H., to Wynn, Susan.

Sept. 17, 1848—Walker, Isaac, to Carner, Nancy.

Sept. 19, 1848—George, Samuel, to Sisk, Charlotte, by F. W. Urey.

Sept. 26, 1848—Satterfield, Thos. F., to Allen, Eliza E., by J. Hawthorne.

Sept. 28, 1848—Lewis, Henry, to Satterfield, S. A.

Oct. 16, 1848—Holeman, John, to Morse, Jane.

Oct. 18, 1848—Guess, John T., to Ritchey, Isabella S., by J. W. Mansfield.

Oct. 24, 1848—Dixon, Tilford, to Fraley, Mary, by T. M. McGough.

Oct. 24, 1848—Fraley, Edmond, to Dickson, Seany, by T. M. McGough.

Oct. 25, 1848—Fralich, Wm. K., to McDowell, (Mrs.) Harriet, by Claiborne Wilson.

Oct. 26, 1848—Ashbridge, Wm., to Young, A. A., by Wm. Cash.

Oct. 30, 1848—Tabor, Joel M., to Cannon, L. F., by J. E. Grace.

Oct. 30, 1848—Morse, J. G., Jr., to Nichols, Melissa E., by Whitnell Jenkins.

Nov. 2, 1848—Stevens, Wm., to Satterfield, Mary, by Wm. Cash.

Nov. 25, 1848—Smith, Jas., to Shannon, Ella.

Dec. 7, 1848—Ward, S. D., to Blue, E. A., by J. Hawthorne.

Dec. 11, 1848—Cobb, G. D., to Webb, F. C., by J. Hawthorne.

Dec. 11, 1848—Bloodworth, Orvill, to Emery, (Mrs.) Margary, by I. N. Wilcox.

Dec. 14, 1848—Chapman, Thos. J., to Hendrickson, M. J., by F. W. Urey.

Dec. 18, 1848—Whittington, Richard, to Mercer, Mary M.

Dec. 18, 1848—Bridges, Berry J., to Bloodworth, S. A., by I. N. Wilcox.

Dec. 21, 1848—Rascoe, John P., to Barnes, E. S., by R. Beard.

Dec. 23, 1848—Wylie, Josiah W., to Harper, E. J., by Eld. S. Scott.

Dec. 27, 1848—Hunter, George, to McLin, N. C., by F. W. Urey.
Dec. 30, 1848—Cook, Joseph P., to Cook, Nancy, by James Vivion.

1849:

Jan. 4, 1849—Matlock, Thos. W., to Martin, Sarah, by J. W. Mansfield.
Jan. 8, 1849—Radcliffe, Thos. C., to Church, Eunice L., by Jno. N. Rucker.
Jan. 8, 1849—Laughter, Jas. H., to Lady, Mary A., by H. Cassidy.
Jan. 9, 1849—Darnall, David, to Houghton, E. M., by F. W. Urey.
Jan. 10, 1849—Jordan, Benj., to Asbridge, Julia A., by W. C. Love.
Jan. 15, 1849—Gray, Wm. F., to Harris, Mary Ann, by Wm. Cash.
Jan. 16, 1849—Samples, Wm. R., to Robinson, Eliz., by W. C. Love.
Jan. 22, 1849—Armstrong, B. F., to McMan, S. W.
Jan. 23, 1849—Vantree, Thos. W., to Hendrickson, M. M.
Feb. 1, 1849—Martin, Edw. J., to Doom, Maris, by R. L. Cobb.
Feb. 5, 1849—Gibson, John, to Ford, Cassandra.
Feb. 13, 1849—Cooper, A. H., to Osborn, Mary, not executed—for want of time, gal would not stand, J. W. Weller, Dep. Clk.
Feb. 10, 1849—McLing, H. D., to Hanford, Martha J., by R. L. Cobb.
Feb. 11, 1849—Nevill, Geo. S., to Rooks, E. S., by Foster Mason.
Feb. 15, 1849—Kilpatrick, P. R., to Campbell, L. C., by Jas. Rufus Dempsey.
Feb. 19, 1849—Thomas, Joseph W., to Colley, Carissa.
Feb. 20, 1849—Scott, Wm., to Lamb, Martha, by Eld. S. Scott.
Feb. 21, 1849—Lawrence, Martin, to Dunlap, Rebecca W., by A. L. Cooper.
Feb. 21, 1849—East, Elihu J., to Coleman, Nancy, by John Barnett.
Feb. 22, 1849—Brooks, A. M., to Weller, C. V., by Wm. Lasley, M. G.
Feb. 22, 1849—Bannister, Simon T., to Wilson, Martha Jane, by H. Cassidy.
Feb. 22, 1849—Williamson, D. B., to Bannister, Martha, by H. Cassidy.
Feb. 22, 1849—Wadley, Francis, to Crowells, Emiline, by Wm. Cash.
Feb. 28, 1849—Jones, Thomas, to Roberts, Rebecca J., by F. W. Urey.
Feb. 3, 1849—Cruise, George, to Tilsey, Cynthia Anne, by John S. Brown, J. P.
Mar. 7, 1849—Pirtle, David, to Alison, Elizabeth.
Mar. 7, 1849—Cotton, Jesse, to Davis, Elizabeth.
Mar. 7, 1849—Harman, Wm. P., to Calvert, Elizabeth A., by Jas. Hawthorne.
Mar. 8, 1849—Lofton, Wm. S., to Drennon, (Mrs.) Eliza G., by Robertson S. Tudor.
Mar. 12, 1849—Helm, Marion, to Henson, Nancy P., by R. R. Marshall.
Mar. 15, 1849—Price, Richen, to Nichols, Sarah J., by F. W. Urey.
Mar. 22, 1849—Gray, Isaac, to Taylor, (Mrs.) A. M., by Rev. A. J. Baird.
Mar. 24, 1849—Dobbs, Wm. H., to Dobbs, M. M., by Wm. Alexander, M. P.
Mar. 28, 1849—Moore, H. F., to Acru, (Mrs.) M. W., by J. W Mansfield.
Mar. 28, 1849—Bradburn, W. C., to Kemp, Prisey, by Robertson S. Tudor.
Mar. 31, 1849—Browning, Williamson, to Vinson, (Mrs.) S. A.
Apr. 4, 1849—Cash, John R., to Cooper, Jane, by Jno. H. Rucker.
Apr. 7, 1849—Glass, Fielding, to Glass, B. A., by Eld. S. Scott.
Apr. 10, 1849—Dillingham, V. J., to Cash, Ann E., by Wm. Cash.

Apr. 11, 1849—Copeland, Joshua, to White, Eliza, by Foster Mason.

Apr. 14, 1849—White, J. N., to Baker, S. F., by Foster Mason.

Apr. 28, 1849—Jackson, C. M., to Flournoy. Rosa. by J. B. Hadden, M. G., Pres. Ch.

May 8, 1849—Scott, Jas., to Gresham, Edna, by F. W. Urey.

May 21, 1849—Brigham, John, to Freeman, A. G., by Rev. A. J. Baird.

May 28, 1849—Gray, Robt., Jr., to Gresham, E., by F. W. Urey.

May 29, 1849—Snack, Henry, to Henson, Martha, by R. R. Marshall.

June 1, 1849—Holland, Wm., to M. J. Hopper.

June 18, 1849—Gray, James, to Ward, Florida. C.

June 18, 1849—O'Hara, Wm., to Cartwright, E., by Richard Beard.

June 19, 1849—Smith, Reuben H., to Lofton, Mildred, by I. N. Wilcox.

June 29, 1849—Everett, A. B., to Everett, (Mrs.) A. E., by I. N. Wilcox.

June 30, 1849—Dunbar, Wm., to McNeily, Rebecca, by F. W. Urey.

July 5, 1849—Richards, Peter, to Frazer, W. J., by Foster Mason.

July 9, 1849—McDowell, Daniel, to McConnell, Mary.

July 17, 1849—Starns, Solomon, to Tyler, (Mrs.) Mary, by John Barnett.

Aug. 8, 1849—Lamar, Joshua, to Kilgore, H.

Aug. 14, 1849—Mitchell, D. D., to Muirs, R. E., by J. W. Mansfield.

Aug. 20, 1849 Grubbs, B. J., to Fowler, Arminta, by Foster Mason.

Aug. 21, 1849—Crider, Daniel, to Rohrer, (Mrs.) Sarah, by W. C. Love.

Aug. 24, 1849—Shoemaker, Wm., to White, Susanna, by H. Cassidy.

Aug. 28, 1849—Galloway, Chas. S. to Parker, Delilah, by F. W. Urey.

Sept. 2, 1849—Holland, Lawson, to Baker, M. R.

Sept. 4, 1849—Litzburgher, John, to Willis, M.

Sept. 15, 1849—Jackson, G. W., to Houghton, Lucinda E., by Whitnell Jenkins.

Sept. 13, 1849—Goodwin, John F., to Cartwright, Serena, by Geo. W. Elley.

Sept. 17, 1849—Davis, John B., to Corns, Hannah, by Wm. Alexander, M. G.

Sept. 20, 1849—Brown, Coleman, to Cannon, (Mrs.) Jane, by T. M. McGough.

Oct. 1, 1849—Weller, James C., to Rucker, (Mrs.) Zerilda, by Rev. S. Scott.

Oct. 6, 1849—Joyner, C. P., to Smiley, Sarah J. (Nancy Jane in return).

Oct. 11, 1849—Christian, John E., to Wheatley, Martha Ann, by H. Cassidy.

Oct. 11, 1849—Faughn, E., to Collie, Nancy M., by Wm. T. McLean, M. G.

Oct. 11, 1849—Given, Wm. W., to McCaslin, C. Jane, by G. Lish.

Oct. 15, 1849—Tier, Wilson, to Ford, Phoebe F.

Oct. 18, 1849—Sharon, Henry, to Hall, P., by John Barnett.

Oct. 21, 1849—Pierce, Robt. R., to Allen, Laura E., by Jas. Hawthorne.

Oct. 24, 1849—Wood, Chas. N., to Archer, Mary 9., by J. W. Mansfield.

Oct. 27, 1849—Krone, David, to Lake, Charlotte, by R. L. Cobb.

Nov. 6, 1849—Holloman, Jas. B., to Osborn, Alcey M., by Jas. Hawthorne.

Nov. 8, 1849—Blaylock, Thos. A., to Martin, S. F., by F. W. Urey.

Nov. 12, 1849—Hodges, Wm., to Salyers, Martha A., by John Barnett.

Nov. 12, 1849—Baker, Wm., to Gray, Mildred, by A. H. Cooper.

Nov. 14, 1849—Park, G. I., to Wagner, (Mrs.) Sarah J., by Jas. Hawthorne.
Nov. 19, 1849—Walker, James, to Hobby, Amanda, by Wm. Cash.
Nov. 26, 1849—Holland, Jas. M., to Early, Caroline, by Alex. McCown, P. C.
Dec. 1, 1849—Gregory, John W., to Hill, Margaret, by R. L. Cobb.
Dec. 3, 1849—Patton, David, to Carson, E. J., by R. L. Love.
Dec. 3, 1849—Shropshire, Benj. to Lindsay, Geor. W.
Dec. 6, 1849—White, David, to Copeland, M. J., by F. W. Urey.
Dec. 7, 1849—Veatch, John M., to Bridges, Chloe A. (Mrs.) by H. Cassidy.
Dec. 11, 1849—Elder, Geo. W., to Leech, Mary A., by W. C. Love.
Dec. 11, 1849—Pickering, E. R., to Hooper, Louisa W., by Rev. S. Scott.
Dec. 15, 1849—Bugg, Jas. H., to Crider, Nancy J., by Geo. Beckett.
Dec. 15, 1849—Griffey, John C., to Gray, F. F., by Geo. Beckett.
Dec. 20, 1849—Franklin, J. W., to Leech, M., by Thos. M. McGough.
Dec. 25, 1849—Witherspoon, Isaac S., to Stallions, M., by Wm. Cash.
Dec. 28, 1849—Bigham, David F., to Yandell (Mrs.) Mary.
Dec. 31, 1849—Wadlington, F., to Moore, Polly, by Foster Mason.
Dec. 31, 1849—Kevil, Manson R., to Cantrell, Martha, by F. W. Urey.

1850:

Jan. 1, 1850—Newcomb, Joseph, to Cain, Mary E., by P. Clinton, J.P.C.C.
Jan. 3, 1850—Brush, James, to Campbell, Nancy, by A. Cannon, M. M. E. C. So.
Jan. 3, 1850—Woodsides, S. M., to Johnson, (Mrs.) M. Sct., by Wm. Cash.
Jan. 3, 1850—Fulks, Noah, to Randalls, Sarah, by I. N. Wilcox.
Jan. 7, 1850—Lester, John M., to Lacey, Mamcy, by F. W. Urey.
Jan. 14, 1850—McElmore, Jas. H., to Parker, (Mrs.) Mary A.
Jan. 14, 1850—Cobb, Giles L., to Catlett, Marion, by Jas. Hawthorne.
Jan. 15, 1850—Butler, John, to Waddell, M. J., by John Barnett.
Jan. 16, 1850—Timmonds, Walter, to Oliver, M. M., by Jas. H. Rucker.
Jan. 16, 1850—Strawmat, Wm. K., to Singleton, M. J., by T. M. McGough.
Jan. 16, 1850—Baker, Leander, to Early, Mary, by John Barnett.
Jan. 19, 1850—Smith, Simeon, to Taylor (Mrs.) Rhoda J., by Rev. S. Scott.
Jan. 21, 1850—Oliver, Joseph, to Garrett, Jane, by John Barnett.
Jan. 23, 1850—Asbridge, Obadiah, to Love, E. A., by Jno. H. Rucker.
Jan. 23, 1850—Lacey, Earl, to Lester, Julia A., by F. W. Urey.
Jan. 26, 1850—Yocum, Isaac D., to Goodall, Eliza D.
Jan. 26, 1850—McCormick, A. J., to Wynn, Paulina, by Jno. H. Rucker.
Jan. 28, 1850—Sizemore, Chas. J., to Ashley, A. A.
Jan. 28, 1850—Kirkpatrick, Wm. D., to Cobb, Aurelia G., by Jas. Hawthorne.
Jan. 28, 1850—Smith, W. W. to Mims, Georgiana.
Jan. 29, 1850—Boneham, Jerome, to Lear, M. L., by R. L. Cobb.
Jan. 30, 1850—Clayton, Jas., to Bashaw, Arrana, by Wm. Cash.
Feb. 4, 1850—Brooks, Jesse P., to Kilgore, Jamima H., by F. W. Urey.
Feb. 9, 1850—Nichols, Nathaniel, to Blaylock, M. A., by Rev. S. Scott.
Feb. 11, 1850—Daniel, E. H., to Perry, Minerva.
Feb. 16, 1850—Darnall, Stallard, to Houghton, Cynthia A., by Wm. Cash.

Fob. 18, 1850—Foley, Mason, to Johnson (Mrs.) Lilly A., by A. H. Cooper.

Feb. 20, 1850—Nichols, Wm., to Phelps, L. J., by F. W. Urey.

Feb. 21, 1850—Thompson, John W., to Dunkerson, M., by Jas. Hawthorne.

Mar. 5, 1850—Harris, John H. S., to Jackson, Delila, by Wm. Cash.

Mar. 9, 1850—Lamb, James, to Lowry, Nancy J., by Geo. W. Bone.

Mar. 11, 1850—Rowland, Casper, to Bronnen, Sarah A., by I. N. Wilcox.

Mar. 13, 1850—Drennan, John, to Wimberly, H., by John H. Rucker.

Mar. 14, 1850—Joyner, Wm., to Smiley, Elizabeth, by F. W. Urey.

Mar. 21, 1850—Galloway, Wm., to Dillingham, M., by Eld. S. Scott.

Mar. 27, 1850—Stevens, Criswell, to Stevens, Ellen, by Elijah Stevens.

Apr. 4, 1850—Sims, Wm. R., to Early, N. G., by John Barnett.

Apr. 4, 1850—Kemp, Dempsey, to Boyd, R. L., by T. M. McGough.

Apr. 12, 1850—Cash, Wm., Jr., to Holloway, M. E., by Willis Champion, P. G.

Apr. 25, 1850—Young, John M., to Harris, (Mrs.) M., by John Barnett.

May 7, 1850—Pearce, Lamberry, to Jones, Ellen, by Thos. J. Early, P. C. C.

May 14, 1850—Gaines, Thos. P., to Hamm, E. W., by T. M. McGough.

May 15, 1850—Howard, F. J., to Smith, Nancy H., by Thos. J. Early, J. P.

May 22, 1850—Clark, David, to Easley, Mary P., by Collin Hodge.

May 25, 1850—Kern, Thos. S., to Oliver, Nancy, by Jno. H. Rucker.

June 11, 1850—Ladd, Henry to McCool, E. J., by Wm. C. Groom, P. C.

Junc 27, 1850—Dunning, Wm., to Dunning, Hannah, by F. W. Urey.

July 3, 1850—Larkins, Henry, to Wilcox, Lucy A., by W. H. Morrison.

July 4, 1850—Huggins, Robertus, to Parker (Mrs.) Armenia.

July 22, 1850—Delaney, W. S., to Shropshire, G. R., by Geo. Beckett.

Aug. 6, 1850—Turner, Matthew to Rochester, Judith, by Foster Mason.

Aug. 6, 1850—Young, D. C., to Sigler, M. J., by Bailous Phelps, M. G.

Aug. 10, 1850—Sivells, D. C., to Hooper, E. J., by Alex. H. McCown, P. C.

Aug. 13, 1850—Dunning, Jesse, to L. C. Dunning, by Wm. Cash.

Aug. 14, 1850—George, Garrett G., to Harris, Cynthia, by F. W. Urey.

Aug. 17, 1850—Brown, Wilson K., to Dare, Amanda E., by T. M. McGough.

Aug. 21, 1050—Franklin, Jas. A., to Wadlington, Mary, by Foster Mason.

Aug. 22, 1850—Franklin, Wm. W., to Hamilton, Lucinda, by F. W. Urey.

Sept. .., 1850—Sizemore, Anderson P., to Naramore, Mary J., by Wm. G. Groom. J. P.

Sept. 25, 1850—Fox, B. S., to McChesney, Sarah C., by Wm. A. McChesney.

Sept. 25, 1850—Hiett, Simeon W., to Bennett, Gracey, by F. W. Urey.

Sept. 30, 1850—Simons, Leonard, to Wells, Amanda H., by F. W. Urey.

Oct. 5, 1850—Leech, Jas. H., to Glenn, Elizabeth, by Rich. Beard.

Oct. 8, 1850—Banister, Jas. H., to Osborn, Mary, by A. H. Cooper.

Oct. 8, 1850—Boyd, Thos., to Daniel, Martha.

Oct. 10, 1850—Hancock, Josiah, to Cherry, Margt. A., by F. W. Urey.

Oct. 14, 1850—Carney, Wm. W., to Robertson, Mary F.

Oct. 15, 1850—Dunning, Jasper, to Young, Mary E., by Wm. Cash.

Oct. 17, 1850—Glass, James, to Salyers, (Mrs.) E., by Eld. Stallard Scott.

Oct. 21, 1850—Brame, Richard A., to Allison, I. A. E., by Richard Beard.

Oct. 23, 1850—Lafield, Wm. R., to Payne, A. B.

Oct. 31, 1850—Hinds, Fingal H., to McCaslin, A. A. by E. Stevens, M. G.
Oct. 31, 1850—Hutchins, Geo. F., to Campbell, (Mrs.) M. E., by Jas. Hawthorne.
Nov. 6, 1850—Riley, Edward, to Northcutt, M. A., by John L. Brown.
Nov. 7, 1850—Lamb, Jesse, to Scott, Sarah M., by F. W. Urey.
Nov. 13, 1850—Oliver, Asberry, to Oliver, Lucinda G., by John Barnett.
Nov. 13, 1850—Oliver, Janus W., to Oliver, Eliza M.
Nov. 13, 1850—McCaslin, Wm. H., to Hinds, A. M., by E. Stevens.
Nov. 13, 1850—Clinton, De Witt, to Moore, China, by I. N. Wilcox.
Nov. 26, 1850—Parks, Jefferson, to Smith, Mary A. E.
Nov. 27, 1850—Hill, Levi W., to Collie, Jinsey T., by Jas. H. Owen.
Dec. 2, 1850—Hyatt, Robert, to Smart, Mary A., by Jno. H. Rucker.
Dec. 3, 1850—Crawford, Wm. H., to Dollins, Sarah J., by W. C. Love.
Dec. 3, 1850—Sessions, L. B. to Adams, (Mrs.) S. E., by Jas. W. Moosfield.
Dec. 10, 1850—Crider, S. F., to Guess, Mary A., by W. C. Love.
Dec. 11, 1850—Griffith, B. C., to McConnell, F. P.
Dec. 12, 1850—Morse, Wm. M., to .... McNely, by F. W. Urey.
Dec. 12, 1850—Stephens, Milton D., to Dunn, A. E., by J. White.
Dec. 13, 1850—Osenbaugh, J. B., to E. Boyd, by F. W. Urey.
Dec. 16, 1850—Campbell, Wm., to McConnell, Sanai.
Dec. 16, 1850—Rice, Wm. L., to Glenn, Sarah, by Jas. W. Hooper.
Dec. 16, 1850—Miller, Isaac, to Dunning, Rebecca, by Eld. S. Scott.
Dec. 18, 1850—Pirtle, Geo. W., to Davis, Martha, by John Barnett.
Dec. 19, 1850—Archer, Wm. B., to Shannon, M. A.
Dec. 20, 1850—Lewis, Benj., to Hammock, Nancy, by F. W. Urey.
Dec. 21, 1850—Wadlington, Thos. B., to Cartwright, M. A.
Dec. 21, 1850—Hughey, Robert to Hughey, (Mrs.) Sarah.
Dec. 24, 1850—Hammond, Chris, to Clark, Mary A., by Jas. H. .........
Dec. 24, 1850—Jones, Andrew J., to Freer, Mary, by F. W. Urey.
Dec. 24, 1850—Soden, Elwood T., to Hildreth, Margt., by H. Cassidy.
Dec. 30, 1850—Keeny, (Heeny), Jas., to Nichols, (Mrs.) Nancy, by F. W. Urey.

---

*Note: Above, the first date given is that of issuance of marriage license, the second date of ceremony, 3rd (if given) is the time of the return made by the minister or J. P.  M. G. is minister of Gospel; J. P. Justice of Peace; C. P. is Cumberland Presbyterian church; M. E. is Methodist Episcopal; Pres. is Presbyterian.  The copying was done with great care but the phonetic spelling creates a puzzle sometimes.  Original spelling was retained, and where there is doubt a ? indicates it.  The use of Mrs. does not denote that all those so given were widows, perhaps an extension of the old-time custom of calling all spinsters "Mrs."  From 1850 to 1860 the Vital Statistics to be found in the Library of the Kentucky Historical Society cover the marriages of this and other counties.  (IEF)

# INDEX

Cobb, Nancy H., 289
Cobb, Persis, 302
Cobb, Robert, 303
Cobb, R. H., 305
Cobb, Robert L. (R. L.), 305, 307
  308, 310-315, 318-325, 332-334
Cobb, Robert S. (R. S.), 303, 304,
  310-312, 315
Cobb, Rose (colored), 137
Cobb, Samuel, 289
Cobb, Sophia M., 320
Cobb, Thomas J., 330
Coburn, Ann W., 115
Coburn, Benjamin W., 136
Coburn, Mrs. Benjamin W., 136
Coburn, Carrie, 115
Coburn, Cornelia, 115
Coburn, Frances, 267
Coburn, Henry William, 267
Coburn, James W., 171
Coburn, John, 115, 267
Coburn, John James, 267
Coburn, Mary, 267
Coburn, Ostrander, 194
Coburn, William, 267
Coburn, Wilson, 115
Cochran (Cochram), Crittenden,
  310
Cochran (Cochram), Eli, 277
Cochran (Cochram), Frances J.,
  138
Cochran (Cochram), George
  Welsh, 137
Cochran (Cochram), Mrs. Hattie
  J., 135
Cochran (Cochram), James H.,
  138
Cochran (Cochram), Jane, 276
Cochran (Cochram), Joseph, 137
Cochran (Cochram), Margaret,
  318
Cochran (Cochram), Martha, 286
Cochran (Cochram), Mary Duf-
  field, 136
Cochran (Cochram), Mary Un-
  derwood, 136
Cochran (Cochram), Morris W.,
  324
Cochran (Cochram), R. A., 135
Cochran (Cochram), Rachel, 282
Cochran (Cochram), Robert A.,
  54, 200
Cochran (Cochram), Thomas,
  274, 324
Cochran (Cochram), Thomas, Jr.,
  317
Cochran (Cochram), Thomas W.,
  284
Cochran (Cochram), William D.,
  137
Cock(e), Elizabeth, 77, 82
Cockran, Henry, 201
Cockran, Hezekiah, 32

Cockran, James, 32
Cockran, William, 32
Cockrell, Addie, 138
Coffee, George G., 136
Coffee, Sally, 210
Coffee, Susan E., 136
Coffey, Kate, 205
Coffey, Moses, 205
Coffey, Nancy, 309
Coffman, Isaac, 60
Colburn, Carl, 138
Colburn, Elizabeth, 136
Colburn, Levi, 137
Colburn, Rosa, 137
Cole, Alfred E., 123
Cole, Allen D., 123
Cole, Benjamin, 185
Cole, Christopher, 200
Cole, Clara Vivian, 123
Cole, Effie, 137
Cole, Elizabeth, 185
Cole, Indiana T., 200
Cole, James R., 293
Cole, John H., 200
Cole, Lucy Jane, 323, 324
Coleman, Archibald, 324
Coleman, B. C., 62
Coleman, Charlotte, 277
Coleman, James, 16, 30, 316, 324
Coleman, Julius G., 173
Coleman, Lucy A., 153, 157
Coleman, M. F., 62
Coleman, N. D., 157
Coleman, Nancy, 293, 332
Coleman, Nicholas D., 153, 186
Coleman, Peach Ann, 325
Coleman, Philipe, 289
Coleman, Robert, 31, 34
Coleraine, Bob
Colgin, William, 201
Coll, Mary, 328
Colle(d)ge, A. B., 135
Colle(d)ge, Mrs. E. A., 136
Colle(d)ge, John A., 136
Colle(d)ge, Lida N., 138
Colley, Arthur, 293
Colley, Carissa, 332
Colley, Cynes, 290
Colley, Elizabeth, 326
Colley, Ellen, 274
Colley, Greenlee, 293
Colley, Larkin, 272
Colley, Phoebe, 282
Collie, Asa, 17
Collie, A. C., 293
Collie, H., 294, 296, 297
Collie, Happy, 325
Collie, Holland E., 328
Collie, Holloway, 284, 291-294
Collie, Isaiah, 309
Collie, Jane, 284
Collie, Jinsey T., 336
Collie, John, 280

Craig, Lewis, 1, 78, 85, 87, 108, 109, 110, 148, 169, 183, 256, 258
Craig, Martha, 224, 298
Craig, Mary, 78, 84
Craig, Mrs. Mary, 183
Craig, Mary T., 183, 184
Craig, Nathaniel, 78, 87
Craig, Phil(1)ip, 78, 86
Craig, Robert, 303
Craig, Sally, 78, 86, 87
Craig, Samuel, 78, 87, 224
Craig, Taliaferro (Tol(1)iver), 67, 69, 78, 84, 85, 87
Craig, Toliver, Jr., 78, 85, 87
Craig, Violet, 11
Craig, William, 11, 290
Crail, Elijah, 19
Crail, Laurence, 110, 256
Crail, Richard, 19
Crandall, C. J., 328
Crane, Ann, 3
Crane, Conrad, 302
Crane, Elizabeth, 1
Crane, John, 1, 137
Crane, Sarah, 1, 3
Cranfield, Eaton, 329
Cravens (Cravins), A., 271
Cravens (Cravins), Andrew, 299
Cravens (Cravins), Elizabeth N., 63
Cravens (Cravins), J., 32
Cravens (Cravins), Jeremiah, 31, 63
Cravens (Cravins), Jesse, 32
Cravens (Cravins), John, 63
Cravens (Cravins), Michael M., 283
Cravens (Cravins), N., 272
Cravens (Cravins), Robert, 31
Cravens (Cravins), William, 33
Cravey, Alberta, 120
Crawford, Bertha, 137
Crawford, Charles, 136
Crawford, Edward, 24
Crawford, Elizabeth, 138
Crawford, George N., 136
Crawford, Henry, 230
Crawford, John, 201
Crawford, Joseph, 136, 230
Crawford, Mary C., 230
Crawford, Mary, 230
Crawford, Thomas, 230
Crawford, William, 267
Crawford, William H., 336
Crawley, Joseph, 61
Craxton, Thomas, 315
Craycraft, Isaac D., 128
Cra(y)craft, Sarah, 165
Crayne, Clarinda, 327
Crayne, James, 323
Creakmur (see Creekmur(e), Bartholomew, 311
Creakmur, Bartlett, 327

Creakmur, Christopher, 287, 327
Creakmur, Margaret, 321
Creakmur, Nancy, 315
Creakmur, Phebe, 319
Creakmur, Priscilla, 292
Creekmur, Ruth, 293
Creakmur, Timothy, 315
Creel, Henry, 19
Creel, Jacob, 19
Creel, John, 19
Creel, Philip, 19
Creighbaum, Allen, 115
Creighbaum, James, 115
Creighbaum, Lida, 115
Creighbaum, Margaret, 115
Creighbaum, Margeret A., 115
Creighbaum, Mary, 115
Creighbaum, Samuel, 115
Crenshaw, Wallace, 67
Cresap, C., 298
Cresap, Elizabeth, 305
Cresap, Hanson B., 308
Cresap, Sally S., 282
Crewdson, Ellen, 104
Crews, David, 210
Crickmur, Ansey, 319
Crider, Abram S., 309
Crider, Daniel, 300, 333
Crider, Finis E., 311
Crider, Jacob, 311
Crider, Jacob, Jr., 282
Crider, James, 271
Crider, John, 298, 328
Crider, Martha M., 305
Crider, Mary Jane, 312
Crider, Nancy J., 334
Crider, Parmilia, 300
Crider, Samuel, 305
Crider, S. F., 336
Crin, William N., 317
Crisp, Alfred, 329
Criswell, Jacob, 32
Criswell, James, 201
Crittenden, Electa, 121
Crittenden, Emily, 121
Crittenden, William, 121
Crockett, Anna Frazer, 122
Croft, Frederick A., 301
Croghan, Lucy, 32
Croghan, William, 26, 32
Cromwell, ——, 20
Cromwell, Alvin, 39
Cromwell, Alvin W., 39
Cromwell, Benjamin, 39
Cromwell, Edward, 39
Cromwell, Elizabeth, 39
Cromwell, Isabella, 39
Cromwell, Jane, 39
Cromwell, Jane L. O., 39
Crow(e), Eli, 32
Crow(e), Elizabeth T., 208
Crow(e), Jackson, 208
Crow(e), James, 208

## F

Fagan, Daniel, 144
Fairbanks, Mrs. Holly, 323
Fairbanks, James B., 302
Faller, Jacob E., 287
Fallis, Isaac, 204
Fansler, John, 142
Fansler, Mrs. Lidia, 142
Fant, Charles F., 142
Fant, James P., 142
Fant, Mrs. James P., 142
Farbush, William, 103
Faris, Elizabeth, 291
Farley, Elizabeth E., 118
Farley, Jeremiah, 299
Farley, J. W., 119
Farley, John W., 118
Farley, Mary, 118
Farley, Thomas J., 118
Farley, Westcott, 118
Farmer, James, 270
Farmer, James W., 304
Farmer, Nancy, 323
Farmer, Sally, 274
Farmer, Sarah, 330
Farrell, J. H., 142
Farrin, Joseph C., 191
Farris, Robert R., 315
Farrow, ——, 46
Farrow, Edna, 121
Farrow, Howard, 143
Farrow, Luella, 121
Farrow, Nannie, 143
Farrow, Sam T., 121
Farrow, William, 48, 49
Farrow, William, Jr., 46
Farrs, George, 29
Farrs, Judy, 29
Farrs, Michael, 29
Farrs, Minny, 29
Farrs, Sarah, 29
Fasiguker?, George, 110
Fate, Peter, 286
Fatherstone, William, 201
Faugher, Elizabeth, 298
Faughn, E., 333
Faughn, Francis, 321
Faughn, James, 304
Faughn, Patsy, 285
Faughn, Sarah, 309
Fauguker, George, 257
Faulkner, Charles G., 318
Faulkner, Jossie, 78
Fauntleroy, David E., 58
Fauntleroy, Griffin T., 57, 58
Fauntleroy, James H., 57, 58
Fauntleroy, John, 57, 58
Fauntleroy, John, Jr., 57
Fauntleroy, John H., 58
Fauntleroy, John R.
Fauntleroy, Margaret, 58

Fauntleroy, Margaret (Harrod), 58
Fauntleroy, Mary, 57, 58
Fauntleroy, Mary Ann, 58
Fauntleroy, Nancy, 57
Fauntleroy, Rebecca, 58
Fauntleroy, Robert, 58
Fauntleroy, Robert W., 58
Fauntleroy, Samuel, 58
Fauntleroy, Samuel K., 58
Fauntleroy, William K., 57
Faw, Elizabeth, 184, 187
Faw, Nancy (Williams), 187
Fearis, George, 170
Feland, Thomas, 207
Felker, Isaac, 325
Felker, Judith Ann, 319
Fenton, Caleb, 257
Fenton, Michael, 146
Fenton, Samuel, 146
Fergeson, Anna B., 143
Ferguson, Deborah (Dans), 26
Ferguson, Isaac, 202
Ferguson, Peter, 26
Fesiale (Fesiate), Polly, 277
Fichter, John, 142
Fic(k)lin, Alice, 142
Fic(k)lin, Horacio N., 142
Fic(k)lin, Mrs. Julia, 114
Fic(k)lin, Robert, 142
Fields, Greenberry, 158
Fields, John R., 156
Fields, Malinda, 146
Fields, Martha, 146
Fields, Rebecca, 157, 158
Fields, Sally R., 158
Fields, Simon, 169
Fields, William, 146
Fike, Elijah, 64
Fike, Rebecca, 60
Fike, Susannah, 175
Filson, Mrs. Elizabeth J., 142
Fincannon, Lovey, 305
Finch, Anderson, 141
Finch, Mrs. Bettie M., 142
Fincher, Otto, 98
Findley, William L., 32
Finirty, James L., 116
Finirty, Lottie, 116
Finirty, Stanley, 116
Finley, Asa, 32
Finley, Dabney, 29, 32
Finley, James, 61
Finley, John E., 169
Finley, John P., 32
Finley, Judith, 32
Finley, William, 32
Finnelly, William, 174
Fischter, Charles L., 142
Fish, Robert, 318
Fishback, Anne Elizabeth, 37
Fisher, Mrs. Jane (Jamison), 26
Fisher, Mary Ann, 122

Good(e), Jenny, 204
Good(e), John, 204-206
Good(e), Joseph, 206
Good(e), Joseph Hoskins, 206
Good(e), J. F., 205
Good(e), J. T., 205
Good(e), Kate, 205
Good(e), Lorenzo D., 204
Good(e), Lorenzo Dow, 204-206
Good(e), Lorenzo Dow, Jr., 207
Good(e), Lorenzy, 206
Good(e), Lucy, 205
Good(e), Maggie G., 205
Good(e), Maria, 204
Good(e), Maria Louise, 207, 208
Good(e), Martha Ann, 207, 208
Good(e), Mary, 204, 205
Good(e), Mary Ann, 207
Good(e), Mattie, 205, 209
Good(e), Micajah, 206
Good(e), Mildred A., 204, 205
Good(e), Mittie, 207
Good(e), Nancy, 204
Good(e), Nancy Ann, 206
Good(e), Nancy Jane, 206
Good(e), Sallie, 206
Good(e), Sally, 205
Good(e), Samuel, 205, 206
Good(e), Sarah, 204, 205, 209
Good(e), Sarah M., 205
Good(e), Timothy, 204
Good(e), Thomas, 204
Good(e), Thomas J., 205
Good(e), Thomas Jefferson, 207
Good(e), Wilbur, 205
Good(e), Wilbur B., 205
Good(e), W. B., 205
Good(e), William, 204, 206
Goodlet, Frances B., 304
Goodlet, John, 305
Goodlet, Spartan, 302
Goodloe, H. S., 62
Goodman, Buckner W., 120
Goodman, C. A., 143
Goodman, Elizabeth, 294
Goodman, Elizabeth Lamar, 120
Goodpaster, ——, 143
Goodpaster, L. A., 143
Goodwin, Andrew, 143
Goodwin, Charles C., 143
Goodwin, Mrs. Charles, 144
Goodwin, Jesse S., 329
Goodwin, John F., 333
Goodwin, John Griffith, 27
Goodwin, Lear, 27
Goodwin, Lydia, 27
Goodwin, Nancy, 27
Goodwin, Samuel, 27
Goodwin, T. F., 144
Gorden, Lewis, 109, 257, 258
Gordlet, Margaret A., 304
Gordon, Ambrose, 28
Gordon, Charles, 174

Gordon, George, 33
Gordon, James, 295
Gordon, John, 28, 33
Gordon, Louise, 299
Gordon, Mary C., 230
Gordon, Patsy, 28
Gordon, Peter, 173
Gordon, Robert, 28
Gordon, Thomas, 272
Gordon, William, 28
Gore, Deborah, 277
Gore, Mastin, 321
Gore, Notley D., 323
Gore, Permelia H., 320
Gore, William, 277
Gore, William H., 308
Gorin, Maria E., 313
Gorman, Henry, 124
Goslin, Benjamin, 45
Goslin, Joseph, 45
Goslin, Nathan, 45
Goslin, Nathaniel, 45
Goslin, Reuben, 45
Gosling, H., 116
Gosset(t), Cyntha, 294
Gosset(t), David, 289
Grace, David, 276
Grace, Elvira, 305
Grace, James, 280, 289
Grace, J. C., 314
Grace, J. E., 313, 325, 331
Grace, Joel E., 314, 315, 317, 318
Grace, Preston, 280
Gracey, George, 276
Gracey, James N., 296
Gracey, Martha, 287
Gracey, Matthew, 297
Gracey, Mildred A., 326
Grady, E., 18
Grady, Trecy, 62
Grafton, Nathan H., 4
Gragg, Hannah, 287
Gragg, William, 288
Graham, Etta F., 121
Graham, Fannie S., 121
Graham, George, 118
Graham, Henry R., 178, 179, 180
Graham, Ivy Duke, 232
Graham, Jane, 118
Graham, John, 49, 202
Graham, John C., 313
Graham, J. P., 232
Graham, Richard, 48, 49
Graham, Sallie, 232
Grant, Charles, 27, 144
Grant, Elizabeth, 122
Grant, Ely, 122
Grant, Fannie, 122
Grant, George, 54, 182
Grant, Hattie E., 122
Grant, John L., 122
Grant, Judith, 230
Grant, Mrs. John T., 143

Hamilton, Benjamin N., 177
Hamilton, Charles, 29
Hamilton, Clifford, 236
Hamilton, Edith Ives Leete, 102
Hamilton, Elizabeth, 275
Hamilton, Jacob, 236
Hamilton, John, 177, 222, 301
Hamilton, Jonathan, 234
Hamilton, J. G., 88
Hamilton, Mrs. Linda, 237
Hamilton, Lucinda, 335
Hamilton, Peggy, 277
Hamilton, Polina E., 323
Hamilton, Polly, 270
Hamilton, Rebecca M., 235
Hamilton, Richard, 307
Hamilton, Waldo, 237
Ham(m), E. W., 335
Ham(m), Polly A., 300
Hamma(o)ck, Hugh, 304
Hamma(o)ck, Jeremiah, 297
Hamma(o)ck, Minney, 271
Hamma(o)ck, Nancy, 336
Hamma(o)ck, Ruth, 269
Hammer, Elizabeth, 262
Hammer, Thomas, 262
Hammock (see Hammack)
Hammond(s), Chris, 336
Hammond(s), James, 78, 87
Hammond(s), John, 272
Hammond(s), Joshua, 281
Hammond(s), Lewis, 300
Hammond(s), Lucy, 303
Hammond(s), Martin, 274
Hammond(s), Mary, 299
Hammond(s), Nancy, 301
Hammond(s), Rhoda, 281
Hammond(s), Ruth C., 302
Hammond(s), Ruth H., 302
Hammond(s), Sarah, 327
Hammond(s), Thomas, 271
Hammond(s), Tymandra, 314
Hampton, Birtie, 235
Hampton, Mrs. Mary, 235
Hampton, R. T., 233
Hampton, Virginia, 236
Hamrick, Carter, 235
Hamrick, Francis, 236
Hamrick, John E., 236
Hamton, William 238
Hanberry, Thomas W., 319
Hance, William, 257
Hancock, C. M., 236
Hancock, Elizabeth T., 112
Hancock, Ezekiel, 314
Hancock, Ezma, 319
Hancock, Eznca, 315
Hancock, George, 124, 263
Hancock, George S., 112, 263
Hancock, John, 112, 269
Hancock, John W., 112, 263
Hancock, Joseph, 202

Hancock, Josiah, 335
Hancock, Julia, 112
Hancock, Mary, 263
Hancock, Mary S., 112
Hancock, Nannie W., 112
Hancock, Nancy Wilkenson, 263
Hancock, Mrs. Sarah B., 237
Hancock, Thomas, 273
Hancock, William, 112
Hand, Mrs. E. F., 102
Hand, Ella Lenore, 102
Hand, Frances, 102
Hand, Harriet Elizabeth, 102
Hand, Hawkins, 262
Haner, James, 202
Hawkins, Mary, 262
Hand, William Thomas, 102
Handley, John, 33, 233
Handley, Joseph, 233
Hanell, Reuben, 283
Haney, Elizabeth, 115
Hanford, Martha J., 332
Hankins, B., 236
Hankins, John, 288
Hankins, Narcissus, 62
Hankins, Tabitha, 295
Hanks, Elizabeth C., 327
Hanks, Henry H., 283
Hanks, Jane, 325
Hanks, Mary, 325
Hanley, James, 303
Hanm, Polly A., 300
Hanna, Adam H., 40
Hanna, Alexander, 30
Hanna, John, 202
Hannah, Elizabeth, 272
Hannington, Agnes, 103
Hannington, William, 103
Hanum, Jonathan, 202
Harber, Mariah, 60
Harbert, Josiah, 110
Harbin, Hettie, 122
Harbin, John, 122
Hardest, Caleb, 41
Hardin, Anthony P., 311
Hardin, Benjamin H., 31
Hardin, Benony, 310, 311
Hardin, Frances (Bartlett) 1
Hardin, Robert, 274
Hardin, Samuel, 26, 28
Hardin, Wesley, 1
Harding, —— 267
Harding, B., 18
Harding, Byram, 218
Harding, Byram, Jr., 59, 162
Harding, David, 267
Harding, Mrs. Elizabeth H., 56, 59, 162, 218
Harding, George, 63, 173
Harding, Lucinda Virginia, 218
Harding, Lucinda V., 56, 218
Harding, Mary Dotson, 236

Hill, Perry, 235
Hill, Samuel, 298
Hill, Sudie, 121
Hill, Thomas, J. C., 325
Hill, William, 174
Hill, William Washington, 307
Hillman, Heathy (Craig), 11
Hillman, Daniel, 11
Hilliard, (see Hillyard)
Hil(l)yard, Alexander, 304
Hil(l)yard, Elizabeth, 303, 313
Hil(l)yard, John J., 300
Hil(l(yard, Thompson, 290
Hil(l)yard, William L., 309
Hil(l)yard, William S., 327
Hilton, Mary, 266
Hinds, A. M., 336
Hinds, Fingal H., 336
Hines, Joseph, 32
Hinkley, Otis, 286
Hinton, John, 46
Hinton, Sarah A., 275
Hiott, Stephen (Steven), 108, 109
Hise, ——, 232
Hitchcock, John V., 323
Hiter, Benjamin, 221
Hiter, Betsy, 221
Hiter, Charles, 221
Hiter, James, 68, 221
Hiter, James, Jr., 221
Hiter, Phebe, 68
Hiter, Polly, 221
Hiter, Richard, 221
Hiter, William, 110
Hitner, Phoebe, 229
Hix, James, 277
Hixon, Nathaniel, 109, 110, 170, 256
Hixon, N., 147
Hoag, Benjamin S., 65
Hoag, Lucy Alice, 65
Hobby, Amanda, 334
Hobby, Delilah, 299
Hobby, Elzy, 330
Hobby, Mary, 312
Hobby, Nancy, 301
Hobby, Willis L., 305
Hobby, William, 329
Hobert, Fanney, 282
Hobert, Jane, 271
Hobert, William, 304
Hocheley, Thomas, 49
Hocker, Alfred, 204
Hocker, Arthur, 209
Hocker, Belle, 209
Hocker, Benjamin D., 208
Hocker, Betsey Helen, 204
Hocker, Catherine, 205
Hocker, Charlie, 205
Hocker, Dorcas, 204, 208
Hocker, E. G., 205
Hocker, Elizabeth, 205
Hocker, Gabriella, 208

Hocker, George, 204
Hocker, Isaiah Dunn, 208
Hocker, Jacob, 204
Hocker, James M., 208
Hocker, Jimmie, 209
Hocker, John, 204, 205
Hocker, Joseph, 204, 205, 208
Hocker, J. D., 205
Hocker, L. G., 205
Hocker, Laura, 209
Hocker, Leslie, 209
Hocker, Maggie, 205
Hocker, Margaret, 204
Hocker, Margaret A., 205
Hocker, Margareta, 208
Hocker, Mary, 204, 206, 208
Hocker, Nancy, 204
Hocker, Nancy Barned, 206
Hocker, Nannie Barnes, 208
Hocker, Nicholas, 204, 205
Hocker, Philip, 204
Hocker, Philip L., 205
Hocker, Philip S., 205
Hocker, Polly, 204
Hocker, R. W., 205
Hocker, Richard W., 208
Hocker, Richard Weaver, 204
Hocker, Samuel, 200, 204, 205, 208, 209
Hocker, Sarah, 204, 209
Hocker, Sarah Myers, 208
Hocker, Sophia, 209
Hocker, S. G., 205
Hocker, Tilman, 208, 209
Hocker, William Dunn, 208
Hocker, W. H., 205
Hockersmith, Florinda J., 306
Hodge, Collin(s), 325, 327, 335
Hodge, Darien, 322
Hodge, Isabella, 116
Hodge, Marath, 307
Hodge, William, 116
Hodges, Alexander M., 301
Hodges, Ann, 323
Hodges, Mary, 106
Hodges, Parmelia J., 194
Hodges, Robert, 303
Hodges, Susan Ann, 104
Hodges. William, 194, 195, 333
Hoensaker, Jacob, 168
Hoffman, Almira, 267
Hoffman, Isaac, 267
Hoffman, Maggie, 267
Hoffman, Mattie, 267
Hoffman, Sallie, 267
Hogan, James P., 319
Hogan, Love, 227, 228
Hogan, Martha, 320
Hogan, Mary J., 21
Hogans, Thos., 32
Hogan, William, 227, 228
Hogg, Stephen, 285
Holawell, Penelope, 281

McCash, David, 202
McCaslin, A. A., 336
McCaslin, C. Jane, 333
McCaslin, James, 284
McCaslin, James, Jr., 312
McCaslin, Mary G., 289
McCaslin, William H., 336
McCastlin, Hugh, 276
McCastlin, Jane, 291
McCatney, Thomas, 145
McCew, Edward, 178, 179
McCew, John, 178
McCew, Selina, 178
McCew, William, 178
McChesney, A. W., 317
McChesney, Elizabeth A., 325
McChesney, Robert, 30
McChesney, Samuel A., 303, 327
McChesney, Sarah C., 335
McChesney, William A., 302, 335
McClain, David, 242
McClain, Mary, 242
McClanahan, Adna, 242
McClanahan, Anne, 38
McClanahan, B. P., 117
McClanahan, Mrs. B. P., 117
McClanahan, C. W., 242
McClanahan, Eliza, 234
McClanahan, M. T., 117
McClanahan, William, 234
McClary, Samuel, 23
McClatchey, John, 168
McClaughlin, Daniel, 261
McClelland, Margaret C., 199
McClelland, Mary, 199
McClelland, Robert P., 199
McClendon, Benjamin, 31
McClung, Mrs. Eliza, 115
McClung, John A., 115
McClure, Andrew, 307
McClure, Francis, 202
McClure, Frank, 31, 184
McClure, James, 285
McClure, Jenny, 270
McClure, Margaret, 205, 276
McClure, Matilda, 184
McClure, Nancey, 273
McClure, William, 31
McClusky, John, 280
McCollough, A. Buley, 119
McCollough, Ann M., 119
McCollough, Hugh, 119
McCollough, Margeret, 119
McCollough, Mary T., 119
McCollough, William, 119
McCollum, Samuel, 295
McConnell, Cerena E., 304
McConnell, F. P., 336
McConnell, Jane A., 307
McConnell, John D., 288
McConnell, John N., 327
McConnell, Joseph A., 310
McConnell, Lucy A, 314

McConnell, Mary, 333
McConnell, Rosannah K., 310
McConnell, Sanai, 336
McConnell, William B., 322
McCool, E. J., 335
McCord, Alta M., 242
McCord, J. W., 18
McCord, Mrs. Peggy, 295
McCormack (see McCormick)
McCormick, A. J., 334
McCormick, Alfred, 242
McCormick, James, 242
McCormick, John, 303
McCormick, John W., 242
McCormick, Mrs. Mary, 241
McCormick, Wesley, 320
McCormack, Wm., 315
McCough (McGough), T. M., 331
McCown, Alex, 334
McCown, Alex H., 335
McCoy, Daniel H., 292
McCoy, Mrs. Huldy, 304
McCoy, Pembrock, 321
McCoy, Wm. D., 293
McCrackin, John, 202
McCrackin, William, 203
McCrary, Martha, 302
McCreary, Elizabeth, 297
McCreery, William Y., 301, 303
McCrory, Hugh, 315
McCullough, James, 130
McCullough, Mary, 130
McDaniel, Alice B., 112
McDaniel, Barbara, 6
McDaniel, Fannie, 113
McDaniel, Florence, 113
McDaniel, George, 99
McDaniel, Polly, 300
McDaniel, Samuel, 307, 326
McDaniel, William T., 241
McDermid, Francis, 176
McDermid, Mary Ann, 190
McDermed, Francis, 176
McDermitt, Mary Ann, 190
McDonald, Edna, 268
McDonald, Edwin, 268
McDonald, Henry, 170
McDonald, Samuel, 242
McDonald, Mrs. Samuel, 111
McDonald, Sarah, 116
McDonald, William, 123, 202
McDoo, Mary, 276
McDougal (McDougle), Harry C., 242
McDougal (McDougle), Mrs. Mary, 242
McDougle (see McDougal)
McDowell, Ailcy, 290
McDowell, Ann, 146
McDowell, Caleb Wallace, 86
McDowell, Clarissa Mira, 77, 85
McDowell, Daniel, 333
McDowell, Elizabeth, 77, 85, 270

Mercer, Charlotte, 270
Mercer, Clemmie W., 243
Mercer, Drury, 278
Mercer, Helen R., 318
Mercer, J., 268
Mercer, James, 278
Mercer, John, Jr., 276
Mercer, Mary M., 331
Meredith, Milly, 60
Merrick, John, 170
Merritt, Jacob M., 302
Merritt, Jemima, 59
Mesner, Conrad, 202
Messinger, Agnes, 196
Messinger, Francis G., 196
Metcalf(e), Charles, 109, 110, 257
Metcalfe, Hiram, 5
Metcalf(e), John, 68. 202
Metcalf(e), Spencer G., 292
Meyars, (see Meyers)
Meyers, Amanda O., 243
Meyers, Claud, 122
Meyers, H. C., 244
Meyers, Jack, 230
Meyers, S. N., 243
Meyers, William R., 267
Middaugh, Hannah, 12
Middleton, James, 73
Middleton. Thomas. 202
Midgett, Pensy, 317
Midgett, Fanny, 281
Midgett, Zilpha, 282
Midyett, Jesse, 279
Milam, Anna Belle, 105
Milam, Annie B., 106
Milam, Ben T., 106
Milam, Ben Tecumseh, 105
Milam, Bettie, 106
Milam, Bettie P., 106
Milam, Bettie Pennington, 105
Milam, Catherine Wilson, 106
Milam, Charles Clark, 105
Milam, E., 105, 106
Milam, E. M., 106
Milam, Elizabeth, 105, 106
Milam, Emma Waide, 105, 106
Milam, James William, 105, 106
Milam, John M., 106
Milam, John Morgan, 105
Milam, J. T. 105, 106
Milam, John Tecumseh, 105, 106
Milam, Katie, 105, 106
Miles, Earnest, 233
Miles, Charles J., 311
Milholland, Catherine, 294
Milker, Catharine, 288
Millar, William, 11
Millbanks, Willis, 16
Miller, ——, 232
Miller, Abraham, 206
Miller, Achiseth, 121
Miller, Alexander, 59

Miller, Amos, 110, 256
Miller, August(us), 122
Miller, Avie, 213
Miller, Barbera, 112
Miller, Catherine F., 112
Miller, Charles Owens, 243
Miller, Charlette, 243
Miller, Mrs. Charlette, 242
Miller, Ebenezer, 204
Miller, Eliza Amanda, 324
Miller, Flora, 118
Miller, Fred B., 112
Miller, Godfry, 112
Miller, Harry A., 112
Miller,, Henry, 103, 112
Miller, Henry A., 243
Miller, Mrs. H. J., 243
Miller, Isaac, 336
Miller, Jacob, 243
Miller, Mrs. Jacob, 243
Miller, James, 118
Miller, James C., 301
Miller, Jane, 273
Miller, John, 50, 112, 270, 279
Miller, John A., 244
Miller, Mrs. John, 242
Miller, Joseph, 268
Miller, Mrs. L., 243
Miller, Louis, 244
Miller, Lucinda, 304
Miller, Margaret, 302
Miller, Martha Jane, 328
Miller, Mary R., 299
Miller, Memos, 206
Miller, Minerva, 282
Miller, Nancy, 293
Miller, Nancy Jane, 325
Miller, O. P., 261
Miller, Peter, 112
Miller, Sally, 288
Miller, Samuel H., 324
Miller, Sarah, 112
Miller, Susannah M., 330
Miller, Thomas, 50
Miller, William, 112, 321
Miller, William D., 296
Miller, Wilson, 243
Milliken, Marie W., 114
Milliken, Morris Hugh, 114
Milliken, Sudie B., 114
Mills, Elizabeth, 315
Mills, James R., 120
Mills, John, 29, 33
Mills, Maria M., 33
Mills, Pearce B., 243
Mills, Mrs. Sophia, 243
Mills, Thomas, 109, 110
Mills, Willa M., 243
Milly, Anna, 232
Milly, Barbara, 232
Mims, Cornelia, 304
Mims, Davis N., 305

Rankin(s), Thomas M., 310
Rankin(s), William, 188, 189
Rannel(l)s, David V., 7, 171
Ranson, Achsah L., 230
Ranson, Bessie, 113
Ranson, Betty B., 113
Ranson, F. B., 230
Ranson, Mary M., 113
Ranson, Matilda G., 230
Ranson, R. H., 230
Rardin, Jacob, 191
Rascal, John P., 318
Rascoe, James E. B., 320
Rascoe, John P., 331
Rascoe, Laban, 16
Rascoe, Laban Taylor, 16
Rascoe, Martha, 320
Rash, James, 59
Rash, Joseph W., 66
Rash, Martha Ruby, 66
Rash, Mary Belle, 66
Rash, Mary W., 62
Rash, Stephen D., 62
Rashels, Valentine, 32
Rasp, Elizabeth, 249
Rasp, Iola J., 249
Rasp, John, 262
Ratcliff(c), C., 297, 299, 301, 302, 310
Ratcliff(e), Coleman, 296, 300, 302, 306, 307, 308, 309, 310, 314
Ratcliff(e), J. C., 298, 299
Ratcliff(e), Mrs. Margaret, 321
Ratcliff(e), Richard S., 311
Ratcliff(e), William, 169
Rathbone, Thomas W., 22
Rathburn, Stephen A., 173
Rathfield, Coleman, 296
Ratliff, (see Ratcliffe)
Ravencraft, ——, 118, 263
Ravencraft, Francis, 118
Ravencraft, Johnny, Jr., 118
Ravencraft, Margeret, 118
Ravencraft, Mrs. Margaret, 118
Rawlins, Fanny, 281
Rawlins, John, 298, 303
Rawlins, Susan, 273
Rawlins, William, 283
Rawls, Silas M., 307
Rawls, William C., 50
Ray, Birdie, 36
Ray, Elizabeth, 58
Ray, Fannie, 281
Ray, Mrs. Georgian H. W., 314
Ray, John, 298
Ray, Isham, 58
Ray, Mary Ann, 57, 58
Ray, William, 283
Ray, William C. B., 310
Raybourne, John, 46
Raybourne, William, 46
Rea, George, 114

Rea, George W., 114
Rea, Henry, 114
Rea, Mary E., 114
Rea, Susan, 114
Rea, Thomas M., 114
Read(e), Christian E., 308
Read(e), James, 285
Read(e), Joseph, 287
Read(e), Margaret E., 21
Read(e), Sally, 285
Reading, William, 31
Reardon, Ann, 180
Reardon, James, 180
Reardon, Milton, 180
Reardon, Philip, 180
Reardon, Rachel, 180
Reasor, Ethel, 76
Redd, Curtis F., 313
Redd, John, 312
Redden, Anna H., 250
Redden, Elizabeth R., 249
Redden, J. M., 248
Redick, Thomas, 32
Reddish, Elvira C., 25, 26
Redmon, Polly, 60
Reece, James, 327
Reece, Presley A., 313
Reece, Willie, 267
Reed, ——, 149, 153
Reed, Adam, 311
Reed, Agnes Lee, 163, 164
Reed, Alice B., 163, 164
Reed, Ann, 42, 44
Reed, Armedda, 158
Reed, Armedda O., 161
Reed, Armida O., 162, 163
Reed, Betsey, 274
Reed, Charles F., 147, 159, 218
Reed, Charles Franklin, 129, 218, 219
Reed, Claud, 250
Reed, Delilah Elizabeth, 163
Reed, Eleanor C., 161
Reed, Eliza Jane, 162
Reed, Elizabeth, 126, 157, 158, 161, 162, 163, 296
Reed, Elizabeth H., 51, 55, 147, 159
Reed, Elizabeth R., 160
Reed, Mrs. Elizabeth, 250
Reed, Mrs. Elizabeth Hildreth (Fristoe), 159, 218, 219
Reed, Emoch, 203
Reed, Emily, 234, 303
Reed, Fannie, 232
Reed, Grace, 249
Reed, Henry Clay, 160
Reed, Ida Virginia, 163
Reed, Isaac, 42, 43, 144, 147, 158, 162, 203
Reed, Isaac S., 158, 161, 163
Reed, Isaac Shelby, 158, 161, 162
Reed, Isabella, 234

Smith, Lucinda, 276
Smith, Lucinda B., 295
Smith, Mrs. Lucy, 214
Smith, Luvenia, 323
Smith, Maggie, 122
Smith, Margeret C., 123
Smith, Maria Burton, 310
Smith, Mary, 10, 112, 119, 121, 288, 322
Smith, Mary A. E., 336
Smith, Mary Ann, 317
Smith, Mary C., 122
Smith, Mary E. 114
Smith, Mary Elizabeth, 112
Smith, Mary Rachel, 73
Smith, Mary (Standiford) 10
Smith, Matilda, 295
Smith, Melissa F., 299
Smith, Mildred, 8
Smith, Minerva, 62
Smith, Mollie, 252
Smith, Morgan. 303
Smith, Moses, 203
Smith, Mourning, 268
Smith, N. B., 123
Smith, Nanc(e)y, 272, 294
Smith, Nancy H., 335
Smith, Nathan, 296
Smith, Pamela, 289
Smith, Paul, 123
Smith, Peggy, 271, 287, 288
Smith, Perney, 295
Smith, Peter, 296
Smith, Pexton, 314
Smith, Polly, 284, 295
Smith, R., 168
Smith, Rachel, 284
Smith, Ransford, 295
Smith, Rebecca, 273
Smith, Reuben Bartholomew, Jr., 165
Smith, Reuben H., 333
Smith, Rhoda, 283
Smith, Ritty, 268
Smith, Robert, 168, 274, 288
Smith, Ruben B., 123
Smith, Sally, 280
Smith, Samuel, 119, 278
Smith, Samuel K., 324
Smith, Sarah, 301
Smith, Sarah Ann, 119
Smith, Sarah Elizabeth, 317
Smith, Simeon, 334
Smith, Simon, 313
Smith, Thomas, 119, 264, 292
Smith, T. H., 114
Smith, Urial, 304
Smith, William, 72, 110, 253, 275, 301
Smith, William Henderson, 72, 73, 76

Smith, William Henderson, Jr., 72, 73, 76
Smith, William Jefferson, 324
Smith, William W., 327
Smith, W. W., 334
Smith, Wilson, 114
Smither, Benjamin, 53
Smott, Bettie Bacon, 252
Smoot, Mrs. Betty, 121
Smoot, Charles S., 251
Smoot, Henry G., 121
Smoot, H. G., 121
Smoot, H. Wall, 253
Smoot, Mary K., 253
Smoot, Retta F., 251
Smoot, William P., 251
Smyley, Samuel, 29
Smyth, Reuben, 278
Snack, Henry, 333
Snapp, Bonnie J., 252
Snapp, Edith E. A., 252
Snedeker (Snediker), Clara E., 251
Snedeker, (Snediker), John, 252
Snelling, Ann, 287
Snelling, Elizabeth E., 322
Snelling, Margaret M. A., 309
Snelling, Reuben, 318
Snelling, Roger B., 318
Snelling, Theodocia, 294
Snoden, William, 318
Snyder, B. F., 74
Snyder, Florence Law Baskett, 74
Soden, Annie E., 320
Soden, Elwood T., 336
Soden, John, 328
Soden, William, 318
Sollinger, John Adam, 323
Son(s), Angeline, 306
Son(s), Arminda, 296
Son(s), Syntha, 266
Son(s), Elizabeth, 271
Son(s), John, 266
Son(s), Mrs. John. 233
Son(s), John F., 279
Son(s), John S., 304
Son(s), Michael, 272
Son(s), Peggy, 272
Son(s), Ruth A., 300
Sorg, Bennett, 282
Sory, Bennett, 282
Sousley, Robert, 113
Sousley, Thomas, 251
Southard, Hezekiah, 203
Soward, Mary Ann, 157
Soward, Richard, 153, 154, 158, 161, 203. 252
Soward, Richard, Jr., 160
Spahr, A. C., 252
Spahr, Eliza Clark, 252
Spain, Nettie, 112